WORLD WAR
HULK

NEVER
STOP MAKING
THEM PAY

WORLD WAR HULK®

TER: GREG PAK WITH PETER DAVID

CILS: JOHN ROMITA JR.

AL RIO, LEE WEEKS, SEAN PHILLIPS,

ARD KIRK, RAFA SANDOVAL

S: KLAUS JANSON WITH SCOTT HANNA,

JEEKS, TOM PALMER, LEONARD KIRK, GARY ERSKINE

RS: CHRISTINA STRAIN, WILLIAM MURAI, MOOSE BAUMANN, GURU eFX

RS: VIRTUAL CALLIGRAPHY'S JOE CARAMAGNA, CHRIS ELIOPOULOS

ART: DAVID FINCH

ANT EDITOR: NATHAN COSBY

R: MARK PANICCIA

R IN CHIEF: JOE QUESADA

SHER: DAN BUCKLEY

ve any comments or queries about World War Hulk? Email us at graphicnovels@panini.co.uk.

Facebook @Panini/Marvel Graphic Novels.

 First printing 2008. Seventeenth impression 2021. Published by Panini Publishing, a division of Panini UK Limited. Mike Riddell, Managing Director. Alan O'Keefe, Managing Editor. Mark Irvine, Production Manager. Marco M. Lupoi, Publishing Director Europe. Brady Webb, Reprint Editor. Luigi Mutti, Assistant Editor, Melanie Wilson, Designer. Office of publication: Brockbourne House, 77 Mount Ephraim, Tunbridge Wells, Kent TN4 8BS. Printed in the United Kingdom by Zenith Media. ISBN: 978-1-90523-977-1

MIX
Paper from responsible sour
FSC® C0103

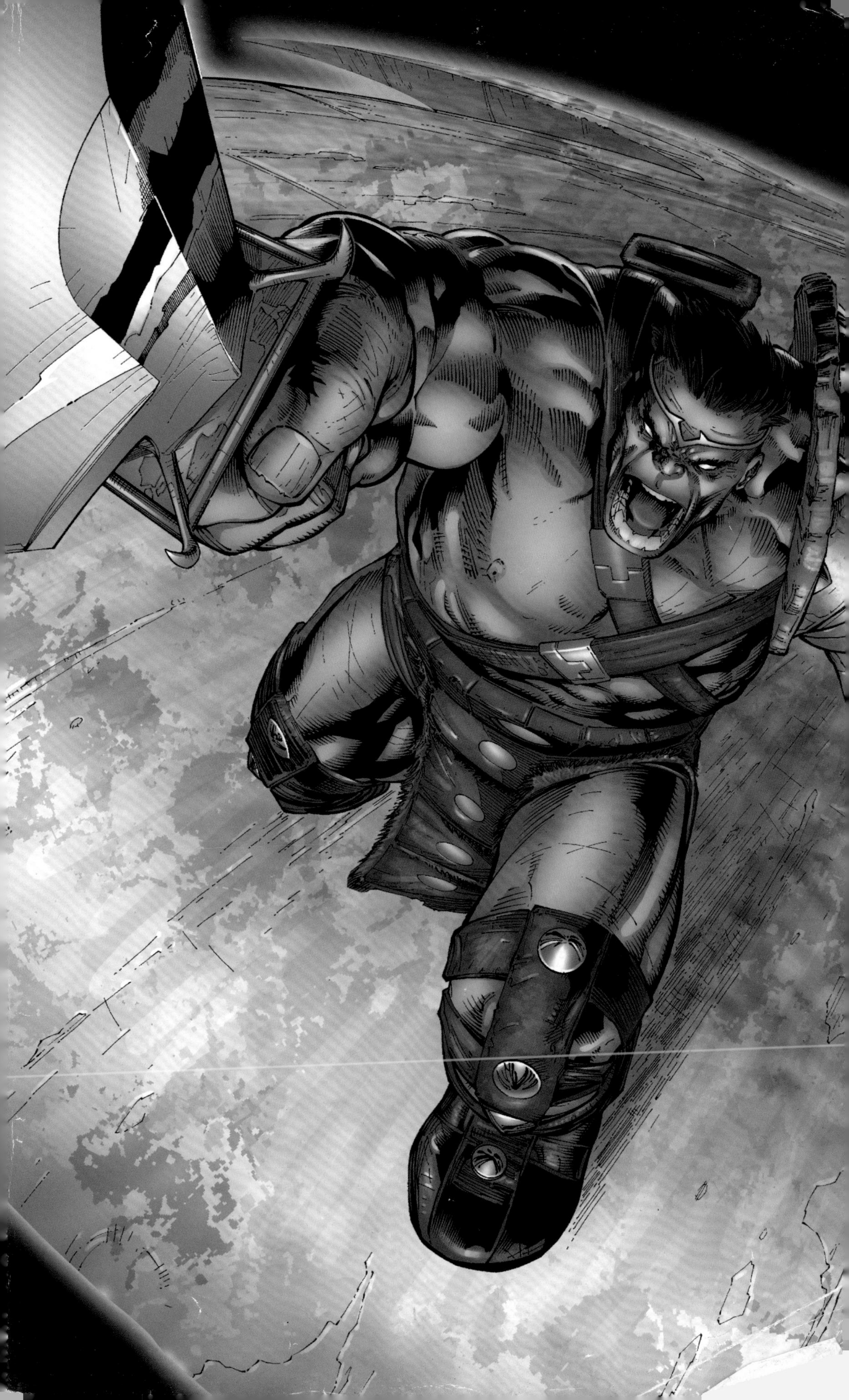

MARVEL GRAPHIC NOVEL

WORLD WAR HULK: PROLOGUE

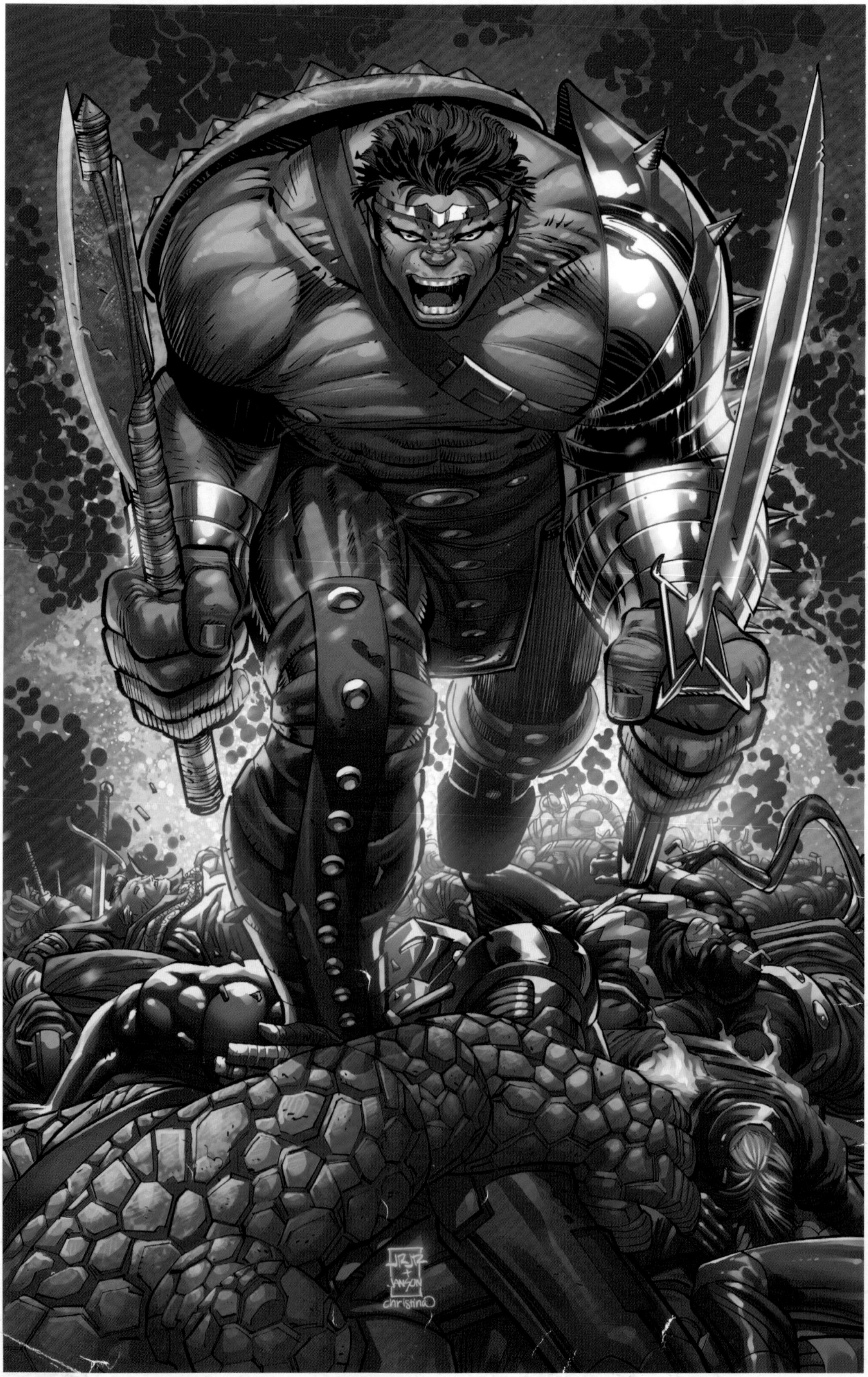

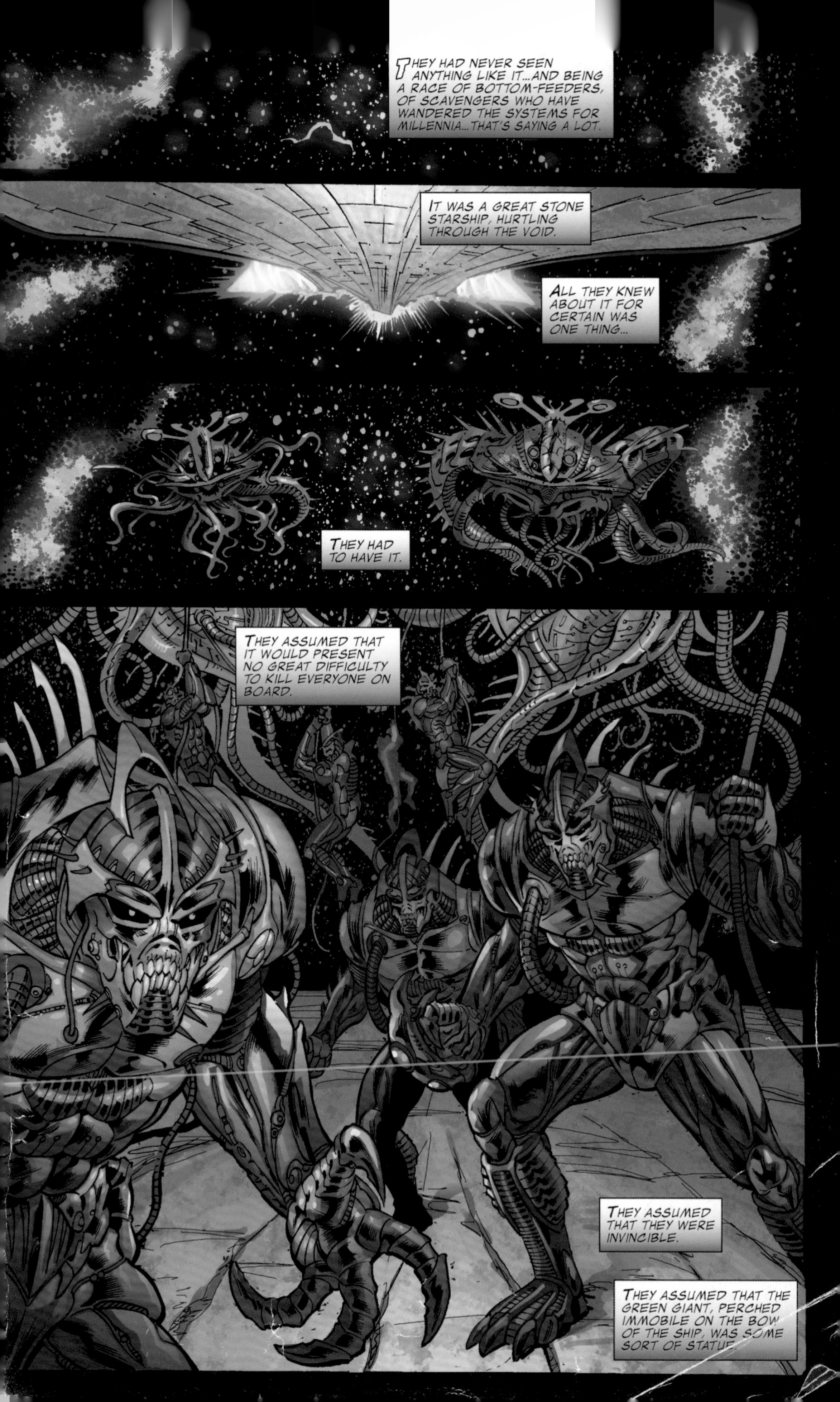

THEY HAD NEVER SEEN ANYTHING LIKE IT...AND BEING A RACE OF BOTTOM-FEEDERS, OF SCAVENGERS WHO HAVE WANDERED THE SYSTEMS FOR MILLENNIA...THAT'S SAYING A LOT.
IT WAS A GREAT STONE STARSHIP, HURTLING THROUGH THE VOID.
ALL THEY KNEW ABOUT IT FOR CERTAIN WAS ONE THING...
THEY HAD TO HAVE IT.
THEY ASSUMED THAT IT WOULD PRESENT NO GREAT DIFFICULTY TO KILL EVERYONE ON BOARD.
THEY ASSUMED THAT THEY WERE INVINCIBLE.
THEY ASSUMED THAT THE GREEN GIANT, PERCHED IMMOBILE ON THE BOW OF THE SHIP, WAS SOME SORT OF STATUE.

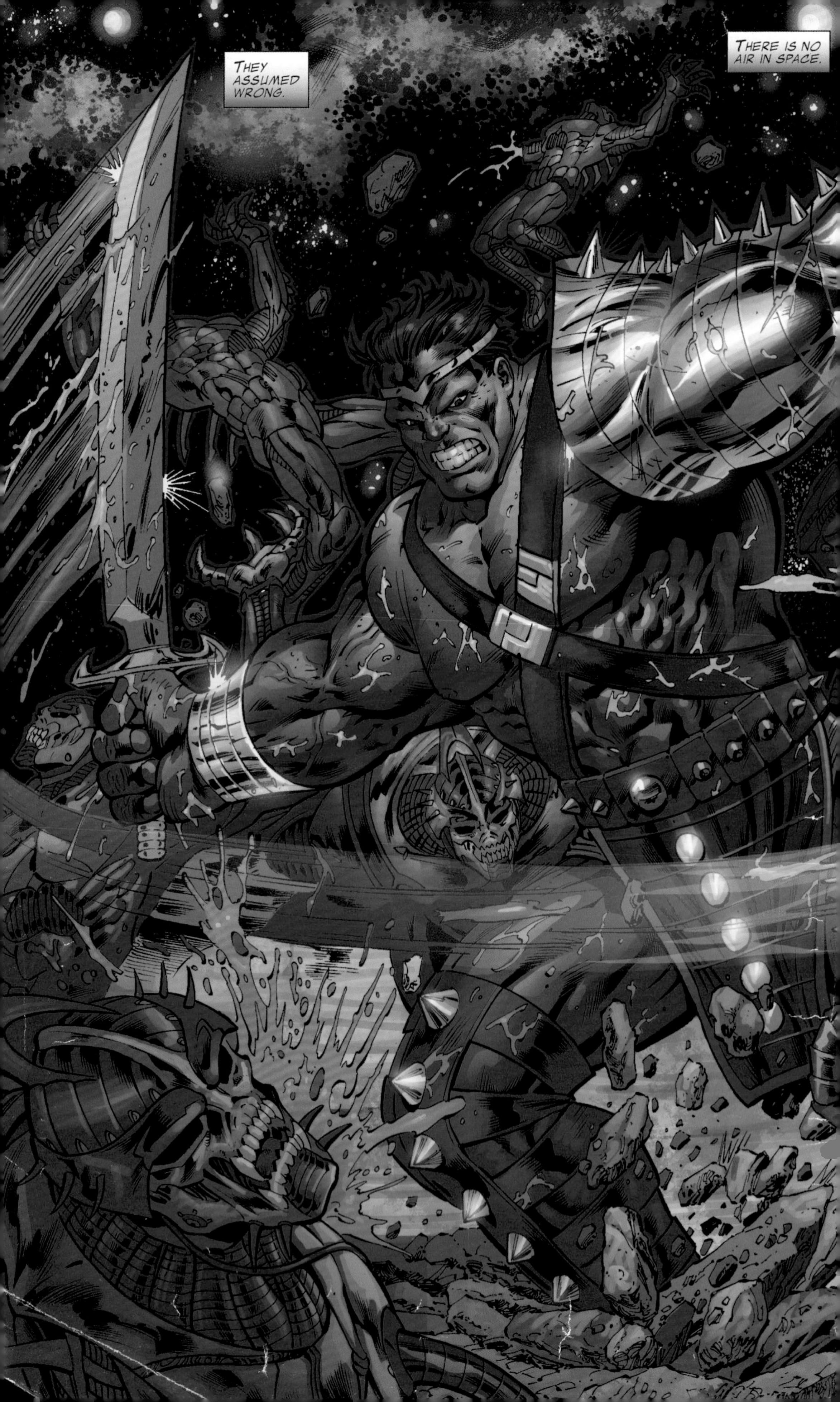

THEY ASSUMED WRONG.
THERE IS NO AIR IN SPACE.

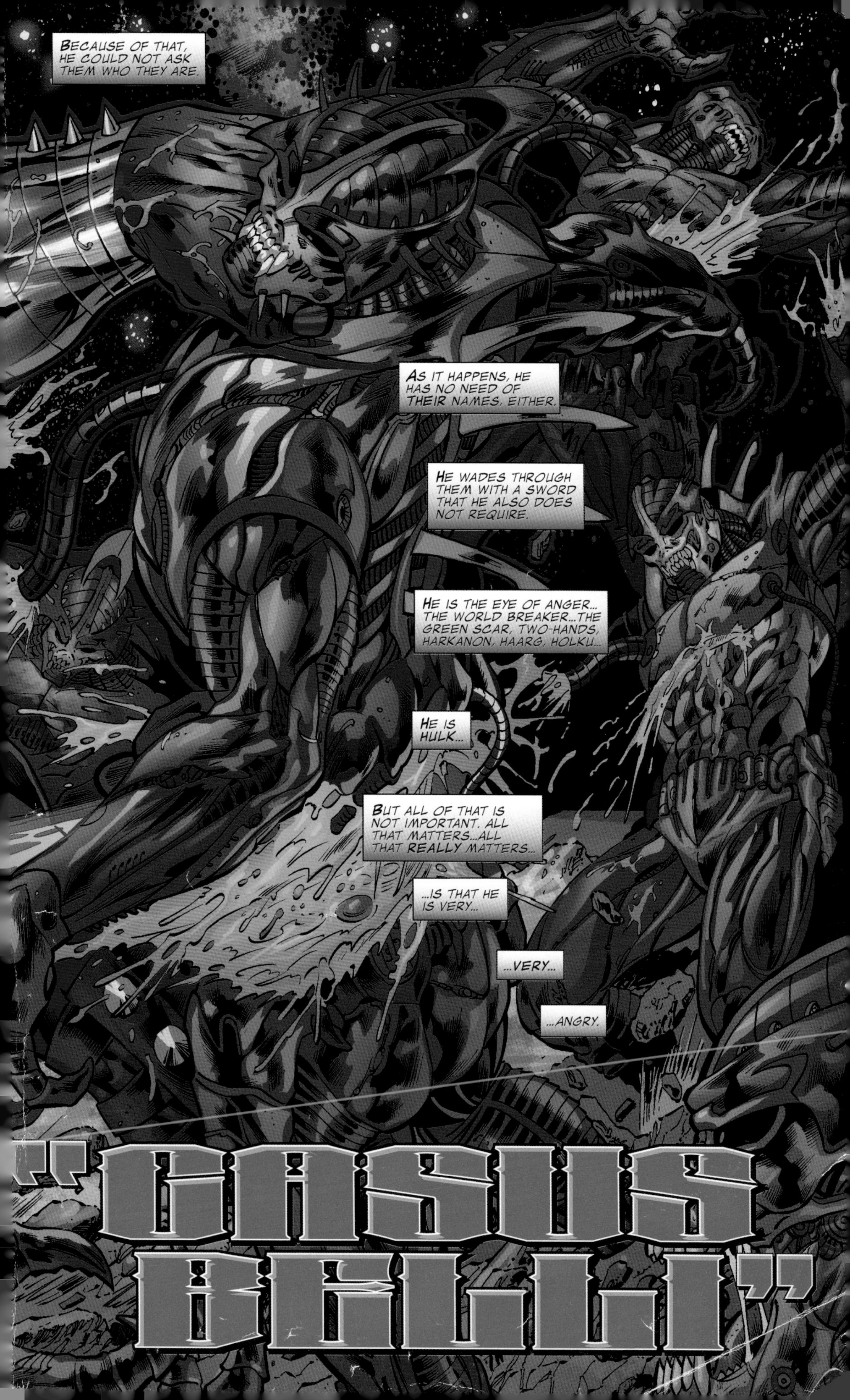
BECAUSE OF THAT, HE COULD NOT ASK THEM WHO THEY ARE.
AS IT HAPPENS, HE HAS NO NEED OF THEIR NAMES, EITHER.
HE WADES THROUGH THEM WITH A SWORD THAT HE ALSO DOES NOT REQUIRE.
HE IS THE EYE OF ANGER... THE WORLD BREAKER...THE GREEN SCAR, TWO-HANDS, HARKANON, HAARG, HOLKU...
HE IS HULK...
BUT ALL OF THAT IS NOT IMPORTANT. ALL THAT MATTERS...ALL THAT REALLY MATTERS...
...IS THAT HE IS VERY...
...VERY...
...ANGRY.
"CASUS BELLI"

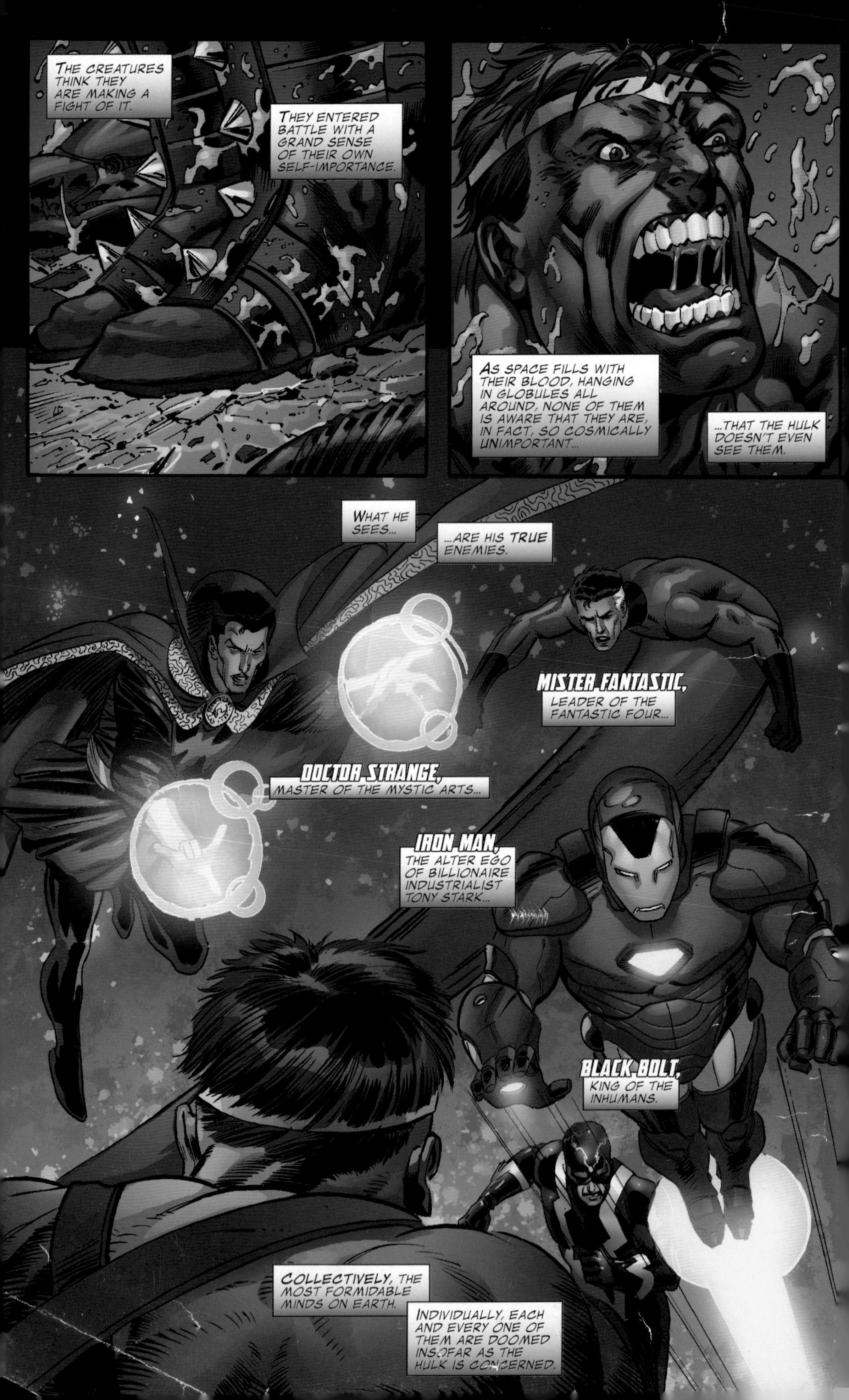
THE CREATURES THINK THEY ARE MAKING A FIGHT OF IT.
THEY ENTERED BATTLE WITH A GRAND SENSE OF THEIR OWN SELF-IMPORTANCE.
AS SPACE FILLS WITH THEIR BLOOD, HANGING IN GLOBULES ALL AROUND, NONE OF THEM IS AWARE THAT THEY ARE, IN FACT, SO COSMICALLY UNIMPORTANT...
...THAT THE HULK DOESN'T EVEN SEE THEM.
WHAT HE SEES...
...ARE HIS TRUE ENEMIES.
MISTER FANTASTIC, LEADER OF THE FANTASTIC FOUR...
DOCTOR STRANGE, MASTER OF THE MYSTIC ARTS...
IRON MAN, THE ALTER EGO OF BILLIONAIRE INDUSTRIALIST TONY STARK...
BLACK BOLT, KING OF THE INHUMANS.
COLLECTIVELY, THE MOST FORMIDABLE MINDS ON EARTH.
INDIVIDUALLY, EACH AND EVERY ONE OF THEM ARE DOOMED INSOFAR AS THE HULK IS CONCERNED.

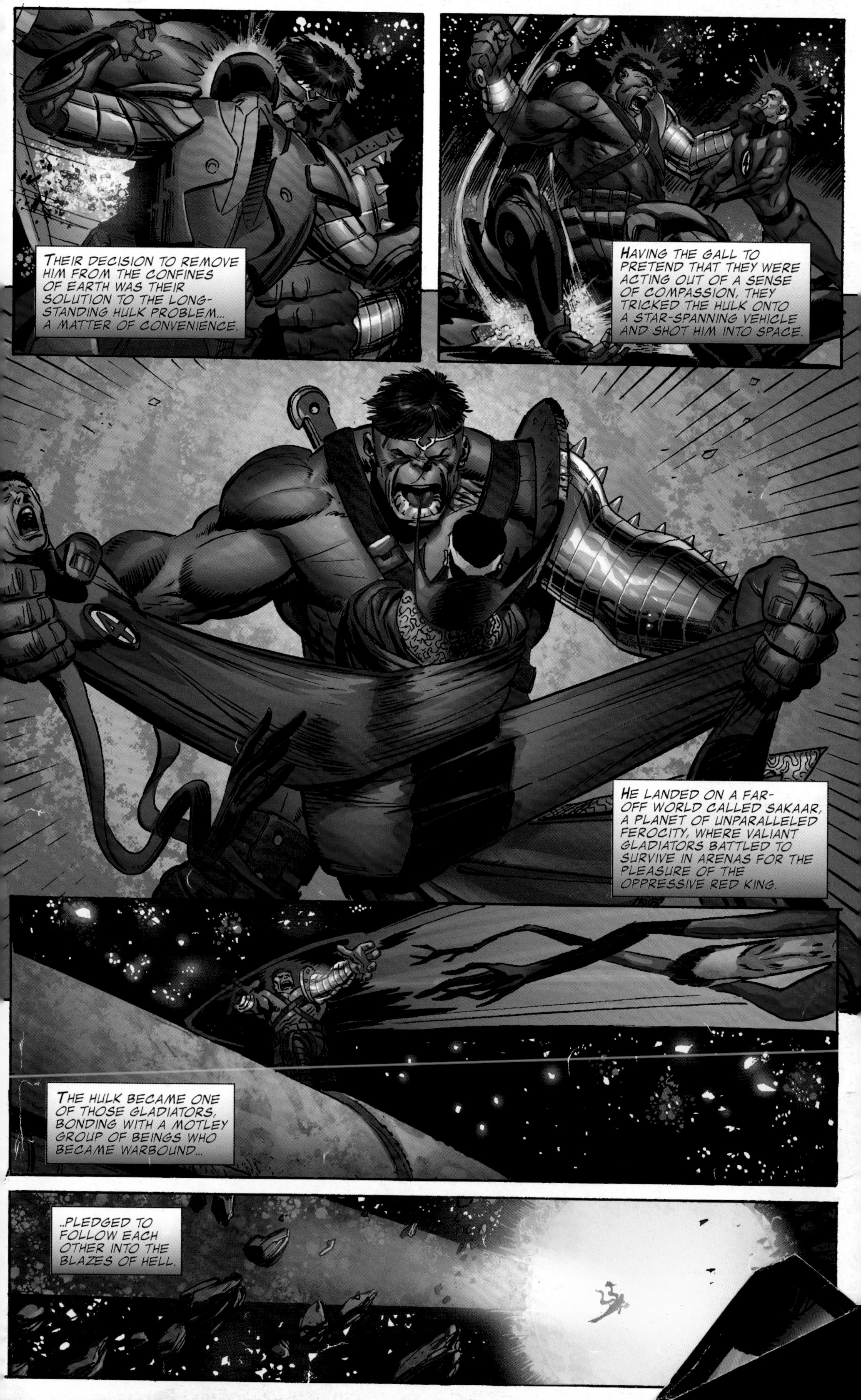
THEIR DECISION TO REMOVE HIM FROM THE CONFINES OF EARTH WAS THEIR SOLUTION TO THE LONG-STANDING HULK PROBLEM... A MATTER OF CONVENIENCE.
HAVING THE GALL TO PRETEND THAT THEY WERE ACTING OUT OF A SENSE OF COMPASSION, THEY TRICKED THE HULK ONTO A STAR-SPANNING VEHICLE AND SHOT HIM INTO SPACE.
HE LANDED ON A FAR-OFF WORLD CALLED SAKAAR, A PLANET OF UNPARALLELED FEROCITY, WHERE VALIANT GLADIATORS BATTLED TO SURVIVE IN ARENAS FOR THE PLEASURE OF THE OPPRESSIVE RED KING.
THE HULK BECAME ONE OF THOSE GLADIATORS, BONDING WITH A MOTLEY GROUP OF BEINGS WHO BECAME WARBOUND...
..PLEDGED TO FOLLOW EACH OTHER INTO THE BLAZES OF HELL.

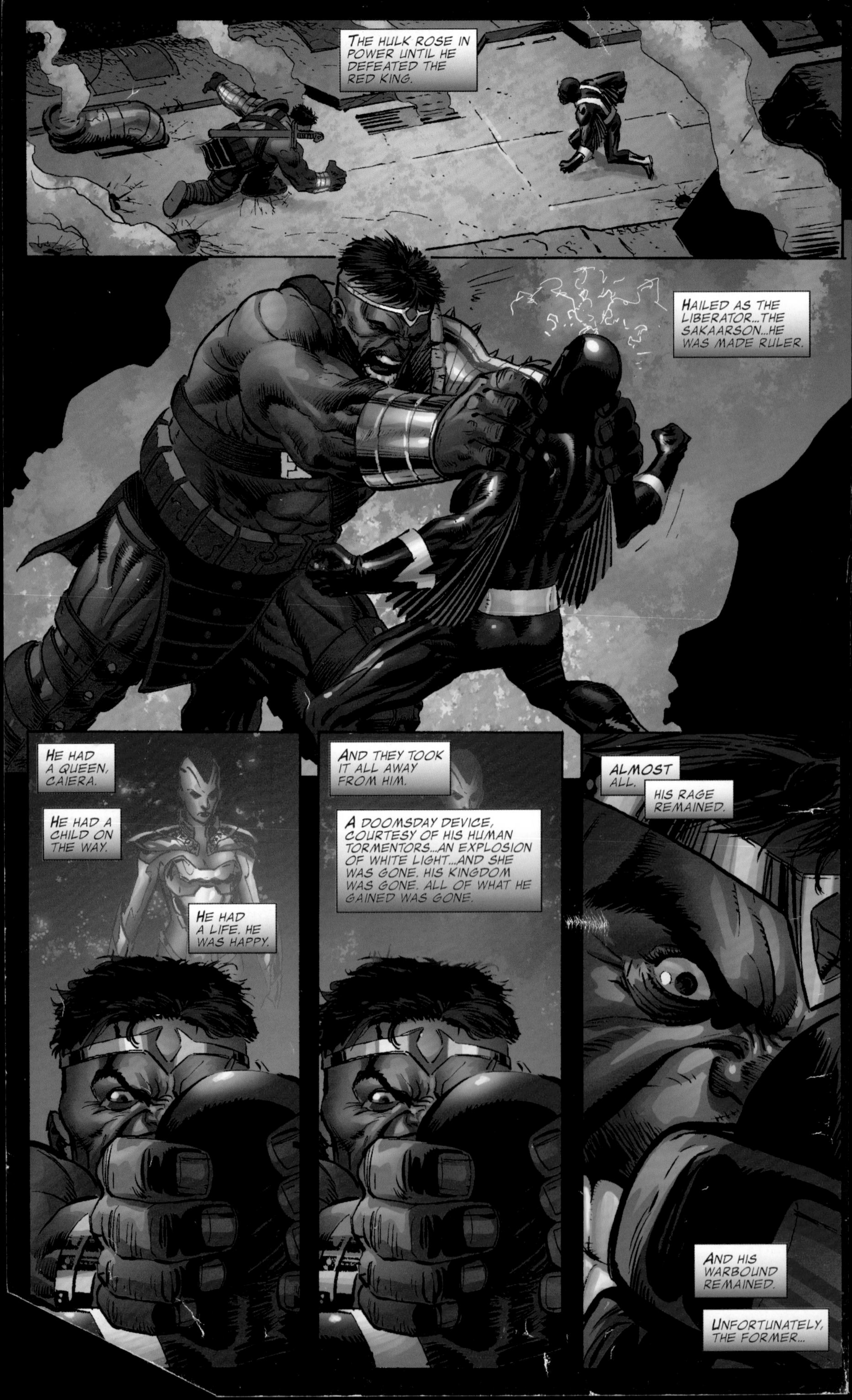
THE HULK ROSE IN POWER UNTIL HE DEFEATED THE RED KING.
HAILED AS THE LIBERATOR...THE SAKAARSON...HE WAS MADE RULER.
HE HAD A QUEEN, CAIERA.
HE HAD A CHILD ON THE WAY.
HE HAD A LIFE. HE WAS HAPPY.
AND THEY TOOK IT ALL AWAY FROM HIM.
A DOOMSDAY DEVICE, COURTESY OF HIS HUMAN TORMENTORS...AN EXPLOSION OF WHITE LIGHT...AND SHE WAS GONE. HIS KINGDOM WAS GONE. ALL OF WHAT HE GAINED WAS GONE.
ALMOST ALL.
HIS RAGE REMAINED.
AND HIS WARBOUND REMAINED.
UNFORTUNATELY, THE FORMER...

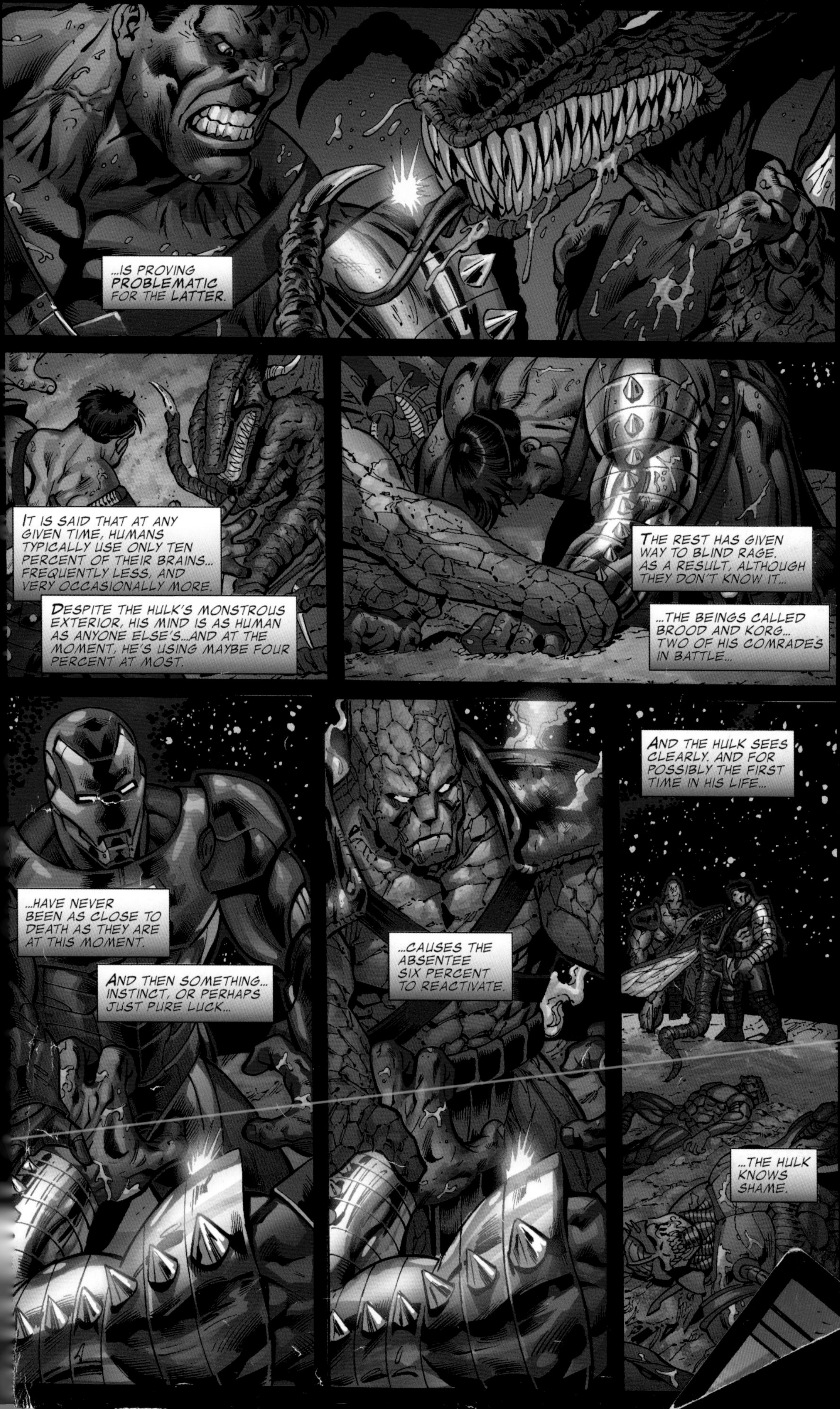
...IS PROVING PROBLEMATIC FOR THE LATTER.
IT IS SAID THAT AT ANY GIVEN TIME, HUMANS TYPICALLY USE ONLY TEN PERCENT OF THEIR BRAINS... FREQUENTLY LESS, AND VERY OCCASIONALLY MORE.
DESPITE THE HULK'S MONSTROUS EXTERIOR, HIS MIND IS AS HUMAN AS ANYONE ELSE'S...AND AT THE MOMENT, HE'S USING MAYBE FOUR PERCENT AT MOST.
THE REST HAS GIVEN WAY TO BLIND RAGE. AS A RESULT, ALTHOUGH THEY DON'T KNOW IT...
...THE BEINGS CALLED BROOD AND KORG... TWO OF HIS COMRADES IN BATTLE...
...HAVE NEVER BEEN AS CLOSE TO DEATH AS THEY ARE AT THIS MOMENT.
AND THEN SOMETHING... INSTINCT, OR PERHAPS JUST PURE LUCK...
...CAUSES THE ABSENTEE SIX PERCENT TO REACTIVATE.
AND THE HULK SEES CLEARLY. AND FOR POSSIBLY THE FIRST TIME IN HIS LIFE...
...THE HULK KNOWS SHAME.

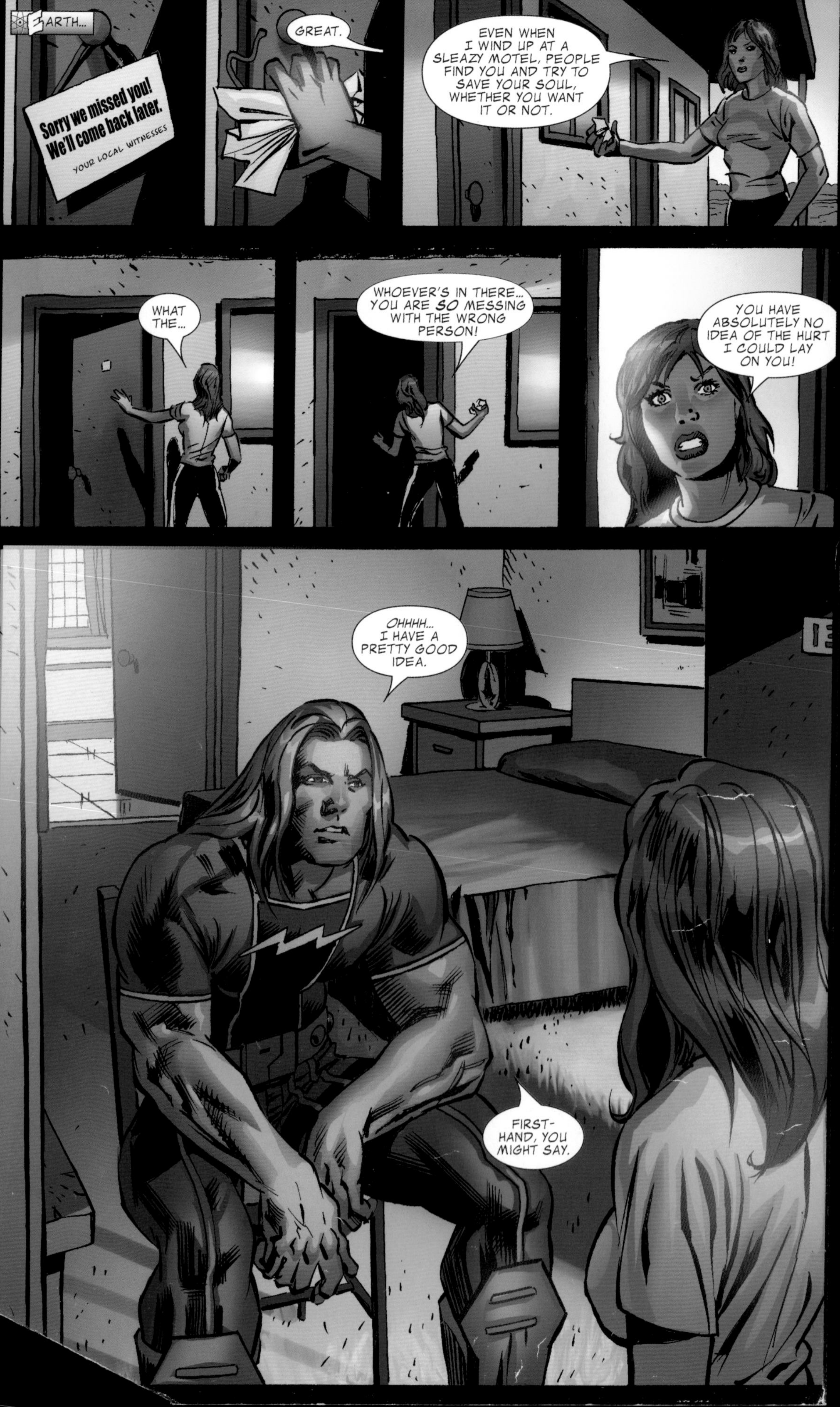
EARTH...
Sorry we missed you! We'll come back later.
YOUR LOCAL WITNESSES
GREAT.
EVEN WHEN I WIND UP AT A SLEAZY MOTEL, PEOPLE FIND YOU AND TRY TO SAVE YOUR SOUL, WHETHER YOU WANT IT OR NOT.
WHAT THE...
WHOEVER'S IN THERE... YOU ARE SO MESSING WITH THE WRONG PERSON!
YOU HAVE ABSOLUTELY NO IDEA OF THE HURT I COULD LAY ON YOU!
OHHHH... I HAVE A PRETTY GOOD IDEA.
FIRST-HAND, YOU MIGHT SAY.

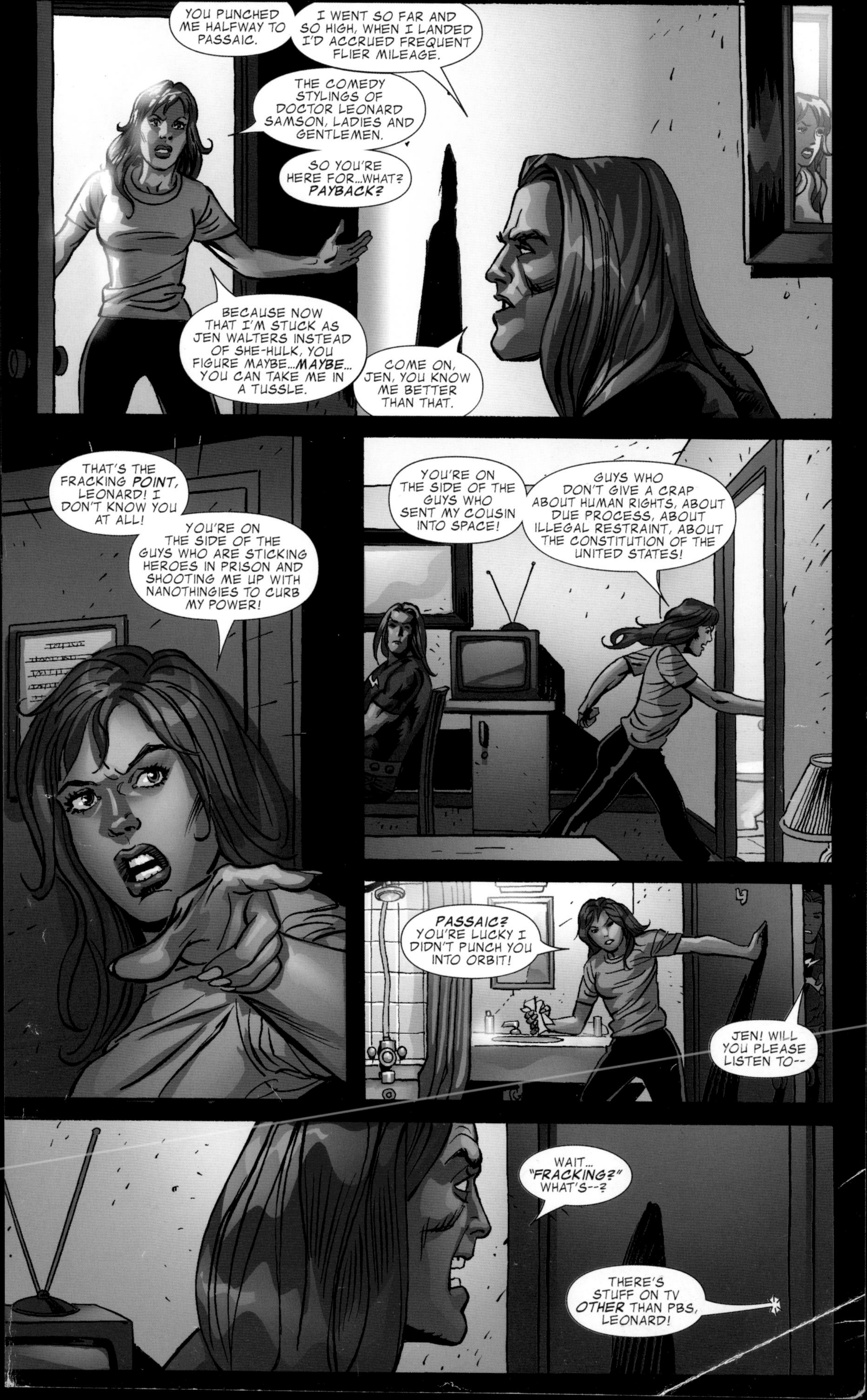
YOU PUNCHED ME HALFWAY TO PASSAIC.
I WENT SO FAR AND SO HIGH, WHEN I LANDED I'D ACCRUED FREQUENT FLIER MILEAGE.
THE COMEDY STYLINGS OF DOCTOR LEONARD SAMSON, LADIES AND GENTLEMEN.
SO YOU'RE HERE FOR...WHAT? PAYBACK?
BECAUSE NOW THAT I'M STUCK AS JEN WALTERS INSTEAD OF SHE-HULK, YOU FIGURE MAYBE...MAYBE... YOU CAN TAKE ME IN A TUSSLE.
COME ON, JEN, YOU KNOW ME BETTER THAN THAT.
THAT'S THE FRACKING POINT, LEONARD! I DON'T KNOW YOU AT ALL!
YOU'RE ON THE SIDE OF THE GUYS WHO ARE STICKING HEROES IN PRISON AND SHOOTING ME UP WITH NANOTHINGIES TO CURB MY POWER!
YOU'RE ON THE SIDE OF THE GUYS WHO SENT MY COUSIN INTO SPACE!
GUYS WHO DON'T GIVE A CRAP ABOUT HUMAN RIGHTS, ABOUT DUE PROCESS, ABOUT ILLEGAL RESTRAINT, ABOUT THE CONSTITUTION OF THE UNITED STATES!
PASSAIC? YOU'RE LUCKY I DIDN'T PUNCH YOU INTO ORBIT!
JEN! WILL YOU PLEASE LISTEN TO--
WAIT... "FRACKING?" WHAT'S--?
THERE'S STUFF ON TV OTHER THAN PBS, LEONARD!

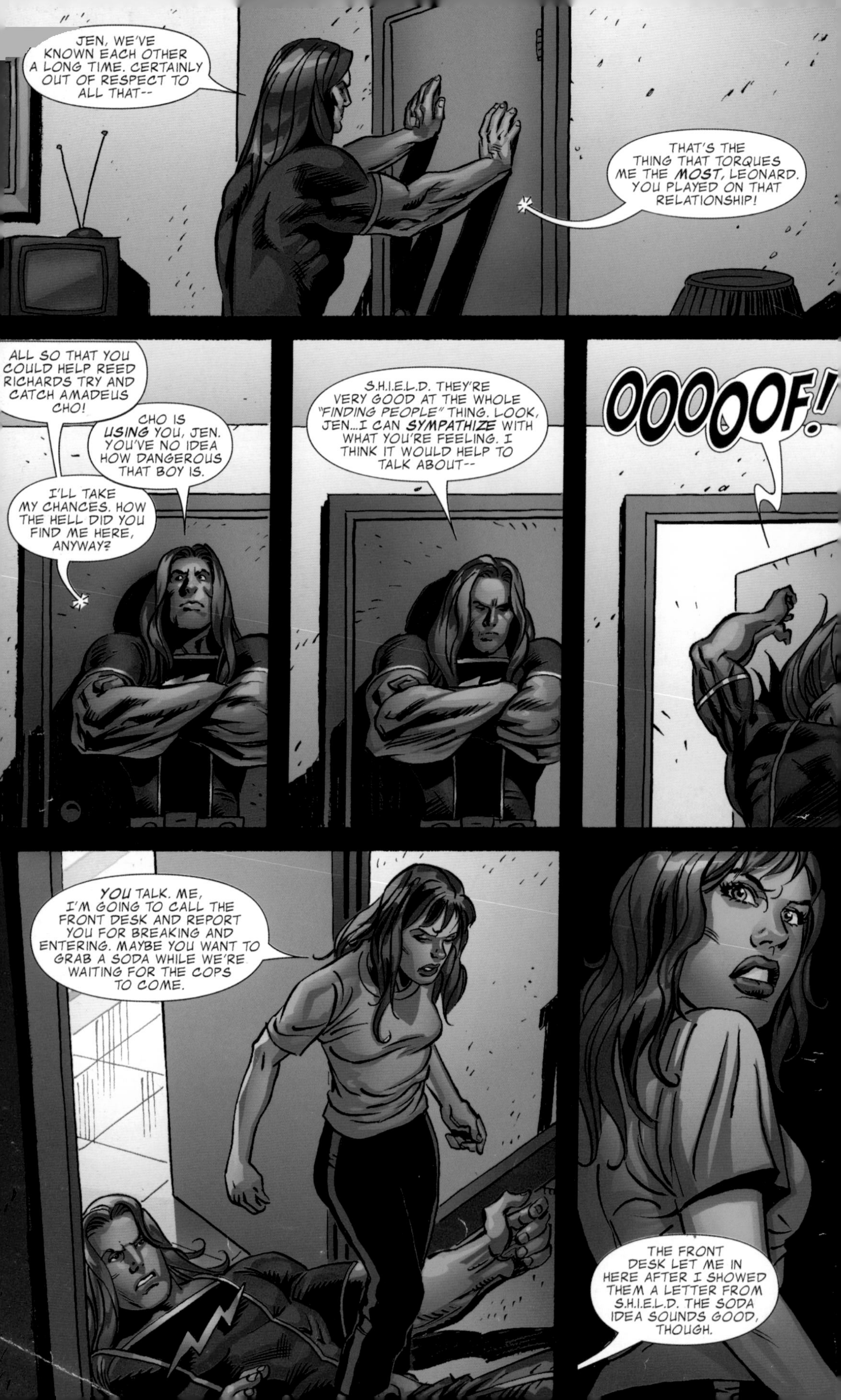
JEN, WE'VE KNOWN EACH OTHER A LONG TIME. CERTAINLY OUT OF RESPECT TO ALL THAT--
THAT'S THE THING THAT TORQUES ME THE MOST, LEONARD. YOU PLAYED ON THAT RELATIONSHIP!
ALL SO THAT YOU COULD HELP REED RICHARDS TRY AND CATCH AMADEUS CHO!
CHO IS USING YOU, JEN. YOU'VE NO IDEA HOW DANGEROUS THAT BOY IS.
I'LL TAKE MY CHANCES. HOW THE HELL DID YOU FIND ME HERE, ANYWAY?
S.H.I.E.L.D. THEY'RE VERY GOOD AT THE WHOLE "FINDING PEOPLE" THING. LOOK, JEN...I CAN SYMPATHIZE WITH WHAT YOU'RE FEELING. I THINK IT WOULD HELP TO TALK ABOUT--
OOOOOF!
YOU TALK. ME, I'M GOING TO CALL THE FRONT DESK AND REPORT YOU FOR BREAKING AND ENTERING. MAYBE YOU WANT TO GRAB A SODA WHILE WE'RE WAITING FOR THE COPS TO COME.
THE FRONT DESK LET ME IN HERE AFTER I SHOWED THEM A LETTER FROM S.H.I.E.L.D. THE SODA IDEA SOUNDS GOOD, THOUGH.

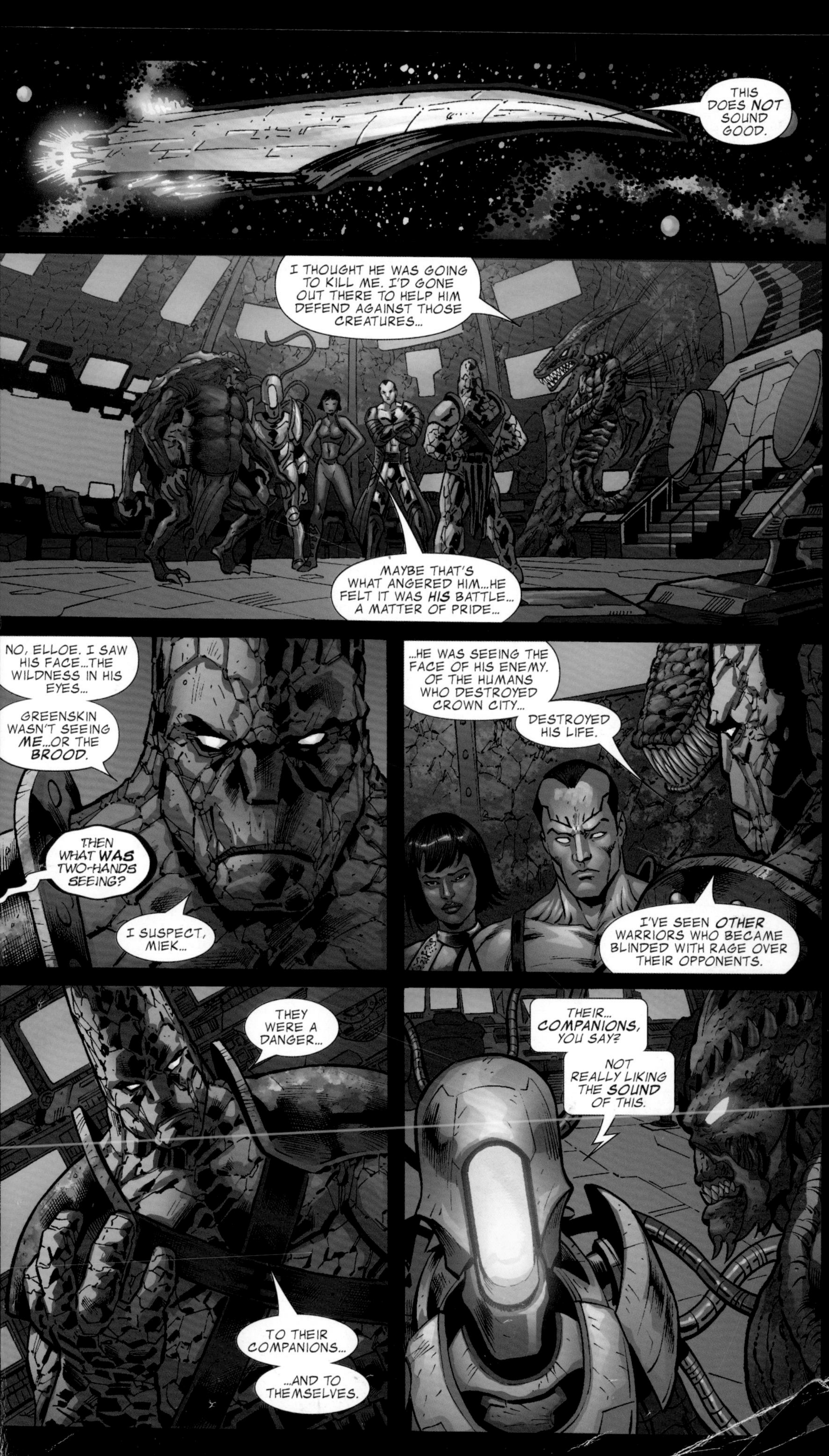
THIS DOES NOT SOUND GOOD.
I THOUGHT HE WAS GOING TO KILL ME. I'D GONE OUT THERE TO HELP HIM DEFEND AGAINST THOSE CREATURES...
MAYBE THAT'S WHAT ANGERED HIM...HE FELT IT WAS HIS BATTLE... A MATTER OF PRIDE...
NO, ELLOE. I SAW HIS FACE...THE WILDNESS IN HIS EYES...
GREENSKIN WASN'T SEEING ME...OR THE BROOD.
THEN WHAT WAS TWO-HANDS SEEING?
I SUSPECT, MIEK...
...HE WAS SEEING THE FACE OF HIS ENEMY. OF THE HUMANS WHO DESTROYED CROWN CITY...
DESTROYED HIS LIFE.
I'VE SEEN OTHER WARRIORS WHO BECAME BLINDED WITH RAGE OVER THEIR OPPONENTS.
THEY WERE A DANGER...
TO THEIR COMPANIONS...
...AND TO THEMSELVES.
THEIR... COMPANIONS, YOU SAY?
NOT REALLY LIKING THE SOUND OF THIS.

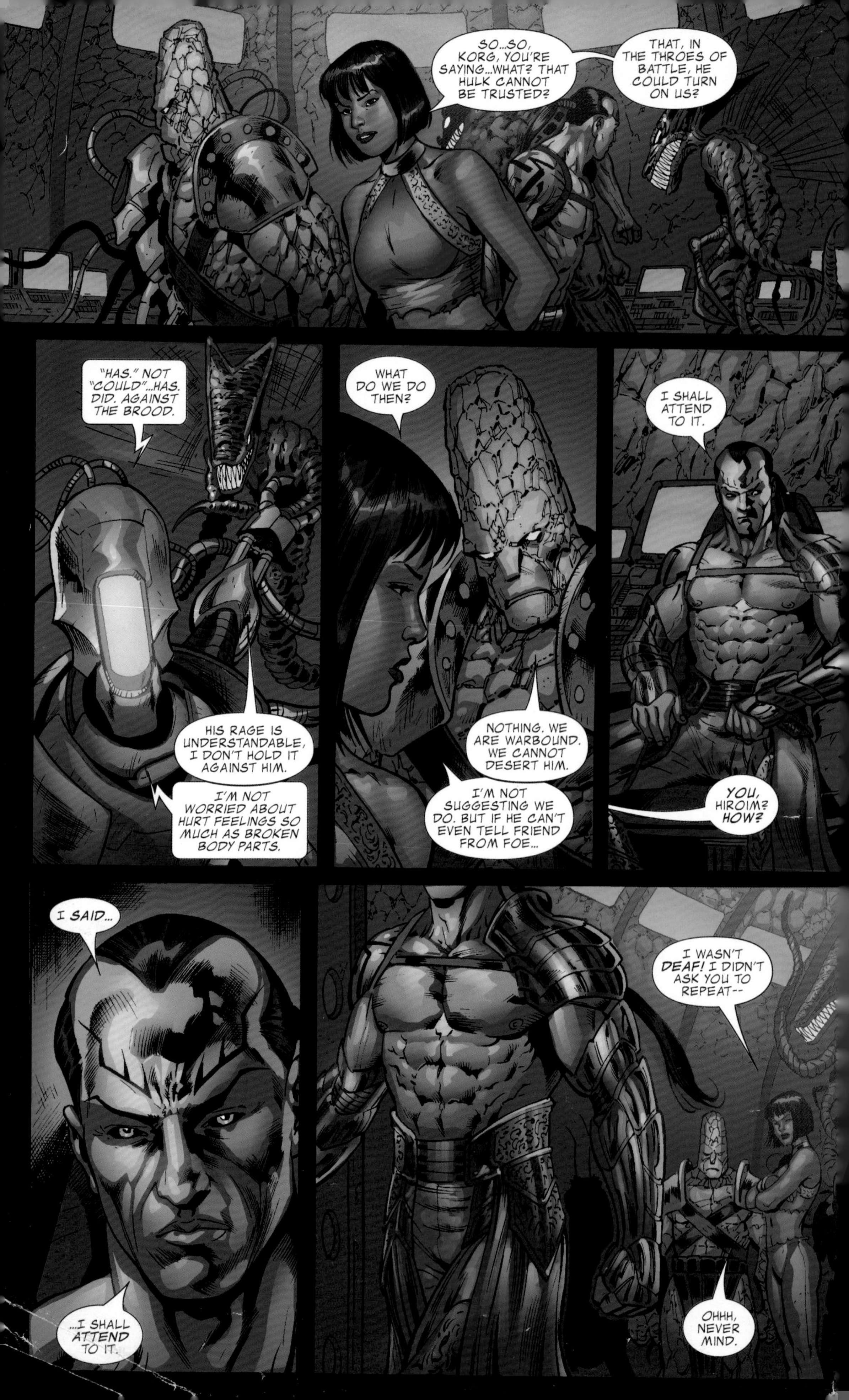
SO...SO, KORG, YOU'RE SAYING...WHAT? THAT HULK CANNOT BE TRUSTED?
THAT, IN THE THROES OF BATTLE, HE COULD TURN ON US?
"HAS." NOT "COULD"...HAS. DID. AGAINST THE BROOD.
HIS RAGE IS UNDERSTANDABLE, I DON'T HOLD IT AGAINST HIM.
I'M NOT WORRIED ABOUT HURT FEELINGS SO MUCH AS BROKEN BODY PARTS.
WHAT DO WE DO THEN?
NOTHING. WE ARE WARBOUND. WE CANNOT DESERT HIM.
I'M NOT SUGGESTING WE DO. BUT IF HE CAN'T EVEN TELL FRIEND FROM FOE...
I SHALL ATTEND TO IT.
YOU, HIROIM? HOW?
I SAID...
...I SHALL ATTEND TO IT.
I WASN'T DEAF! I DIDN'T ASK YOU TO REPEAT--
OHHH, NEVER MIND.

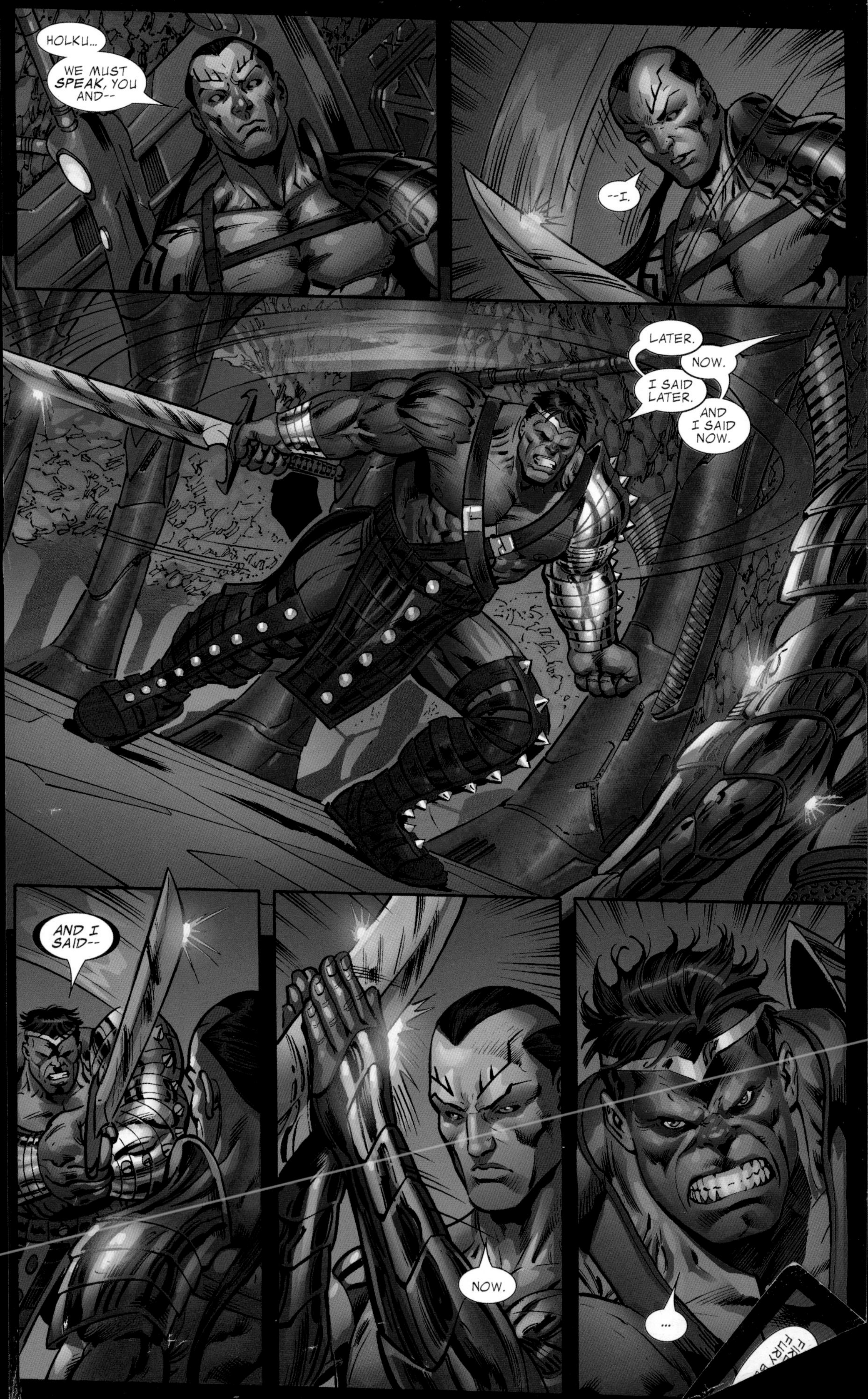
HOLKU...
WE MUST SPEAK, YOU AND--
--I.
LATER.
NOW.
I SAID LATER.
AND I SAID NOW.
AND I SAID--
NOW.
...

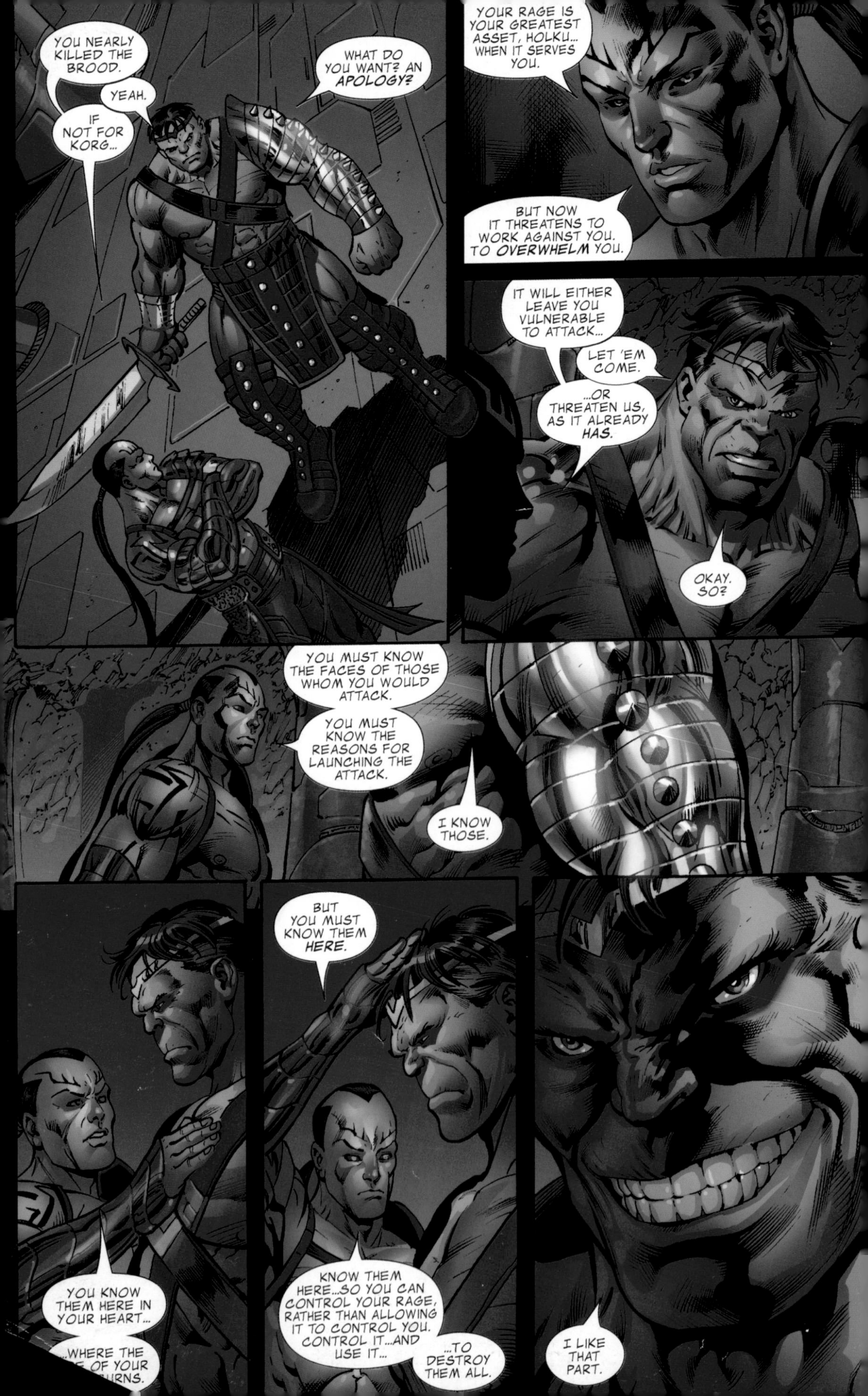
YOU NEARLY KILLED THE BROOD.
YEAH.
IF NOT FOR KORG...
WHAT DO YOU WANT? AN APOLOGY?
YOUR RAGE IS YOUR GREATEST ASSET, HOLKU... WHEN IT SERVES YOU.
BUT NOW IT THREATENS TO WORK AGAINST YOU. TO OVERWHELM YOU.
IT WILL EITHER LEAVE YOU VULNERABLE TO ATTACK...
LET 'EM COME.
...OR THREATEN US, AS IT ALREADY HAS.
OKAY. SO?
YOU MUST KNOW THE FACES OF THOSE WHOM YOU WOULD ATTACK.
YOU MUST KNOW THE REASONS FOR LAUNCHING THE ATTACK.
I KNOW THOSE.
BUT YOU MUST KNOW THEM HERE.
YOU KNOW THEM HERE IN YOUR HEART...
...WHERE THE OF YOUR
KNOW THEM HERE...SO YOU CAN CONTROL YOUR RAGE, RATHER THAN ALLOWING IT TO CONTROL YOU. CONTROL IT...AND USE IT...
...TO DESTROY THEM ALL.
I LIKE THAT PART.

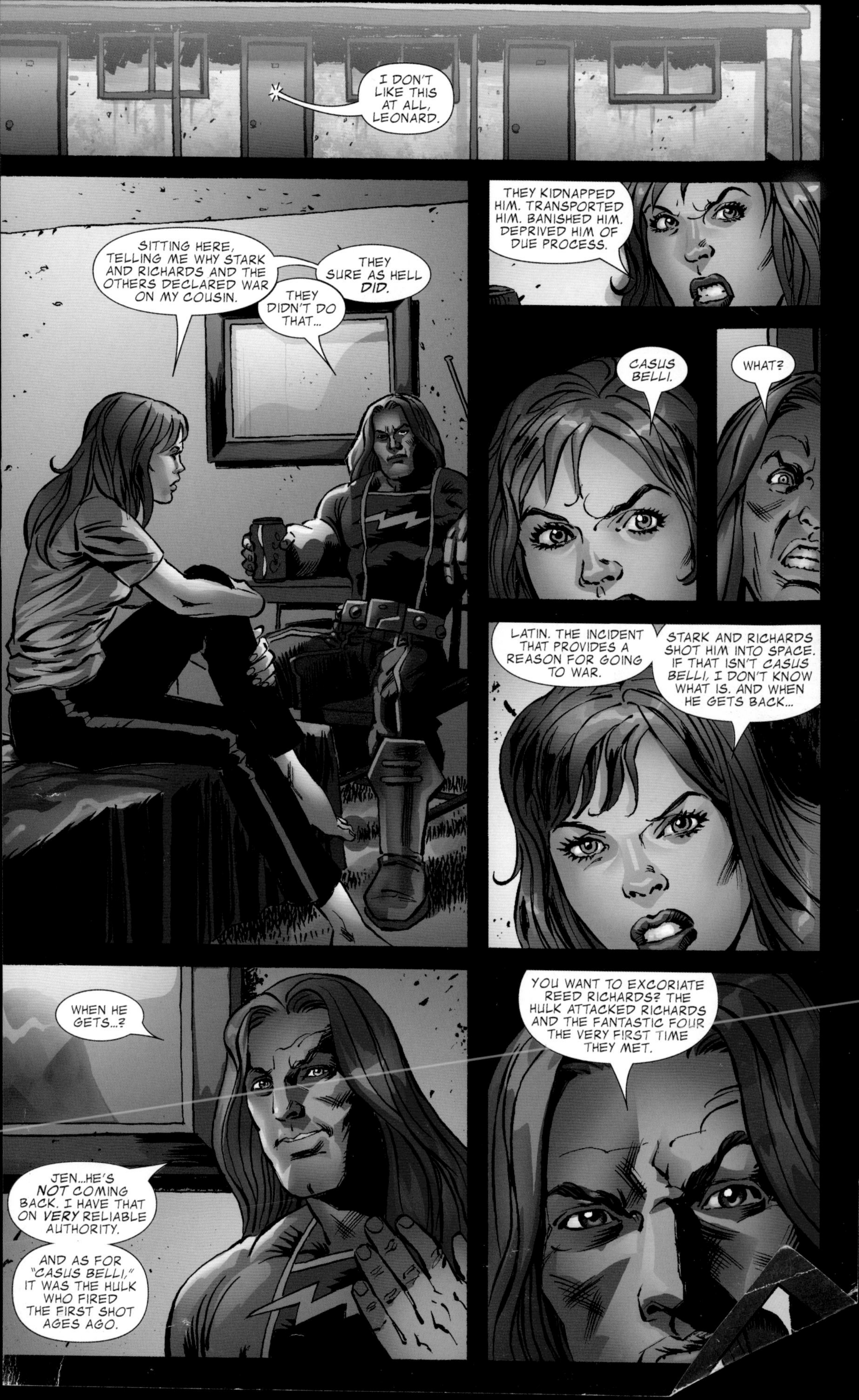
I DON'T LIKE THIS AT ALL, LEONARD.
SITTING HERE, TELLING ME WHY STARK AND RICHARDS AND THE OTHERS DECLARED WAR ON MY COUSIN.
THEY DIDN'T DO THAT...
THEY SURE AS HELL *DID*.
THEY KIDNAPPED HIM. TRANSPORTED HIM. BANISHED HIM. DEPRIVED HIM OF DUE PROCESS.
CASUS BELLI.
WHAT?
LATIN. THE INCIDENT THAT PROVIDES A REASON FOR GOING TO WAR.
STARK AND RICHARDS SHOT HIM INTO SPACE. IF THAT ISN'T *CASUS BELLI*, I DON'T KNOW WHAT IS. AND WHEN HE GETS BACK...
WHEN HE GETS...?
JEN...HE'S *NOT* COMING BACK. I HAVE THAT ON *VERY* RELIABLE AUTHORITY.
AND AS FOR *"CASUS BELLI,"* IT WAS THE HULK WHO FIRED THE FIRST SHOT AGES AGO.
YOU WANT TO EXCORIATE REED RICHARDS? THE HULK ATTACKED RICHARDS AND THE FANTASTIC FOUR THE VERY FIRST TIME THEY MET.

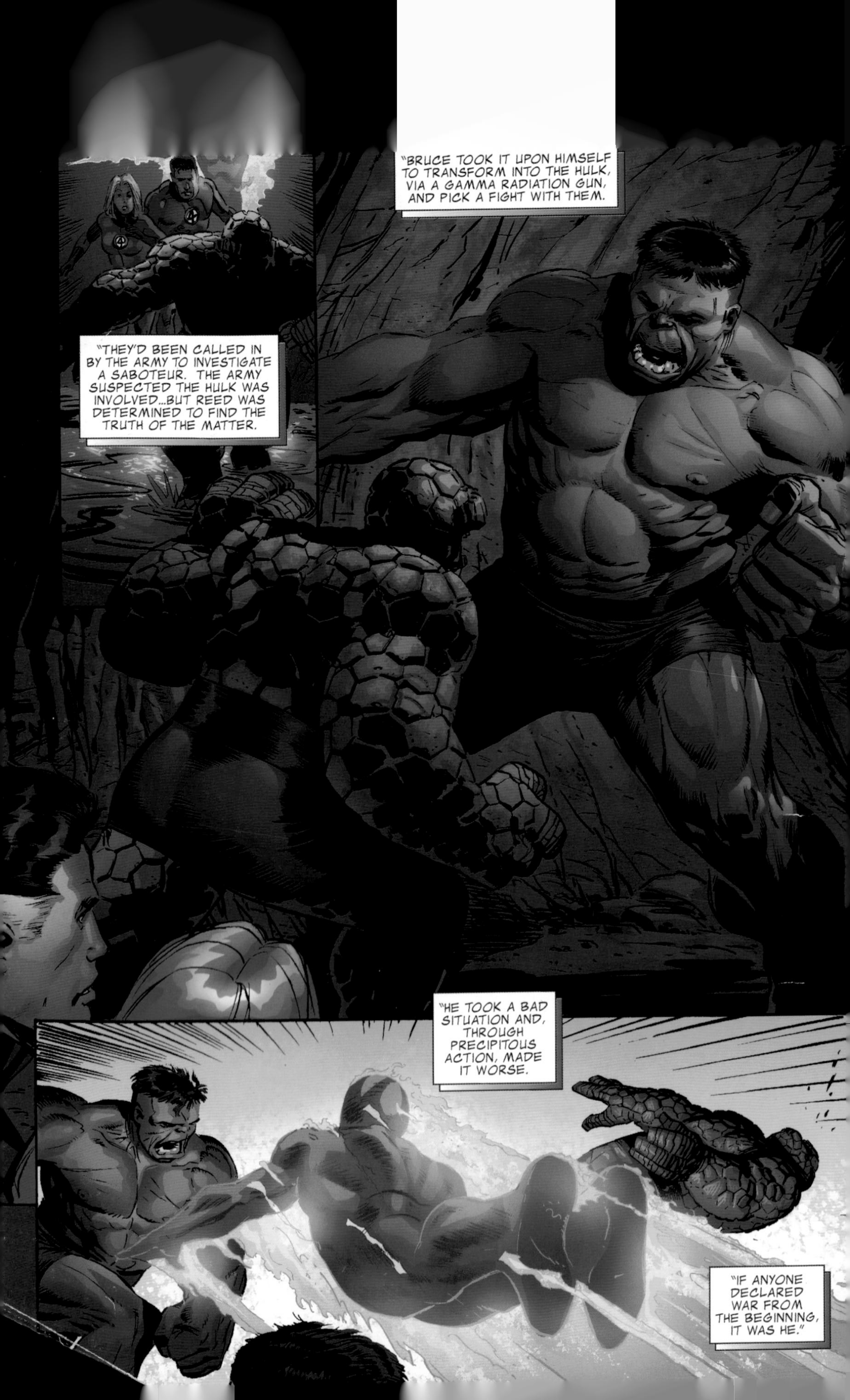
"THEY'D BEEN CALLED IN BY THE ARMY TO INVESTIGATE A SABOTEUR. THE ARMY SUSPECTED THE HULK WAS INVOLVED...BUT REED WAS DETERMINED TO FIND THE TRUTH OF THE MATTER.
"BRUCE TOOK IT UPON HIMSELF TO TRANSFORM INTO THE HULK, VIA A GAMMA RADIATION GUN, AND PICK A FIGHT WITH THEM.
"HE TOOK A BAD SITUATION AND, THROUGH PRECIPITOUS ACTION, MADE IT WORSE.
"IF ANYONE DECLARED WAR FROM THE BEGINNING, IT WAS HE."

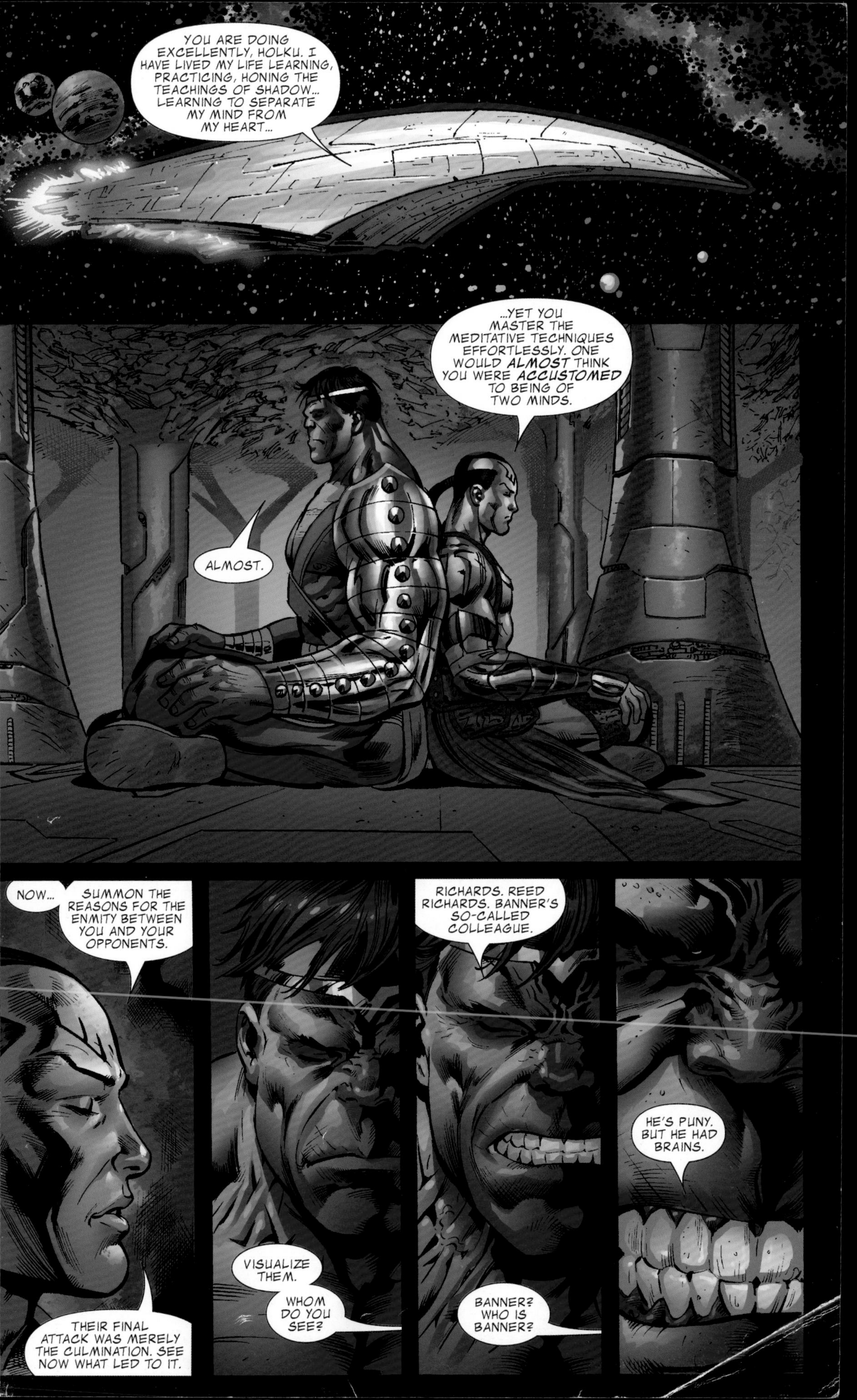
YOU ARE DOING EXCELLENTLY, HOLKU. I HAVE LIVED MY LIFE LEARNING, PRACTICING, HONING THE TEACHINGS OF SHADOW... LEARNING TO SEPARATE MY MIND FROM MY HEART...
...YET YOU MASTER THE MEDITATIVE TECHNIQUES EFFORTLESSLY. ONE WOULD ALMOST THINK YOU WERE ACCUSTOMED TO BEING OF TWO MINDS.
ALMOST.
NOW...
SUMMON THE REASONS FOR THE ENMITY BETWEEN YOU AND YOUR OPPONENTS.
THEIR FINAL ATTACK WAS MERELY THE CULMINATION. SEE NOW WHAT LED TO IT.
VISUALIZE THEM.
WHOM DO YOU SEE?
RICHARDS. REED RICHARDS. BANNER'S SO-CALLED COLLEAGUE.
BANNER? WHO IS BANNER?
HE'S PUNY. BUT HE HAD BRAINS.

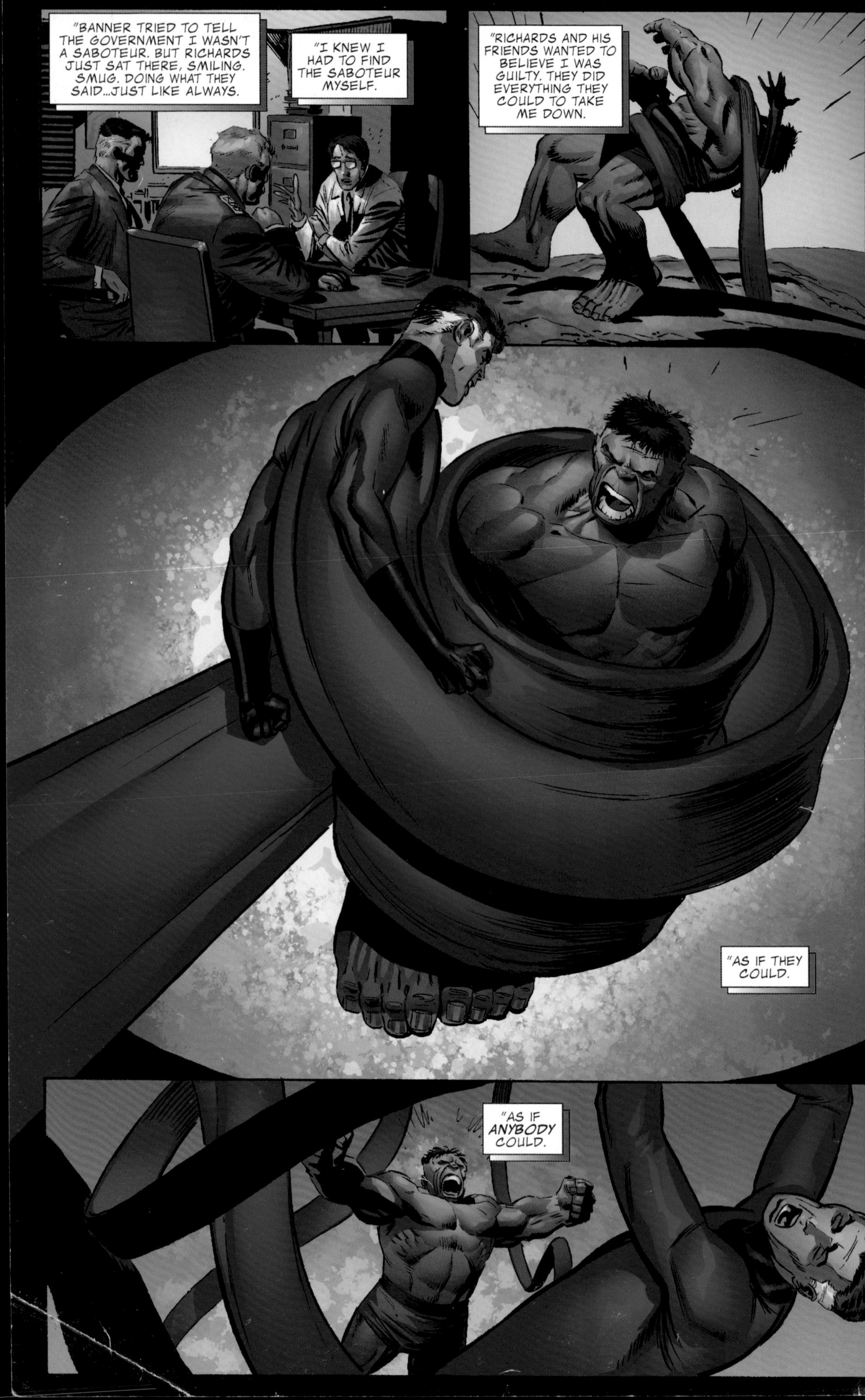
"BANNER TRIED TO TELL THE GOVERNMENT I WASN'T A SABOTEUR. BUT RICHARDS JUST SAT THERE, SMILING. SMUG. DOING WHAT THEY SAID...JUST LIKE ALWAYS.
"I KNEW I HAD TO FIND THE SABOTEUR MYSELF.
"RICHARDS AND HIS FRIENDS WANTED TO BELIEVE I WAS GUILTY. THEY DID EVERYTHING THEY COULD TO TAKE ME DOWN.
"AS IF THEY COULD.
"AS IF ANYBODY COULD.

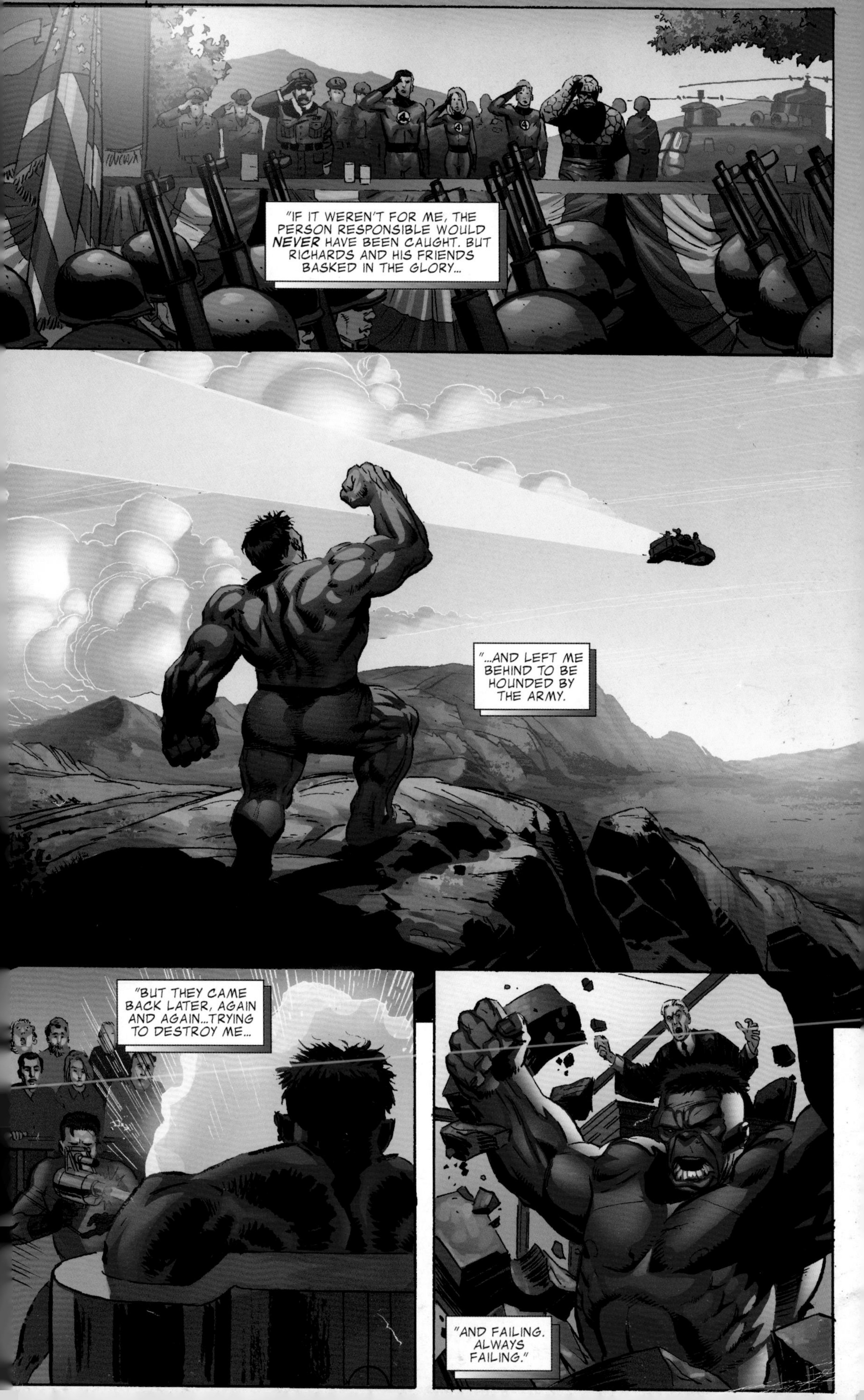
"IF IT WEREN'T FOR ME, THE PERSON RESPONSIBLE WOULD **NEVER** HAVE BEEN CAUGHT. BUT RICHARDS AND HIS FRIENDS BASKED IN THE GLORY...
"...AND LEFT ME BEHIND TO BE HOUNDED BY THE ARMY.
"BUT THEY CAME BACK LATER, AGAIN AND AGAIN...TRYING TO DESTROY ME...
"AND FAILING. ALWAYS FAILING."

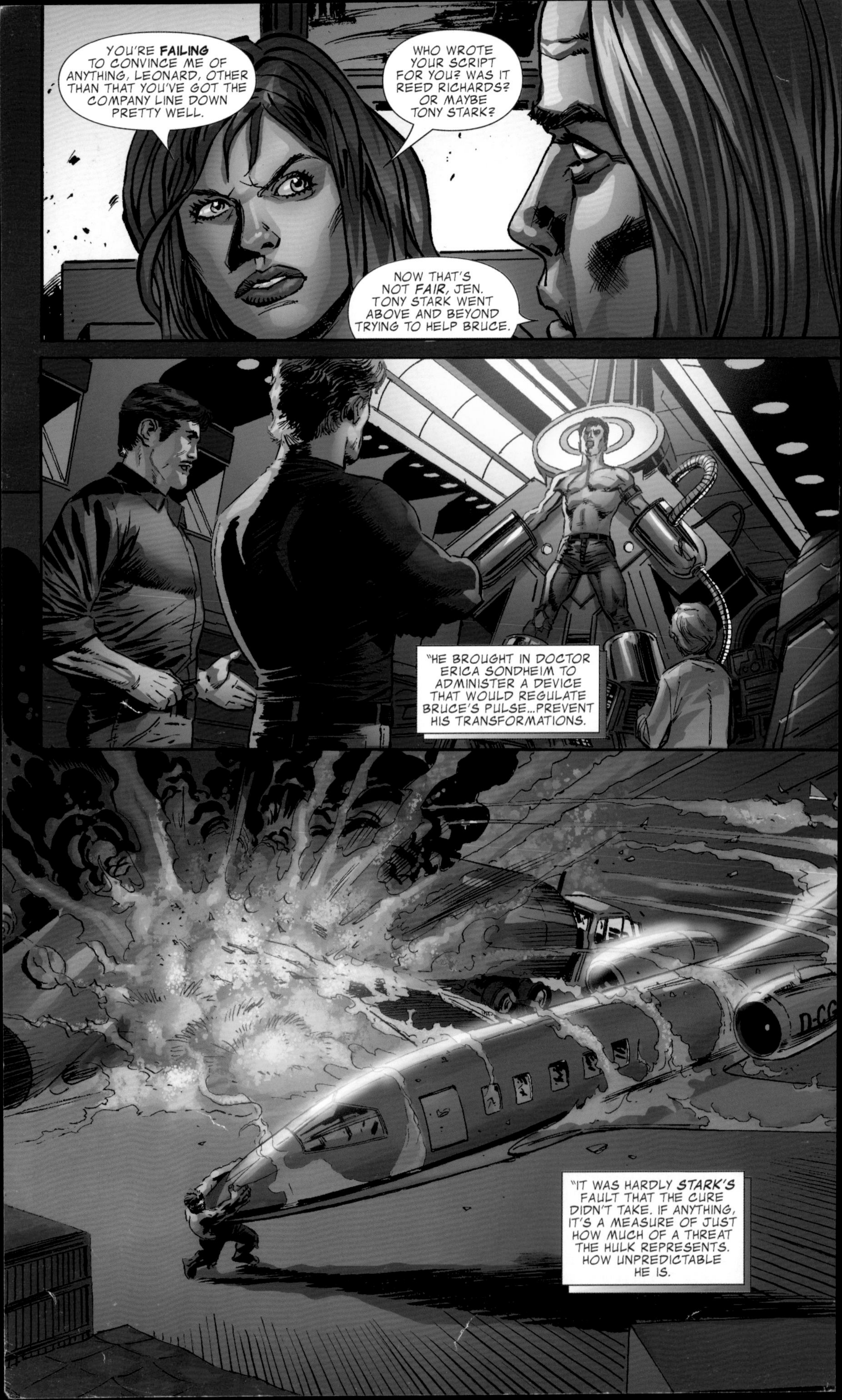

YOU'RE **FAILING** TO CONVINCE ME OF ANYTHING, LEONARD, OTHER THAN THAT YOU'VE GOT THE COMPANY LINE DOWN PRETTY WELL.
WHO WROTE YOUR SCRIPT FOR YOU? WAS IT REED RICHARDS? OR MAYBE TONY STARK?
NOW THAT'S NOT ***FAIR***, JEN. TONY STARK WENT ABOVE AND BEYOND TRYING TO HELP BRUCE.
"HE BROUGHT IN DOCTOR ERICA SONDHEIM TO ADMINISTER A DEVICE THAT WOULD REGULATE BRUCE'S PULSE...PREVENT HIS TRANSFORMATIONS.
"IT WAS HARDLY ***STARK'S*** FAULT THAT THE CURE DIDN'T TAKE. IF ANYTHING, IT'S A MEASURE OF JUST HOW MUCH OF A THREAT THE HULK REPRESENTS. HOW UNPREDICTABLE HE IS.

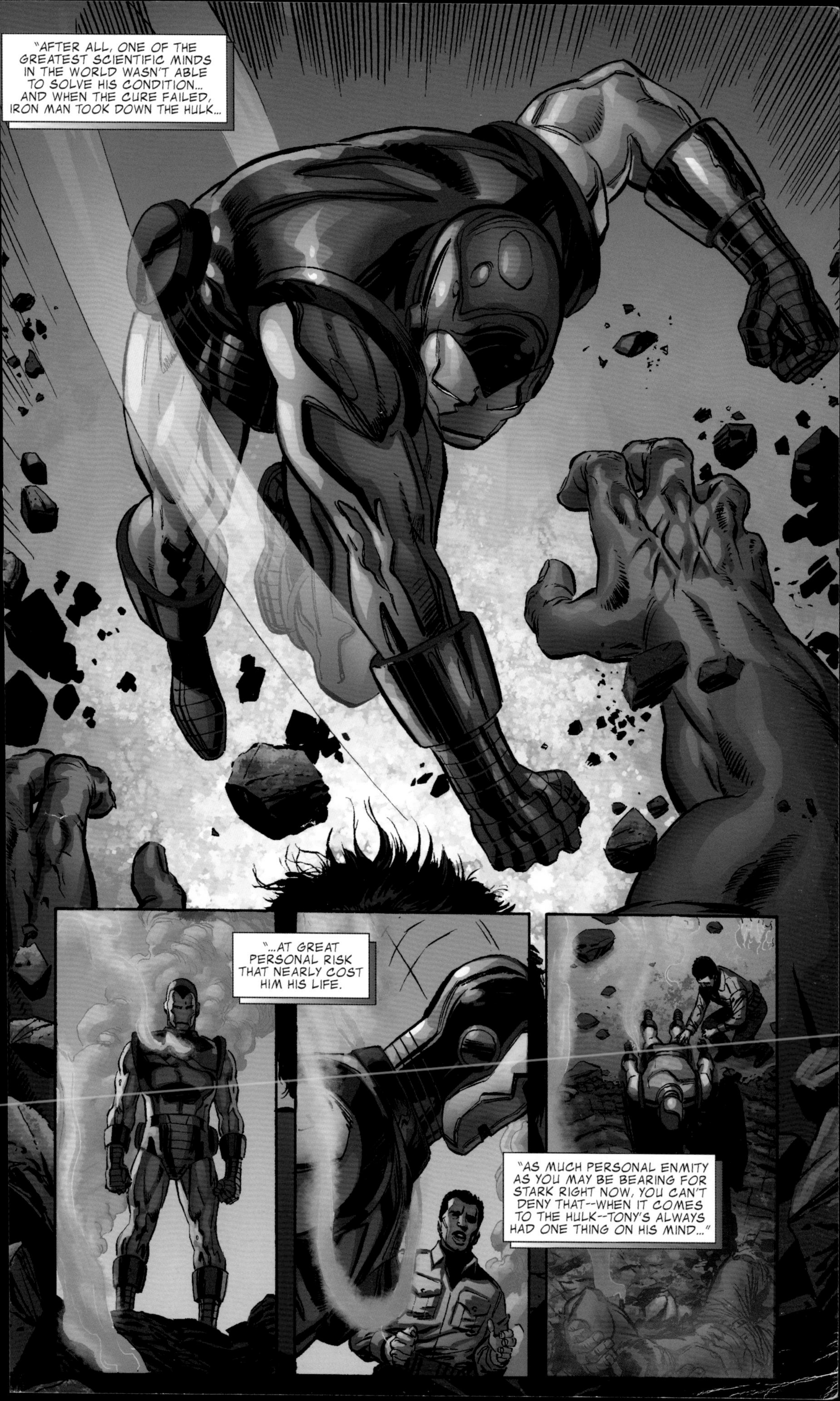
"AFTER ALL, ONE OF THE GREATEST SCIENTIFIC MINDS IN THE WORLD WASN'T ABLE TO SOLVE HIS CONDITION... AND WHEN THE CURE FAILED, IRON MAN TOOK DOWN THE HULK...
"...AT GREAT PERSONAL RISK THAT NEARLY COST HIM HIS LIFE.
"AS MUCH PERSONAL ENMITY AS YOU MAY BE BEARING FOR STARK RIGHT NOW, YOU CAN'T DENY THAT--WHEN IT COMES TO THE HULK--TONY'S ALWAYS HAD ONE THING ON HIS MIND..."

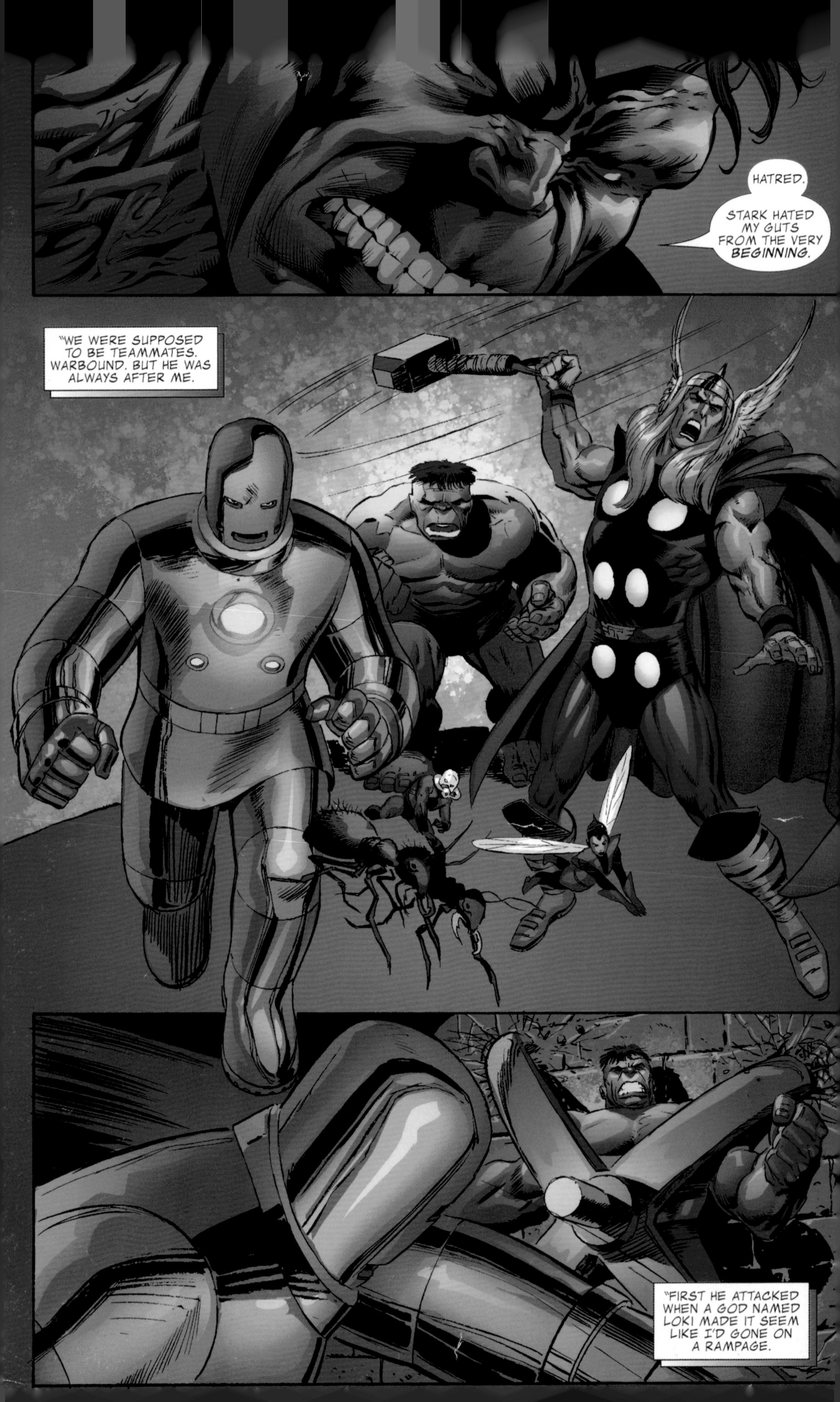
HATRED.
STARK HATED MY GUTS FROM THE VERY BEGINNING.
"WE WERE SUPPOSED TO BE TEAMMATES. WARBOUND. BUT HE WAS ALWAYS AFTER ME.
"FIRST HE ATTACKED WHEN A GOD NAMED LOKI MADE IT SEEM LIKE I'D GONE ON A RAMPAGE.

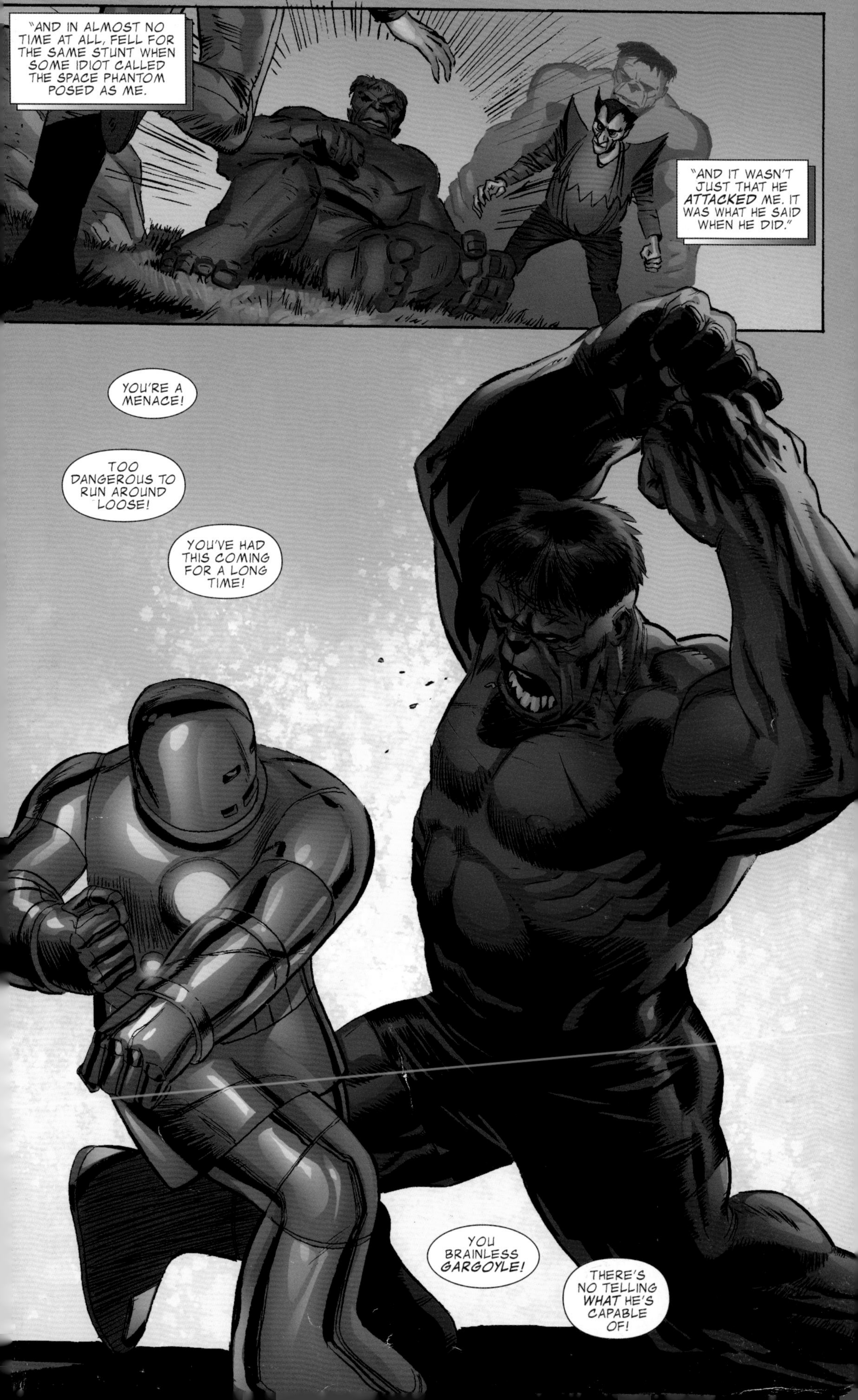
"AND IN ALMOST NO TIME AT ALL, FELL FOR THE SAME STUNT WHEN SOME IDIOT CALLED THE SPACE PHANTOM POSED AS ME.
"AND IT WASN'T JUST THAT HE ATTACKED ME. IT WAS WHAT HE SAID WHEN HE DID."
YOU'RE A MENACE!
TOO DANGEROUS TO RUN AROUND LOOSE!
YOU'VE HAD THIS COMING FOR A LONG TIME!
YOU BRAINLESS GARGOYLE!
THERE'S NO TELLING WHAT HE'S CAPABLE OF!

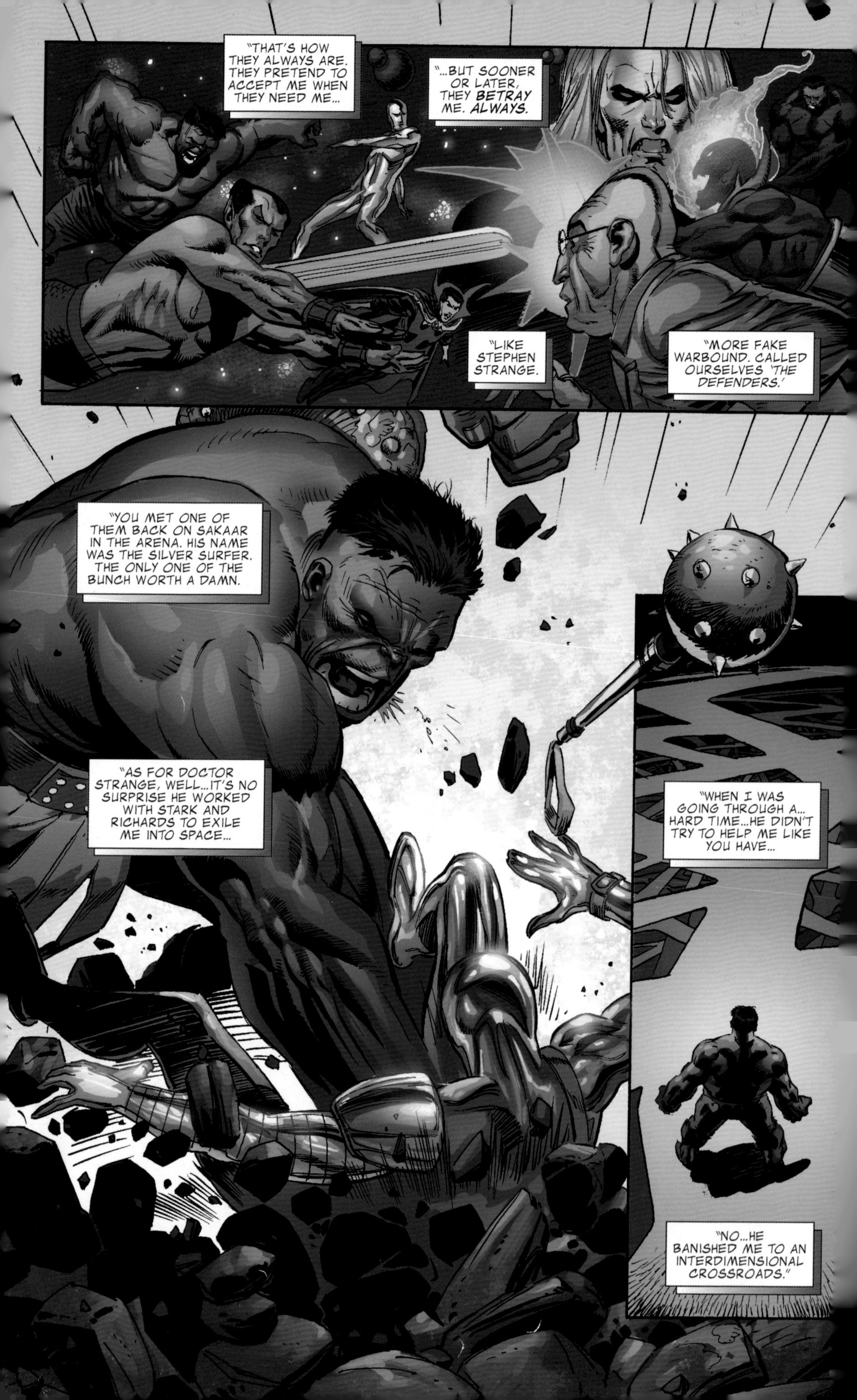

"THAT'S HOW THEY ALWAYS ARE. THEY PRETEND TO ACCEPT ME WHEN THEY NEED ME...
"...BUT SOONER OR LATER, THEY *BETRAY* ME. *ALWAYS.*
"LIKE STEPHEN STRANGE.
"MORE FAKE WARBOUND. CALLED OURSELVES 'THE DEFENDERS.'
"YOU MET ONE OF THEM BACK ON SAKAAR IN THE ARENA. HIS NAME WAS THE SILVER SURFER. THE ONLY ONE OF THE BUNCH WORTH A DAMN.
"AS FOR DOCTOR STRANGE, WELL...IT'S NO SURPRISE HE WORKED WITH STARK AND RICHARDS TO EXILE ME INTO SPACE...
"WHEN I WAS GOING THROUGH A... HARD TIME...HE DIDN'T TRY TO HELP ME LIKE YOU HAVE...
"NO...HE BANISHED ME TO AN INTERDIMENSIONAL CROSSROADS."

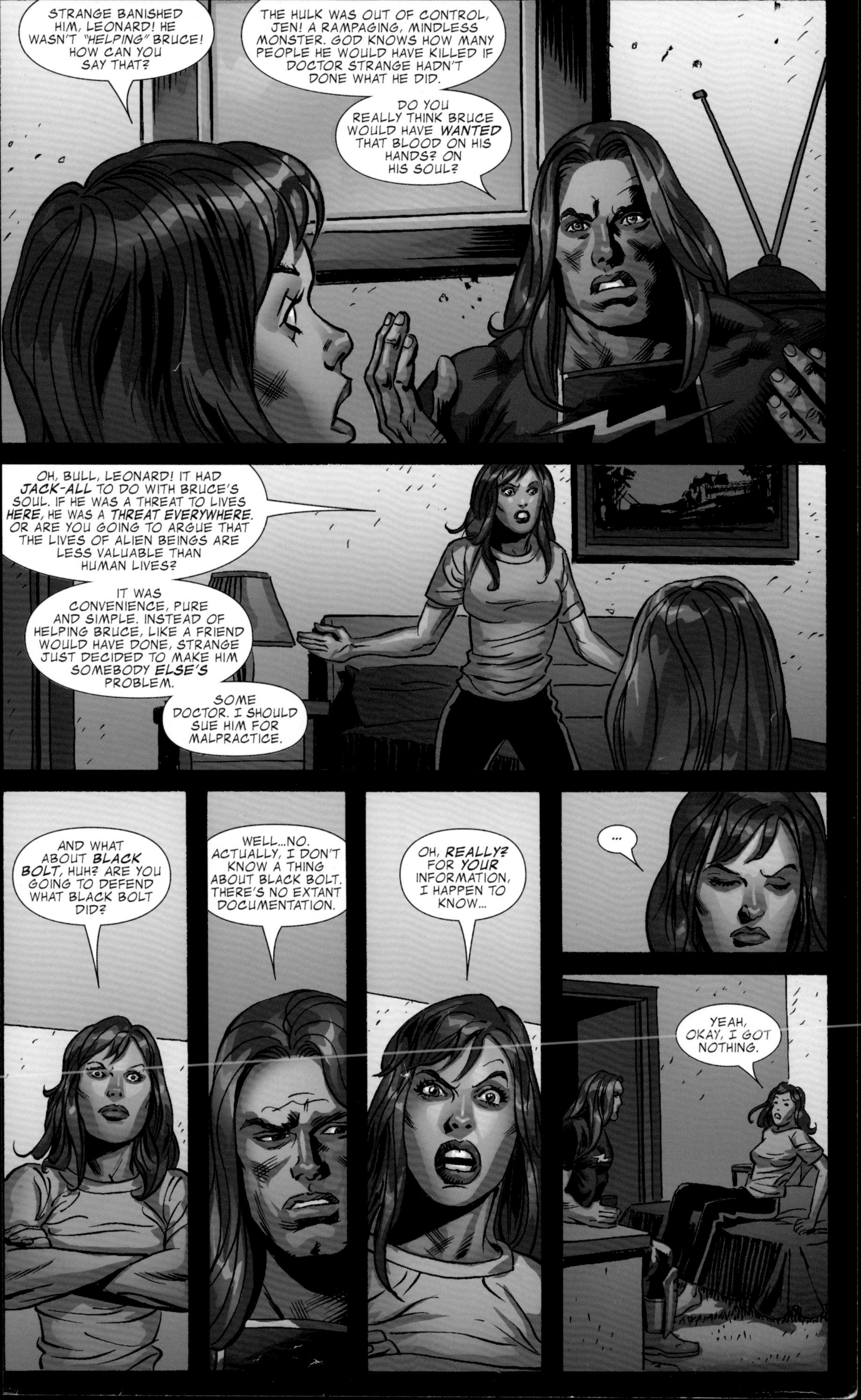
STRANGE BANISHED HIM, LEONARD! HE WASN'T "HELPING" BRUCE! HOW CAN YOU SAY THAT?
THE HULK WAS OUT OF CONTROL, JEN! A RAMPAGING, MINDLESS MONSTER. GOD KNOWS HOW MANY PEOPLE HE WOULD HAVE KILLED IF DOCTOR STRANGE HADN'T DONE WHAT HE DID.
DO YOU REALLY THINK BRUCE WOULD HAVE WANTED THAT BLOOD ON HIS HANDS? ON HIS SOUL?
OH, BULL, LEONARD! IT HAD JACK-ALL TO DO WITH BRUCE'S SOUL. IF HE WAS A THREAT TO LIVES HERE, HE WAS A THREAT EVERYWHERE. OR ARE YOU GOING TO ARGUE THAT THE LIVES OF ALIEN BEINGS ARE LESS VALUABLE THAN HUMAN LIVES?
IT WAS CONVENIENCE, PURE AND SIMPLE. INSTEAD OF HELPING BRUCE, LIKE A FRIEND WOULD HAVE DONE, STRANGE JUST DECIDED TO MAKE HIM SOMEBODY ELSE'S PROBLEM.
SOME DOCTOR. I SHOULD SUE HIM FOR MALPRACTICE.
AND WHAT ABOUT BLACK BOLT, HUH? ARE YOU GOING TO DEFEND WHAT BLACK BOLT DID?
WELL...NO. ACTUALLY, I DON'T KNOW A THING ABOUT BLACK BOLT. THERE'S NO EXTANT DOCUMENTATION.
OH, REALLY? FOR YOUR INFORMATION, I HAPPEN TO KNOW...
...
YEAH, OKAY, I GOT NOTHING.

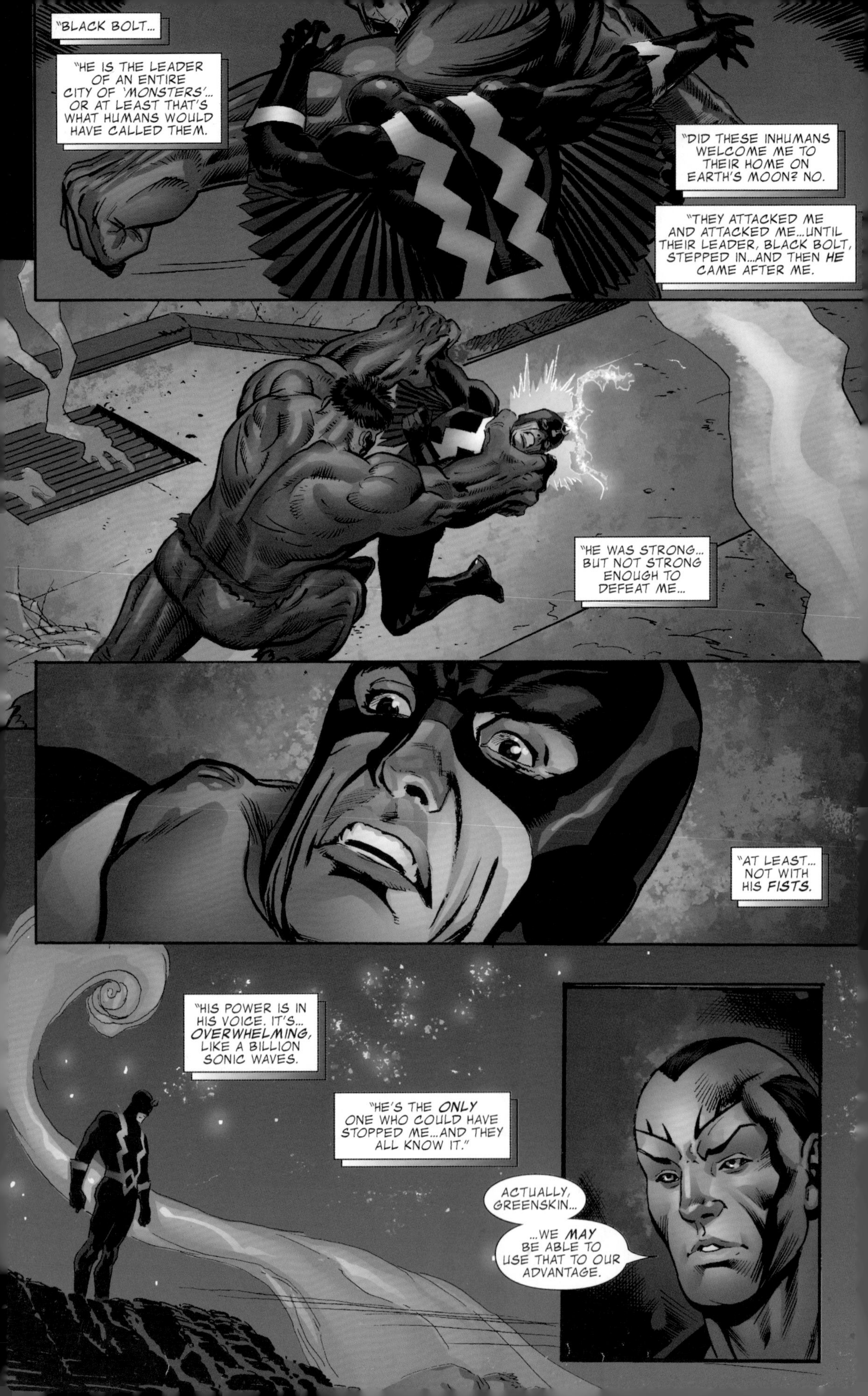
"BLACK BOLT...
"HE IS THE LEADER OF AN ENTIRE CITY OF 'MONSTERS'... OR AT LEAST THAT'S WHAT HUMANS WOULD HAVE CALLED THEM.
"DID THESE INHUMANS WELCOME ME TO THEIR HOME ON EARTH'S MOON? NO.
"THEY ATTACKED ME AND ATTACKED ME...UNTIL THEIR LEADER, BLACK BOLT, STEPPED IN...AND THEN *HE* CAME AFTER ME.
"HE WAS STRONG... BUT NOT STRONG ENOUGH TO DEFEAT ME...
"AT LEAST... NOT WITH HIS *FISTS*.
"HIS POWER IS IN HIS VOICE. IT'S... *OVERWHELMING*, LIKE A BILLION SONIC WAVES.
"HE'S THE *ONLY* ONE WHO COULD HAVE STOPPED ME...AND THEY ALL KNOW IT."
ACTUALLY, GREENSKIN...
...WE *MAY* BE ABLE TO USE THAT TO OUR ADVANTAGE.

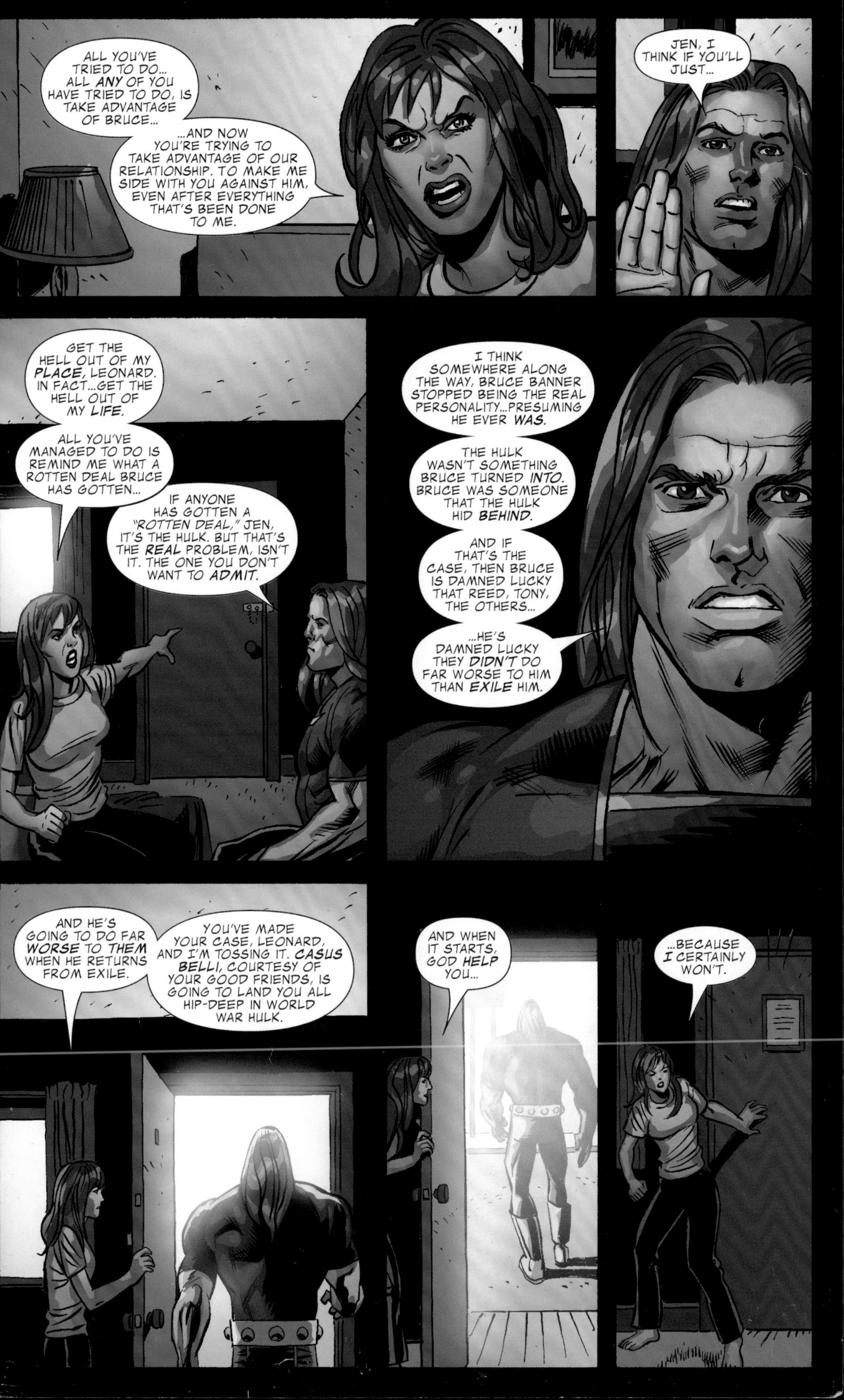
ALL YOU'VE TRIED TO DO... ALL ANY OF YOU HAVE TRIED TO DO, IS TAKE ADVANTAGE OF BRUCE...
...AND NOW YOU'RE TRYING TO TAKE ADVANTAGE OF OUR RELATIONSHIP. TO MAKE ME SIDE WITH YOU AGAINST HIM, EVEN AFTER EVERYTHING THAT'S BEEN DONE TO ME.
JEN, I THINK IF YOU'LL JUST...
GET THE HELL OUT OF MY PLACE, LEONARD. IN FACT...GET THE HELL OUT OF MY LIFE.
ALL YOU'VE MANAGED TO DO IS REMIND ME WHAT A ROTTEN DEAL BRUCE HAS GOTTEN...
IF ANYONE HAS GOTTEN A "ROTTEN DEAL," JEN, IT'S THE HULK. BUT THAT'S THE REAL PROBLEM, ISN'T IT. THE ONE YOU DON'T WANT TO ADMIT.
I THINK SOMEWHERE ALONG THE WAY, BRUCE BANNER STOPPED BEING THE REAL PERSONALITY...PRESUMING HE EVER WAS.
THE HULK WASN'T SOMETHING BRUCE TURNED INTO. BRUCE WAS SOMEONE THAT THE HULK HID BEHIND.
AND IF THAT'S THE CASE, THEN BRUCE IS DAMNED LUCKY THAT REED, TONY, THE OTHERS...
...HE'S DAMNED LUCKY THEY DIDN'T DO FAR WORSE TO HIM THAN EXILE HIM.
AND HE'S GOING TO DO FAR WORSE TO THEM WHEN HE RETURNS FROM EXILE.
YOU'VE MADE YOUR CASE, LEONARD, AND I'M TOSSING IT. CASUS BELLI, COURTESY OF YOUR GOOD FRIENDS, IS GOING TO LAND YOU ALL HIP-DEEP IN WORLD WAR HULK.
AND WHEN IT STARTS, GOD HELP YOU...
...BECAUSE I CERTAINLY WON'T.

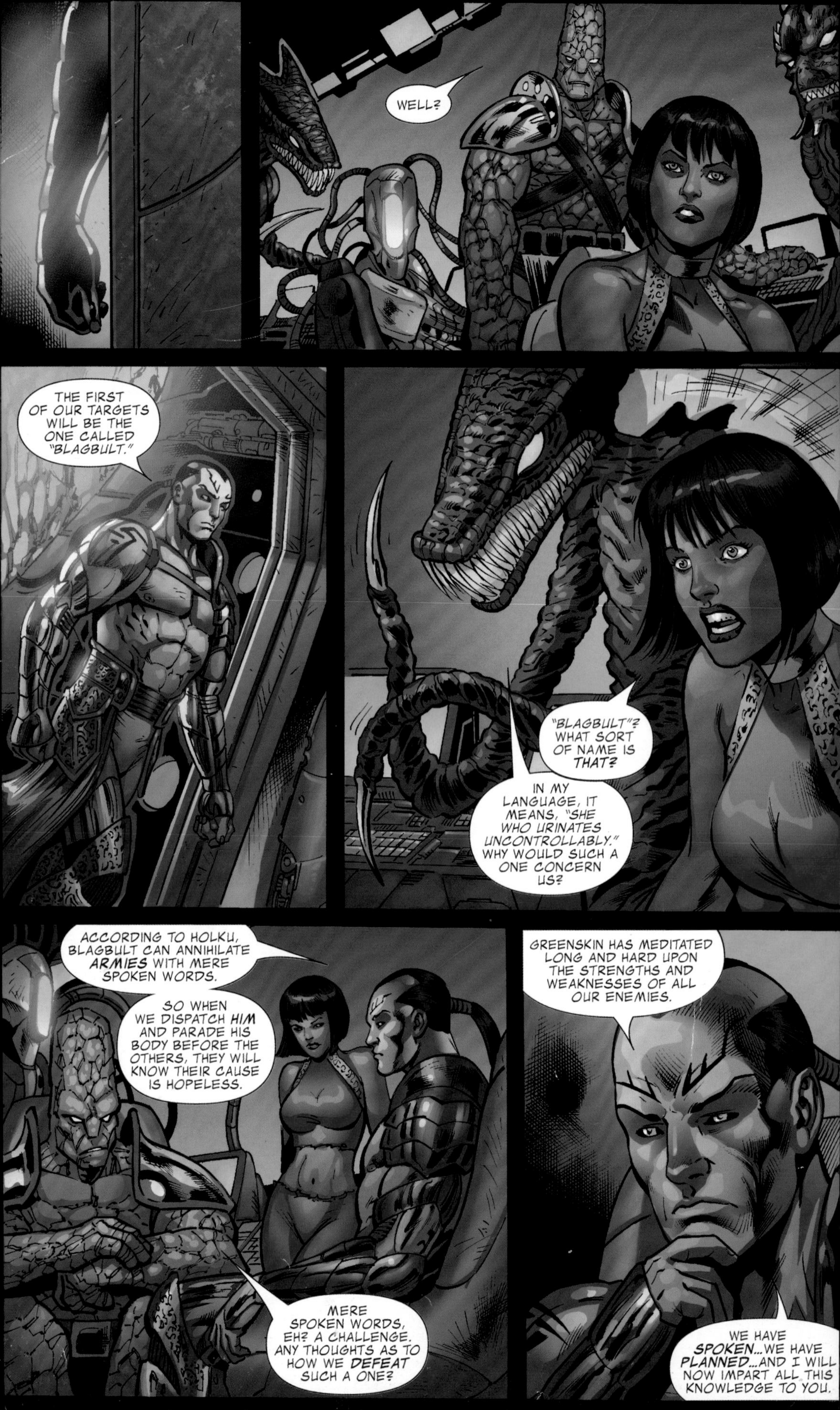
WELL?
THE FIRST OF OUR TARGETS WILL BE THE ONE CALLED "BLAGBULT."
"BLAGBULT"? WHAT SORT OF NAME IS THAT?
IN MY LANGUAGE, IT MEANS, "SHE WHO URINATES UNCONTROLLABLY." WHY WOULD SUCH A ONE CONCERN US?
ACCORDING TO HOLKU, BLAGBULT CAN ANNIHILATE ARMIES WITH MERE SPOKEN WORDS.
SO WHEN WE DISPATCH HIM AND PARADE HIS BODY BEFORE THE OTHERS, THEY WILL KNOW THEIR CAUSE IS HOPELESS.
MERE SPOKEN WORDS, EH? A CHALLENGE. ANY THOUGHTS AS TO HOW WE DEFEAT SUCH A ONE?
GREENSKIN HAS MEDITATED LONG AND HARD UPON THE STRENGTHS AND WEAKNESSES OF ALL OUR ENEMIES.
WE HAVE SPOKEN...WE HAVE PLANNED...AND I WILL NOW IMPART ALL THIS KNOWLEDGE TO YOU.

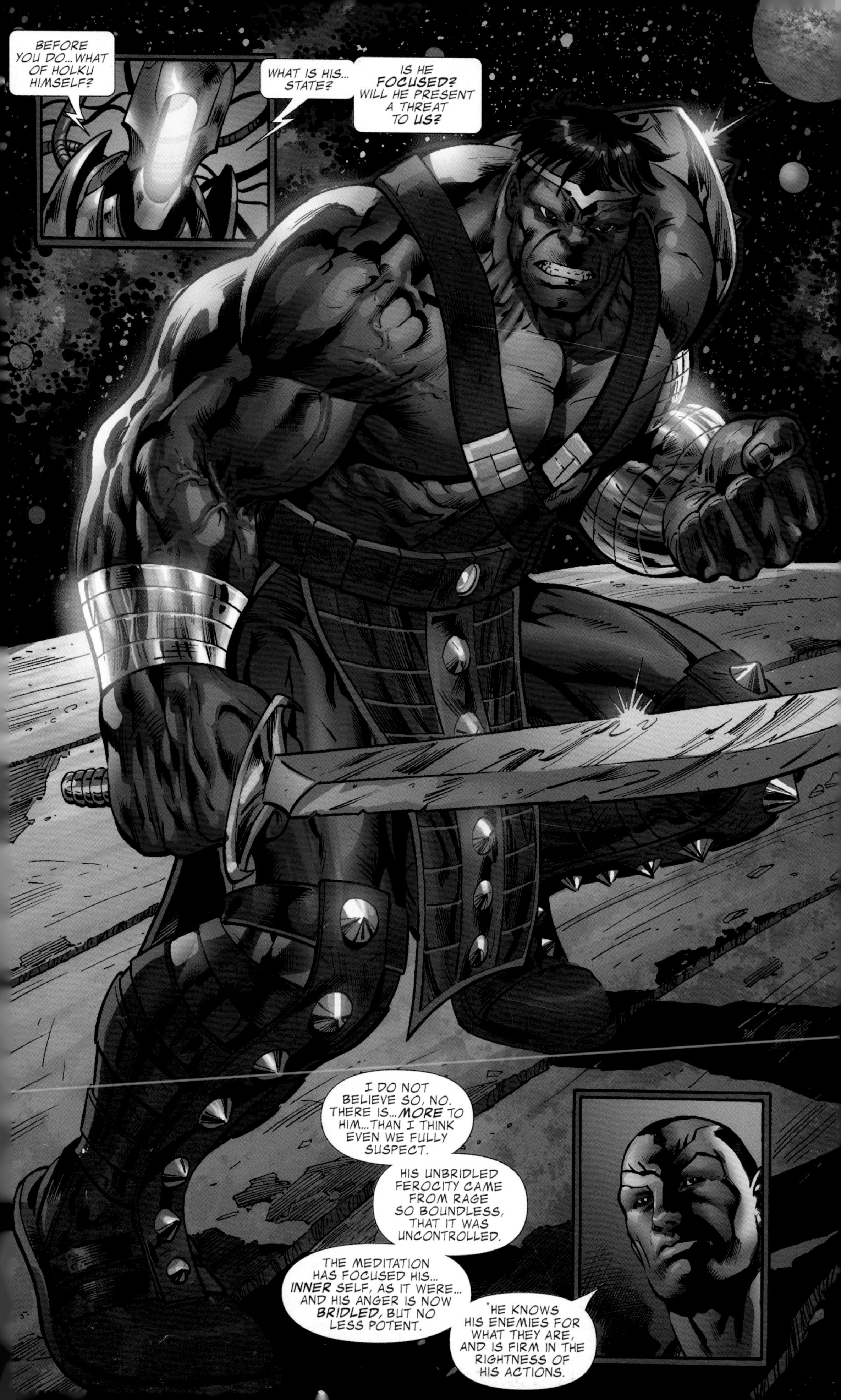

BEFORE YOU DO...WHAT OF HOLKU HIMSELF?
WHAT IS HIS... STATE?
IS HE FOCUSED? WILL HE PRESENT A THREAT TO US?
I DO NOT BELIEVE SO, NO. THERE IS...MORE TO HIM...THAN I THINK EVEN WE FULLY SUSPECT.
HIS UNBRIDLED FEROCITY CAME FROM RAGE SO BOUNDLESS, THAT IT WAS UNCONTROLLED.
THE MEDITATION HAS FOCUSED HIS... INNER SELF, AS IT WERE... AND HIS ANGER IS NOW BRIDLED, BUT NO LESS POTENT.
HE KNOWS HIS ENEMIES FOR WHAT THEY ARE, AND IS FIRM IN THE RIGHTNESS OF HIS ACTIONS.

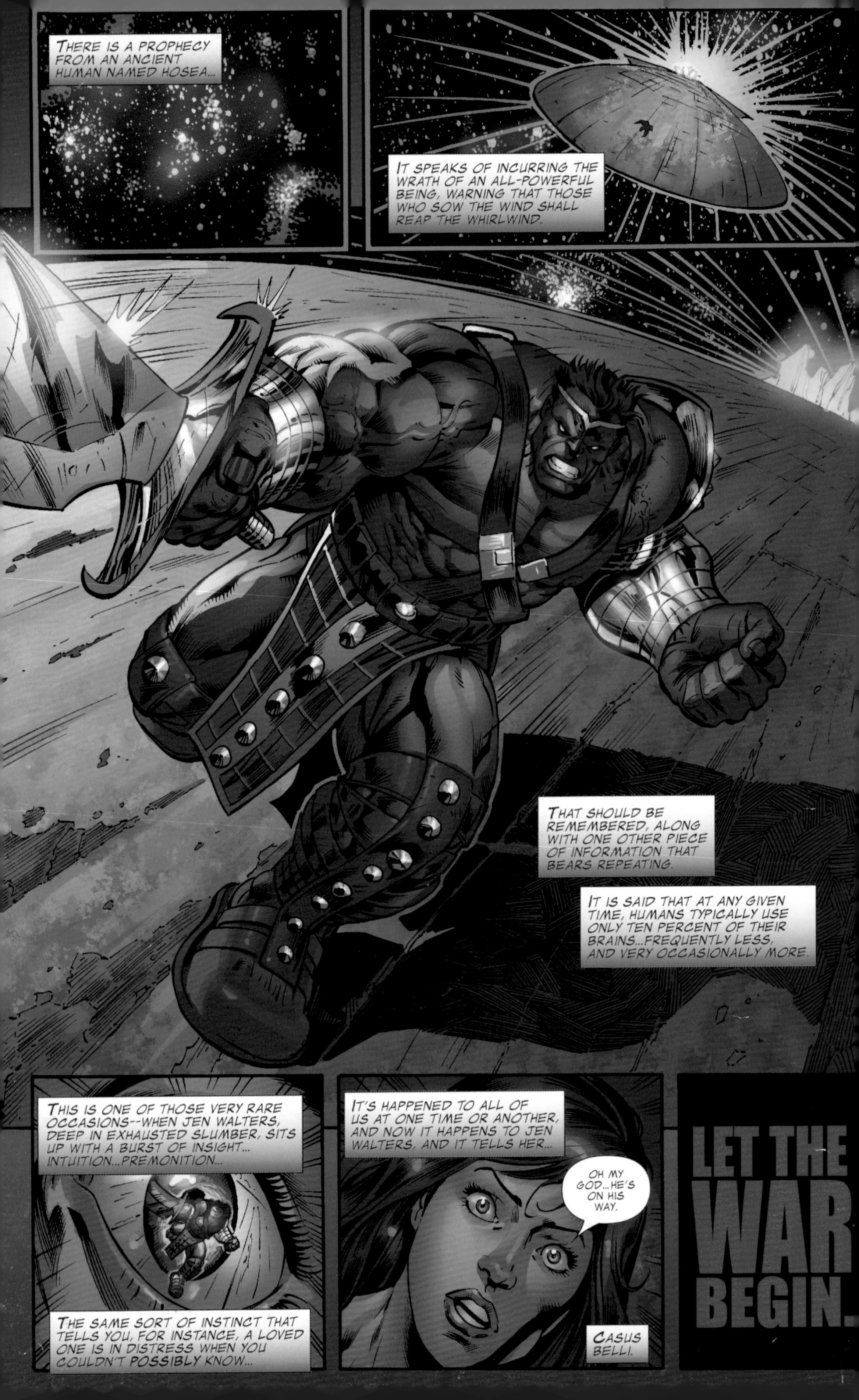

THERE IS A PROPHECY FROM AN ANCIENT HUMAN NAMED HOSEA...
IT SPEAKS OF INCURRING THE WRATH OF AN ALL-POWERFUL BEING, WARNING THAT THOSE WHO SOW THE WIND SHALL REAP THE WHIRLWIND.
THAT SHOULD BE REMEMBERED, ALONG WITH ONE OTHER PIECE OF INFORMATION THAT BEARS REPEATING.
IT IS SAID THAT AT ANY GIVEN TIME, HUMANS TYPICALLY USE ONLY TEN PERCENT OF THEIR BRAINS...FREQUENTLY LESS, AND VERY OCCASIONALLY MORE.
THIS IS ONE OF THOSE VERY RARE OCCASIONS--WHEN JEN WALTERS, DEEP IN EXHAUSTED SLUMBER, SITS UP WITH A BURST OF INSIGHT... INTUITION...PREMONITION...
THE SAME SORT OF INSTINCT THAT TELLS YOU, FOR INSTANCE, A LOVED ONE IS IN DISTRESS WHEN YOU COULDN'T POSSIBLY KNOW...
IT'S HAPPENED TO ALL OF US AT ONE TIME OR ANOTHER, AND NOW IT HAPPENS TO JEN WALTERS, AND IT TELLS HER...
OH MY GOD...HE'S ON HIS WAY.
CASUS BELLI.
LET THE WAR BEGIN.

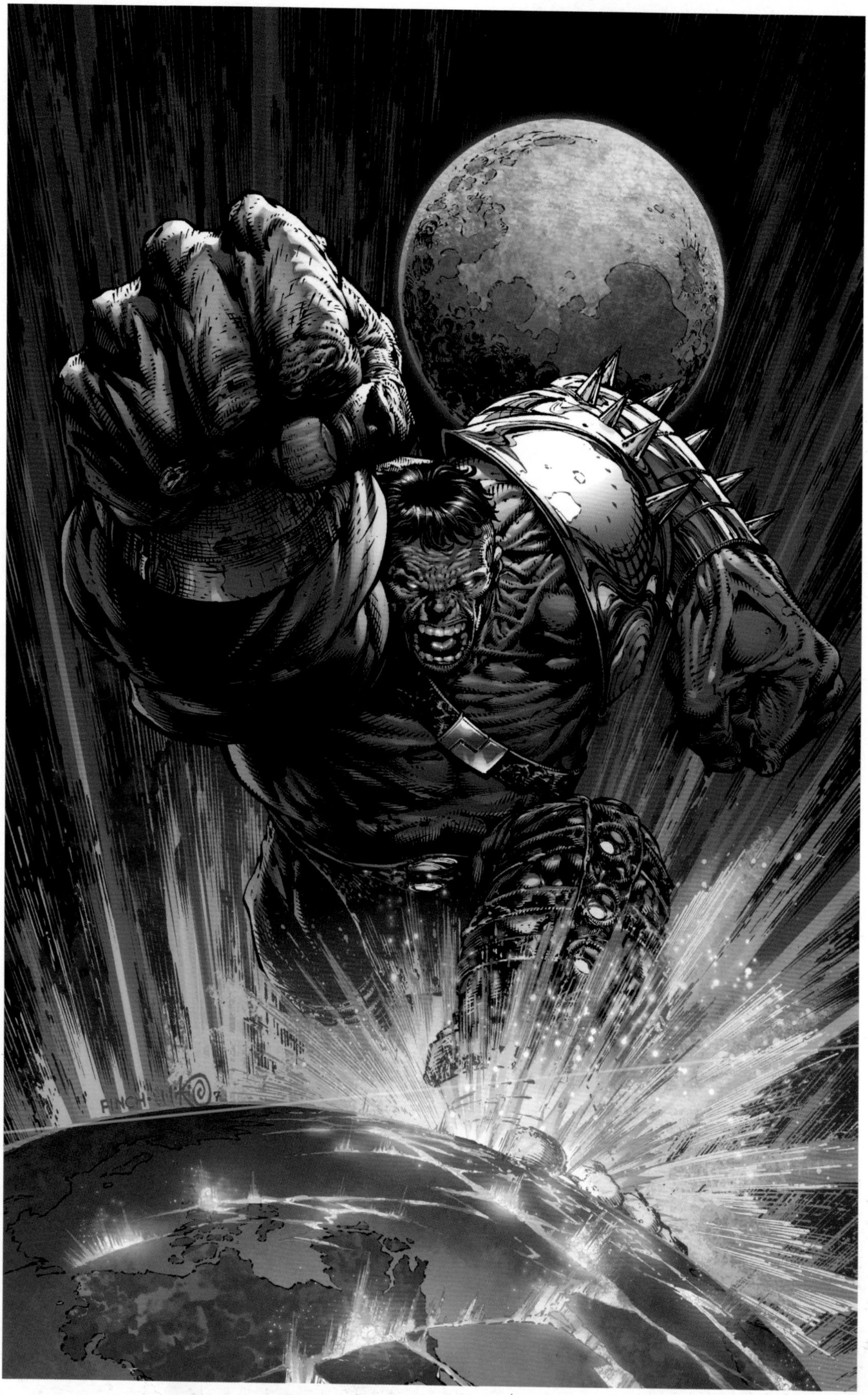

THIS IS THE STORY OF THE HULK.

A MONSTER WHO FELL FROM THE SKY TO THE SAVAGE PLANET OF SAKAAR...

...A WHOLE WORLD OF MONSTERS.

BUT WHILE THEY STABBED HIM...

...BURNED HIM...

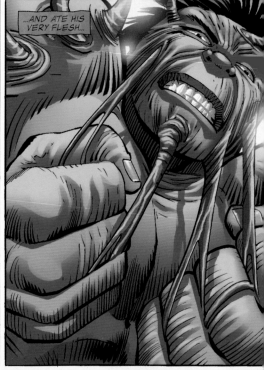

...AND ATE HIS VERY FLESH...

...HE NEVER FORGOT THE REAL MONSTERS...

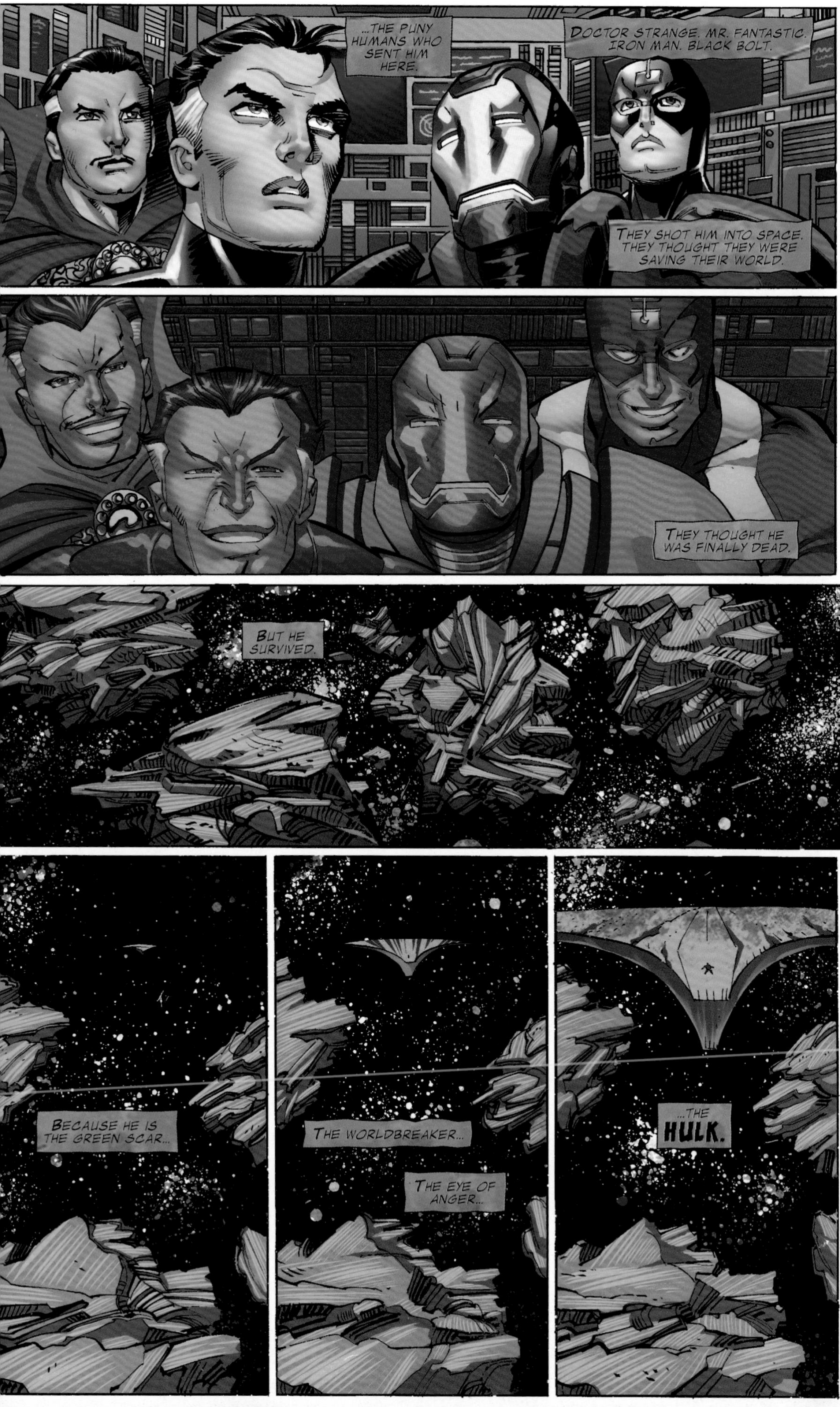
...THE PUNY HUMANS WHO SENT HIM HERE.
DOCTOR STRANGE. MR. FANTASTIC. IRON MAN. BLACK BOLT.
THEY SHOT HIM INTO SPACE. THEY THOUGHT THEY WERE SAVING THEIR WORLD.
THEY THOUGHT HE WAS FINALLY DEAD.
BUT HE SURVIVED.
BECAUSE HE IS THE GREEN SCAR...
THE WORLDBREAKER...
THE EYE OF ANGER...
...THE HULK.

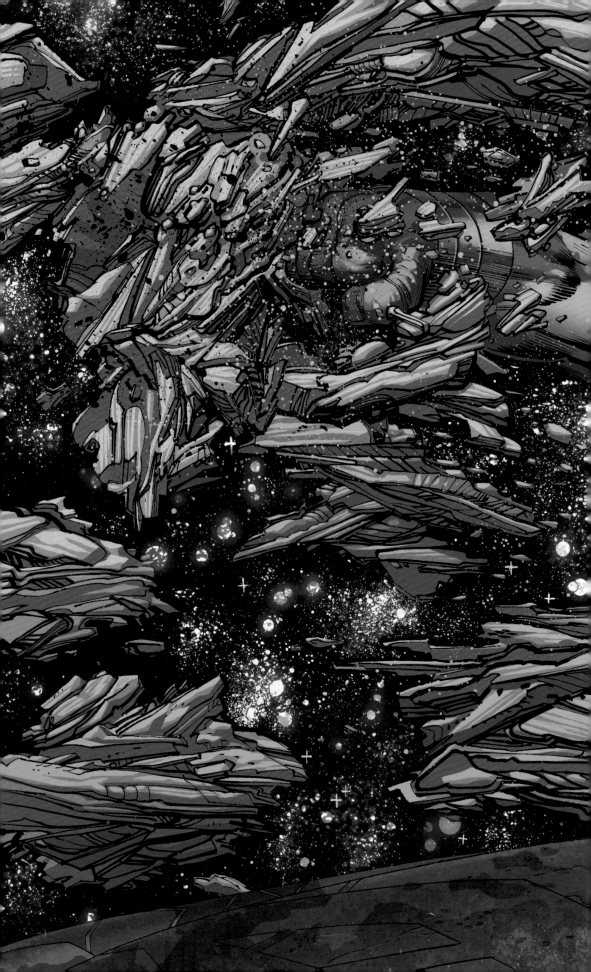

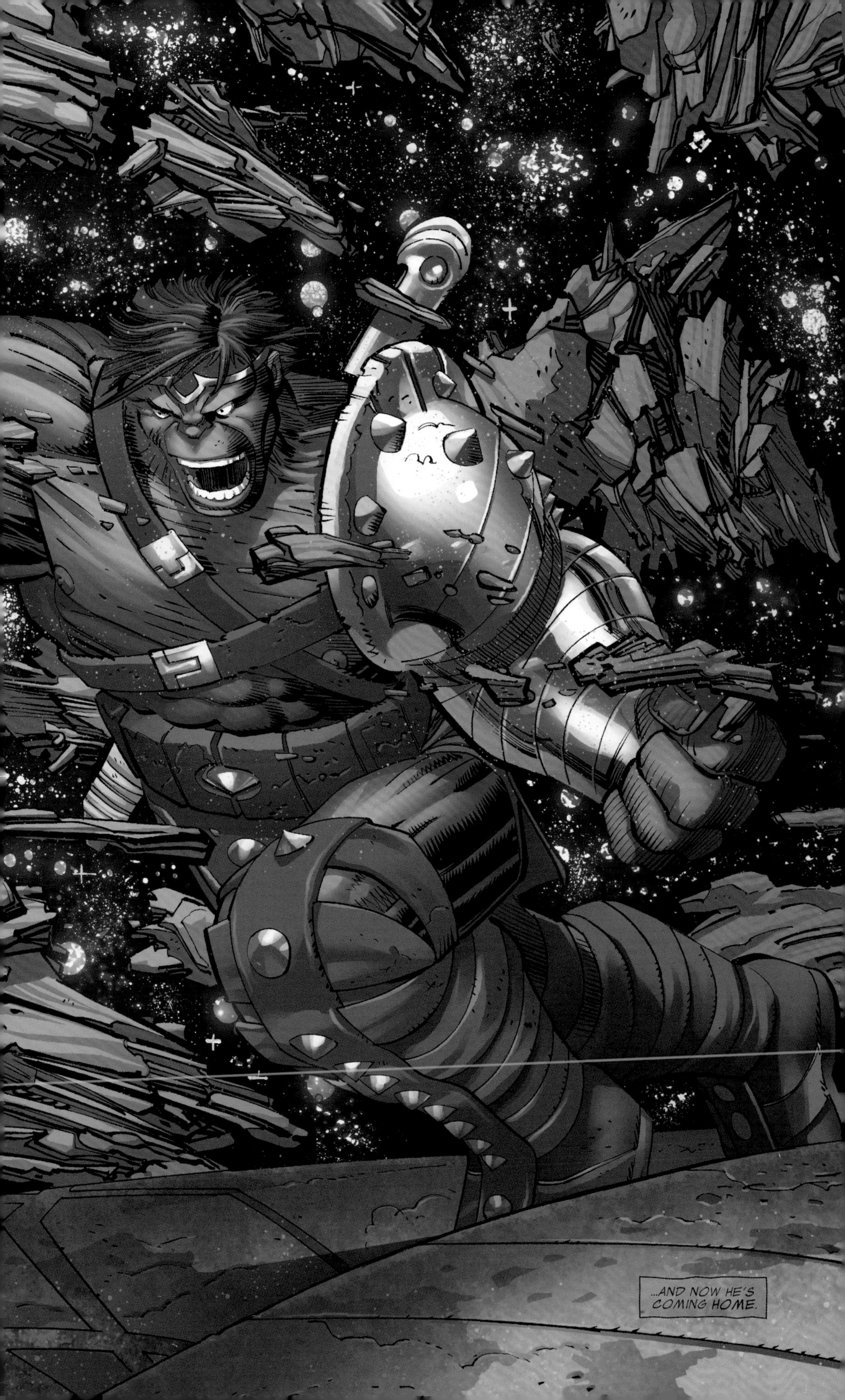
...AND NOW HE'S COMING HOME.

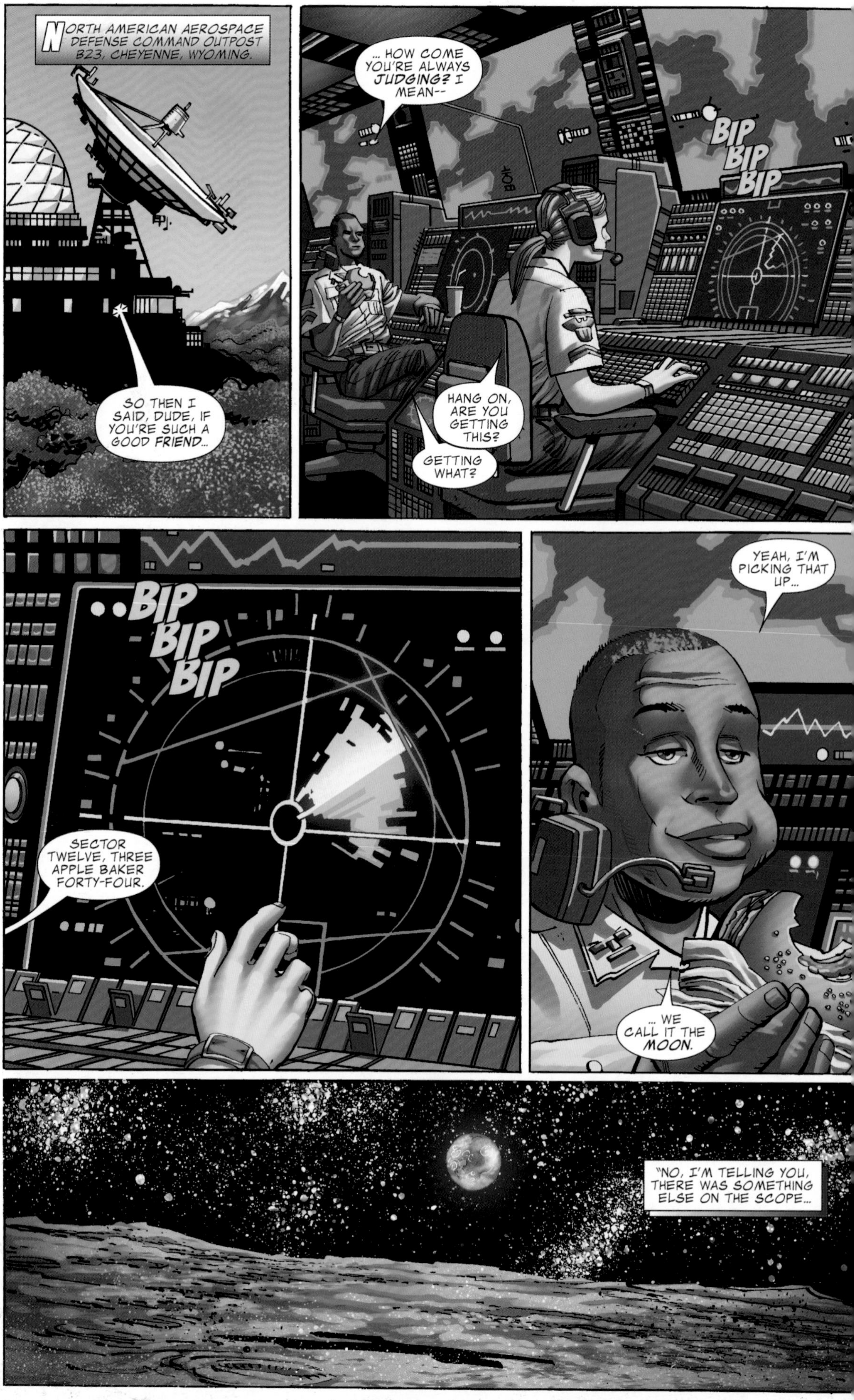
NORTH AMERICAN AEROSPACE DEFENSE COMMAND OUTPOST B23, CHEYENNE, WYOMING.
SO THEN I SAID, DUDE, IF YOU'RE SUCH A GOOD FRIEND...
... HOW COME YOU'RE ALWAYS JUDGING? I MEAN--
BIP BIP BIP
HANG ON, ARE YOU GETTING THIS?
GETTING WHAT?
BIP BIP BIP
SECTOR TWELVE, THREE APPLE BAKER FORTY-FOUR.
YEAH, I'M PICKING THAT UP...
... WE CALL IT THE MOON.
"NO, I'M TELLING YOU, THERE WAS SOMETHING ELSE ON THE SCOPE...

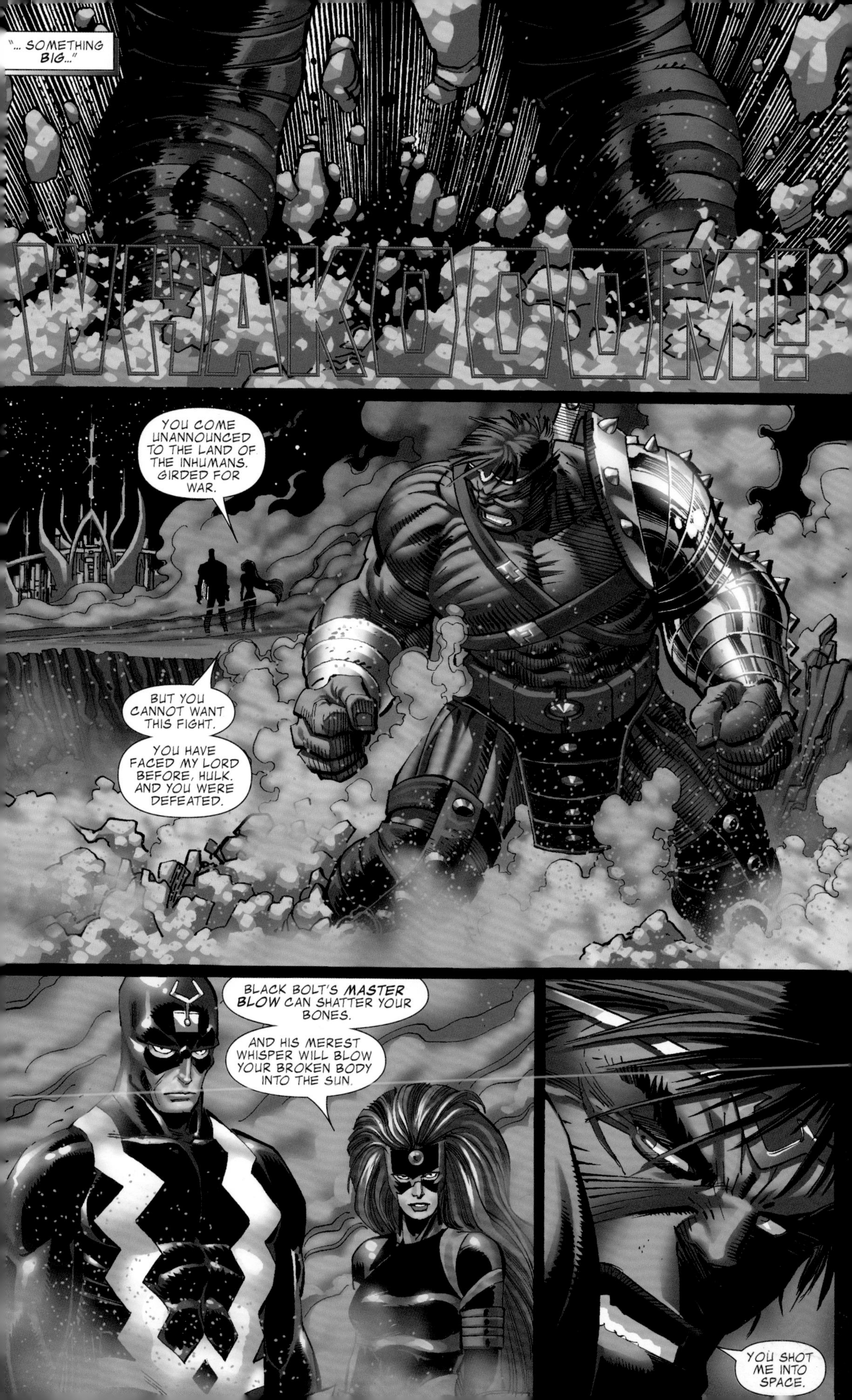
"... SOMETHING BIG..."
WHAKOOOM!
YOU COME UNANNOUNCED TO THE LAND OF THE INHUMANS. GIRDED FOR WAR.
BUT YOU CANNOT WANT THIS FIGHT.
YOU HAVE FACED MY LORD BEFORE, HULK. AND YOU WERE DEFEATED.
BLACK BOLT'S MASTER BLOW CAN SHATTER YOUR BONES.
AND HIS MEREST WHISPER WILL BLOW YOUR BROKEN BODY INTO THE SUN.
YOU SHOT ME INTO SPACE.

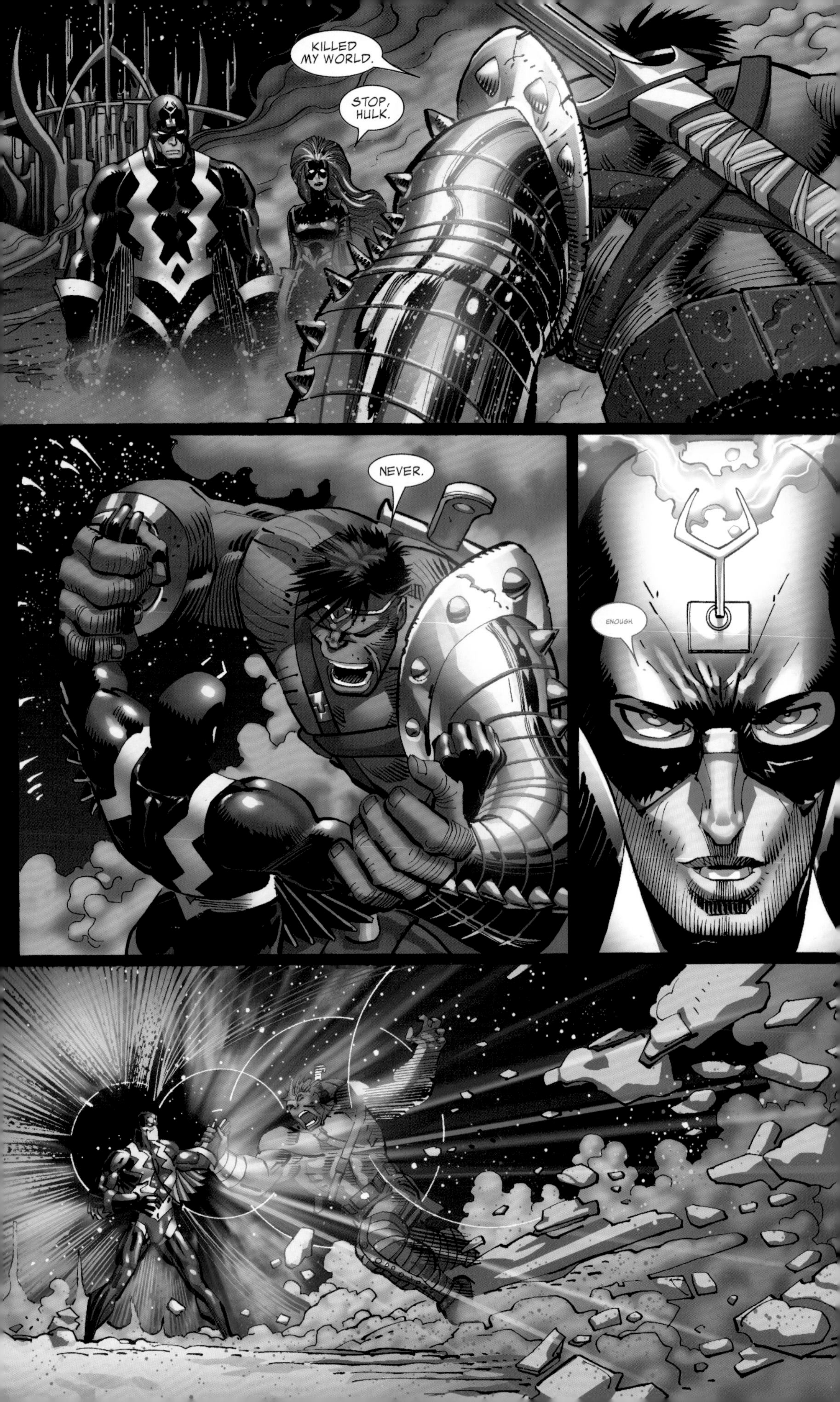
KILLED MY WORLD.
STOP, HULK.
NEVER.
ENOUGH.

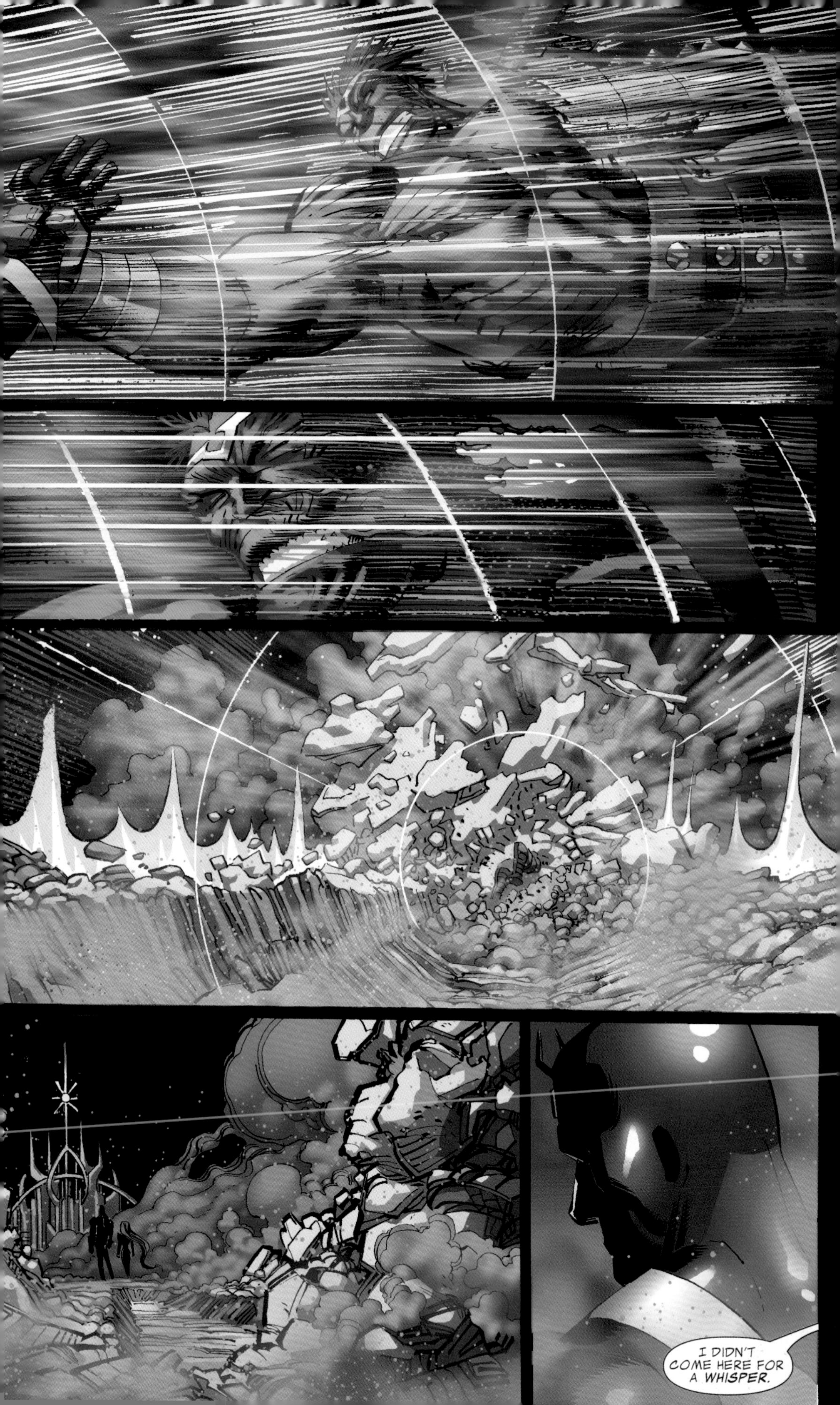
I DIDN'T COME HERE FOR A WHISPER.

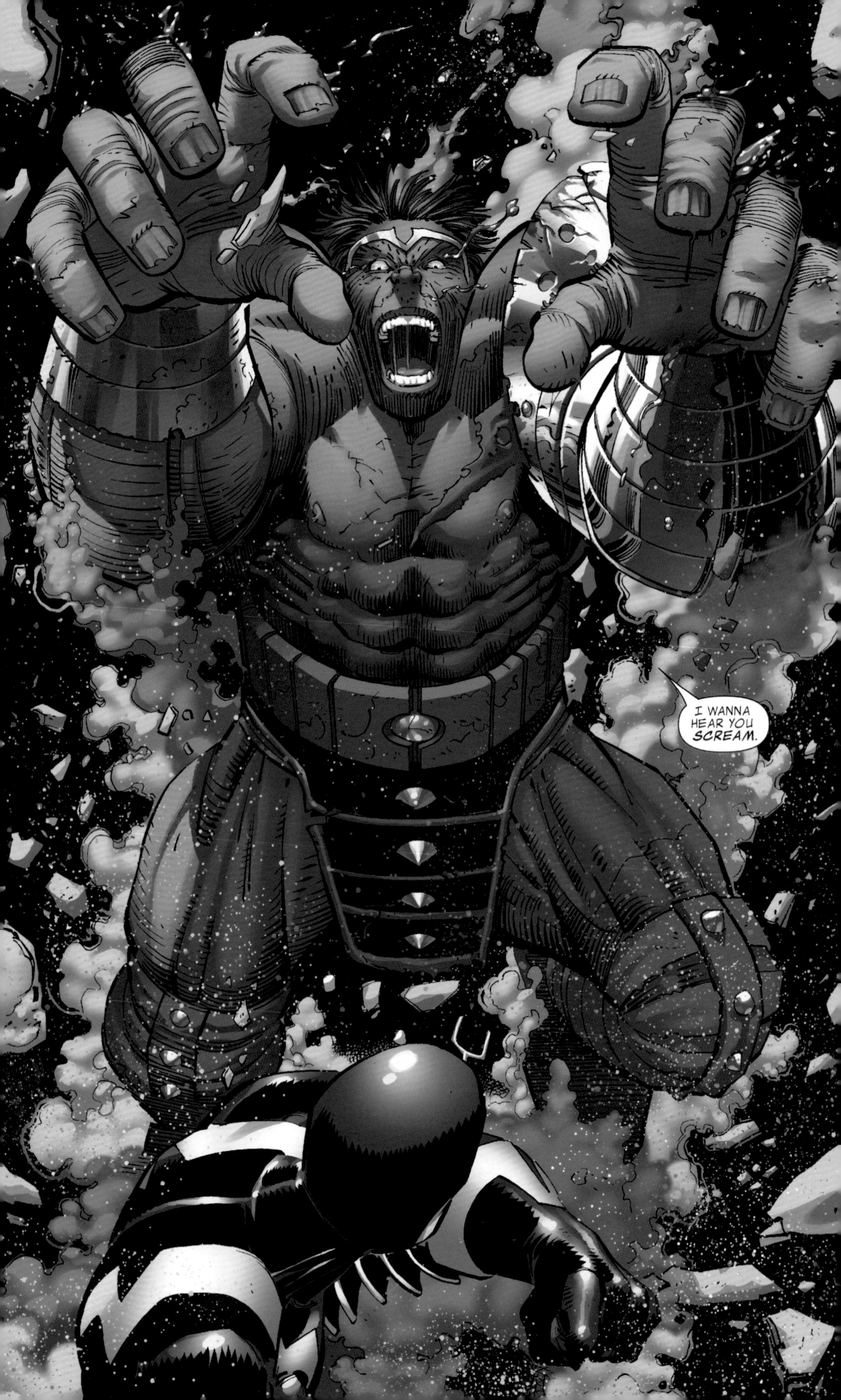
I WANNA HEAR YOU SCREAM.

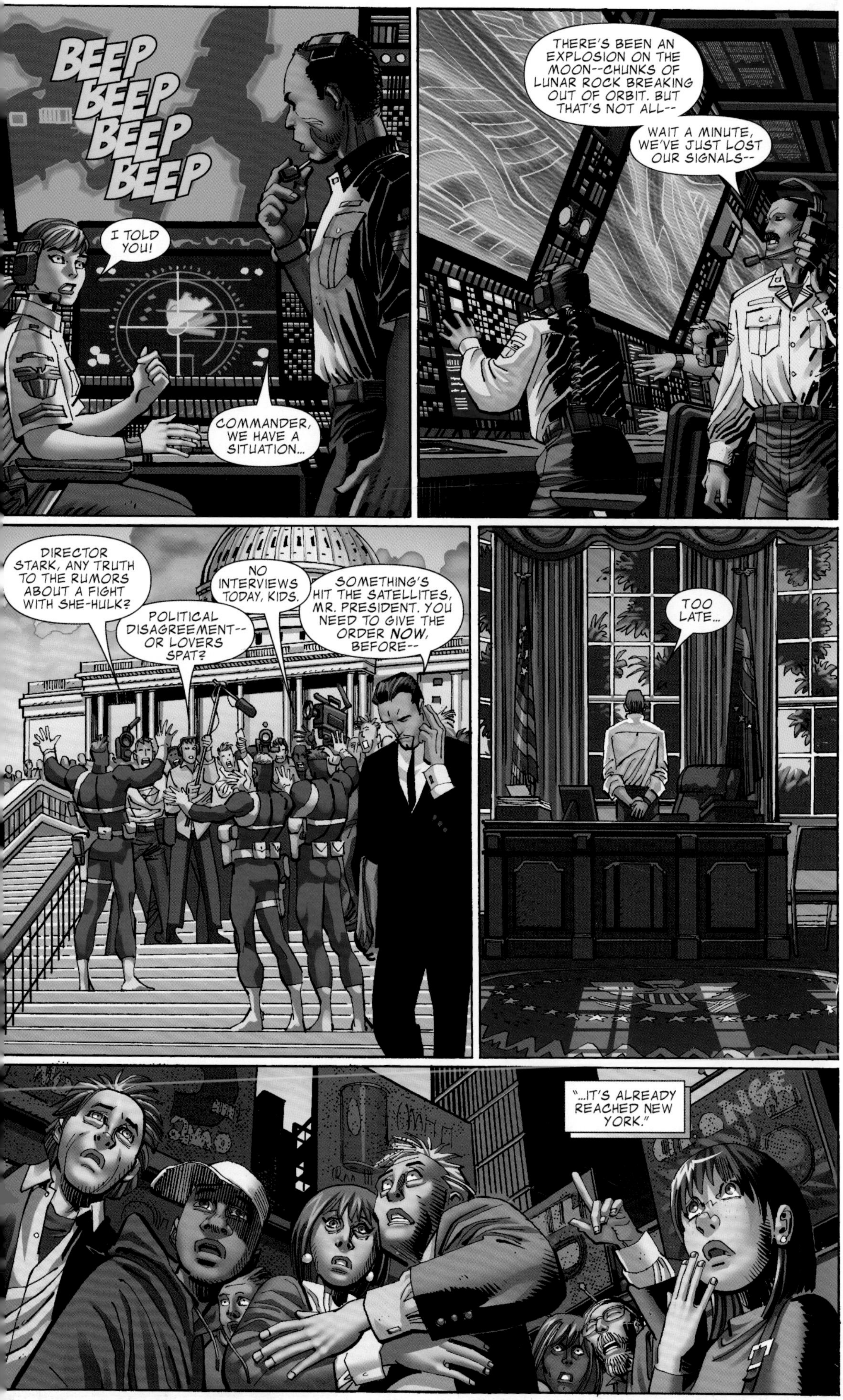
BEEP BEEP BEEP BEEP
I TOLD YOU!
COMMANDER, WE HAVE A SITUATION...
THERE'S BEEN AN EXPLOSION ON THE MOON--CHUNKS OF LUNAR ROCK BREAKING OUT OF ORBIT. BUT THAT'S NOT ALL--
WAIT A MINUTE, WE'VE JUST LOST OUR SIGNALS--
DIRECTOR STARK, ANY TRUTH TO THE RUMORS ABOUT A FIGHT WITH SHE-HULK?
POLITICAL DISAGREEMENT--OR LOVERS SPAT?
NO INTERVIEWS TODAY, KIDS.
SOMETHING'S HIT THE SATELLITES, MR. PRESIDENT. YOU NEED TO GIVE THE ORDER NOW, BEFORE--
TOO LATE...
"...IT'S ALREADY REACHED NEW YORK."

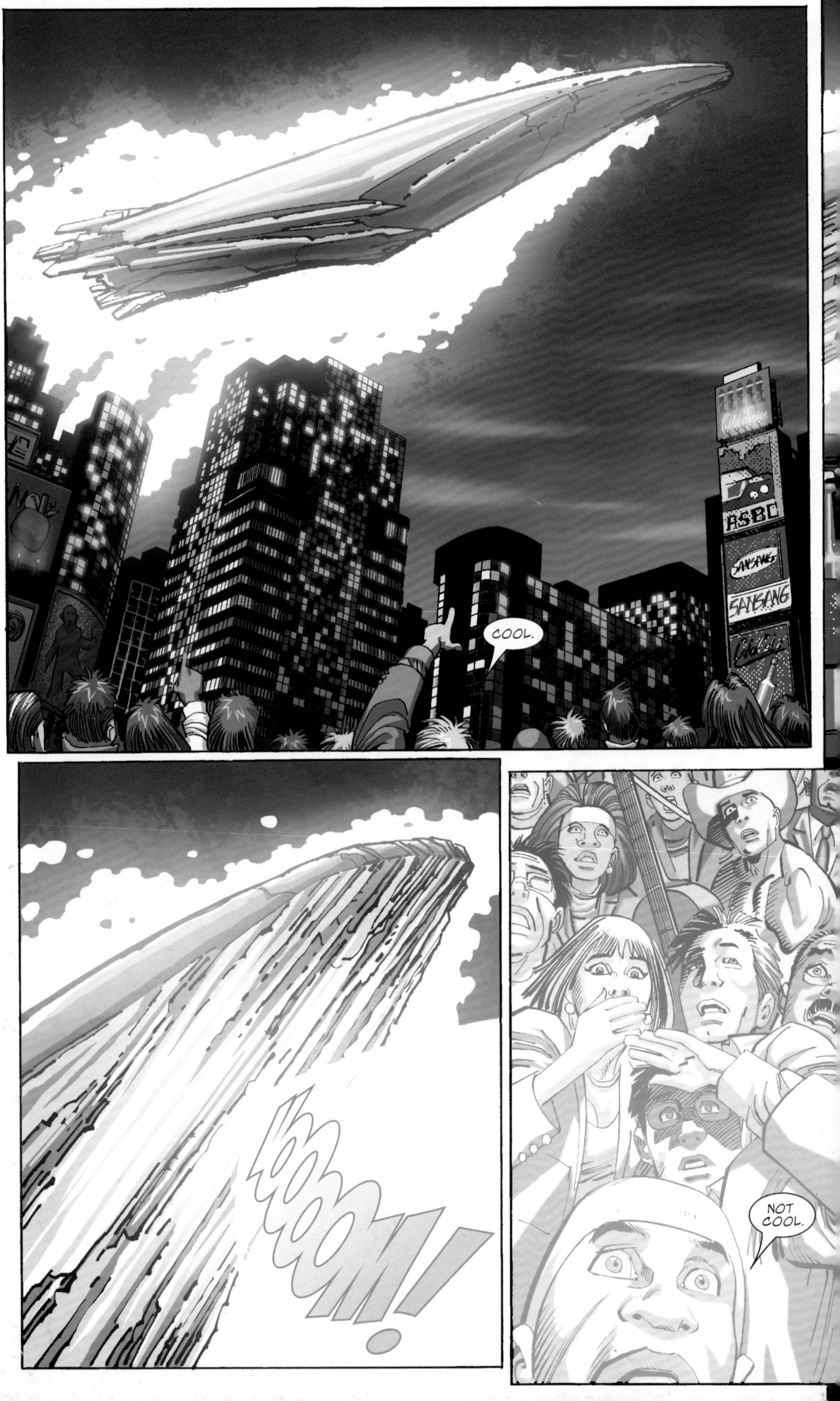
ASBC
SANSANG
SANSANG
COOL.
WOOOOM!
NOT COOL.

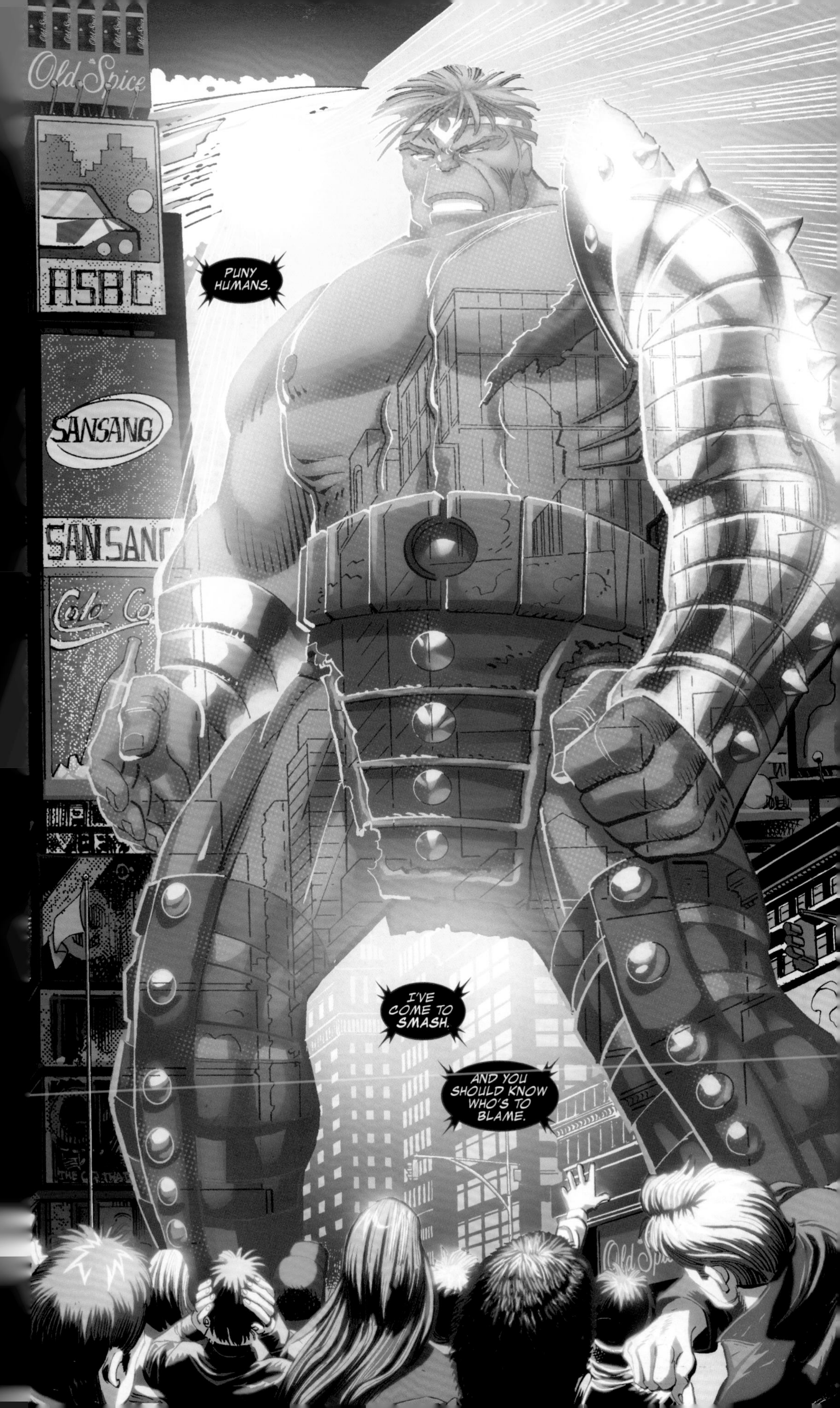
Old Spice
ASBC
PUNY HUMANS.
SANSANG
SANSANG
I'VE COME TO SMASH.
AND YOU SHOULD KNOW WHO'S TO BLAME.

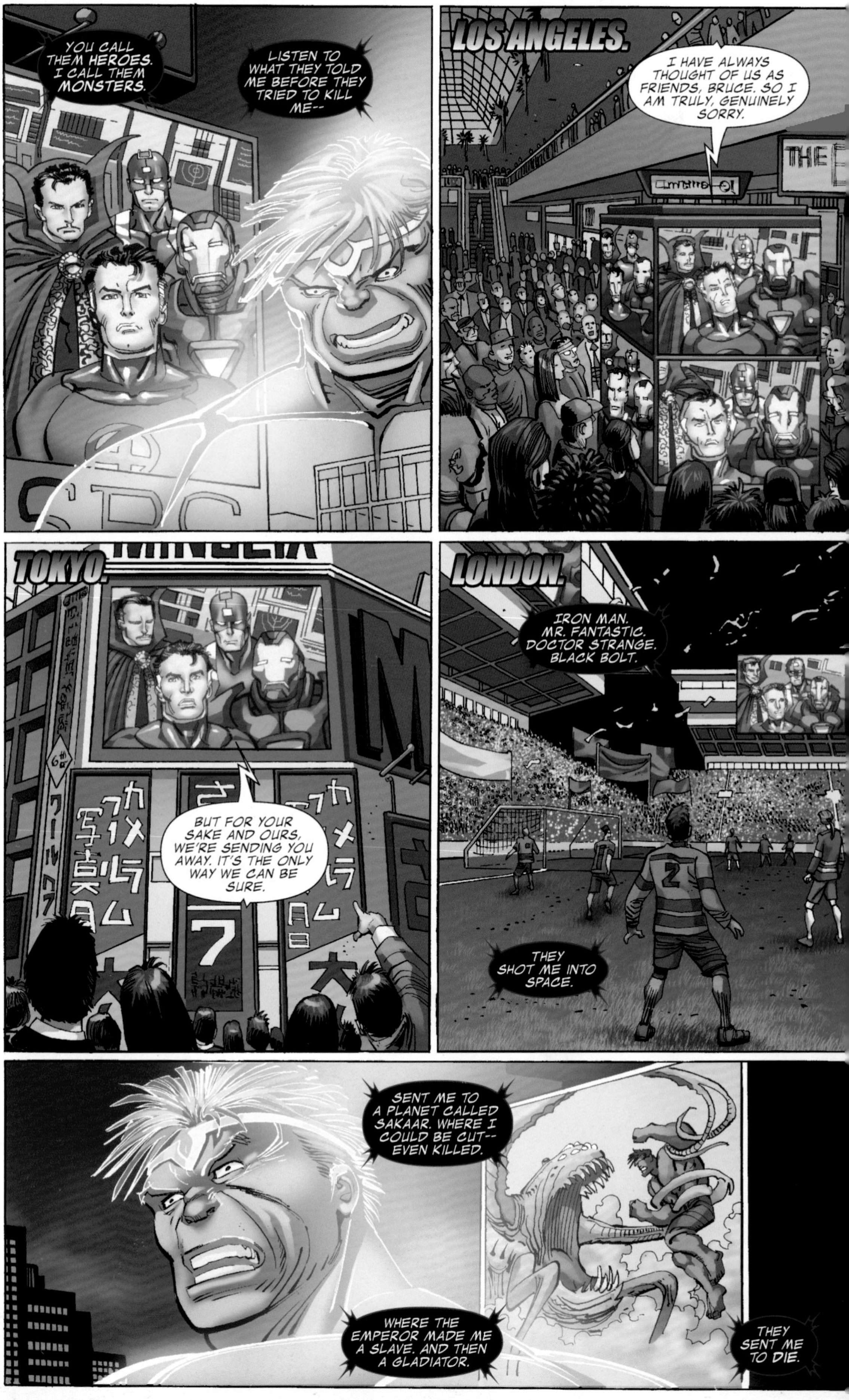
YOU CALL THEM HEROES. I CALL THEM MONSTERS.
LISTEN TO WHAT THEY TOLD ME BEFORE THEY TRIED TO KILL ME--
LOS ANGELES.
I HAVE ALWAYS THOUGHT OF US AS FRIENDS, BRUCE. SO I AM TRULY, GENUINELY SORRY.
TOKYO.
BUT FOR YOUR SAKE AND OURS, WE'RE SENDING YOU AWAY. IT'S THE ONLY WAY WE CAN BE SURE.
LONDON.
IRON MAN. MR. FANTASTIC. DOCTOR STRANGE. BLACK BOLT.
THEY SHOT ME INTO SPACE.
SENT ME TO A PLANET CALLED SAKAAR. WHERE I COULD BE CUT-- EVEN KILLED.
WHERE THE EMPEROR MADE ME A SLAVE. AND THEN A GLADIATOR.
THEY SENT ME TO DIE.

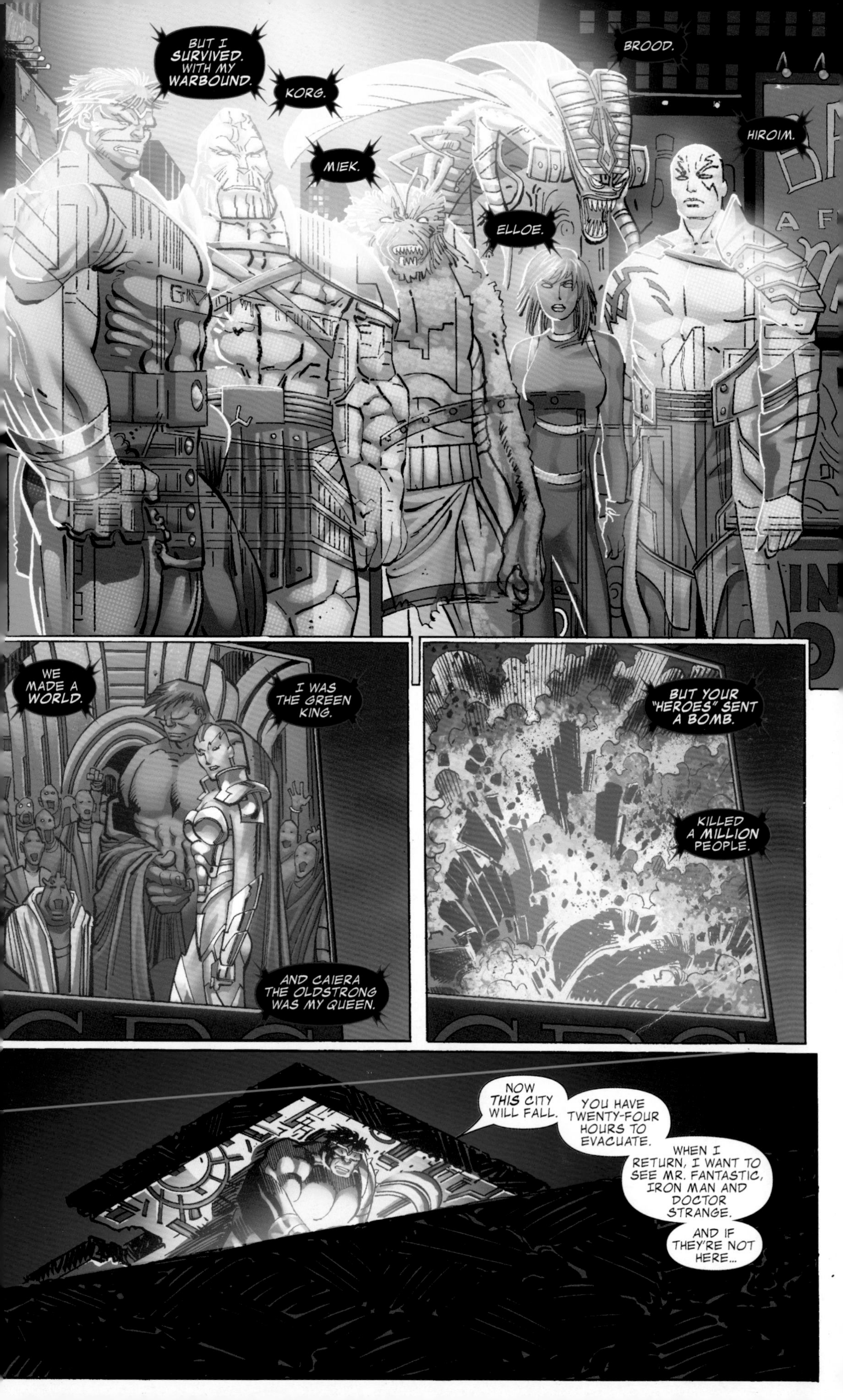
BUT I SURVIVED. WITH MY WARBOUND.
KORG.
MIEK.
BROOD.
ELLOE.
HIROIM.
WE MADE A WORLD.
I WAS THE GREEN KING.
AND CAIERA THE OLDSTRONG WAS MY QUEEN.
BUT YOUR "HEROES" SENT A BOMB.
KILLED A MILLION PEOPLE.
NOW THIS CITY WILL FALL.
YOU HAVE TWENTY-FOUR HOURS TO EVACUATE.
WHEN I RETURN, I WANT TO SEE MR. FANTASTIC, IRON MAN AND DOCTOR STRANGE.
AND IF THEY'RE NOT HERE...

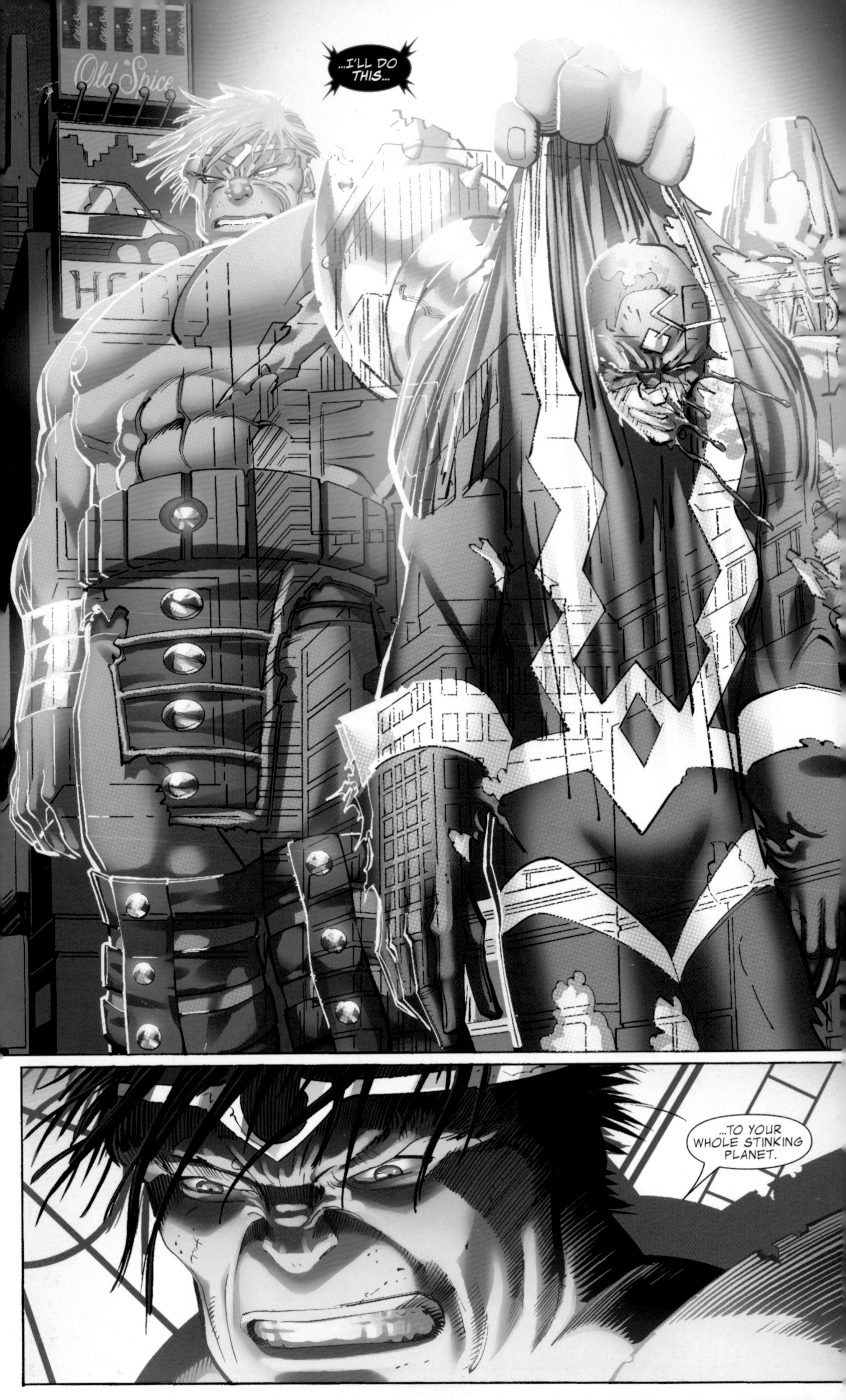
Old Spice
...I'LL DO THIS...
...TO YOUR WHOLE STINKING PLANET.

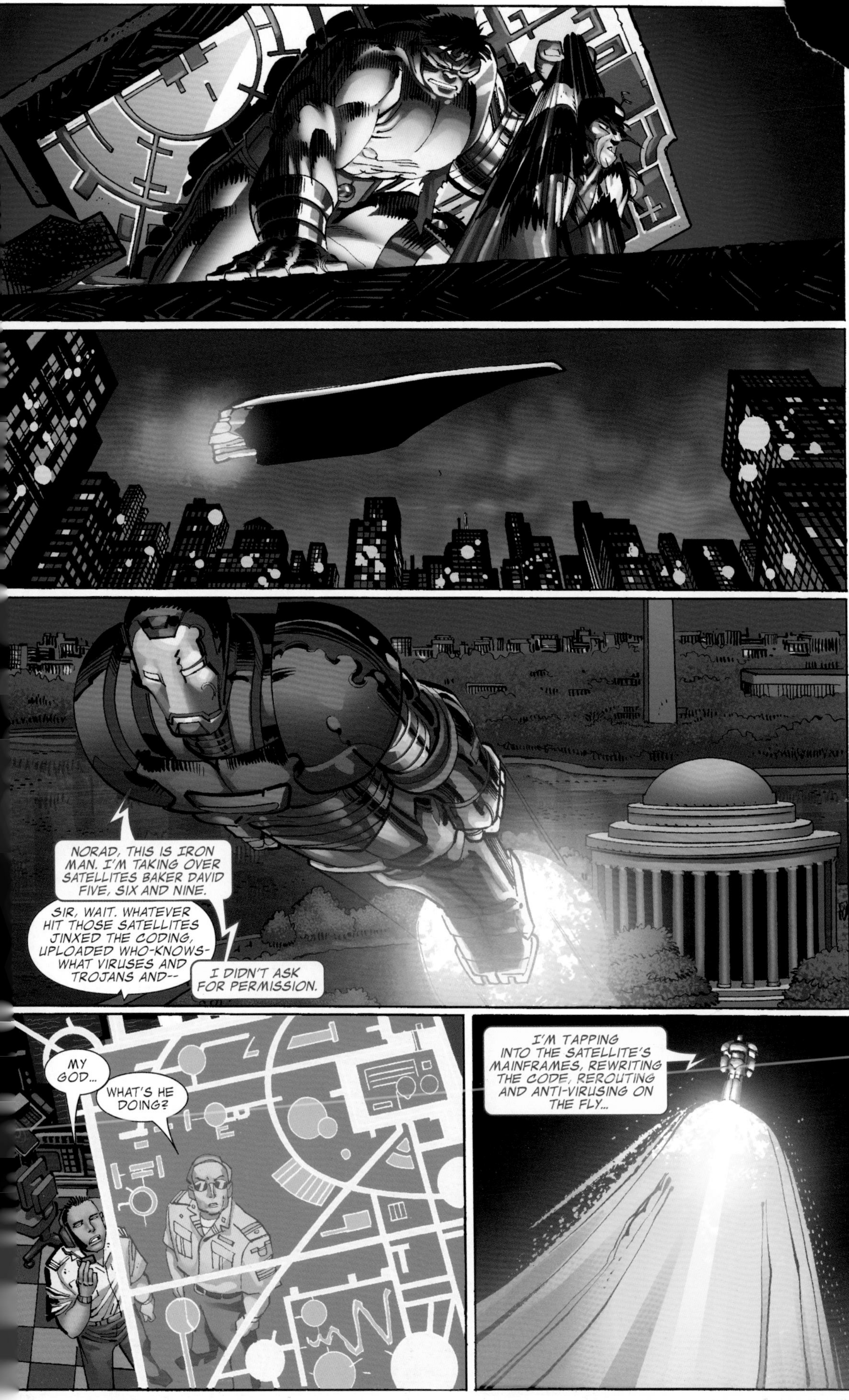
NORAD, THIS IS IRON MAN. I'M TAKING OVER SATELLITES BAKER DAVID FIVE, SIX AND NINE.
SIR, WAIT. WHATEVER HIT THOSE SATELLITES JINXED THE CODING, UPLOADED WHO-KNOWS-WHAT VIRUSES AND TROJANS AND--
I DIDN'T ASK FOR PERMISSION.
MY GOD...
WHAT'S HE DOING?
I'M TAPPING INTO THE SATELLITE'S MAINFRAMES, REWRITING THE CODE, REROUTING AND ANTI-VIRUSING ON THE FLY...

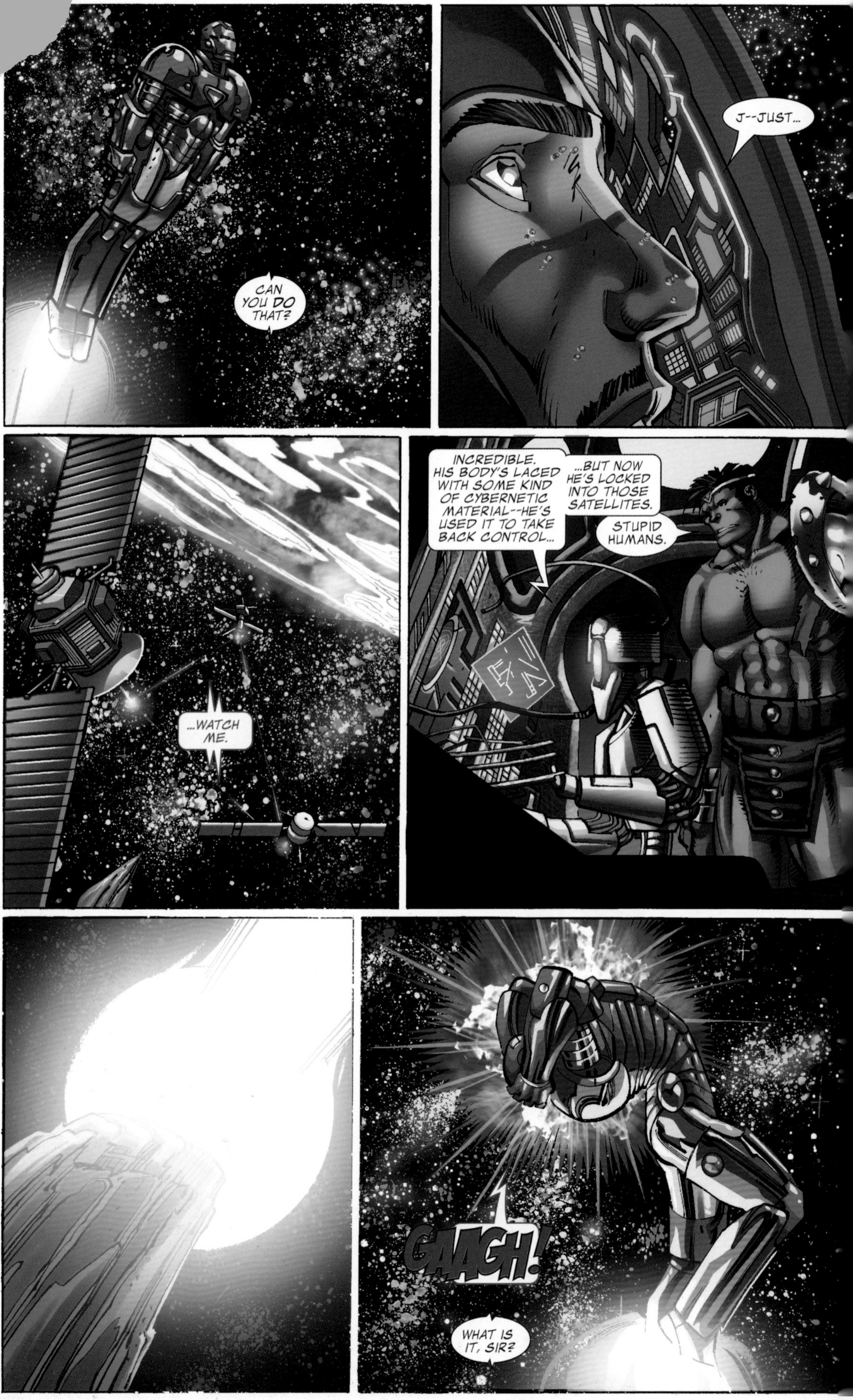
CAN YOU DO THAT?
J--JUST...
...WATCH ME.
INCREDIBLE. HIS BODY'S LACED WITH SOME KIND OF CYBERNETIC MATERIAL--HE'S USED IT TO TAKE BACK CONTROL...
...BUT NOW HE'S LOCKED INTO THOSE SATELLITES.
STUPID HUMANS.
GAAGH!
WHAT IS IT, SIR?

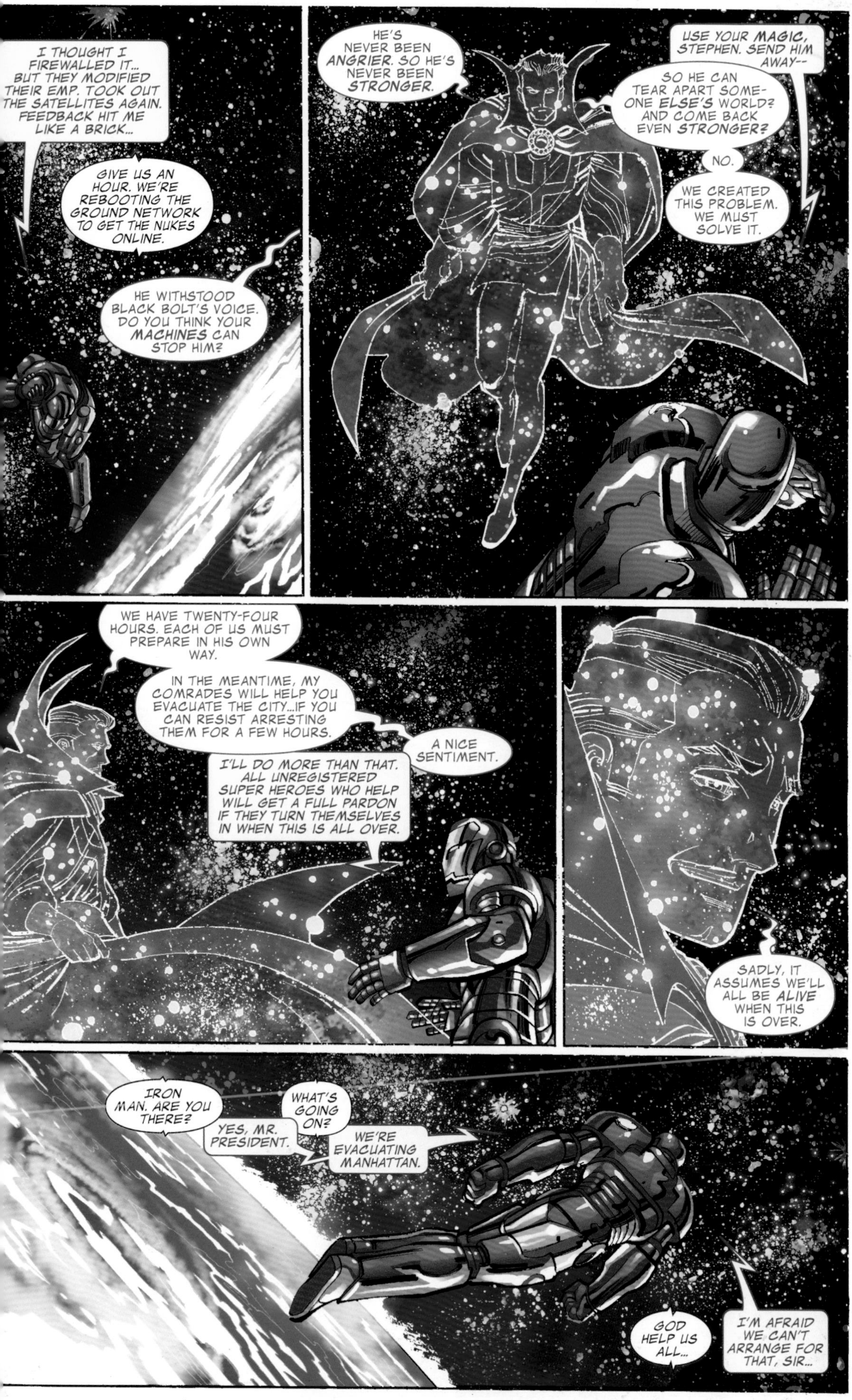
I THOUGHT I FIREWALLED IT... BUT THEY MODIFIED THEIR EMP. TOOK OUT THE SATELLITES AGAIN. FEEDBACK HIT ME LIKE A BRICK...
GIVE US AN HOUR. WE'RE REBOOTING THE GROUND NETWORK TO GET THE NUKES ONLINE.
HE WITHSTOOD BLACK BOLT'S VOICE. DO YOU THINK YOUR MACHINES CAN STOP HIM?
HE'S NEVER BEEN ANGRIER. SO HE'S NEVER BEEN STRONGER.
USE YOUR MAGIC, STEPHEN. SEND HIM AWAY--
SO HE CAN TEAR APART SOME-ONE ELSE'S WORLD? AND COME BACK EVEN STRONGER?
NO.
WE CREATED THIS PROBLEM. WE MUST SOLVE IT.
WE HAVE TWENTY-FOUR HOURS. EACH OF US MUST PREPARE IN HIS OWN WAY.
IN THE MEANTIME, MY COMRADES WILL HELP YOU EVACUATE THE CITY...IF YOU CAN RESIST ARRESTING THEM FOR A FEW HOURS.
A NICE SENTIMENT.
I'LL DO MORE THAN THAT. ALL UNREGISTERED SUPER HEROES WHO HELP WILL GET A FULL PARDON IF THEY TURN THEMSELVES IN WHEN THIS IS ALL OVER.
SADLY, IT ASSUMES WE'LL ALL BE ALIVE WHEN THIS IS OVER.
IRON MAN. ARE YOU THERE?
YES, MR. PRESIDENT.
WHAT'S GOING ON?
WE'RE EVACUATING MANHATTAN.
GOD HELP US ALL...
I'M AFRAID WE CAN'T ARRANGE FOR THAT, SIR...

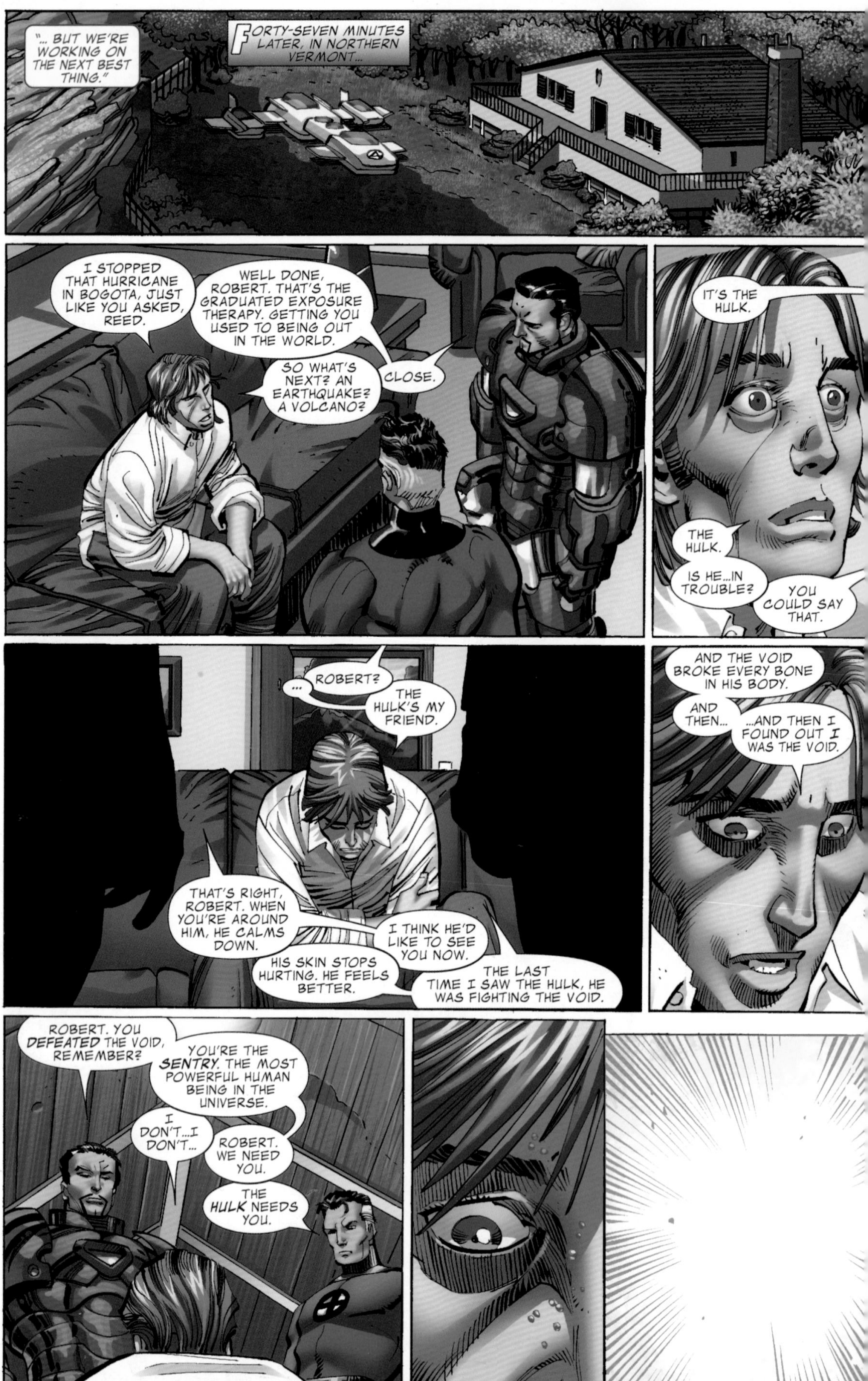
"... BUT WE'RE WORKING ON THE NEXT BEST THING."
FORTY-SEVEN MINUTES LATER, IN NORTHERN VERMONT...
I STOPPED THAT HURRICANE IN BOGOTA, JUST LIKE YOU ASKED, REED.
WELL DONE, ROBERT. THAT'S THE GRADUATED EXPOSURE THERAPY. GETTING YOU USED TO BEING OUT IN THE WORLD.
SO WHAT'S NEXT? AN EARTHQUAKE? A VOLCANO?
CLOSE.
IT'S THE HULK.
THE HULK.
IS HE...IN TROUBLE?
YOU COULD SAY THAT.
...
ROBERT?
THE HULK'S MY FRIEND.
THAT'S RIGHT, ROBERT. WHEN YOU'RE AROUND HIM, HE CALMS DOWN.
HIS SKIN STOPS HURTING. HE FEELS BETTER.
I THINK HE'D LIKE TO SEE YOU NOW.
THE LAST TIME I SAW THE HULK, HE WAS FIGHTING THE VOID.
AND THE VOID BROKE EVERY BONE IN HIS BODY.
AND THEN...
...AND THEN I FOUND OUT I WAS THE VOID.
ROBERT. YOU DEFEATED THE VOID, REMEMBER?
YOU'RE THE SENTRY. THE MOST POWERFUL HUMAN BEING IN THE UNIVERSE.
I DON'T...I DON'T...
ROBERT. WE NEED YOU.
THE HULK NEEDS YOU.

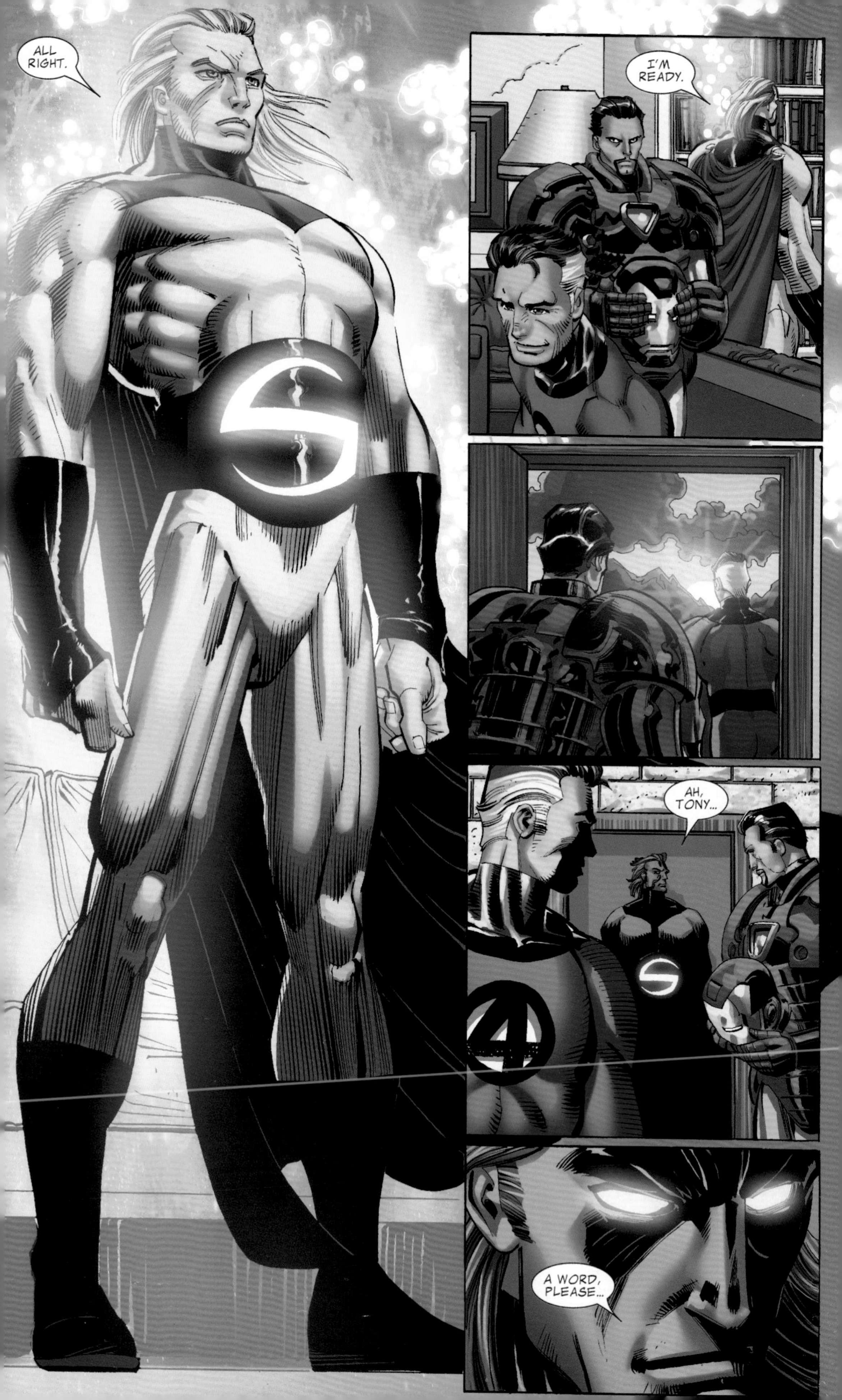
ALL RIGHT.
I'M READY.
AH, TONY...
A WORD, PLEASE...

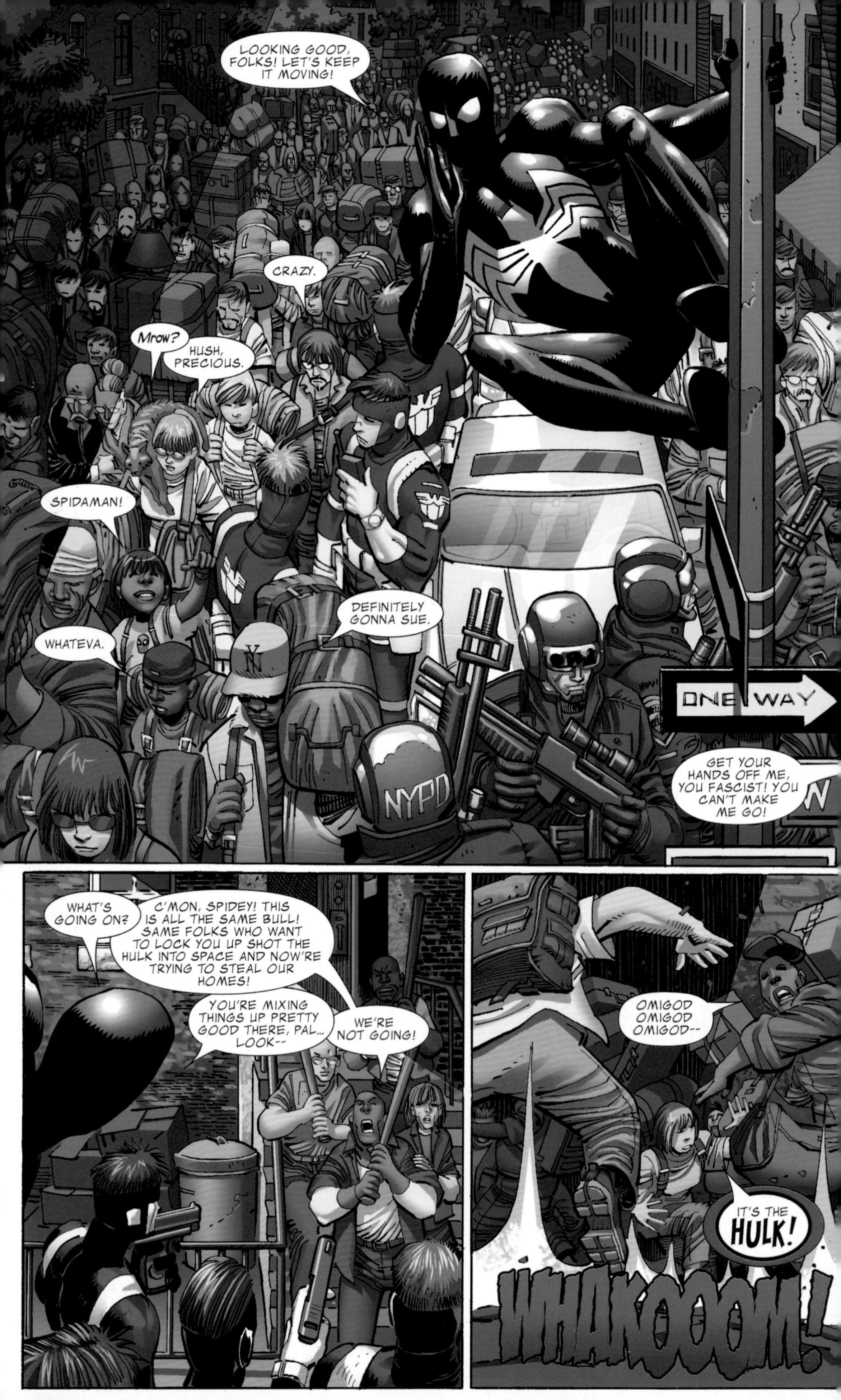
LOOKING GOOD, FOLKS! LET'S KEEP IT MOVING!
CRAZY.
Mrow?
HUSH, PRECIOUS.
SPIDAMAN!
DEFINITELY GONNA SUE.
WHATEVA.
ONE WAY
NYPD
GET YOUR HANDS OFF ME, YOU FASCIST! YOU CAN'T MAKE ME GO!
WHAT'S GOING ON?
C'MON, SPIDEY! THIS IS ALL THE SAME BULL! SAME FOLKS WHO WANT TO LOCK YOU UP SHOT THE HULK INTO SPACE AND NOW'RE TRYING TO STEAL OUR HOMES!
YOU'RE MIXING THINGS UP PRETTY GOOD THERE, PAL... LOOK--
WE'RE NOT GOING!
OMIGOD OMIGOD OMIGOD--
IT'S THE HULK!
WHAKOOOM!

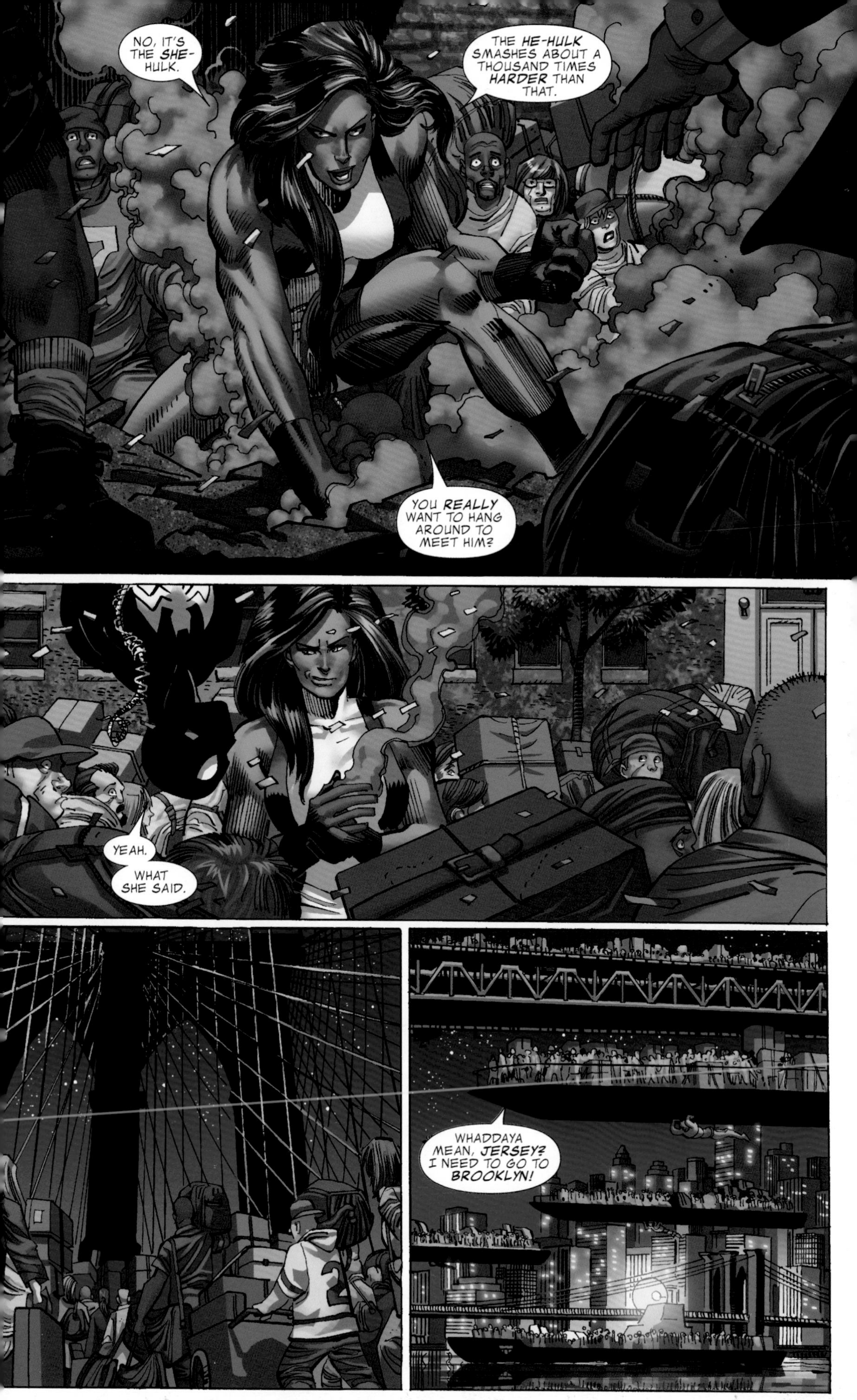
NO, IT'S THE SHE-HULK.
THE HE-HULK SMASHES ABOUT A THOUSAND TIMES HARDER THAN THAT.
YOU REALLY WANT TO HANG AROUND TO MEET HIM?
YEAH.
WHAT SHE SAID.
WHADDAYA MEAN, JERSEY? I NEED TO GO TO BROOKLYN!

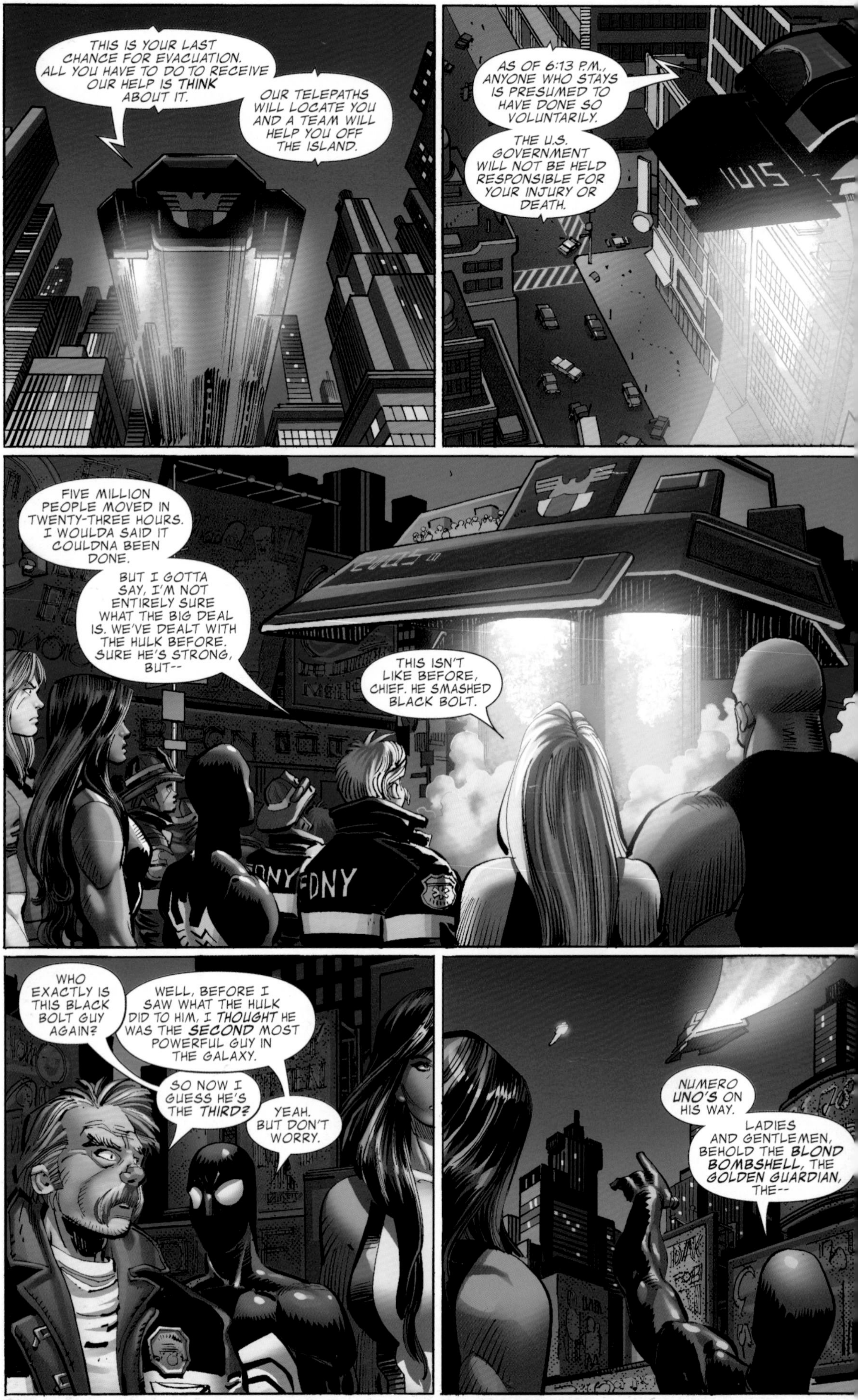
THIS IS YOUR LAST CHANCE FOR EVACUATION. ALL YOU HAVE TO DO TO RECEIVE OUR HELP IS THINK ABOUT IT.
OUR TELEPATHS WILL LOCATE YOU AND A TEAM WILL HELP YOU OFF THE ISLAND.
AS OF 6:13 P.M., ANYONE WHO STAYS IS PRESUMED TO HAVE DONE SO VOLUNTARILY.
THE U.S. GOVERNMENT WILL NOT BE HELD RESPONSIBLE FOR YOUR INJURY OR DEATH.
FIVE MILLION PEOPLE MOVED IN TWENTY-THREE HOURS. I WOULDA SAID IT COULDNA BEEN DONE.
BUT I GOTTA SAY, I'M NOT ENTIRELY SURE WHAT THE BIG DEAL IS. WE'VE DEALT WITH THE HULK BEFORE. SURE HE'S STRONG, BUT--
THIS ISN'T LIKE BEFORE, CHIEF. HE SMASHED BLACK BOLT.
FDNY
FDNY
WHO EXACTLY IS THIS BLACK BOLT GUY AGAIN?
WELL, BEFORE I SAW WHAT THE HULK DID TO HIM, I THOUGHT HE WAS THE SECOND MOST POWERFUL GUY IN THE GALAXY.
SO NOW I GUESS HE'S THE THIRD?
YEAH. BUT DON'T WORRY.
NUMERO UNO'S ON HIS WAY.
LADIES AND GENTLEMEN, BEHOLD THE BLOND BOMBSHELL, THE GOLDEN GUARDIAN, THE--

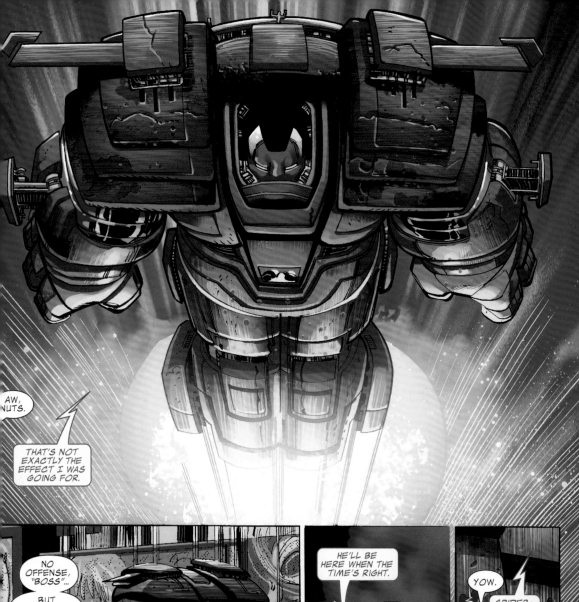

AW, NUTS.

THAT'S NOT EXACTLY THE EFFECT I WAS GOING FOR.

NO OFFENSE, "BOSS"...

...BUT WE WERE EXPECTING THE SENTRY.

HE'LL BE HERE WHEN THE TIME'S RIGHT.

DUDE, IS GALACTUS BACK IN TOWN? BECAUSE OTHERWISE--

YOW.

SPIDER-SENSE?

LIKE YOU WOULDN'T BELIEVE.

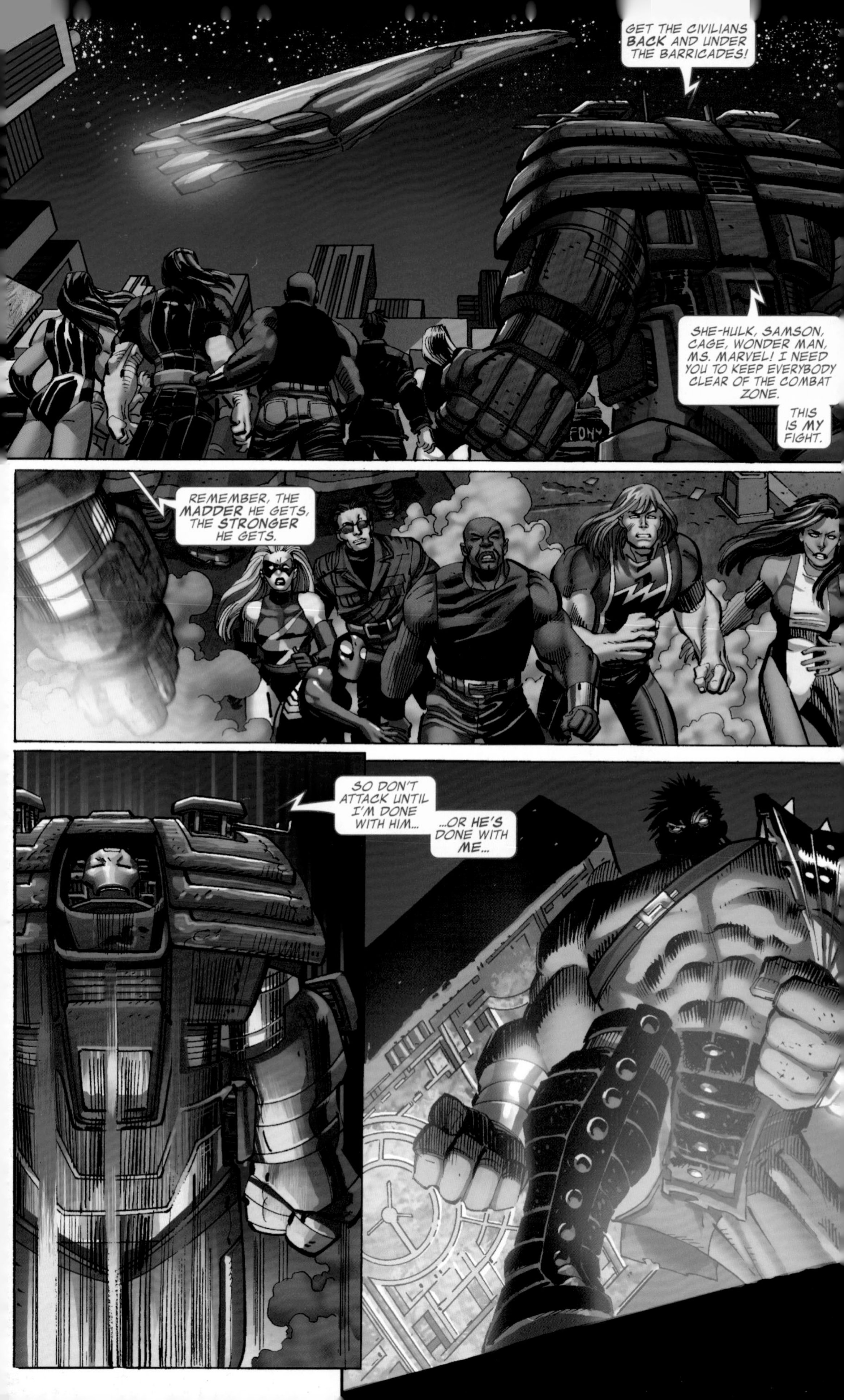
GET THE CIVILIANS BACK AND UNDER THE BARRICADES!
SHE-HULK, SAMSON, CAGE, WONDER MAN, MS. MARVEL! I NEED YOU TO KEEP EVERYBODY CLEAR OF THE COMBAT ZONE.
THIS IS MY FIGHT.
REMEMBER, THE MADDER HE GETS, THE STRONGER HE GETS.
SO DON'T ATTACK UNTIL I'M DONE WITH HIM...
...OR HE'S DONE WITH ME...

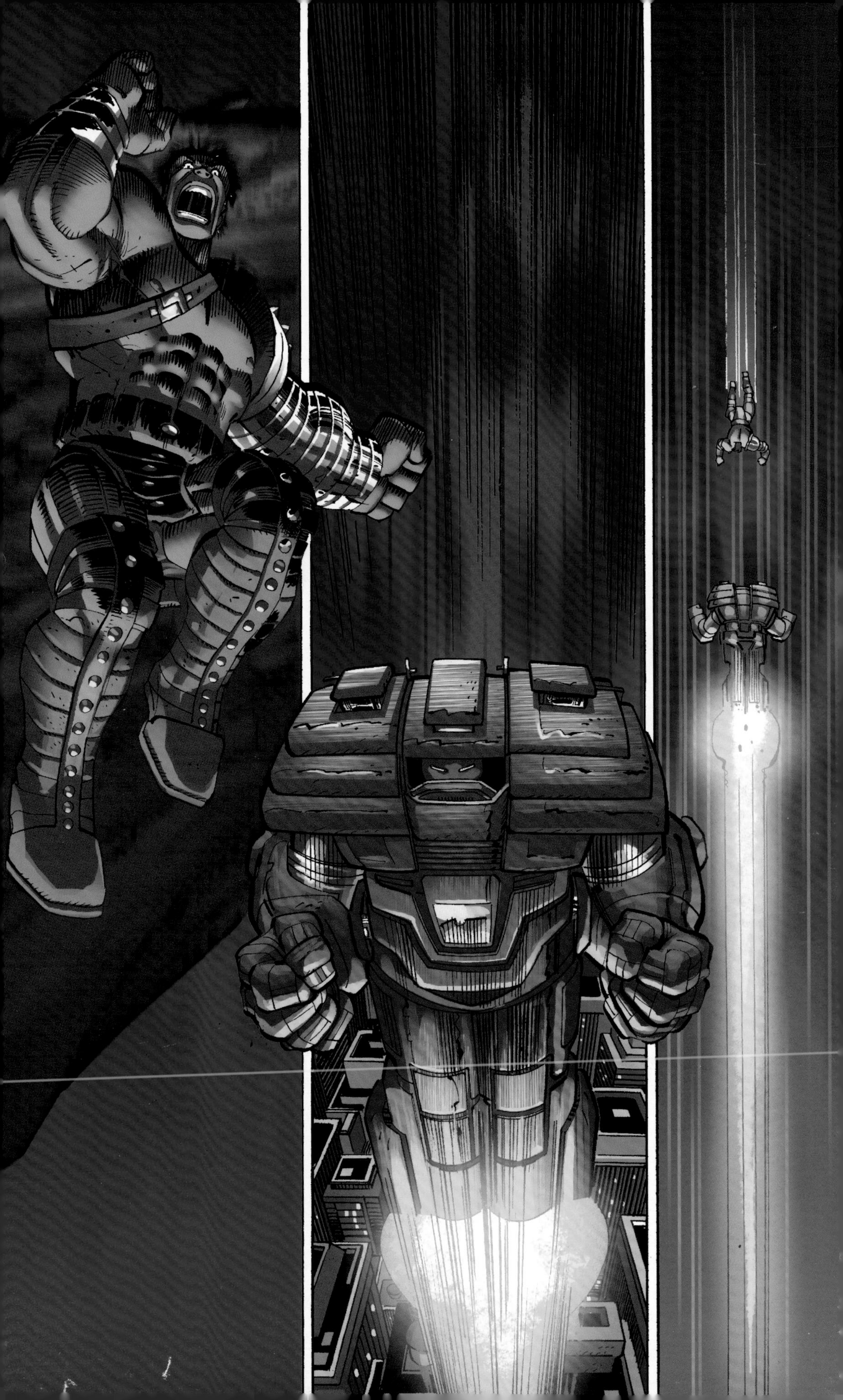

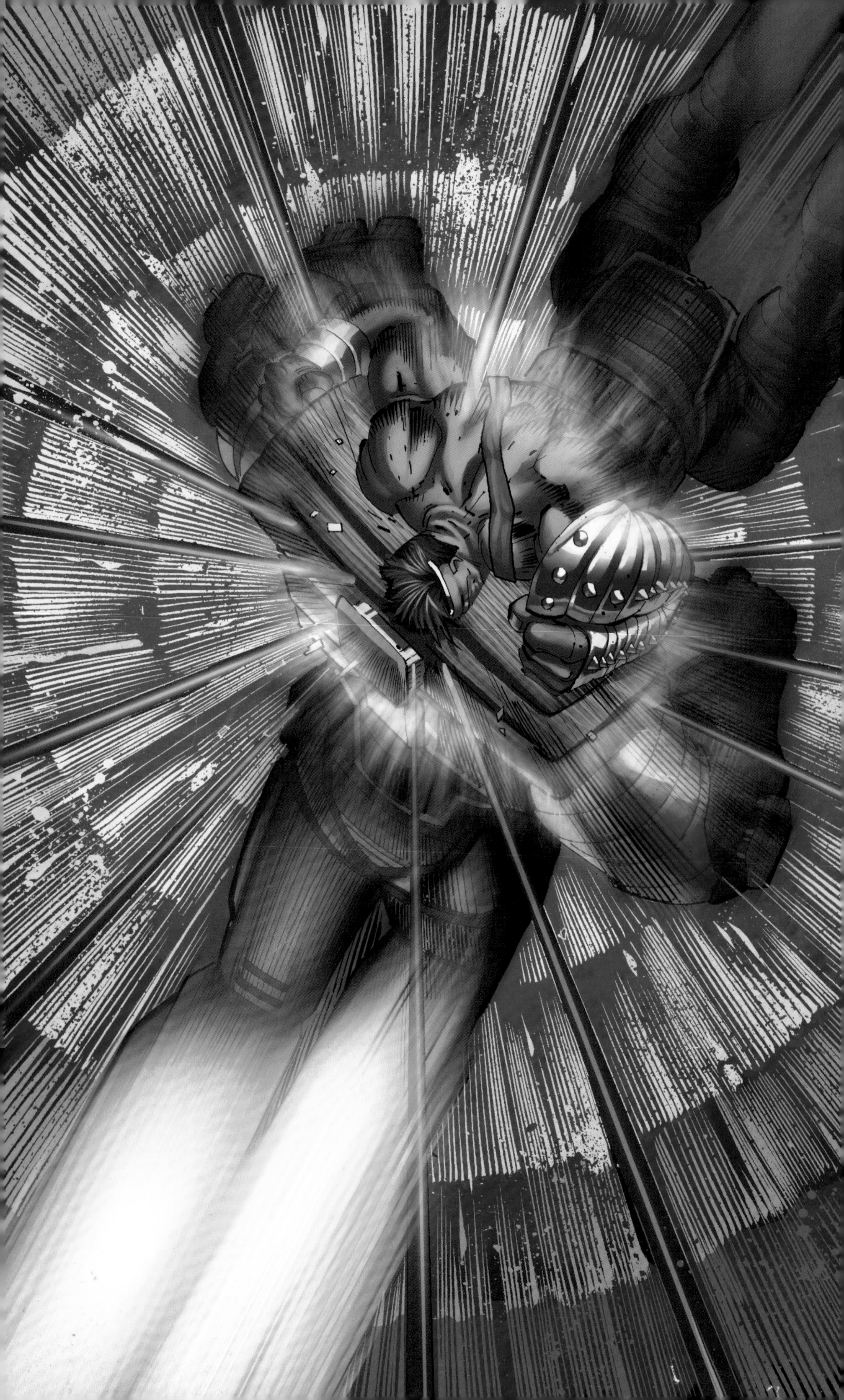

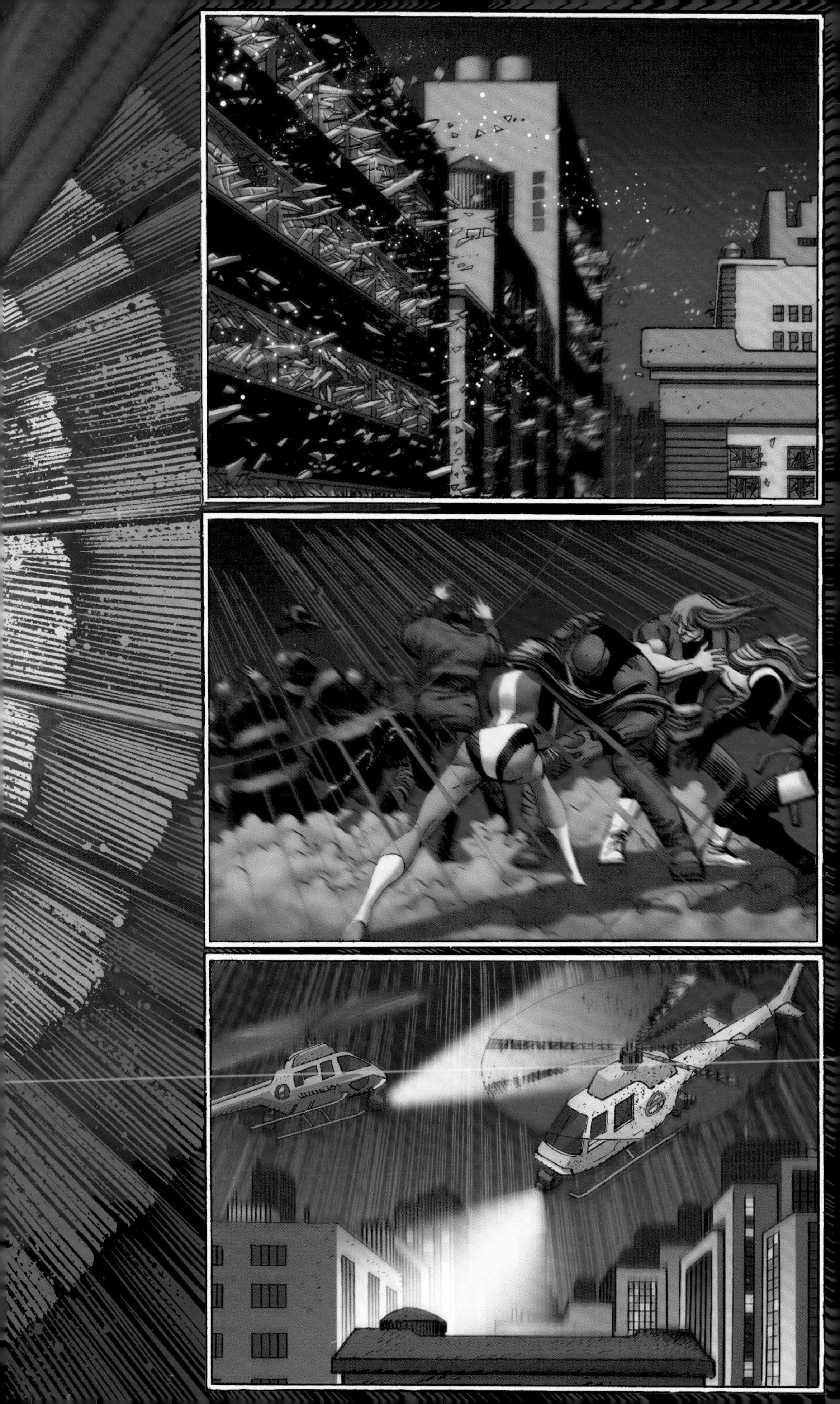

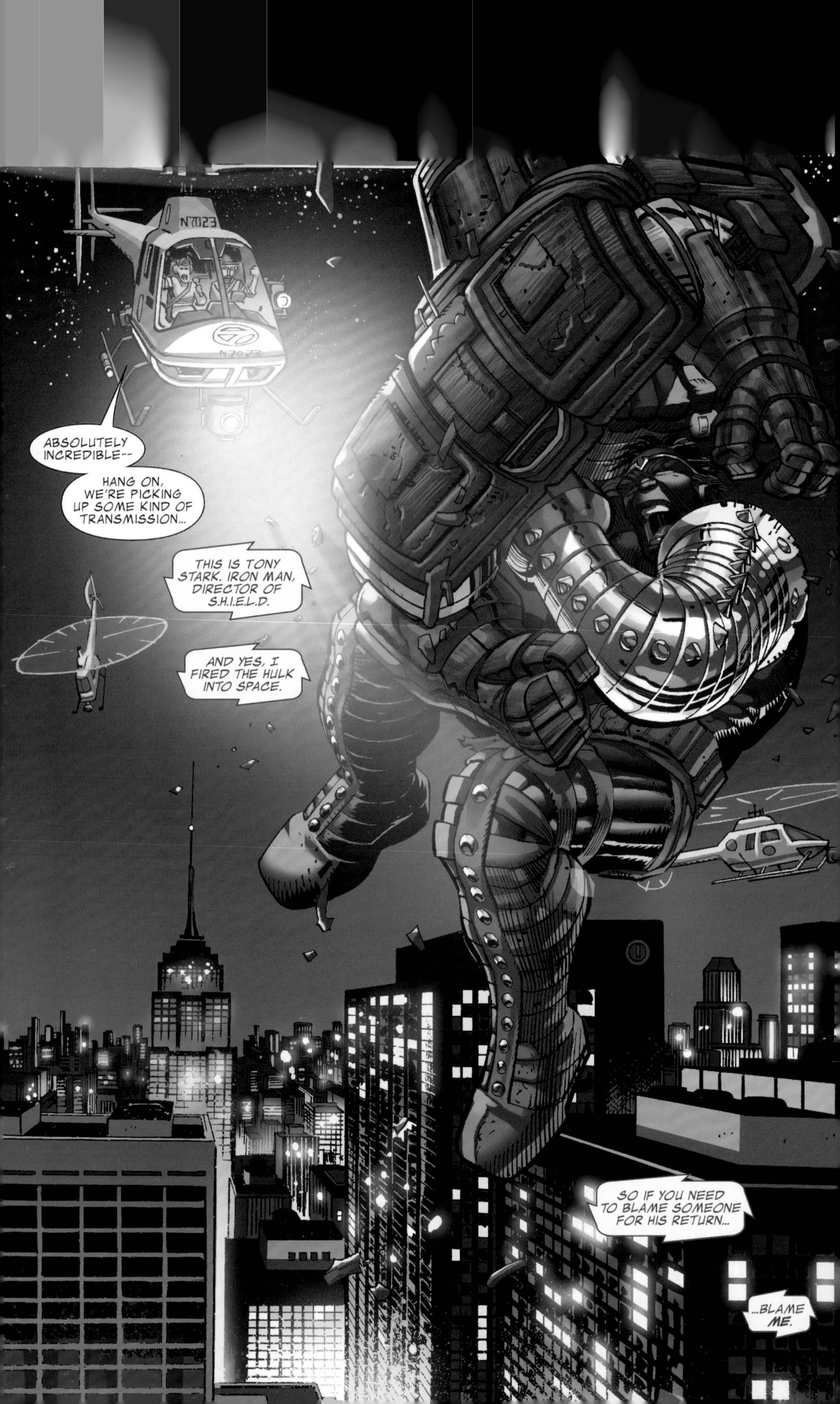

ABSOLUTELY INCREDIBLE--
HANG ON, WE'RE PICKING UP SOME KIND OF TRANSMISSION...
THIS IS TONY STARK. IRON MAN, DIRECTOR OF S.H.I.E.L.D.
AND YES, I FIRED THE HULK INTO SPACE.
SO IF YOU NEED TO BLAME SOMEONE FOR HIS RETURN...
...BLAME ME.

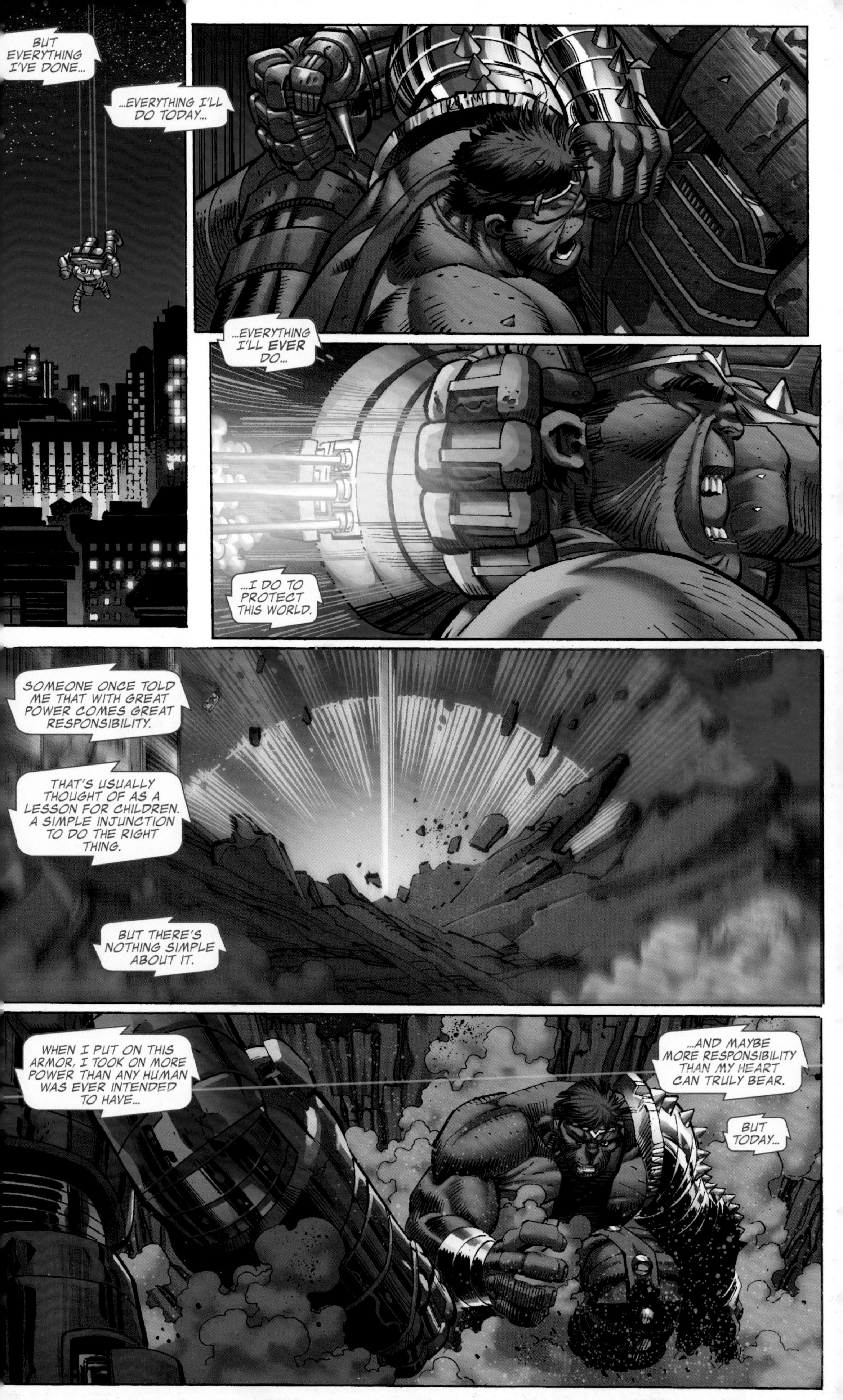
BUT EVERYTHING I'VE DONE...
...EVERYTHING I'LL DO TODAY...
...EVERYTHING I'LL EVER DO...
...I DO TO PROTECT THIS WORLD.
SOMEONE ONCE TOLD ME THAT WITH GREAT POWER COMES GREAT RESPONSIBILITY.
THAT'S USUALLY THOUGHT OF AS A LESSON FOR CHILDREN. A SIMPLE INJUNCTION TO DO THE RIGHT THING.
BUT THERE'S NOTHING SIMPLE ABOUT IT.
WHEN I PUT ON THIS ARMOR, I TOOK ON MORE POWER THAN ANY HUMAN WAS EVER INTENDED TO HAVE...
...AND MAYBE MORE RESPONSIBILITY THAN MY HEART CAN TRULY BEAR.
BUT TODAY...

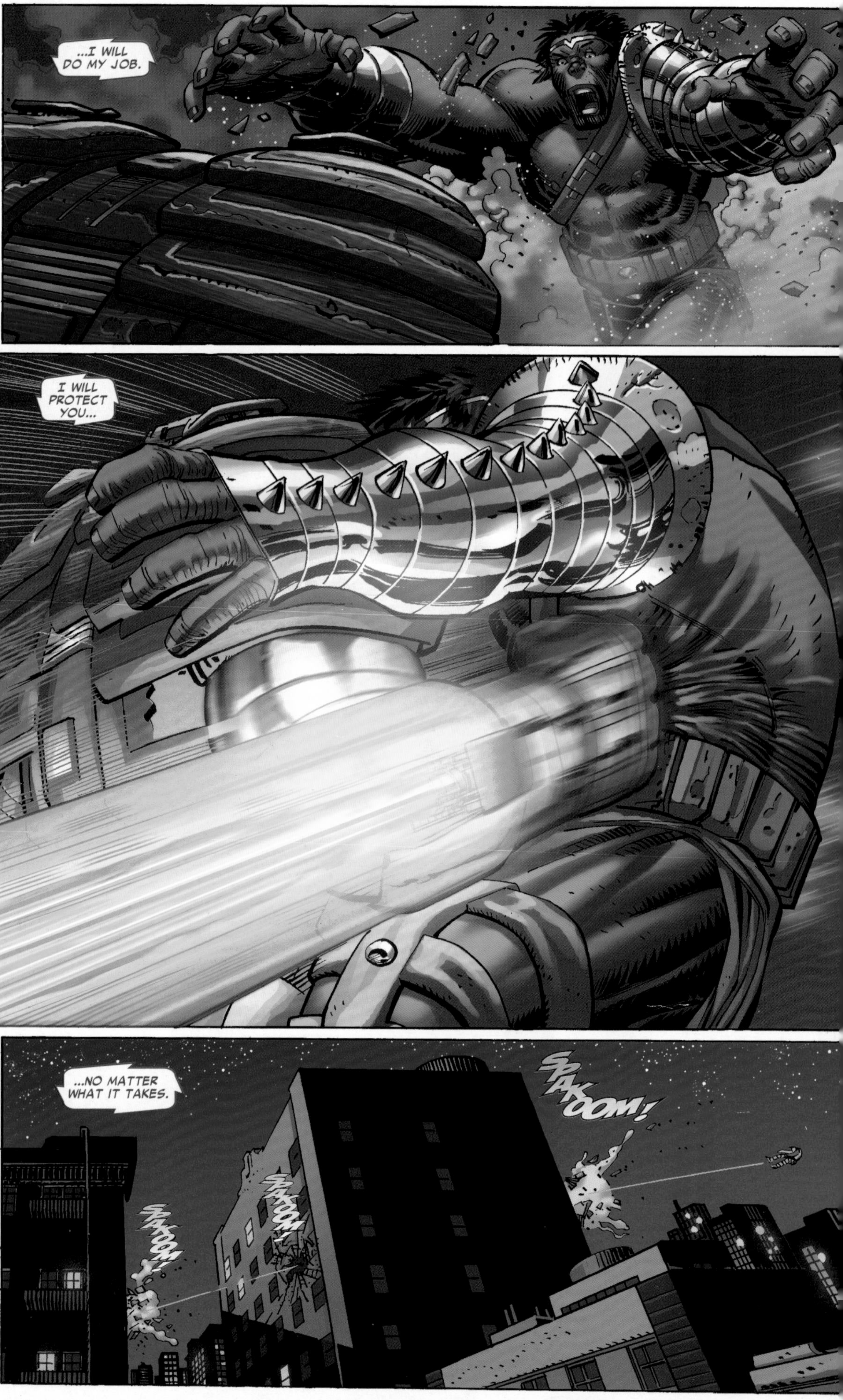
...I WILL DO MY JOB.
I WILL PROTECT YOU...
...NO MATTER WHAT IT TAKES.
SPAKOOM!
SPAKOOM!
SPAKOOM!

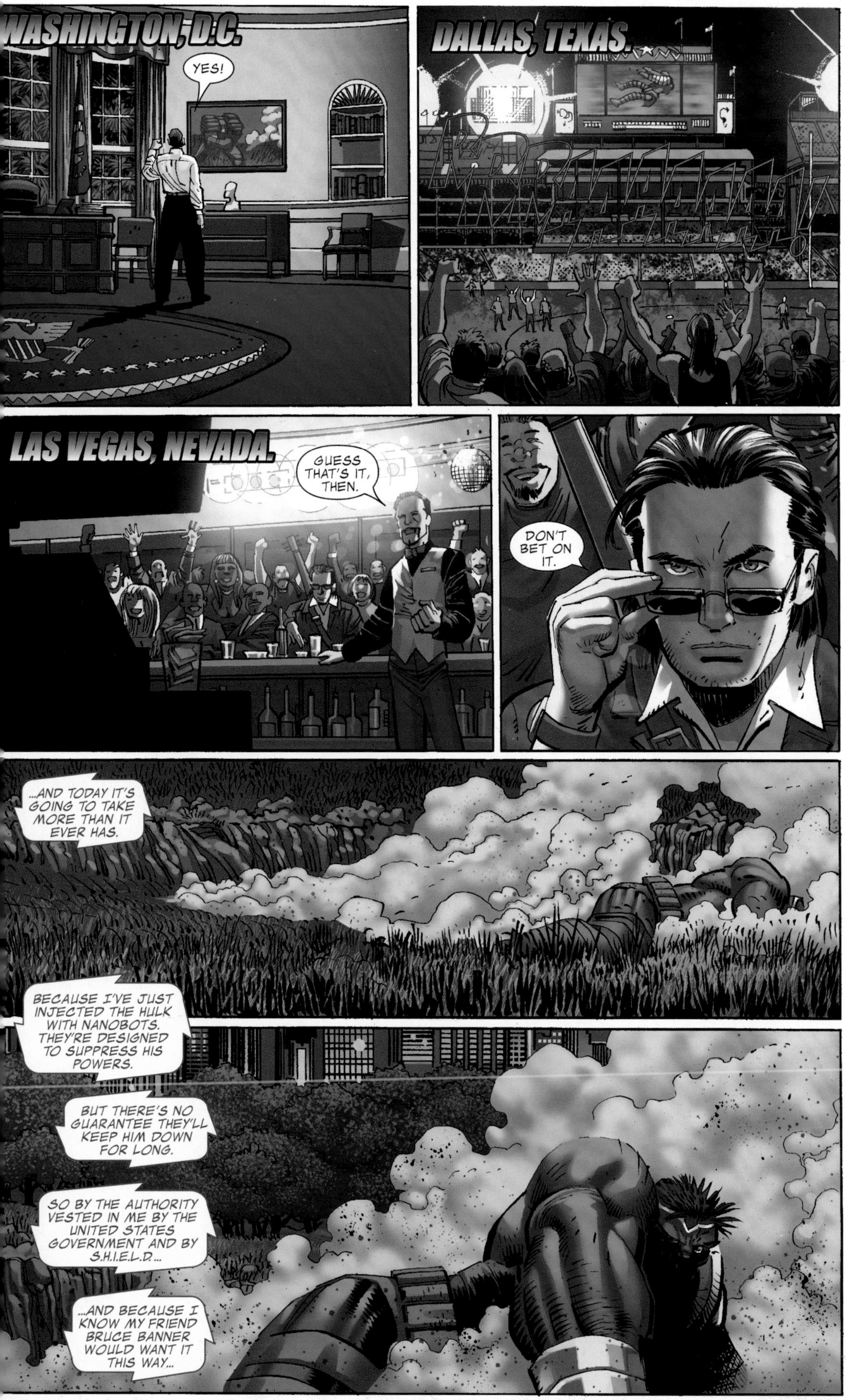
WASHINGTON, D.C.
YES!
DALLAS, TEXAS.
LAS VEGAS, NEVADA.
GUESS THAT'S IT, THEN.
DON'T BET ON IT.
...AND TODAY IT'S GOING TO TAKE MORE THAN IT EVER HAS.
BECAUSE I'VE JUST INJECTED THE HULK WITH NANOBOTS. THEY'RE DESIGNED TO SUPPRESS HIS POWERS.
BUT THERE'S NO GUARANTEE THEY'LL KEEP HIM DOWN FOR LONG.
SO BY THE AUTHORITY VESTED IN ME BY THE UNITED STATES GOVERNMENT AND BY S.H.I.E.L.D...
...AND BECAUSE I KNOW MY FRIEND BRUCE BANNER WOULD WANT IT THIS WAY...

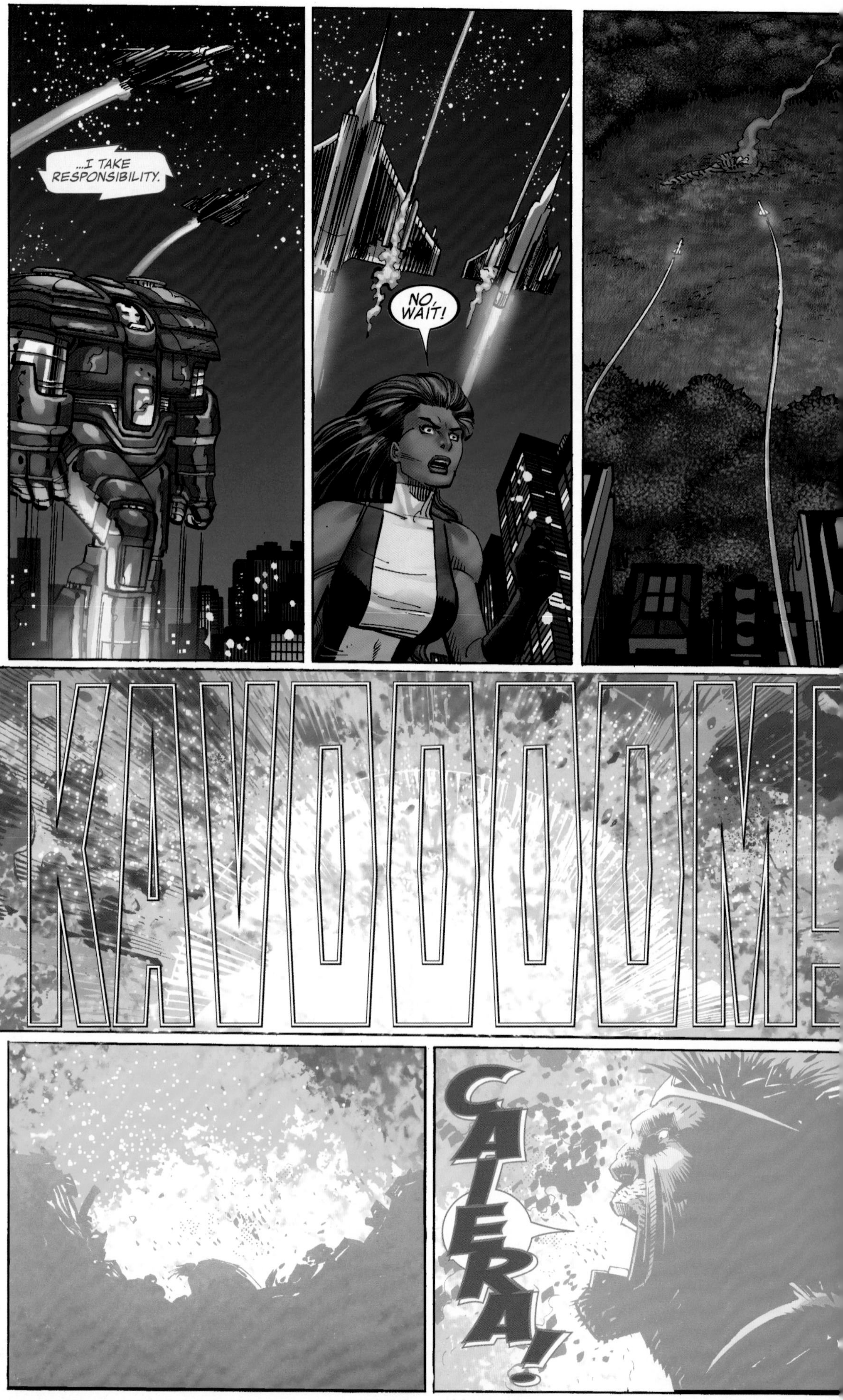
...I TAKE RESPONSIBILITY.
NO, WAIT!
KAVOOOOM
CAIERA!

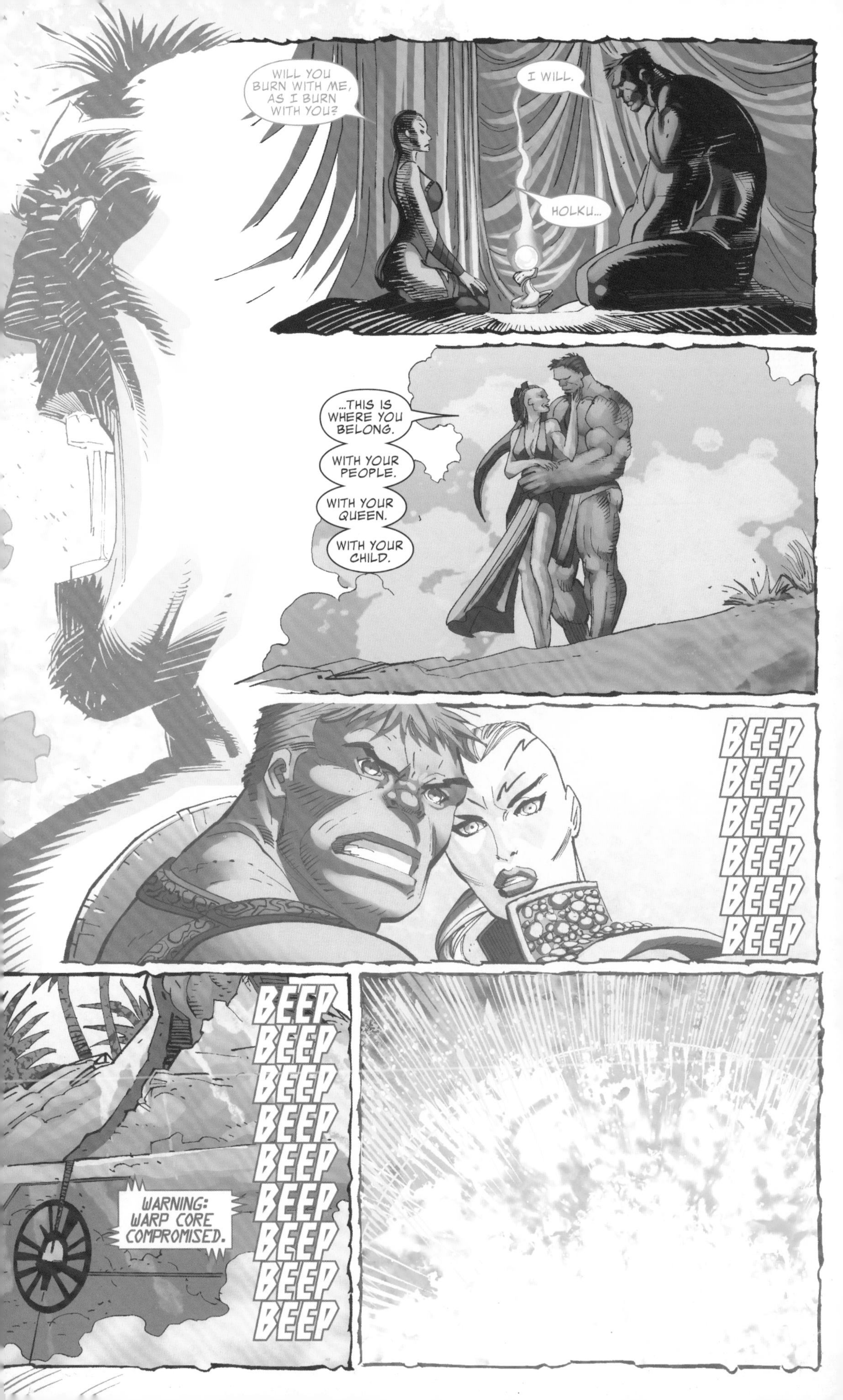
WILL YOU BURN WITH ME, AS I BURN WITH YOU?
I WILL.
HOLKU...
...THIS IS WHERE YOU BELONG.
WITH YOUR PEOPLE.
WITH YOUR QUEEN.
WITH YOUR CHILD.
BEEP BEEP BEEP BEEP BEEP BEEP
BEEP BEEP BEEP BEEP BEEP BEEP BEEP BEEP BEEP
WARNING: WARP CORE COMPROMISED.

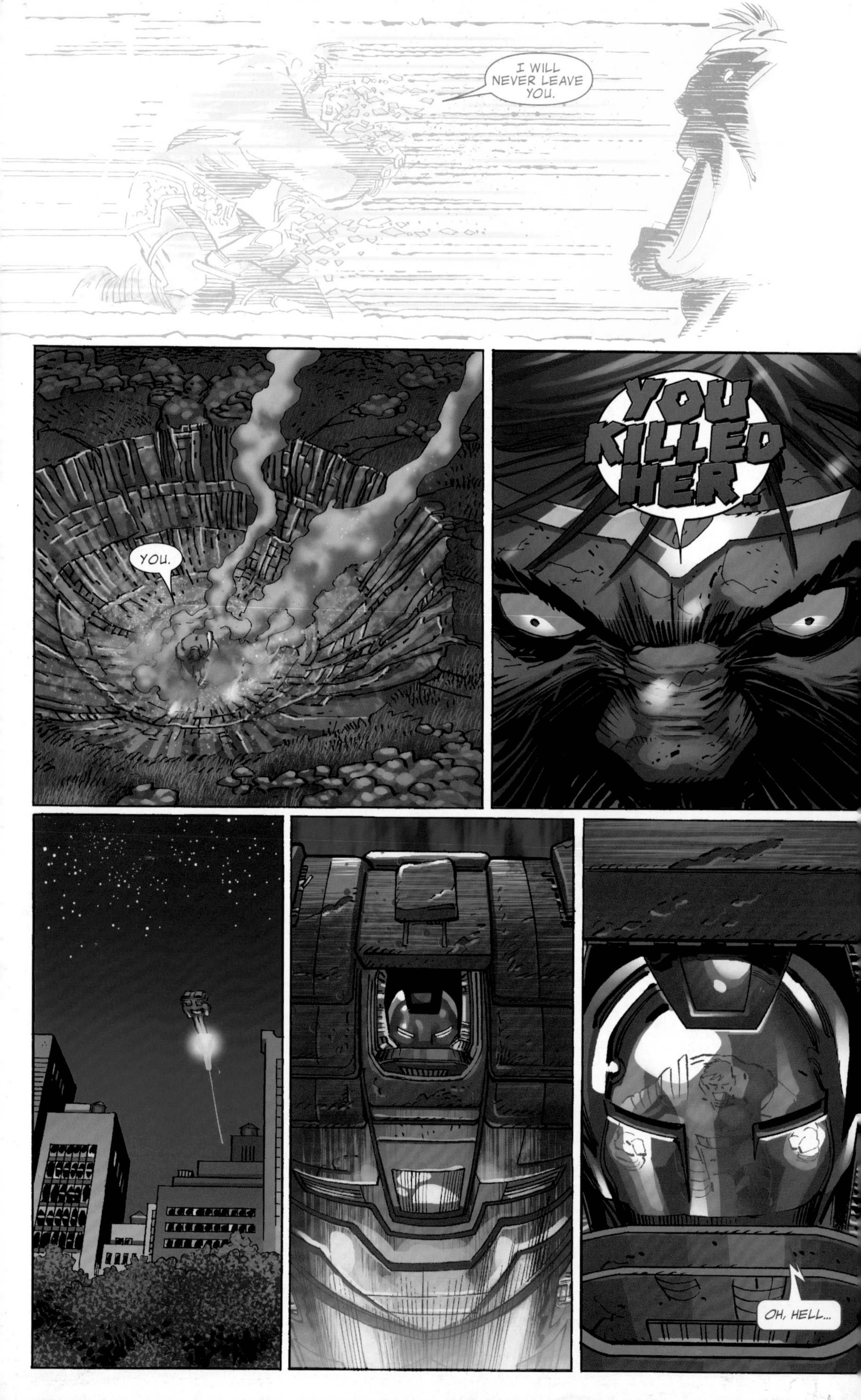
I WILL NEVER LEAVE YOU.
YOU.
YOU KILLED HER.
OH, HELL...

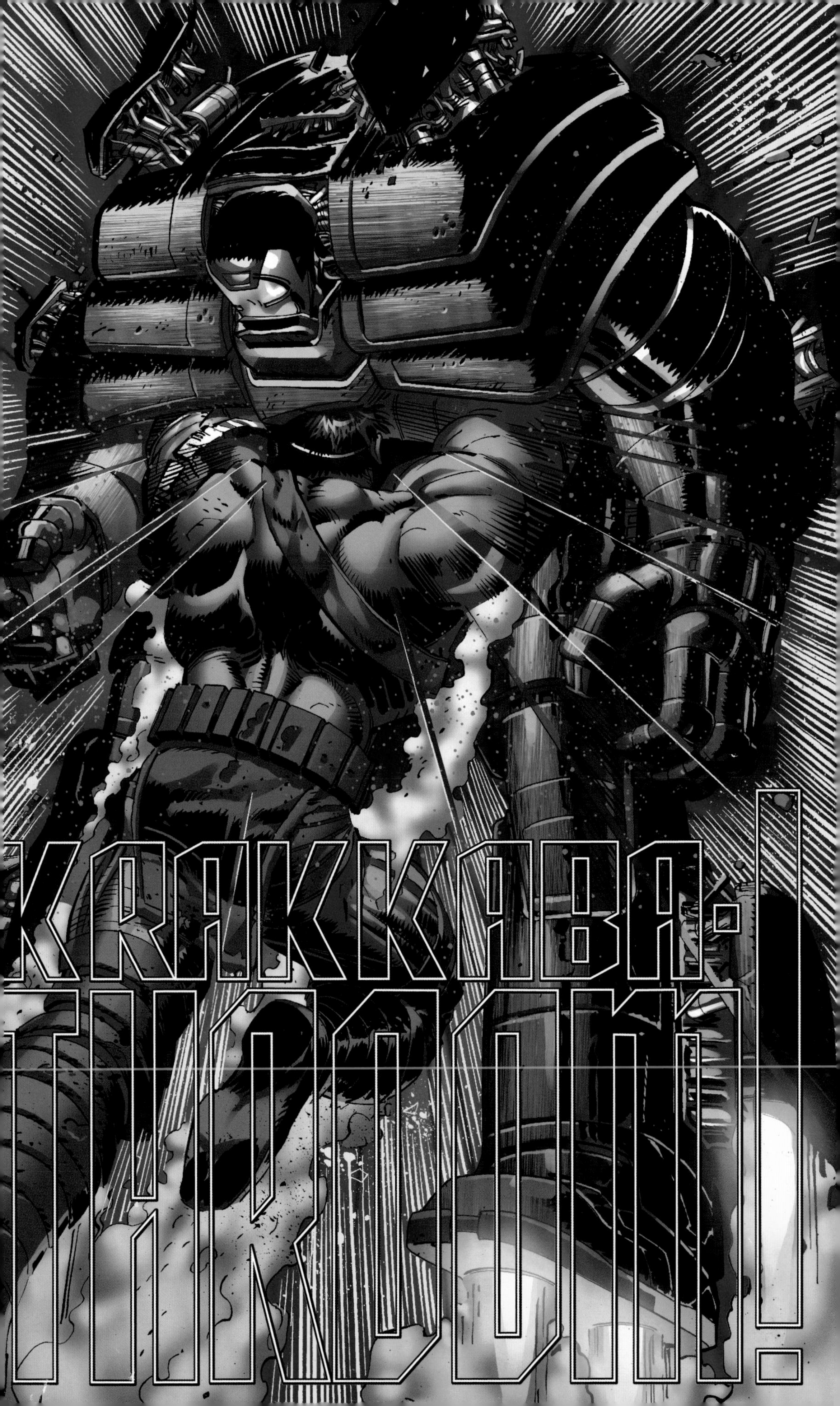
KRAKKABA-
THROOM!

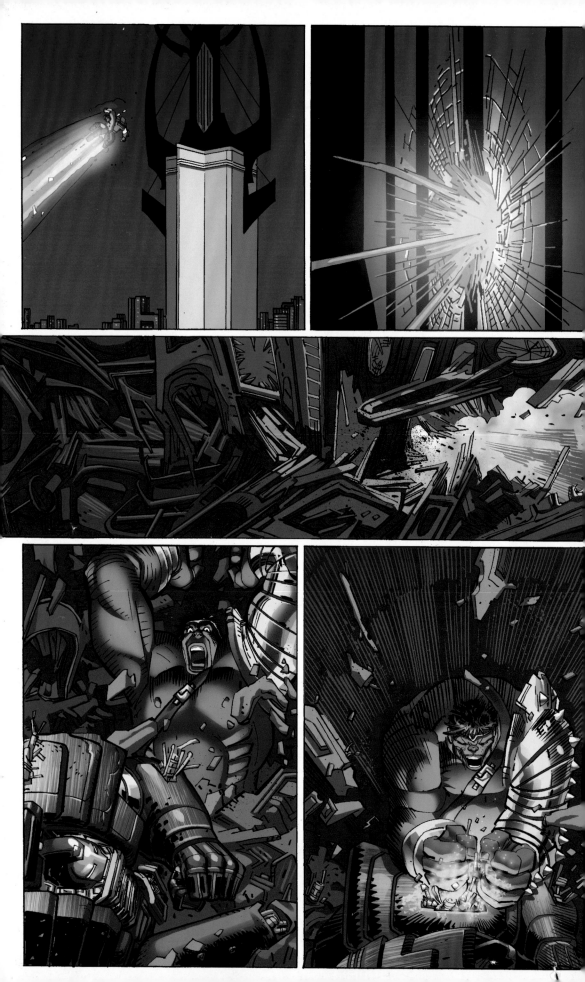

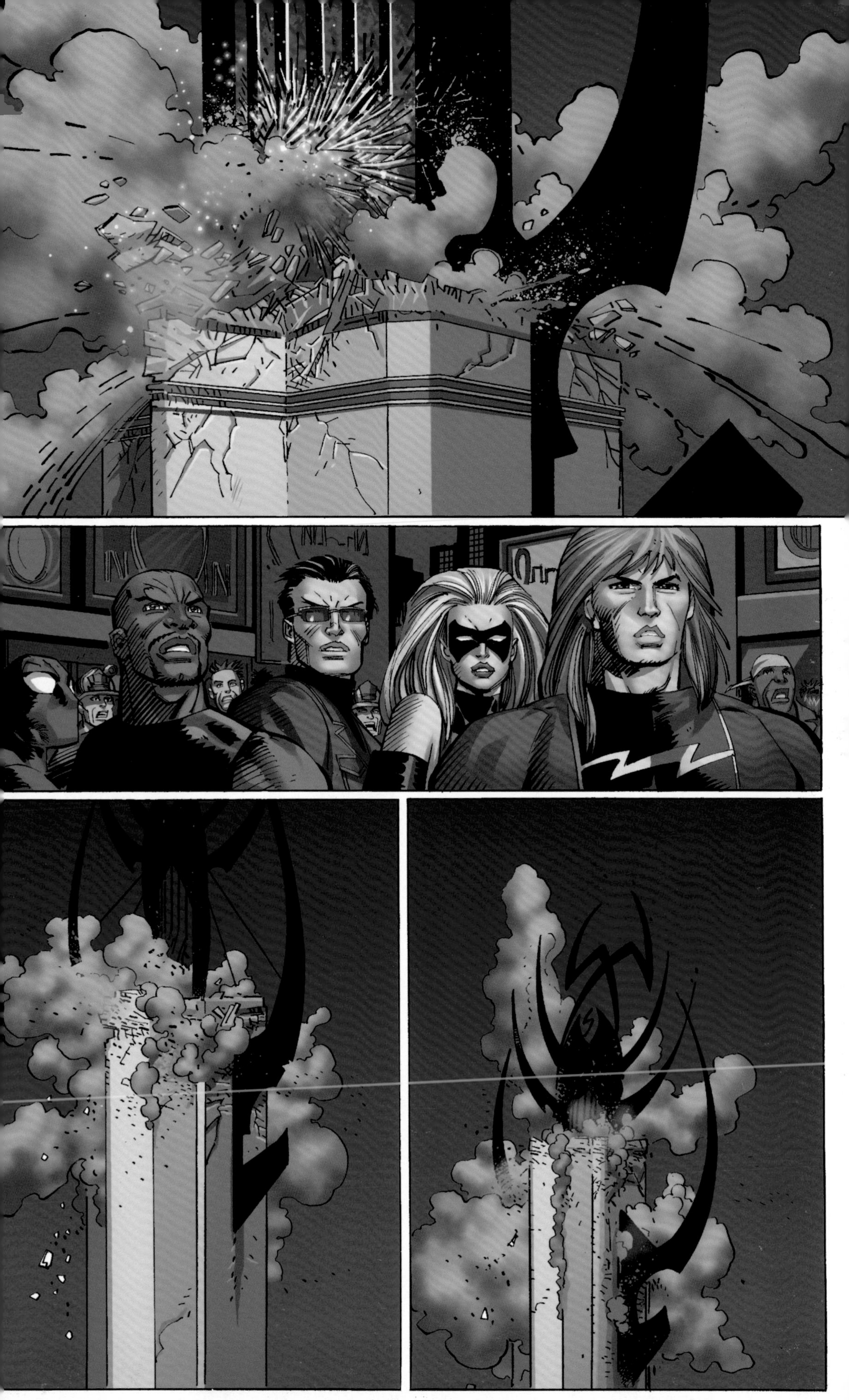

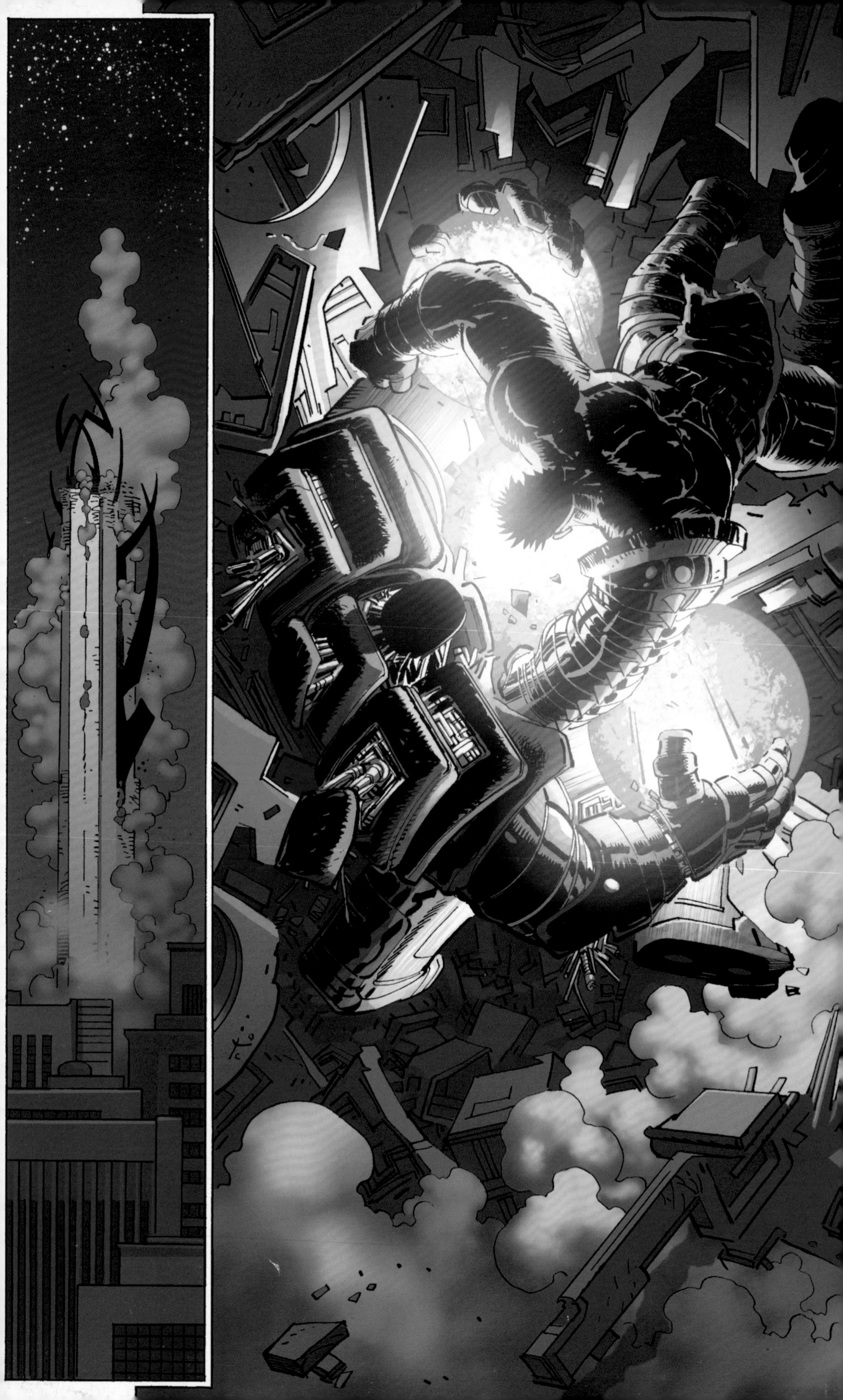

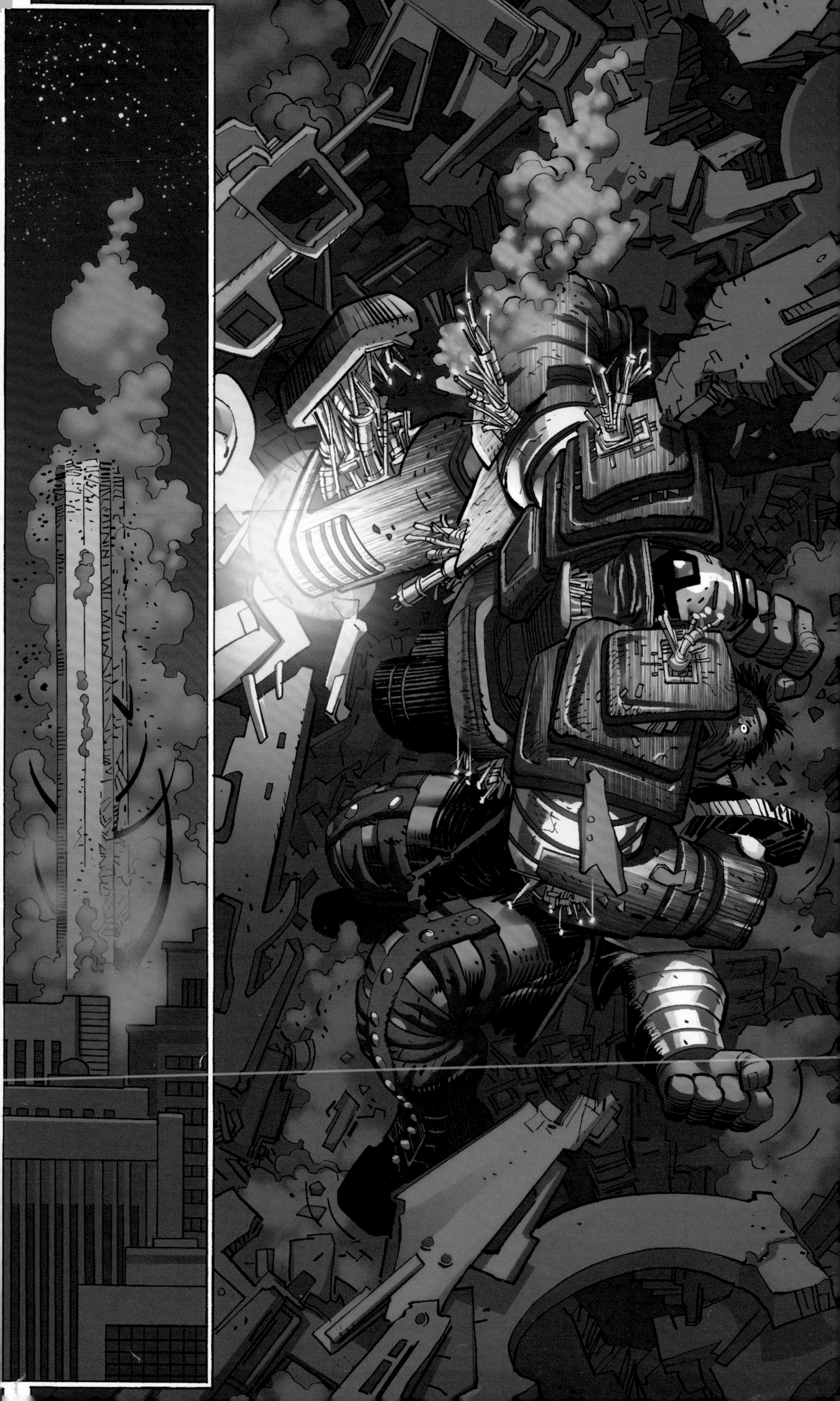

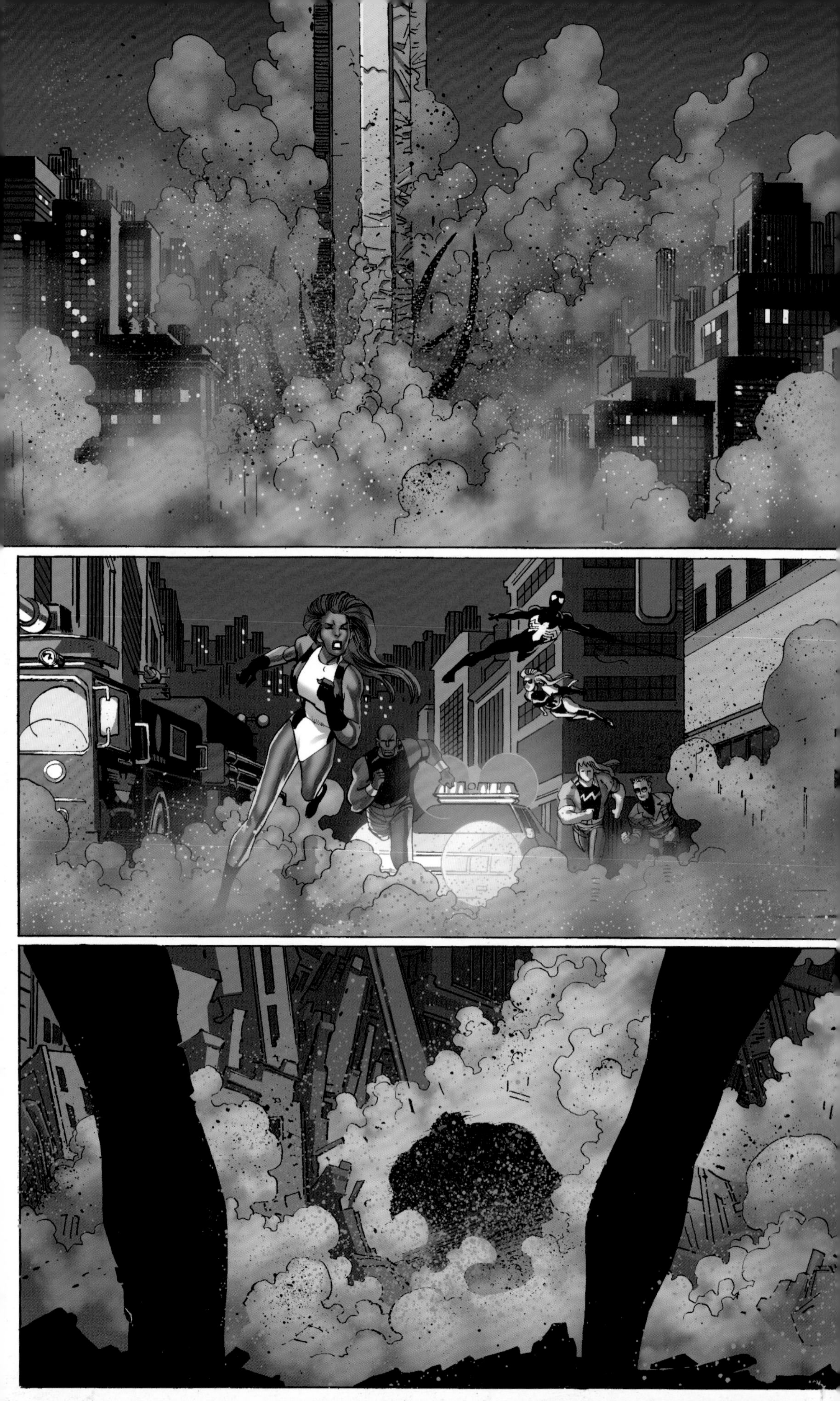

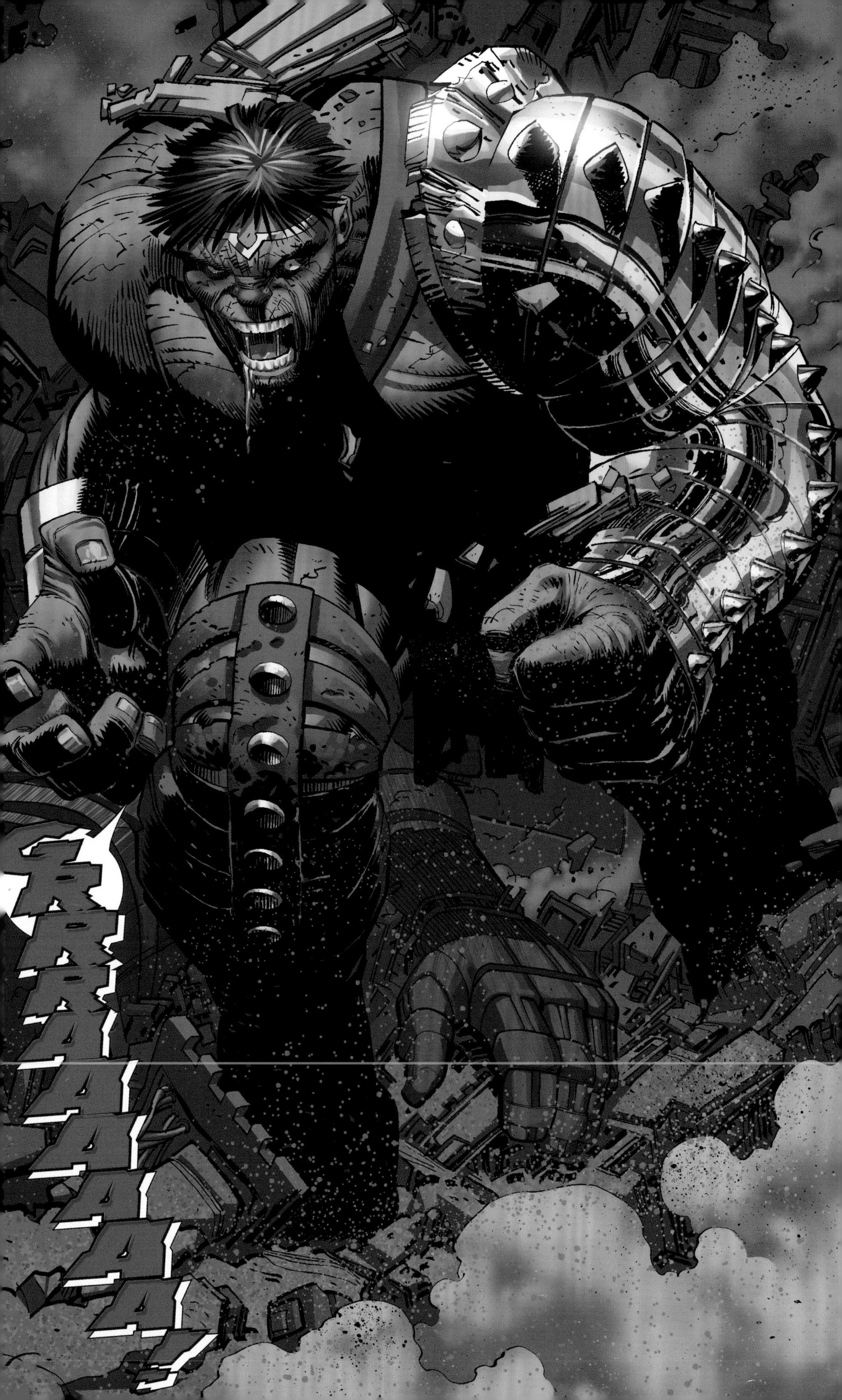
RRAAAAAA!

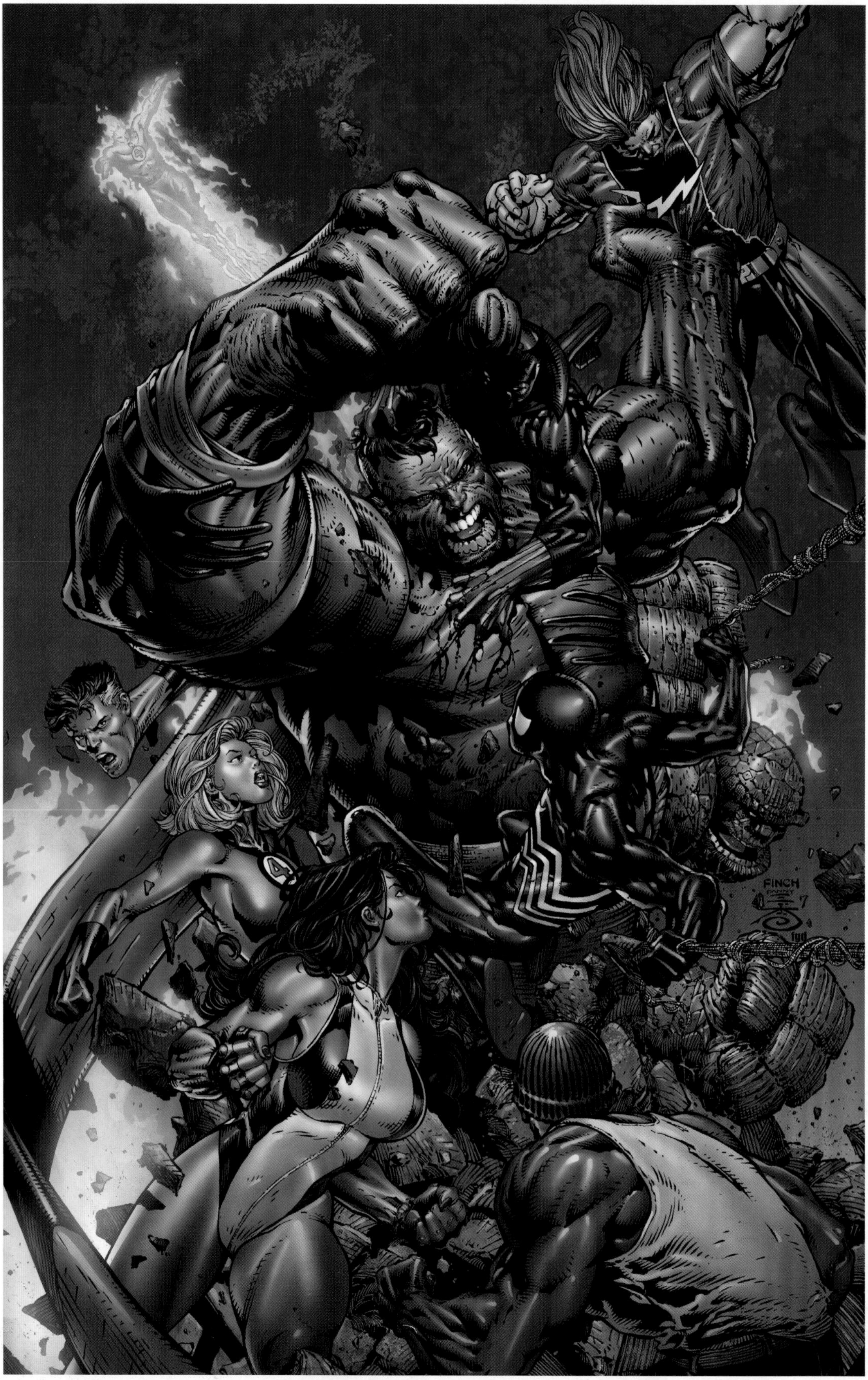
FINCH

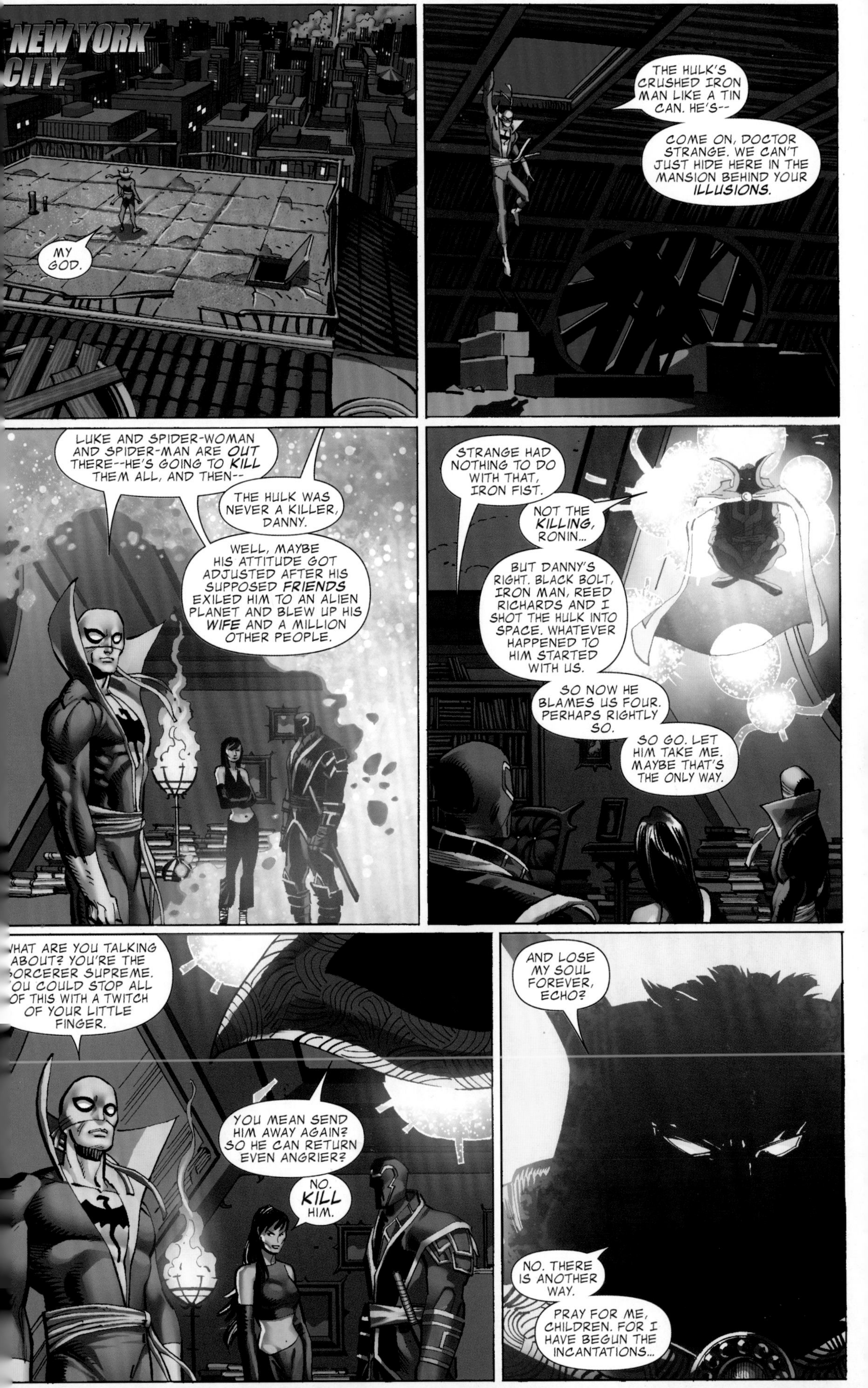
NEW YORK CITY.
MY GOD.
THE HULK'S CRUSHED IRON MAN LIKE A TIN CAN. HE'S--
COME ON, DOCTOR STRANGE. WE CAN'T JUST HIDE HERE IN THE MANSION BEHIND YOUR ILLUSIONS.
LUKE AND SPIDER-WOMAN AND SPIDER-MAN ARE OUT THERE--HE'S GOING TO KILL THEM ALL, AND THEN--
THE HULK WAS NEVER A KILLER, DANNY.
WELL, MAYBE HIS ATTITUDE GOT ADJUSTED AFTER HIS SUPPOSED FRIENDS EXILED HIM TO AN ALIEN PLANET AND BLEW UP HIS WIFE AND A MILLION OTHER PEOPLE.
STRANGE HAD NOTHING TO DO WITH THAT, IRON FIST.
NOT THE KILLING, RONIN...
BUT DANNY'S RIGHT. BLACK BOLT, IRON MAN, REED RICHARDS AND I SHOT THE HULK INTO SPACE. WHATEVER HAPPENED TO HIM STARTED WITH US.
SO NOW HE BLAMES US FOUR. PERHAPS RIGHTLY SO.
SO GO. LET HIM TAKE ME. MAYBE THAT'S THE ONLY WAY.
WHAT ARE YOU TALKING ABOUT? YOU'RE THE SORCERER SUPREME. YOU COULD STOP ALL OF THIS WITH A TWITCH OF YOUR LITTLE FINGER.
YOU MEAN SEND HIM AWAY AGAIN? SO HE CAN RETURN EVEN ANGRIER?
NO. KILL HIM.
AND LOSE MY SOUL FOREVER, ECHO?
NO. THERE IS ANOTHER WAY.
PRAY FOR ME, CHILDREN. FOR I HAVE BEGUN THE INCANTATIONS...

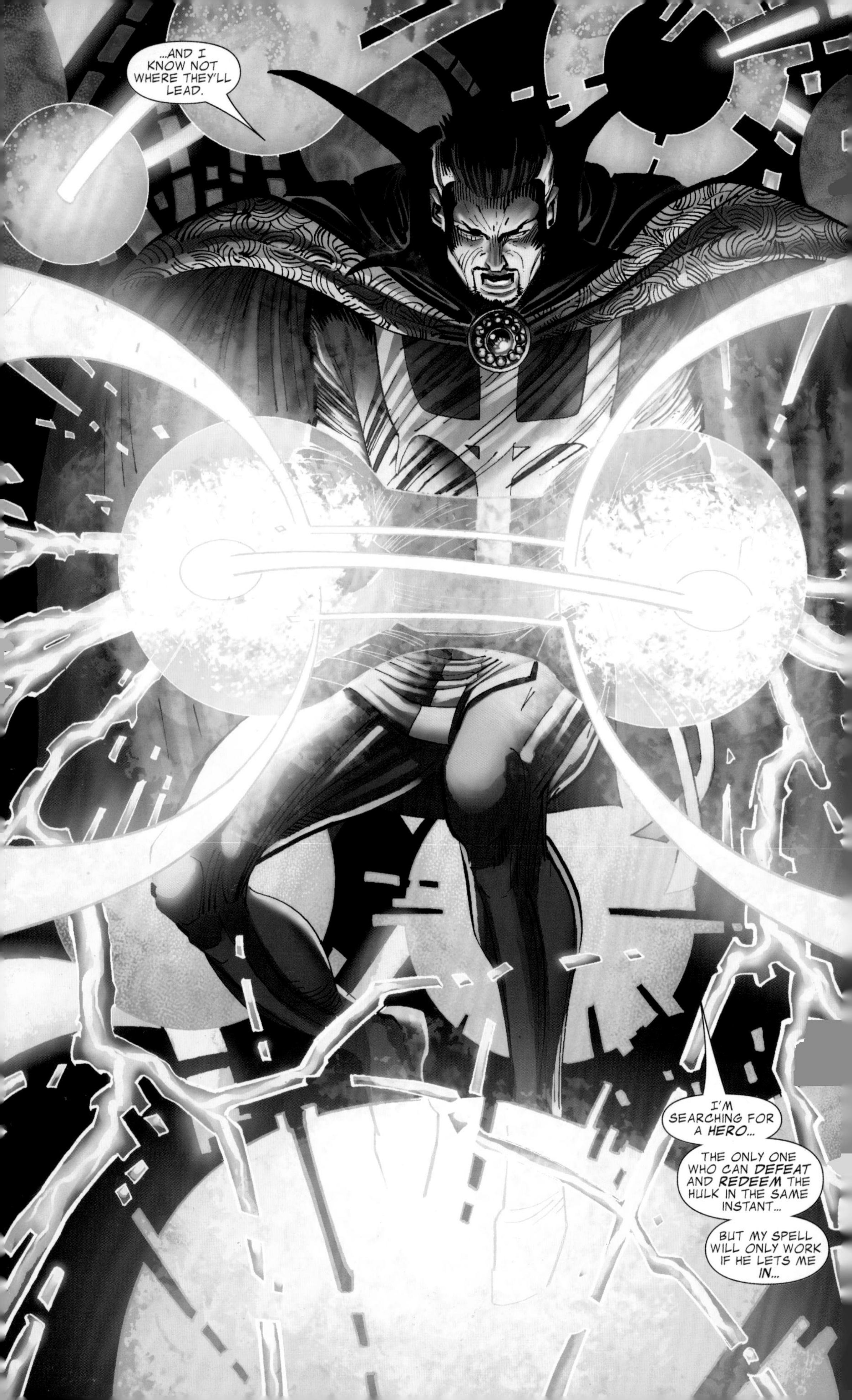
...AND I KNOW NOT WHERE THEY'LL LEAD.
I'M SEARCHING FOR A HERO...
THE ONLY ONE WHO CAN DEFEAT AND REDEEM THE HULK IN THE SAME INSTANT...
BUT MY SPELL WILL ONLY WORK IF HE LETS ME IN...

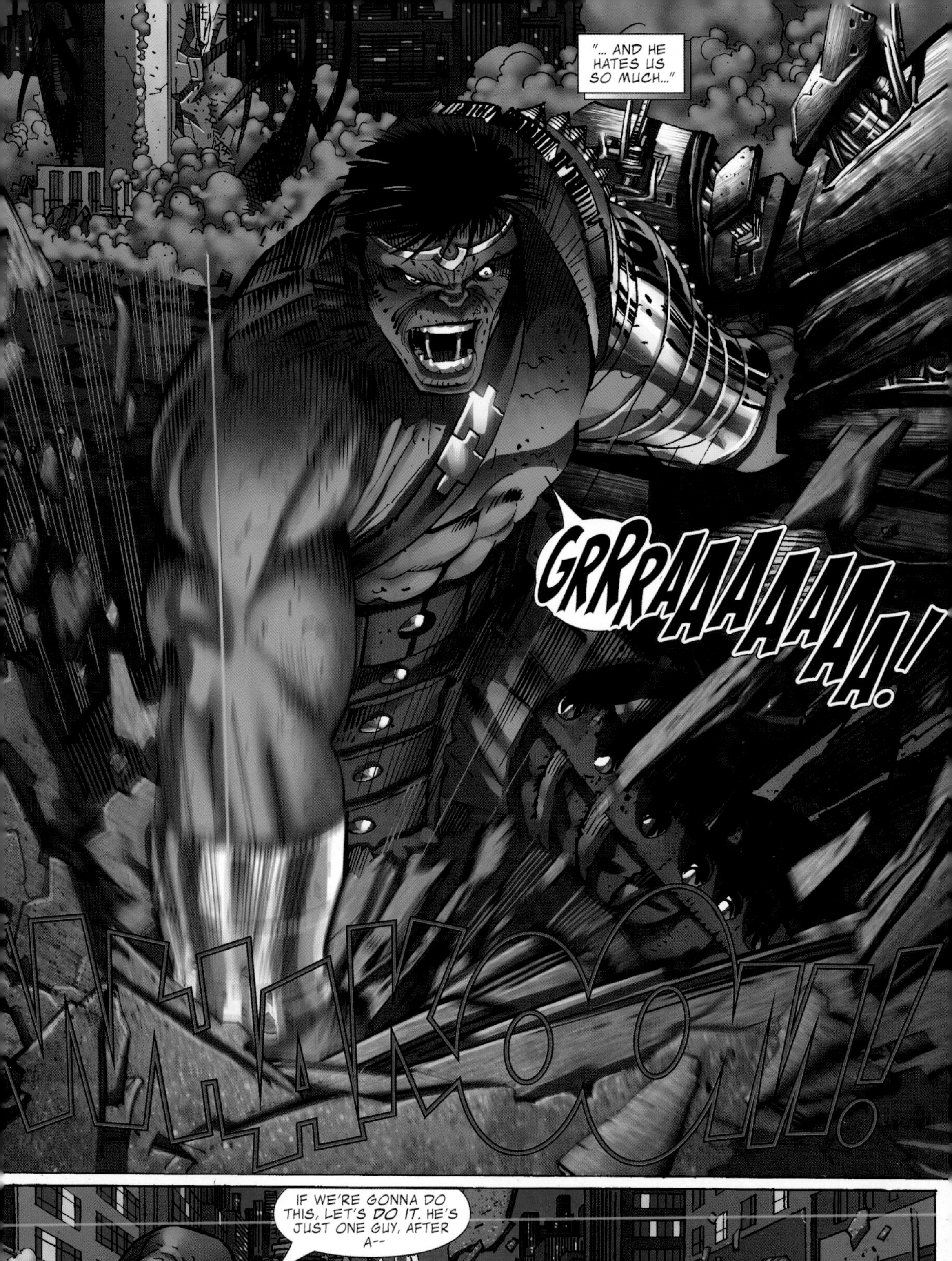
"... AND HE HATES US SO MUCH..."
GRRRAAAAAAAA!
WHAKOOOM!

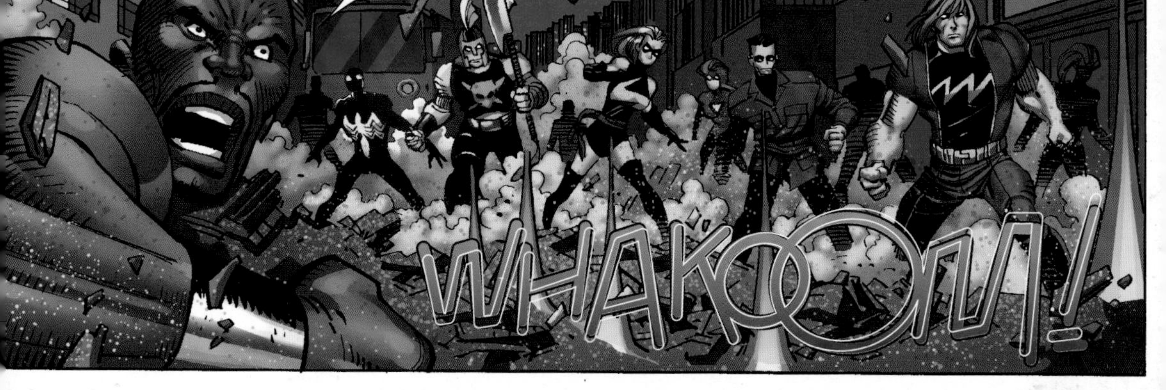
IF WE'RE GONNA DO THIS, LET'S DO IT. HE'S JUST ONE GUY, AFTER A--
WHAKOOOM!

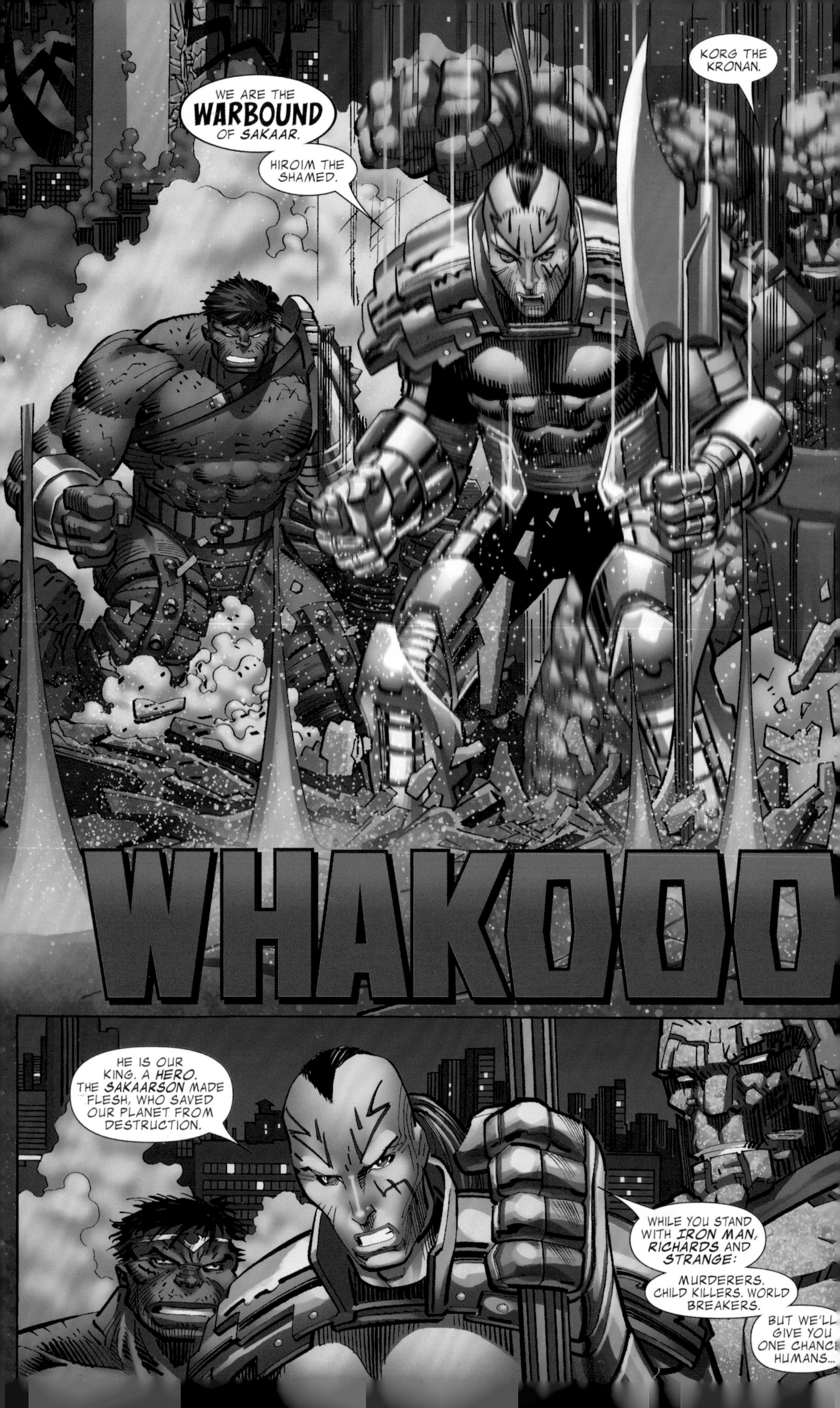
WE ARE THE WARBOUND OF SAKAAR.
HIROIM THE SHAMED.
KORG THE KRONAN.
WHAKOOO
HE IS OUR KING. A HERO. THE SAKAARSON MADE FLESH, WHO SAVED OUR PLANET FROM DESTRUCTION.
WHILE YOU STAND WITH IRON MAN, RICHARDS AND STRANGE:
MURDERERS. CHILD KILLERS. WORLD BREAKERS.
BUT WE'LL GIVE YOU ONE CHANC HUMANS...

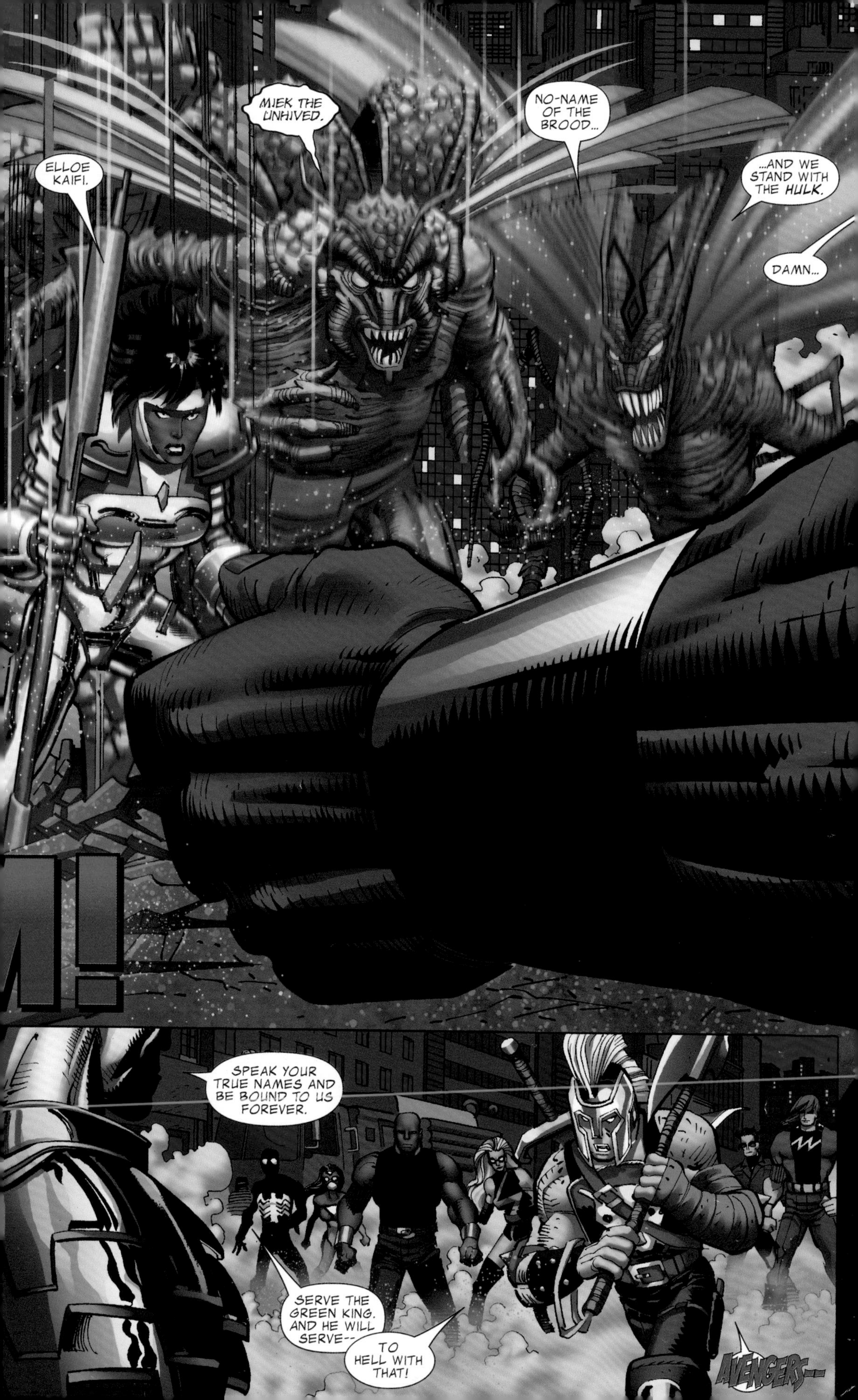
ELLOE KAIFI.
MIEK THE UNHIVED.
NO-NAME OF THE BROOD...
...AND WE STAND WITH THE HULK.
DAMN...
SPEAK YOUR TRUE NAMES AND BE BOUND TO US FOREVER.
SERVE THE GREEN KING. AND HE WILL SERVE--
TO HELL WITH THAT!
AVENGERS--

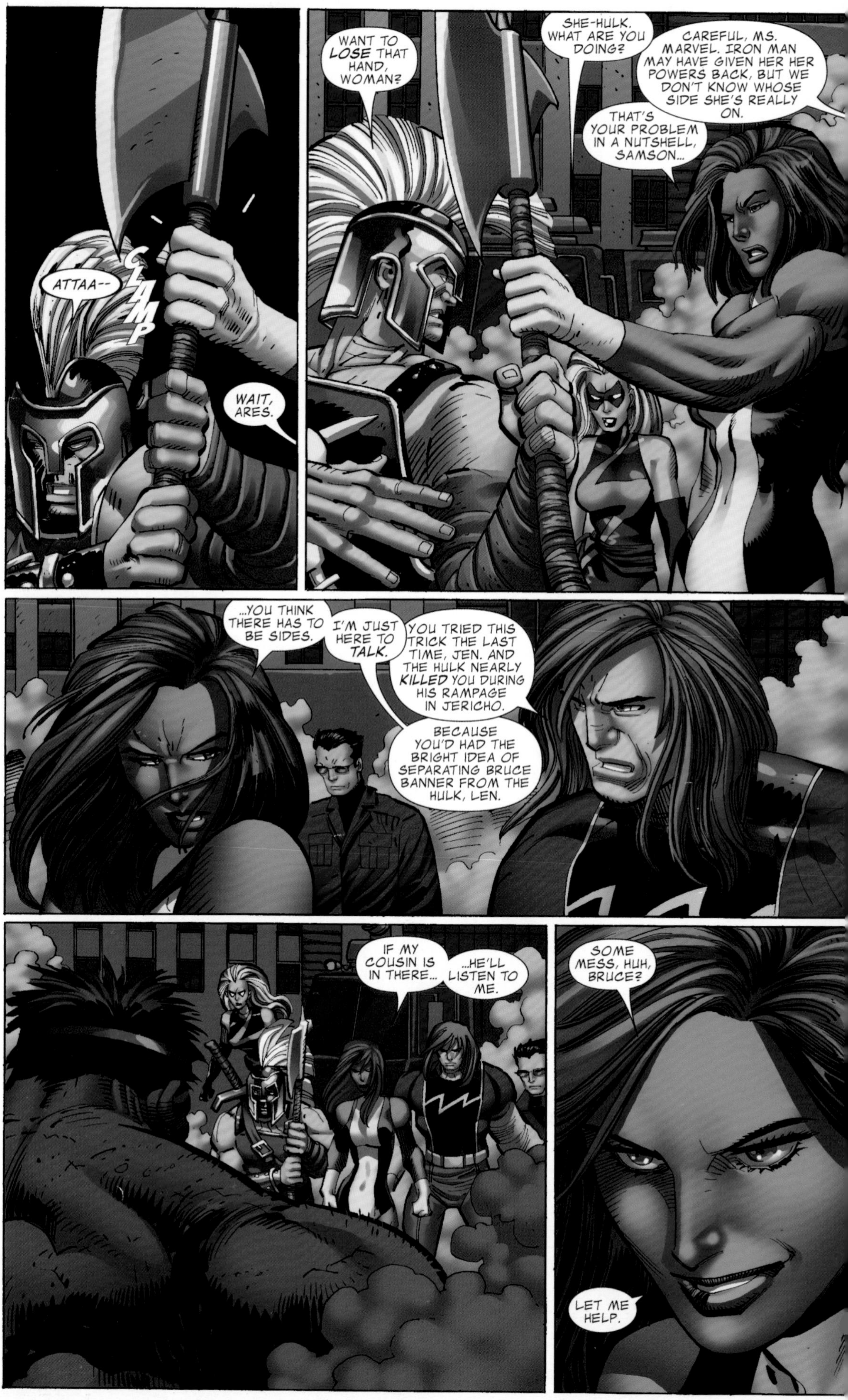
ATTAA--
CLAMP
WAIT, ARES.
WANT TO LOSE THAT HAND, WOMAN?
SHE-HULK. WHAT ARE YOU DOING?
CAREFUL, MS. MARVEL. IRON MAN MAY HAVE GIVEN HER HER POWERS BACK, BUT WE DON'T KNOW WHOSE SIDE SHE'S REALLY ON.
THAT'S YOUR PROBLEM IN A NUTSHELL, SAMSON...
...YOU THINK THERE HAS TO BE SIDES.
I'M JUST HERE TO TALK.
YOU TRIED THIS TRICK THE LAST TIME, JEN. AND THE HULK NEARLY KILLED YOU DURING HIS RAMPAGE IN JERICHO.
BECAUSE YOU'D HAD THE BRIGHT IDEA OF SEPARATING BRUCE BANNER FROM THE HULK, LEN.
IF MY COUSIN IS IN THERE...
...HE'LL LISTEN TO ME.
SOME MESS, HUH, BRUCE?
LET ME HELP.

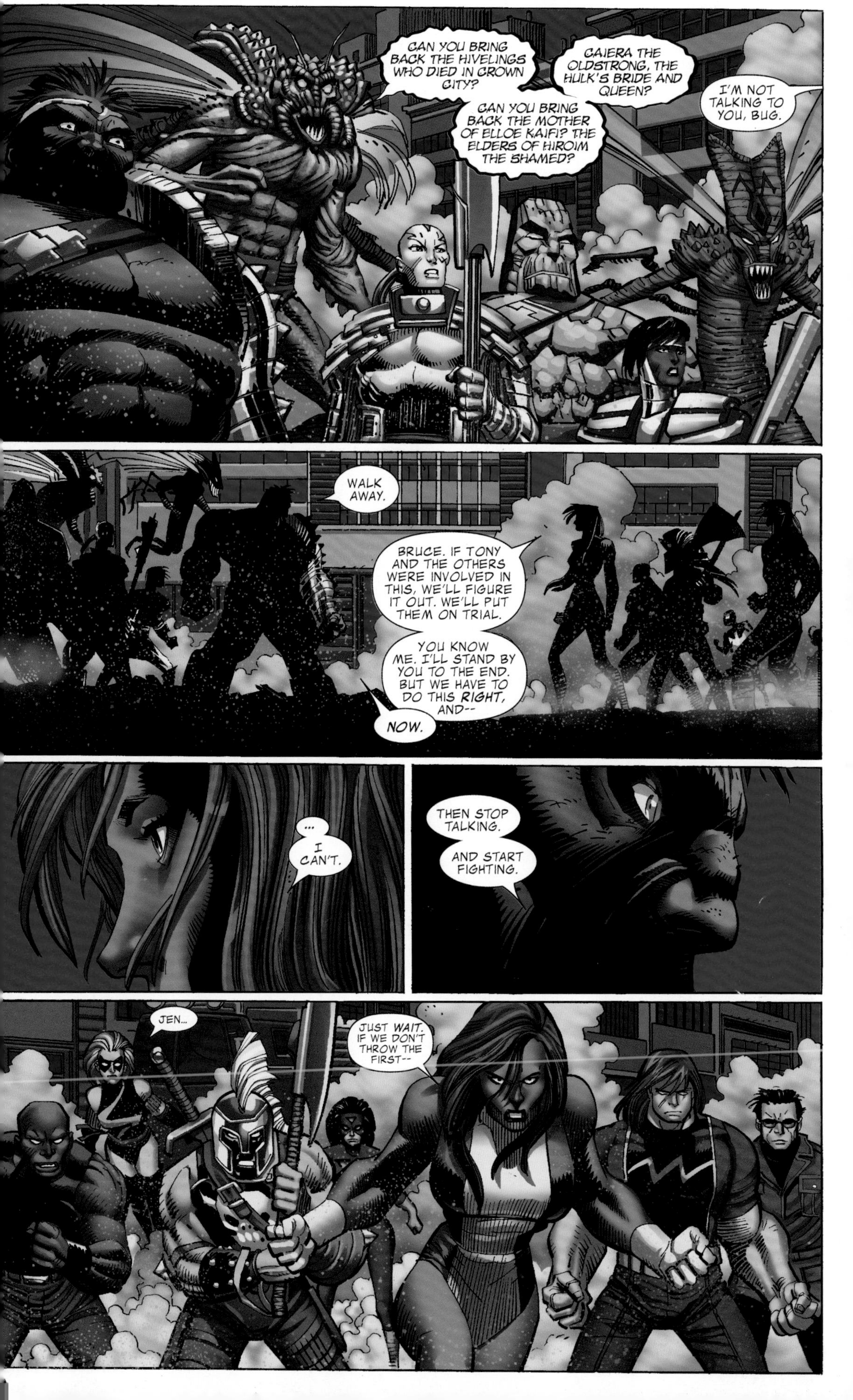
CAN YOU BRING BACK THE HIVELINGS WHO DIED IN CROWN CITY?
CAN YOU BRING BACK THE MOTHER OF ELLOE KAIFI? THE ELDERS OF HIROIM THE SHAMED?
CAIERA THE OLDSTRONG, THE HULK'S BRIDE AND QUEEN?
I'M NOT TALKING TO YOU, BUG.
WALK AWAY.
BRUCE. IF TONY AND THE OTHERS WERE INVOLVED IN THIS, WE'LL FIGURE IT OUT. WE'LL PUT THEM ON TRIAL.
YOU KNOW ME. I'LL STAND BY YOU TO THE END. BUT WE HAVE TO DO THIS RIGHT, AND--
NOW.
... I CAN'T.
THEN STOP TALKING.
AND START FIGHTING.
JEN...
JUST WAIT. IF WE DON'T THROW THE FIRST--

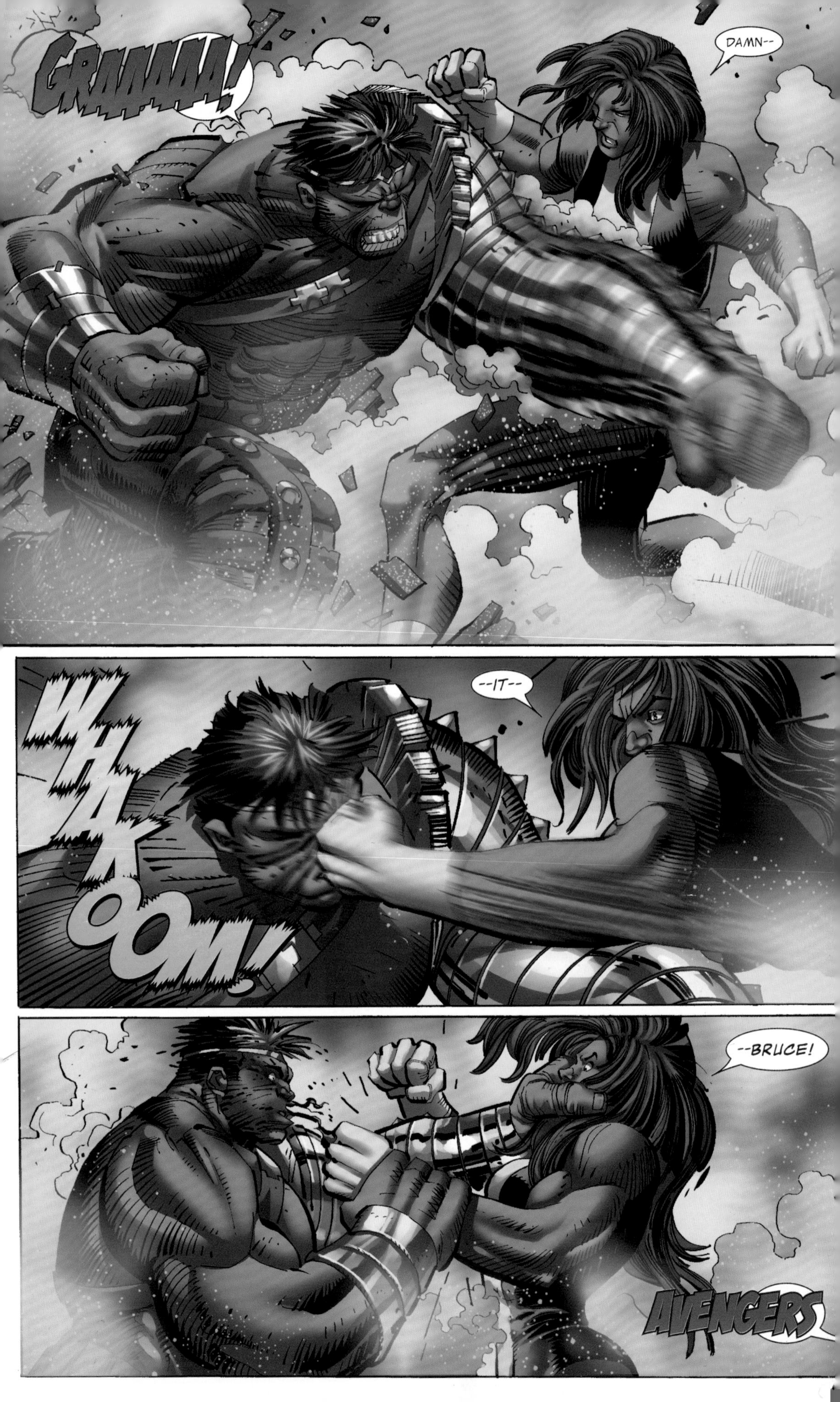
GRAAAAA!
DAMN--
WHAKOOM!
--IT--
--BRUCE!
AVENGERS

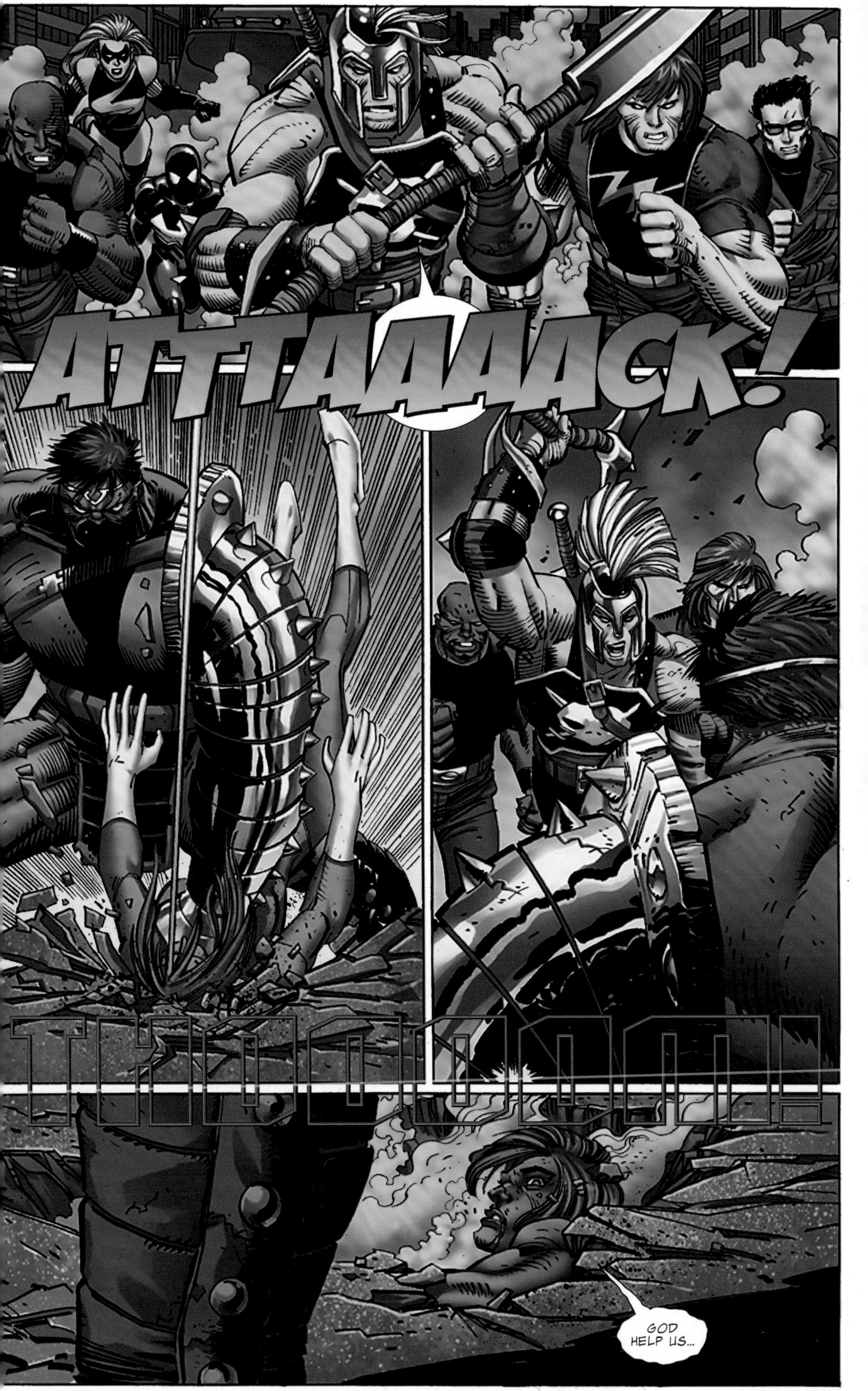
ATTAAAACK!
THOOOOM!
GOD HELP US...

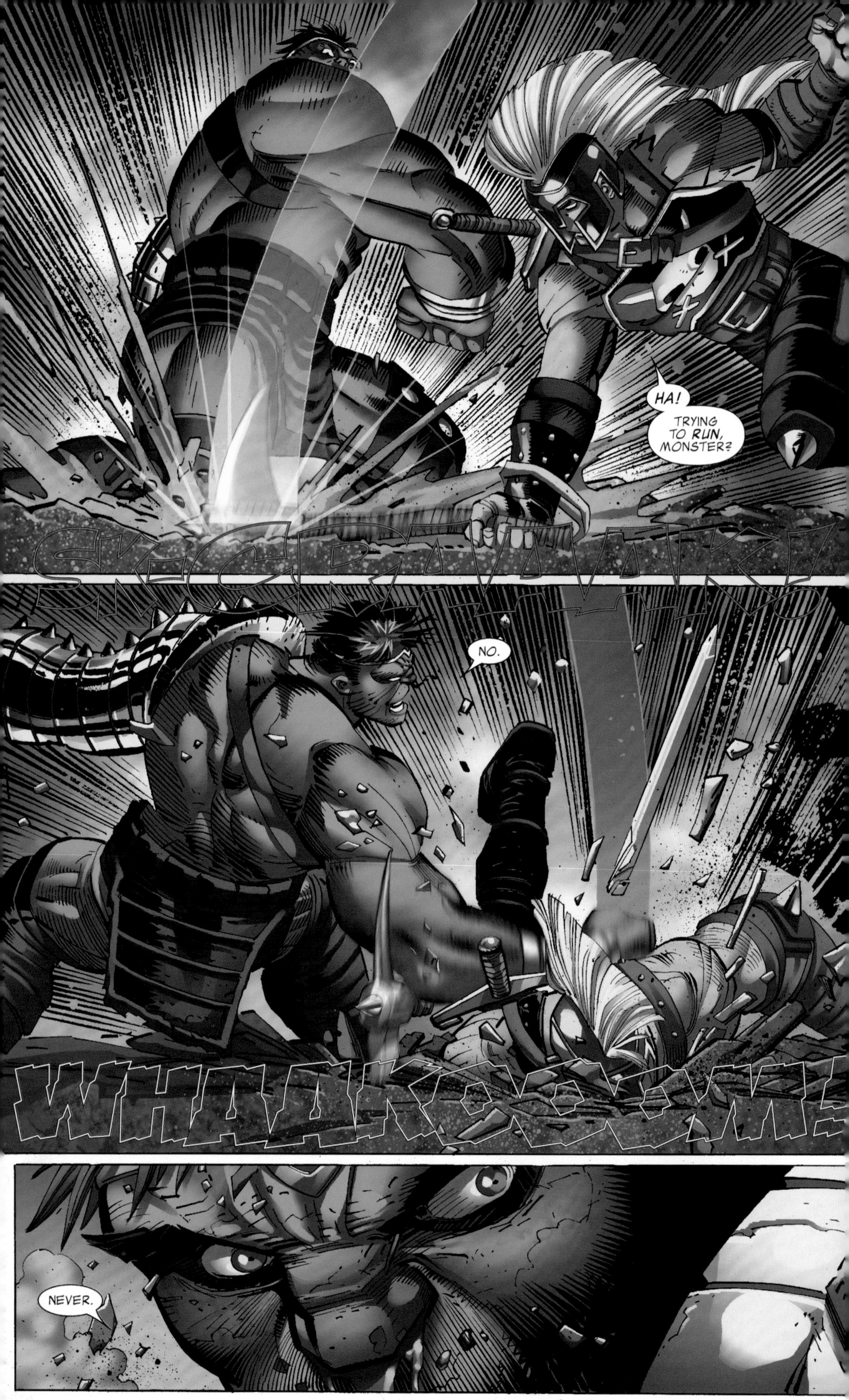
HA!
TRYING TO RUN, MONSTER?
NO.
NEVER.

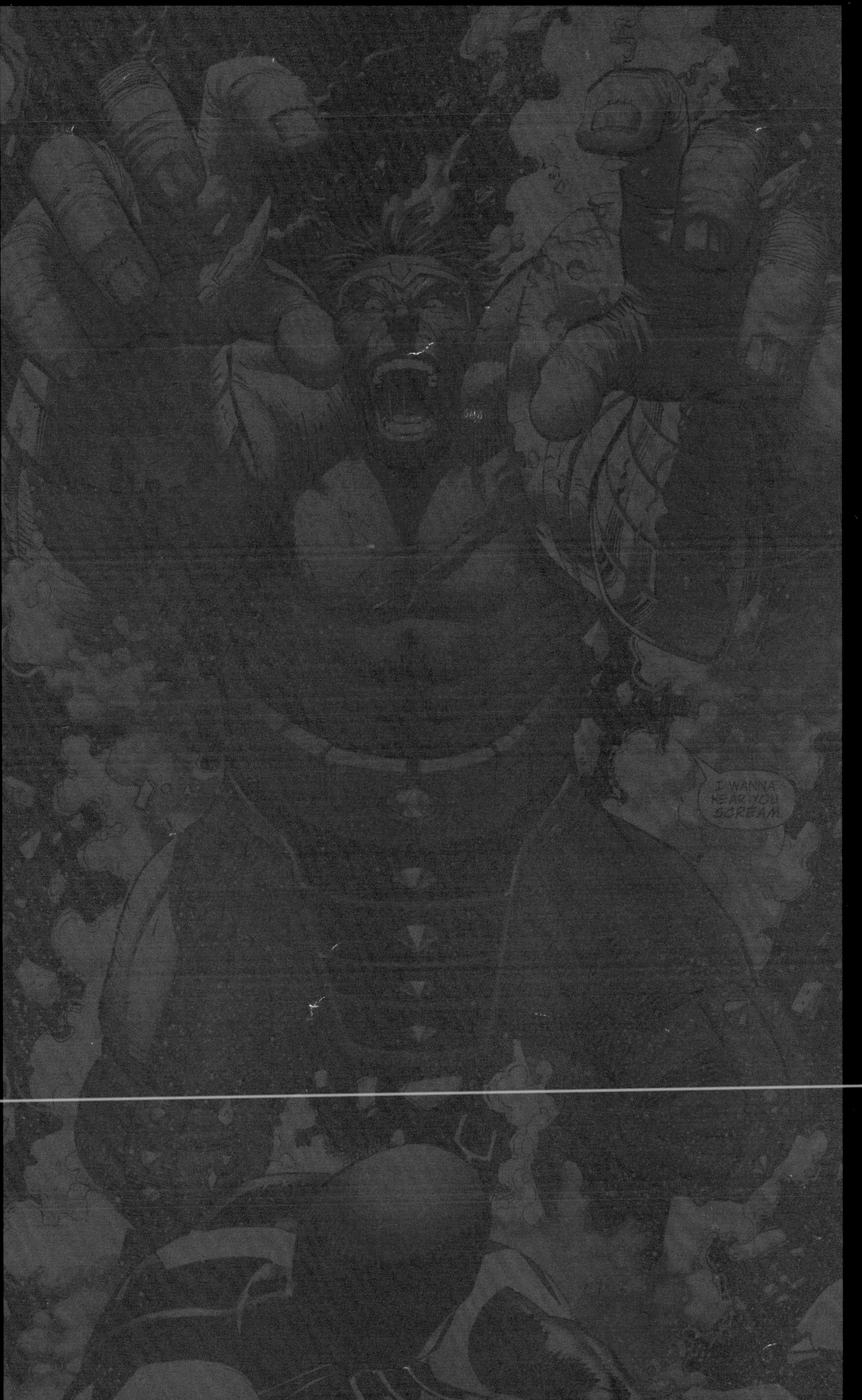
I WANNA HEAR YOU SCREAM.

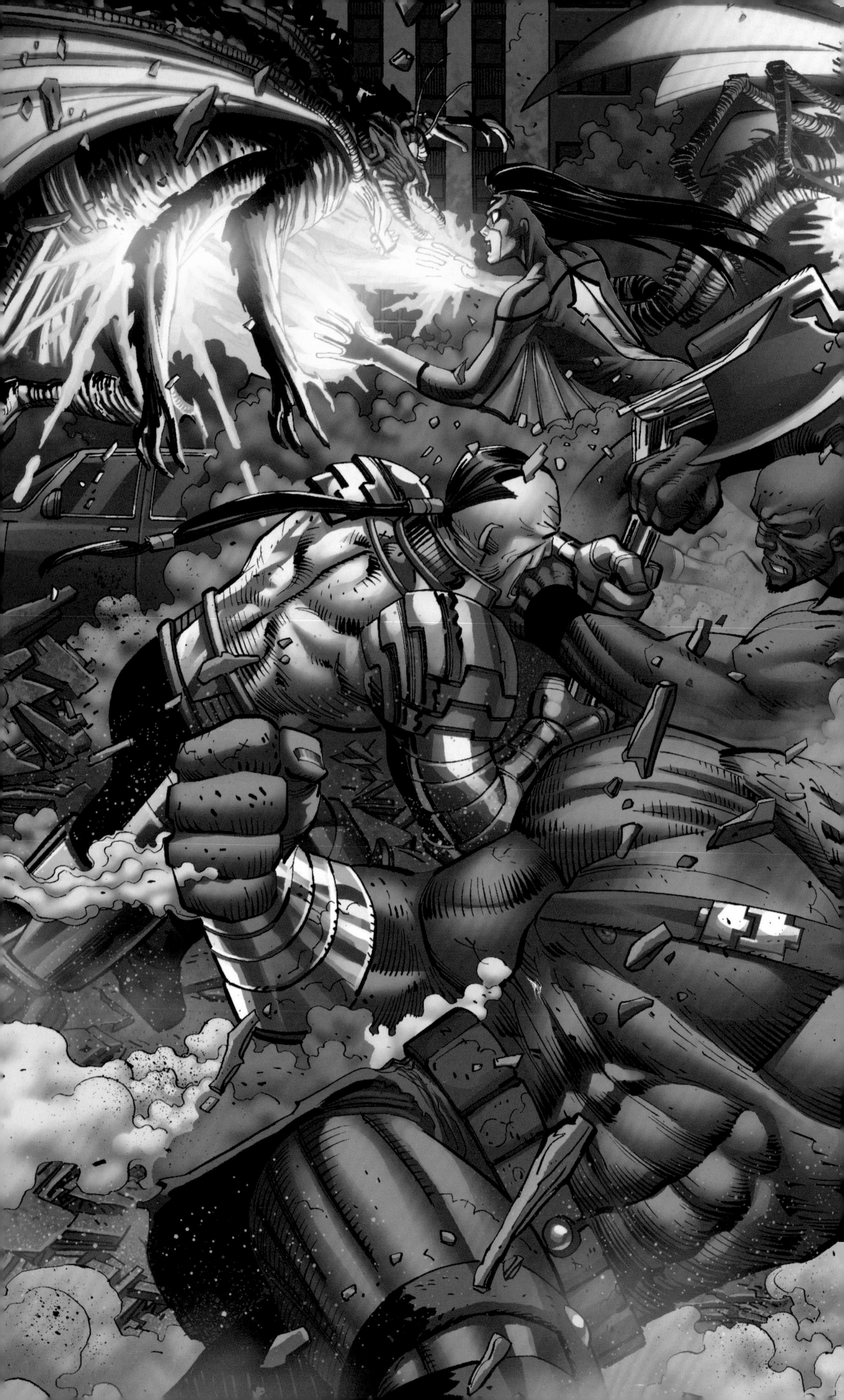

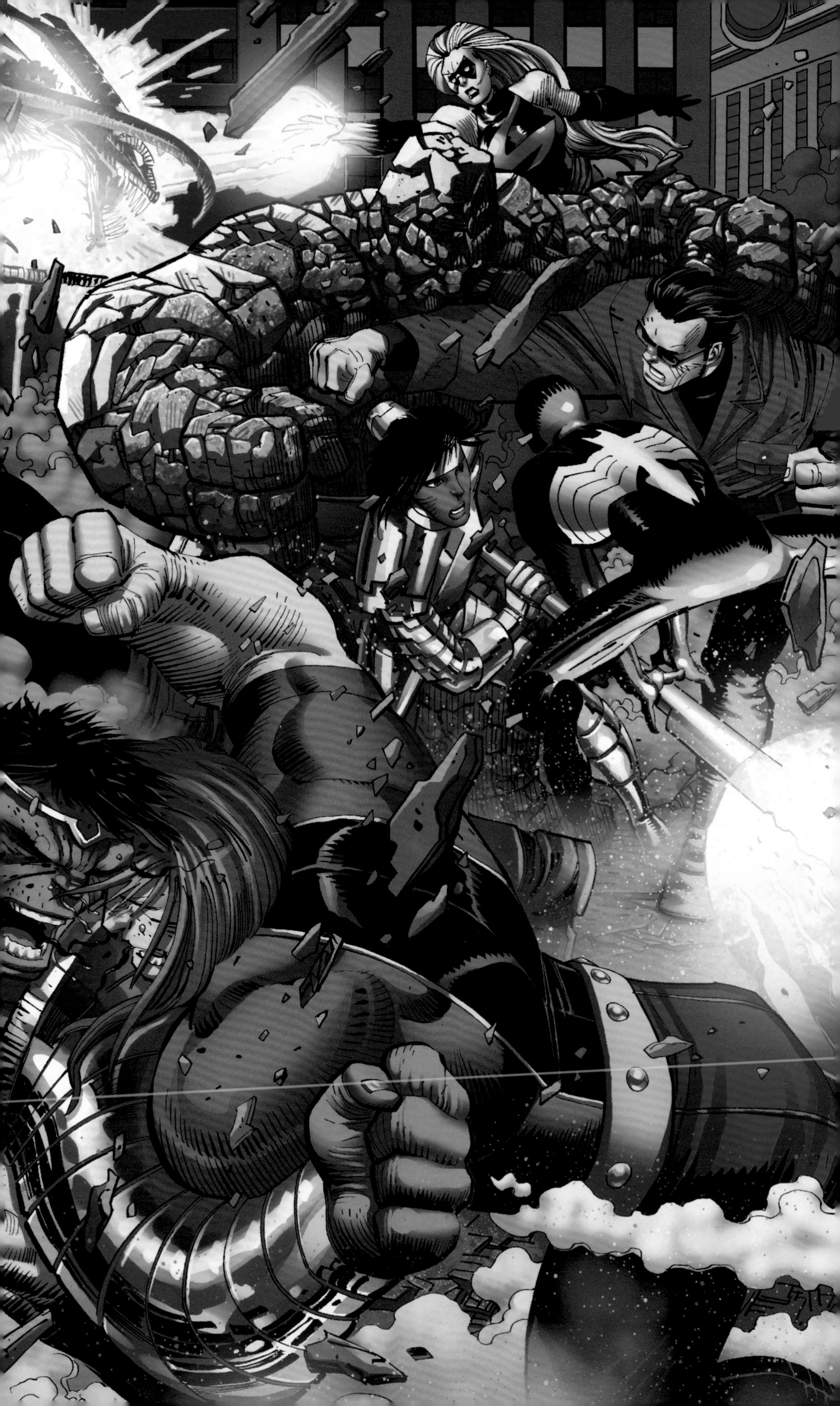

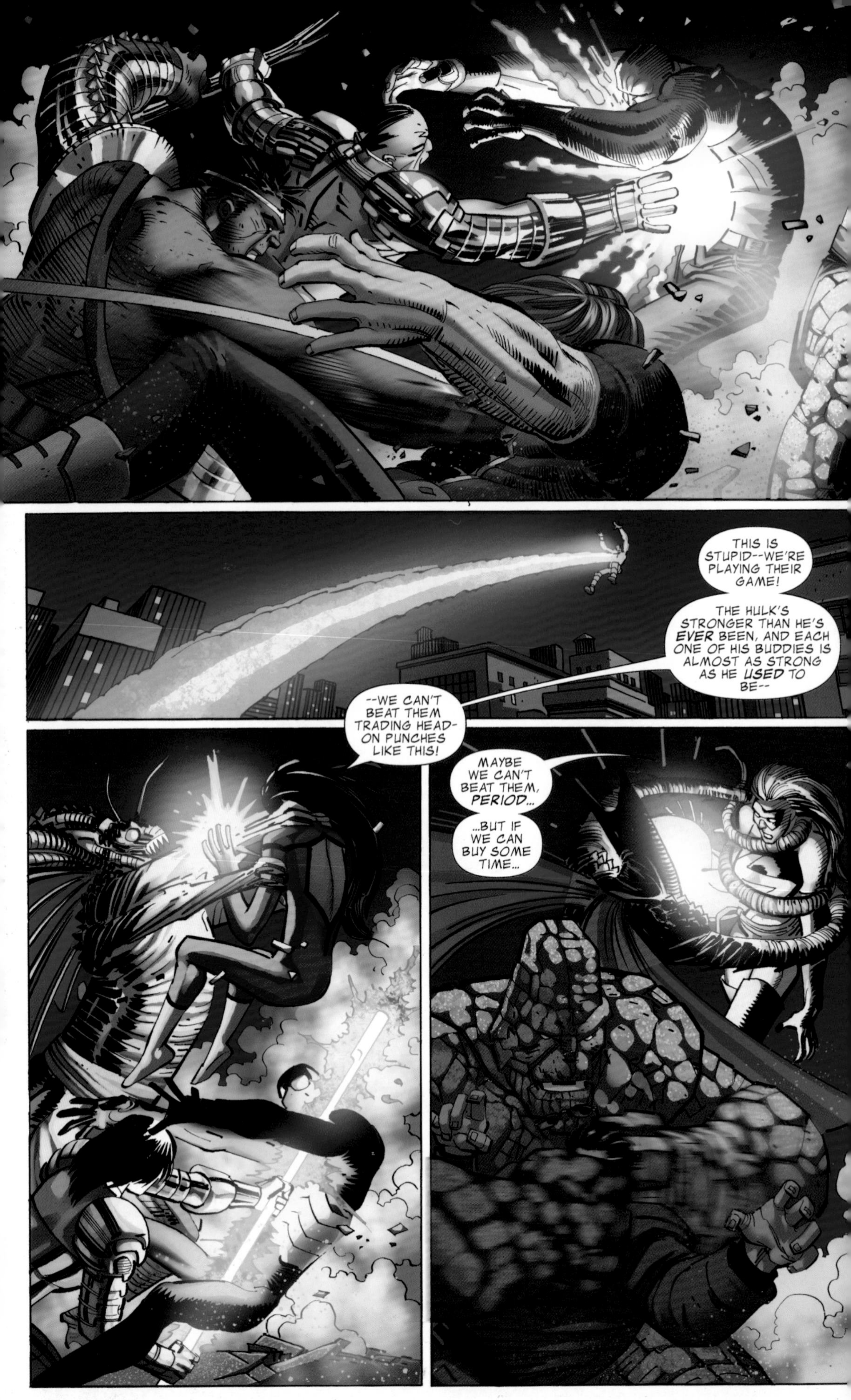
THIS IS STUPID--WE'RE PLAYING THEIR GAME!
THE HULK'S STRONGER THAN HE'S EVER BEEN, AND EACH ONE OF HIS BUDDIES IS ALMOST AS STRONG AS HE USED TO BE--
--WE CAN'T BEAT THEM TRADING HEAD-ON PUNCHES LIKE THIS!
MAYBE WE CAN'T BEAT THEM, PERIOD...
...BUT IF WE CAN BUY SOME TIME...

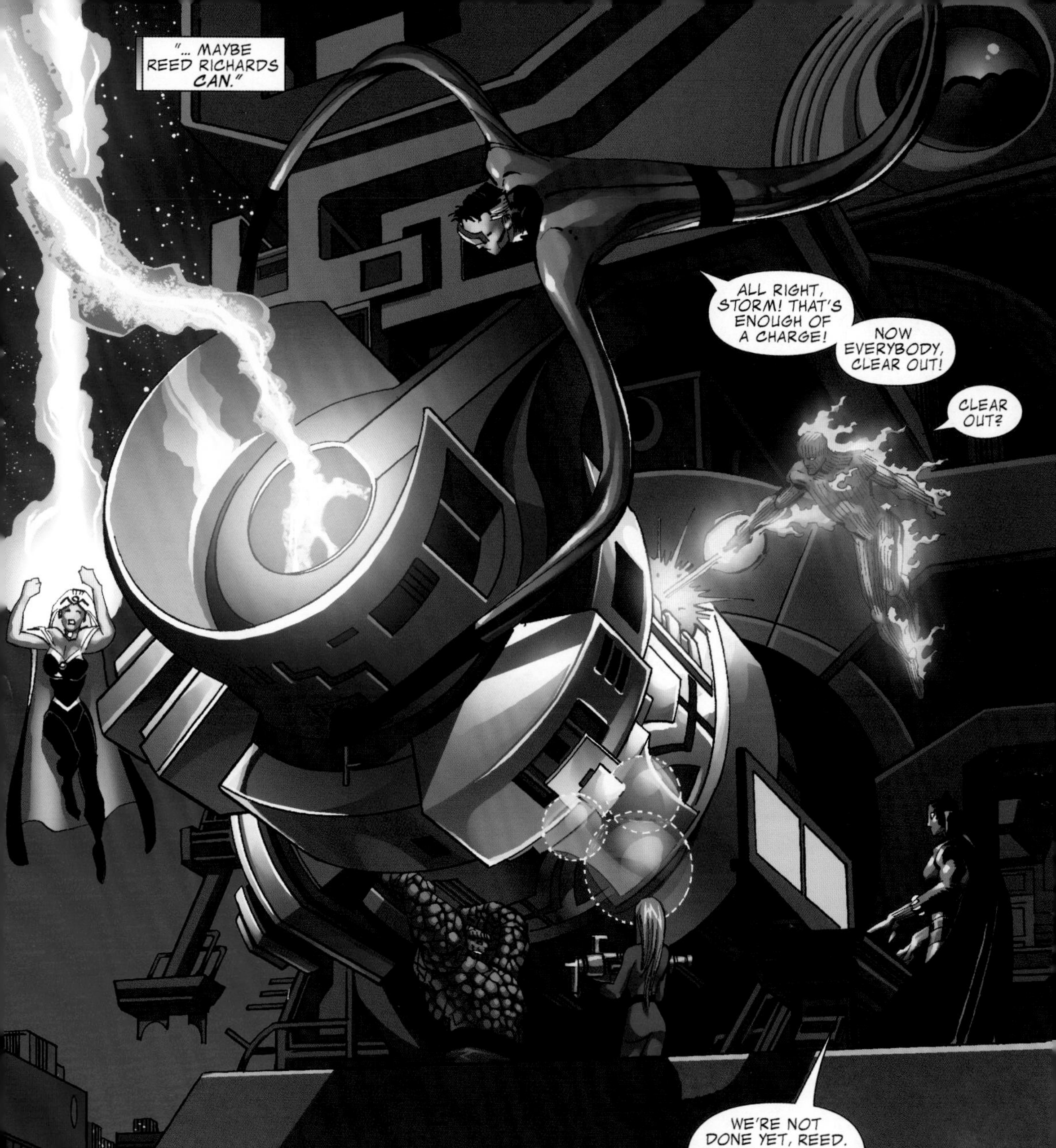
"... MAYBE REED RICHARDS CAN."
ALL RIGHT, STORM! THAT'S ENOUGH OF A CHARGE!
NOW EVERYBODY, CLEAR OUT!
CLEAR OUT?
WE'RE NOT DONE YET, REED. THERE ARE THREE MORE LAYERS OF CIRCUITRY YET TO--

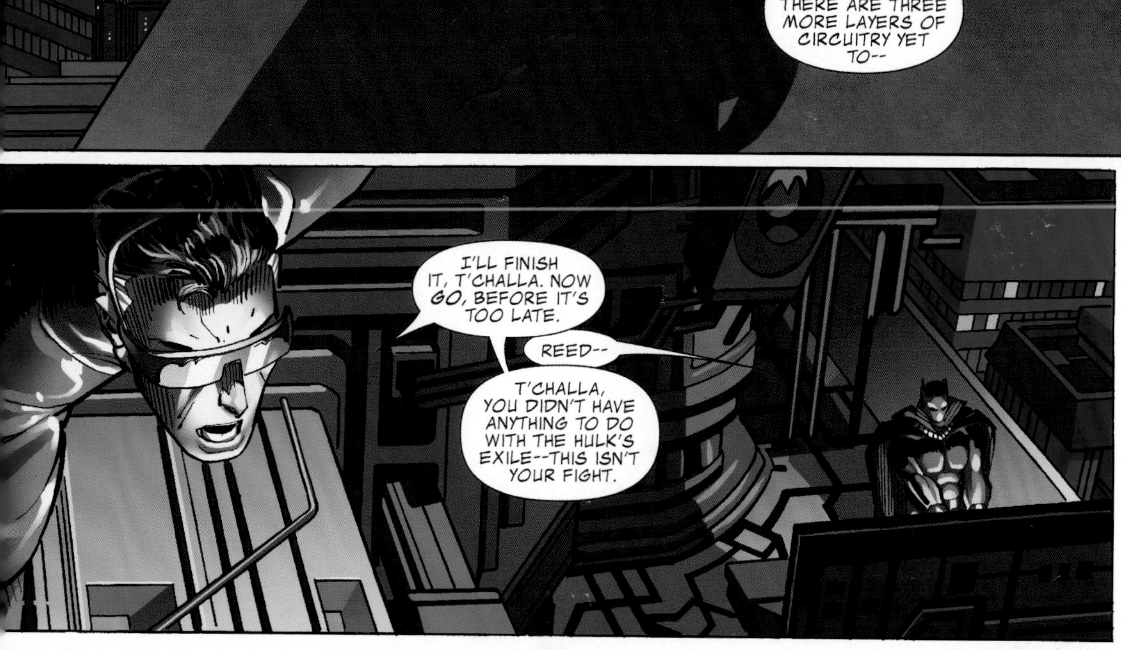
I'LL FINISH IT, T'CHALLA. NOW GO, BEFORE IT'S TOO LATE.
REED--
T'CHALLA, YOU DIDN'T HAVE ANYTHING TO DO WITH THE HULK'S EXILE--THIS ISN'T YOUR FIGHT.

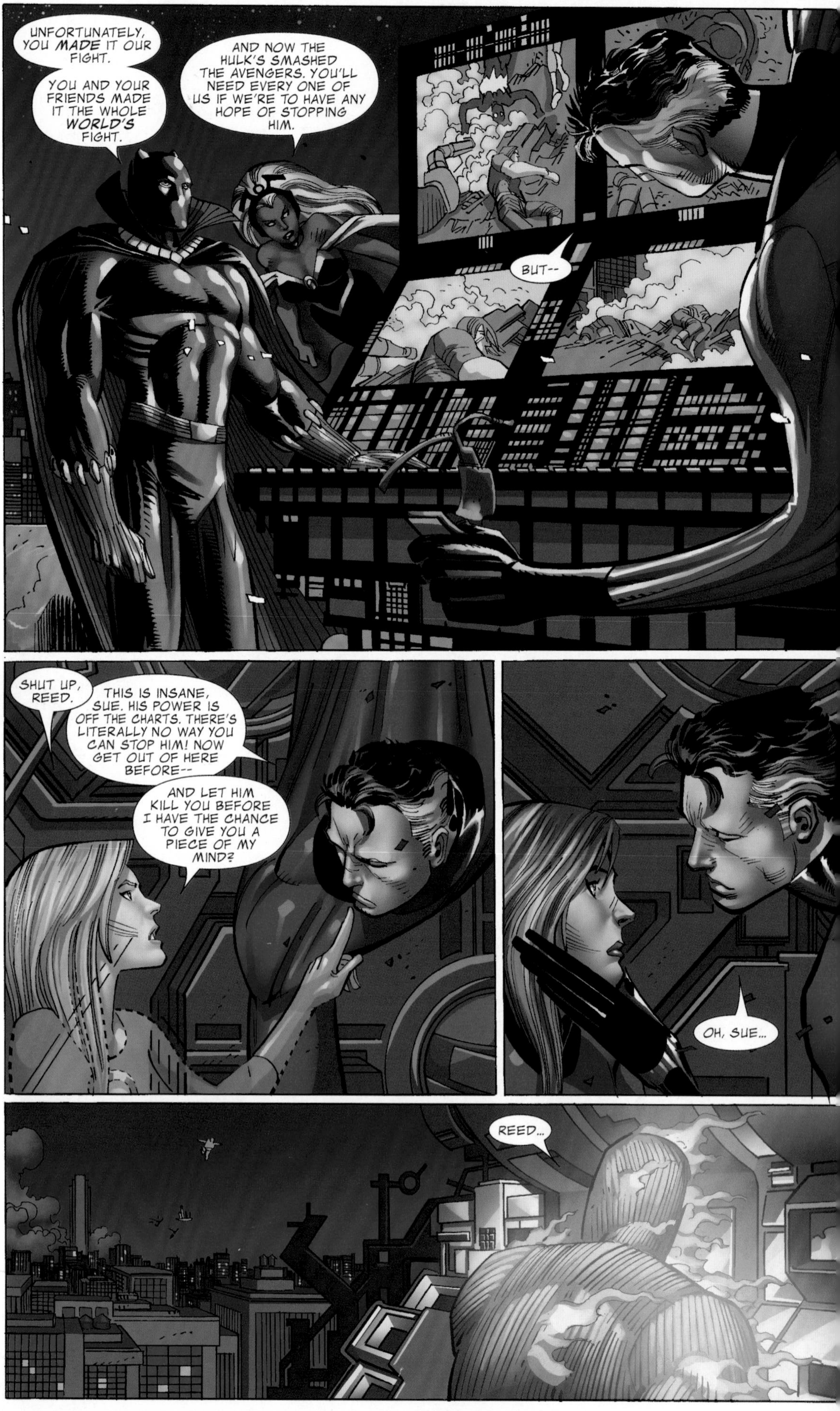
UNFORTUNATELY, YOU MADE IT OUR FIGHT.
YOU AND YOUR FRIENDS MADE IT THE WHOLE WORLD'S FIGHT.
AND NOW THE HULK'S SMASHED THE AVENGERS. YOU'LL NEED EVERY ONE OF US IF WE'RE TO HAVE ANY HOPE OF STOPPING HIM.
BUT--
SHUT UP, REED.
THIS IS INSANE, SUE. HIS POWER IS OFF THE CHARTS. THERE'S LITERALLY NO WAY YOU CAN STOP HIM! NOW GET OUT OF HERE BEFORE--
AND LET HIM KILL YOU BEFORE I HAVE THE CHANCE TO GIVE YOU A PIECE OF MY MIND?
OH, SUE...
REED...

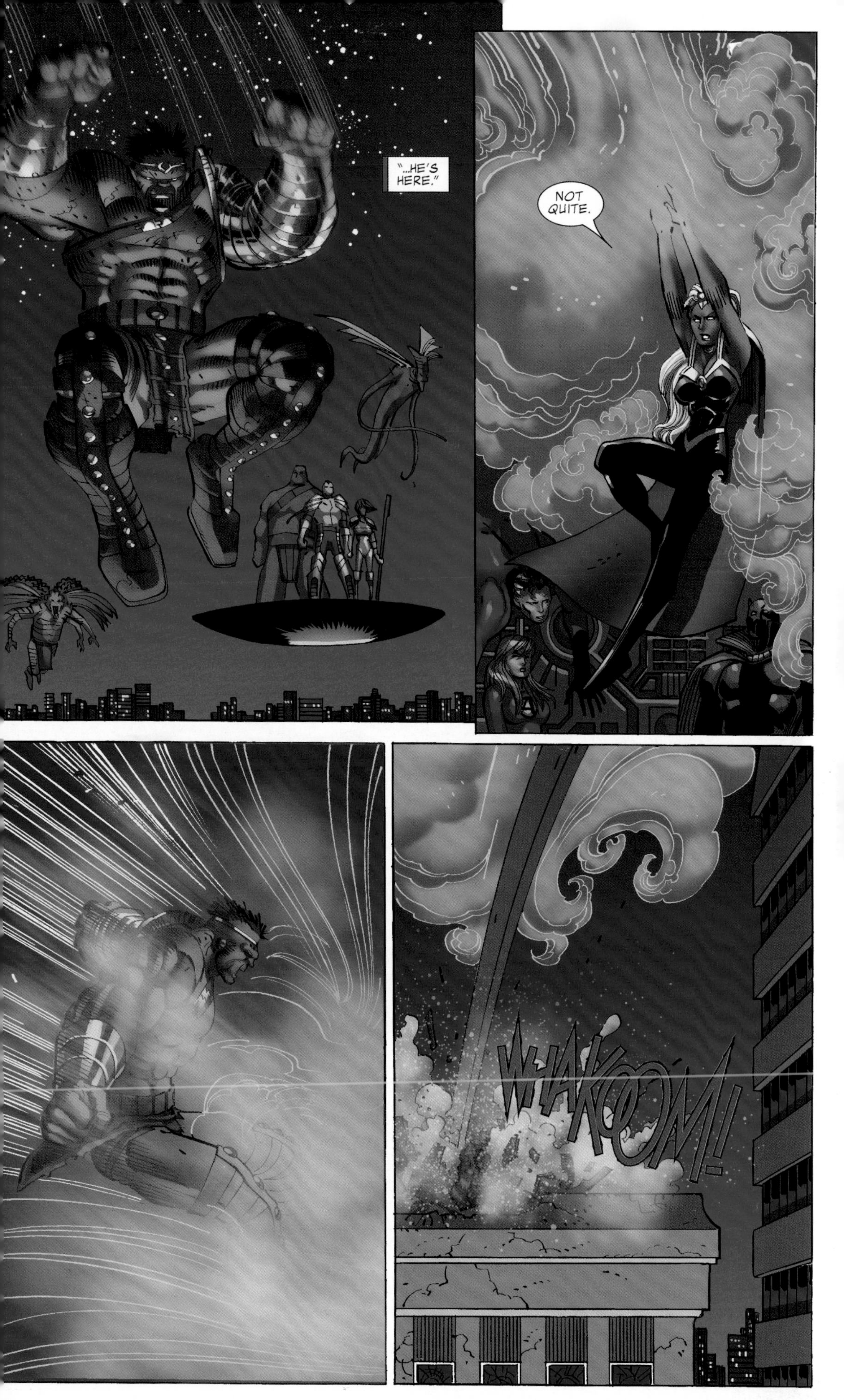
"...HE'S HERE."
NOT QUITE.
WHAKOOM!

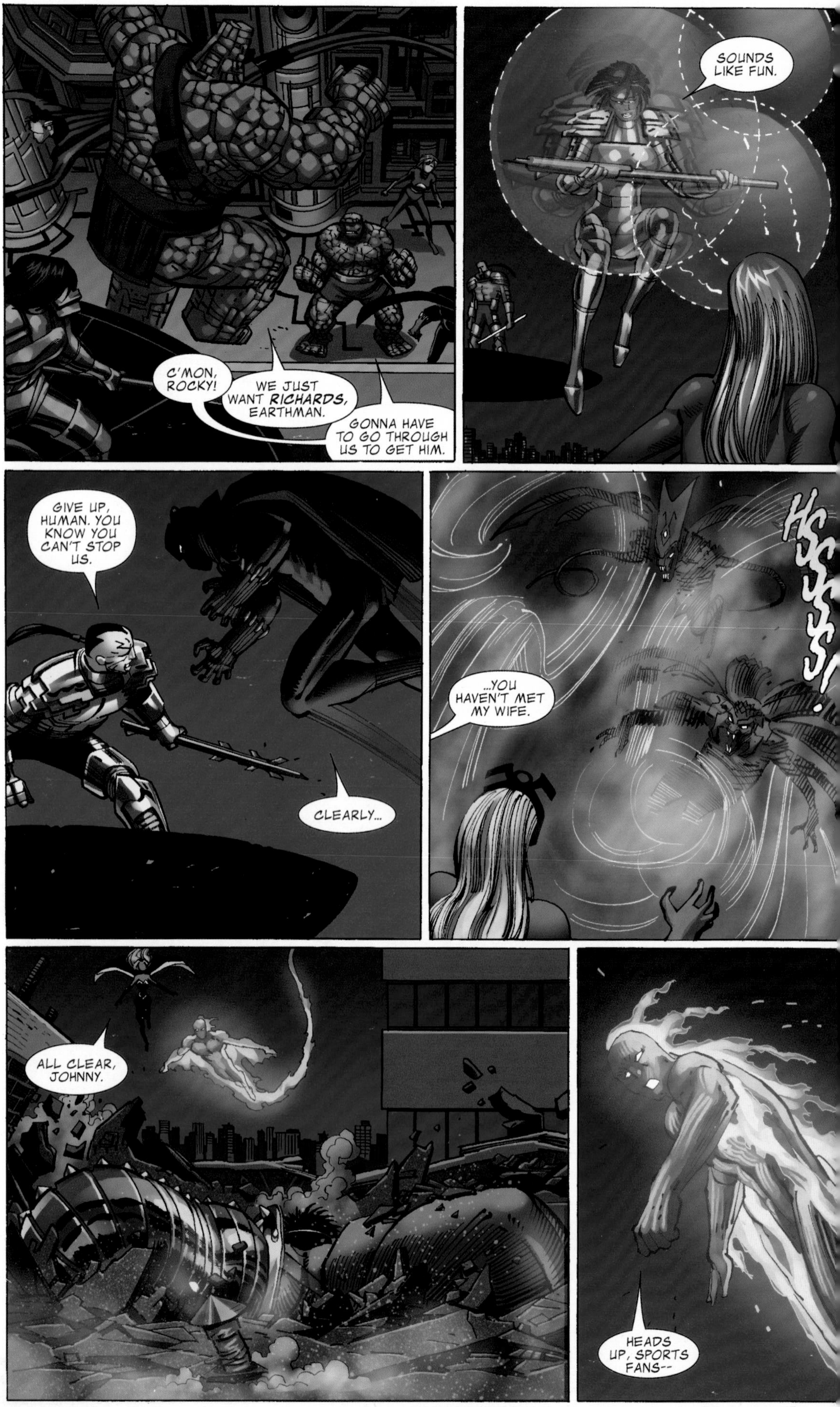
C'MON, ROCKY!
WE JUST WANT RICHARDS, EARTHMAN.
GONNA HAVE TO GO THROUGH US TO GET HIM.
SOUNDS LIKE FUN.
GIVE UP, HUMAN. YOU KNOW YOU CAN'T STOP US.
CLEARLY...
...YOU HAVEN'T MET MY WIFE.
HSSSSS!
ALL CLEAR, JOHNNY.
HEADS UP, SPORTS FANS--

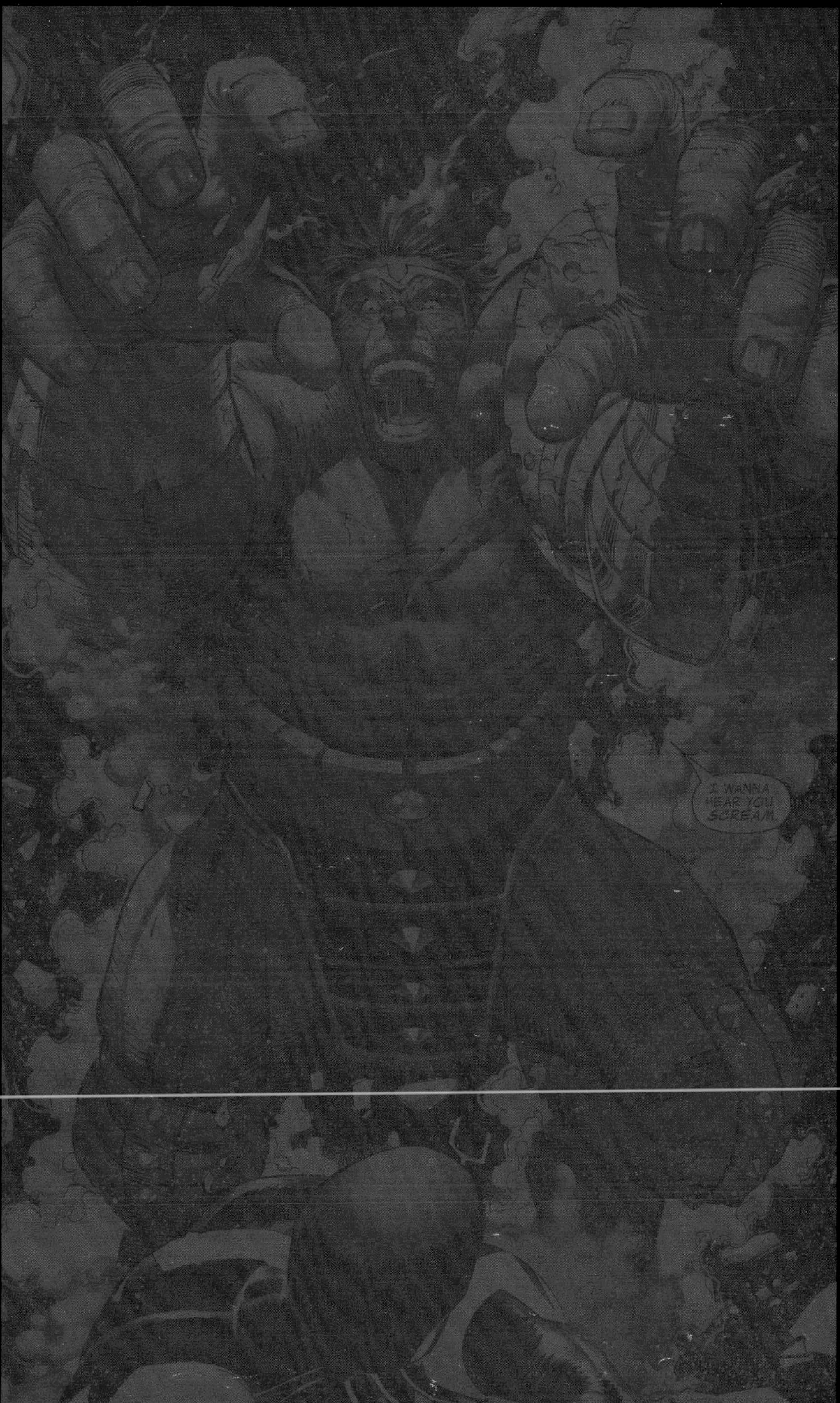
I WANNA HEAR YOU SCREAM.

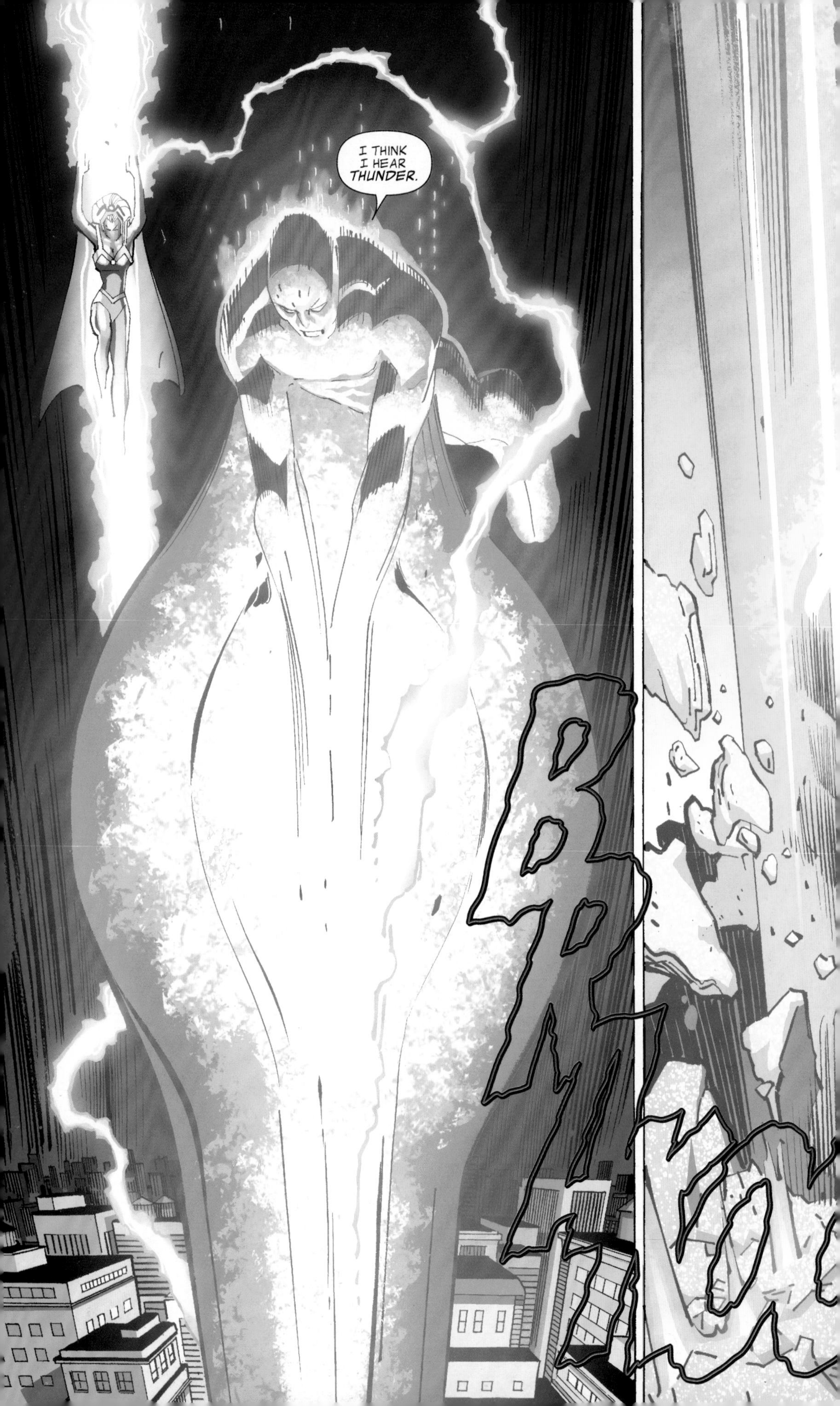
I THINK I HEAR THUNDER.

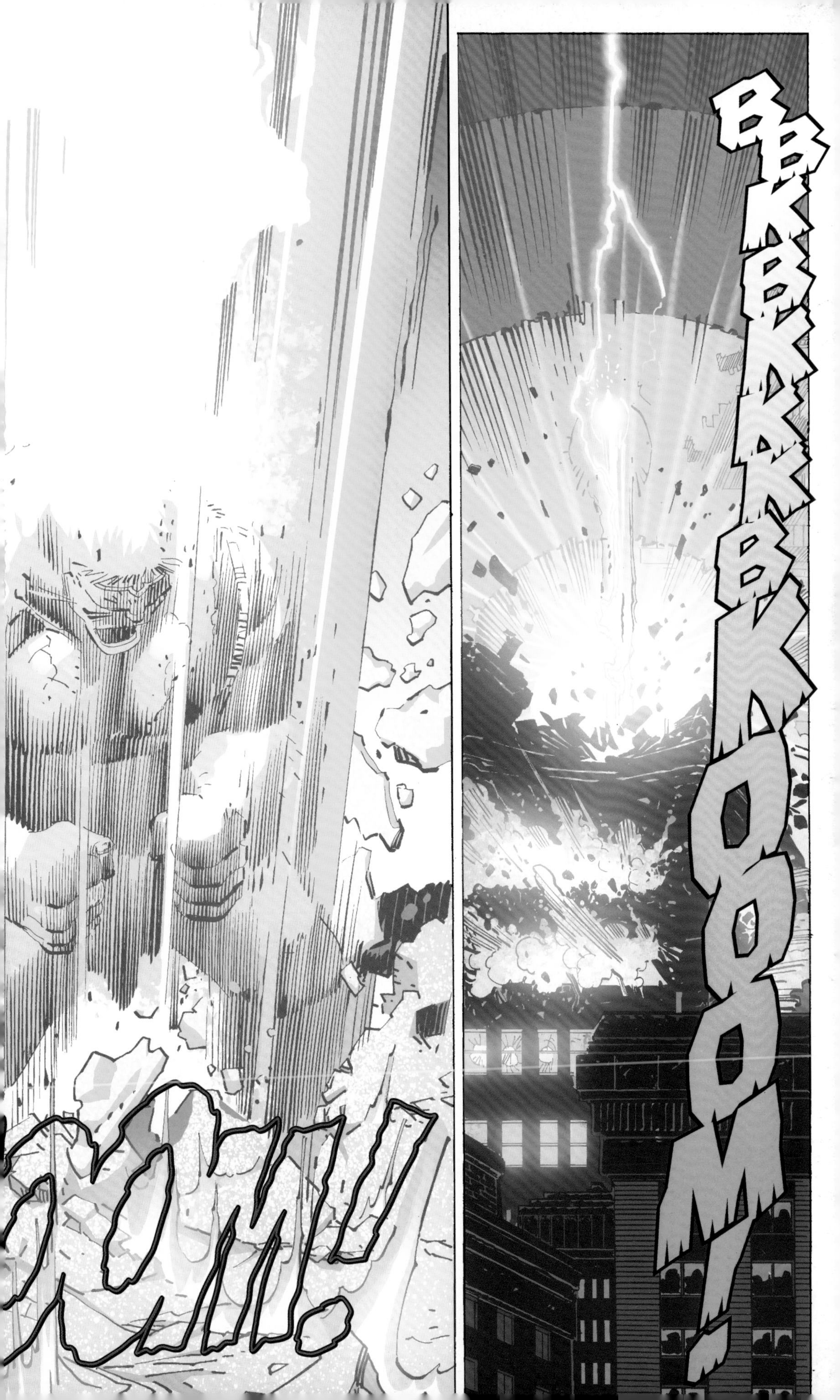

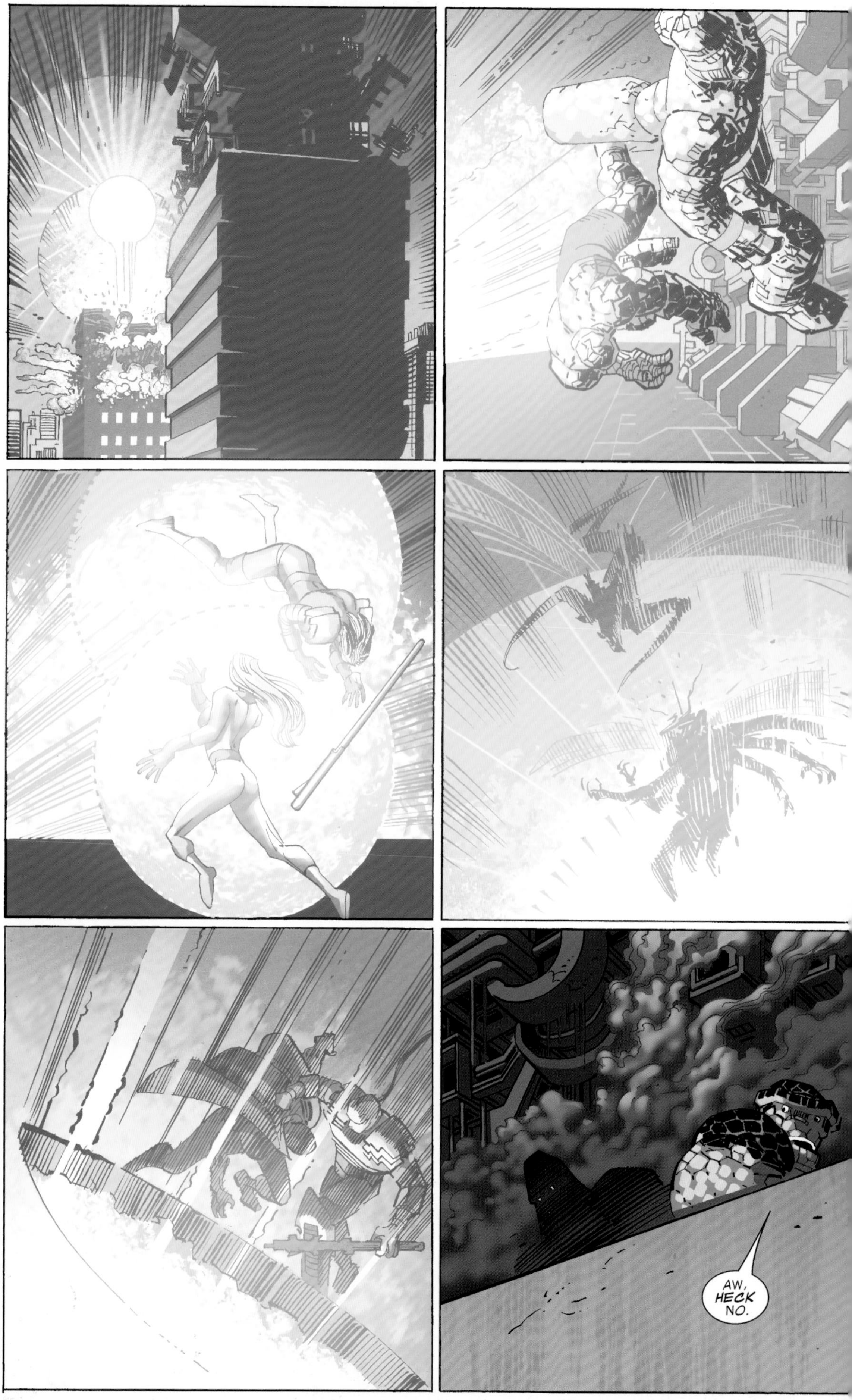
AW, HECK NO.

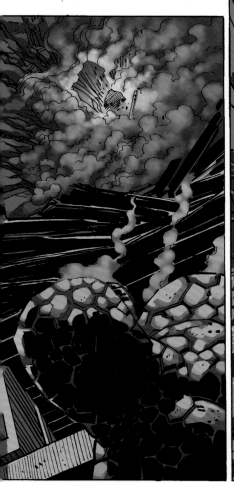

EARTHMAN, WAIT!

YOU'VE ALREADY LOST!

PEOPLE BEEN TELLING ME THAT ALL MY LIFE, FELLA.

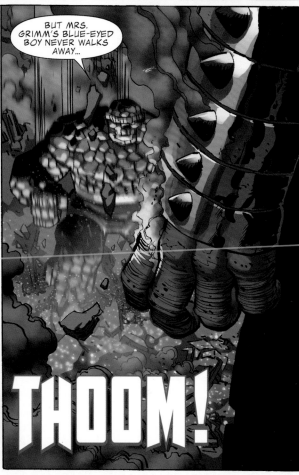

BUT MRS. GRIMM'S BLUE-EYED BOY NEVER WALKS AWAY...

THOOM!

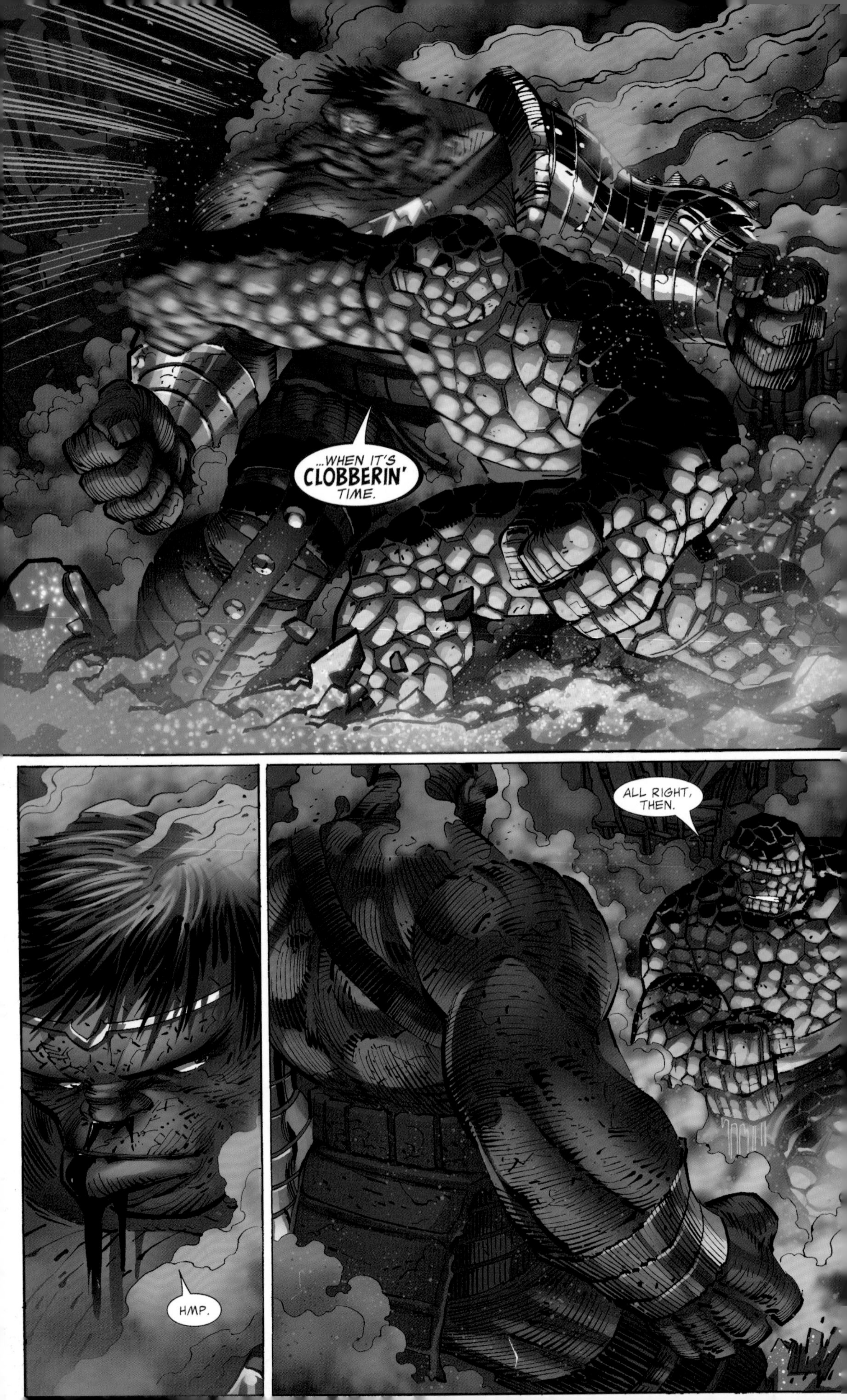
...WHEN IT'S CLOBBERIN' TIME.
HMP.
ALL RIGHT, THEN.

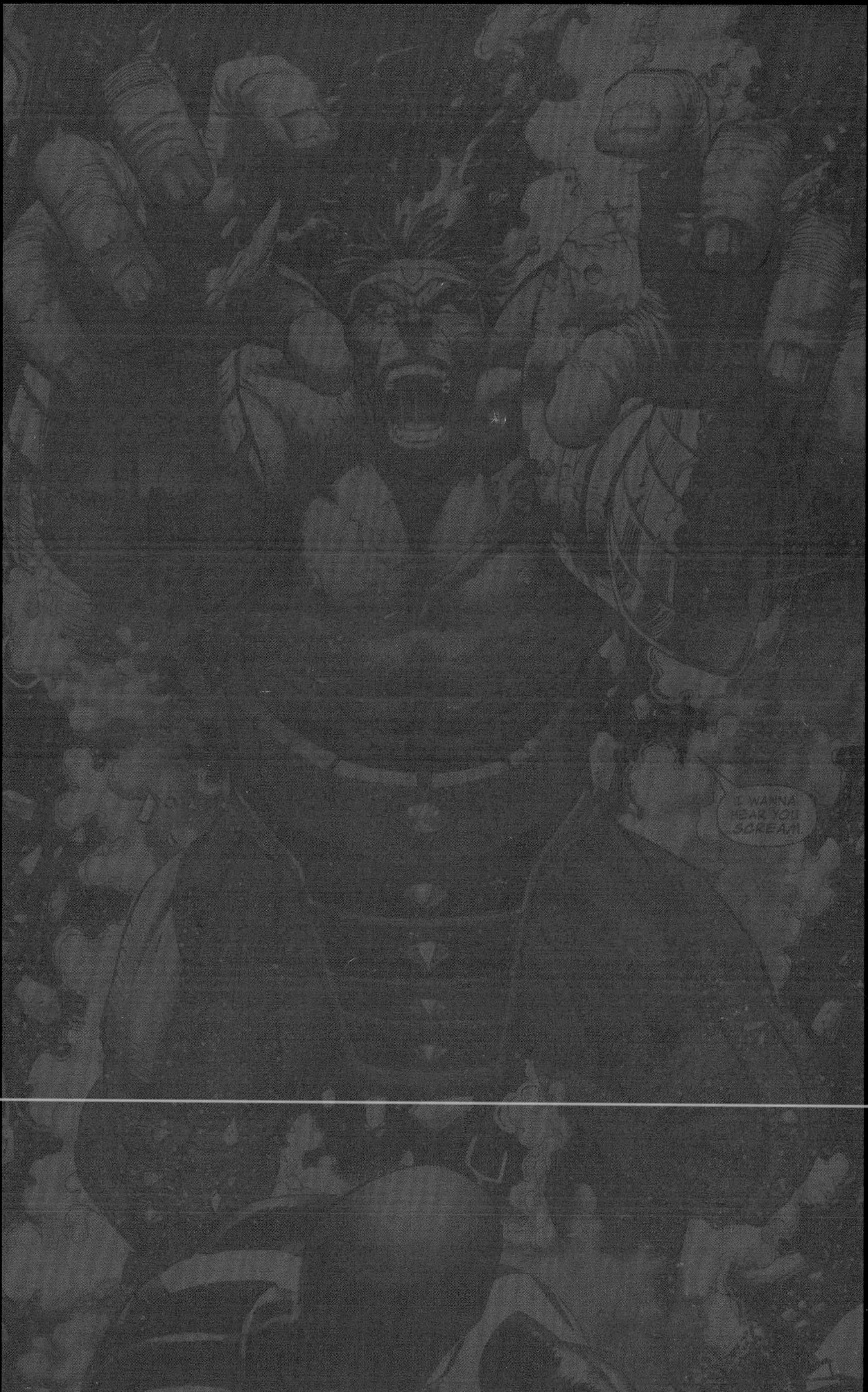
I WANNA HEAR YOU SCREAM.

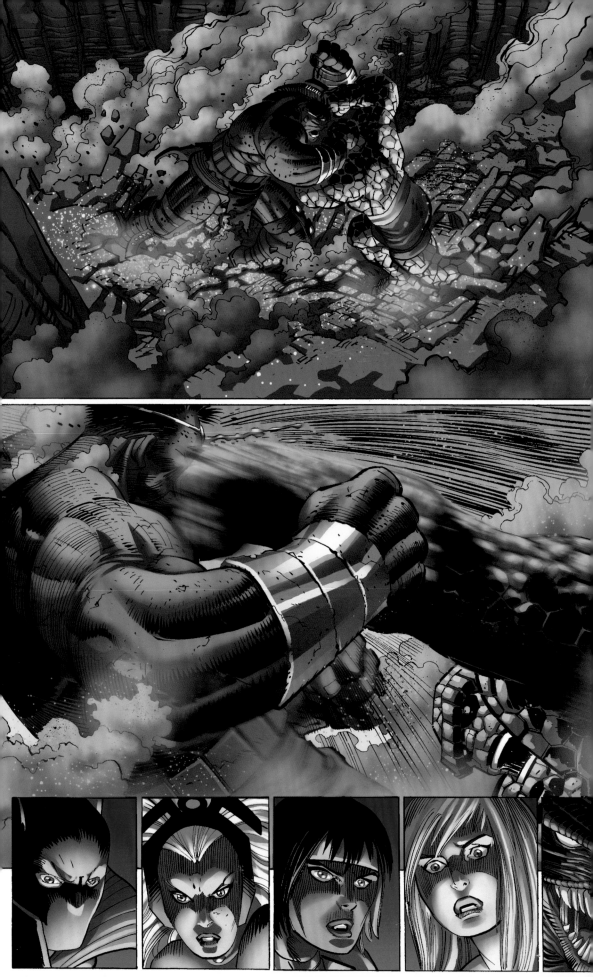

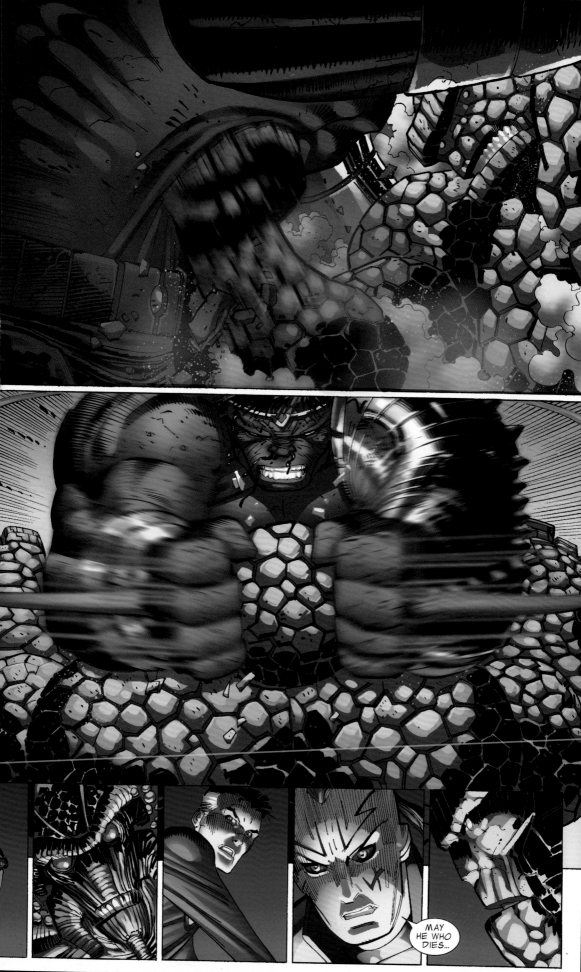

MAY
HE WHO
DIES...

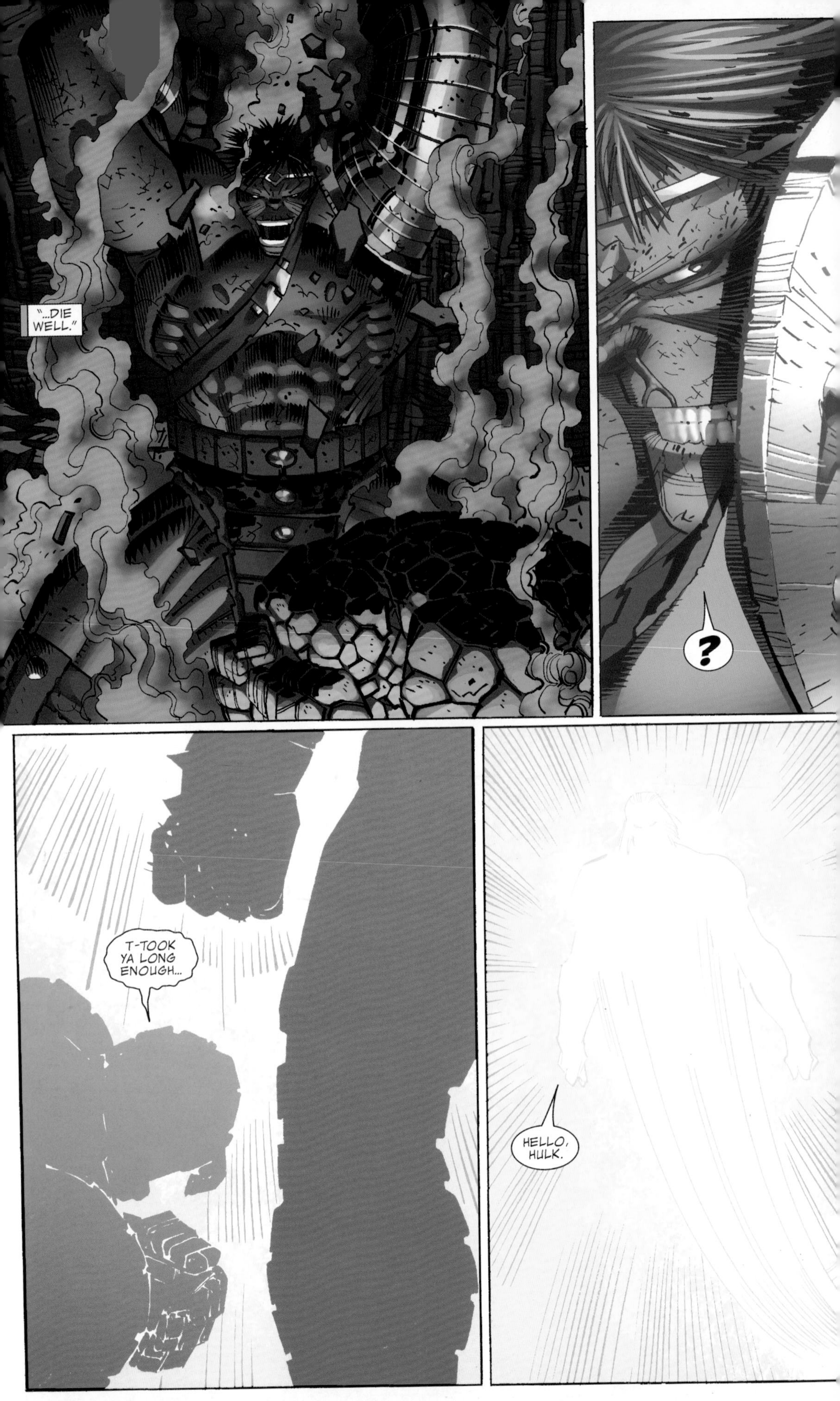
"...DIE WELL."
?
T-TOOK YA LONG ENOUGH...
HELLO, HULK.

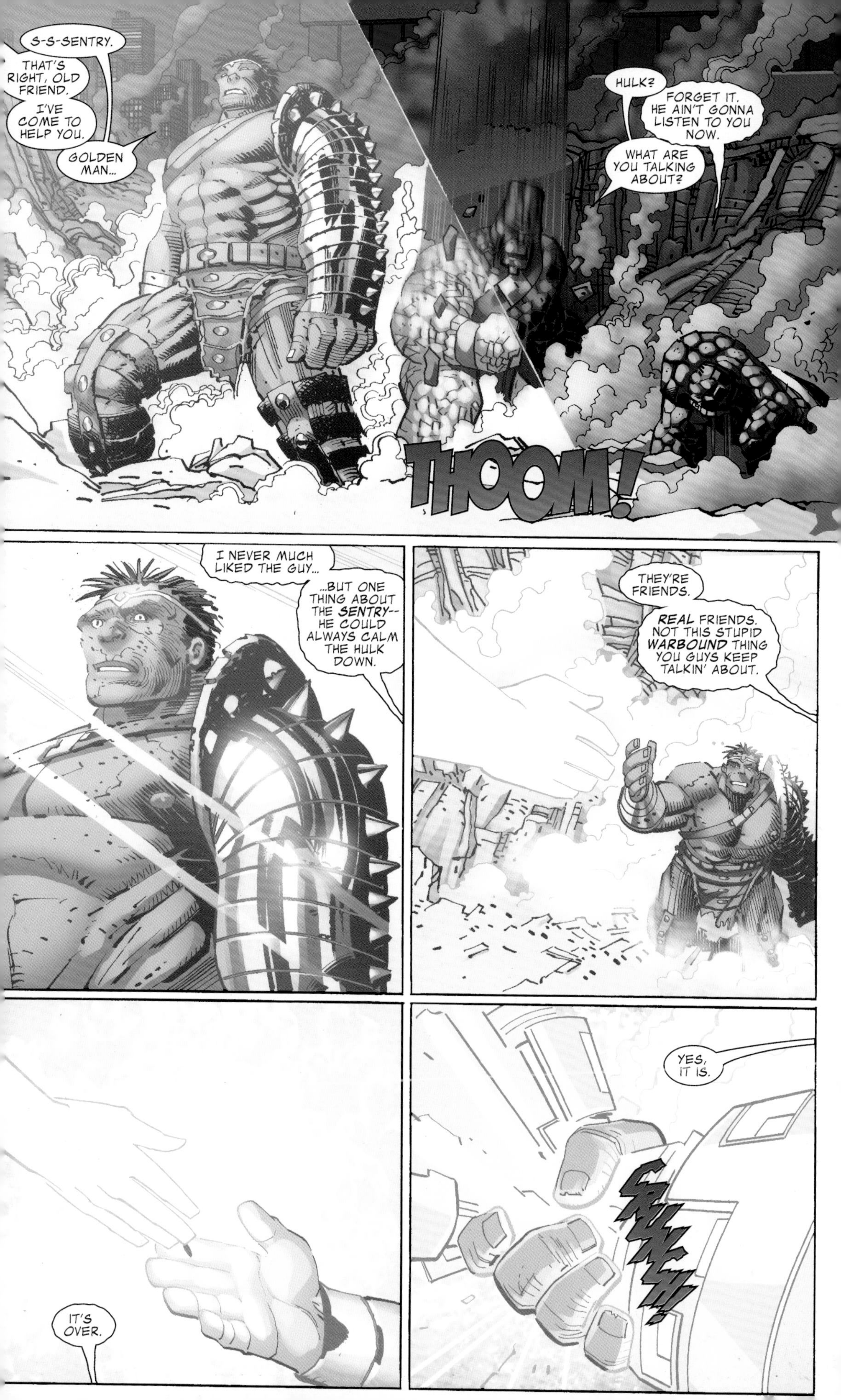
S-S-SENTRY.
THAT'S RIGHT, OLD FRIEND.
I'VE COME TO HELP YOU.
GOLDEN MAN...
HULK?
FORGET IT. HE AIN'T GONNA LISTEN TO YOU NOW.
WHAT ARE YOU TALKING ABOUT?
THOOM!
I NEVER MUCH LIKED THE GUY...
...BUT ONE THING ABOUT THE SENTRY-- HE COULD ALWAYS CALM THE HULK DOWN.
THEY'RE FRIENDS.
REAL FRIENDS. NOT THIS STUPID WARBOUND THING YOU GUYS KEEP TALKIN' ABOUT.
IT'S OVER.
YES, IT IS.
CRUNCH!

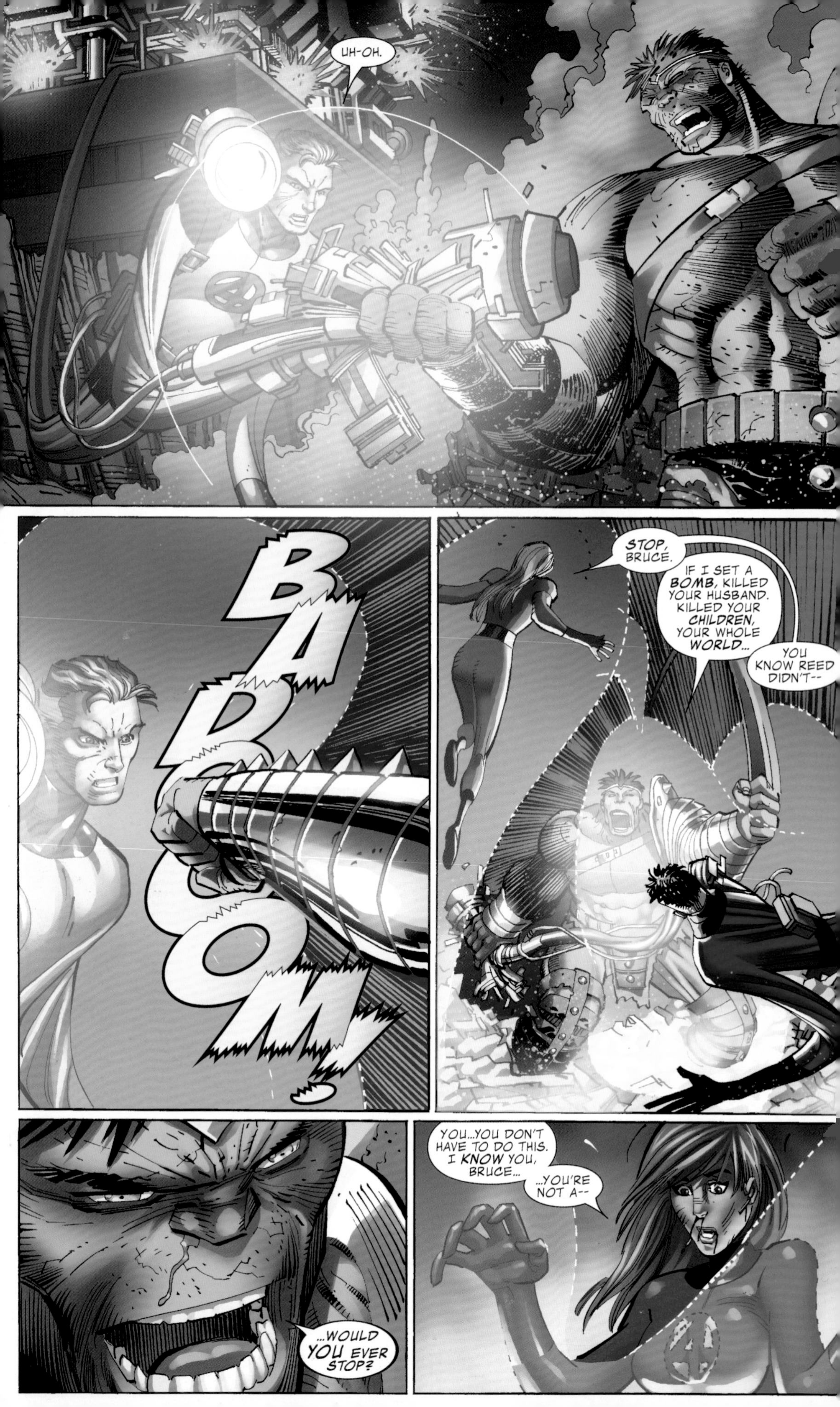
UH-OH.
BADOOOM!
STOP, BRUCE.
IF I SET A BOMB, KILLED YOUR HUSBAND. KILLED YOUR CHILDREN, YOUR WHOLE WORLD...
YOU KNOW REED DIDN'T--
...WOULD YOU EVER STOP?
YOU...YOU DON'T HAVE TO DO THIS. I KNOW YOU, BRUCE...
...YOU'RE NOT A--

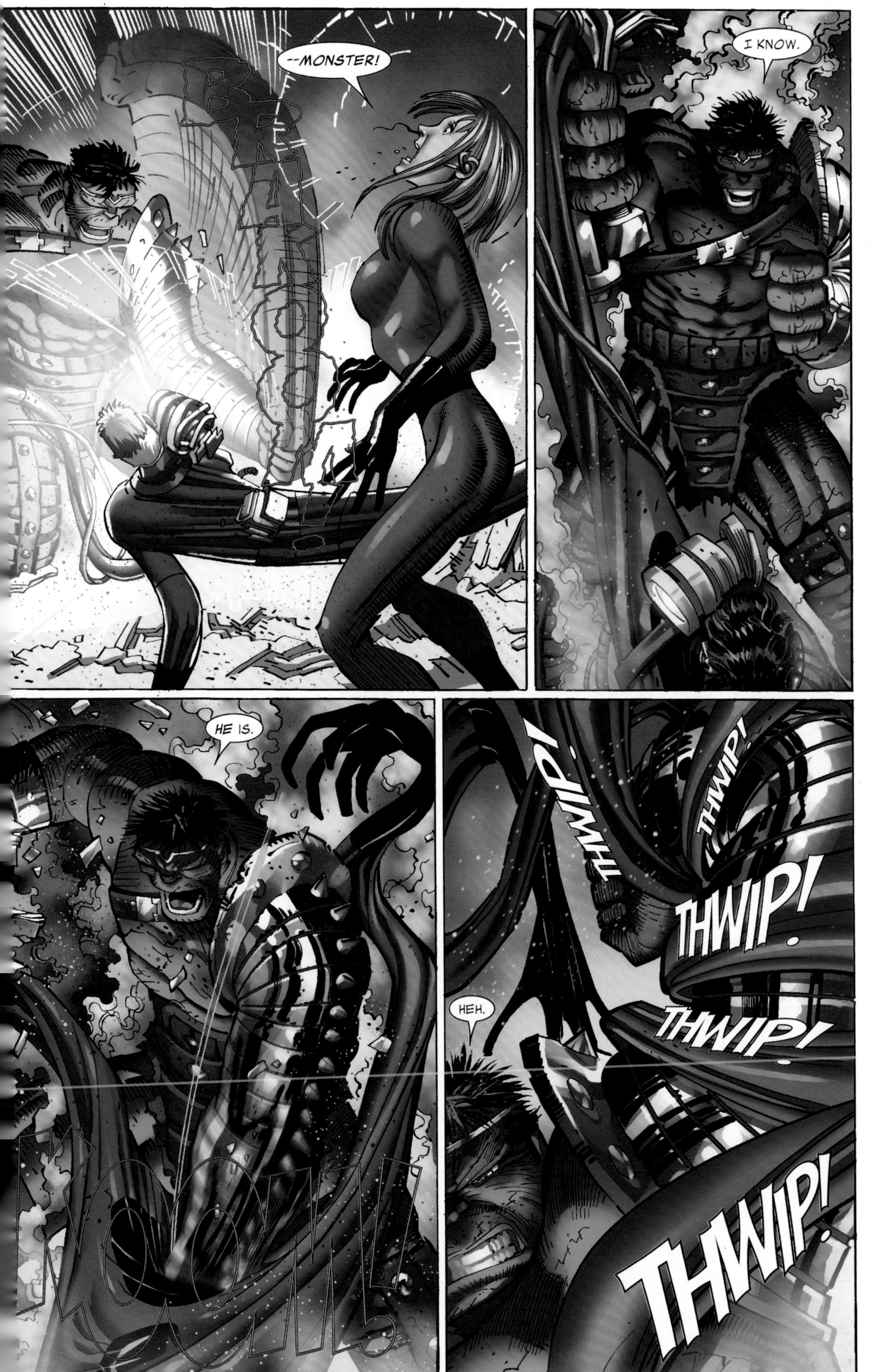
--MONSTER!
I KNOW.
HE IS.
THWIP!
THWIP!
THWIP!
THWIP!
HEH.
THWIP!

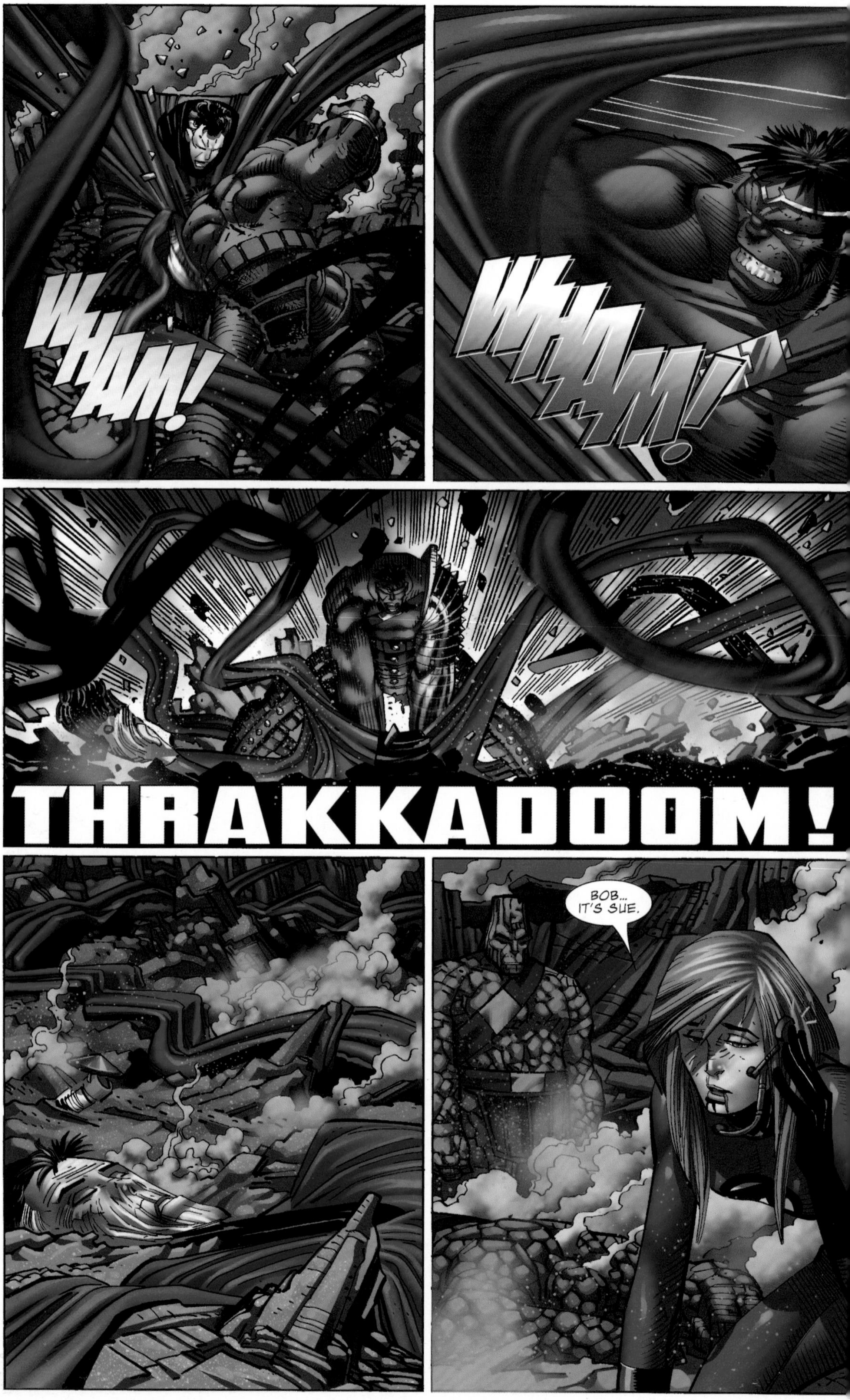
WHAM!
WHAM!
THRAKKADOOOM!
BOB... IT'S SUE.

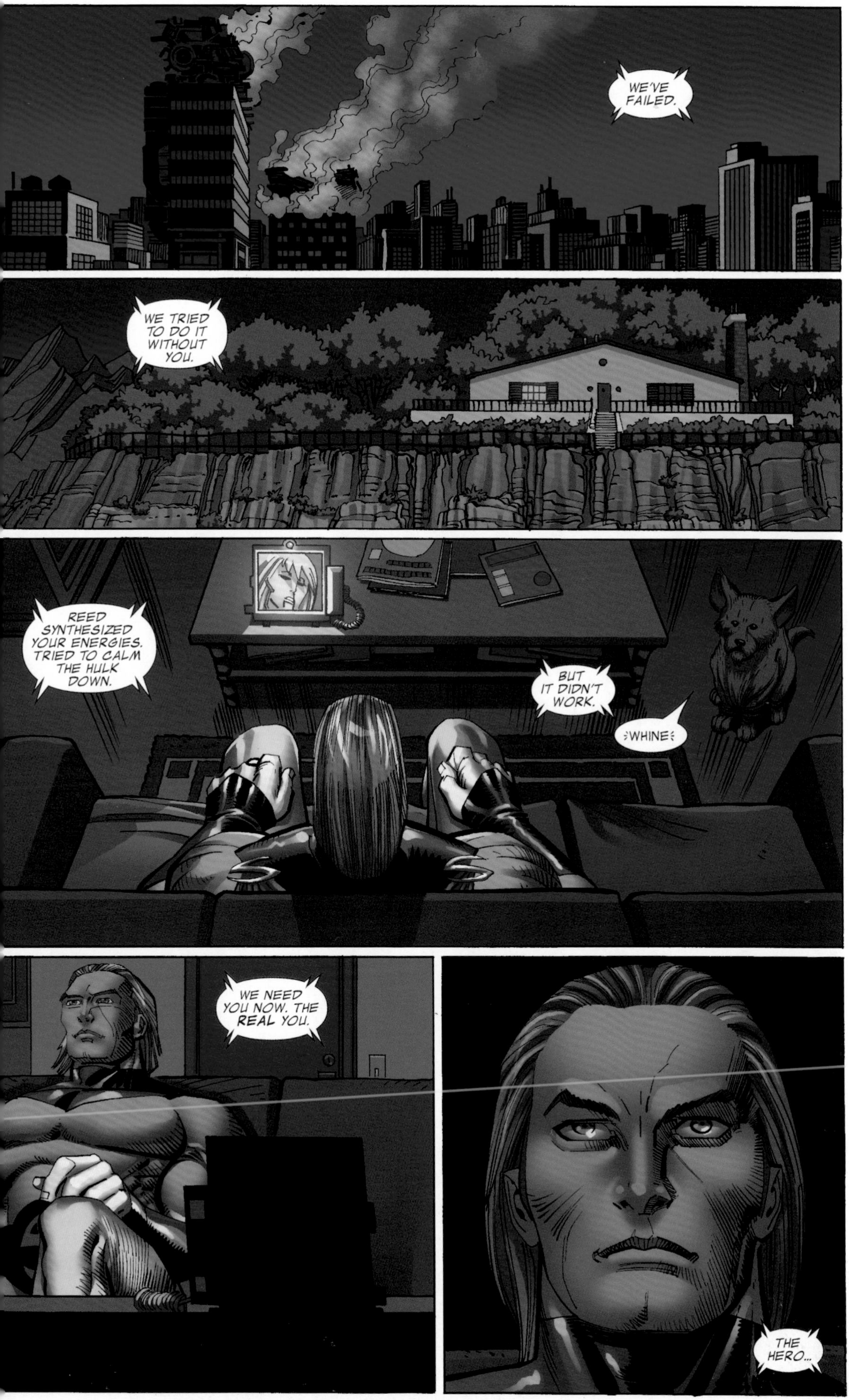
WE'VE FAILED.
WE TRIED TO DO IT WITHOUT YOU.
REED SYNTHESIZED YOUR ENERGIES. TRIED TO CALM THE HULK DOWN.
BUT IT DIDN'T WORK.
WHINE
WE NEED YOU NOW. THE REAL YOU.
THE HERO...

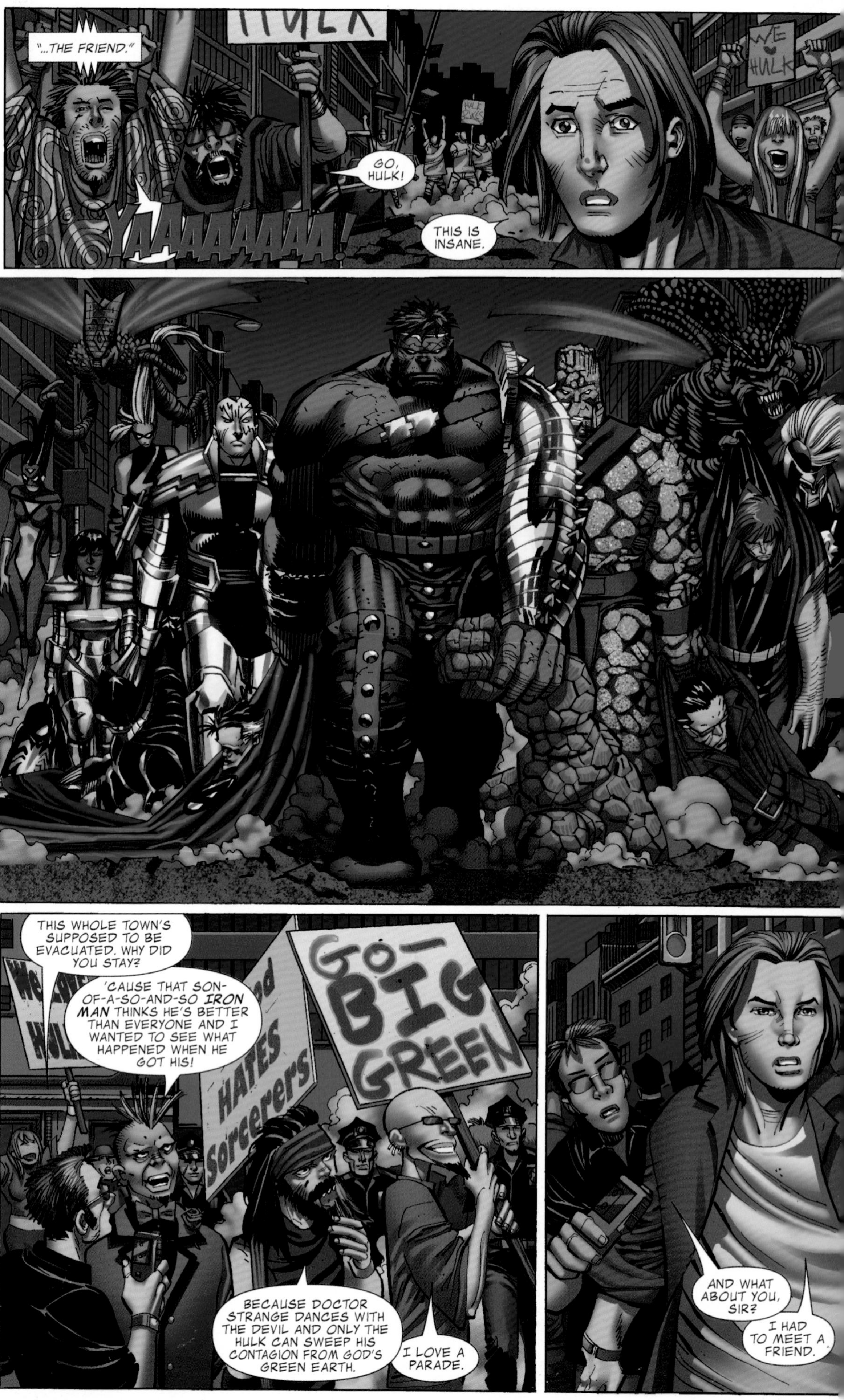
"...THE FRIEND."
YAAAAAAAA!
GO, HULK!
THIS IS INSANE.
WE HULK
THIS WHOLE TOWN'S SUPPOSED TO BE EVACUATED. WHY DID YOU STAY?
'CAUSE THAT SON-OF-A-SO-AND-SO IRON MAN THINKS HE'S BETTER THAN EVERYONE AND I WANTED TO SEE WHAT HAPPENED WHEN HE GOT HIS!
GO— BIG GREEN
HATES Sorcerers
BECAUSE DOCTOR STRANGE DANCES WITH THE DEVIL AND ONLY THE HULK CAN SWEEP HIS CONTAGION FROM GOD'S GREEN EARTH.
I LOVE A PARADE.
AND WHAT ABOUT YOU, SIR?
I HAD TO MEET A FRIEND.

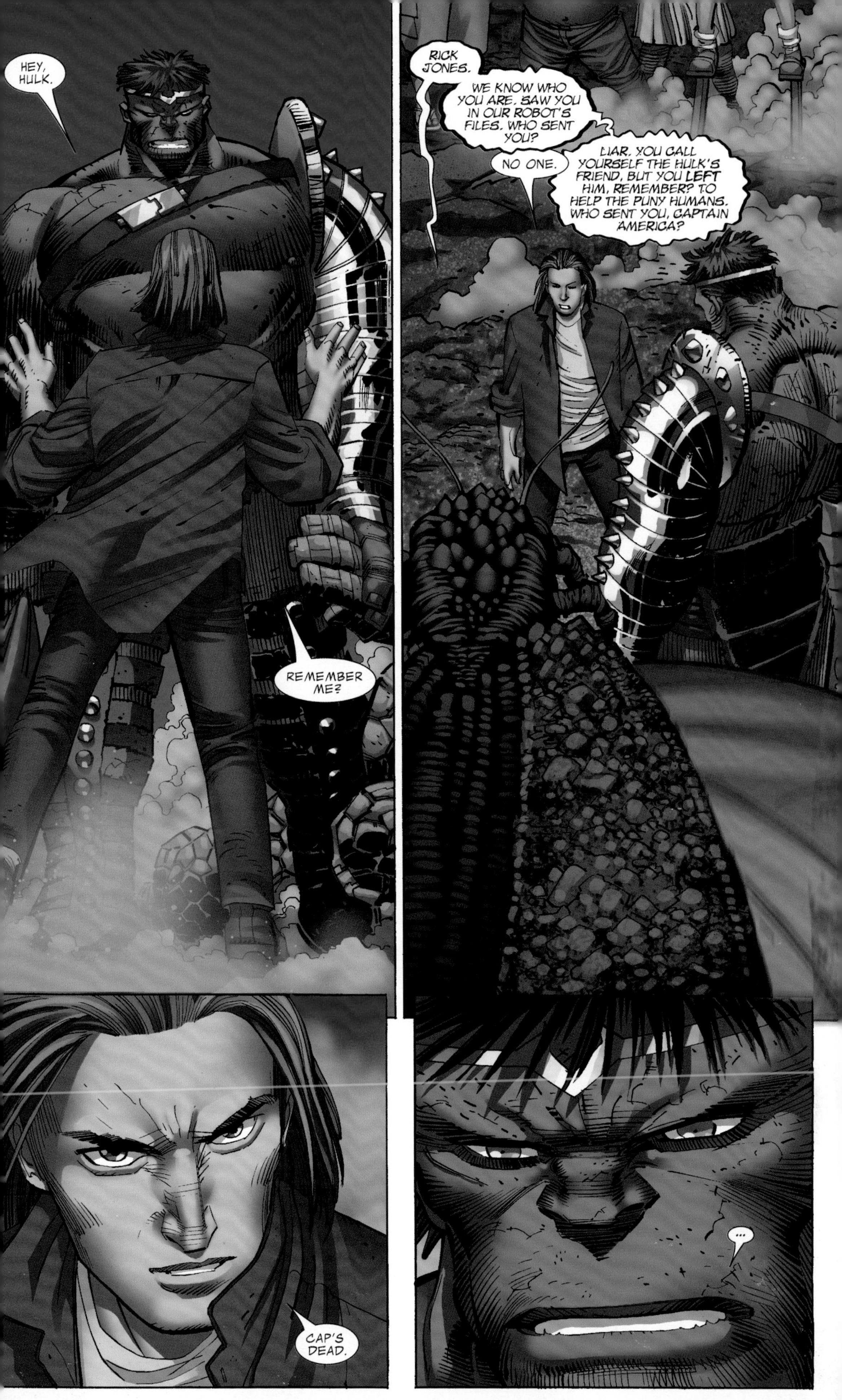
HEY, HULK.
REMEMBER ME?
RICK JONES.
WE KNOW WHO YOU ARE. SAW YOU IN OUR ROBOT'S FILES. WHO SENT YOU?
NO ONE.
LIAR. YOU CALL YOURSELF THE HULK'S FRIEND, BUT YOU LEFT HIM, REMEMBER? TO HELP THE PUNY HUMANS. WHO SENT YOU, CAPTAIN AMERICA?
CAP'S DEAD.
...

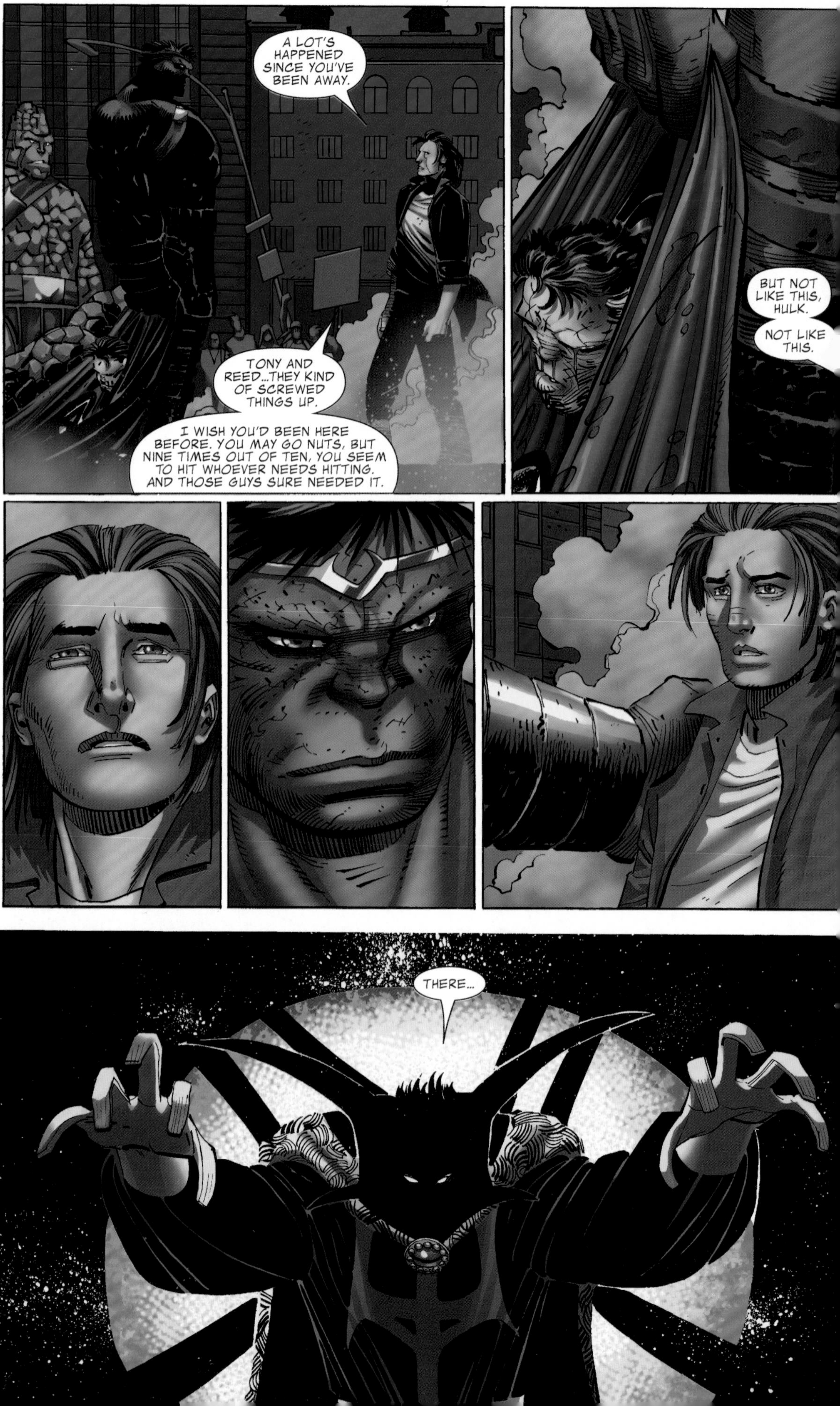
A LOT'S HAPPENED SINCE YOU'VE BEEN AWAY.
TONY AND REED...THEY KIND OF SCREWED THINGS UP.
I WISH YOU'D BEEN HERE BEFORE. YOU MAY GO NUTS, BUT NINE TIMES OUT OF TEN, YOU SEEM TO HIT WHOEVER NEEDS HITTING. AND THOSE GUYS SURE NEEDED IT.
BUT NOT LIKE THIS, HULK.
NOT LIKE THIS.
THERE...

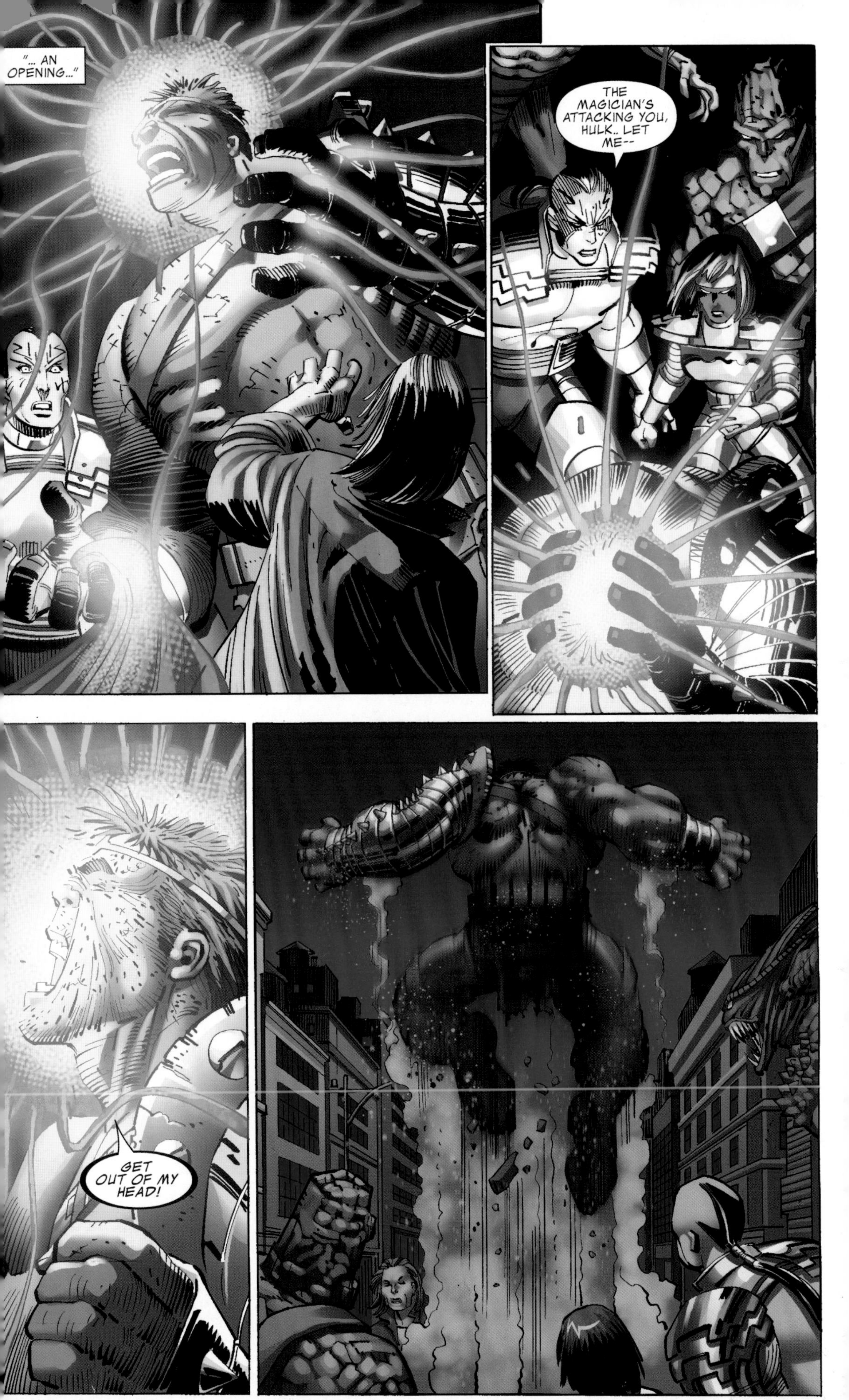
"... AN OPENING..."
THE MAGICIAN'S ATTACKING YOU, HULK.. LET ME--
GET OUT OF MY HEAD!

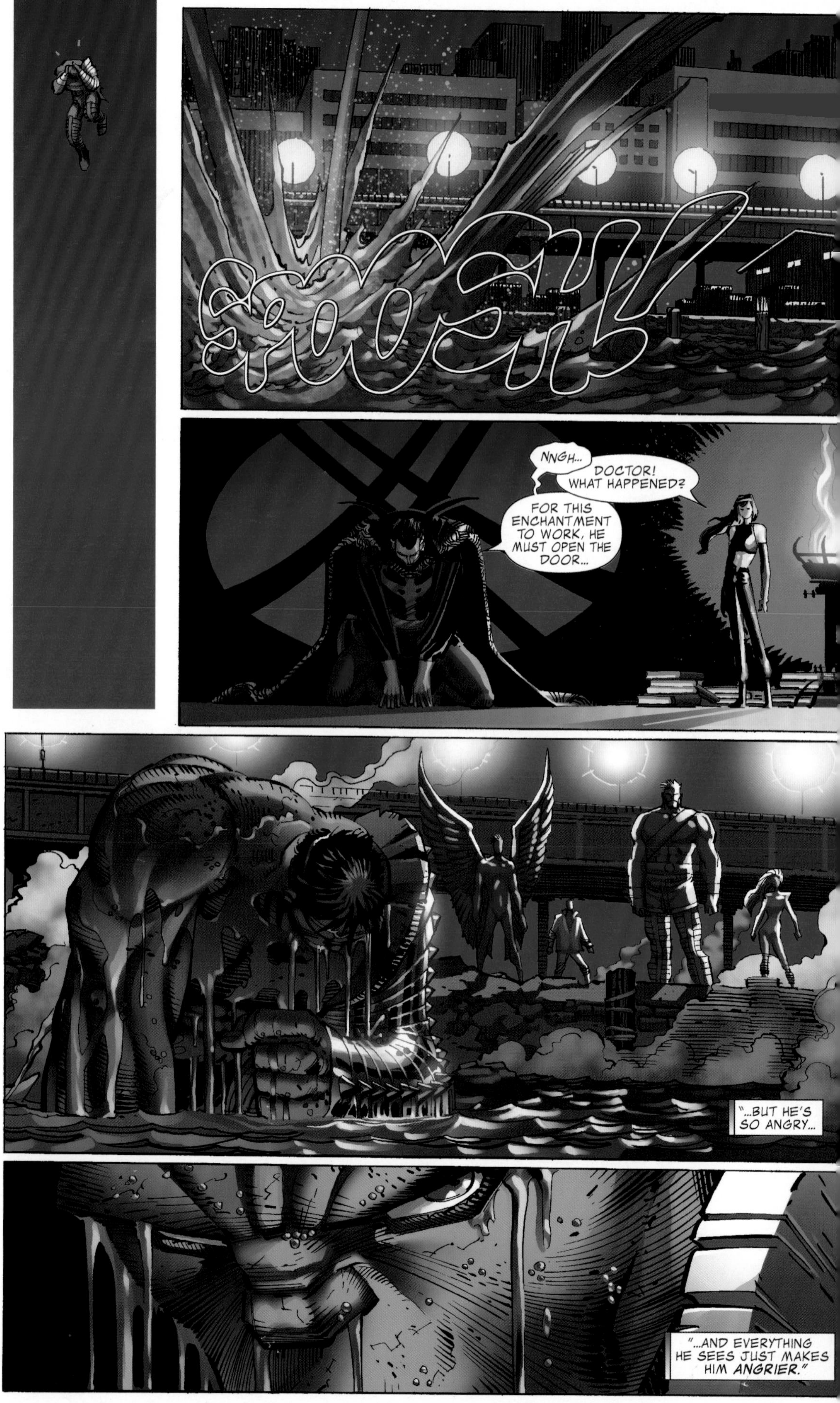
SPOOSH!
NNGH...
DOCTOR! WHAT HAPPENED?
FOR THIS ENCHANTMENT TO WORK, HE MUST OPEN THE DOOR...
"...BUT HE'S SO ANGRY...
"...AND EVERYTHING HE SEES JUST MAKES HIM ANGRIER."

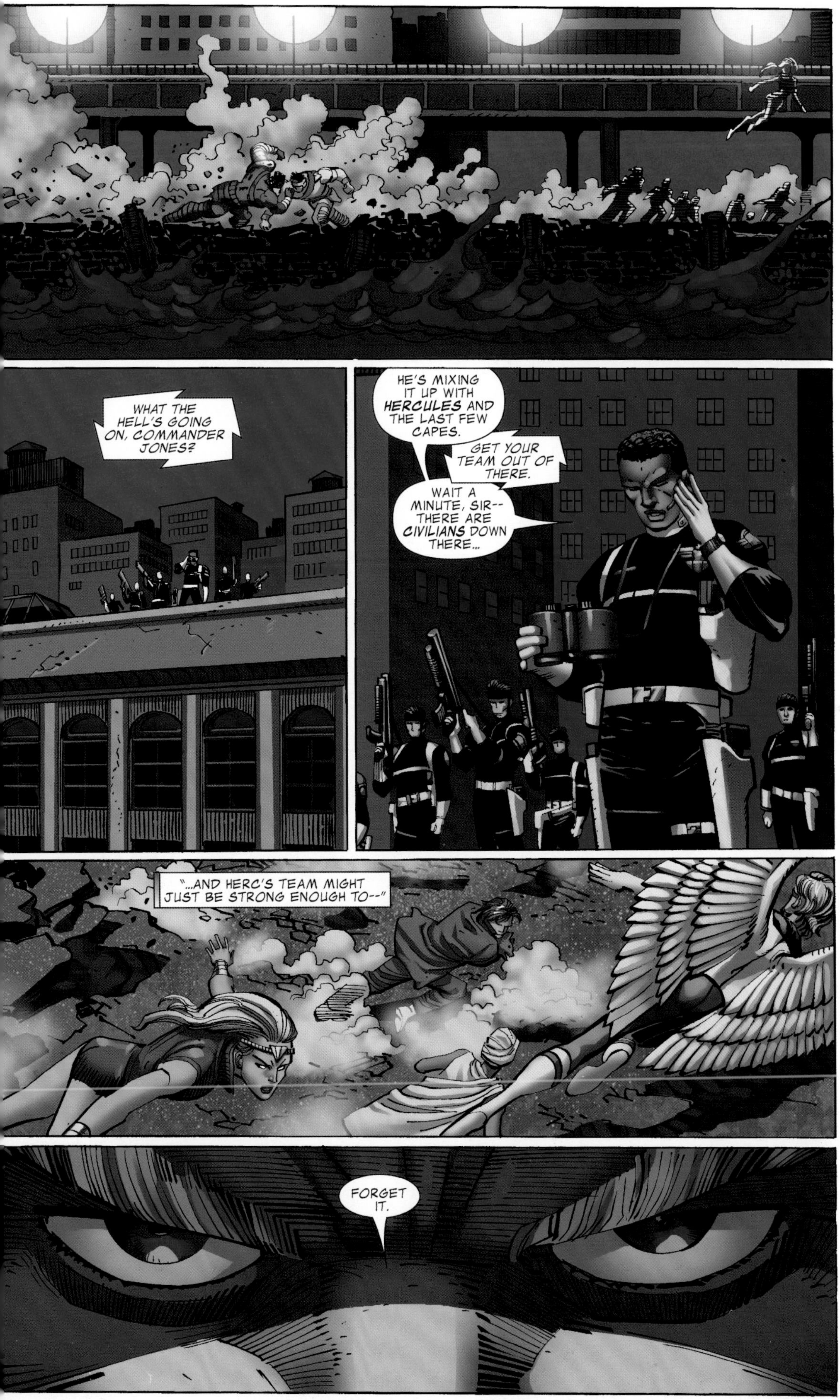

WHAT THE HELL'S GOING ON, COMMANDER JONES?
HE'S MIXING IT UP WITH HERCULES AND THE LAST FEW CAPES.
GET YOUR TEAM OUT OF THERE.
WAIT A MINUTE, SIR-- THERE ARE CIVILIANS DOWN THERE...
"...AND HERC'S TEAM MIGHT JUST BE STRONG ENOUGH TO--"
FORGET IT.

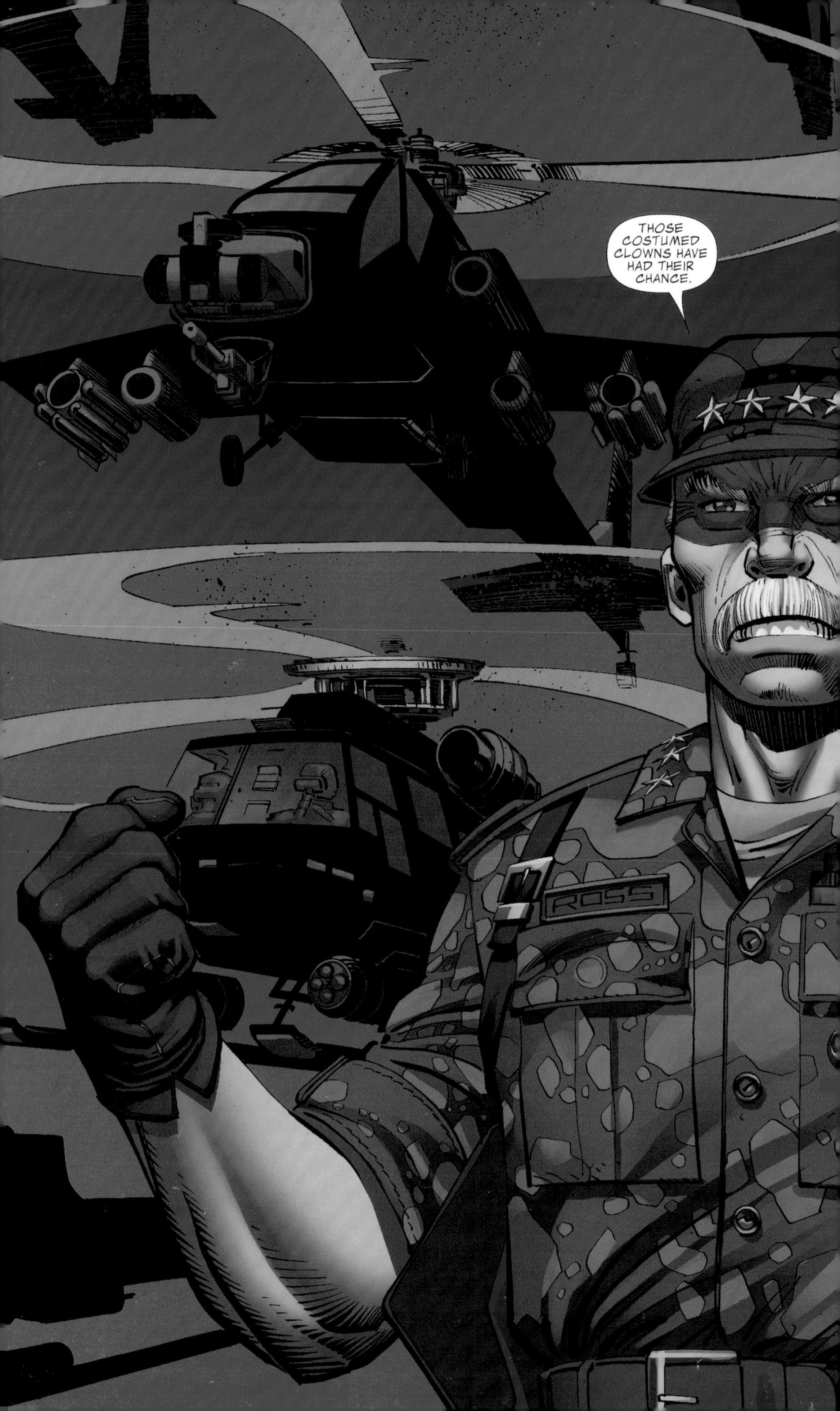
THOSE COSTUMED CLOWNS HAVE HAD THEIR CHANCE.
ROSS

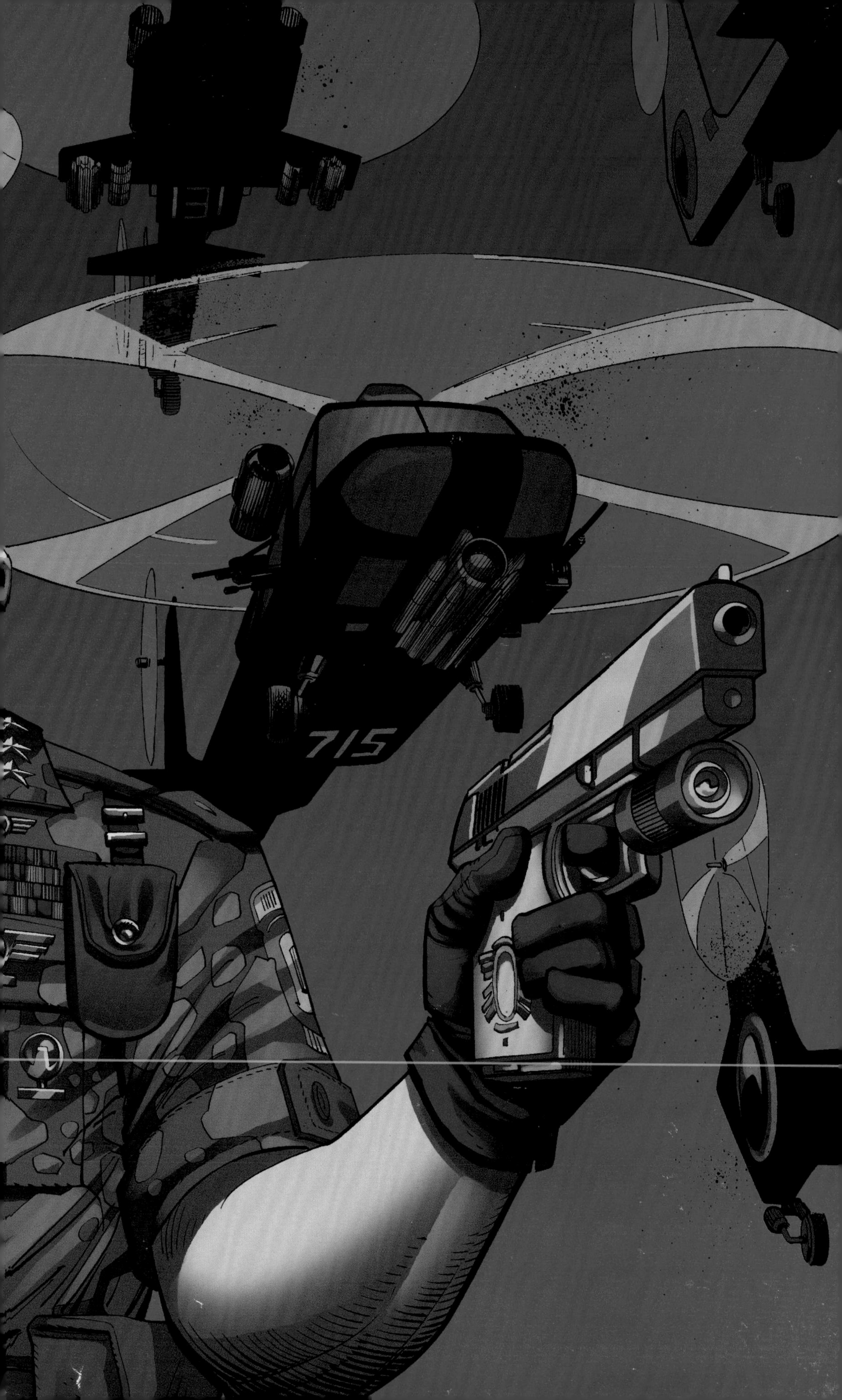
131
715

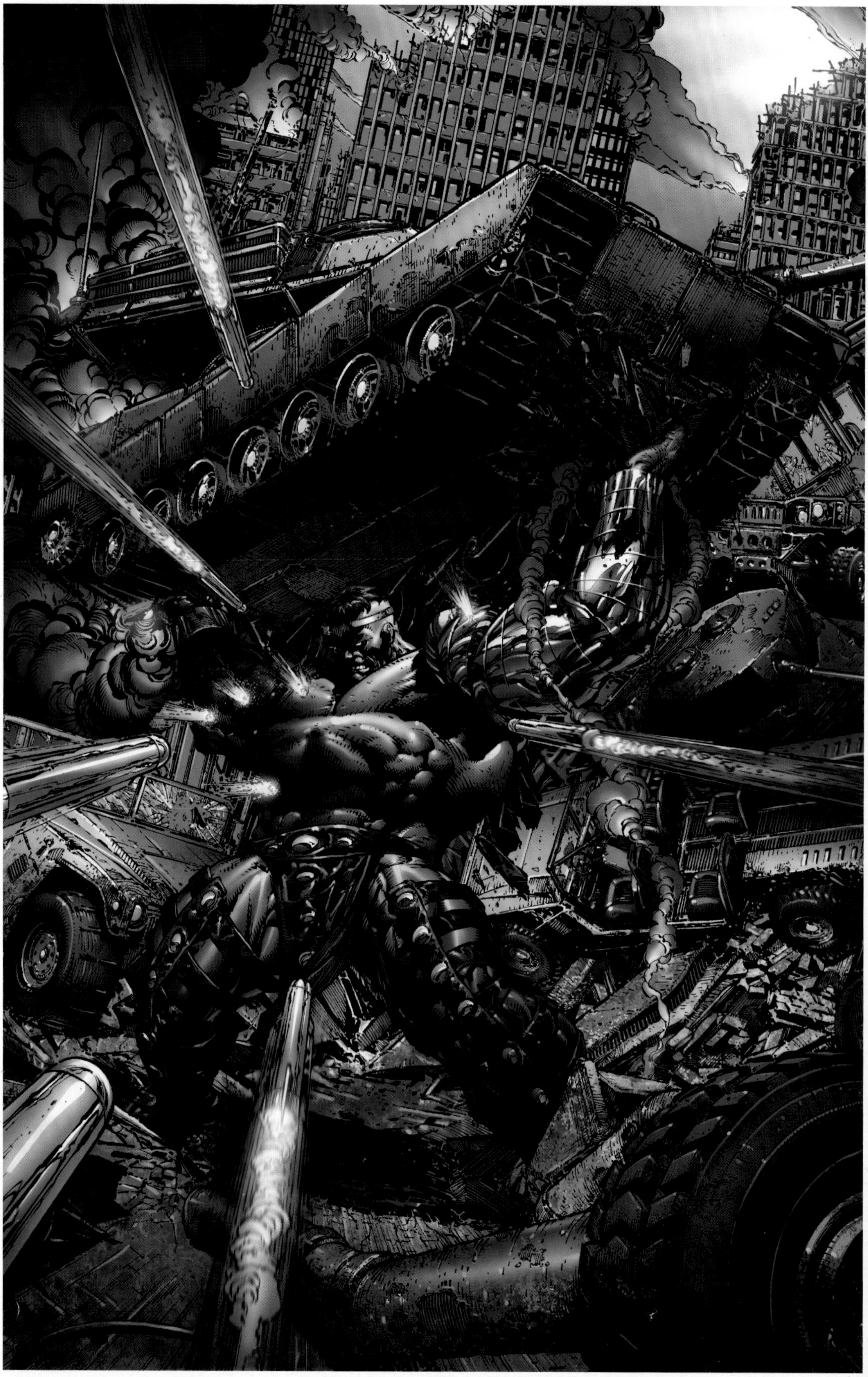

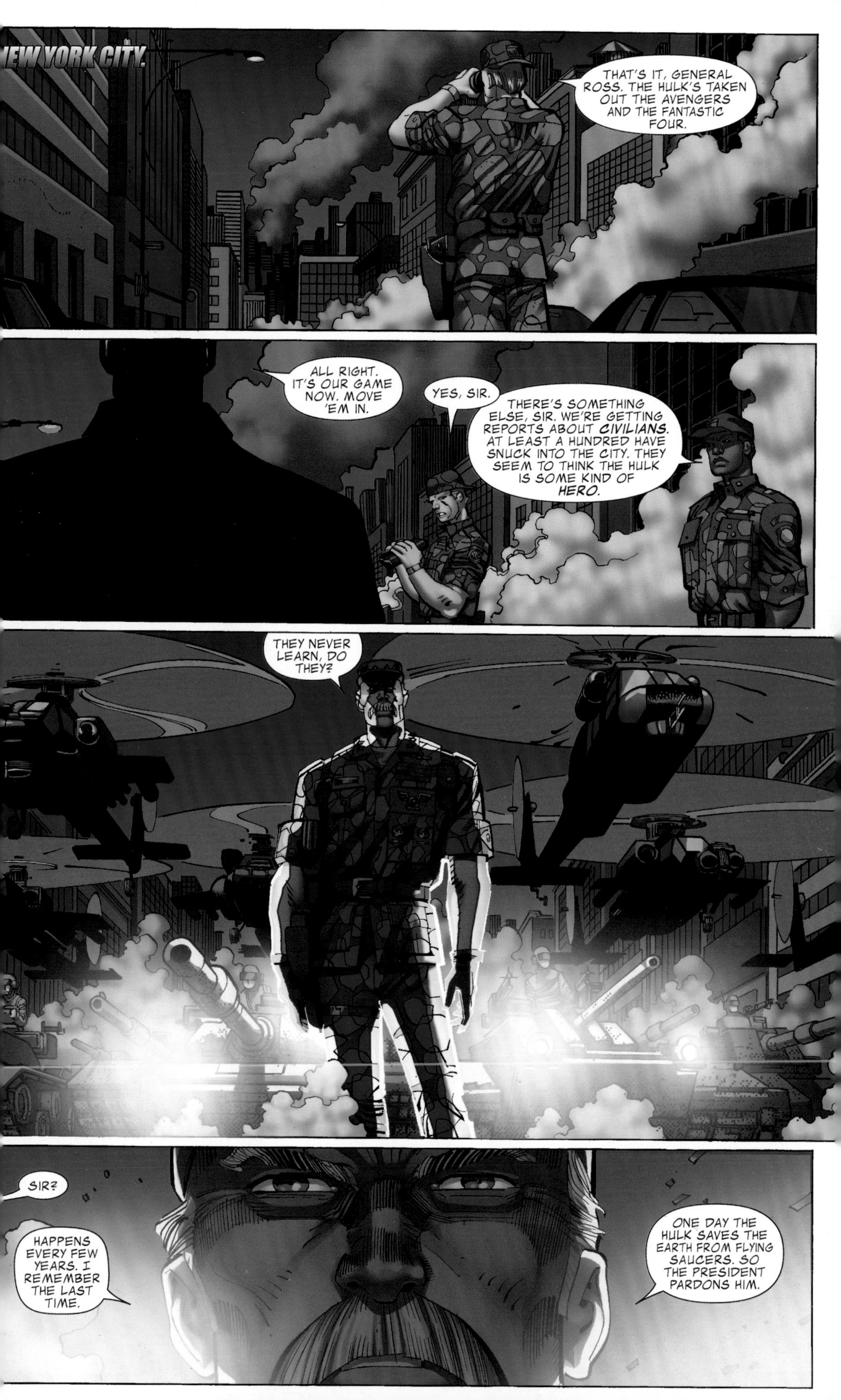
NEW YORK CITY.
THAT'S IT, GENERAL ROSS. THE HULK'S TAKEN OUT THE AVENGERS AND THE FANTASTIC FOUR.
ALL RIGHT. IT'S OUR GAME NOW. MOVE 'EM IN.
YES, SIR.
THERE'S SOMETHING ELSE, SIR. WE'RE GETTING REPORTS ABOUT CIVILIANS. AT LEAST A HUNDRED HAVE SNUCK INTO THE CITY. THEY SEEM TO THINK THE HULK IS SOME KIND OF HERO.
THEY NEVER LEARN, DO THEY?
SIR?
HAPPENS EVERY FEW YEARS. I REMEMBER THE LAST TIME.
ONE DAY THE HULK SAVES THE EARTH FROM FLYING SAUCERS. SO THE PRESIDENT PARDONS HIM.

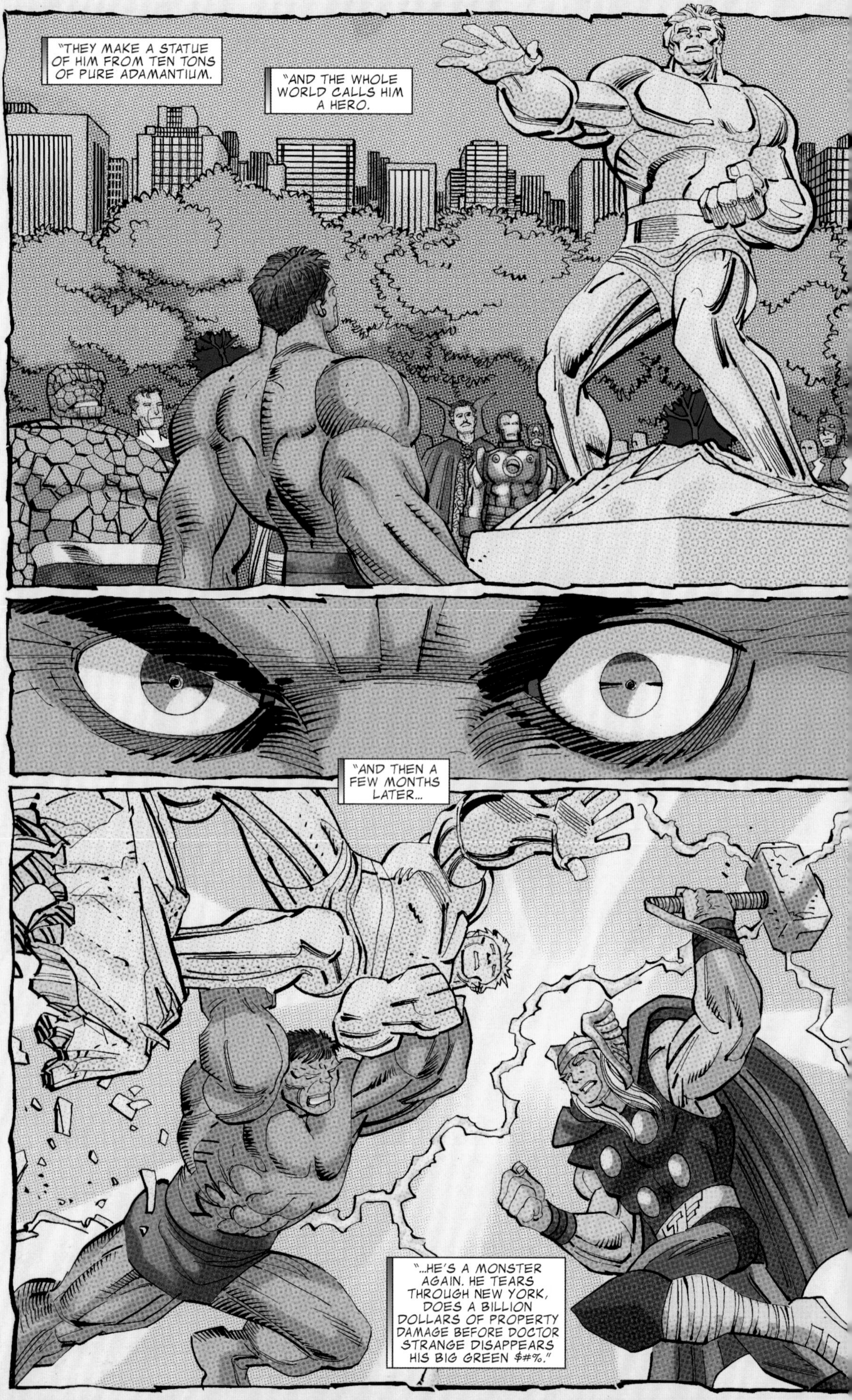
"THEY MAKE A STATUE OF HIM FROM TEN TONS OF PURE ADAMANTIUM.
"AND THE WHOLE WORLD CALLS HIM A HERO.
"AND THEN A FEW MONTHS LATER...
"...HE'S A MONSTER AGAIN. HE TEARS THROUGH NEW YORK, DOES A BILLION DOLLARS OF PROPERTY DAMAGE BEFORE DOCTOR STRANGE DISAPPEARS HIS BIG GREEN $#%."

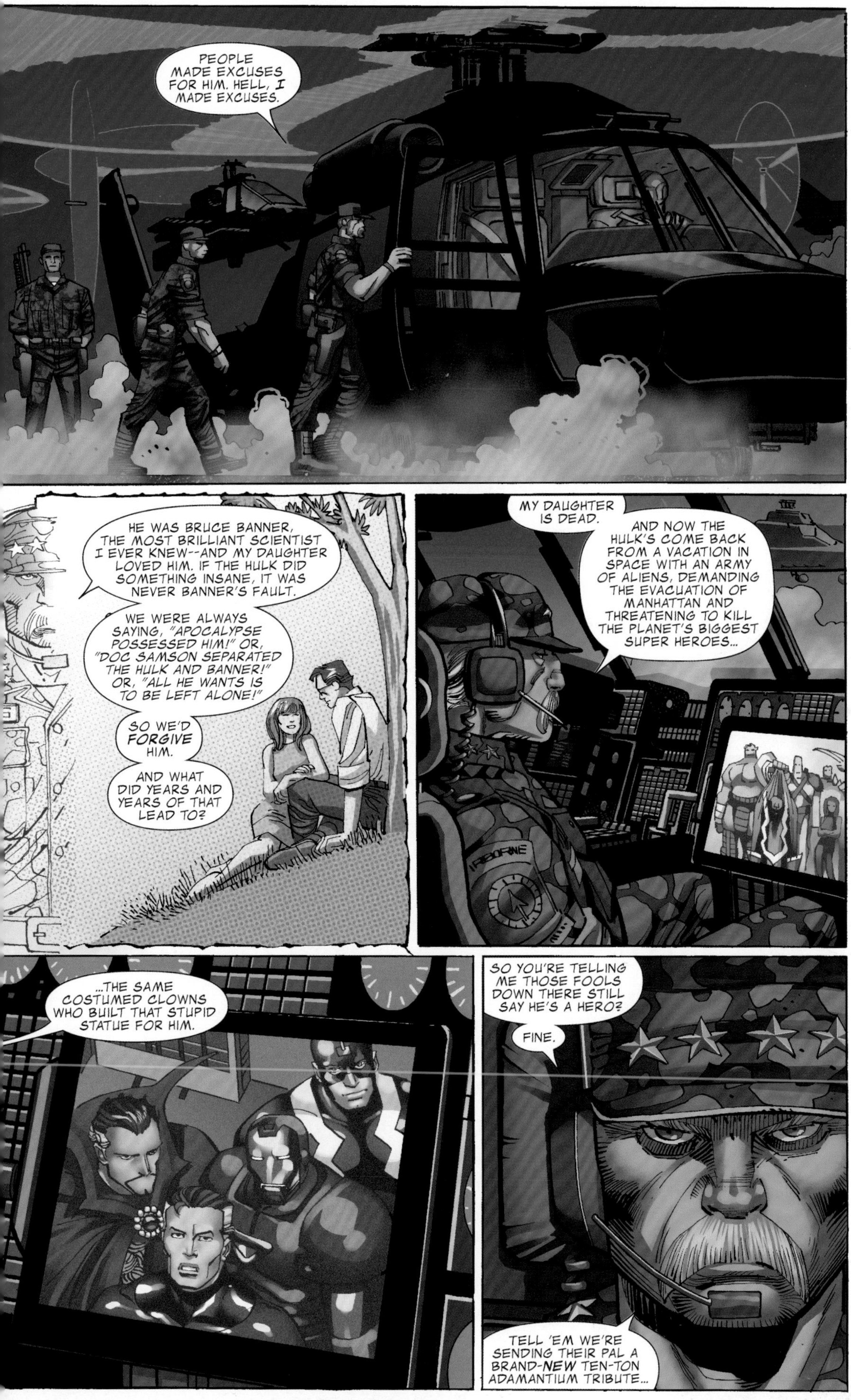
PEOPLE MADE EXCUSES FOR HIM. HELL, I MADE EXCUSES.
HE WAS BRUCE BANNER, THE MOST BRILLIANT SCIENTIST I EVER KNEW--AND MY DAUGHTER LOVED HIM. IF THE HULK DID SOMETHING INSANE, IT WAS NEVER BANNER'S FAULT.
WE WERE ALWAYS SAYING, "APOCALYPSE POSSESSED HIM!" OR, "DOC SAMSON SEPARATED THE HULK AND BANNER!" OR, "ALL HE WANTS IS TO BE LEFT ALONE!"
SO WE'D FORGIVE HIM.
AND WHAT DID YEARS AND YEARS OF THAT LEAD TO?
MY DAUGHTER IS DEAD.
AND NOW THE HULK'S COME BACK FROM A VACATION IN SPACE WITH AN ARMY OF ALIENS, DEMANDING THE EVACUATION OF MANHATTAN AND THREATENING TO KILL THE PLANET'S BIGGEST SUPER HEROES...
...THE SAME COSTUMED CLOWNS WHO BUILT THAT STUPID STATUE FOR HIM.
SO YOU'RE TELLING ME THOSE FOOLS DOWN THERE STILL SAY HE'S A HERO?
FINE.
TELL 'EM WE'RE SENDING THEIR PAL A BRAND-NEW TEN-TON ADAMANTIUM TRIBUTE...

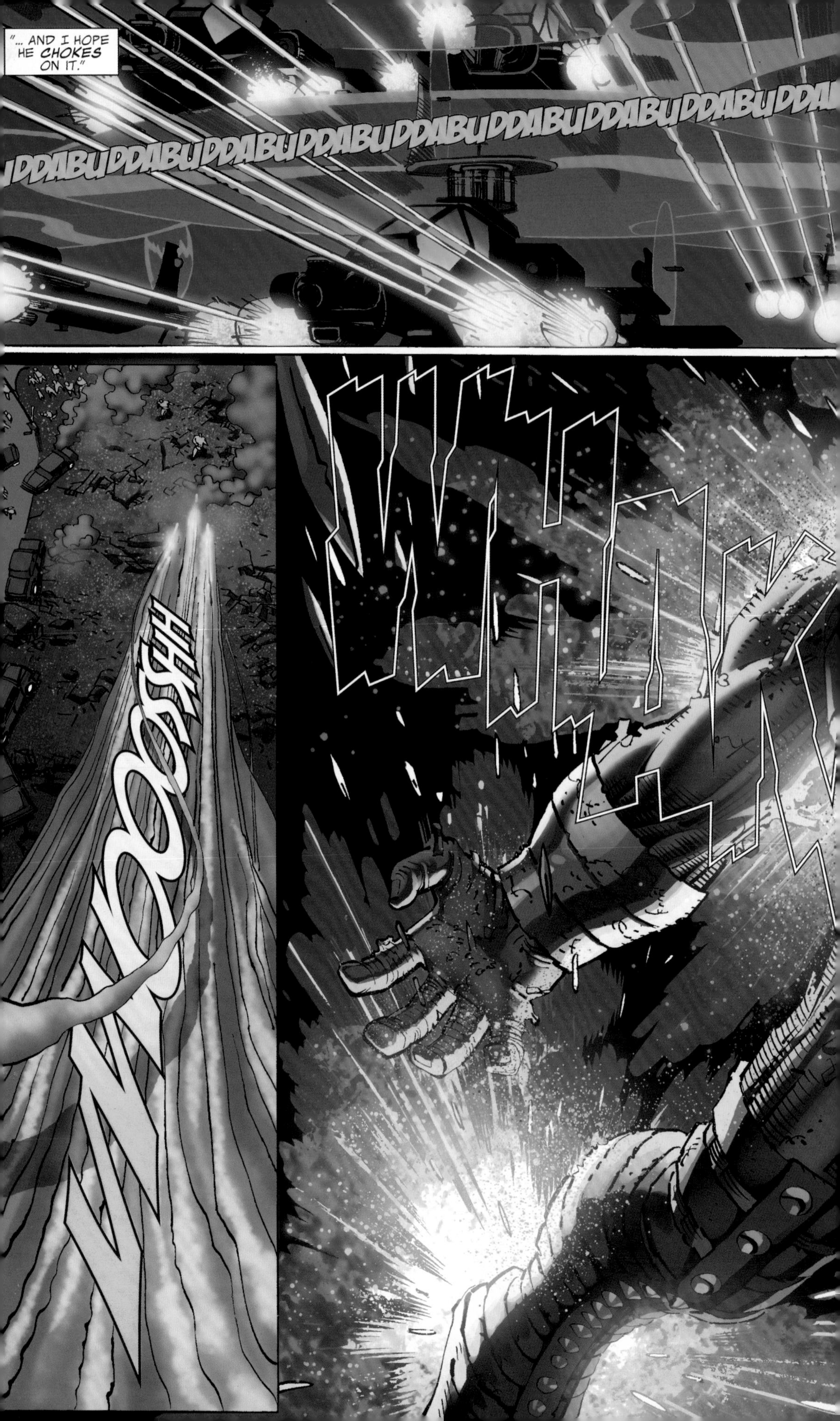
"... AND I HOPE HE CHOKES ON IT."
WHOOSH

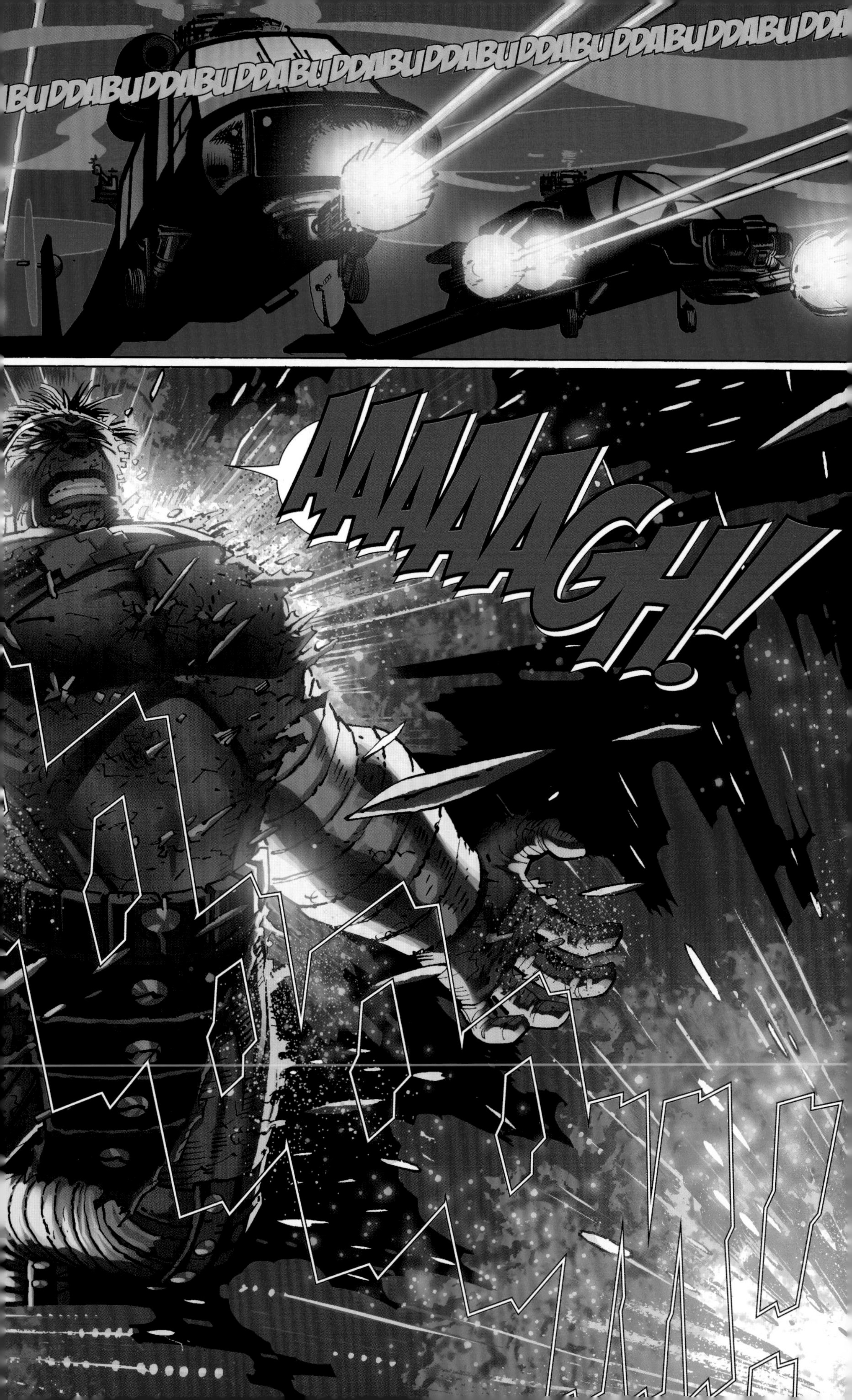
BUDDABUDDABUDDABUDDABUDDABUDDABUDDABUDDA
AAAAAGH!

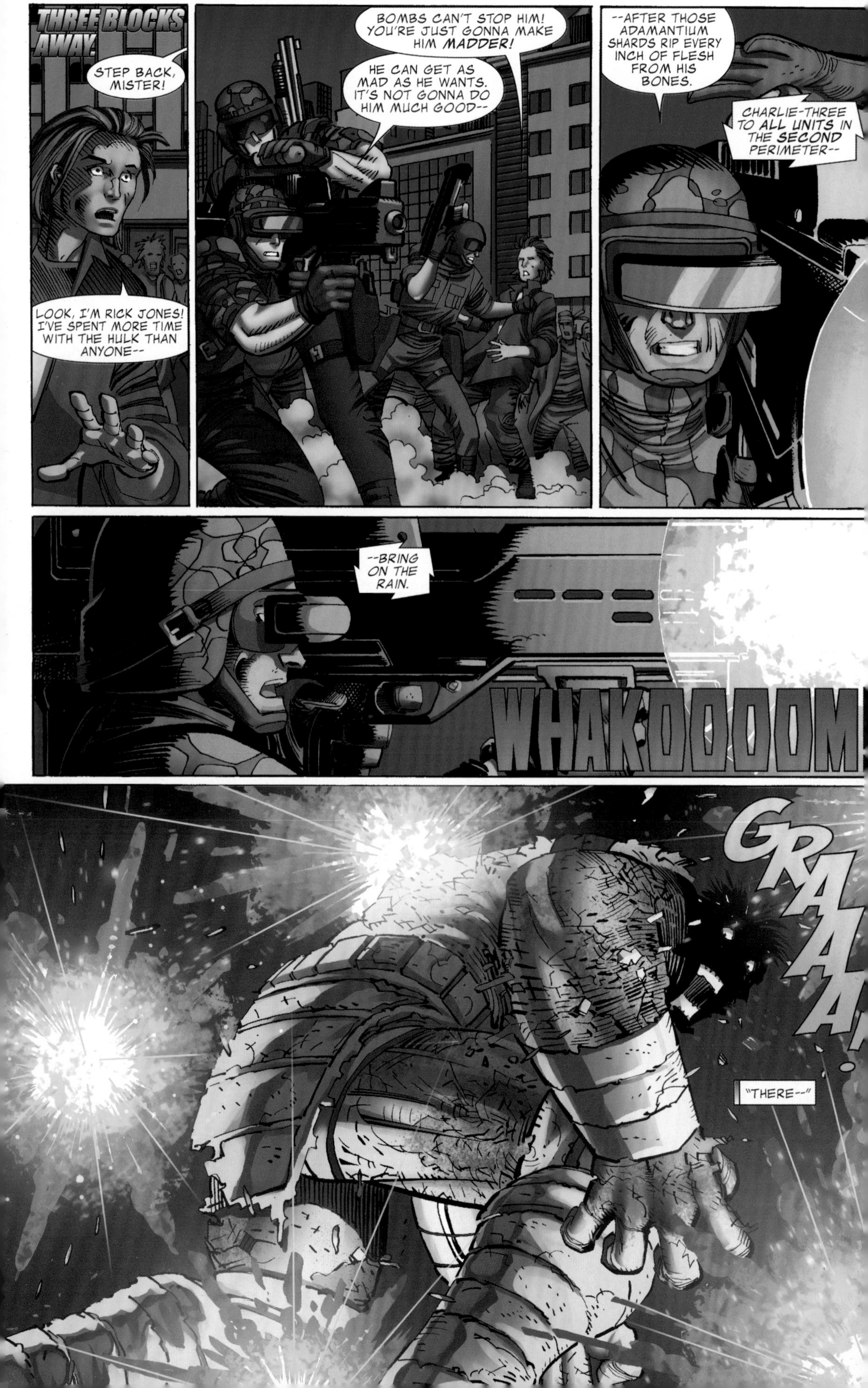
THREE BLOCKS AWAY.
STEP BACK, MISTER!
LOOK, I'M RICK JONES! I'VE SPENT MORE TIME WITH THE HULK THAN ANYONE--
BOMBS CAN'T STOP HIM! YOU'RE JUST GONNA MAKE HIM MADDER!
HE CAN GET AS MAD AS HE WANTS. IT'S NOT GONNA DO HIM MUCH GOOD--
--AFTER THOSE ADAMANTIUM SHARDS RIP EVERY INCH OF FLESH FROM HIS BONES.
CHARLIE-THREE TO ALL UNITS IN THE SECOND PERIMETER--
--BRING ON THE RAIN.
WHAKOOOOM
"THERE--"

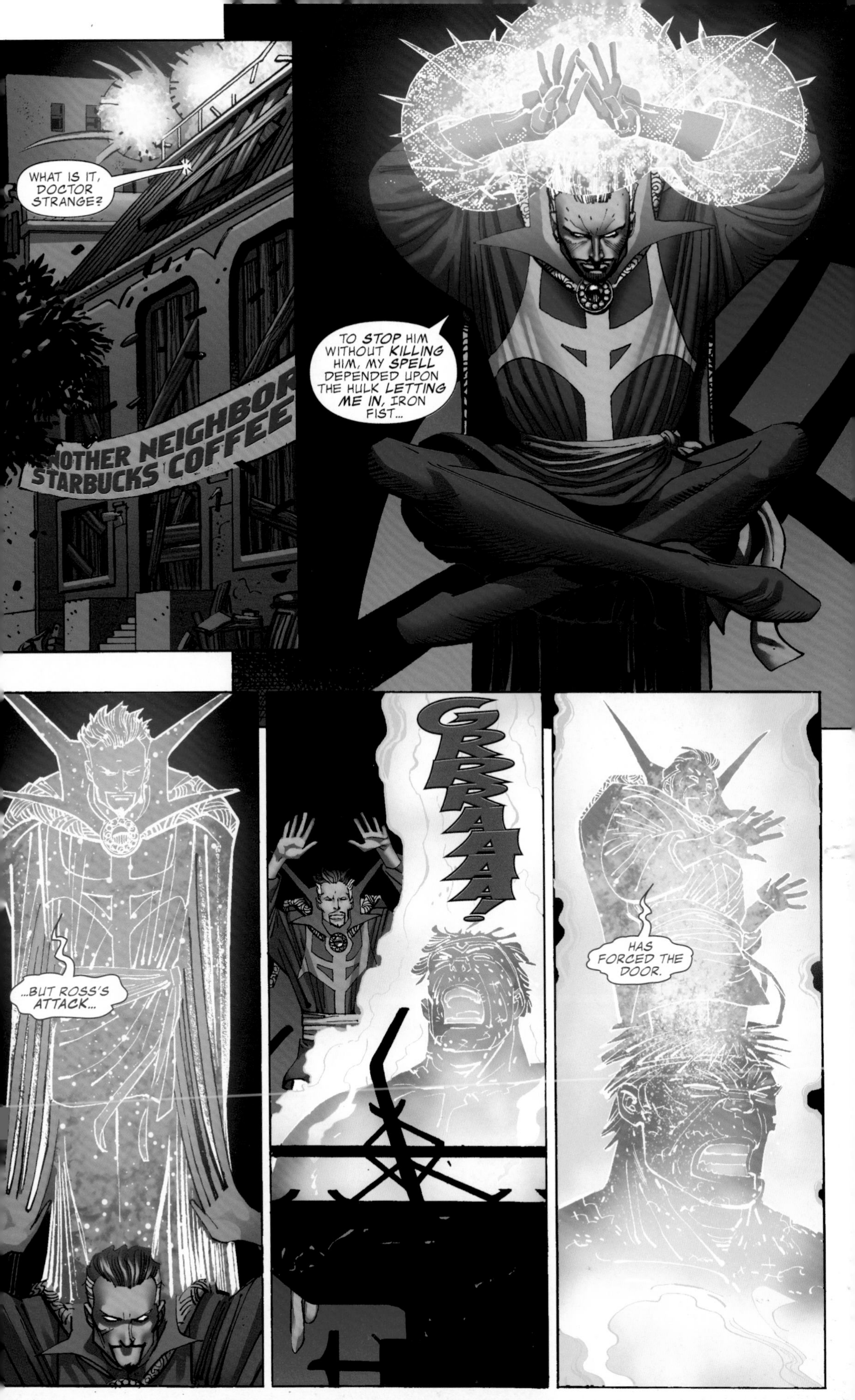
WHAT IS IT, DOCTOR STRANGE?
ANOTHER NEIGHBOR STARBUCKS COFFEE
TO STOP HIM WITHOUT KILLING HIM, MY SPELL DEPENDED UPON THE HULK LETTING ME IN, IRON FIST...
...BUT ROSS'S ATTACK...
GRRAAAA!
HAS FORCED THE DOOR.

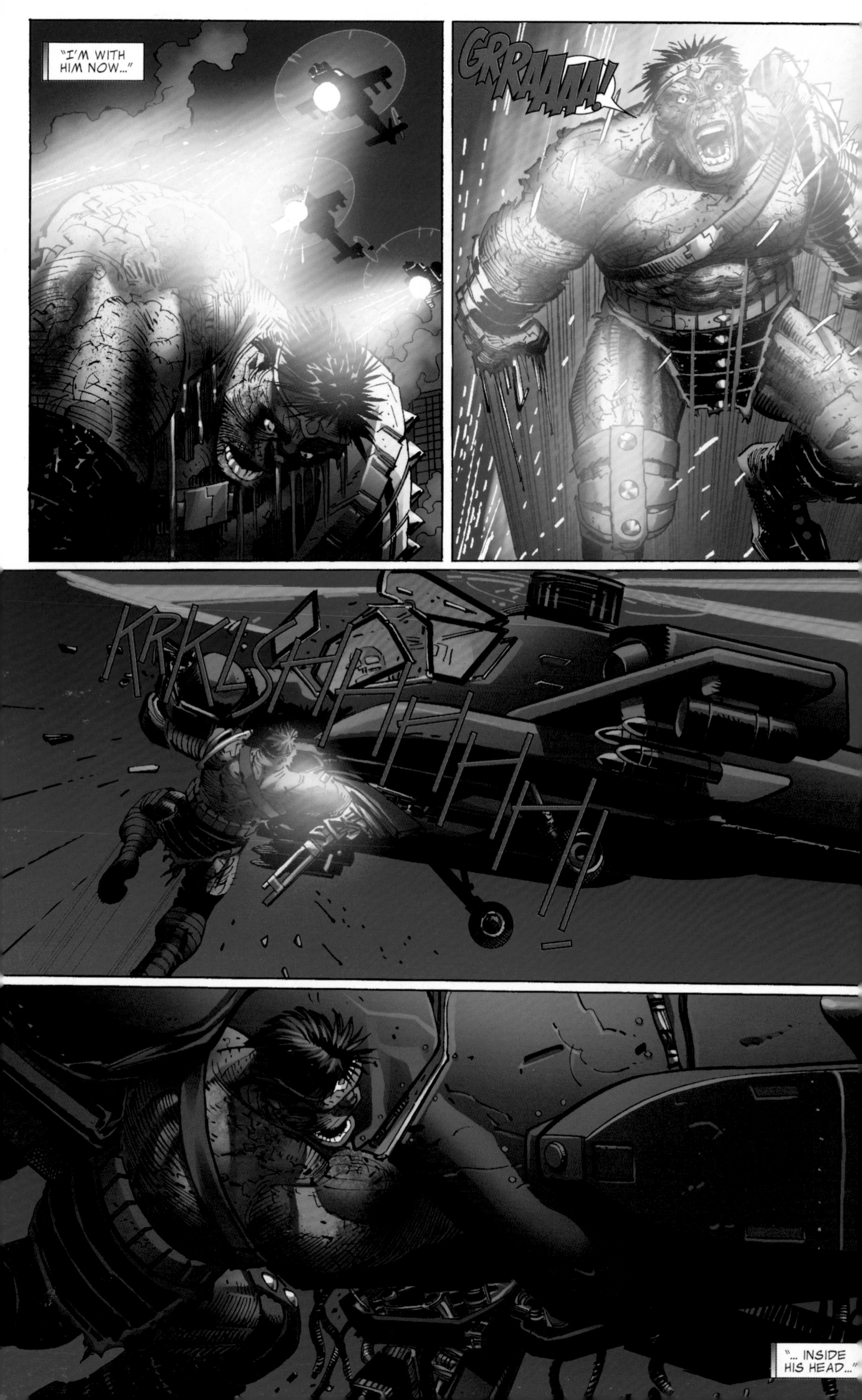
"I'M WITH HIM NOW..."
GRRAAAAA!
KRKLSHHHHHH
"... INSIDE HIS HEAD..."

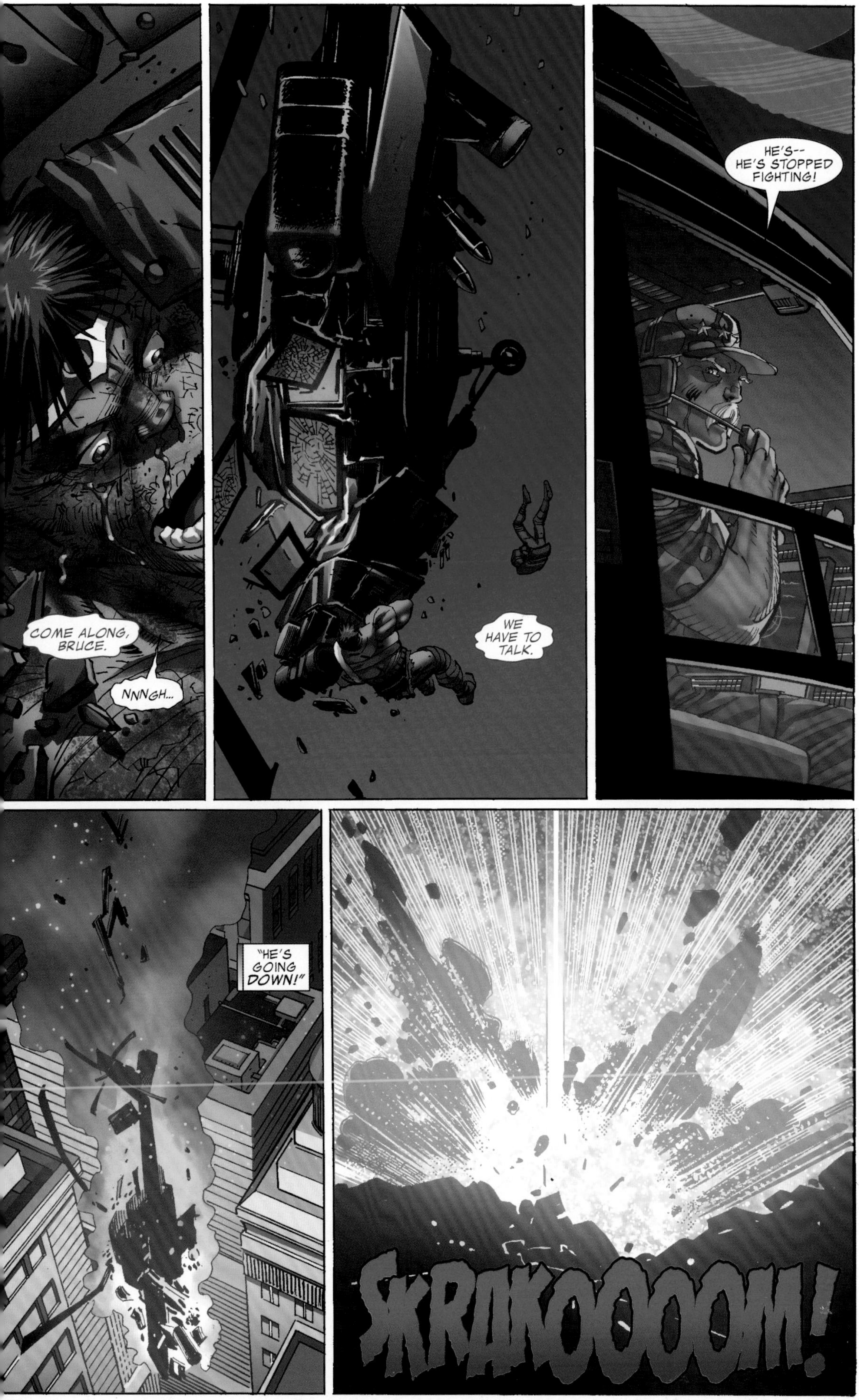

COME ALONG, BRUCE.
NNNGH...
WE HAVE TO TALK.
HE'S-- HE'S STOPPED FIGHTING!
"HE'S GOING DOWN!"
SKRAKOOOOM!

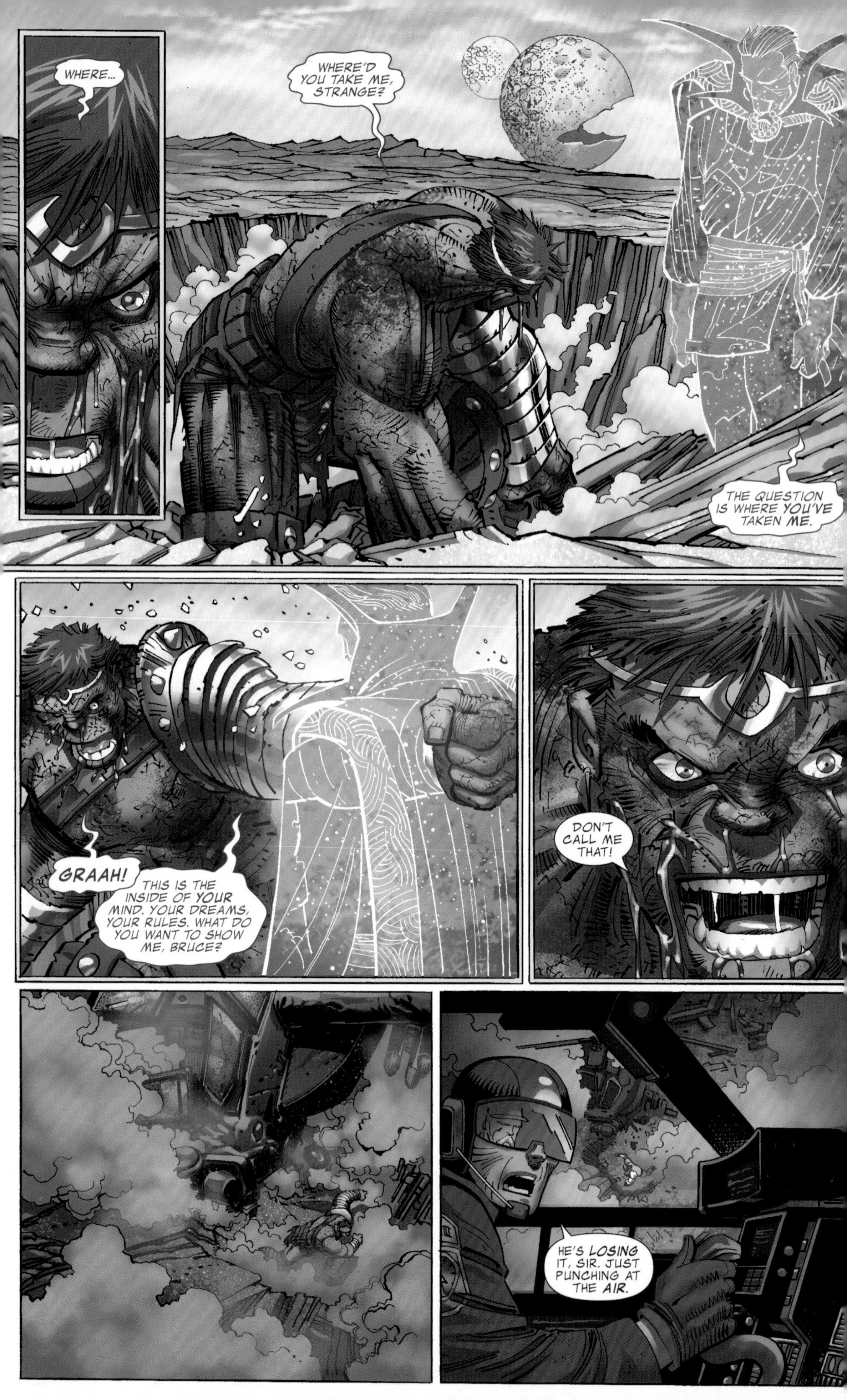
WHERE...
WHERE'D YOU TAKE ME, STRANGE?
THE QUESTION IS WHERE YOU'VE TAKEN ME.
GRAAH!
THIS IS THE INSIDE OF YOUR MIND. YOUR DREAMS, YOUR RULES. WHAT DO YOU WANT TO SHOW ME, BRUCE?
DON'T CALL ME THAT!
HE'S LOSING IT, SIR. JUST PUNCHING AT THE AIR.

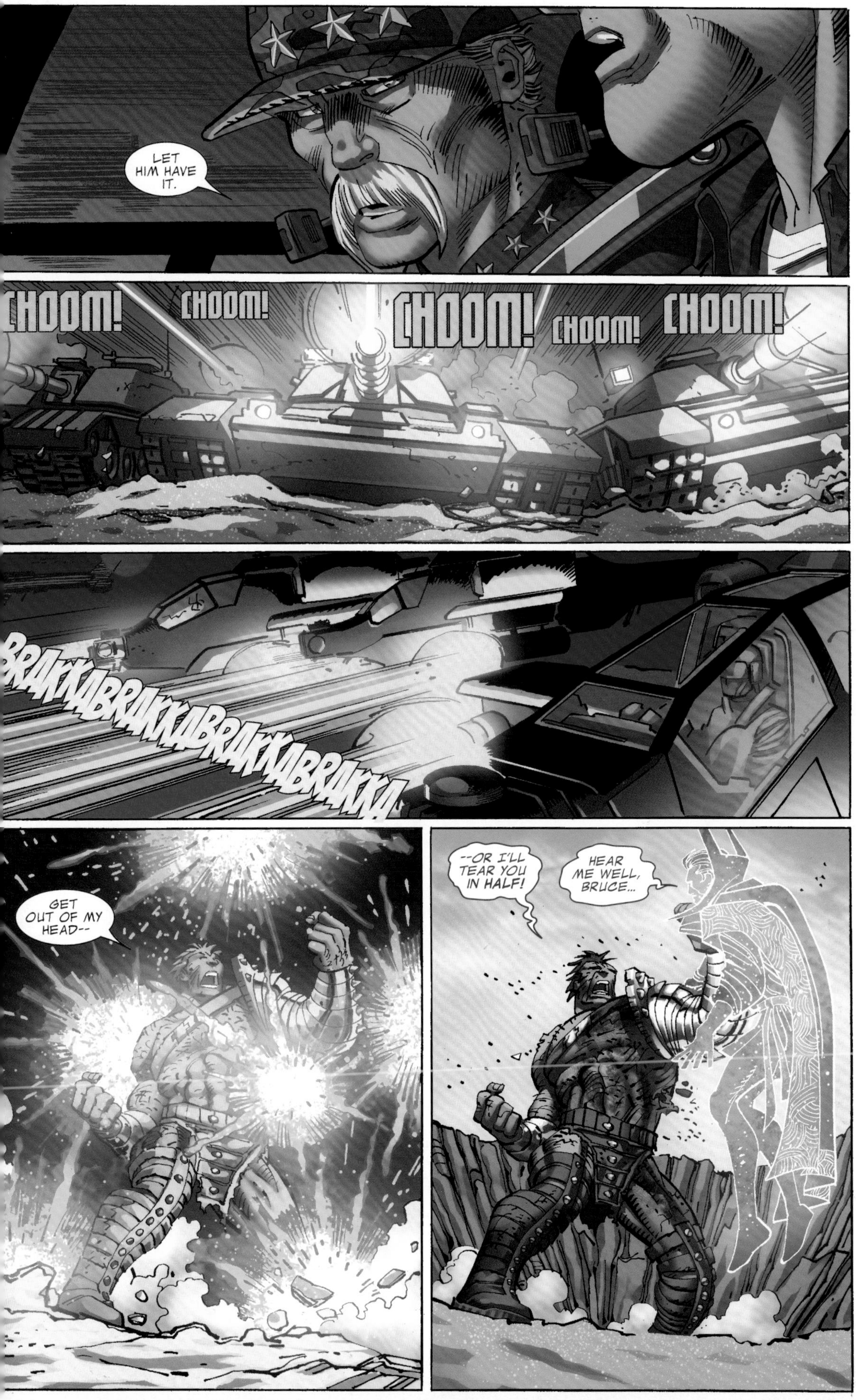
LET HIM HAVE IT.
CHOOM! CHOOM! CHOOM! CHOOM! CHOOM!
BRAKKABRAKKABRAKKABRAKKA
GET OUT OF MY HEAD--
--OR I'LL TEAR YOU IN HALF!
HEAR ME WELL, BRUCE...

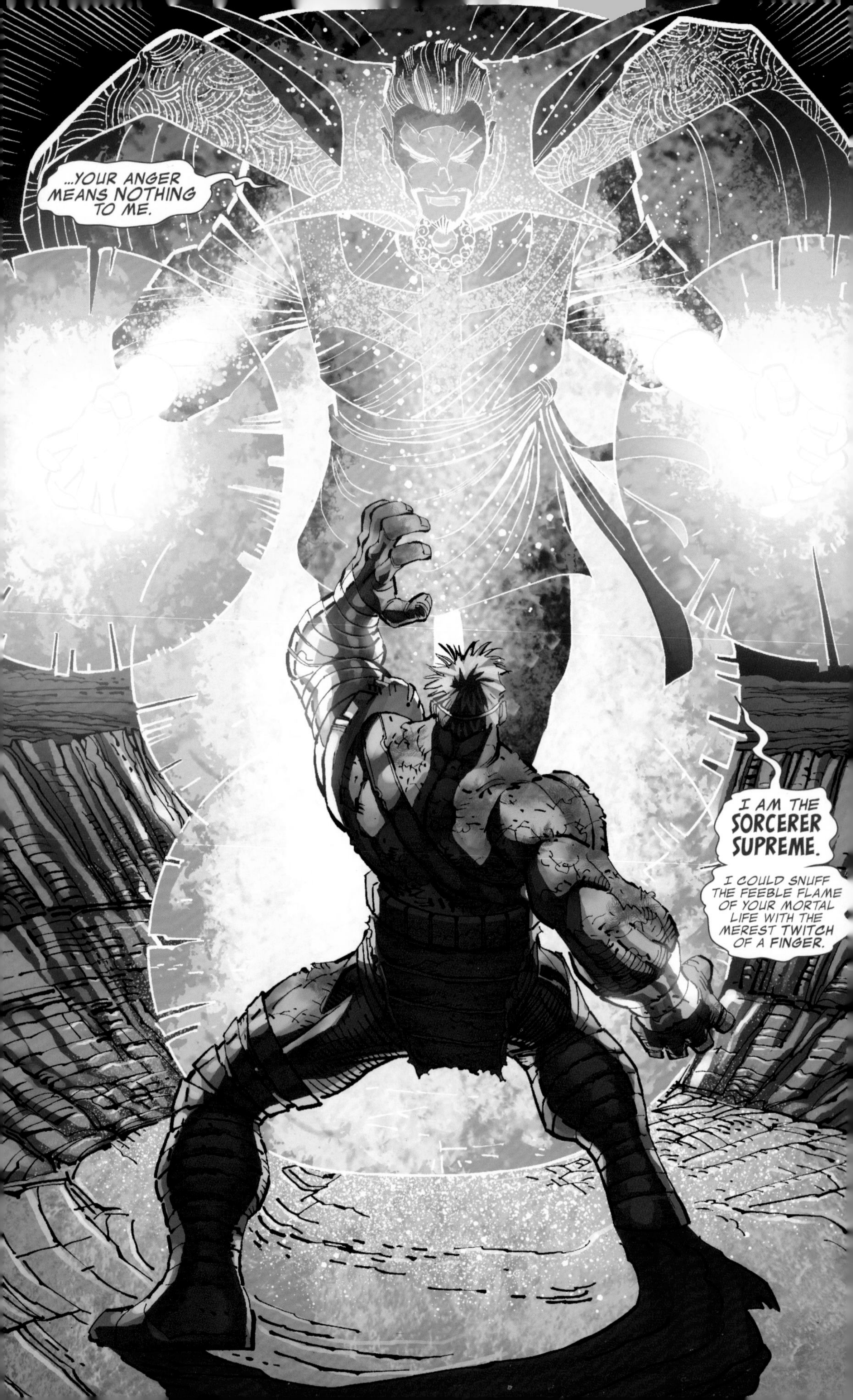
...YOUR ANGER MEANS NOTHING TO ME.
I AM THE SORCERER SUPREME.
I COULD SNUFF THE FEEBLE FLAME OF YOUR MORTAL LIFE WITH THE MEREST TWITCH OF A FINGER.

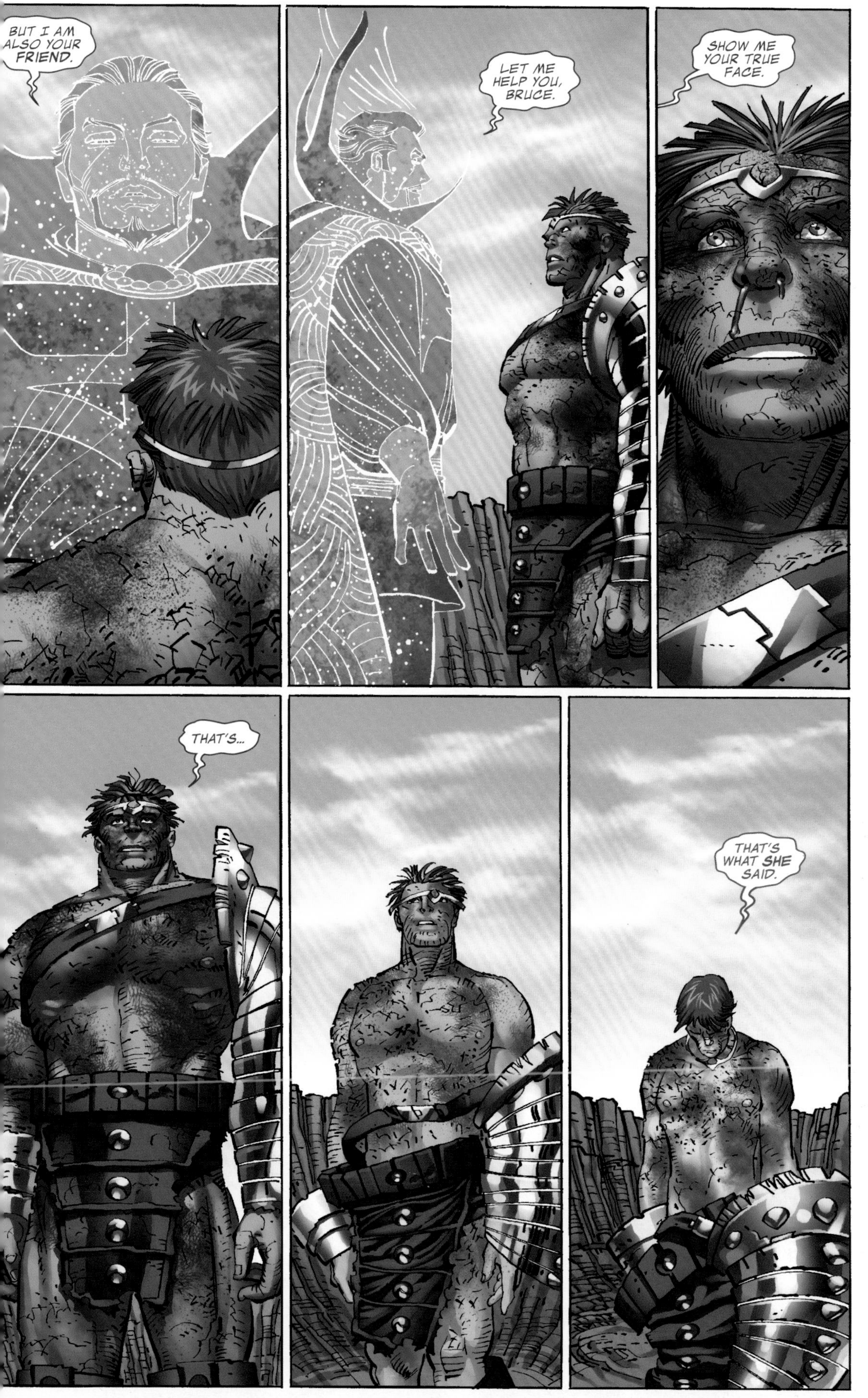
BUT I AM ALSO YOUR FRIEND.
LET ME HELP YOU, BRUCE.
SHOW ME YOUR TRUE FACE.
THAT'S...
THAT'S WHAT SHE SAID.

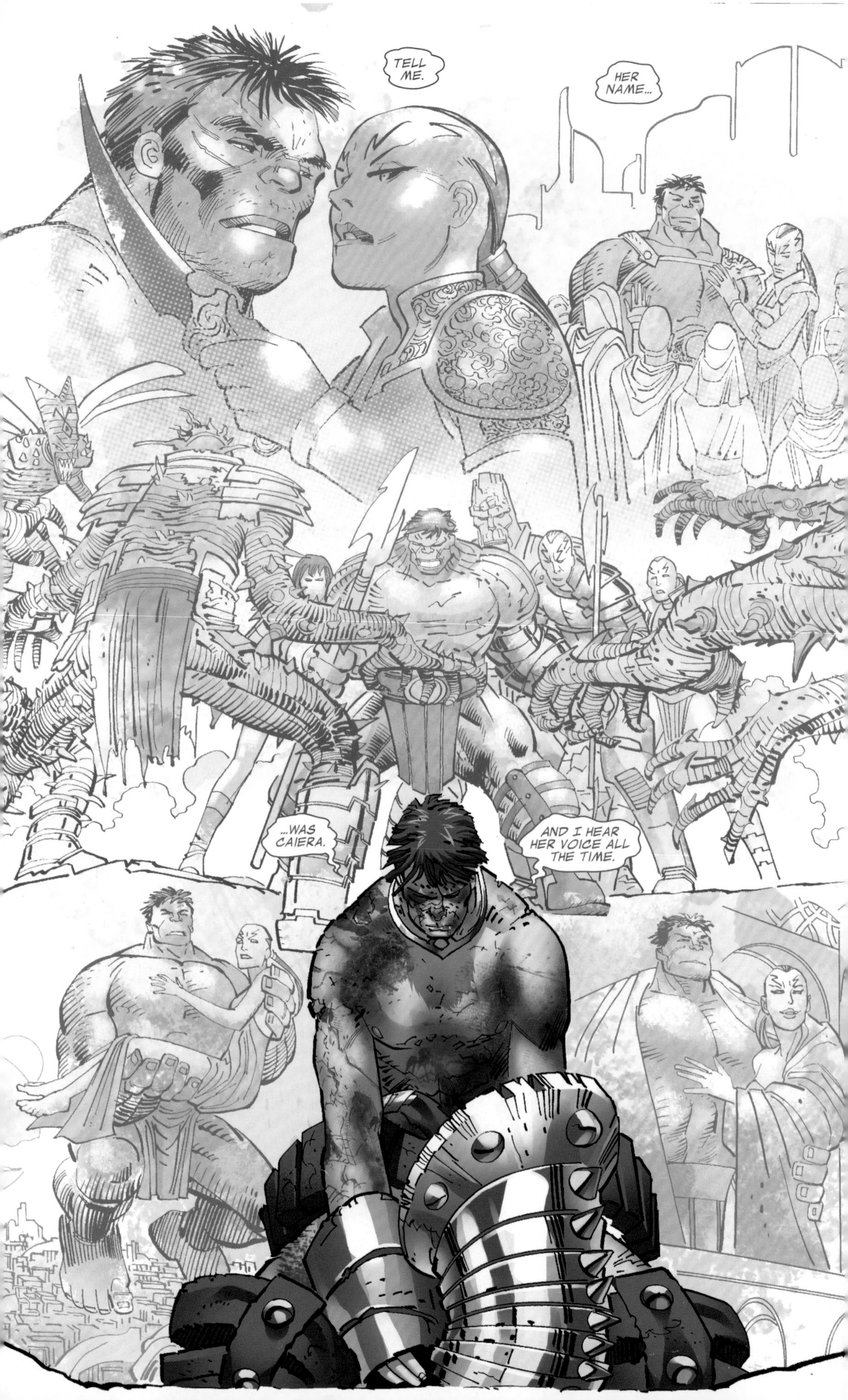
TELL ME.
HER NAME...
...WAS CAIERA.
AND I HEAR HER VOICE ALL THE TIME.

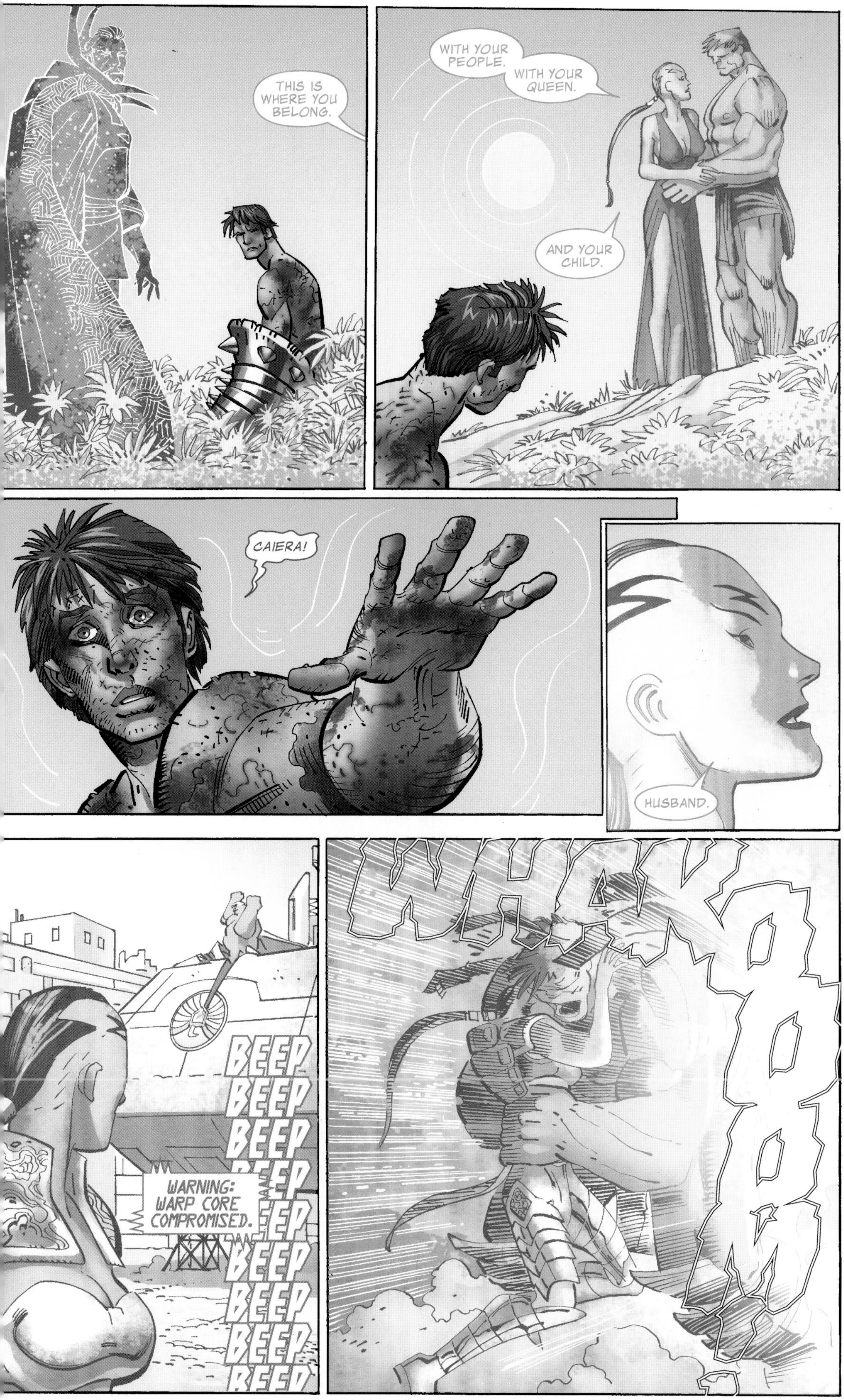
THIS IS WHERE YOU BELONG.
WITH YOUR PEOPLE.
WITH YOUR QUEEN.
AND YOUR CHILD.
CAIERA!
HUSBAND.
BEEP BEEP BEEP BEEP BEEP BEEP BEEP BEEP BEEP BEEP
WARNING: WARP CORE COMPROMISED.

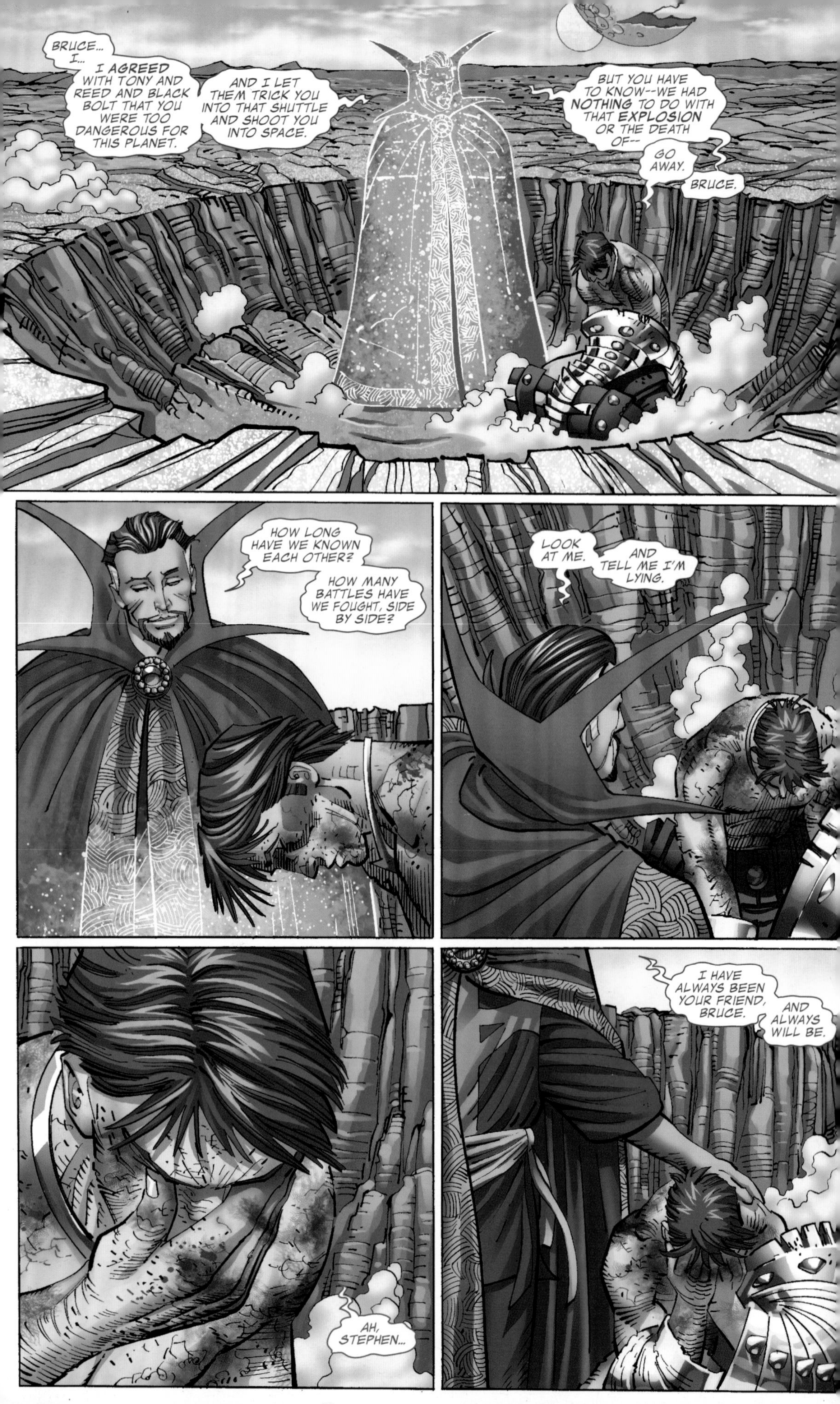
BRUCE... I... I AGREED WITH TONY AND REED AND BLACK BOLT THAT YOU WERE TOO DANGEROUS FOR THIS PLANET.
AND I LET THEM TRICK YOU INTO THAT SHUTTLE AND SHOOT YOU INTO SPACE.
BUT YOU HAVE TO KNOW--WE HAD NOTHING TO DO WITH THAT EXPLOSION OR THE DEATH OF--
GO AWAY.
BRUCE.
HOW LONG HAVE WE KNOWN EACH OTHER?
HOW MANY BATTLES HAVE WE FOUGHT, SIDE BY SIDE?
LOOK AT ME.
AND TELL ME I'M LYING.
AH, STEPHEN...
I HAVE ALWAYS BEEN YOUR FRIEND, BRUCE.
AND ALWAYS WILL BE.

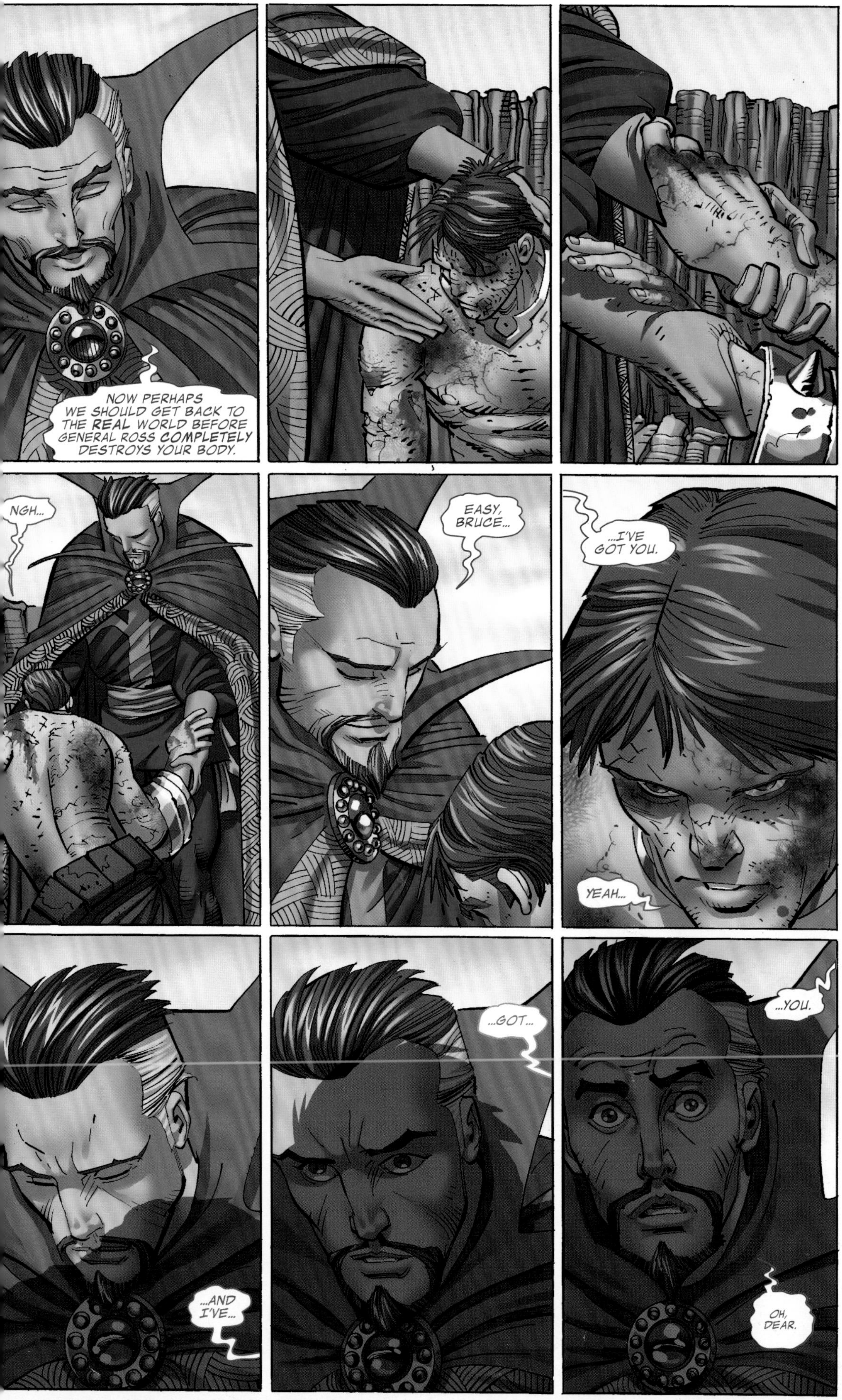
NOW PERHAPS WE SHOULD GET BACK TO THE REAL WORLD BEFORE GENERAL ROSS COMPLETELY DESTROYS YOUR BODY.
NGH...
EASY, BRUCE...
...I'VE GOT YOU.
YEAH...
...AND I'VE...
...GOT...
...YOU.
OH, DEAR.

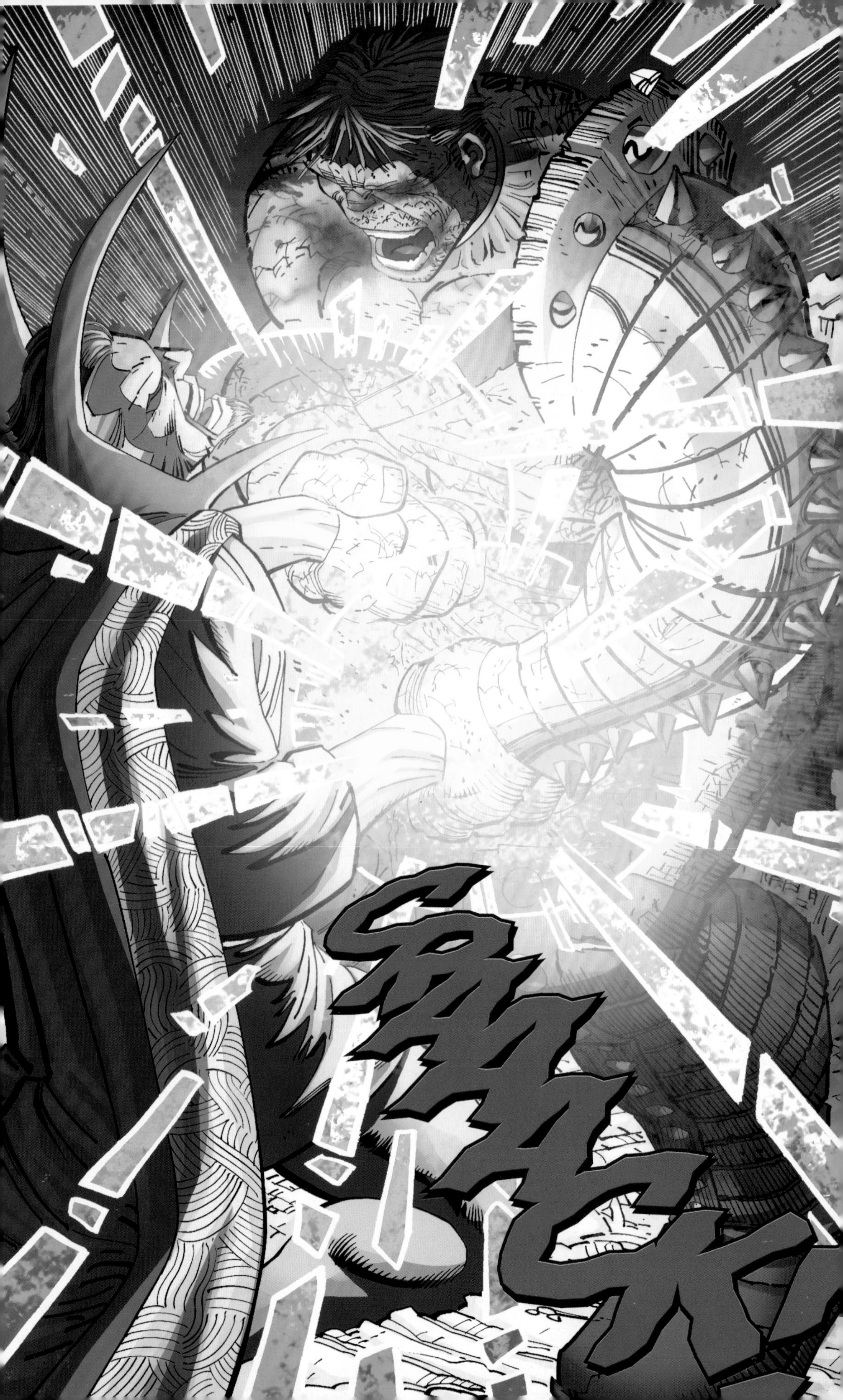
CRAACK!

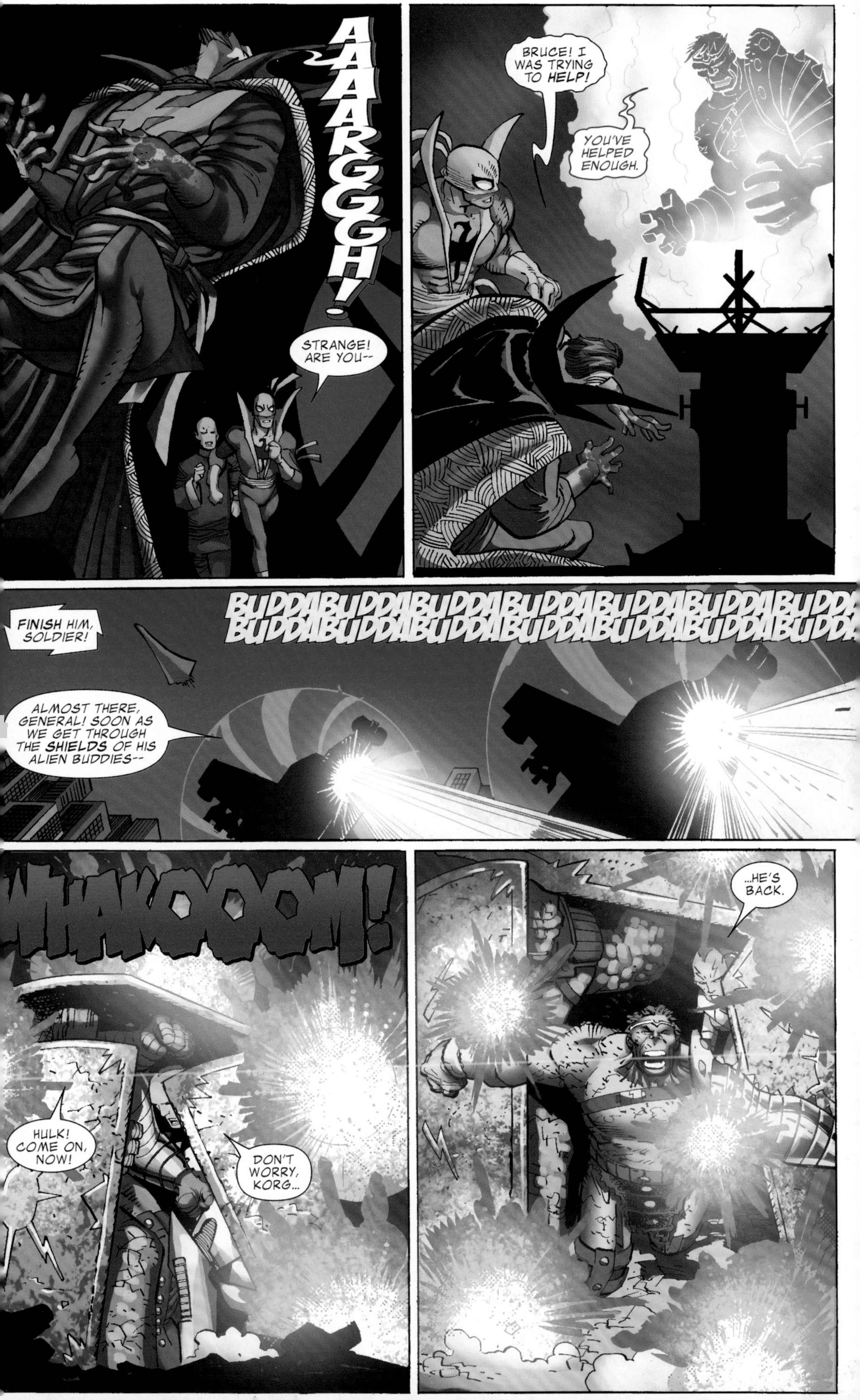
AAAARGGGH!
STRANGE! ARE YOU--
BRUCE! I WAS TRYING TO HELP!
YOU'VE HELPED ENOUGH.
FINISH HIM, SOLDIER!
BUDDABUDDABUDDABUDDABUDDABUDDABUDDA
BUDDABUDDABUDDABUDDABUDDABUDDABUDDA
ALMOST THERE, GENERAL! SOON AS WE GET THROUGH THE SHIELDS OF HIS ALIEN BUDDIES--
WHAKOOOM!
HULK! COME ON, NOW!
DON'T WORRY, KORG...
...HE'S BACK.

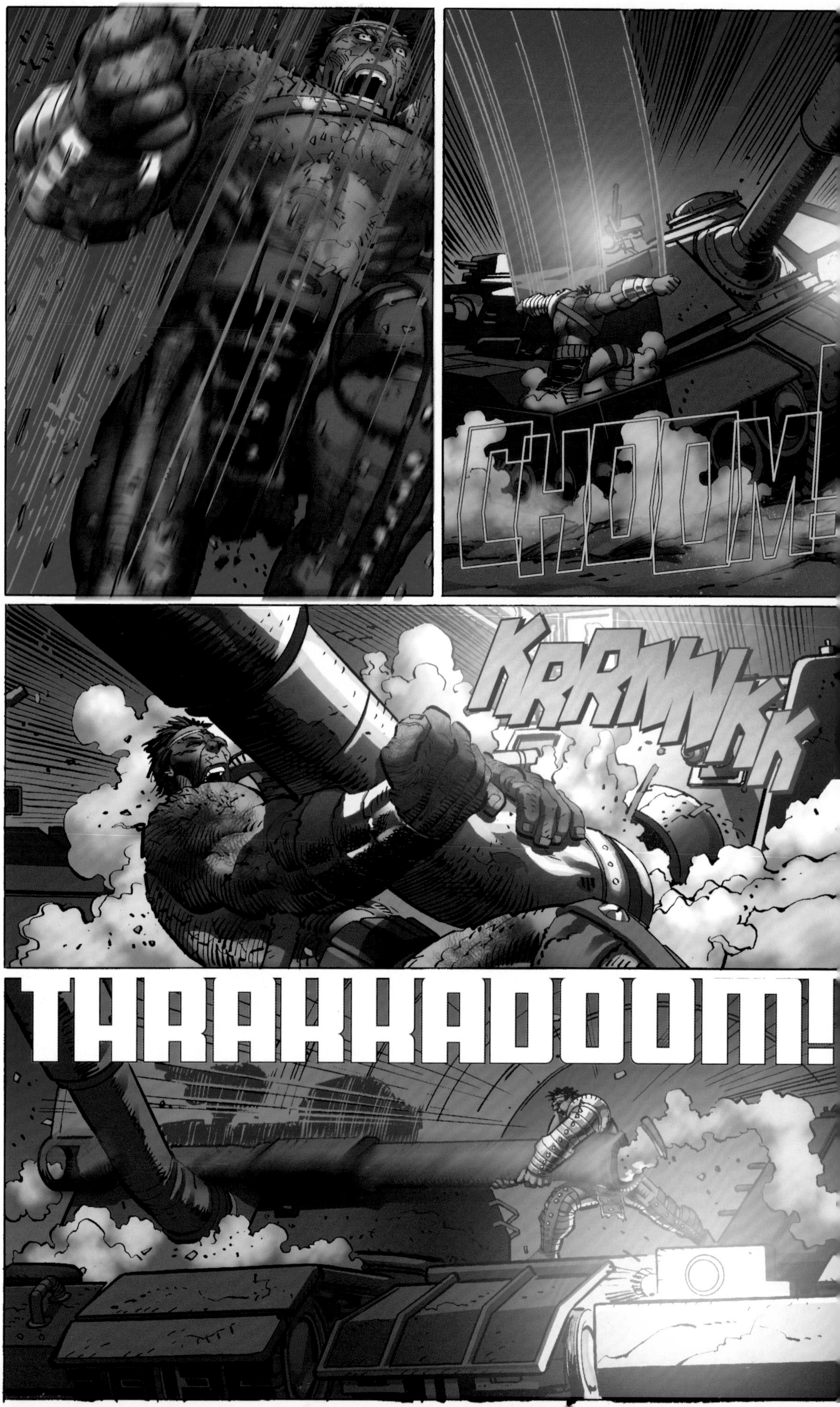
CHOOOM!
KRANNKK
THRAKKADOOOM!

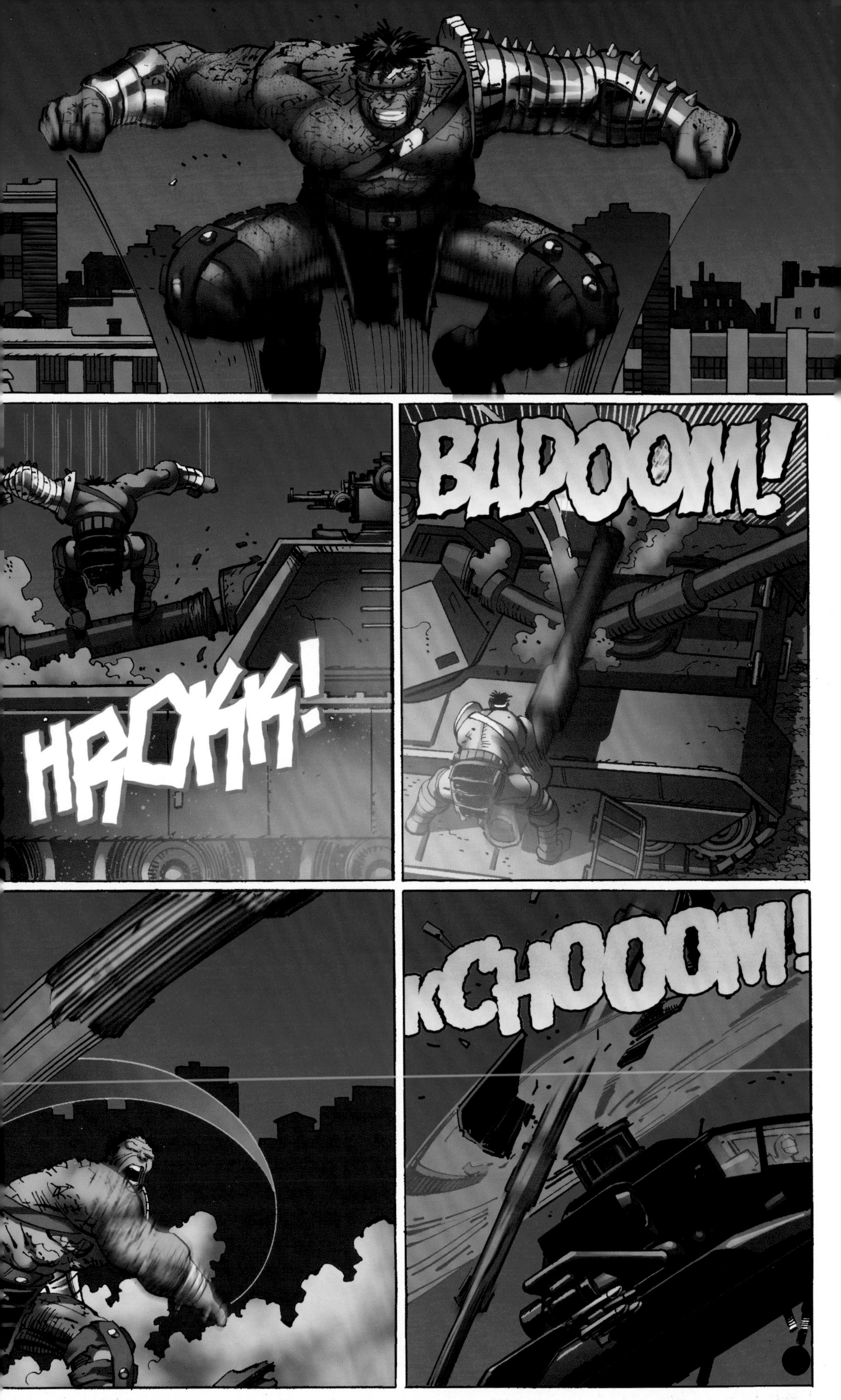
HROKK!
BADOOM!
KCHOOOM!

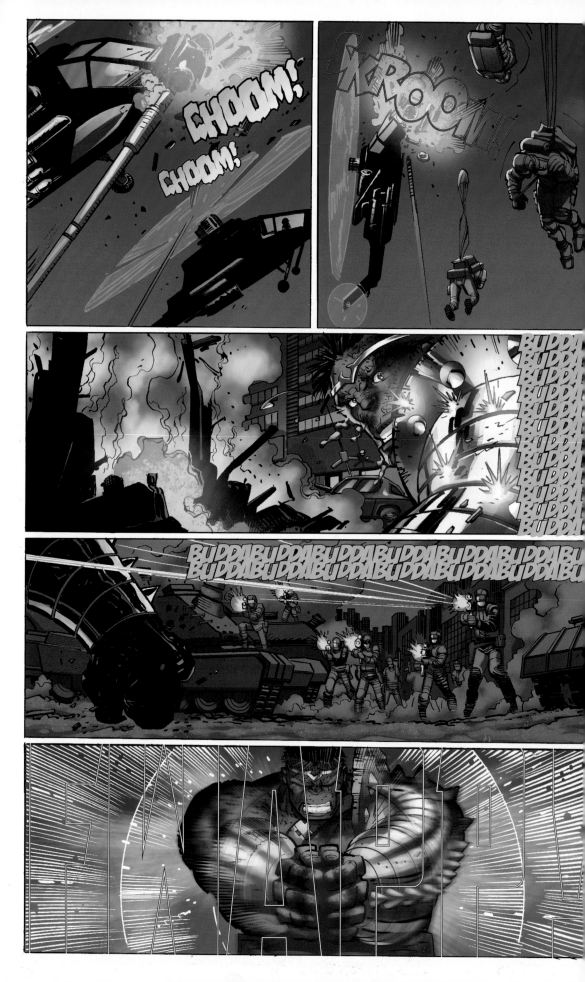

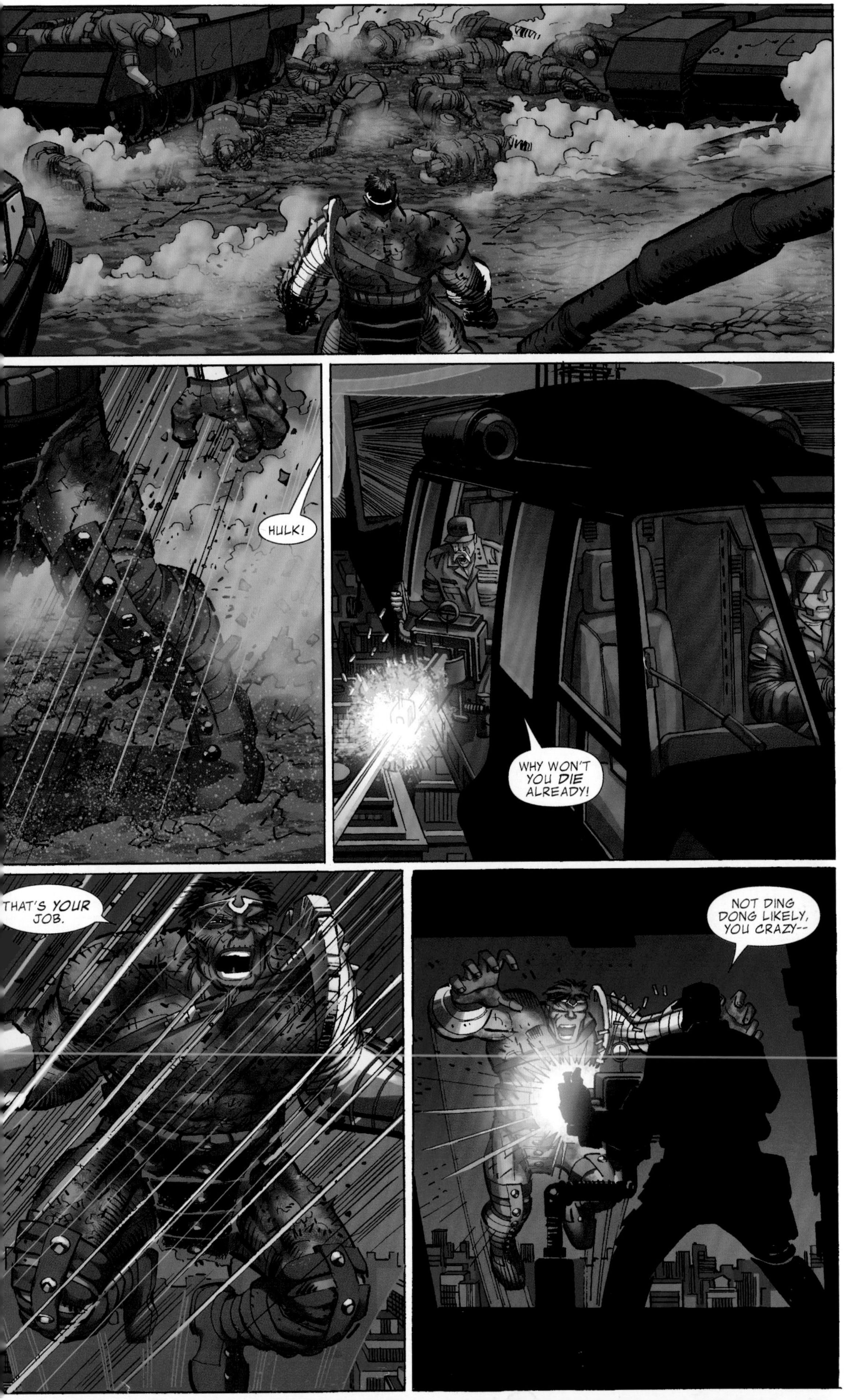
HULK!
WHY WON'T YOU DIE ALREADY!
THAT'S YOUR JOB.
NOT DING DONG LIKELY, YOU CRAZY--

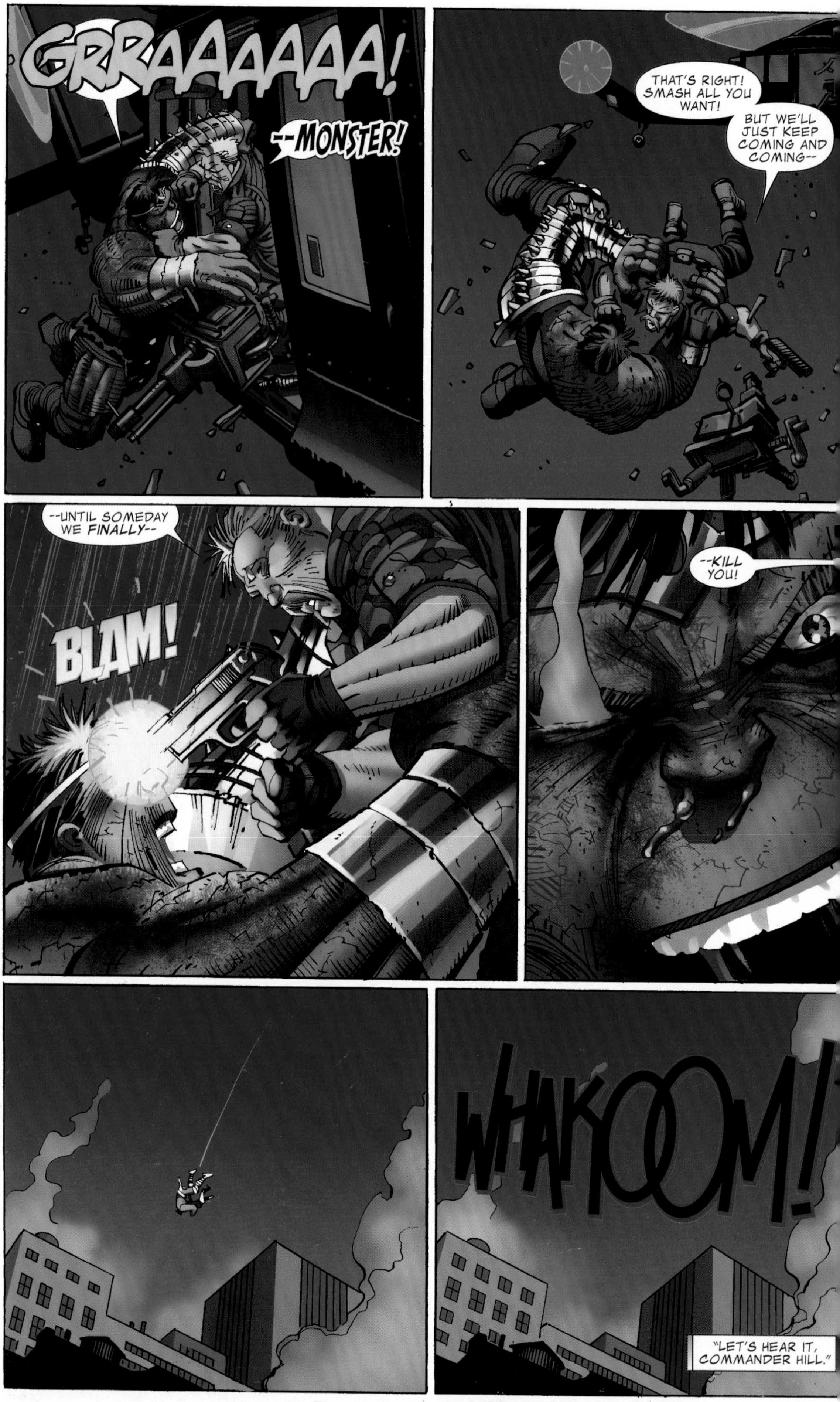
GRRAAAAAA!
--MONSTER!
THAT'S RIGHT! SMASH ALL YOU WANT!
BUT WE'LL JUST KEEP COMING AND COMING--
--UNTIL SOMEDAY WE FINALLY--
BLAM!
--KILL YOU!
WHAKOOOM!
"LET'S HEAR IT, COMMANDER HILL."

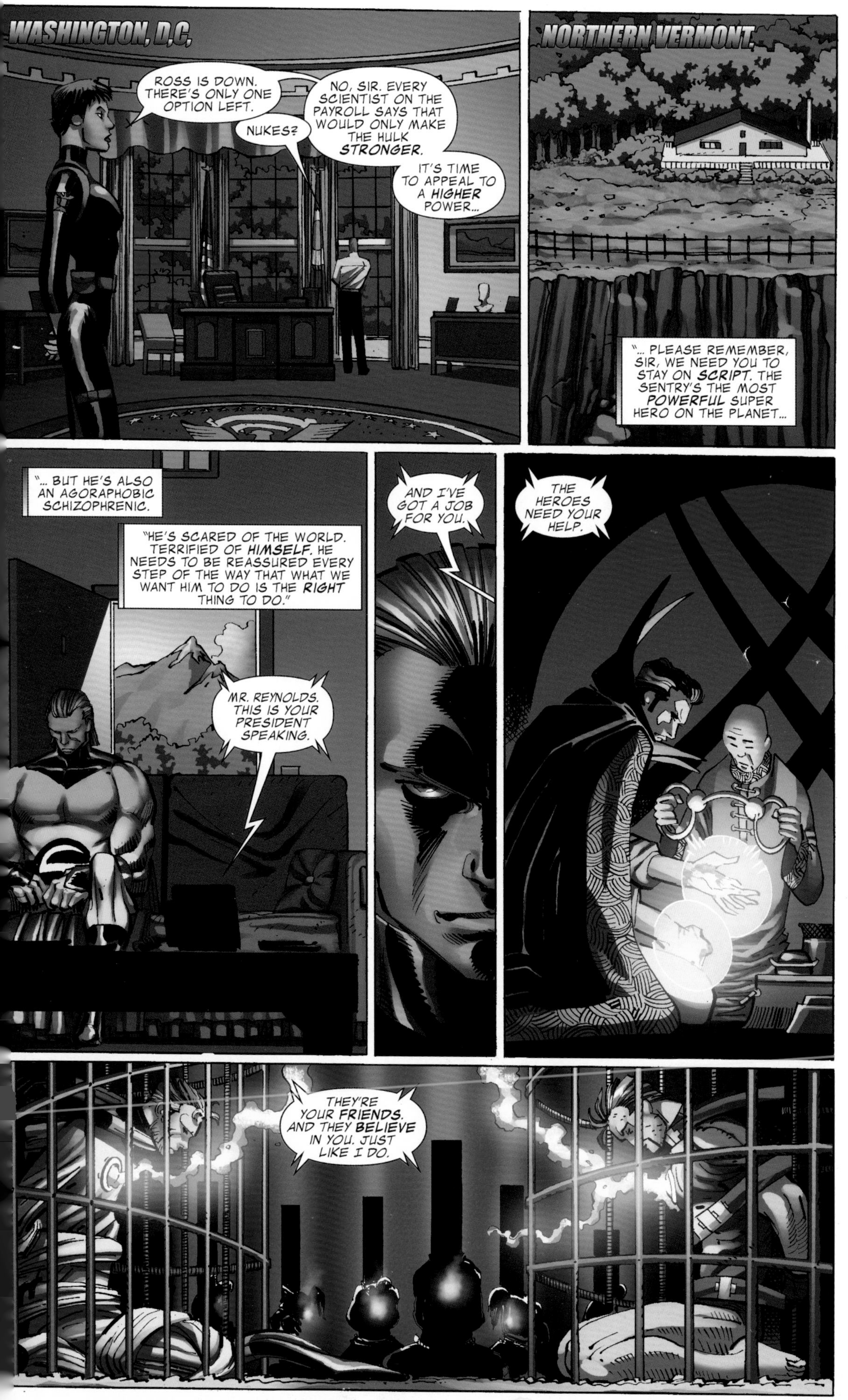
WASHINGTON, D.C.
ROSS IS DOWN. THERE'S ONLY ONE OPTION LEFT.
NUKES?
NO, SIR. EVERY SCIENTIST ON THE PAYROLL SAYS THAT WOULD ONLY MAKE THE HULK STRONGER.
IT'S TIME TO APPEAL TO A HIGHER POWER...
NORTHERN VERMONT.
"... PLEASE REMEMBER, SIR, WE NEED YOU TO STAY ON SCRIPT. THE SENTRY'S THE MOST POWERFUL SUPER HERO ON THE PLANET...
"... BUT HE'S ALSO AN AGORAPHOBIC SCHIZOPHRENIC.
"HE'S SCARED OF THE WORLD. TERRIFIED OF HIMSELF. HE NEEDS TO BE REASSURED EVERY STEP OF THE WAY THAT WHAT WE WANT HIM TO DO IS THE RIGHT THING TO DO."
MR. REYNOLDS. THIS IS YOUR PRESIDENT SPEAKING.
AND I'VE GOT A JOB FOR YOU.
THE HEROES NEED YOUR HELP.
THEY'RE YOUR FRIENDS. AND THEY BELIEVE IN YOU. JUST LIKE I DO.

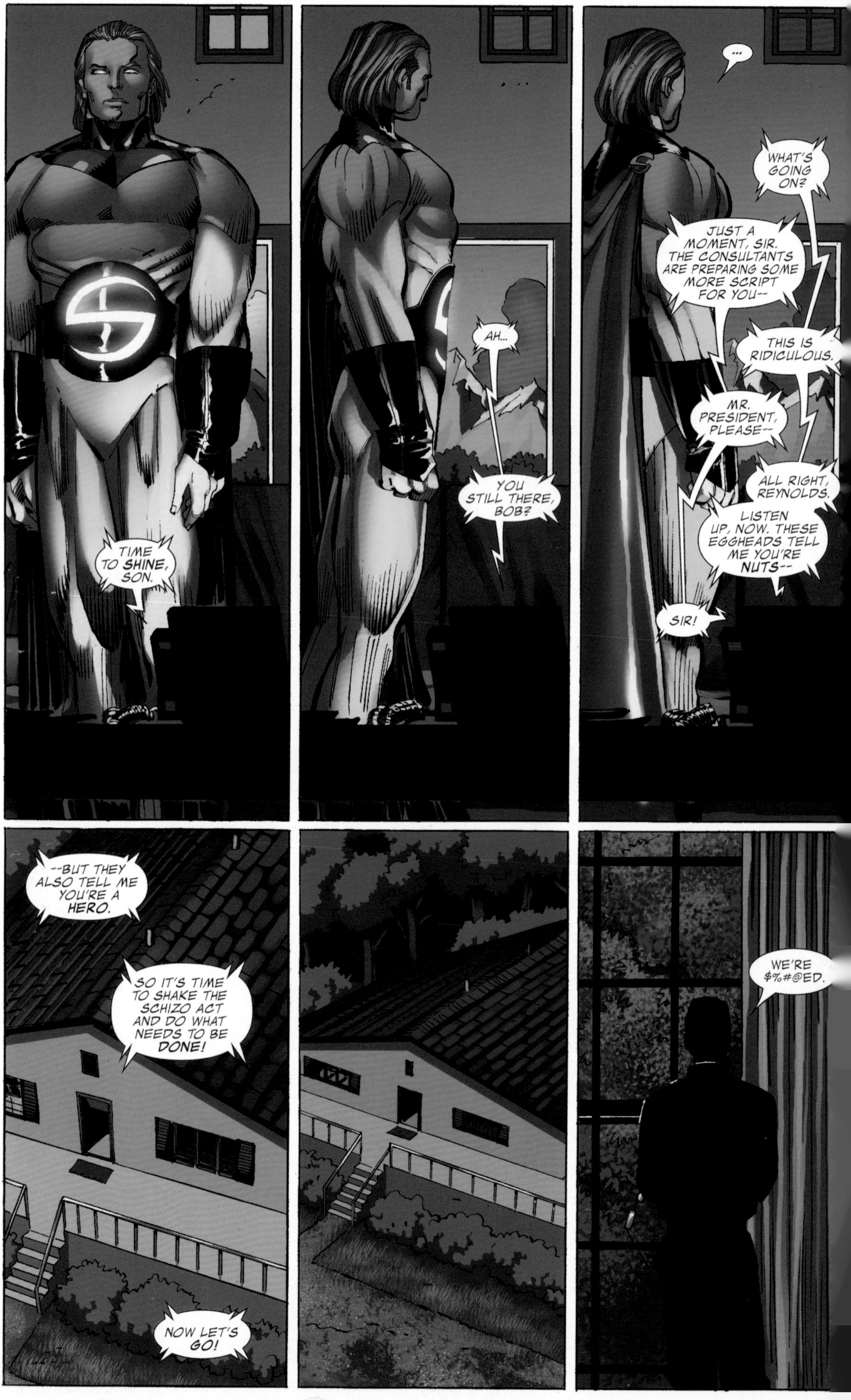
TIME TO SHINE, SON.
...
AH...
YOU STILL THERE, BOB?
...
WHAT'S GOING ON?
JUST A MOMENT, SIR. THE CONSULTANTS ARE PREPARING SOME MORE SCRIPT FOR YOU--
THIS IS RIDICULOUS.
MR. PRESIDENT, PLEASE--
ALL RIGHT, REYNOLDS.
LISTEN UP, NOW. THESE EGGHEADS TELL ME YOU'RE NUTS--
SIR!
--BUT THEY ALSO TELL ME YOU'RE A HERO.
SO IT'S TIME TO SHAKE THE SCHIZO ACT AND DO WHAT NEEDS TO BE DONE!
NOW LET'S GO!
WE'RE $%#@ED.

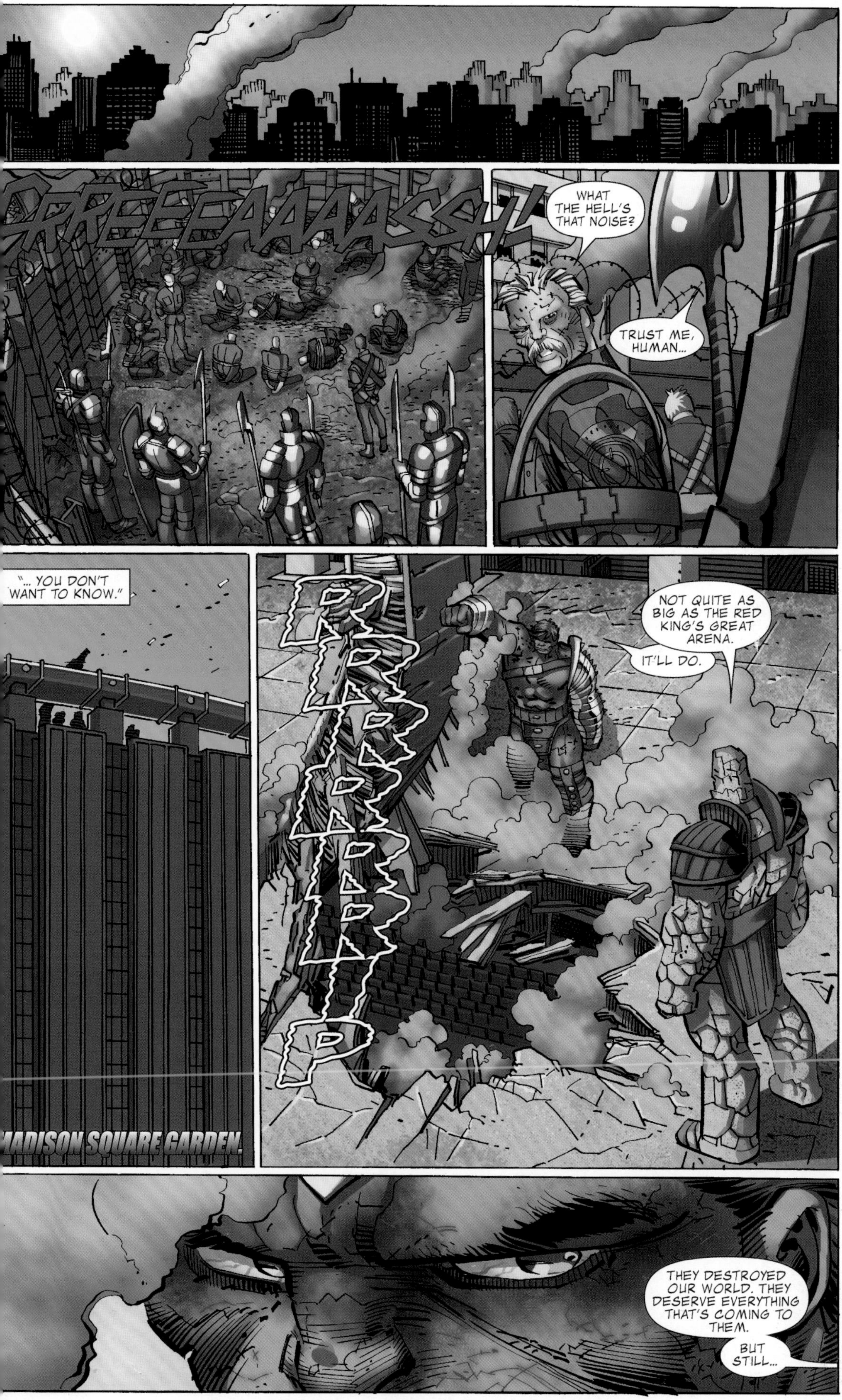

KRREEEAAAAASSH!
WHAT THE HELL'S THAT NOISE?
TRUST ME, HUMAN...
"... YOU DON'T WANT TO KNOW."
MADISON SQUARE GARDEN.
NOT QUITE AS BIG AS THE RED KING'S GREAT ARENA.
IT'LL DO.
THEY DESTROYED OUR WORLD. THEY DESERVE EVERYTHING THAT'S COMING TO THEM.
BUT STILL...

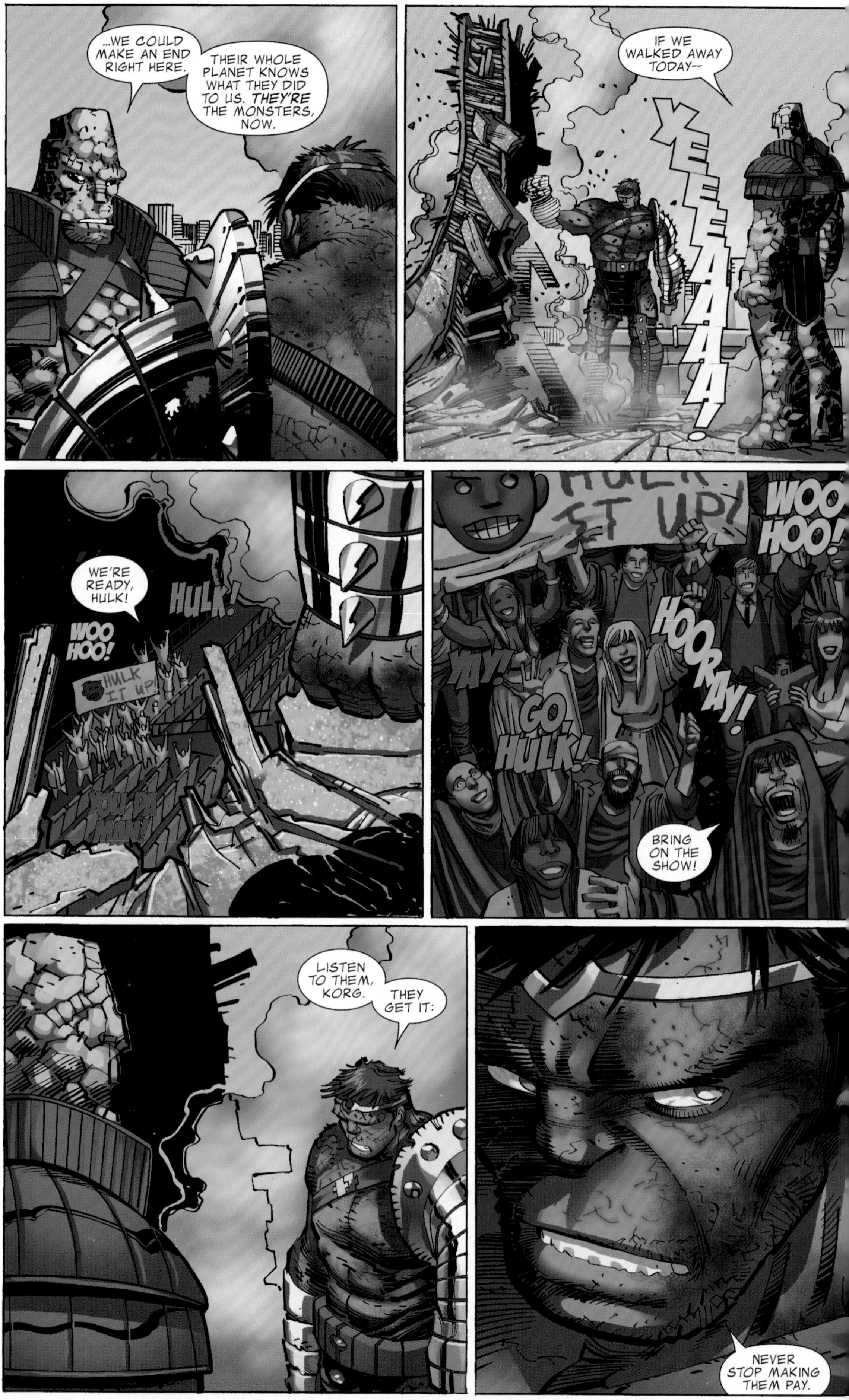

...WE COULD MAKE AN END RIGHT HERE.
THEIR WHOLE PLANET KNOWS WHAT THEY DID TO US. *THEY'RE* THE MONSTERS, NOW.
IF WE WALKED AWAY TODAY--
YEEEEAAAAA!
WE'RE READY, HULK!
HULK!
WOO HOO!
HULK IT UP!
YOU DA MAN!
HULK IT UP!
WOO HOO!
HOORAY!
YAY!
GO, HULK!
BRING ON THE SHOW!
LISTEN TO THEM, KORG.
THEY GET IT:
NEVER STOP MAKING THEM PAY.

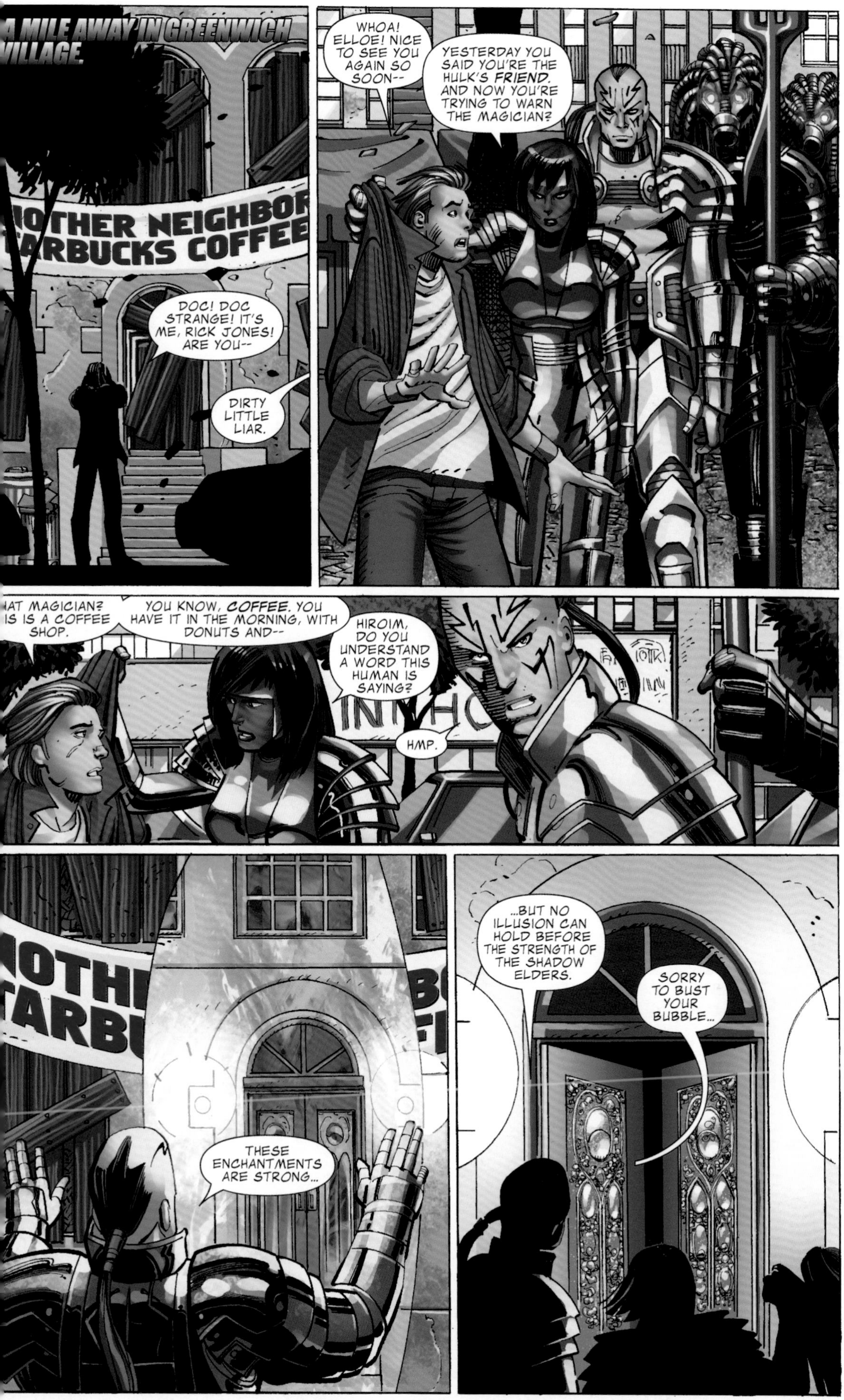
A MILE AWAY IN GREENWICH VILLAGE.
NOTHER NEIGHBOR
TARBUCKS COFFEE
DOC! DOC STRANGE! IT'S ME, RICK JONES! ARE YOU--
DIRTY LITTLE LIAR.
WHOA! ELLOE! NICE TO SEE YOU AGAIN SO SOON--
YESTERDAY YOU SAID YOU'RE THE HULK'S FRIEND. AND NOW YOU'RE TRYING TO WARN THE MAGICIAN?
HAT MAGICIAN? IS IS A COFFEE SHOP.
YOU KNOW, COFFEE. YOU HAVE IT IN THE MORNING, WITH DONUTS AND--
HIROIM, DO YOU UNDERSTAND A WORD THIS HUMAN IS SAYING?
HMP.
THESE ENCHANTMENTS ARE STRONG...
...BUT NO ILLUSION CAN HOLD BEFORE THE STRENGTH OF THE SHADOW ELDERS.
SORRY TO BUST YOUR BUBBLE...

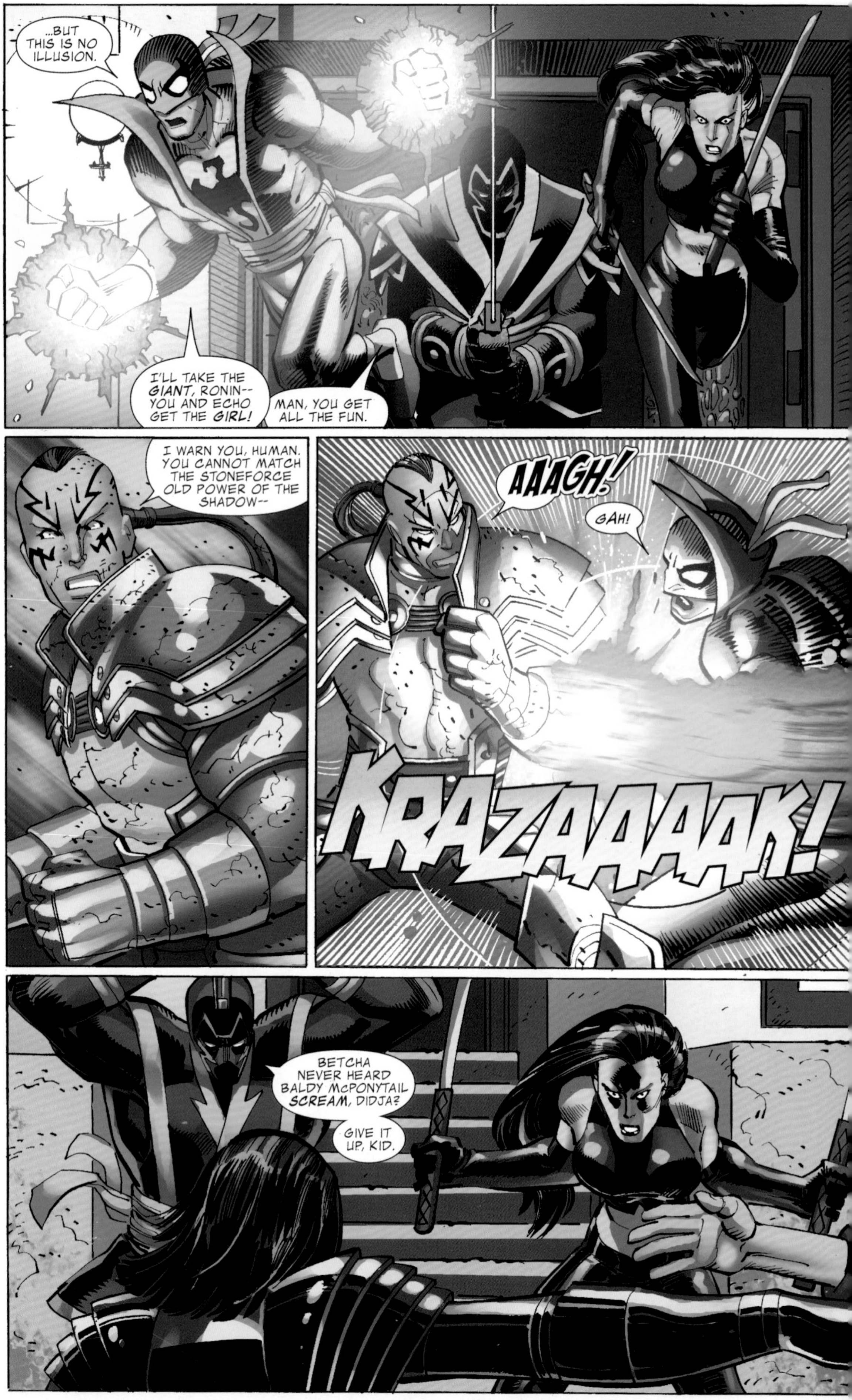

...BUT THIS IS NO ILLUSION.
I'LL TAKE THE GIANT, RONIN-- YOU AND ECHO GET THE GIRL!
MAN, YOU GET ALL THE FUN.
I WARN YOU, HUMAN. YOU CANNOT MATCH THE STONEFORCE OLD POWER OF THE SHADOW--
AAAGH!
GAH!
KRAZAAAAK!
BETCHA NEVER HEARD BALDY McPONYTAIL SCREAM, DIDJA?
GIVE IT UP, KID.

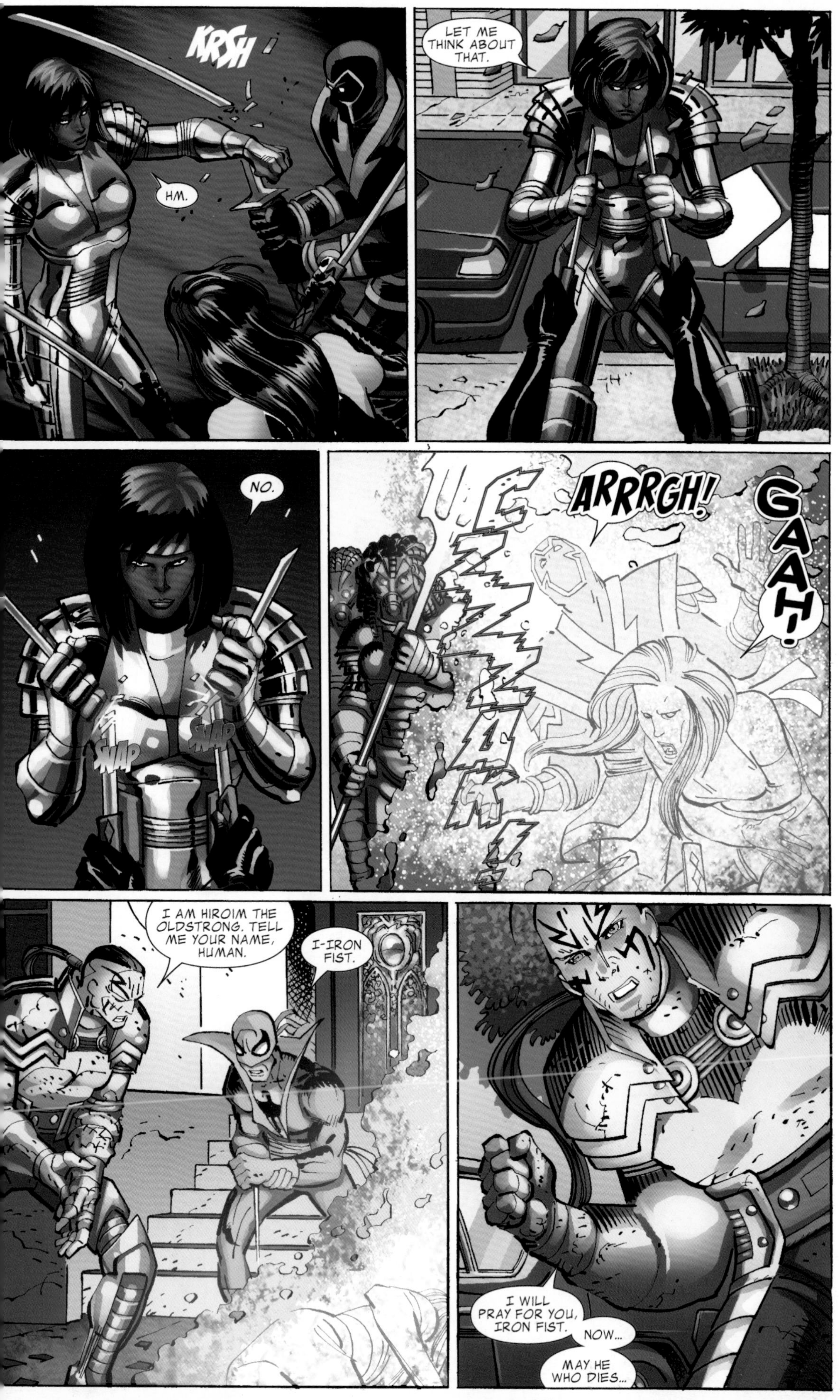
KRSH
HM.
LET ME THINK ABOUT THAT.
NO.
SNAP
SNAP
ARRRGH!
GAAH!
I AM HIROIM THE OLDSTRONG. TELL ME YOUR NAME, HUMAN.
I-IRON FIST.
I WILL PRAY FOR YOU, IRON FIST.
NOW...
MAY HE WHO DIES...

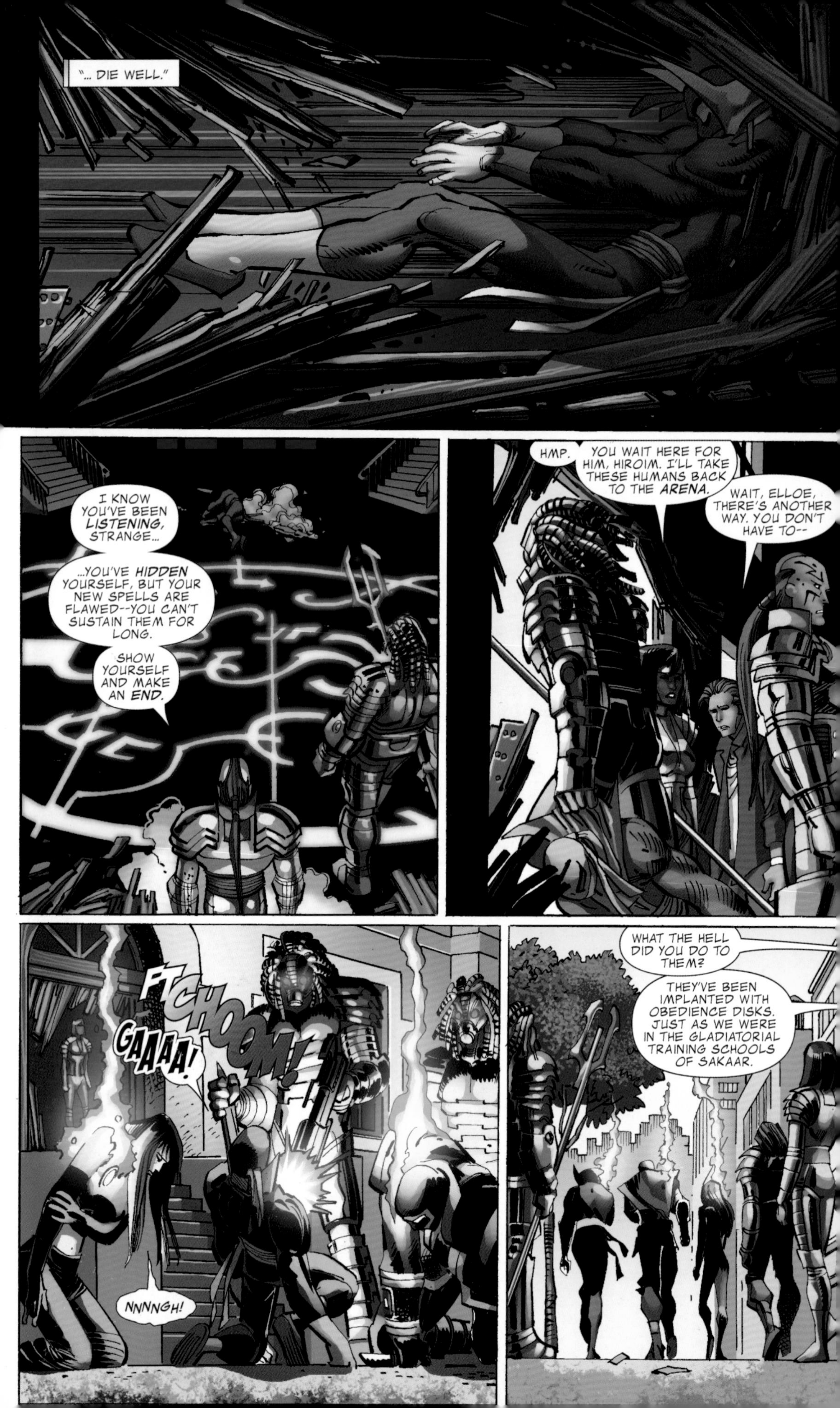
"... DIE WELL."
I KNOW YOU'VE BEEN LISTENING, STRANGE...
...YOU'VE HIDDEN YOURSELF, BUT YOUR NEW SPELLS ARE FLAWED--YOU CAN'T SUSTAIN THEM FOR LONG.
SHOW YOURSELF AND MAKE AN END.
HMP.
YOU WAIT HERE FOR HIM, HIROIM. I'LL TAKE THESE HUMANS BACK TO THE ARENA.
WAIT, ELLOE, THERE'S ANOTHER WAY. YOU DON'T HAVE TO--
FTCHOOM!
GAAAA!
NNNNGH!
WHAT THE HELL DID YOU DO TO THEM?
THEY'VE BEEN IMPLANTED WITH OBEDIENCE DISKS. JUST AS WE WERE IN THE GLADIATORIAL TRAINING SCHOOLS OF SAKAAR.

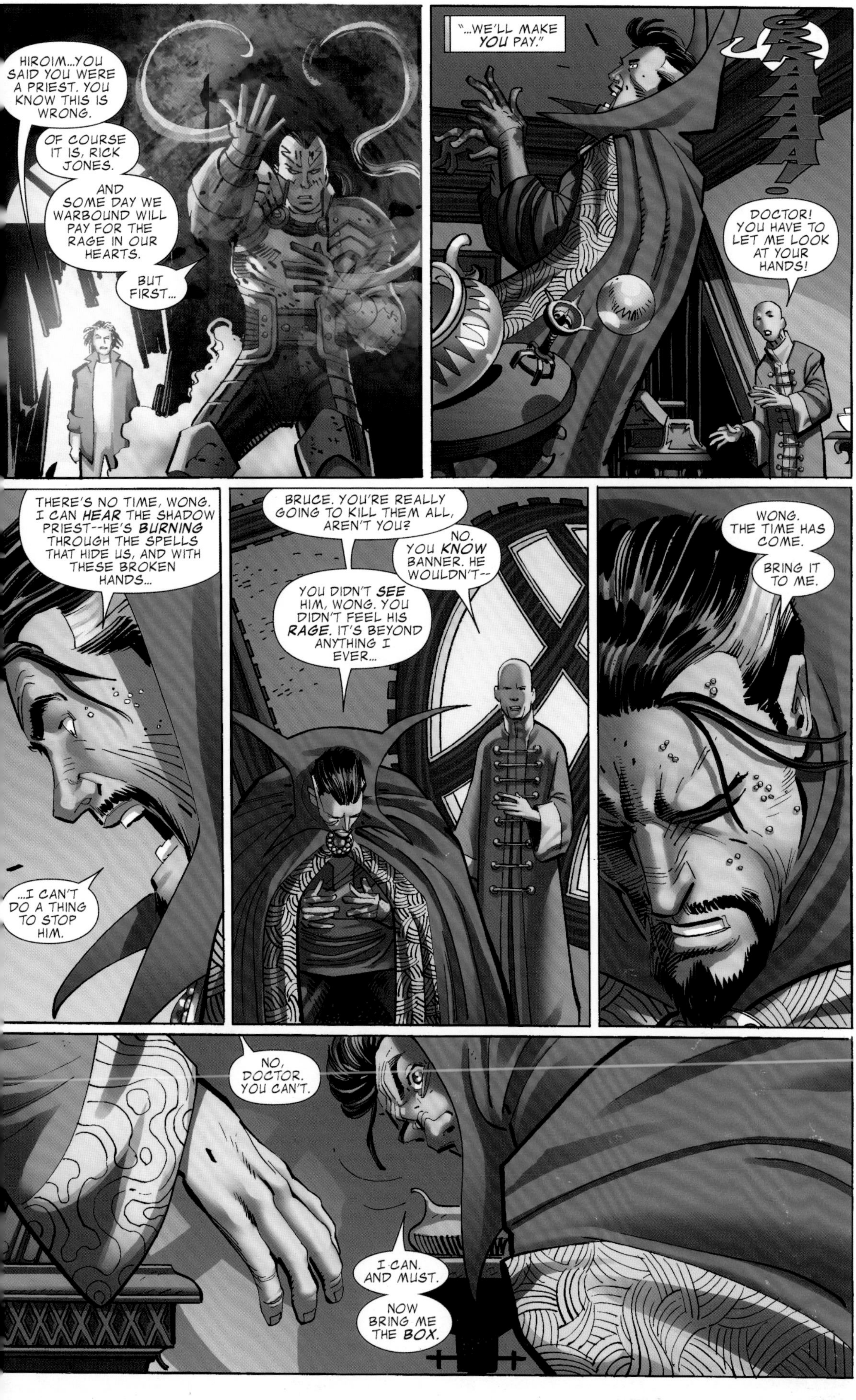

HIROIM...YOU SAID YOU WERE A PRIEST. YOU KNOW THIS IS WRONG.
OF COURSE IT IS, RICK JONES.
AND SOME DAY WE WARBOUND WILL PAY FOR THE RAGE IN OUR HEARTS.
BUT FIRST...
"...WE'LL MAKE YOU PAY."
GRAAAAA!
DOCTOR! YOU HAVE TO LET ME LOOK AT YOUR HANDS!
THERE'S NO TIME, WONG. I CAN HEAR THE SHADOW PRIEST--HE'S BURNING THROUGH THE SPELLS THAT HIDE US, AND WITH THESE BROKEN HANDS...
...I CAN'T DO A THING TO STOP HIM.
BRUCE. YOU'RE REALLY GOING TO KILL THEM ALL, AREN'T YOU?
NO. YOU KNOW BANNER. HE WOULDN'T--
YOU DIDN'T SEE HIM, WONG. YOU DIDN'T FEEL HIS RAGE. IT'S BEYOND ANYTHING I EVER...
WONG. THE TIME HAS COME.
BRING IT TO ME.
NO, DOCTOR. YOU CAN'T.
I CAN. AND MUST.
NOW BRING ME THE BOX.

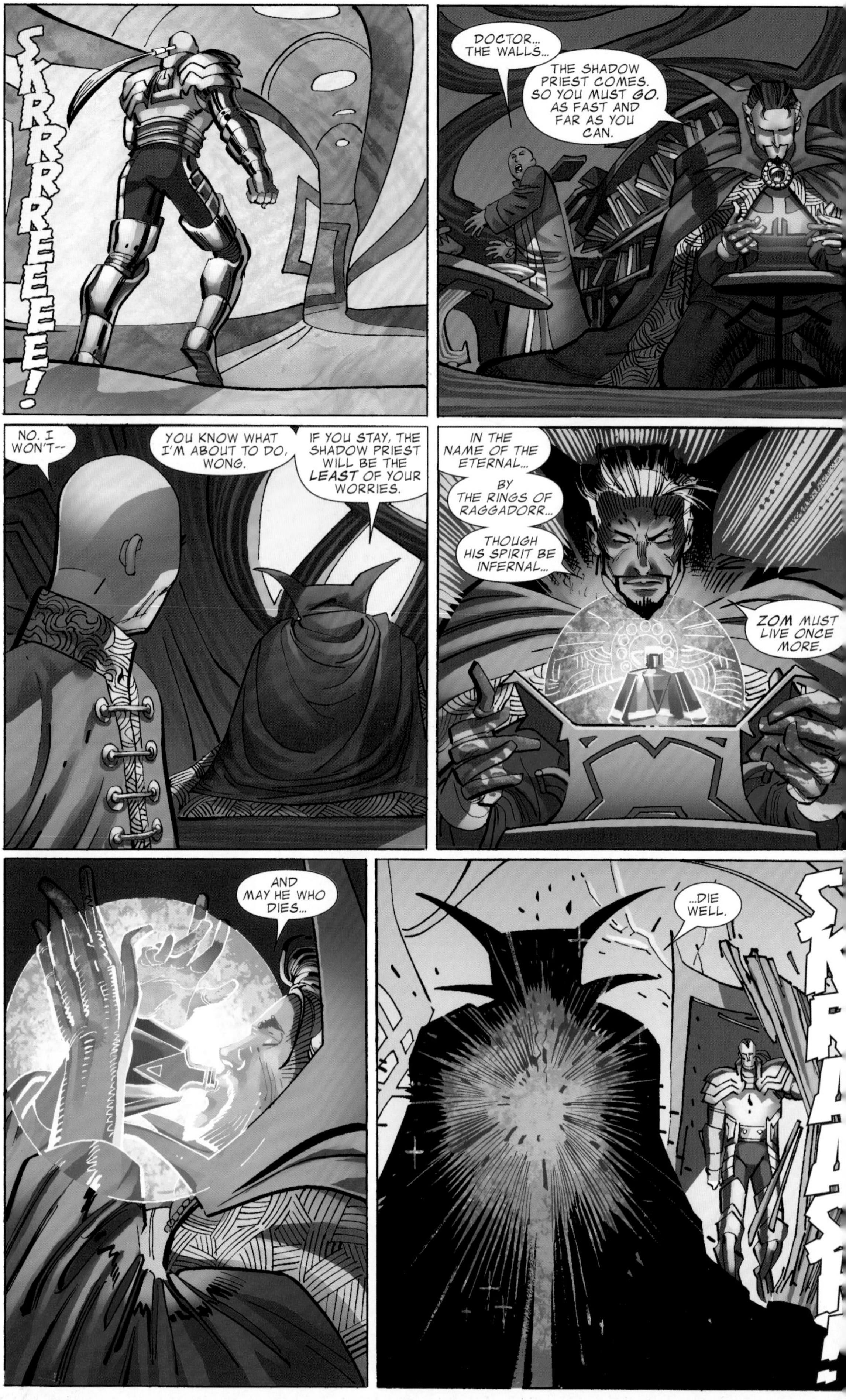
SKRRRREEEEE!
DOCTOR... THE WALLS...
THE SHADOW PRIEST COMES. SO YOU MUST GO. AS FAST AND FAR AS YOU CAN.
NO. I WON'T--
YOU KNOW WHAT I'M ABOUT TO DO, WONG.
IF YOU STAY, THE SHADOW PRIEST WILL BE THE LEAST OF YOUR WORRIES.
IN THE NAME OF THE ETERNAL...
BY THE RINGS OF RAGGADORR...
THOUGH HIS SPIRIT BE INFERNAL...
ZOM MUST LIVE ONCE MORE.
AND MAY HE WHO DIES...
...DIE WELL.

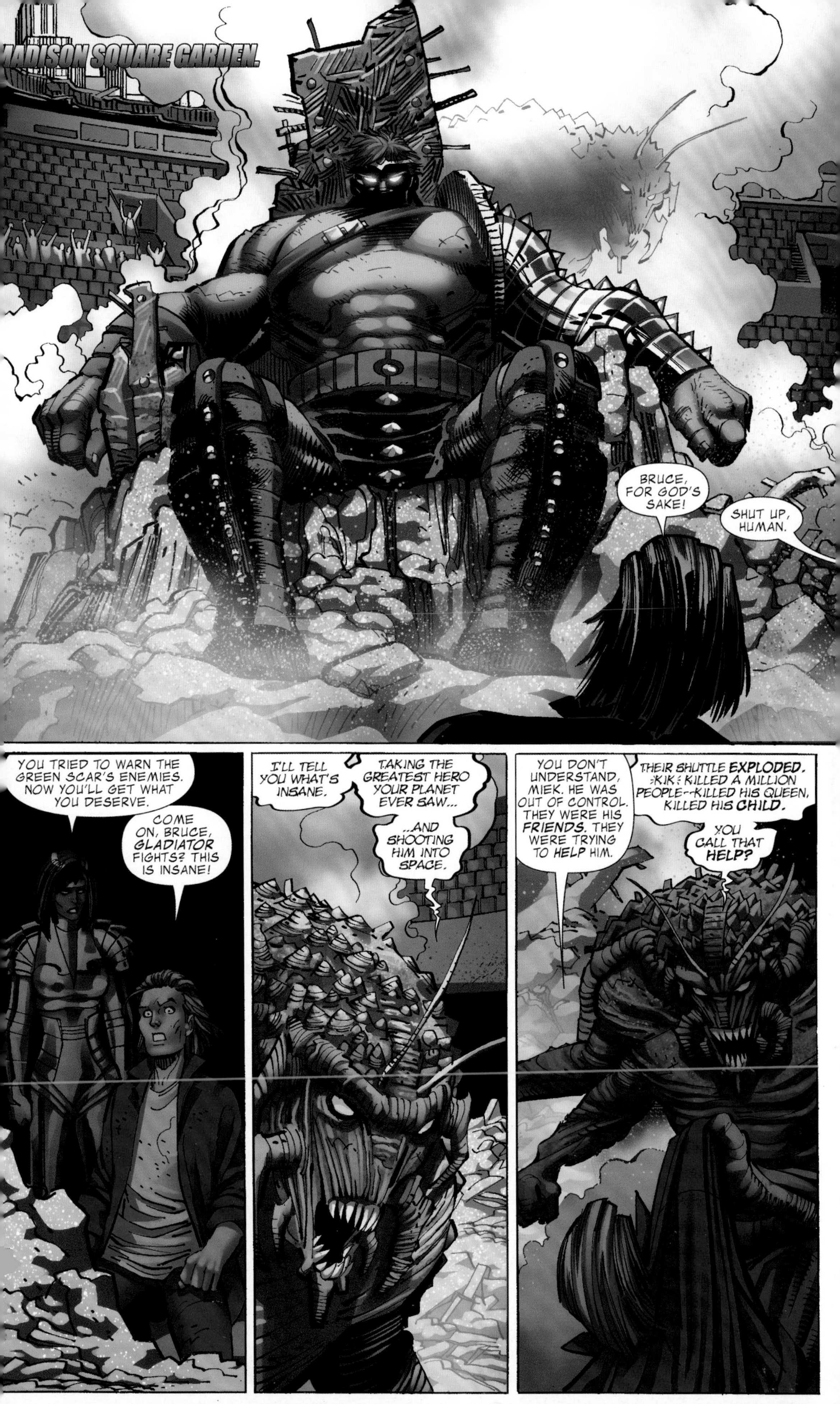
MADISON SQUARE GARDEN.
BRUCE, FOR GOD'S SAKE!
SHUT UP, HUMAN.
YOU TRIED TO WARN THE GREEN SCAR'S ENEMIES. NOW YOU'LL GET WHAT YOU DESERVE.
COME ON, BRUCE, GLADIATOR FIGHTS? THIS IS INSANE!
I'LL TELL YOU WHAT'S INSANE.
TAKING THE GREATEST HERO YOUR PLANET EVER SAW...
...AND SHOOTING HIM INTO SPACE.
YOU DON'T UNDERSTAND, MIEK. HE WAS OUT OF CONTROL. THEY WERE HIS FRIENDS. THEY WERE TRYING TO HELP HIM.
THEIR SHUTTLE EXPLODED. :KIK: KILLED A MILLION PEOPLE--KILLED HIS QUEEN, KILLED HIS CHILD.
YOU CALL THAT HELP?

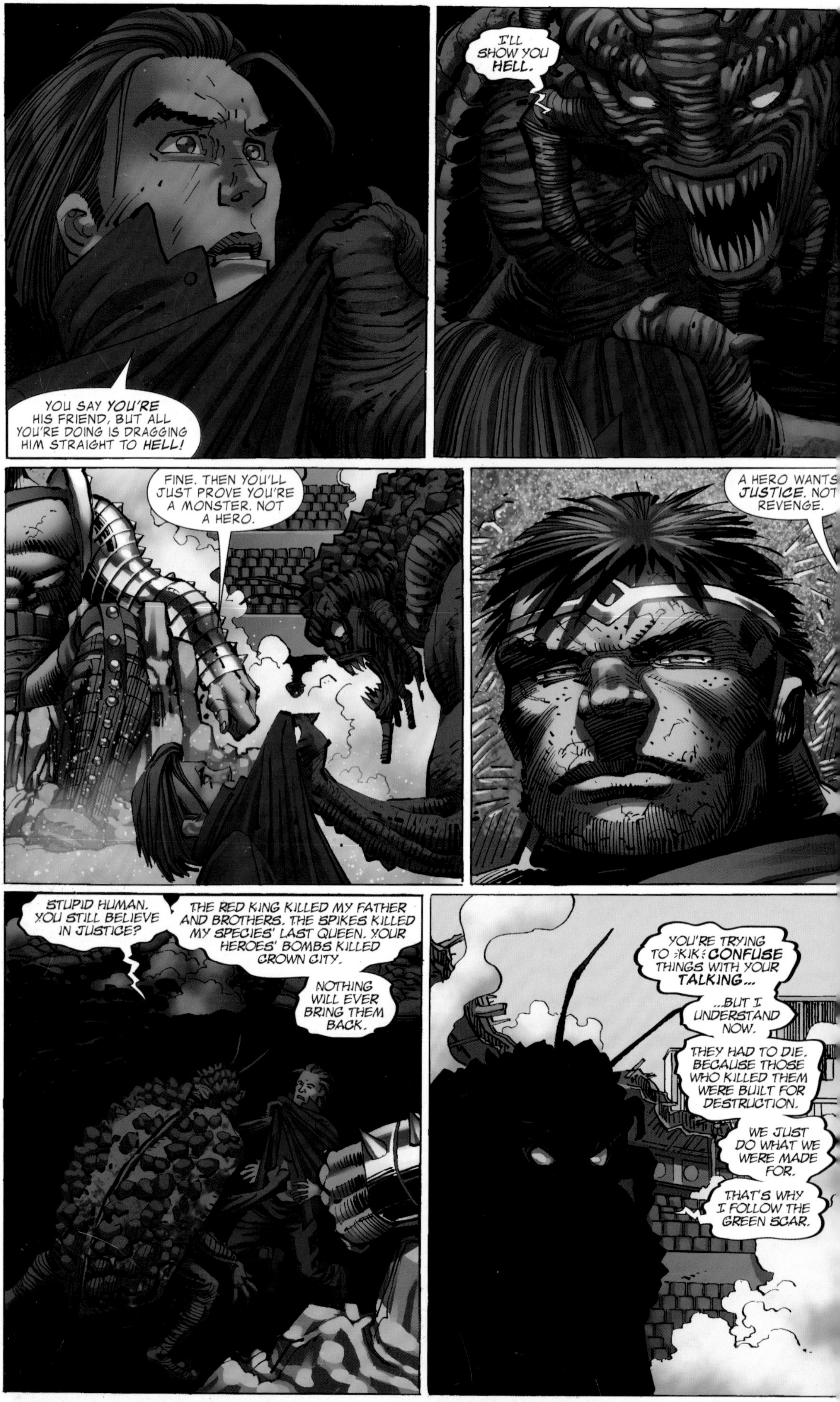
YOU SAY YOU'RE HIS FRIEND, BUT ALL YOU'RE DOING IS DRAGGING HIM STRAIGHT TO HELL!
I'LL SHOW YOU HELL.
FINE. THEN YOU'LL JUST PROVE YOU'RE A MONSTER. NOT A HERO.
A HERO WANTS JUSTICE. NOT REVENGE.
STUPID HUMAN. YOU STILL BELIEVE IN JUSTICE?
THE RED KING KILLED MY FATHER AND BROTHERS. THE SPIKES KILLED MY SPECIES' LAST QUEEN. YOUR HEROES' BOMBS KILLED CROWN CITY.
NOTHING WILL EVER BRING THEM BACK.
YOU'RE TRYING TO KIK CONFUSE THINGS WITH YOUR TALKING...
...BUT I UNDERSTAND NOW.
THEY HAD TO DIE. BECAUSE THOSE WHO KILLED THEM WERE BUILT FOR DESTRUCTION.
WE JUST DO WHAT WE WERE MADE FOR.
THAT'S WHY I FOLLOW THE GREEN SCAR.

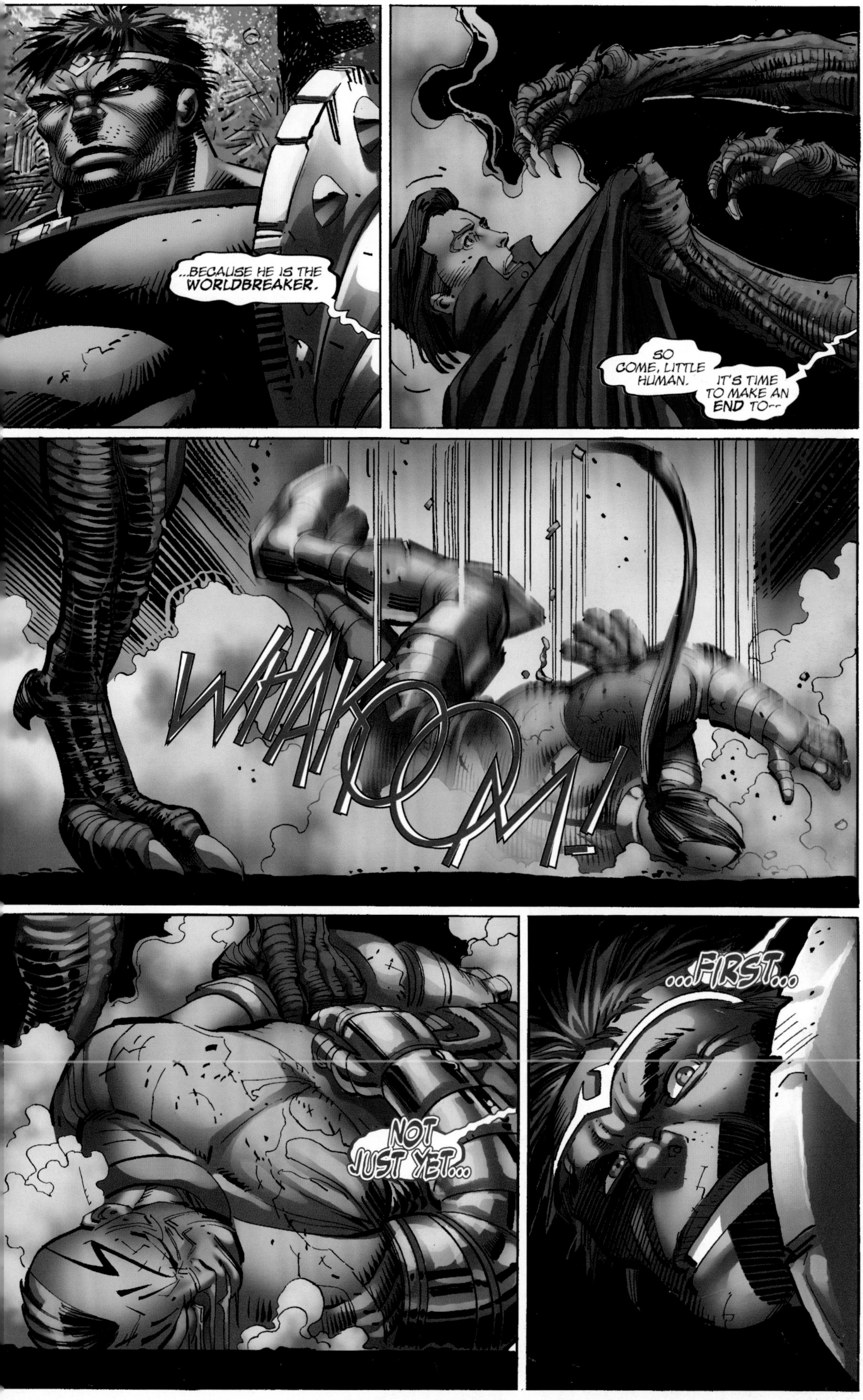
...BECAUSE HE IS THE WORLDBREAKER.
SO COME, LITTLE HUMAN.
IT'S TIME TO MAKE AN END TO--
WHAKOOM!
NOT JUST YET...
...FIRST...

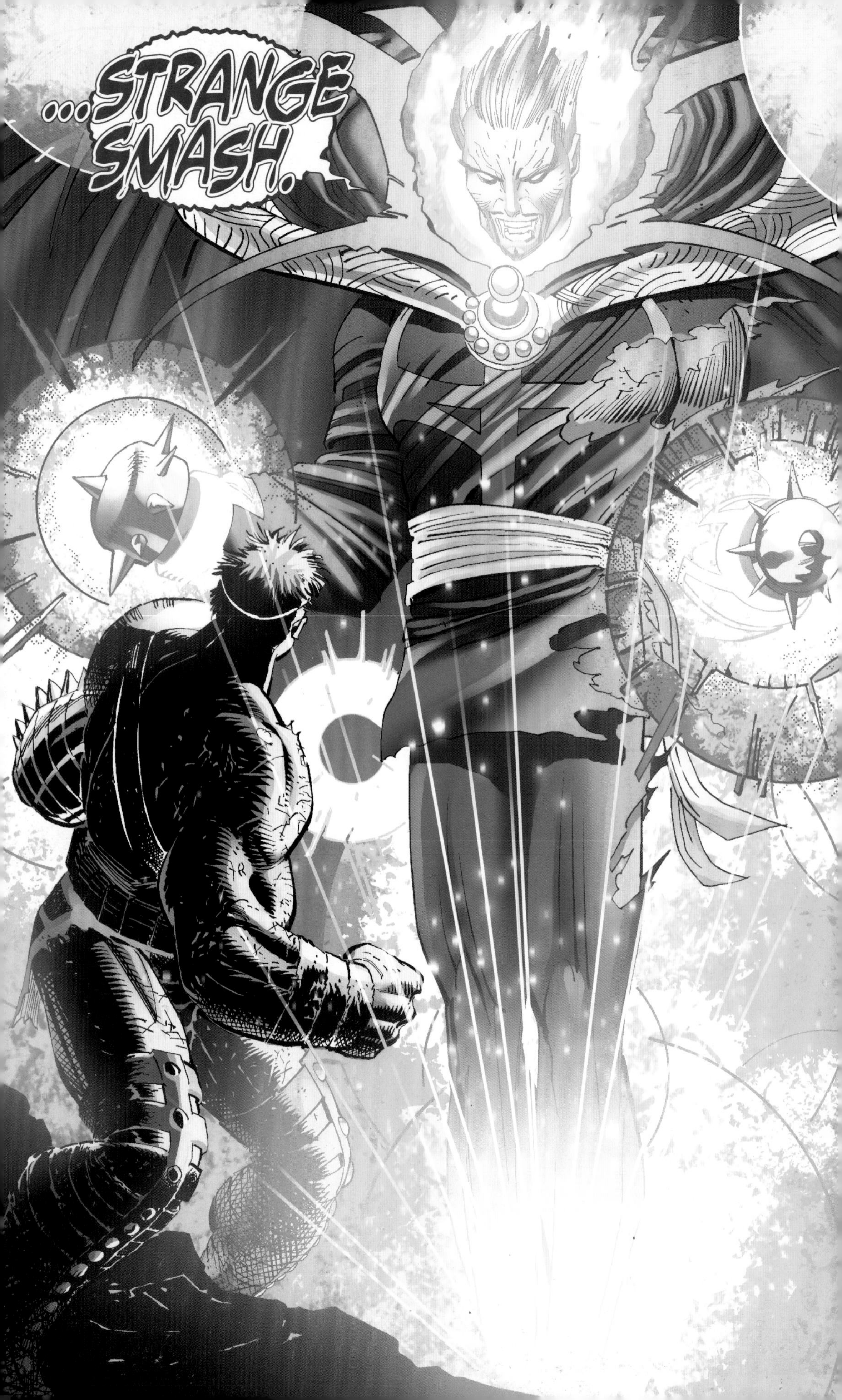
...STRANGE SMASH.

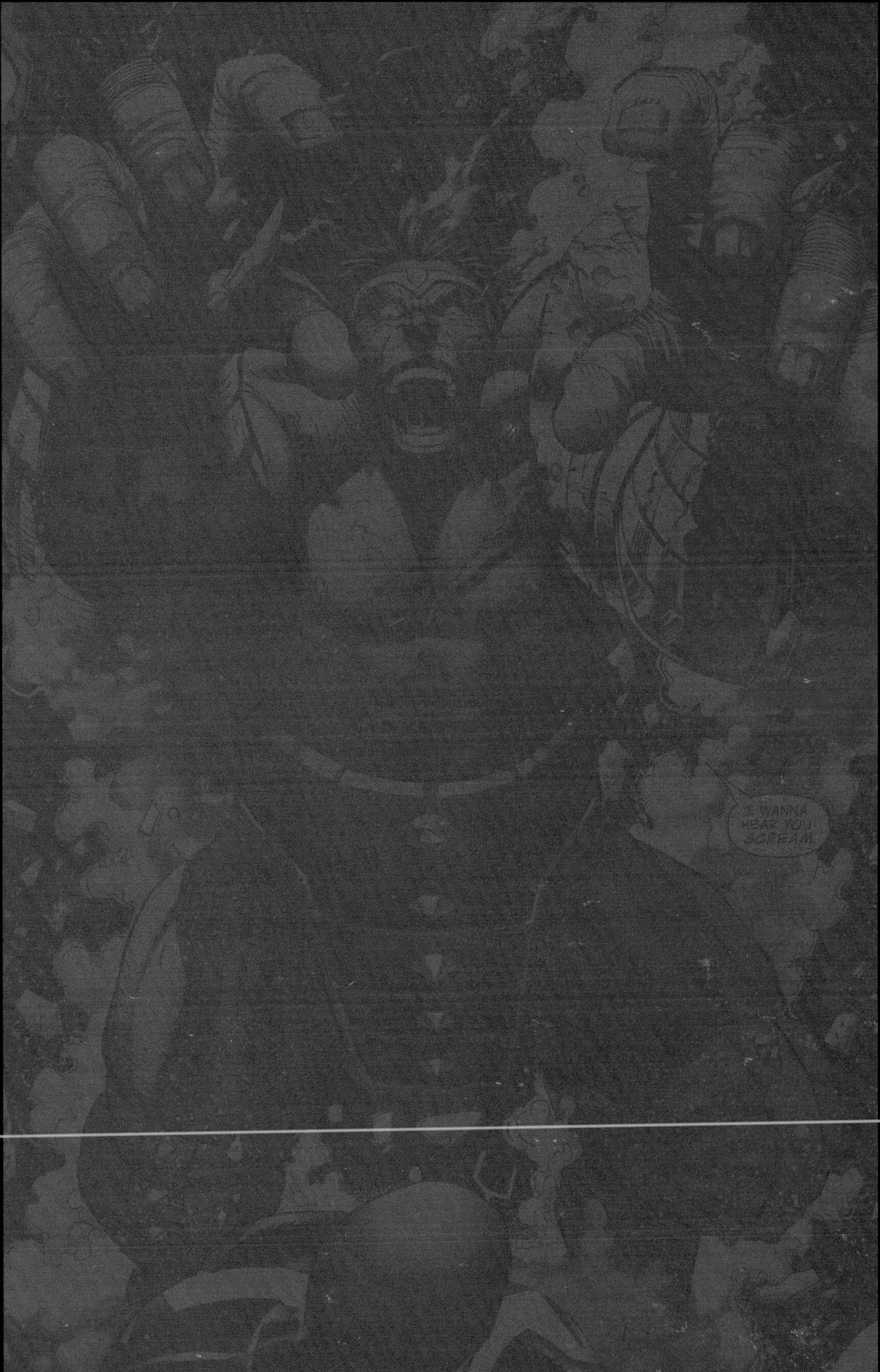
I WANNA HEAR YOU SCREAM.

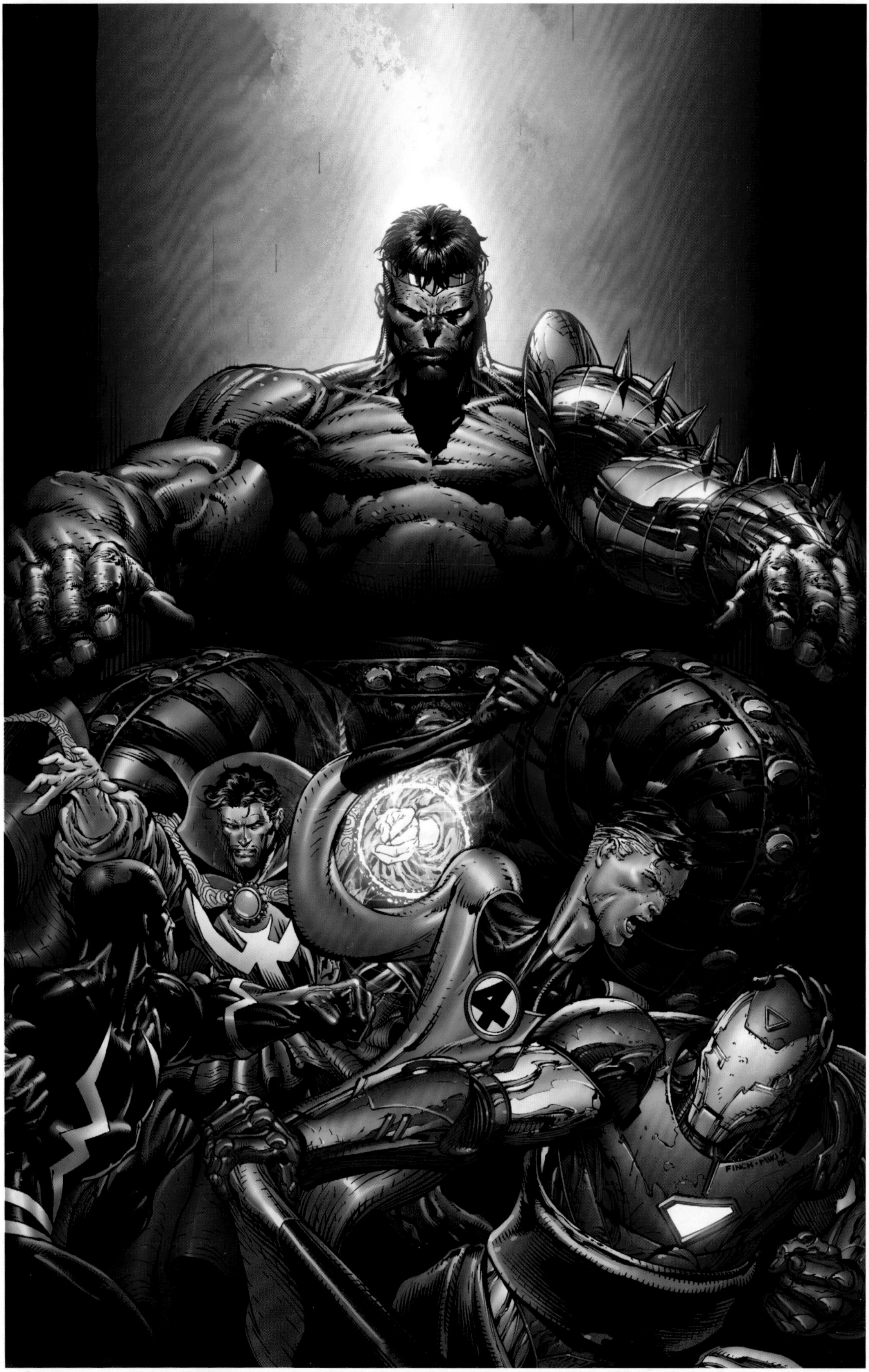

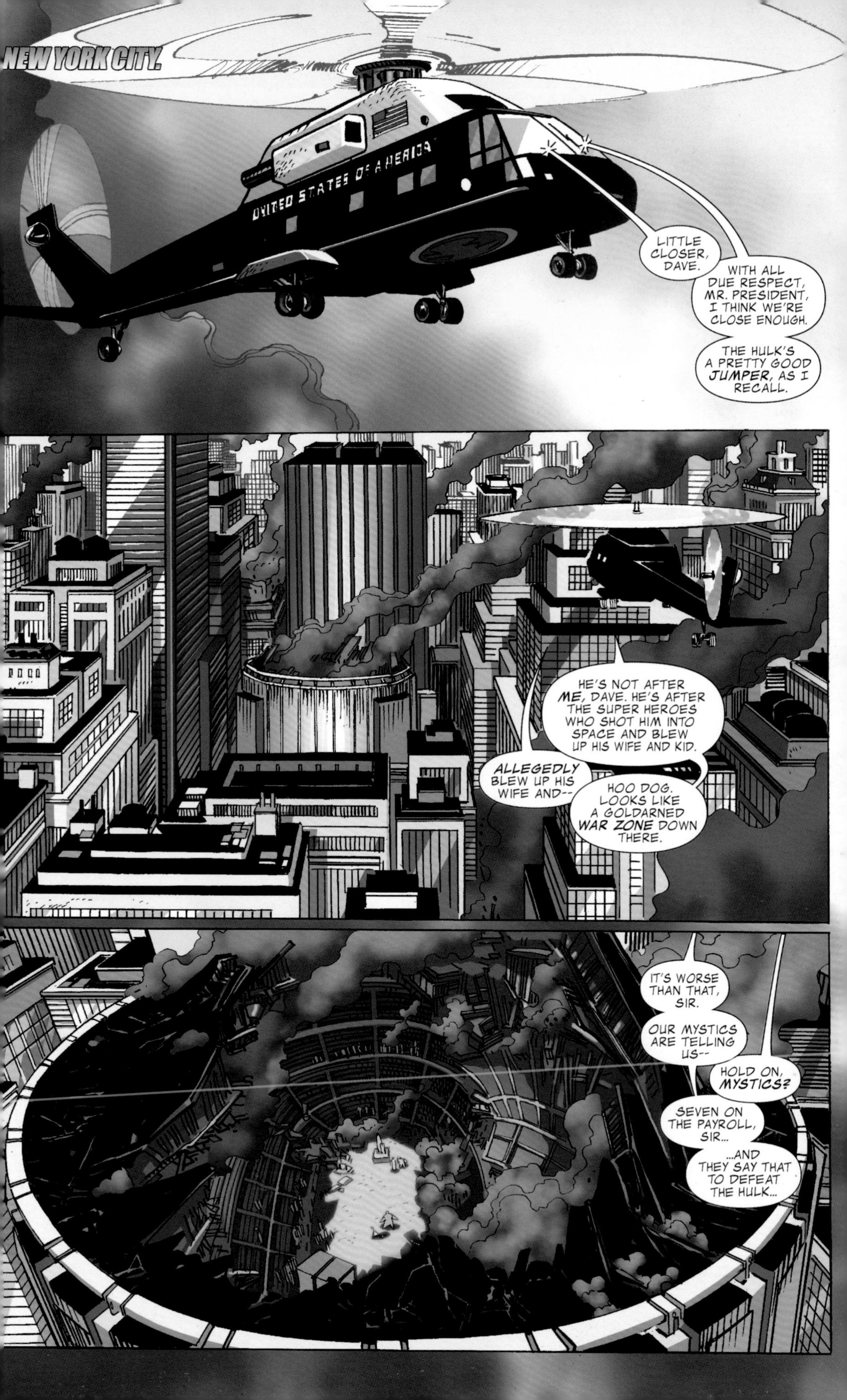
NEW YORK CITY.
UNITED STATES OF AMERICA
LITTLE CLOSER, DAVE.
WITH ALL DUE RESPECT, MR. PRESIDENT, I THINK WE'RE CLOSE ENOUGH.
THE HULK'S A PRETTY GOOD JUMPER, AS I RECALL.
HE'S NOT AFTER ME, DAVE. HE'S AFTER THE SUPER HEROES WHO SHOT HIM INTO SPACE AND BLEW UP HIS WIFE AND KID.
ALLEGEDLY BLEW UP HIS WIFE AND--
HOO DOG. LOOKS LIKE A GOLDARNED WAR ZONE DOWN THERE.
IT'S WORSE THAN THAT, SIR.
OUR MYSTICS ARE TELLING US--
HOLD ON, MYSTICS?
SEVEN ON THE PAYROLL, SIR...
...AND THEY SAY THAT TO DEFEAT THE HULK...

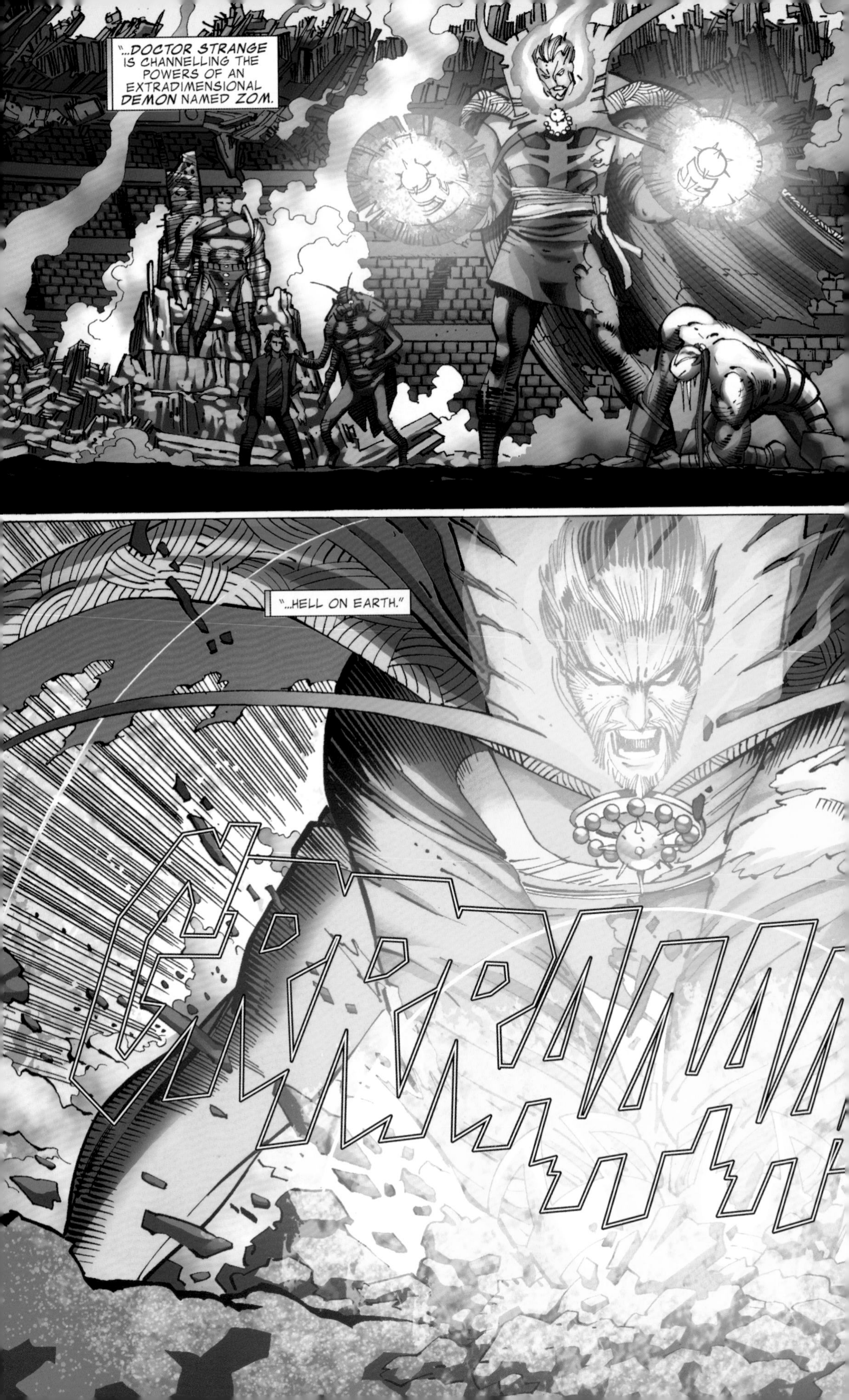
"...DOCTOR STRANGE IS CHANNELLING THE POWERS OF AN EXTRADIMENSIONAL DEMON NAMED ZOM.
"...HELL ON EARTH."

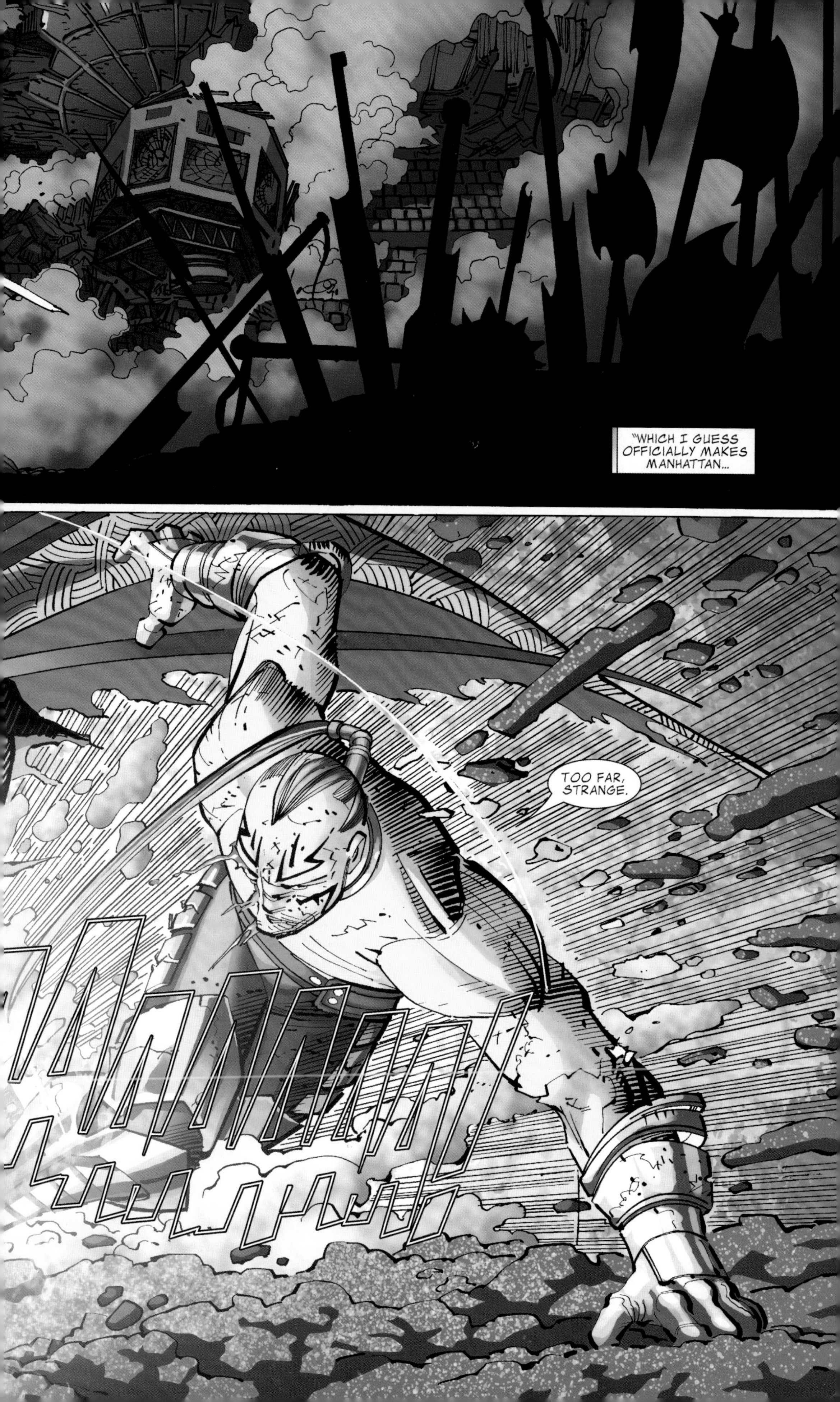
"WHICH I GUESS OFFICIALLY MAKES MANHATTAN...
TOO FAR, STRANGE.

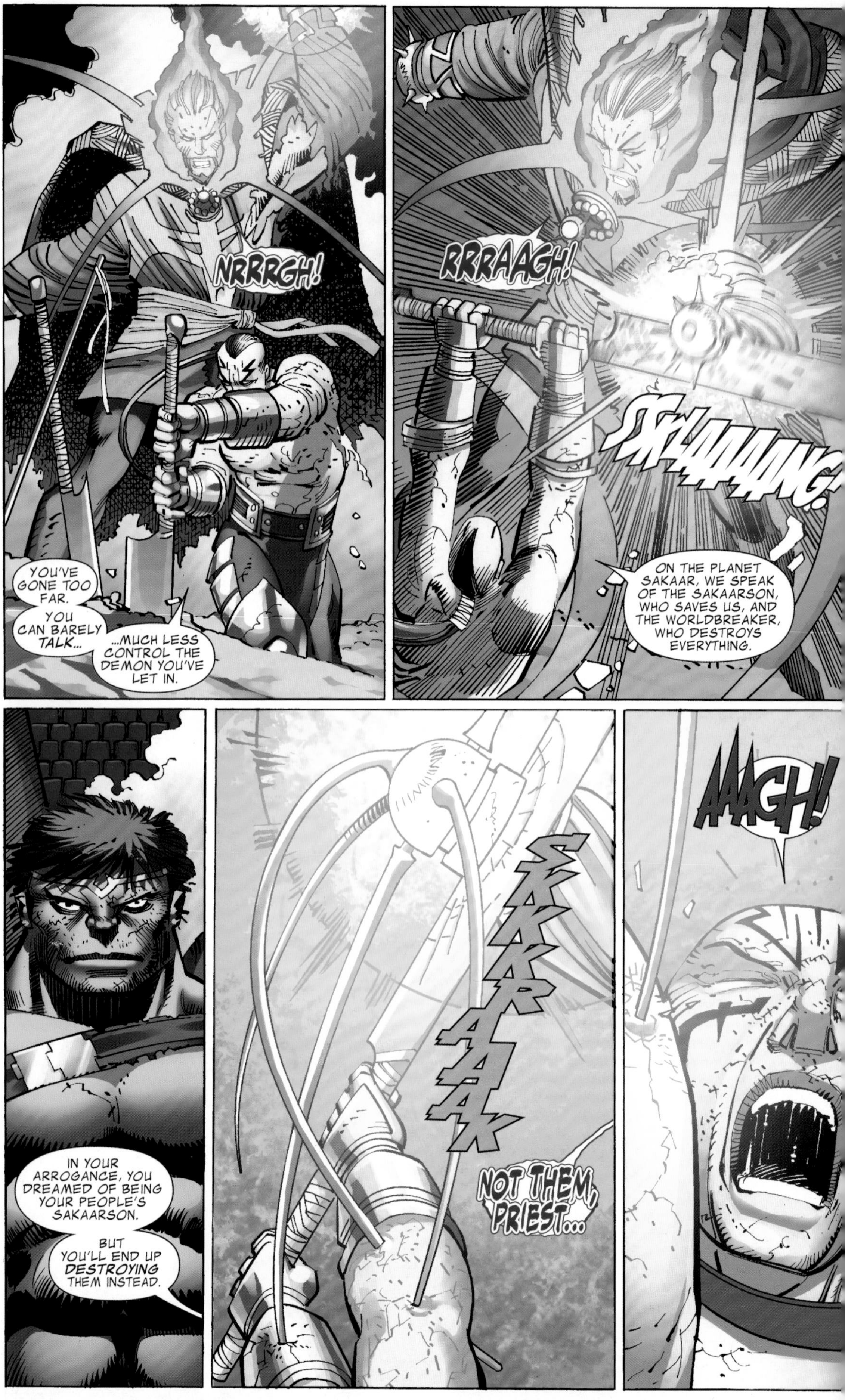
NRRRGH!
YOU'VE GONE TOO FAR.
YOU CAN BARELY TALK...
...MUCH LESS CONTROL THE DEMON YOU'VE LET IN.
RRRAAGH!
SKLAAAAANG!
ON THE PLANET SAKAAR, WE SPEAK OF THE SAKAARSON, WHO SAVES US, AND THE WORLDBREAKER, WHO DESTROYS EVERYTHING.
IN YOUR ARROGANCE, YOU DREAMED OF BEING YOUR PEOPLE'S SAKAARSON.
BUT YOU'LL END UP DESTROYING THEM INSTEAD.
SKAKRAAAK
NOT THEM, PRIEST...
AAAGH!

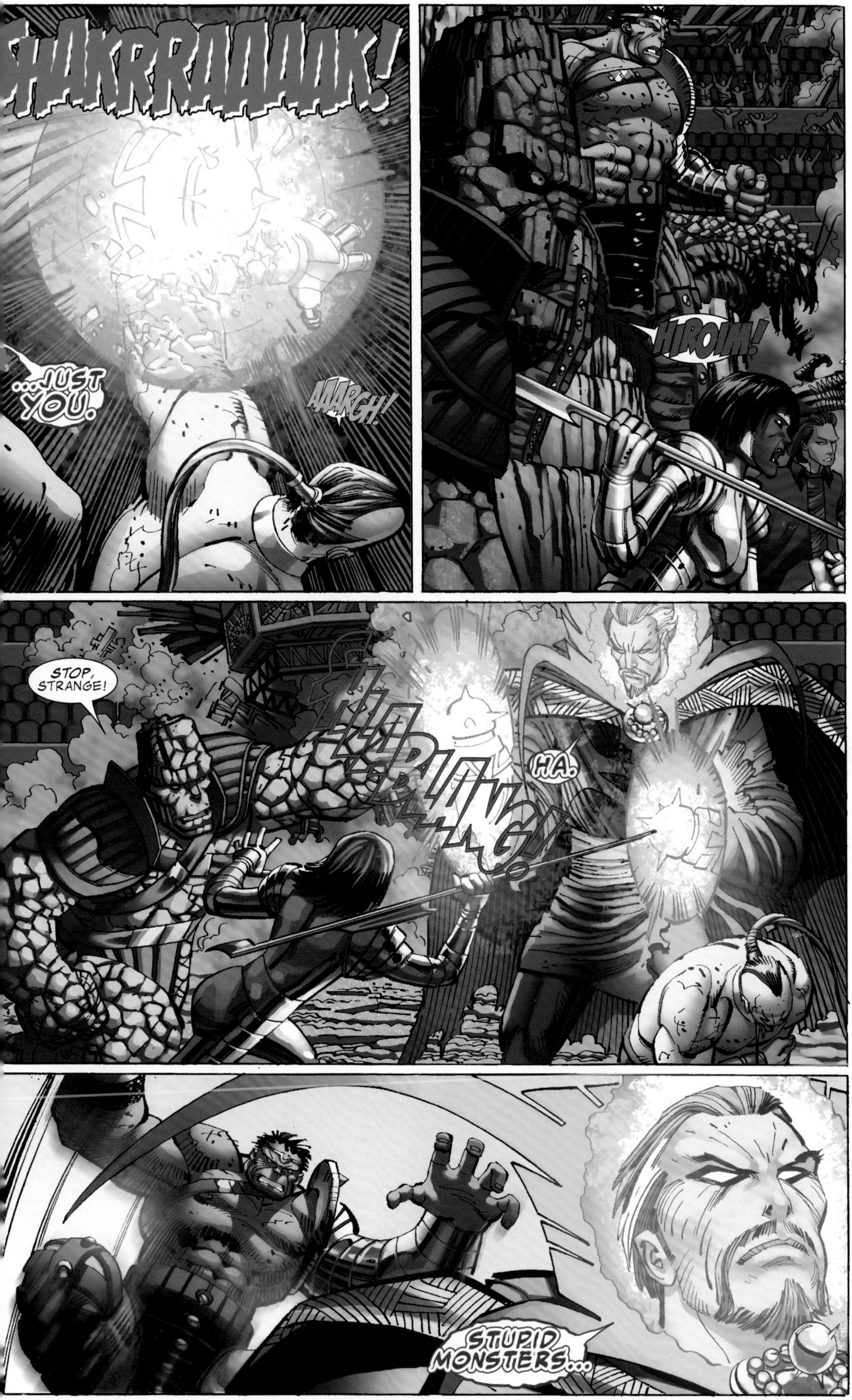
SHAKRRAAAAK!
...JUST YOU.
AAARGH!
HIROIM!
STOP, STRANGE!
HA.
STUPID MONSTERS...

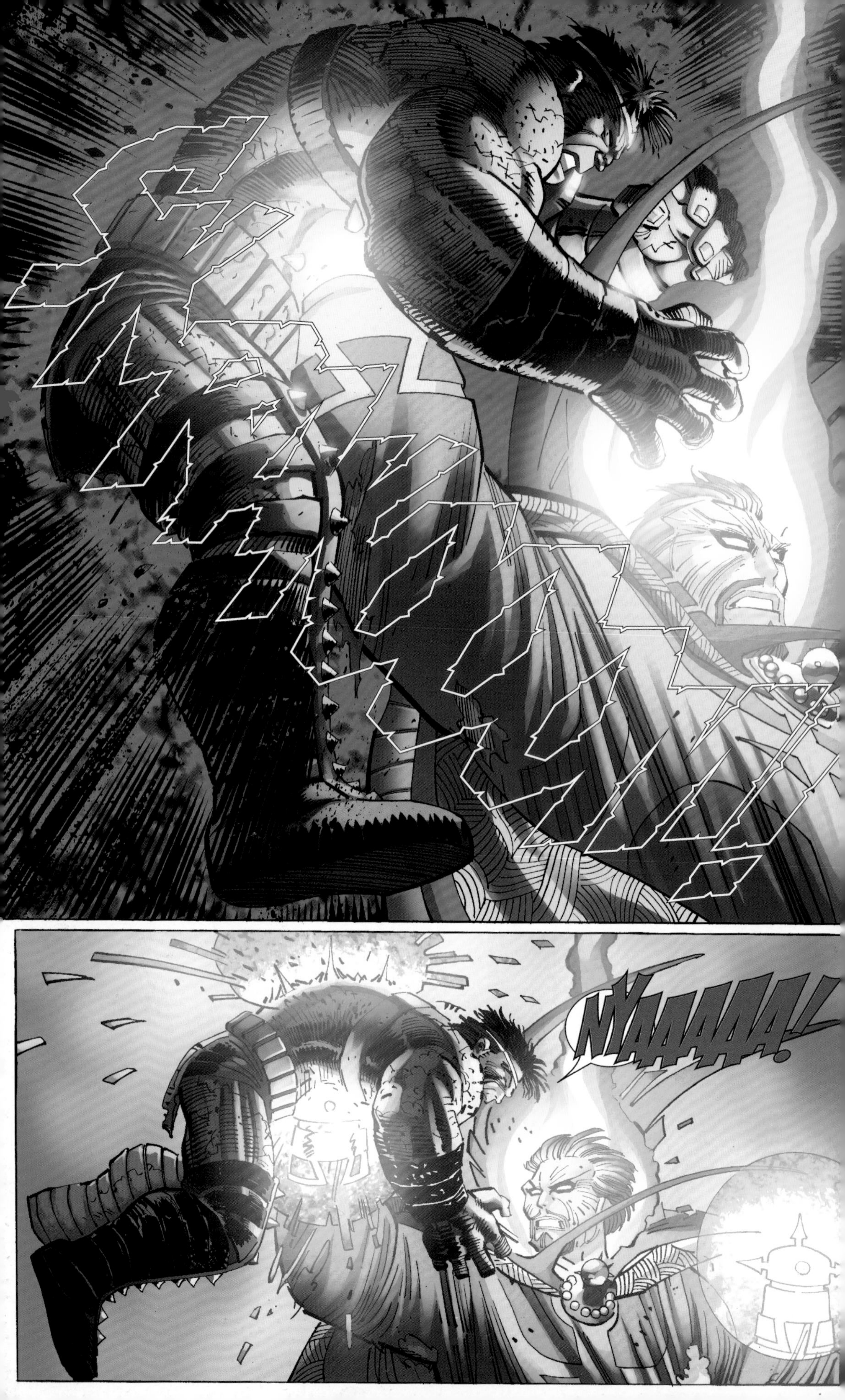
NYAAAAAA!!

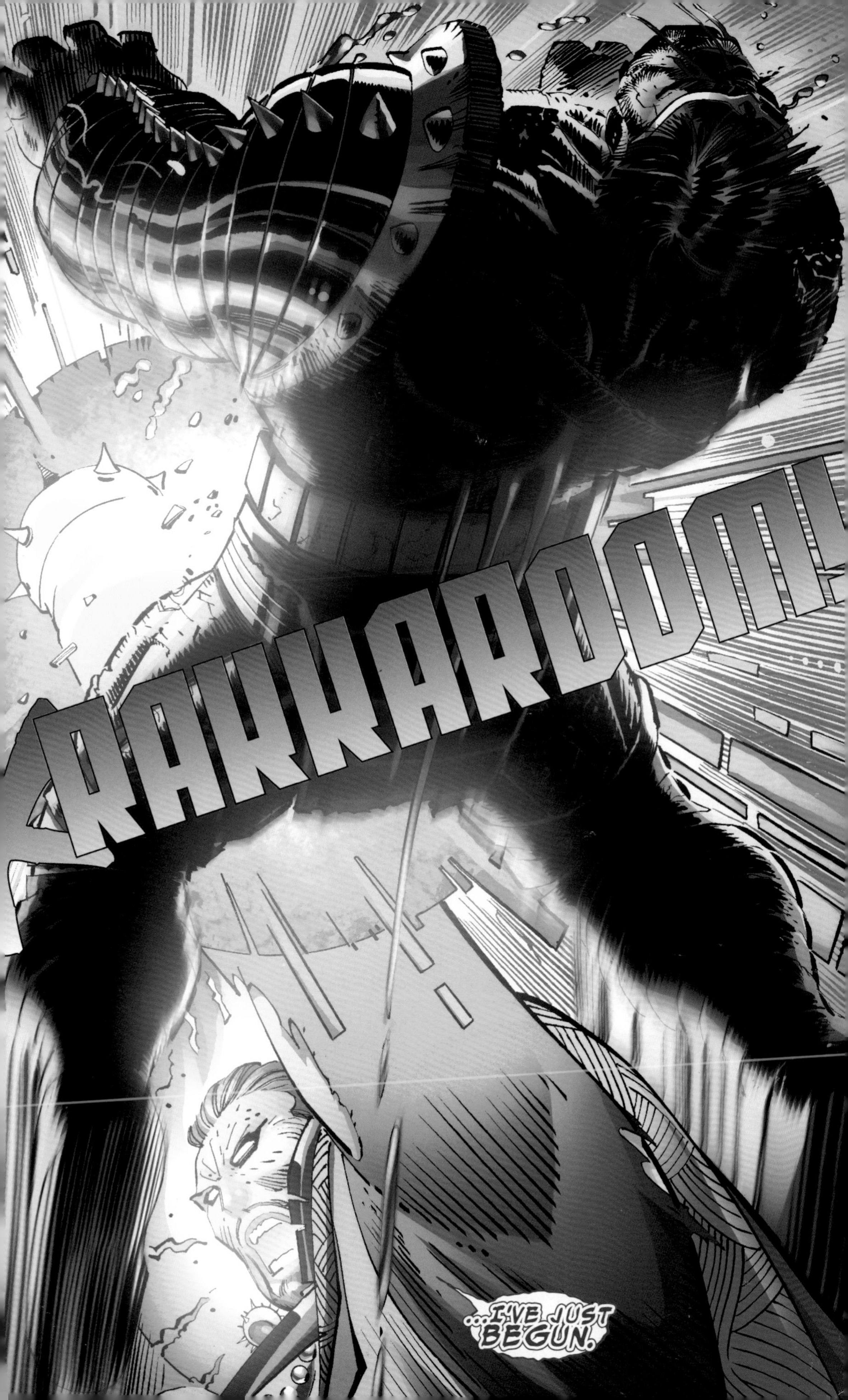
RAKKAROOM!
...I'VE JUST BEGUN.

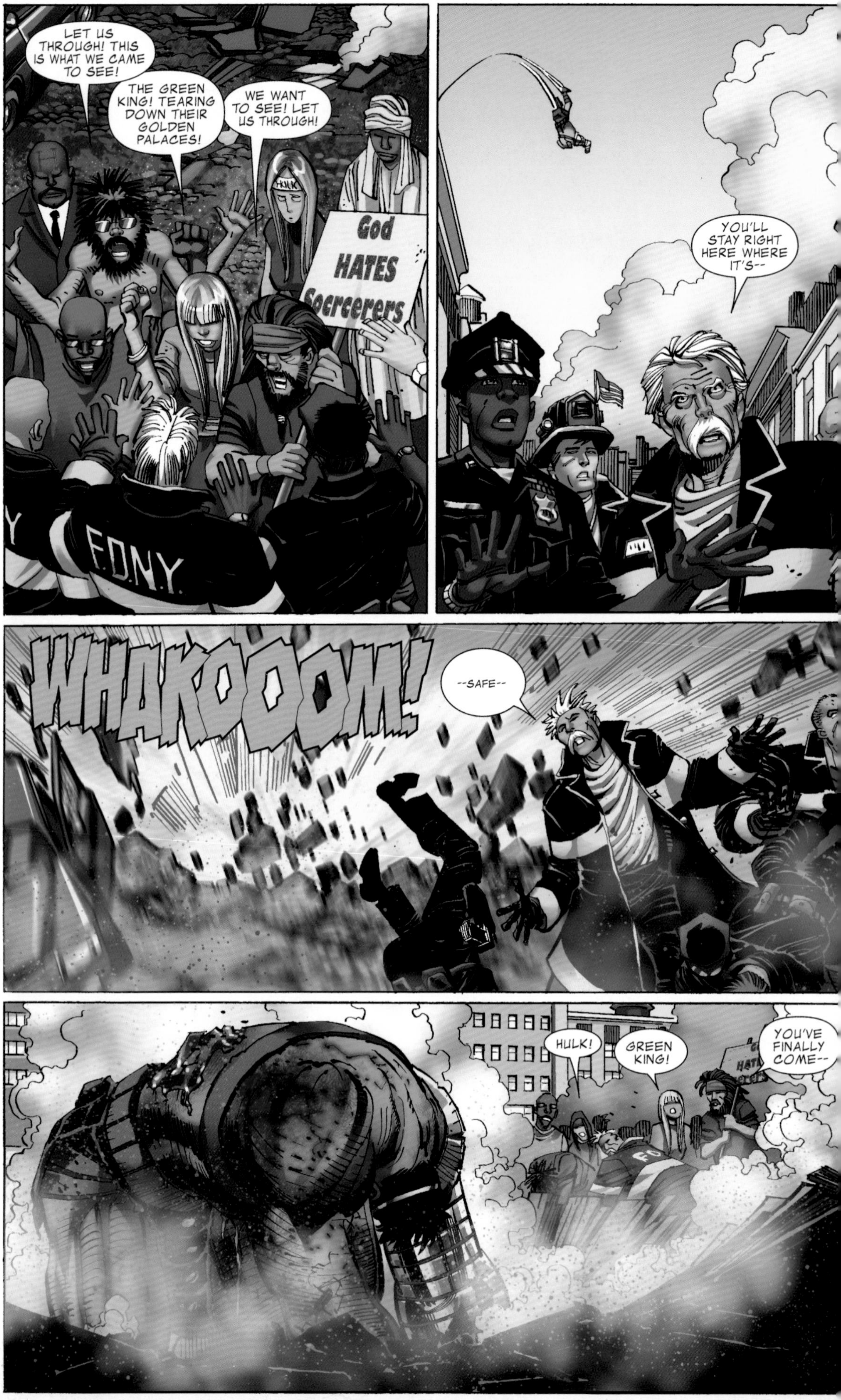
LET US THROUGH! THIS IS WHAT WE CAME TO SEE!
THE GREEN KING! TEARING DOWN THEIR GOLDEN PALACES!
WE WANT TO SEE! LET US THROUGH!
HULK
God HATES Socrcerers
F.D.N.Y.
YOU'LL STAY RIGHT HERE WHERE IT'S--
WHAKOOOM!
--SAFE--
HULK!
GREEN KING!
YOU'VE FINALLY COME--

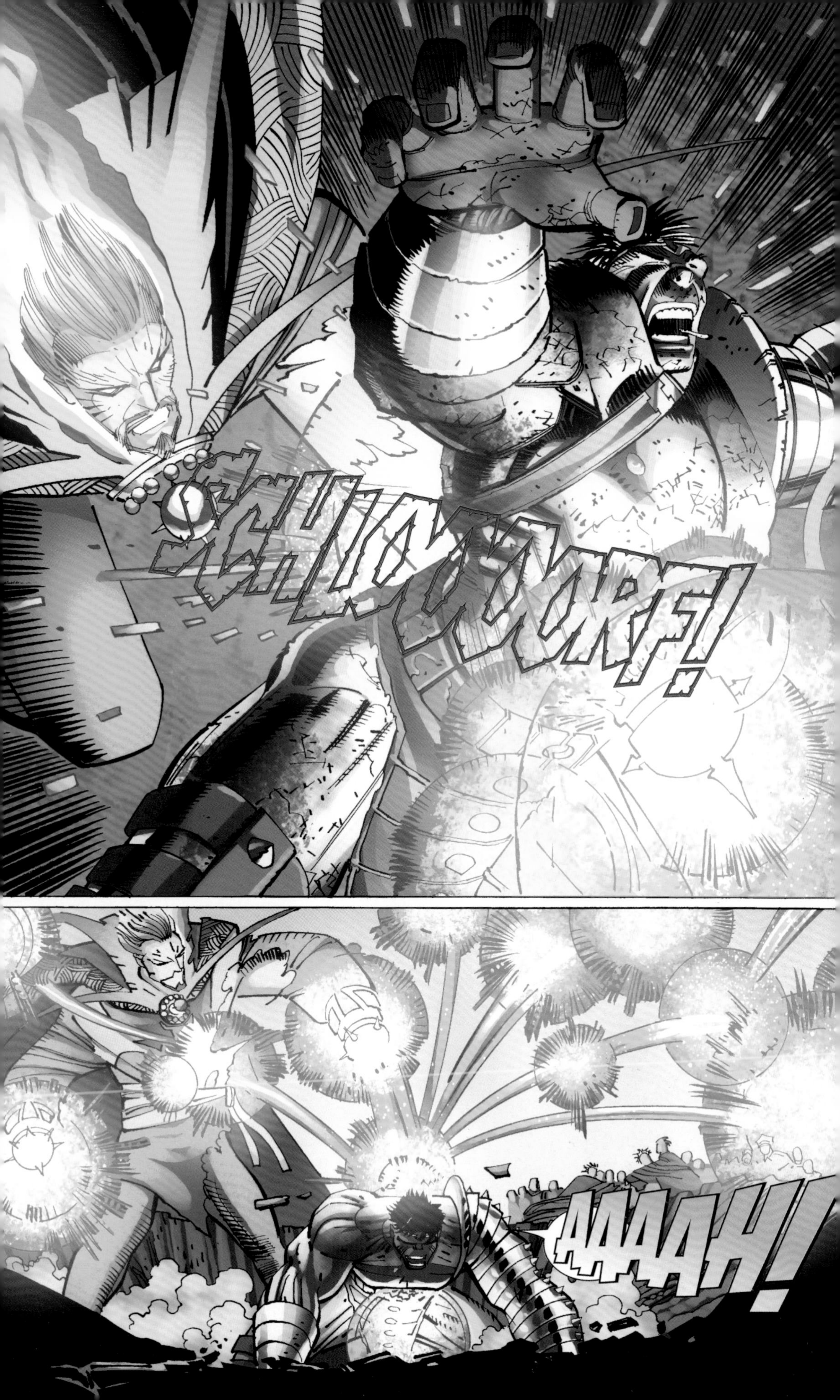
SCHLOOOORF!
AAAAH!

--TO SAVE US...

CRRAAACK!

WHAKOOOM!

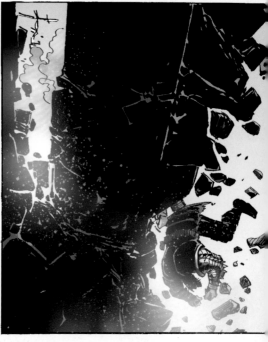

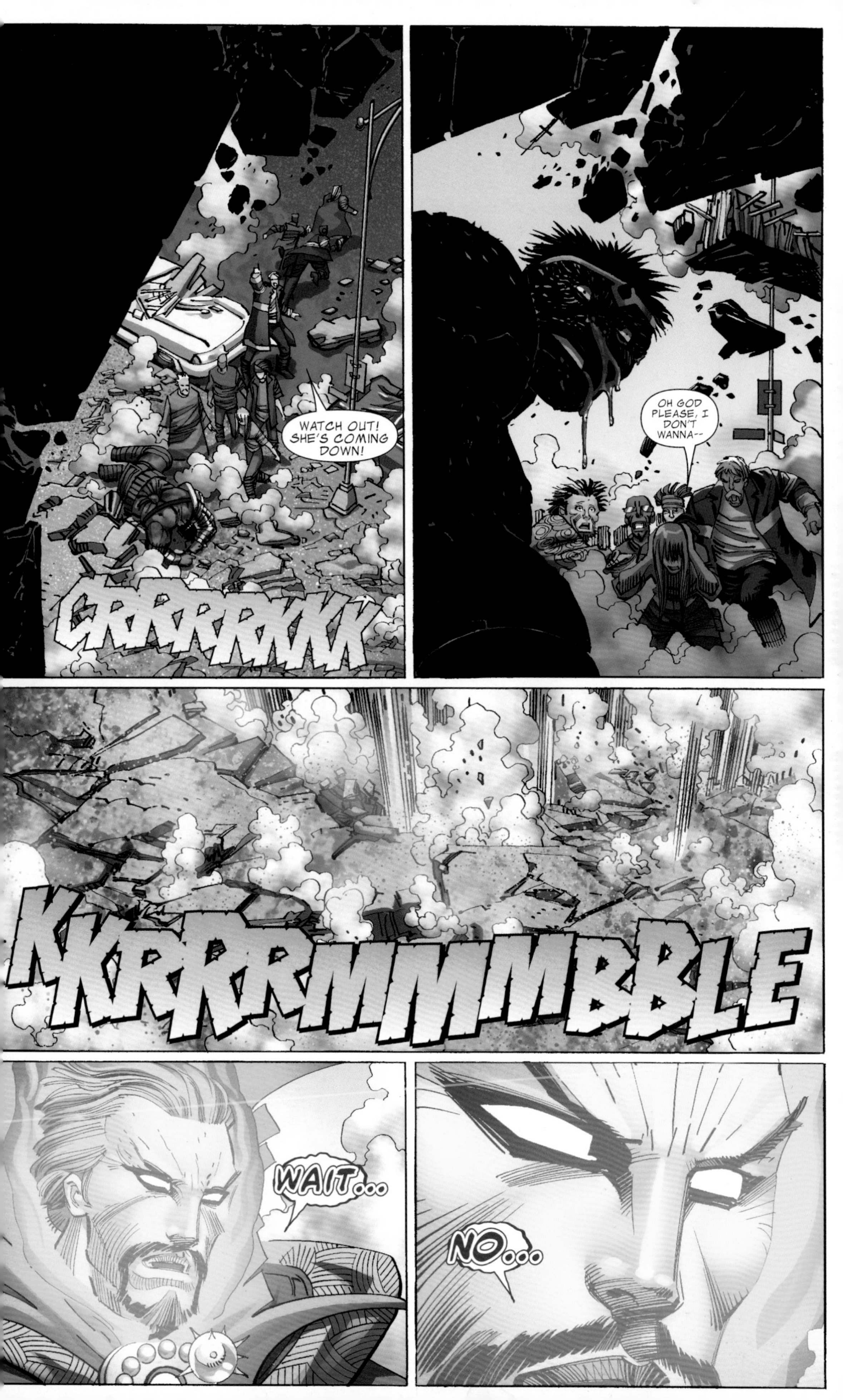
WATCH OUT! SHE'S COMING DOWN!
CRRRRRKKK
OH GOD PLEASE, I DON'T WANNA--
KKRRRRMMMMBBLE
WAIT...
NO...

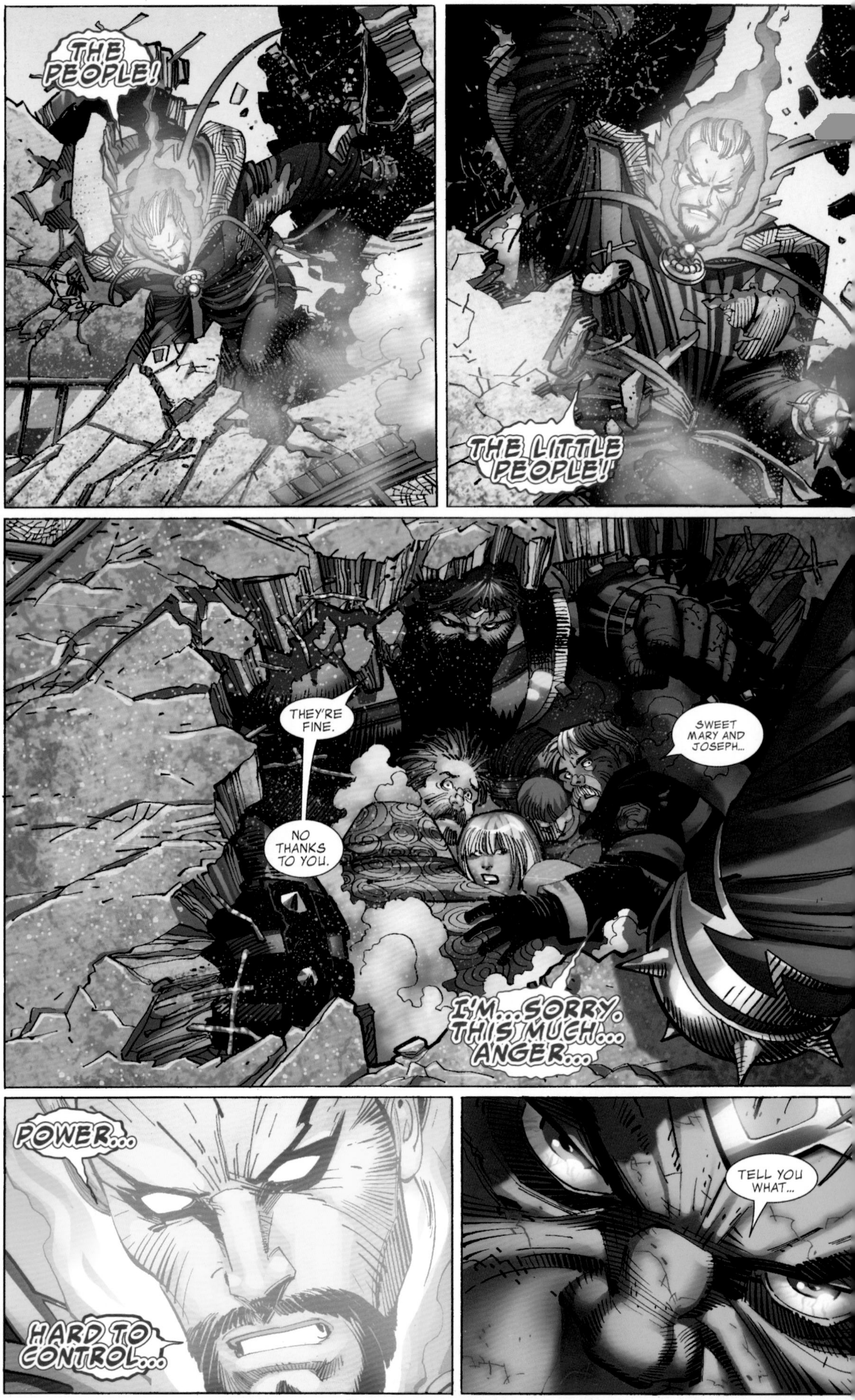
THE PEOPLE!
THE LITTLE PEOPLE!
THEY'RE FINE.
NO THANKS TO YOU.
SWEET MARY AND JOSEPH...
I'M... SORRY. THIS MUCH... ANGER...
POWER...
HARD TO CONTROL...
TELL YOU WHAT...

...I'LL GIVE YOU A LESSON.

SHWAUUUM!

BLAAAAAACHOOOM!

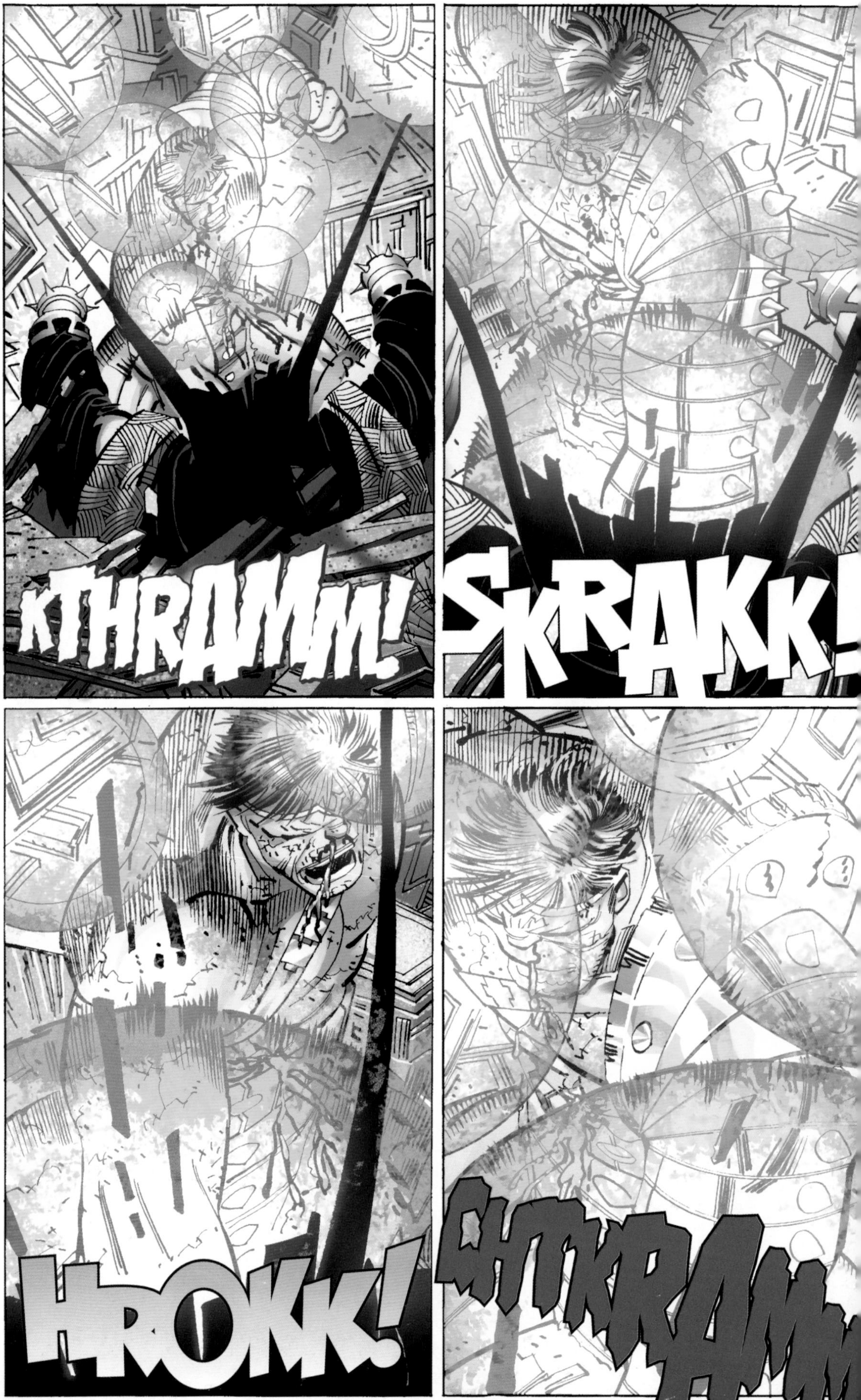
KTHRAMM!
SKRAKK!
HROKK!
CHTKRAMM

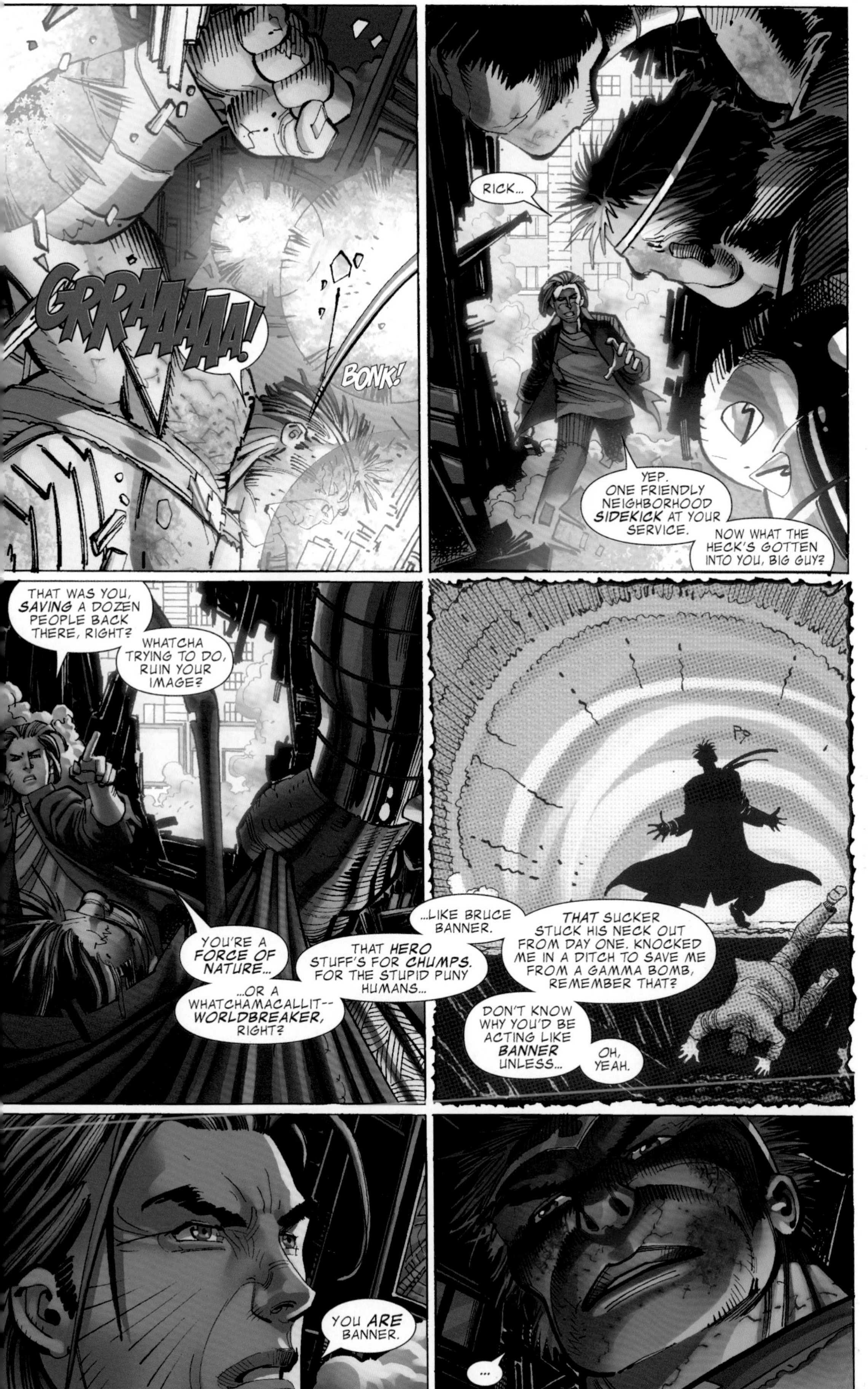
GRRAAAAAA!
BONK!
RICK...
YEP. ONE FRIENDLY NEIGHBORHOOD SIDEKICK AT YOUR SERVICE.
NOW WHAT THE HECK'S GOTTEN INTO YOU, BIG GUY?
THAT WAS YOU, SAVING A DOZEN PEOPLE BACK THERE, RIGHT?
WHATCHA TRYING TO DO, RUIN YOUR IMAGE?
YOU'RE A FORCE OF NATURE...
...OR A WHATCHAMACALLIT-- WORLDBREAKER, RIGHT?
THAT HERO STUFF'S FOR CHUMPS. FOR THE STUPID PUNY HUMANS...
...LIKE BRUCE BANNER.
THAT SUCKER STUCK HIS NECK OUT FROM DAY ONE. KNOCKED ME IN A DITCH TO SAVE ME FROM A GAMMA BOMB, REMEMBER THAT?
DON'T KNOW WHY YOU'D BE ACTING LIKE BANNER UNLESS...
OH, YEAH.
YOU ARE BANNER.
...

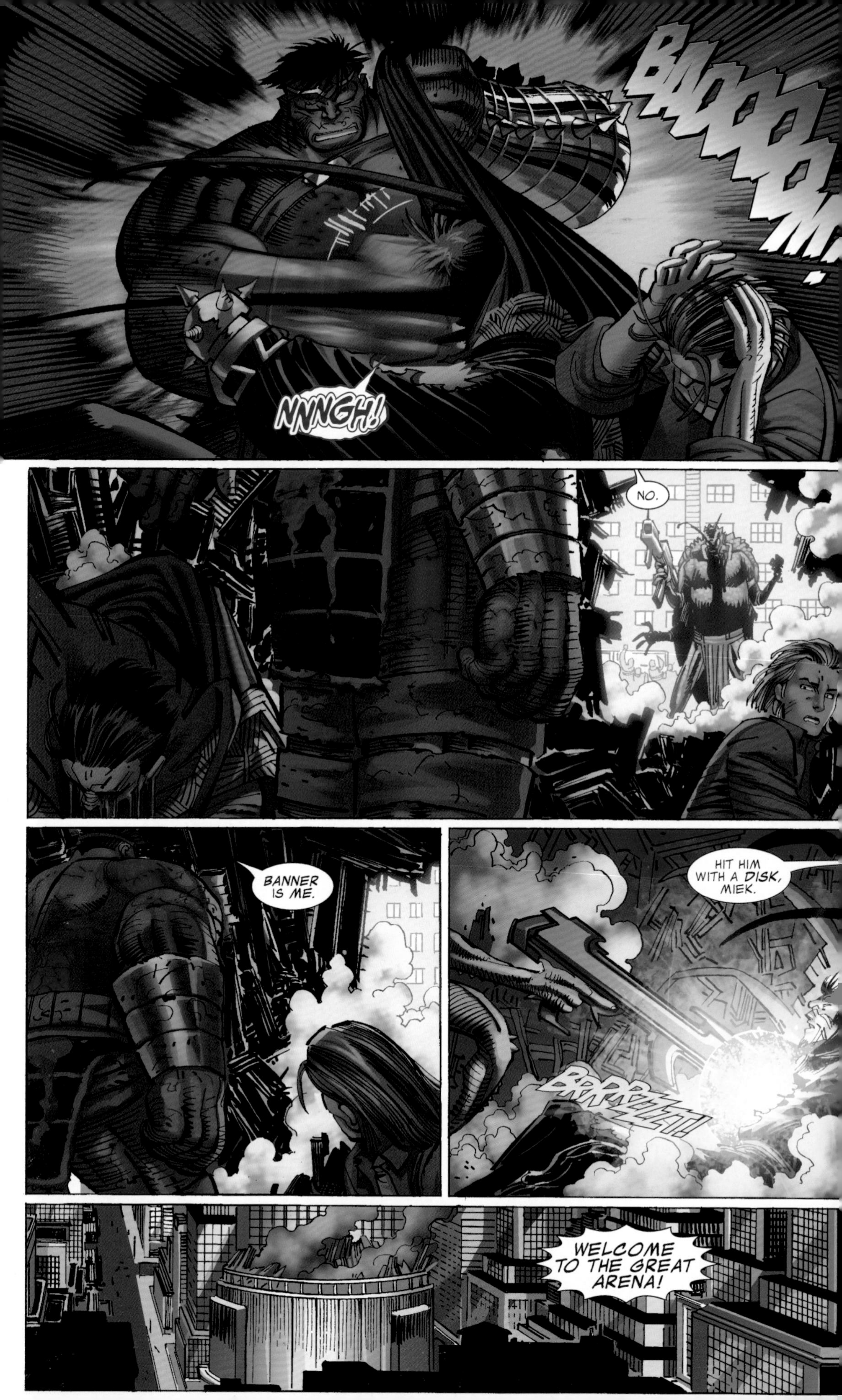
BADOOOM!
NNNGH!
NO.
BANNER IS ME.
HIT HIM WITH A DISK, MIEK.
BRRRZZZZT!
WELCOME TO THE GREAT ARENA!

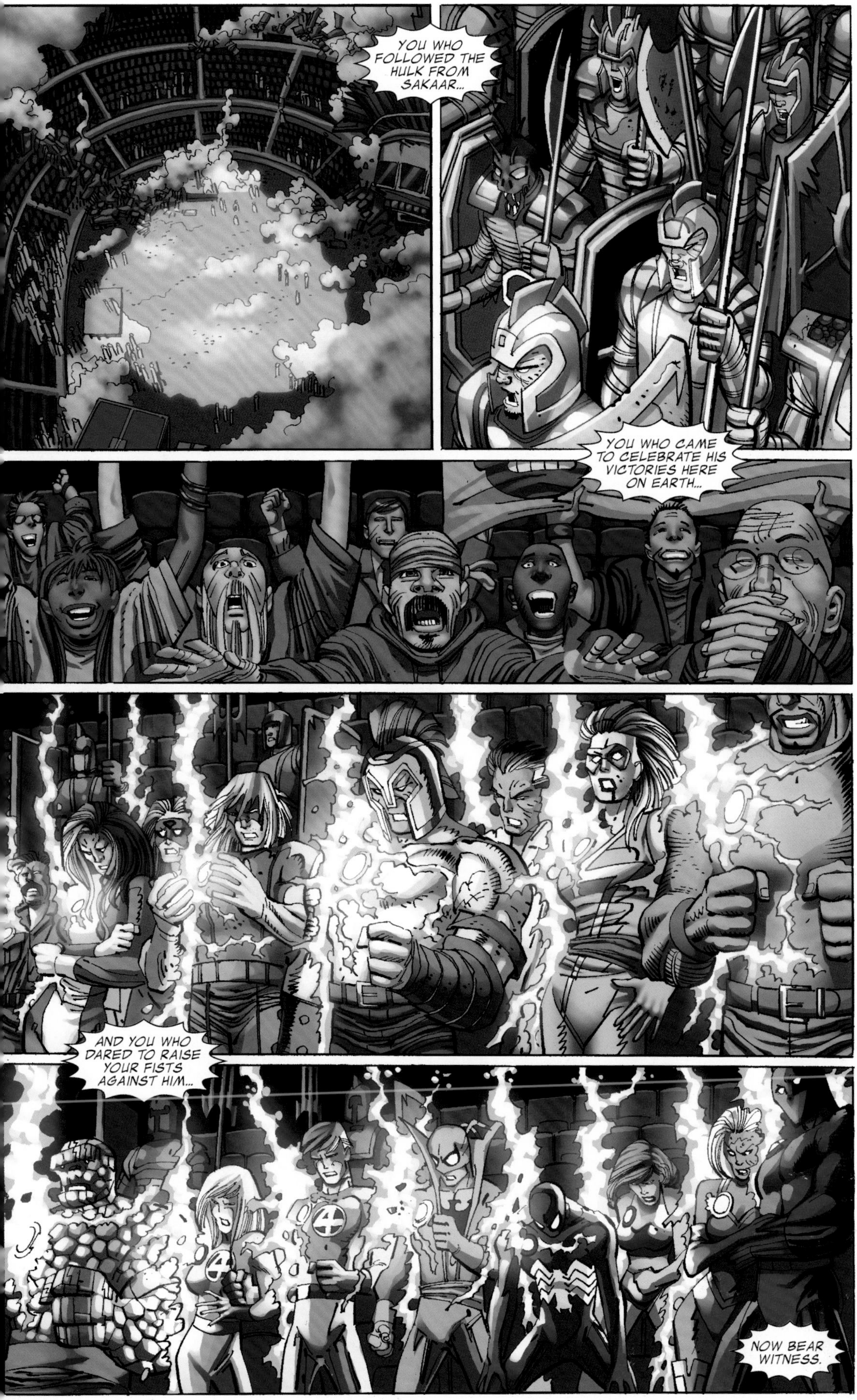
YOU WHO FOLLOWED THE HULK FROM SAKAAR...
YOU WHO CAME TO CELEBRATE HIS VICTORIES HERE ON EARTH...
AND YOU WHO DARED TO RAISE YOUR FISTS AGAINST HIM...
NOW BEAR WITNESS.

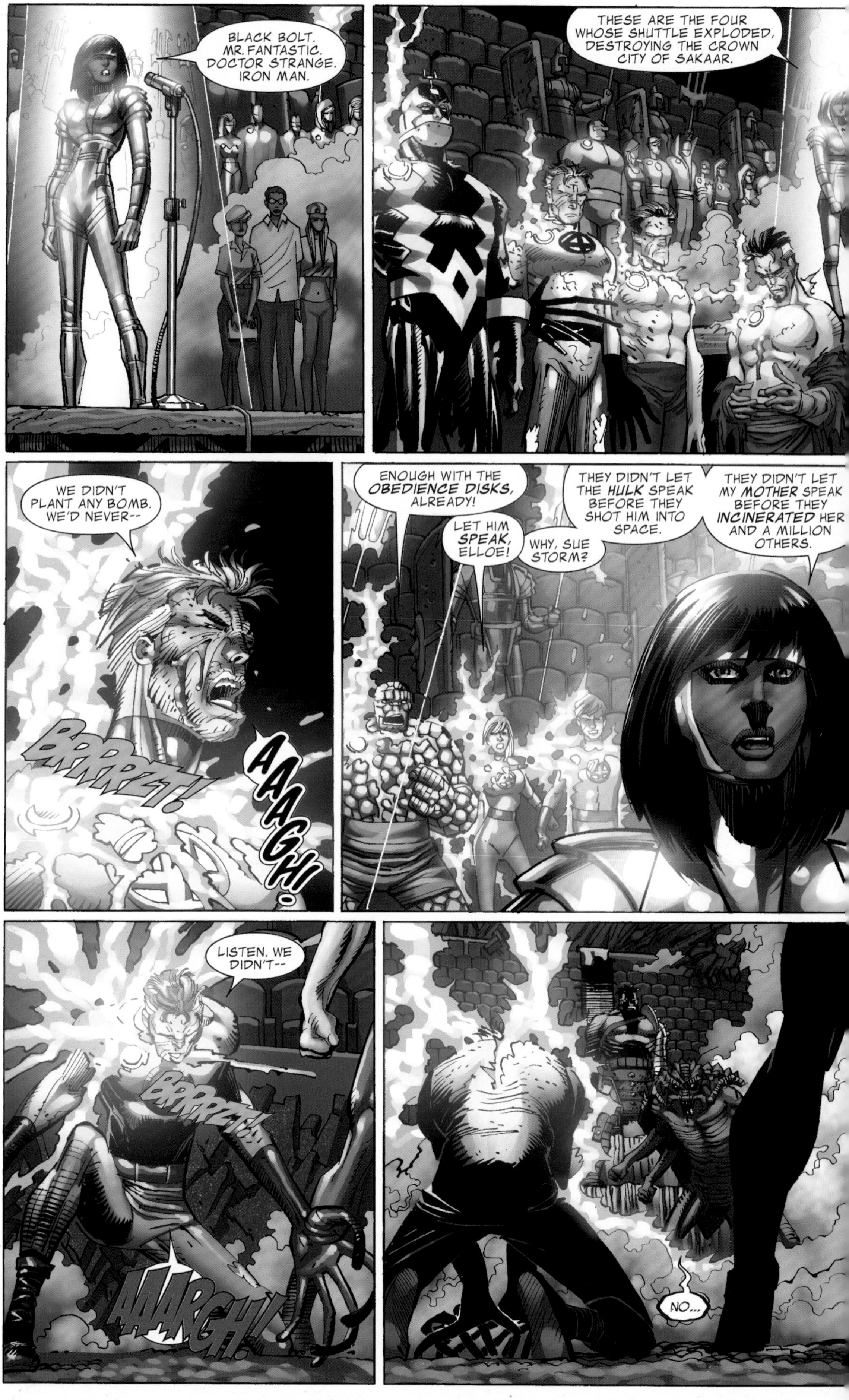
BLACK BOLT. MR. FANTASTIC. DOCTOR STRANGE. IRON MAN.
THESE ARE THE FOUR WHOSE SHUTTLE EXPLODED, DESTROYING THE CROWN CITY OF SAKAAR.
WE DIDN'T PLANT ANY BOMB. WE'D NEVER--
BRRRZT!
AAAGH!
ENOUGH WITH THE OBEDIENCE DISKS, ALREADY!
LET HIM SPEAK, ELLOE!
WHY, SUE STORM?
THEY DIDN'T LET THE HULK SPEAK BEFORE THEY SHOT HIM INTO SPACE.
THEY DIDN'T LET MY MOTHER SPEAK BEFORE THEY INCINERATED HER AND A MILLION OTHERS.
LISTEN. WE DIDN'T--
BRRRZT!
AAARGH!
NO...

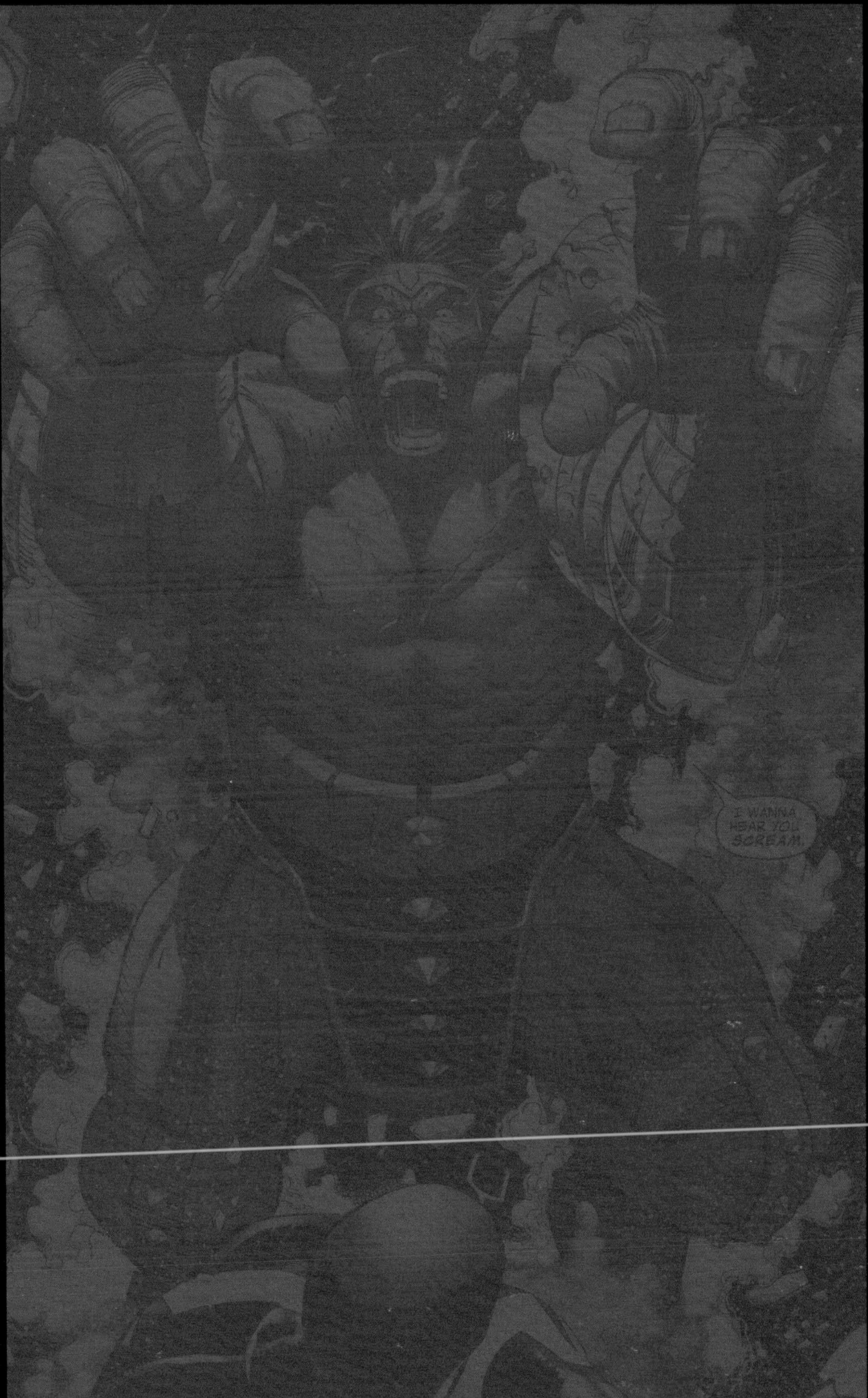
I WANNA HEAR YOU SCREAM.

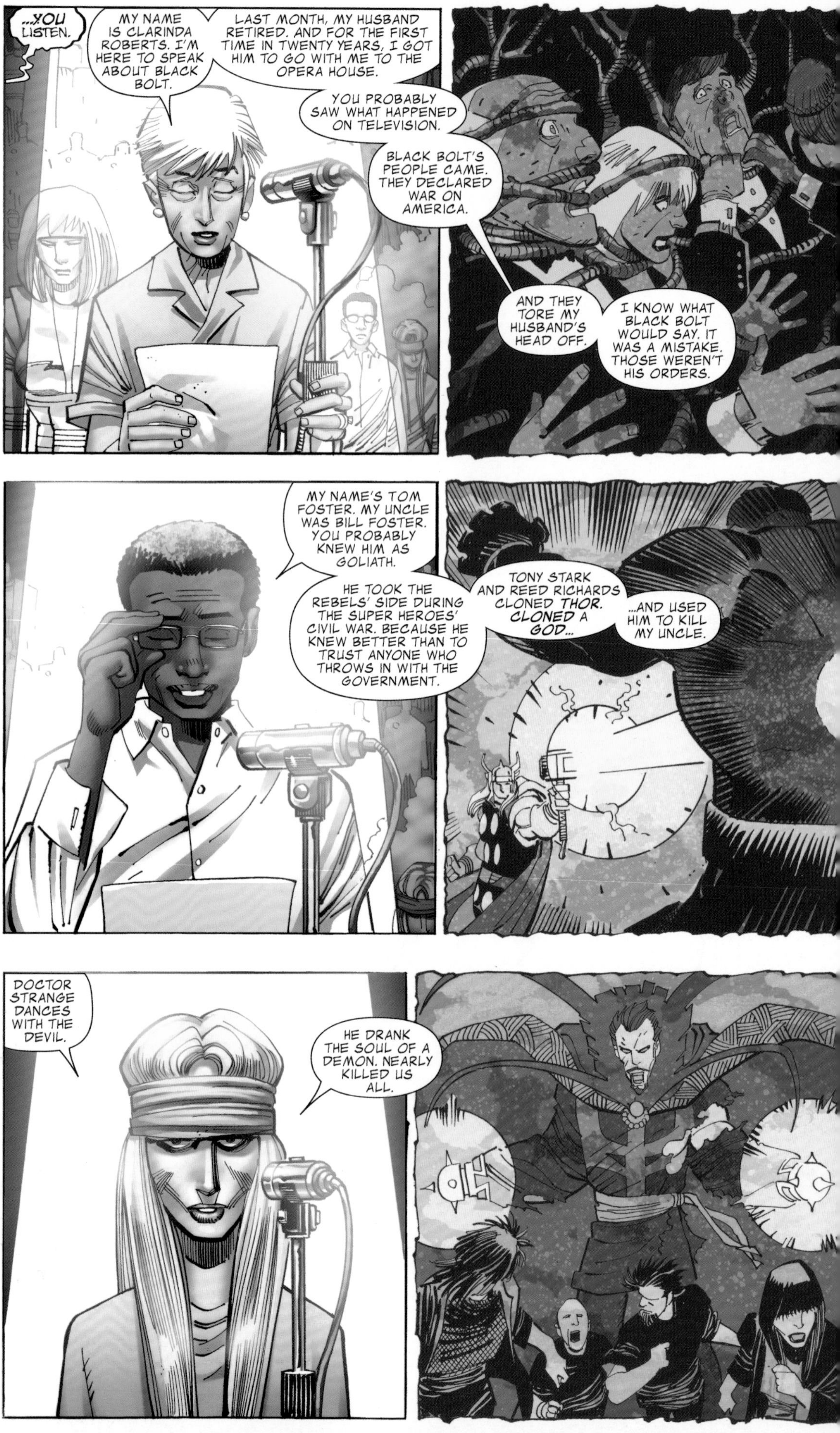
...YOU LISTEN.
MY NAME IS CLARINDA ROBERTS. I'M HERE TO SPEAK ABOUT BLACK BOLT.
LAST MONTH, MY HUSBAND RETIRED. AND FOR THE FIRST TIME IN TWENTY YEARS, I GOT HIM TO GO WITH ME TO THE OPERA HOUSE.
YOU PROBABLY SAW WHAT HAPPENED ON TELEVISION.
BLACK BOLT'S PEOPLE CAME. THEY DECLARED WAR ON AMERICA.
AND THEY TORE MY HUSBAND'S HEAD OFF.
I KNOW WHAT BLACK BOLT WOULD SAY. IT WAS A MISTAKE. THOSE WEREN'T HIS ORDERS.
MY NAME'S TOM FOSTER. MY UNCLE WAS BILL FOSTER. YOU PROBABLY KNEW HIM AS GOLIATH.
HE TOOK THE REBELS' SIDE DURING THE SUPER HEROES' CIVIL WAR. BECAUSE HE KNEW BETTER THAN TO TRUST ANYONE WHO THROWS IN WITH THE GOVERNMENT.
TONY STARK AND REED RICHARDS CLONED *THOR.* *CLONED* A *GOD*...
...AND USED HIM TO KILL MY UNCLE.
DOCTOR STRANGE DANCES WITH THE DEVIL.
HE DRANK THE SOUL OF A DEMON. NEARLY KILLED US ALL.

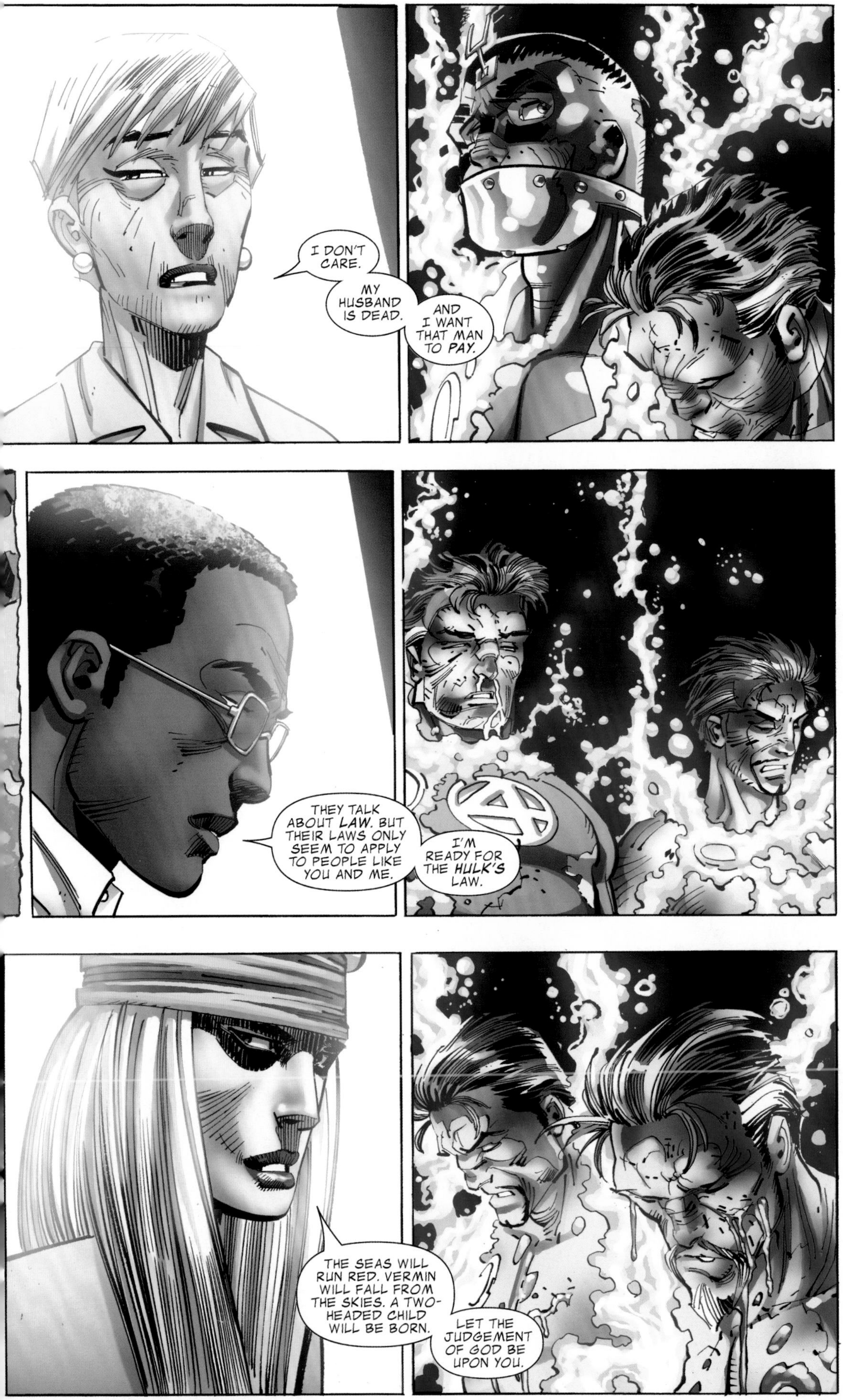
I DON'T CARE.
MY HUSBAND IS DEAD.
AND I WANT THAT MAN TO PAY.
THEY TALK ABOUT LAW. BUT THEIR LAWS ONLY SEEM TO APPLY TO PEOPLE LIKE YOU AND ME.
I'M READY FOR THE HULK'S LAW.
THE SEAS WILL RUN RED. VERMIN WILL FALL FROM THE SKIES. A TWO-HEADED CHILD WILL BE BORN.
LET THE JUDGEMENT OF GOD BE UPON YOU.

DON'T LIKE IT, DO YOU? IT'S NOT FAIR. NOT THE WHOLE STORY.

YOU HAVE EXCUSES. EXPLANATIONS. YOU'RE INNOCENT.

THESE PEOPLE DON'T KNOW WHAT REALLY HAPPENED. THEY DON'T KNOW WHAT'S IN YOUR HEART.

NOW YOU KNOW HOW IT FEELS.

AND NOW...

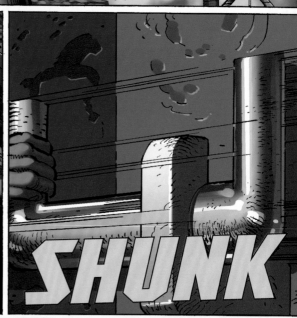

SHUNK

HRRLLLAAAOO

...YOU'RE GONNA FIND OUT HOW THIS FEELS.

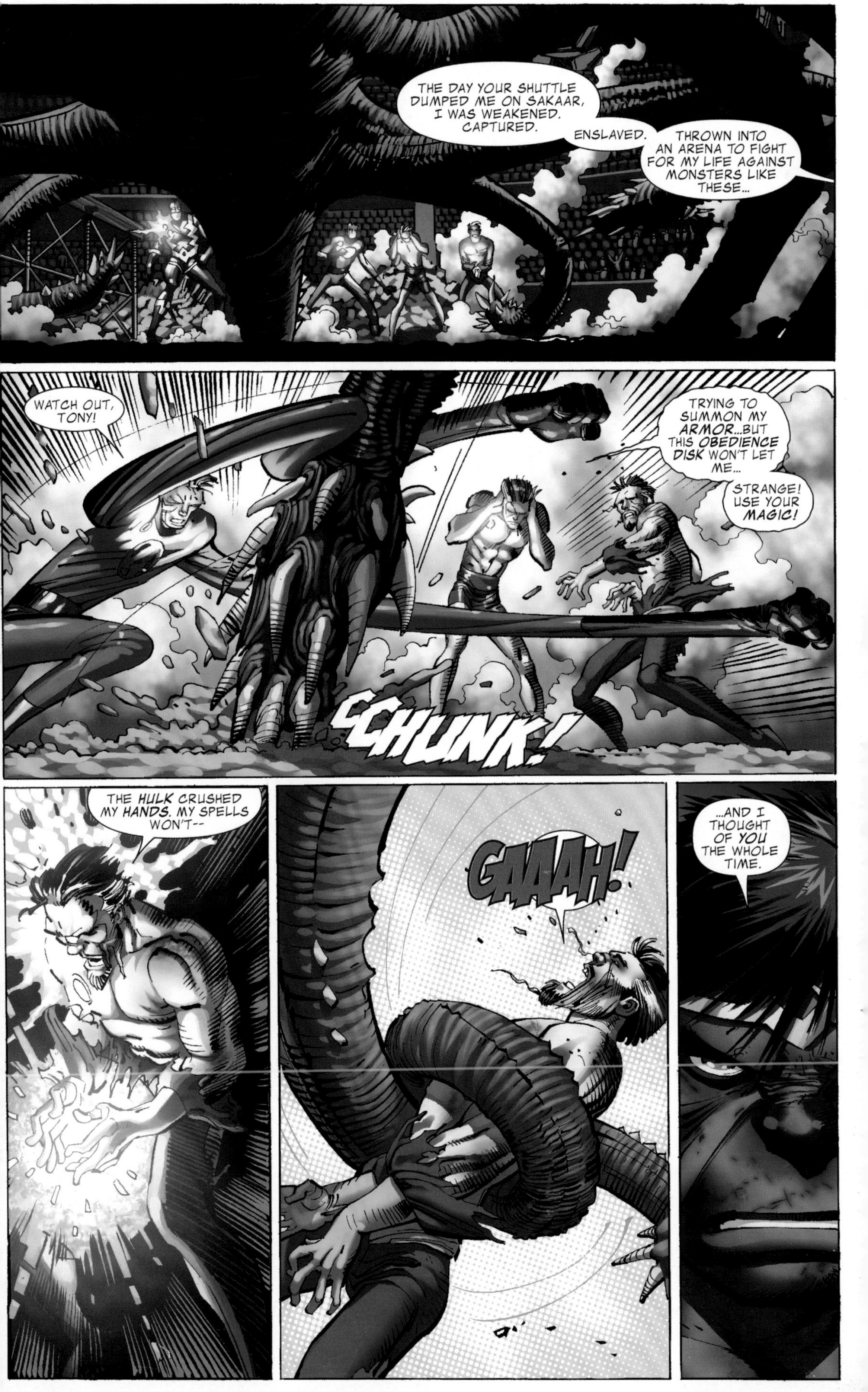
THE DAY YOUR SHUTTLE DUMPED ME ON SAKAAR, I WAS WEAKENED. CAPTURED.
ENSLAVED.
THROWN INTO AN ARENA TO FIGHT FOR MY LIFE AGAINST MONSTERS LIKE THESE...
WATCH OUT, TONY!
TRYING TO SUMMON MY ARMOR...BUT THIS OBEDIENCE DISK WON'T LET ME...
STRANGE! USE YOUR MAGIC!
CCHUNK!
THE HULK CRUSHED MY HANDS. MY SPELLS WON'T--
GAAAH!
...AND I THOUGHT OF YOU THE WHOLE TIME.

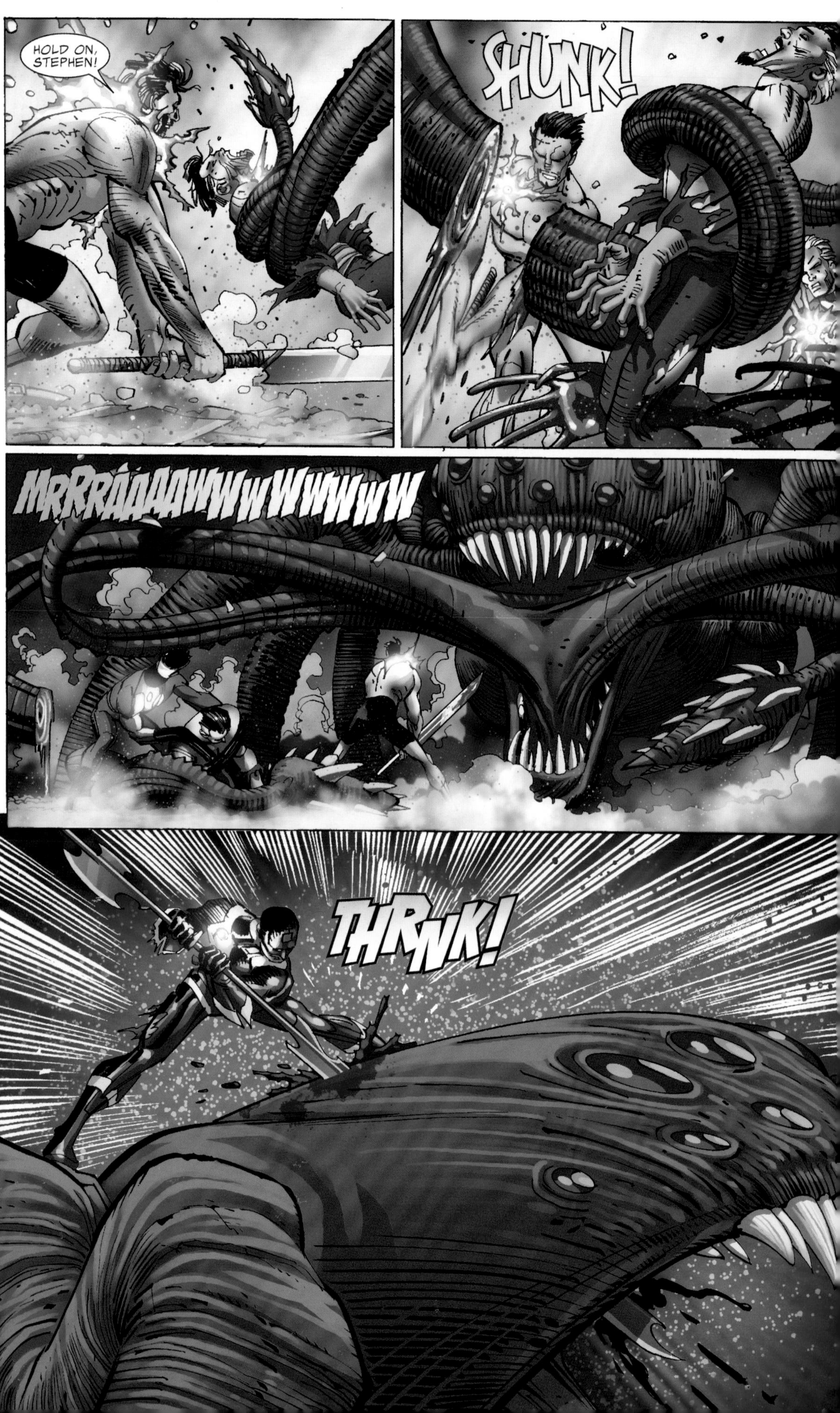

HOLD ON, STEPHEN!
SHUNK!
MRRRAAAAWWWWWWWWW
THRNK!

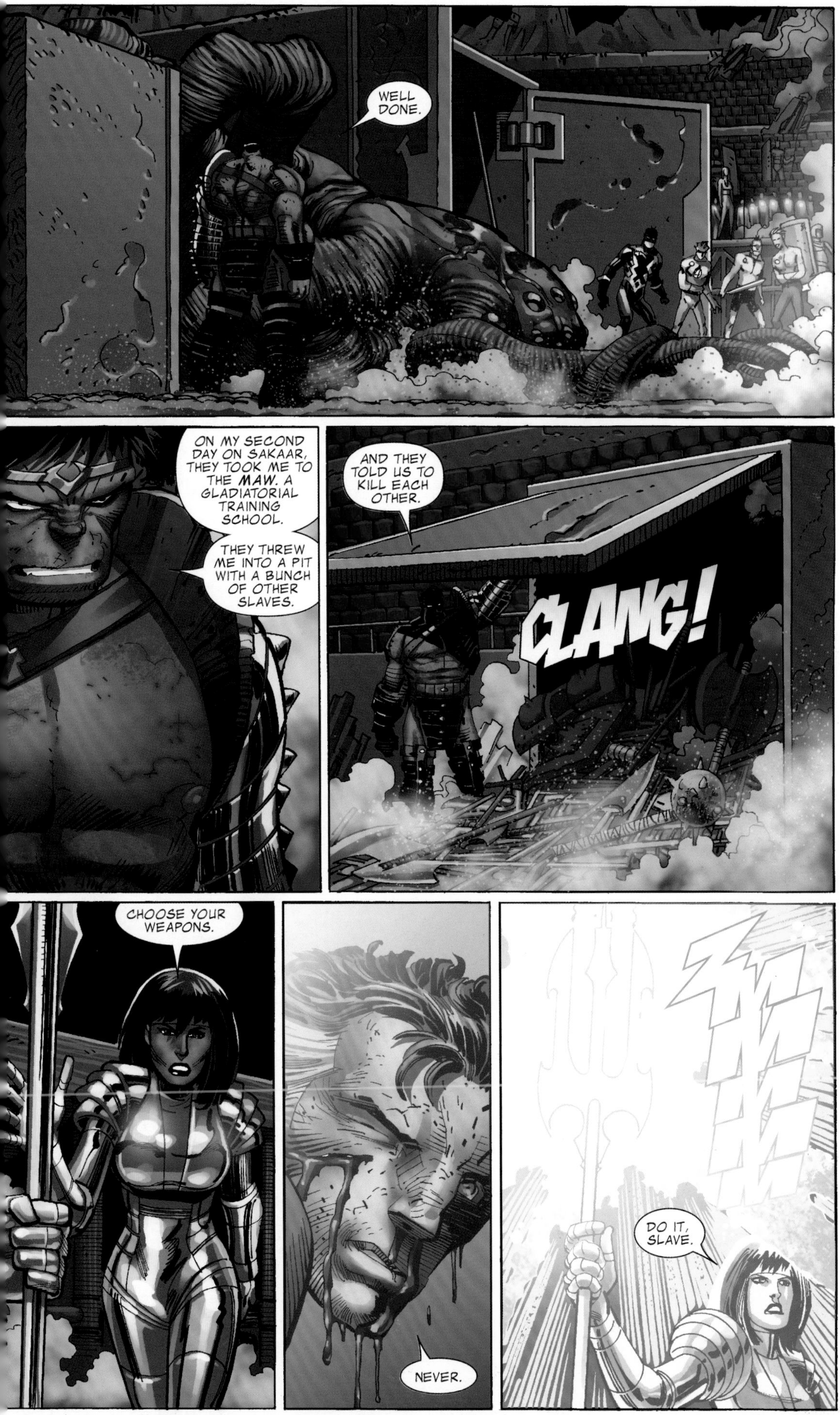
WELL DONE.
ON MY SECOND DAY ON SAKAAR, THEY TOOK ME TO THE MAW. A GLADIATORIAL TRAINING SCHOOL.
THEY THREW ME INTO A PIT WITH A BUNCH OF OTHER SLAVES.
AND THEY TOLD US TO KILL EACH OTHER.
CLANG!
CHOOSE YOUR WEAPONS.
NEVER.
DO IT, SLAVE.

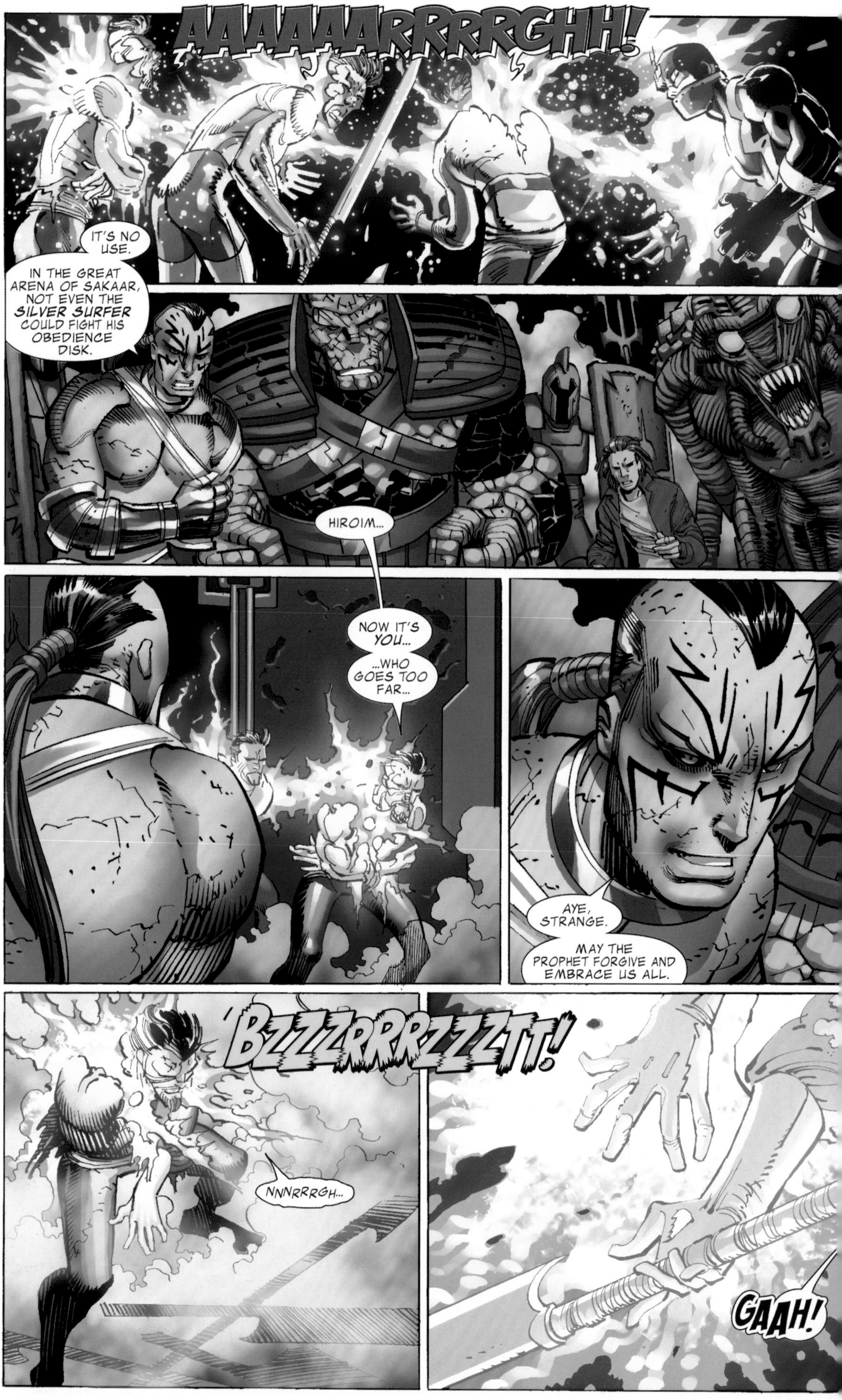
AAAAAARRRRGHH!
IT'S NO USE.
IN THE GREAT ARENA OF SAKAAR, NOT EVEN THE SILVER SURFER COULD FIGHT HIS OBEDIENCE DISK.
HIROIM...
NOW IT'S YOU...
...WHO GOES TOO FAR...
AYE, STRANGE.
MAY THE PROPHET FORGIVE AND EMBRACE US ALL.
BZZZRRRZZZTT!
NNNRRRGH...
GAAH!

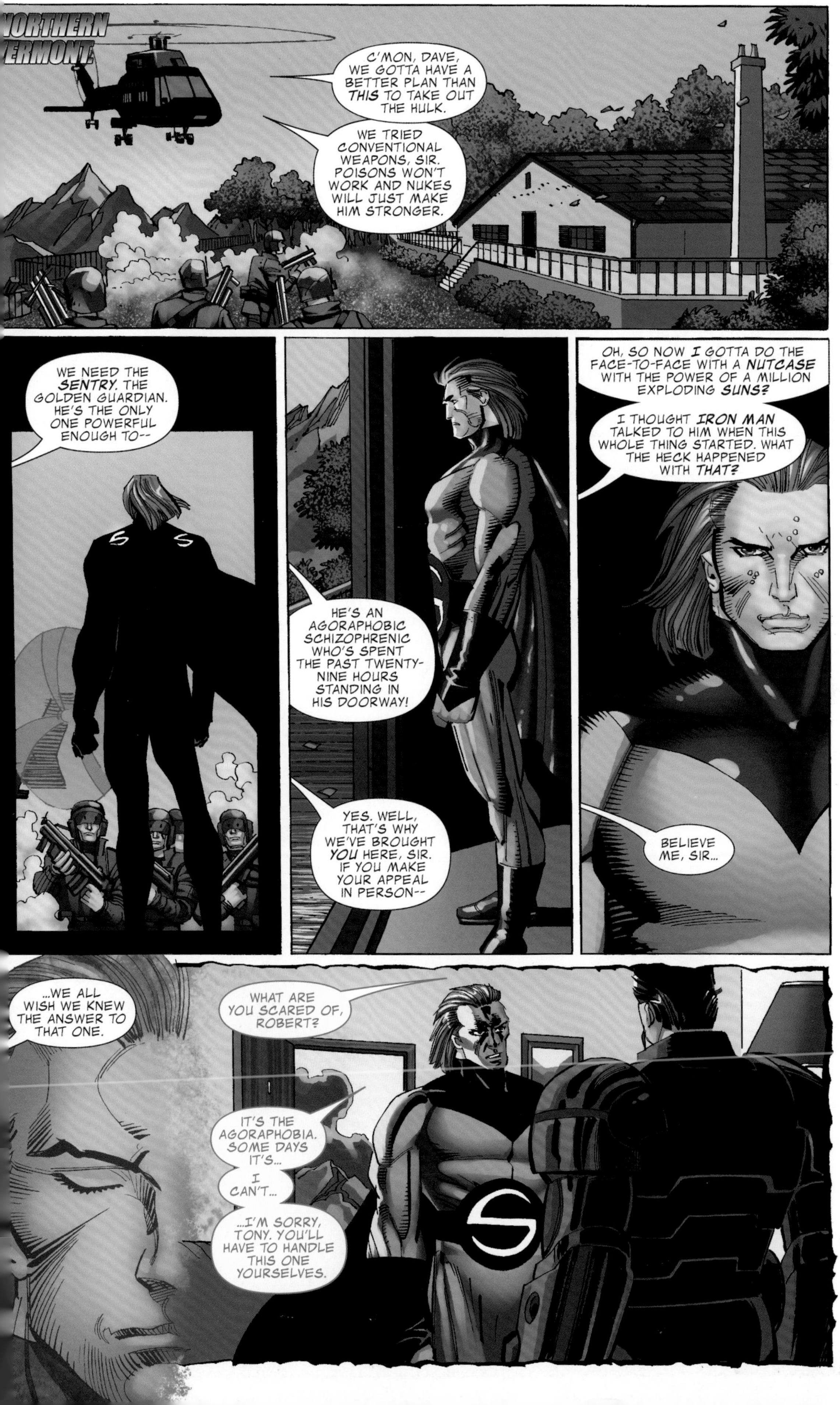
NORTHERN VERMONT
C'MON, DAVE, WE GOTTA HAVE A BETTER PLAN THAN THIS TO TAKE OUT THE HULK.
WE TRIED CONVENTIONAL WEAPONS, SIR. POISONS WON'T WORK AND NUKES WILL JUST MAKE HIM STRONGER.
WE NEED THE SENTRY. THE GOLDEN GUARDIAN. HE'S THE ONLY ONE POWERFUL ENOUGH TO--
HE'S AN AGORAPHOBIC SCHIZOPHRENIC WHO'S SPENT THE PAST TWENTY-NINE HOURS STANDING IN HIS DOORWAY!
YES. WELL, THAT'S WHY WE'VE BROUGHT YOU HERE, SIR. IF YOU MAKE YOUR APPEAL IN PERSON--
OH, SO NOW I GOTTA DO THE FACE-TO-FACE WITH A NUTCASE WITH THE POWER OF A MILLION EXPLODING SUNS?
I THOUGHT IRON MAN TALKED TO HIM WHEN THIS WHOLE THING STARTED. WHAT THE HECK HAPPENED WITH THAT?
BELIEVE ME, SIR...
...WE ALL WISH WE KNEW THE ANSWER TO THAT ONE.
WHAT ARE YOU SCARED OF, ROBERT?
IT'S THE AGORAPHOBIA. SOME DAYS IT'S...
I CAN'T...
...I'M SORRY, TONY. YOU'LL HAVE TO HANDLE THIS ONE YOURSELVES.

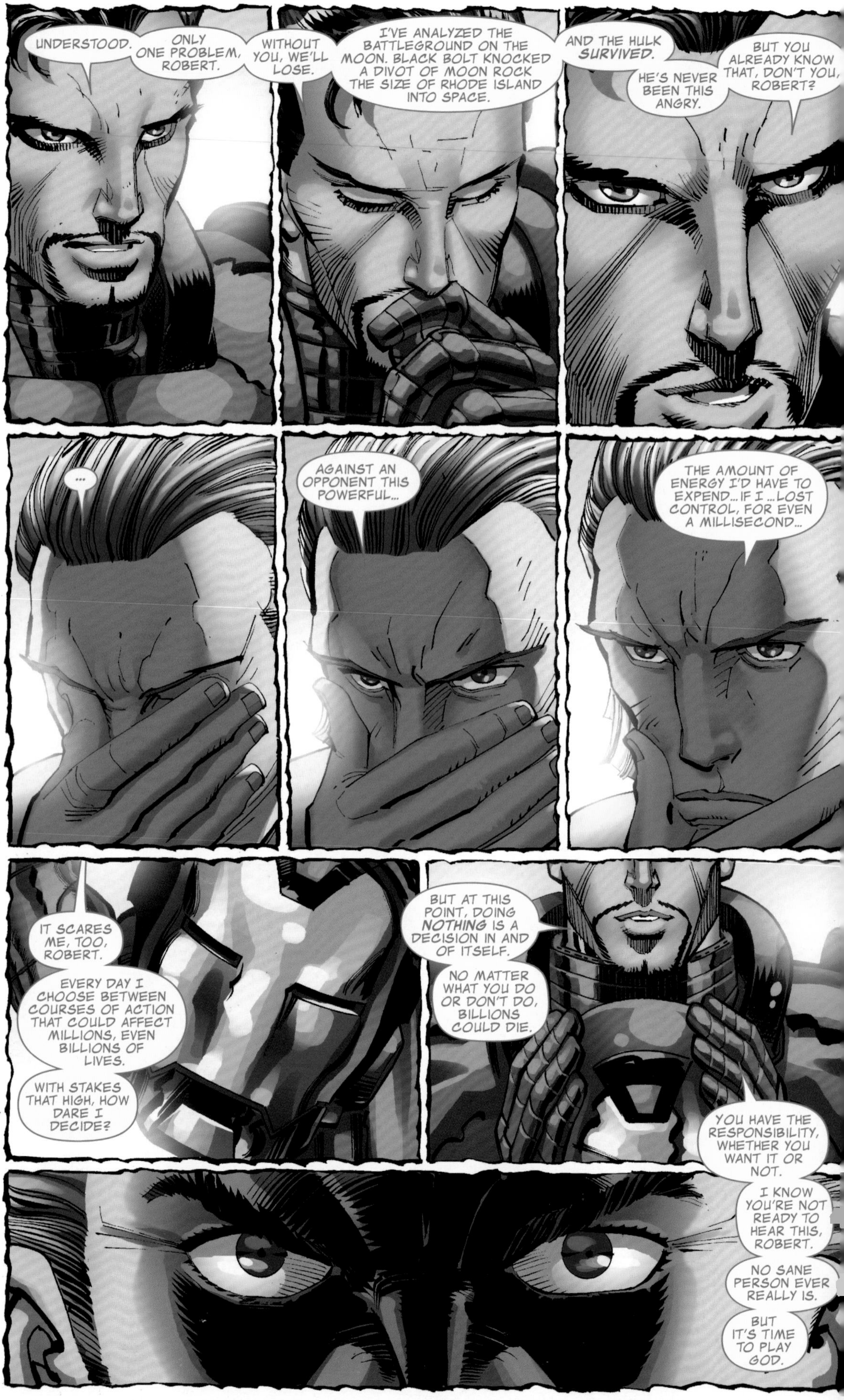
UNDERSTOOD.
ONLY ONE PROBLEM, ROBERT.
WITHOUT YOU, WE'LL LOSE.
I'VE ANALYZED THE BATTLEGROUND ON THE MOON. BLACK BOLT KNOCKED A DIVOT OF MOON ROCK THE SIZE OF RHODE ISLAND INTO SPACE.
AND THE HULK *SURVIVED.*
HE'S NEVER BEEN THIS ANGRY.
BUT YOU ALREADY KNOW THAT, DON'T YOU, ROBERT?
...
AGAINST AN OPPONENT THIS POWERFUL...
THE AMOUNT OF ENERGY I'D HAVE TO EXPEND... IF I ...LOST CONTROL, FOR EVEN A MILLISECOND...
IT SCARES ME, TOO, ROBERT.
EVERY DAY I CHOOSE BETWEEN COURSES OF ACTION THAT COULD AFFECT MILLIONS, EVEN BILLIONS OF LIVES.
WITH STAKES THAT HIGH, HOW DARE I DECIDE?
BUT AT THIS POINT, DOING **NOTHING** IS A DECISION IN AND OF ITSELF.
NO MATTER WHAT YOU DO OR DON'T DO, BILLIONS COULD DIE.
YOU HAVE THE RESPONSIBILITY, WHETHER YOU WANT IT OR NOT.
I KNOW YOU'RE NOT READY TO HEAR THIS, ROBERT.
NO SANE PERSON EVER REALLY IS.
BUT IT'S TIME TO PLAY GOD.

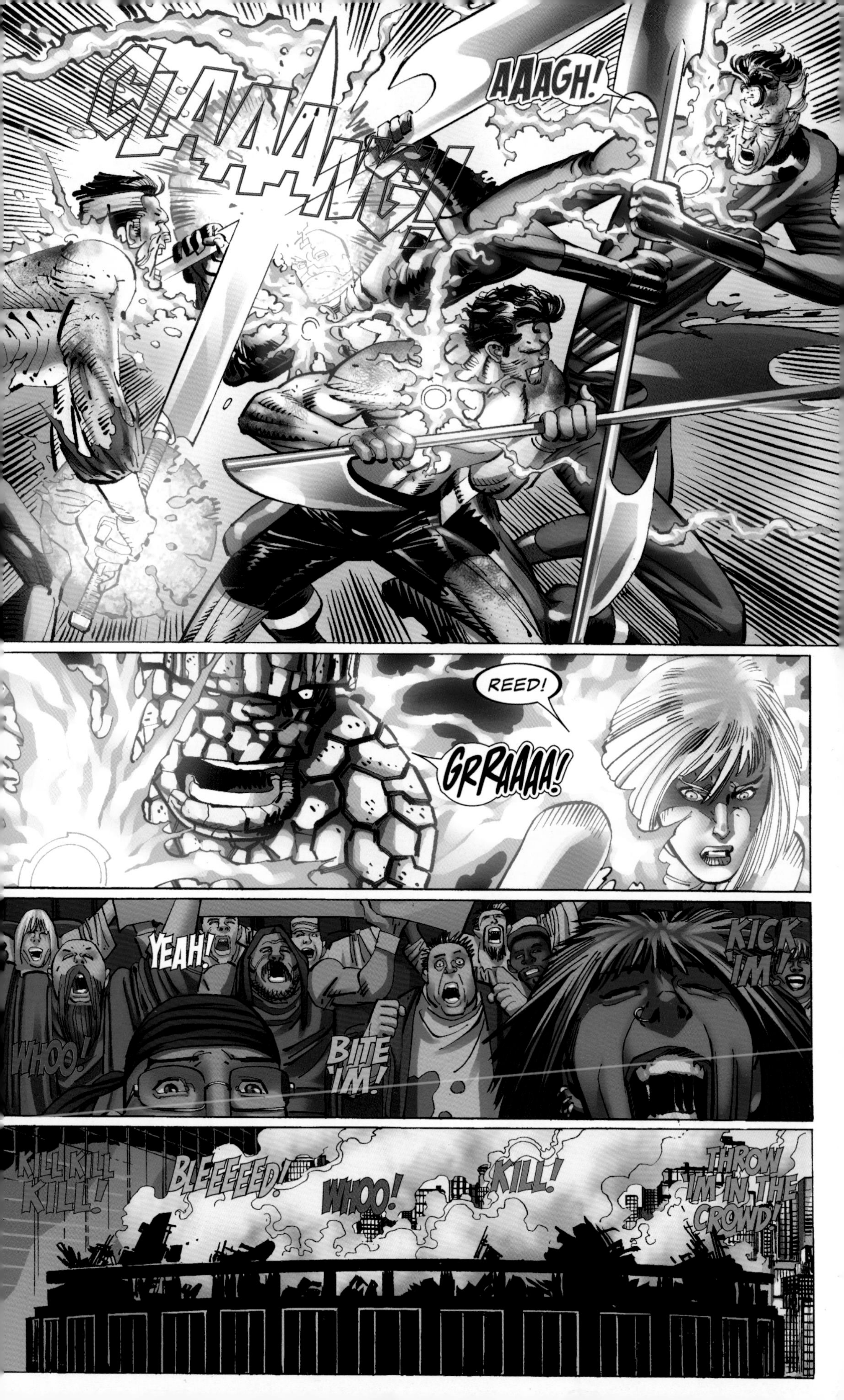
CLANNNG!
AAAGH!
REED!
GRRAAAA!
YEAH!
KICK 'IM!
WHOO!
BITE 'IM!
KILL KILL KILL!
BLEEEEED!
WHOO!
KILL!
THROW 'IM IN THE CROWD!

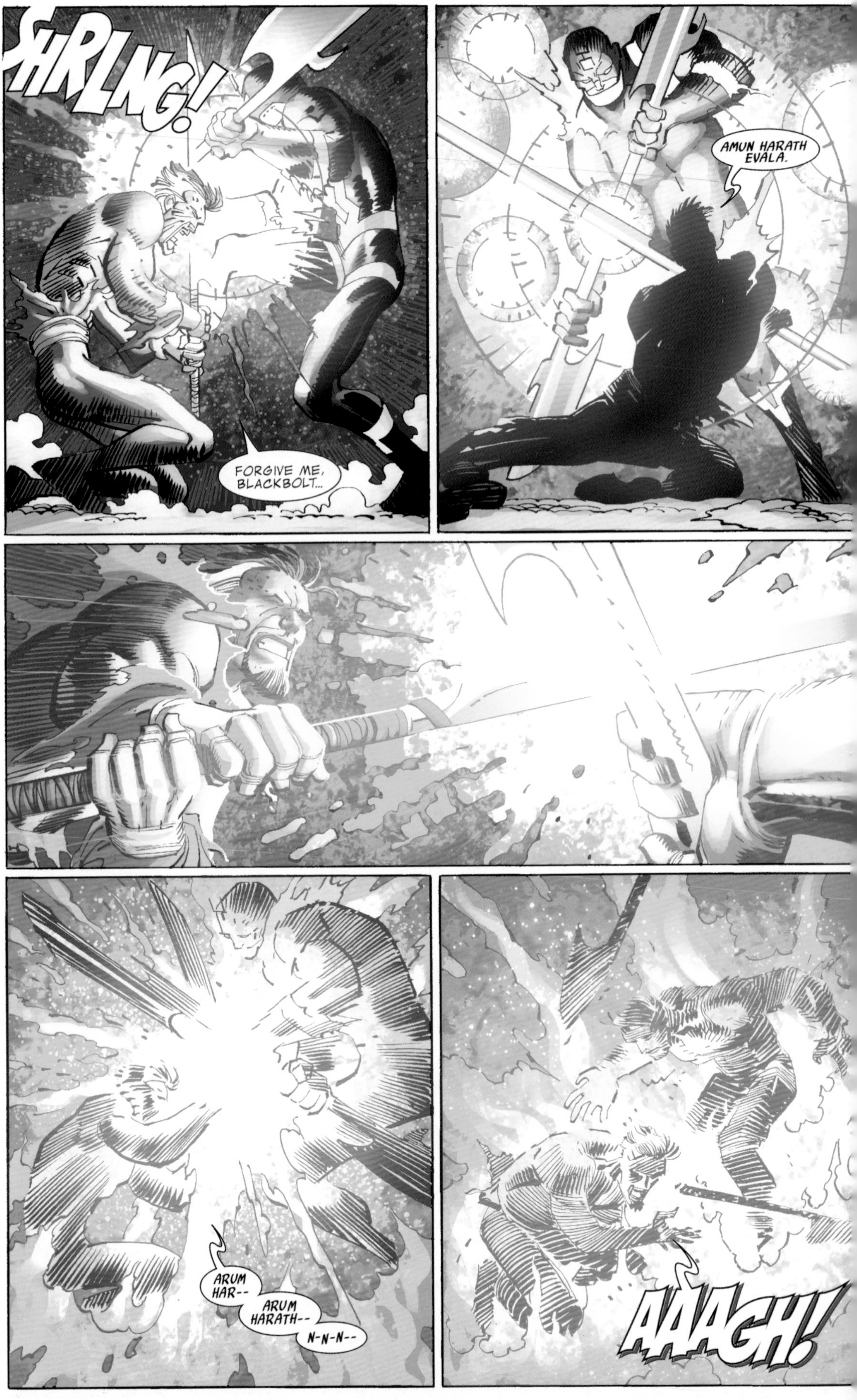
SHRLNG!
FORGIVE ME, BLACKBOLT...
AMUN HARATH EVALA.
ARUM HAR--
ARUM HARATH--
N-N-N--
AAAGH!

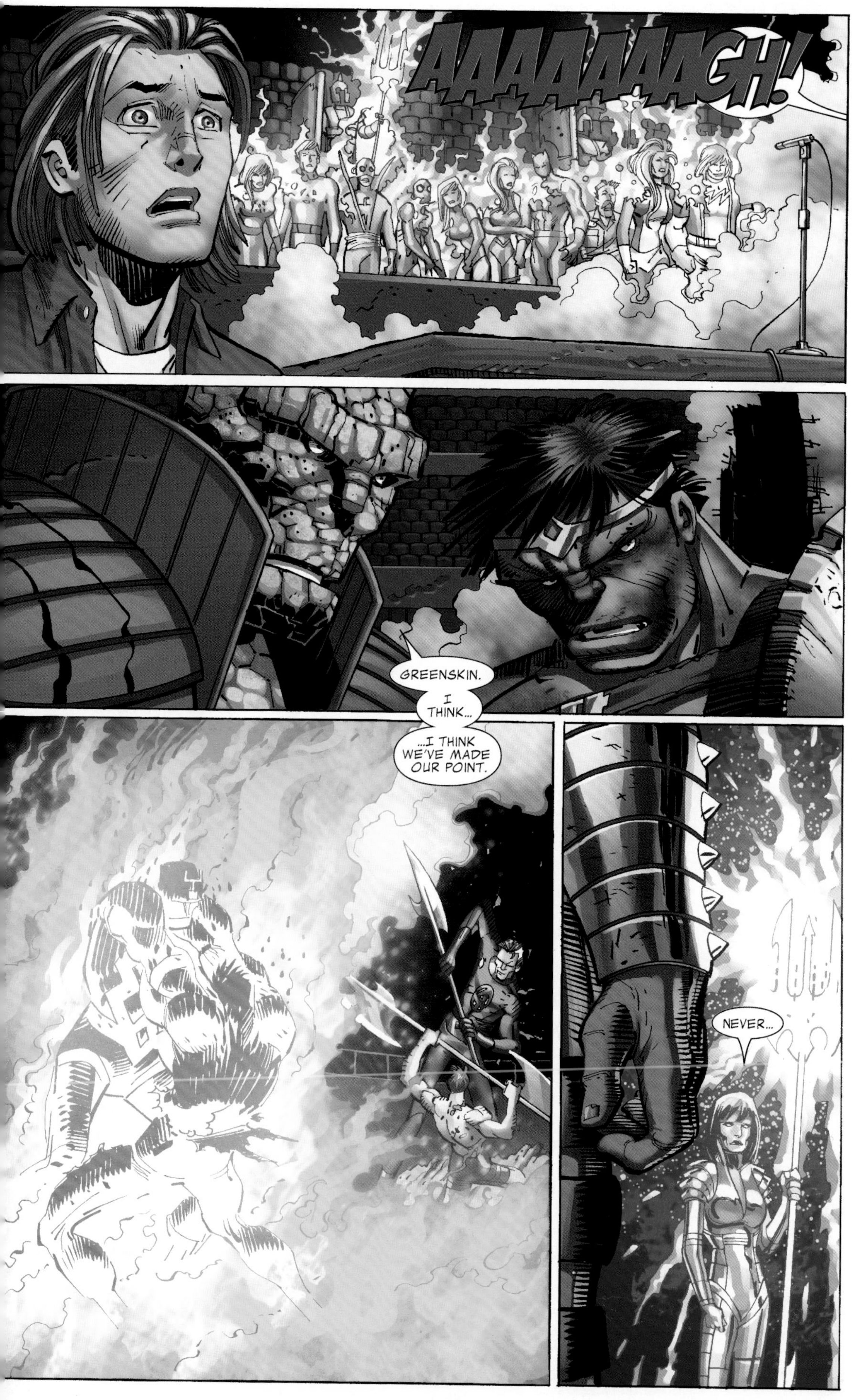
AAAAAAAAGH!
GREENSKIN.
I THINK...
...I THINK WE'VE MADE OUR POINT.
NEVER...

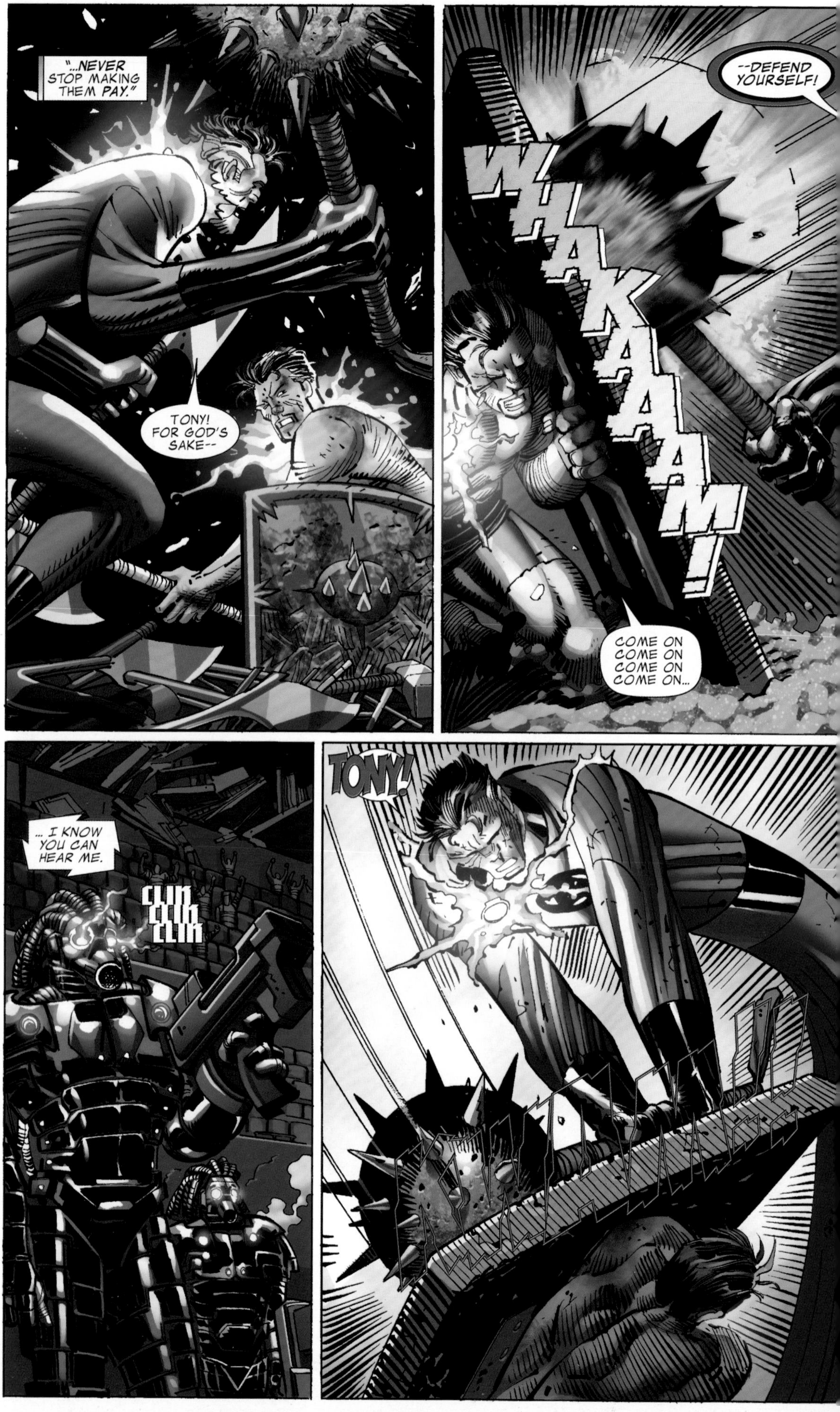
"...NEVER STOP MAKING THEM PAY."
TONY! FOR GOD'S SAKE--
--DEFEND YOURSELF!
WHAKAAAM!
COME ON COME ON COME ON COME ON...
... I KNOW YOU CAN HEAR ME.
TONY!

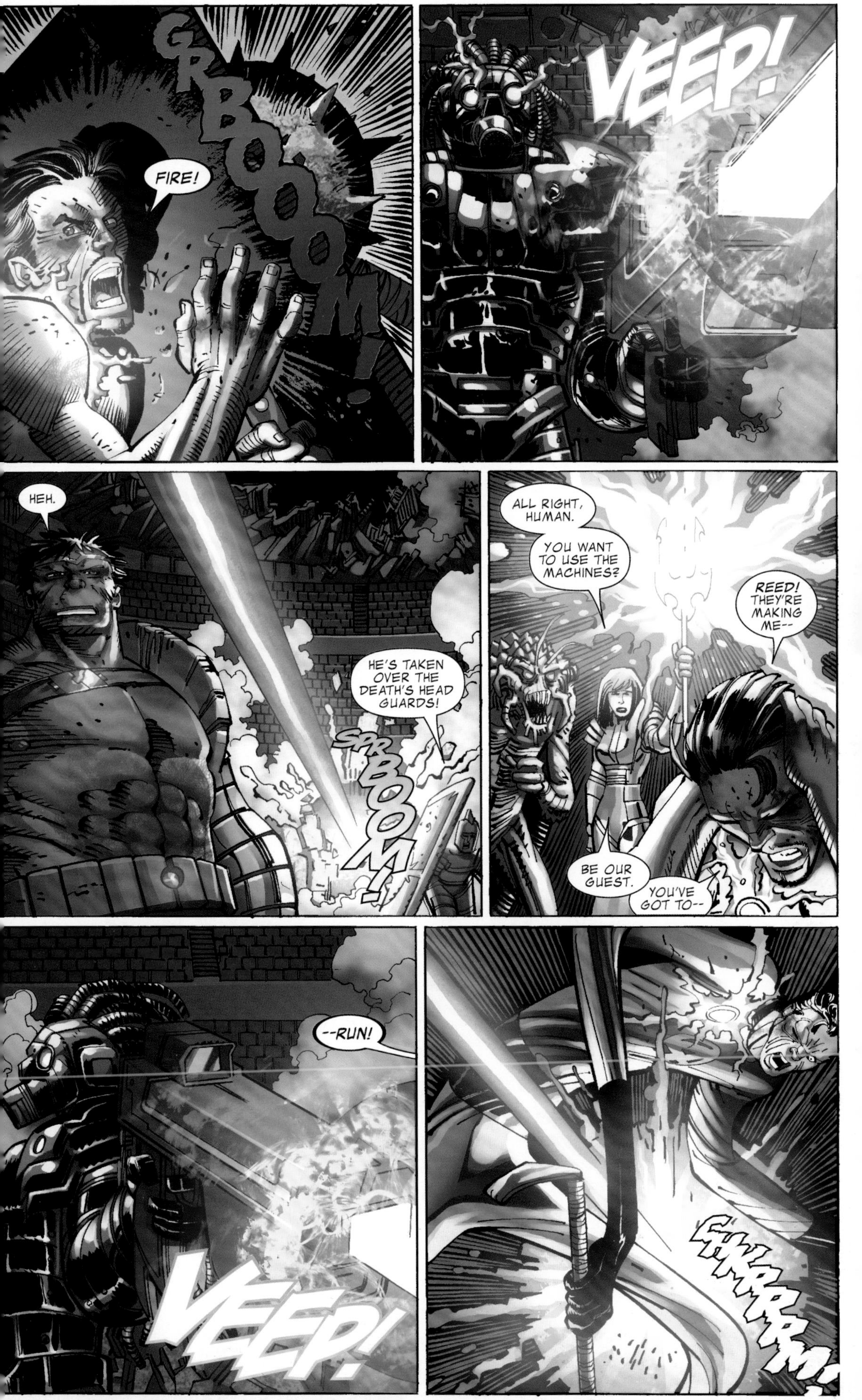

GRBOOOOM
FIRE!
VEEP!
HEH.
HE'S TAKEN OVER THE DEATH'S HEAD GUARDS!
SPRBOOOM!
ALL RIGHT, HUMAN.
YOU WANT TO USE THE MACHINES?
BE OUR GUEST.
REED! THEY'RE MAKING ME--
YOU'VE GOT TO--
--RUN!
VEEP!
SHKRRRM!

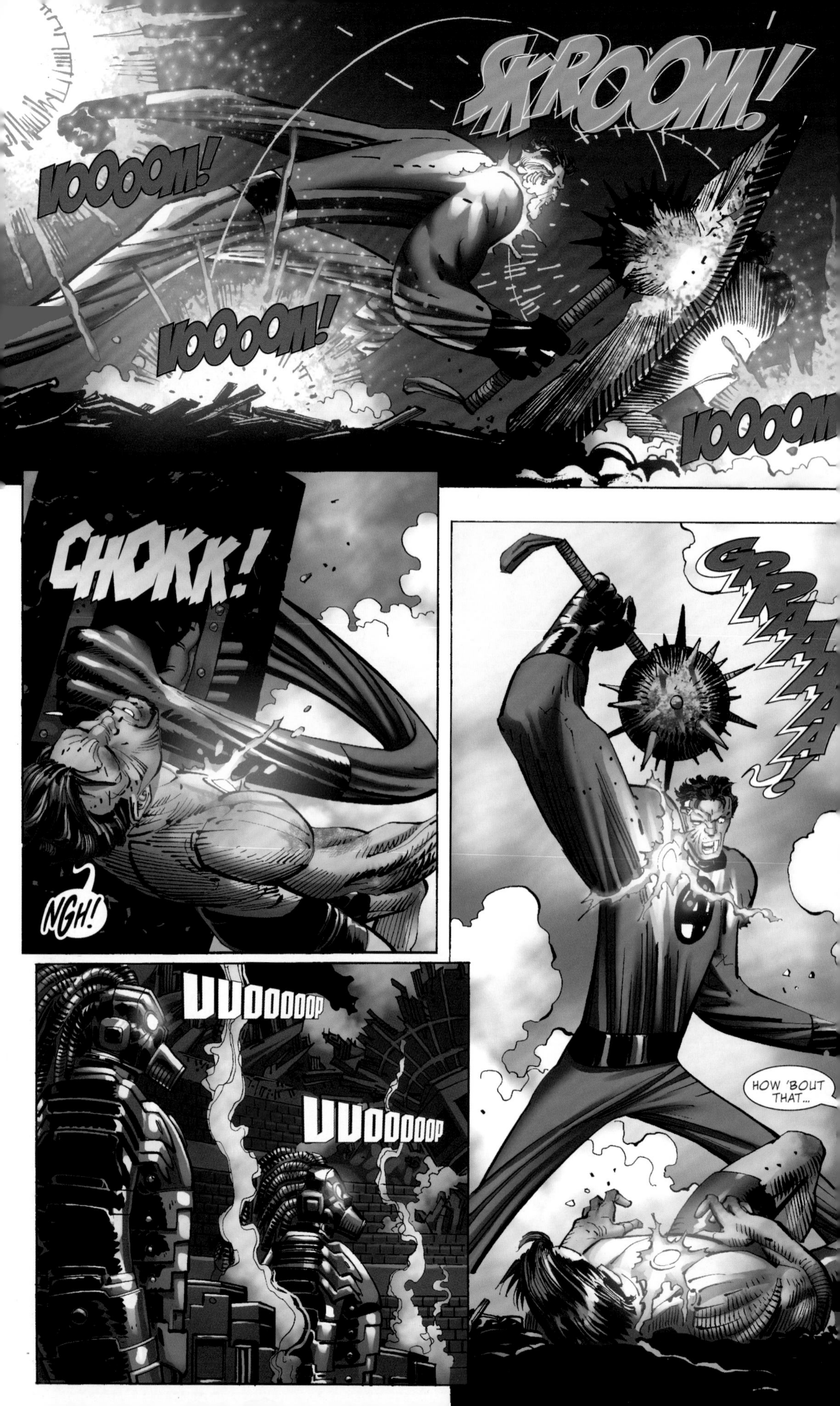
SKROOM!
VOOOOM!
VOOOOM!
VOOOOM
CHOKK!
NGH!
GRRAAAAAA!
UVOOOOOOP
UVOOOOOOP
HOW 'BOUT THAT...

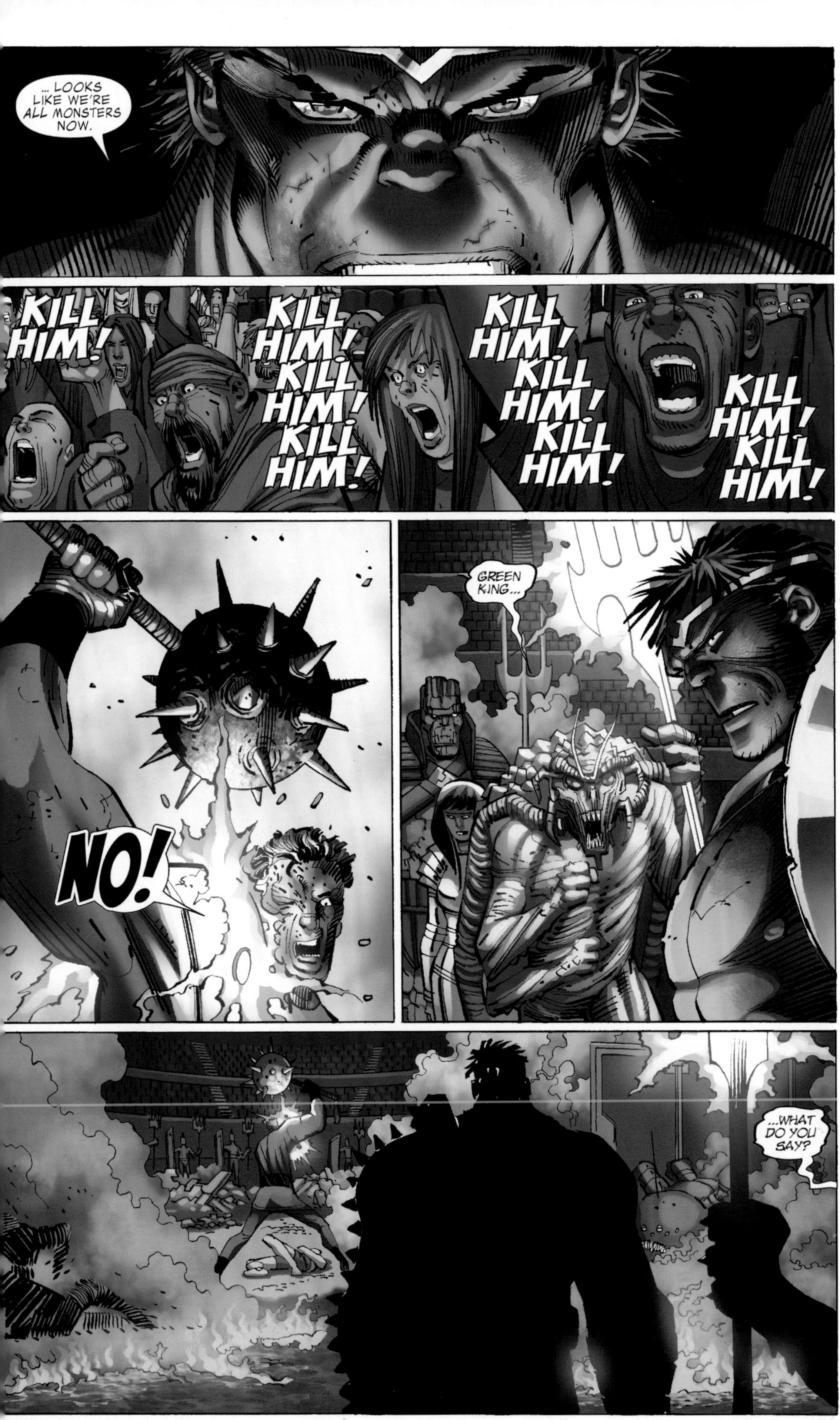
...LOOKS LIKE WE'RE ALL MONSTERS NOW.
KILL HIM!
KILL HIM! KILL HIM! KILL HIM!
KILL HIM! KILL HIM! KILL HIM!
KILL HIM! KILL HIM!
NO!
GREEN KING...
...WHAT DO YOU SAY?

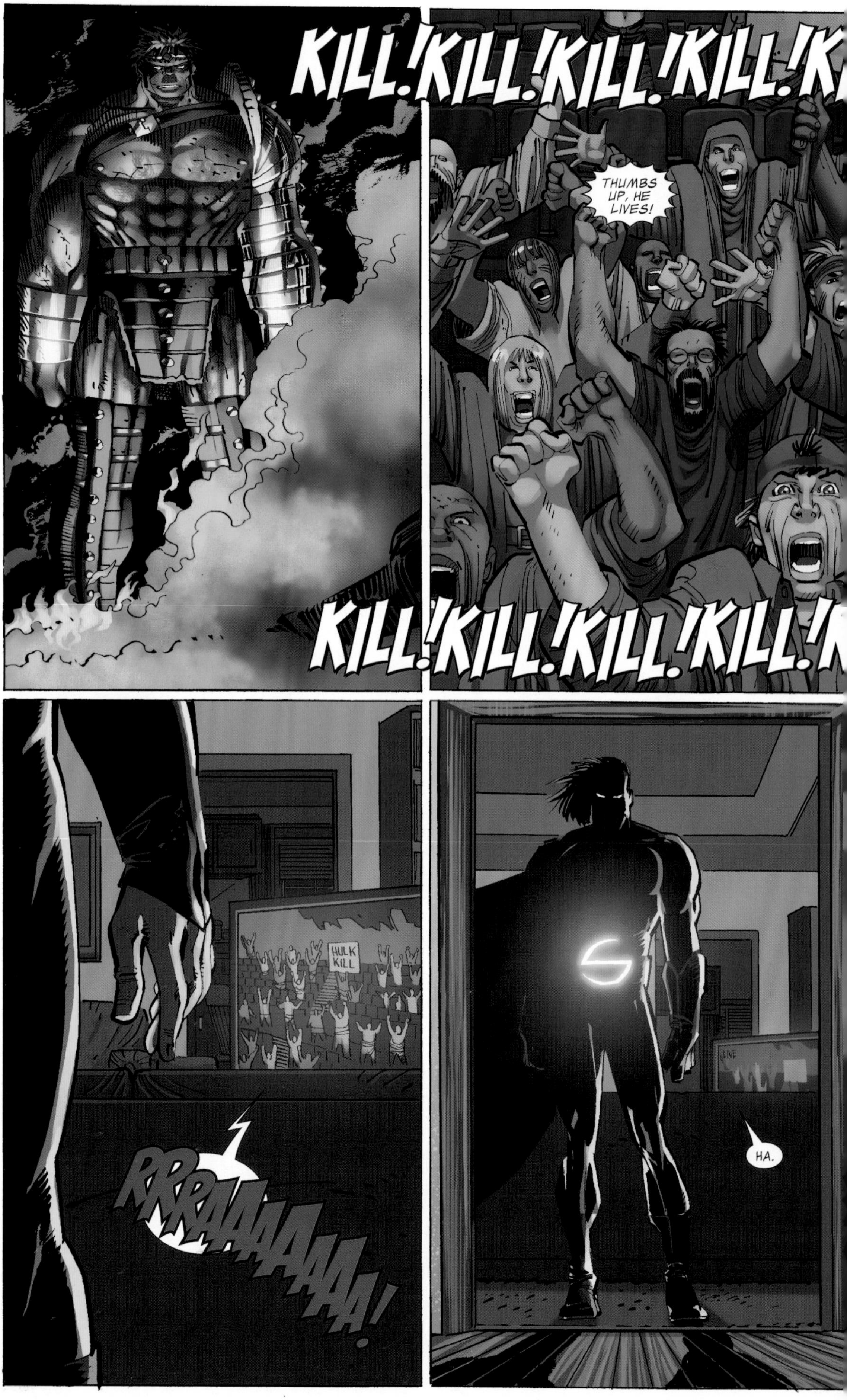

KILL! KILL! KILL! KILL! K
THUMBS UP, HE LIVES!
KILL! KILL! KILL! KILL! K
HULK KILL
RRRAAAAAAAAA!
LIVE
HA.

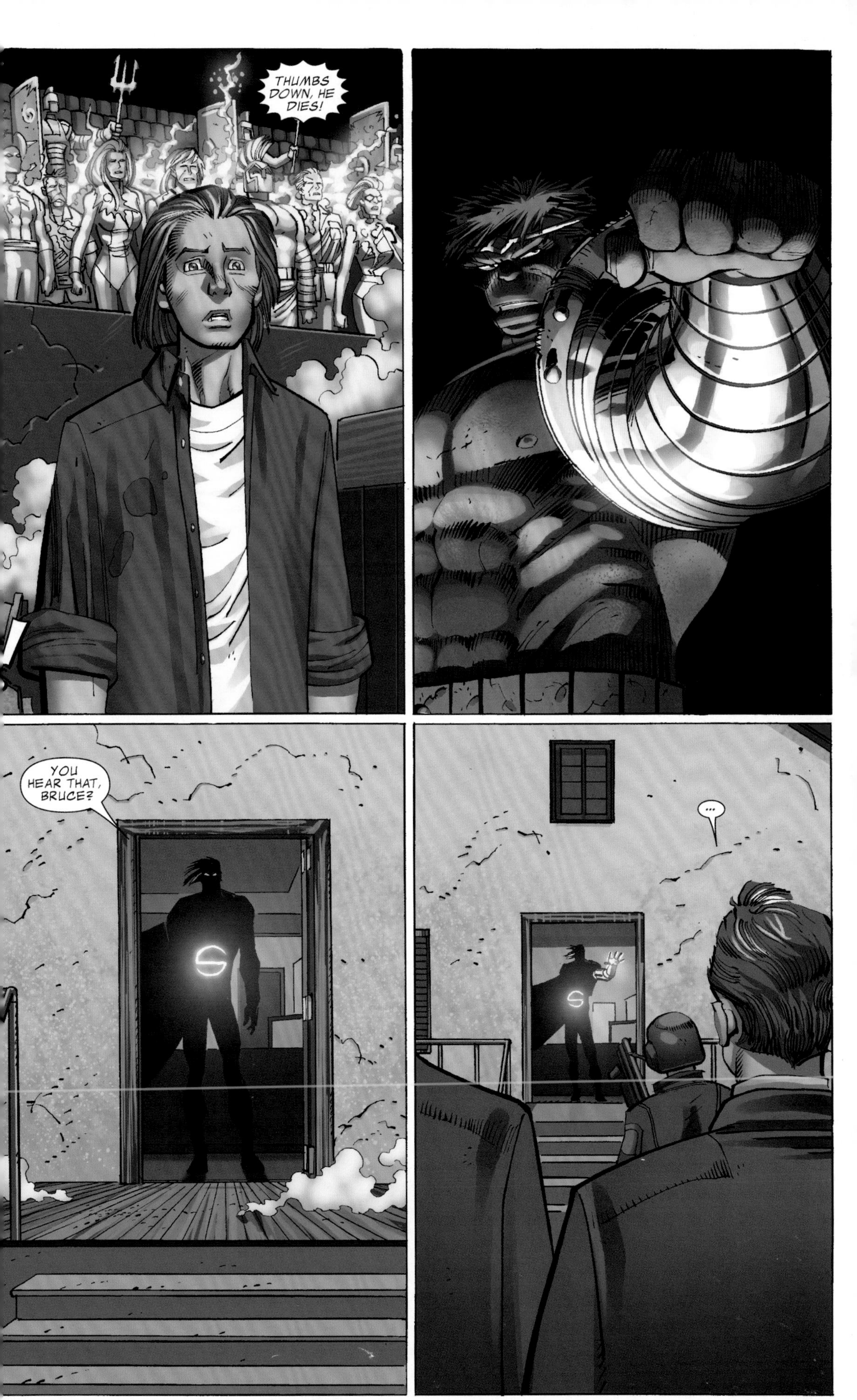
THUMBS DOWN, HE DIES!
YOU HEAR THAT, BRUCE?
...

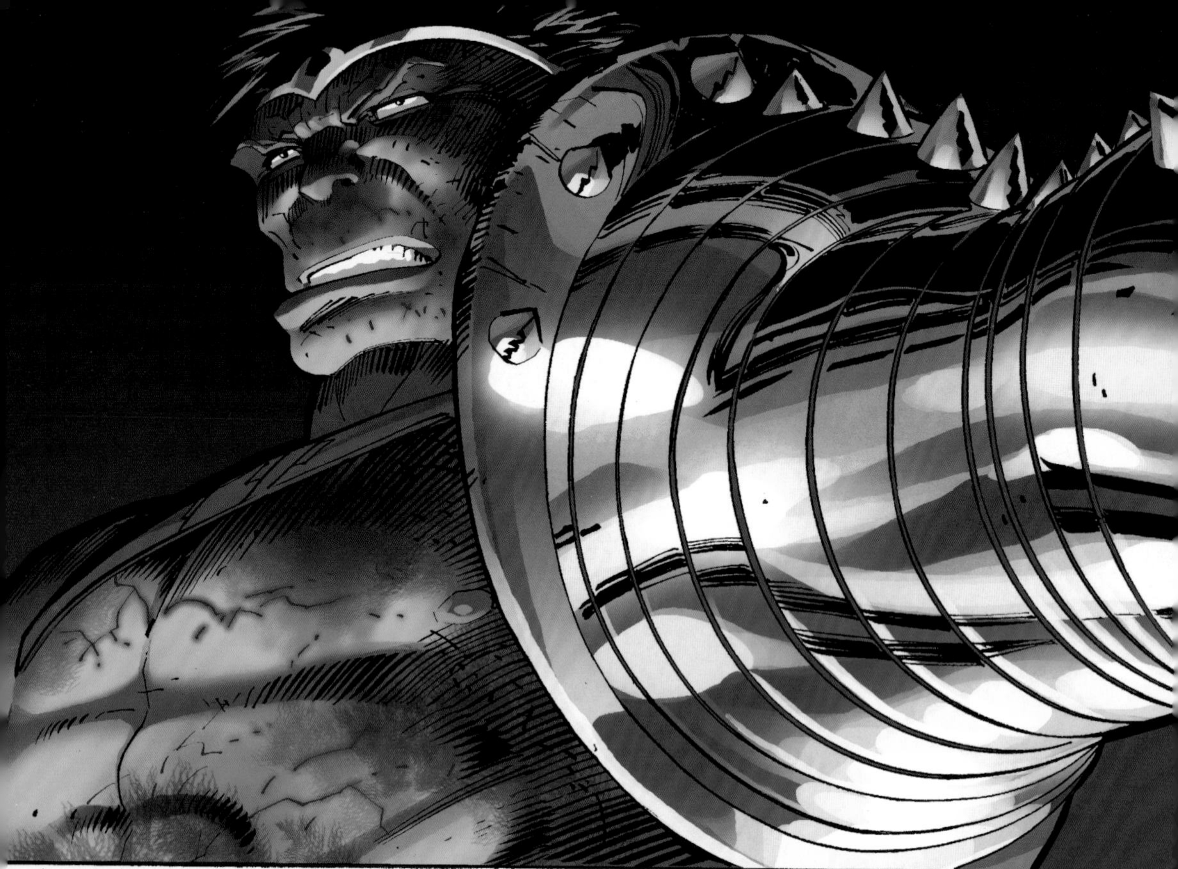

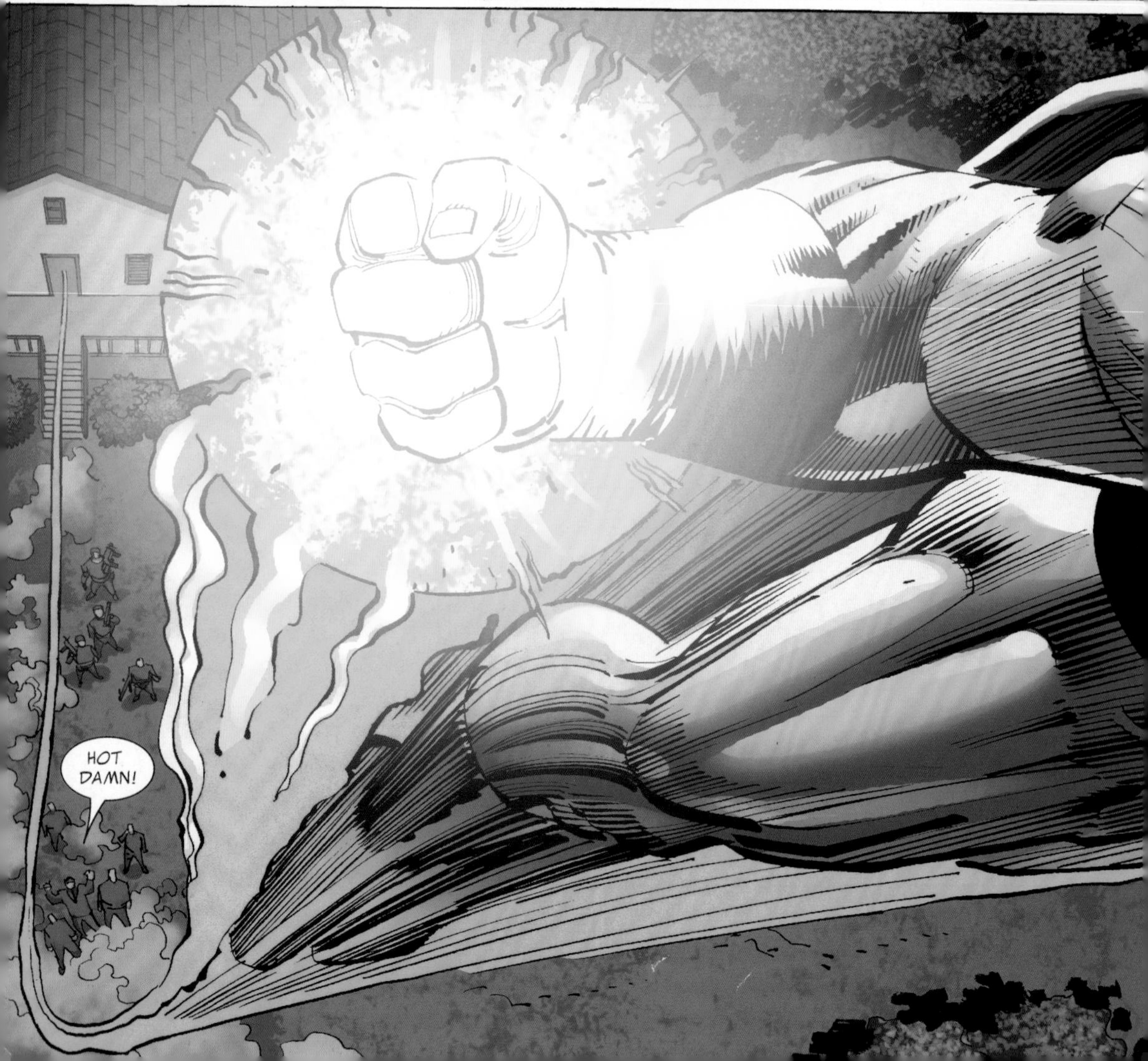
HOT DAMN!

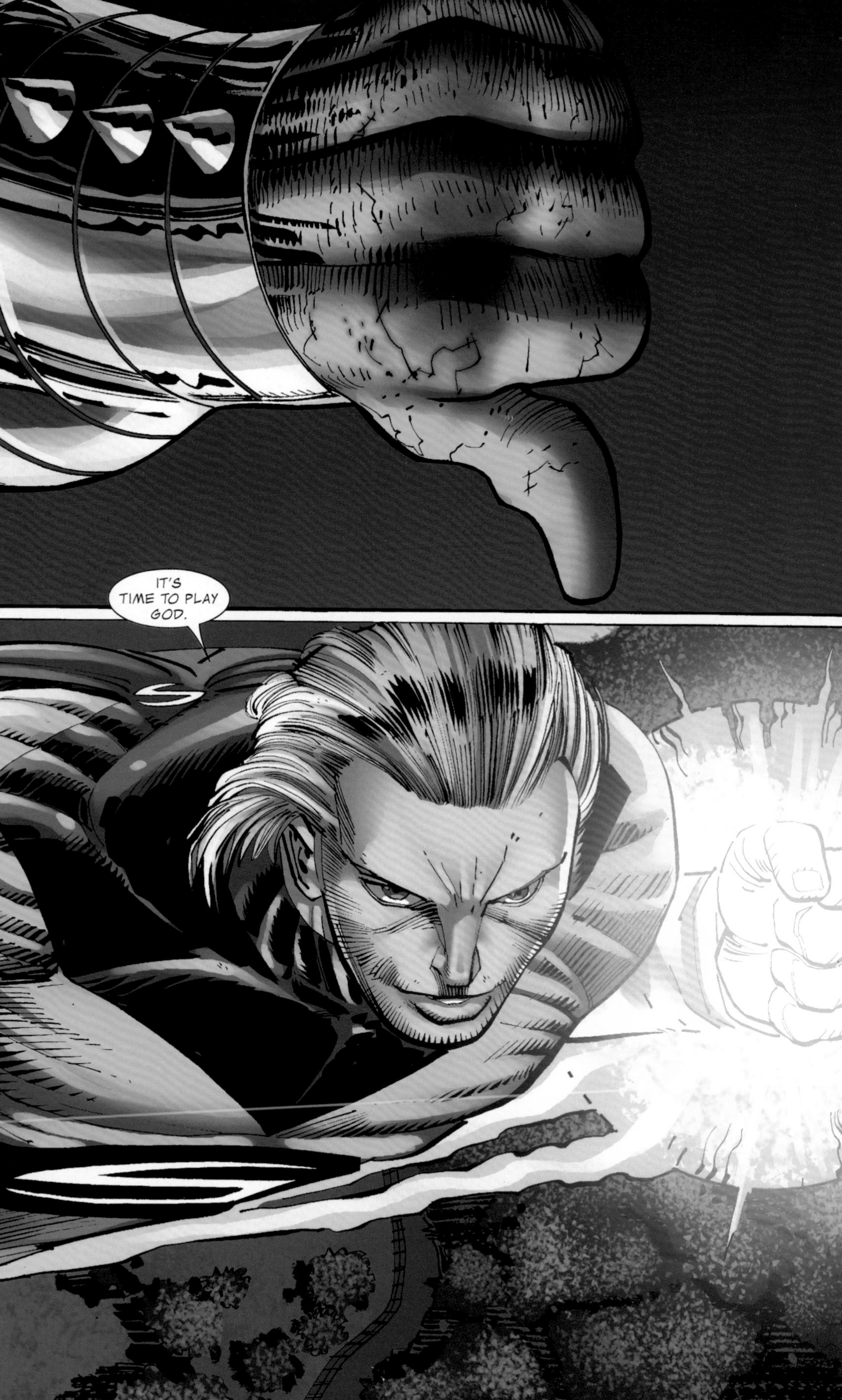
IT'S TIME TO PLAY GOD.

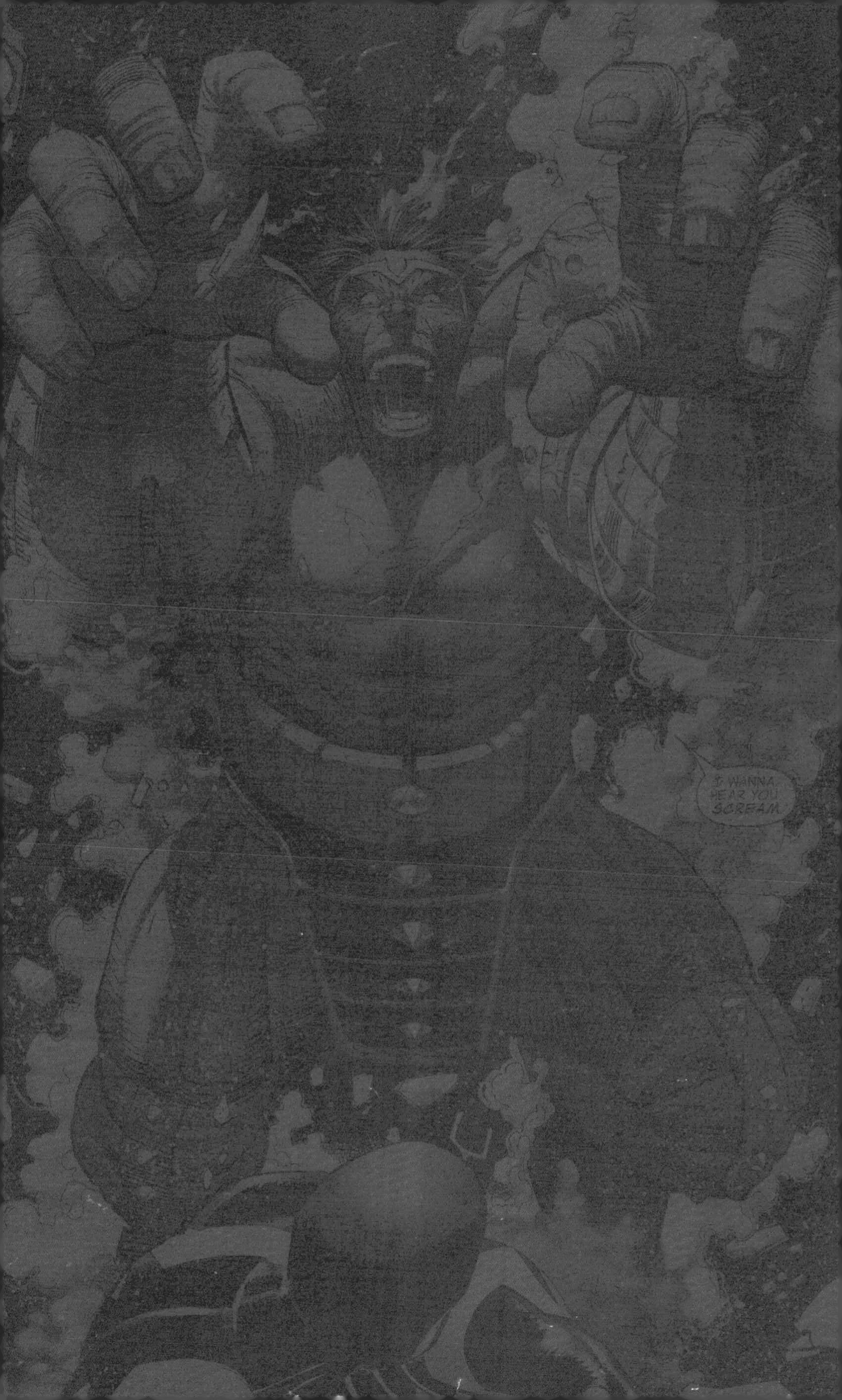
I WANNA HEAR YOU SCREAM

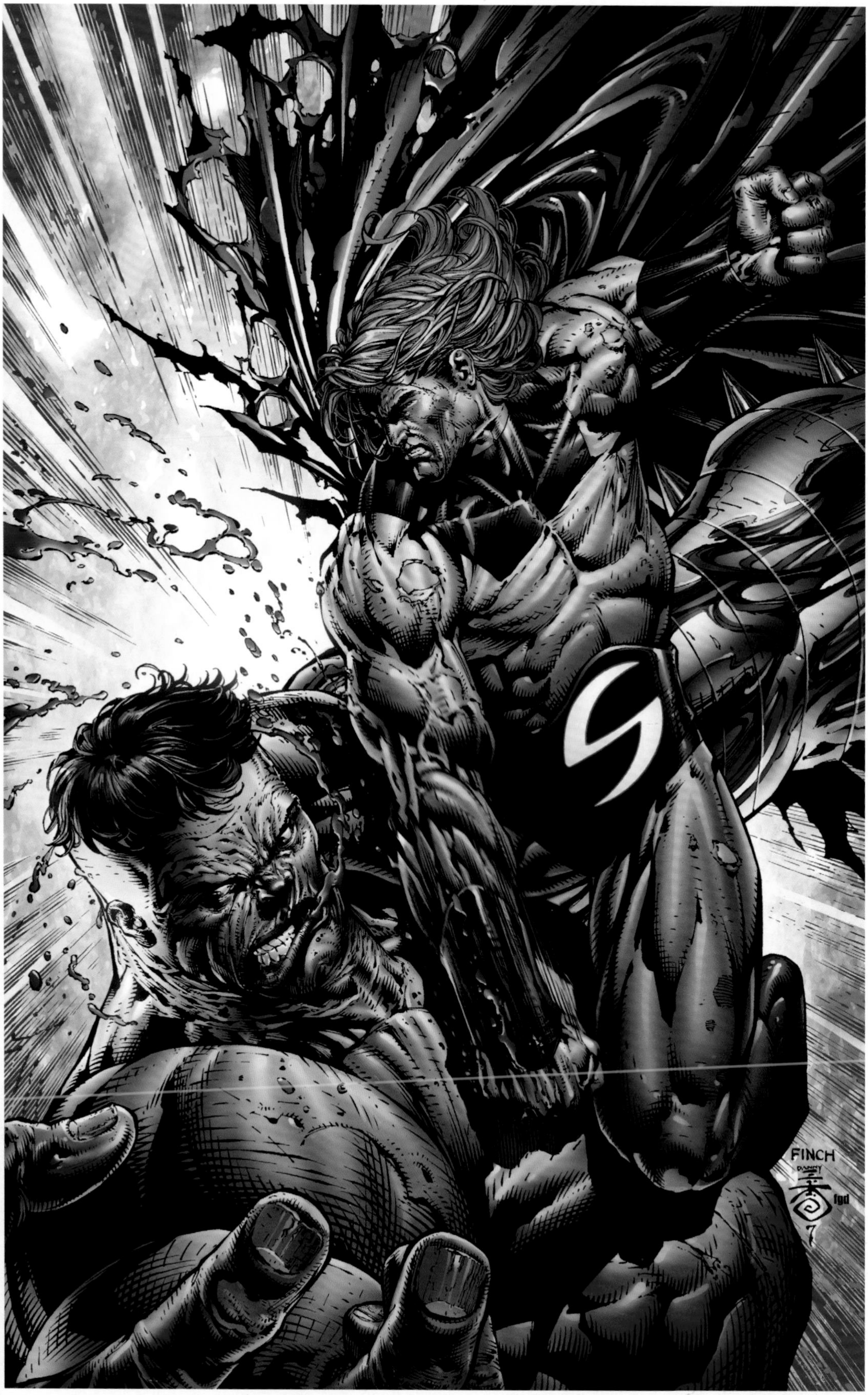
FINCH

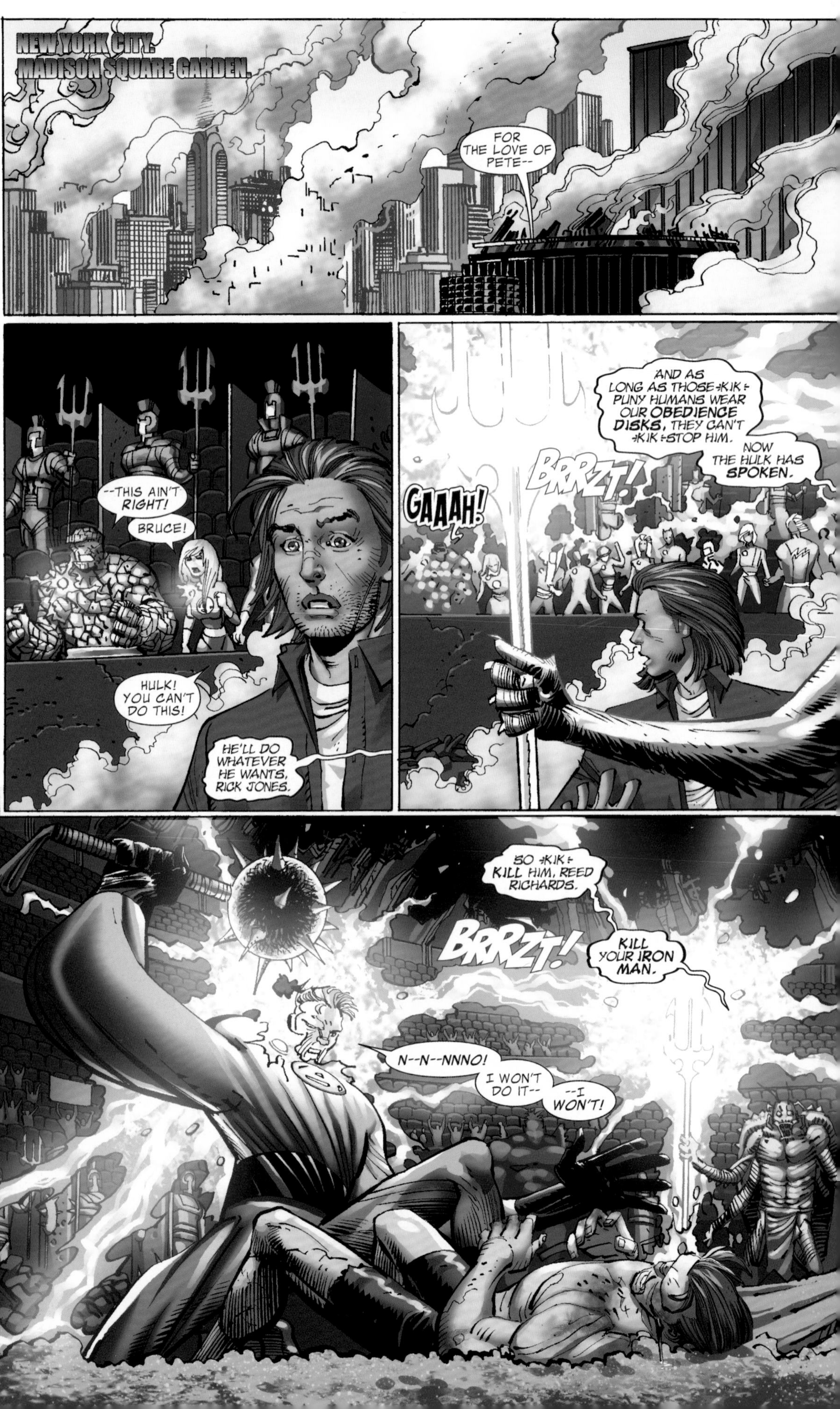
NEW YORK CITY.
MADISON SQUARE GARDEN.
FOR THE LOVE OF PETE--
--THIS AIN'T RIGHT!
BRUCE!
HULK! YOU CAN'T DO THIS!
HE'LL DO WHATEVER HE WANTS, RICK JONES.
AND AS LONG AS THOSE *KIK* PUNY HUMANS WEAR OUR OBEDIENCE DISKS, THEY CAN'T *KIK* STOP HIM.
NOW THE HULK HAS SPOKEN.
BRRZT!
GAAAH!
SO *KIK* KILL HIM, REED RICHARDS.
BRRZT!
KILL YOUR IRON MAN.
N--N--NNNO!
I WON'T DO IT--
--I WON'T!

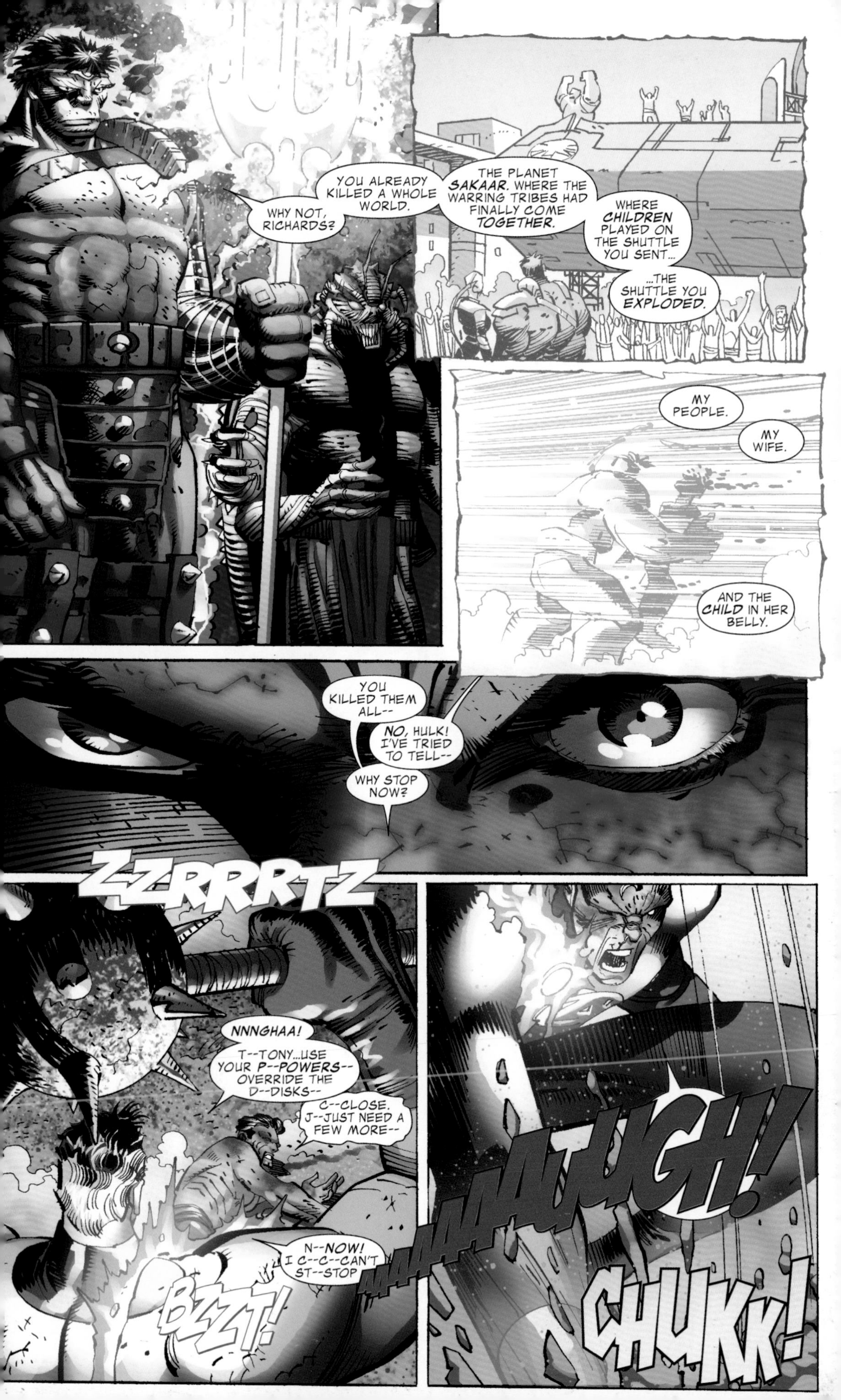

WHY NOT, RICHARDS?
YOU ALREADY KILLED A WHOLE WORLD.
THE PLANET SAKAAR. WHERE THE WARRING TRIBES HAD FINALLY COME TOGETHER.
WHERE CHILDREN PLAYED ON THE SHUTTLE YOU SENT...
...THE SHUTTLE YOU EXPLODED.
MY PEOPLE.
MY WIFE.
AND THE CHILD IN HER BELLY.
YOU KILLED THEM ALL--
NO, HULK! I'VE TRIED TO TELL--
WHY STOP NOW?
ZZRRRRTZ
NNNGHAA!
T--TONY...USE YOUR P--POWERS-- OVERRIDE THE D--DISKS--
C--CLOSE. J--JUST NEED A FEW MORE--
N--NOW! I C--C--CAN'T ST--STOP
BZZT!
AAAAAAAAAUUGH!
CHUKK!

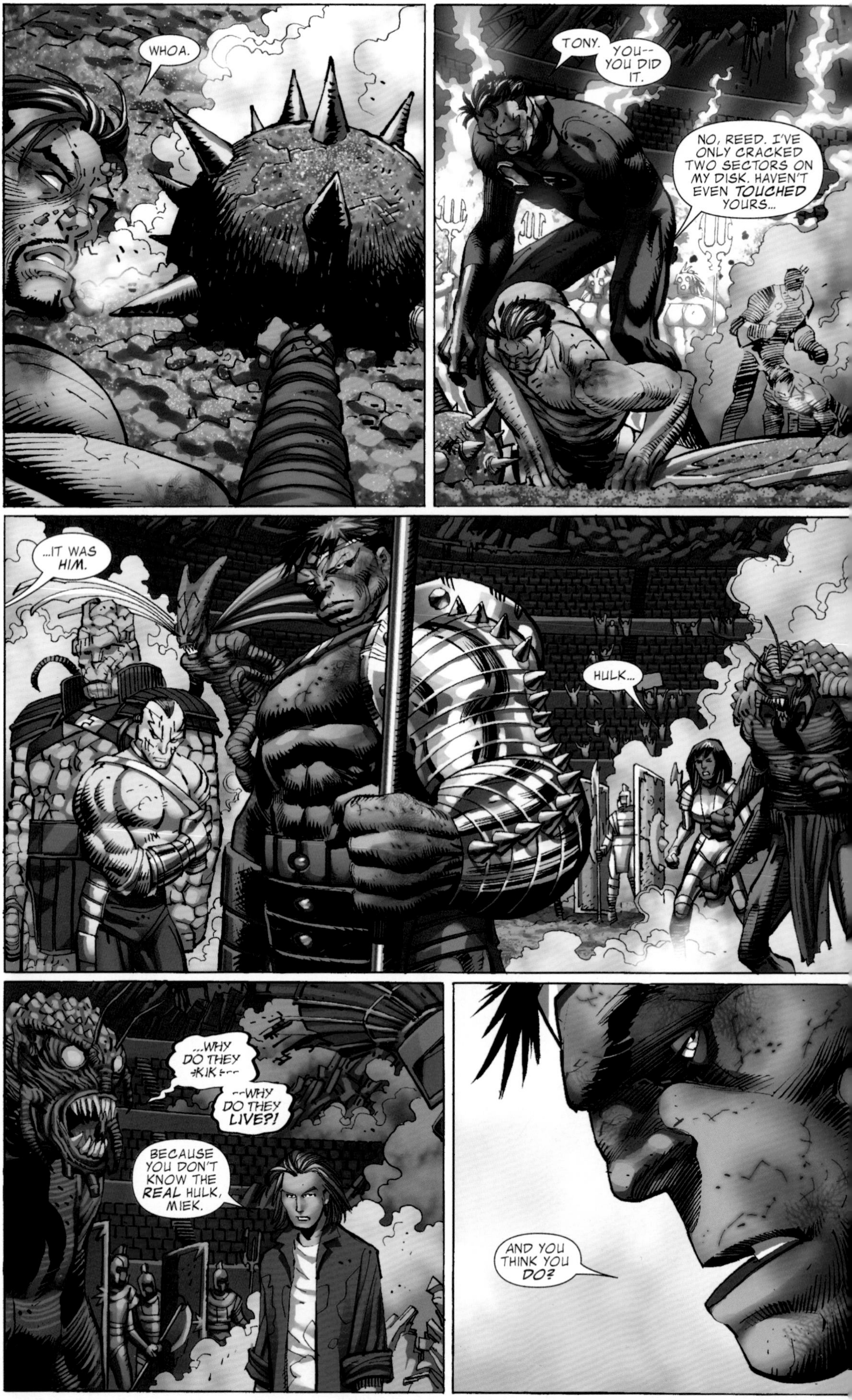
WHOA.
TONY.
YOU-- YOU DID IT.
NO, REED. I'VE ONLY CRACKED TWO SECTORS ON MY DISK. HAVEN'T EVEN TOUCHED YOURS...
...IT WAS HIM.
HULK...
...WHY DO THEY KIK---
--WHY DO THEY LIVE?!
BECAUSE YOU DON'T KNOW THE REAL HULK, MIEK.
AND YOU THINK YOU DO?

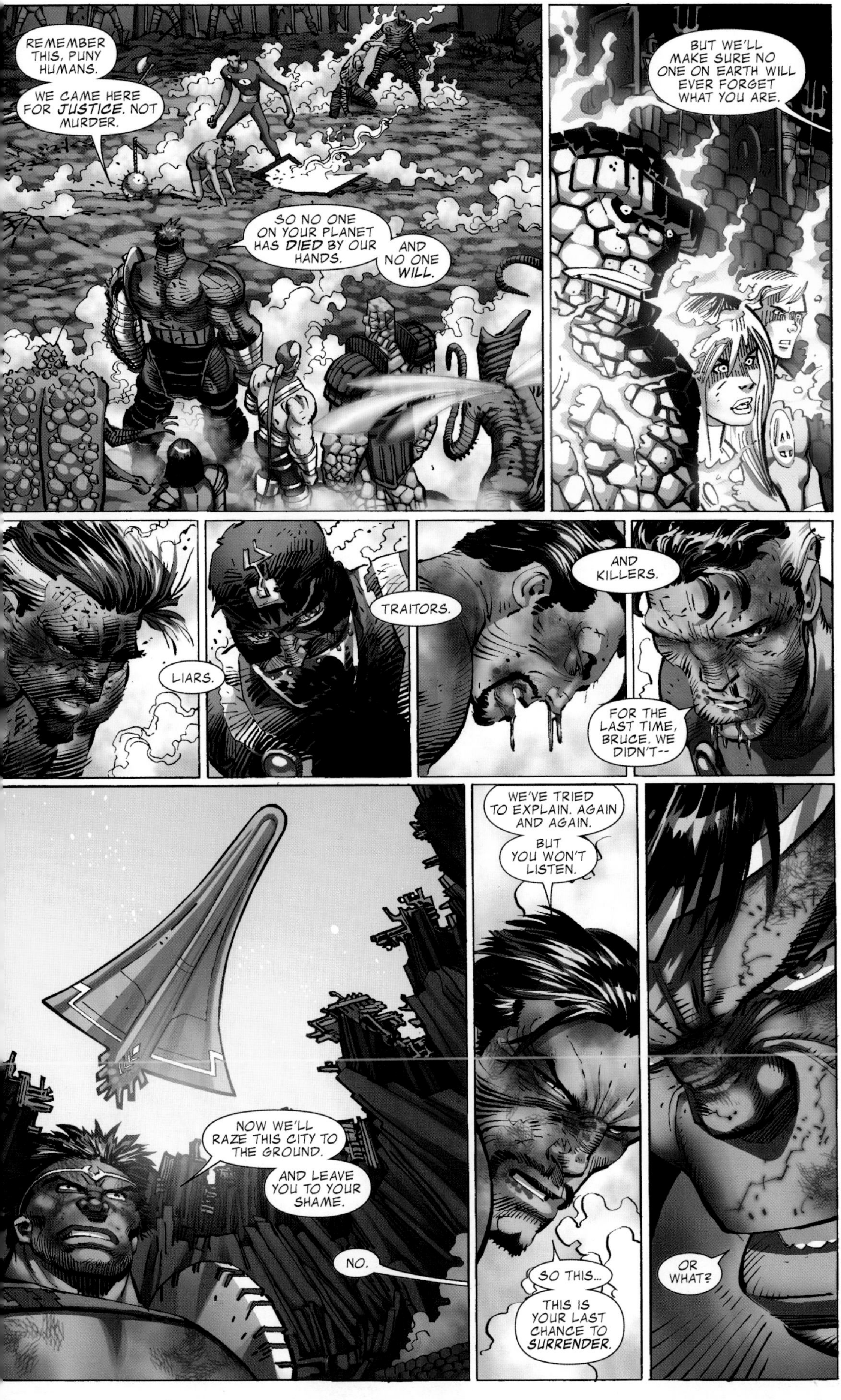
REMEMBER THIS, PUNY HUMANS.
WE CAME HERE FOR JUSTICE. NOT MURDER.
SO NO ONE ON YOUR PLANET HAS DIED BY OUR HANDS.
AND NO ONE WILL.
BUT WE'LL MAKE SURE NO ONE ON EARTH WILL EVER FORGET WHAT YOU ARE.
LIARS.
TRAITORS.
AND KILLERS.
FOR THE LAST TIME, BRUCE. WE DIDN'T--
NOW WE'LL RAZE THIS CITY TO THE GROUND.
AND LEAVE YOU TO YOUR SHAME.
NO.
WE'VE TRIED TO EXPLAIN. AGAIN AND AGAIN.
BUT YOU WON'T LISTEN.
SO THIS...
THIS IS YOUR LAST CHANCE TO SURRENDER.
OR WHAT?

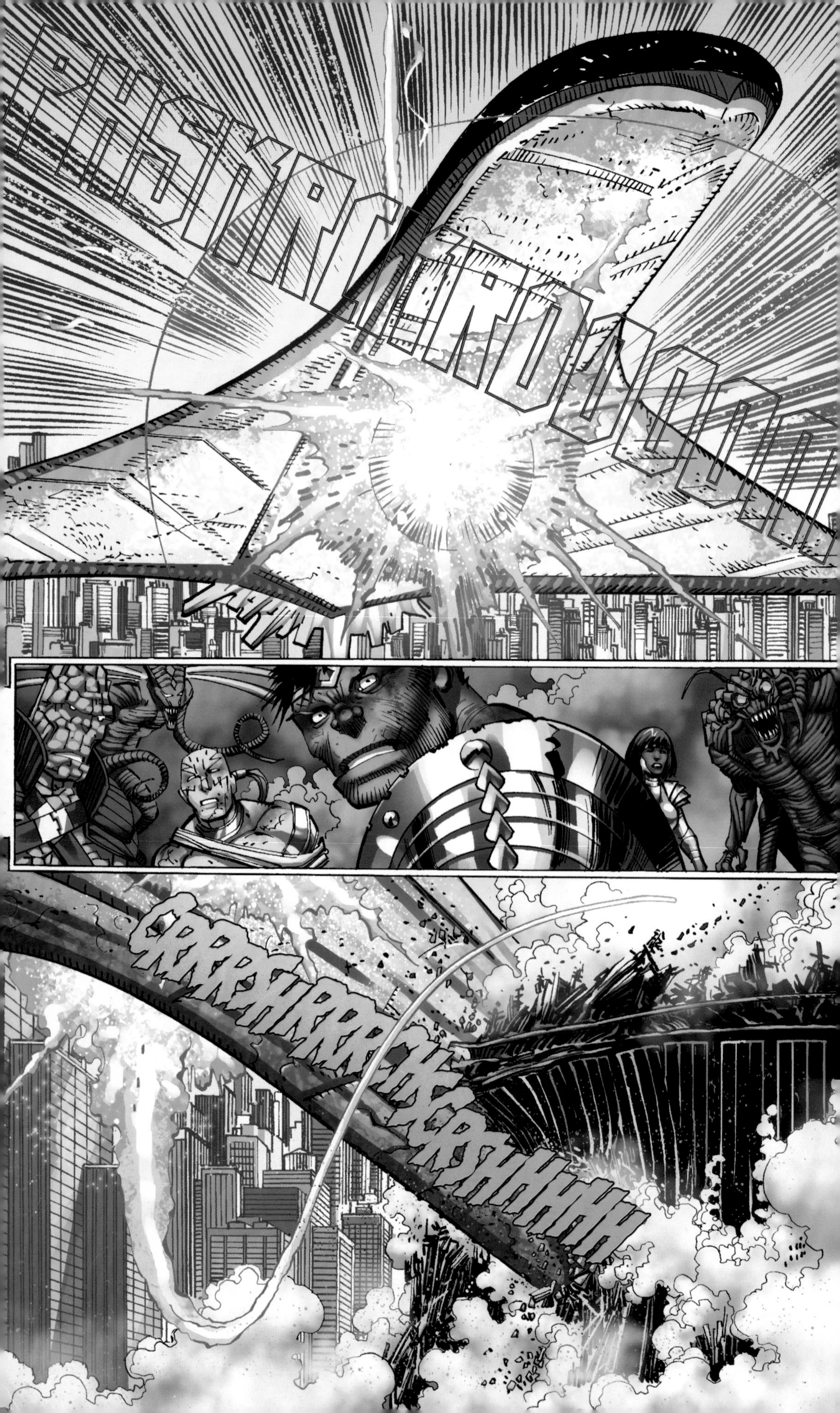
GRRRCHRRRRCHKRSHHHHH

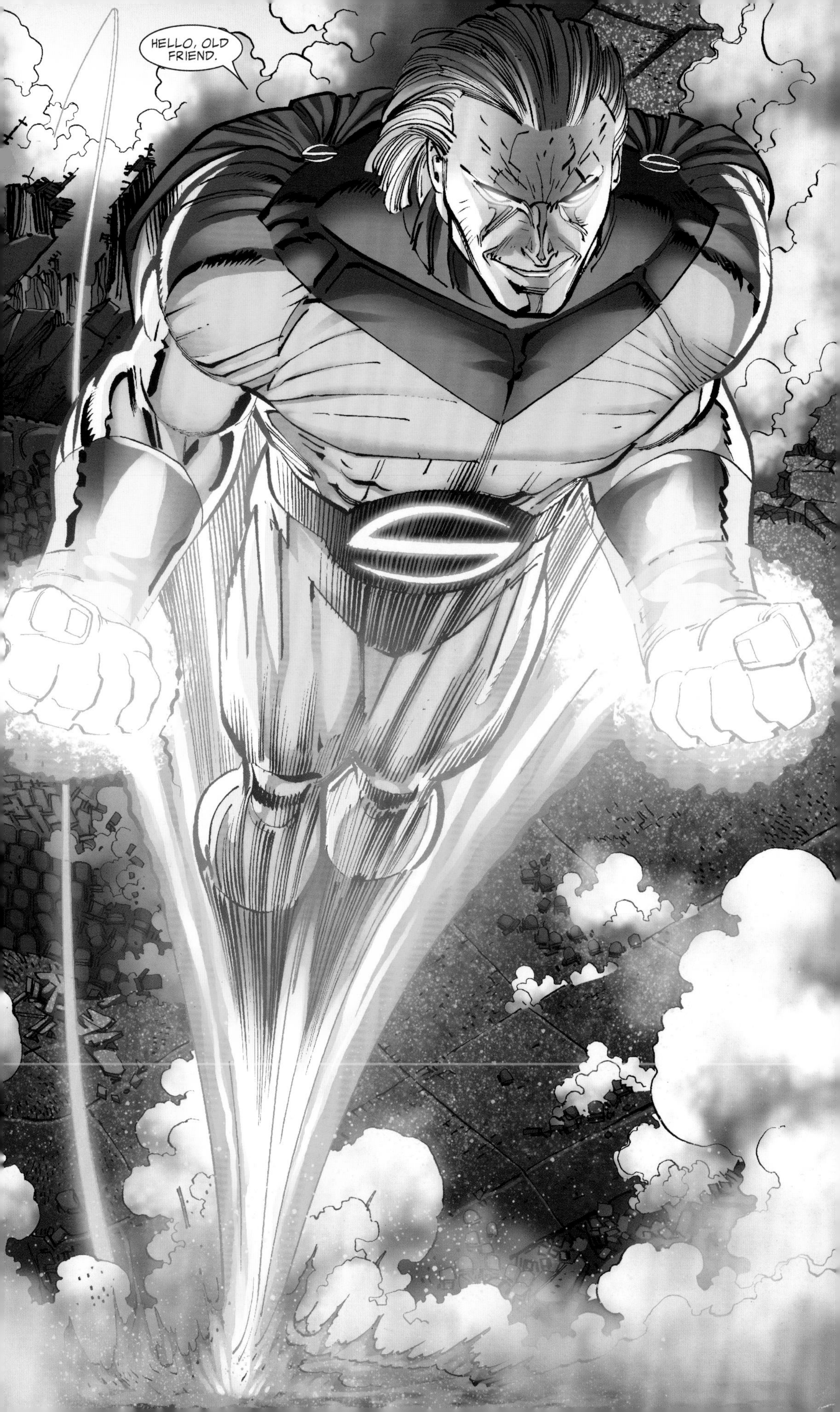
HELLO, OLD FRIEND.

KWAGLOO

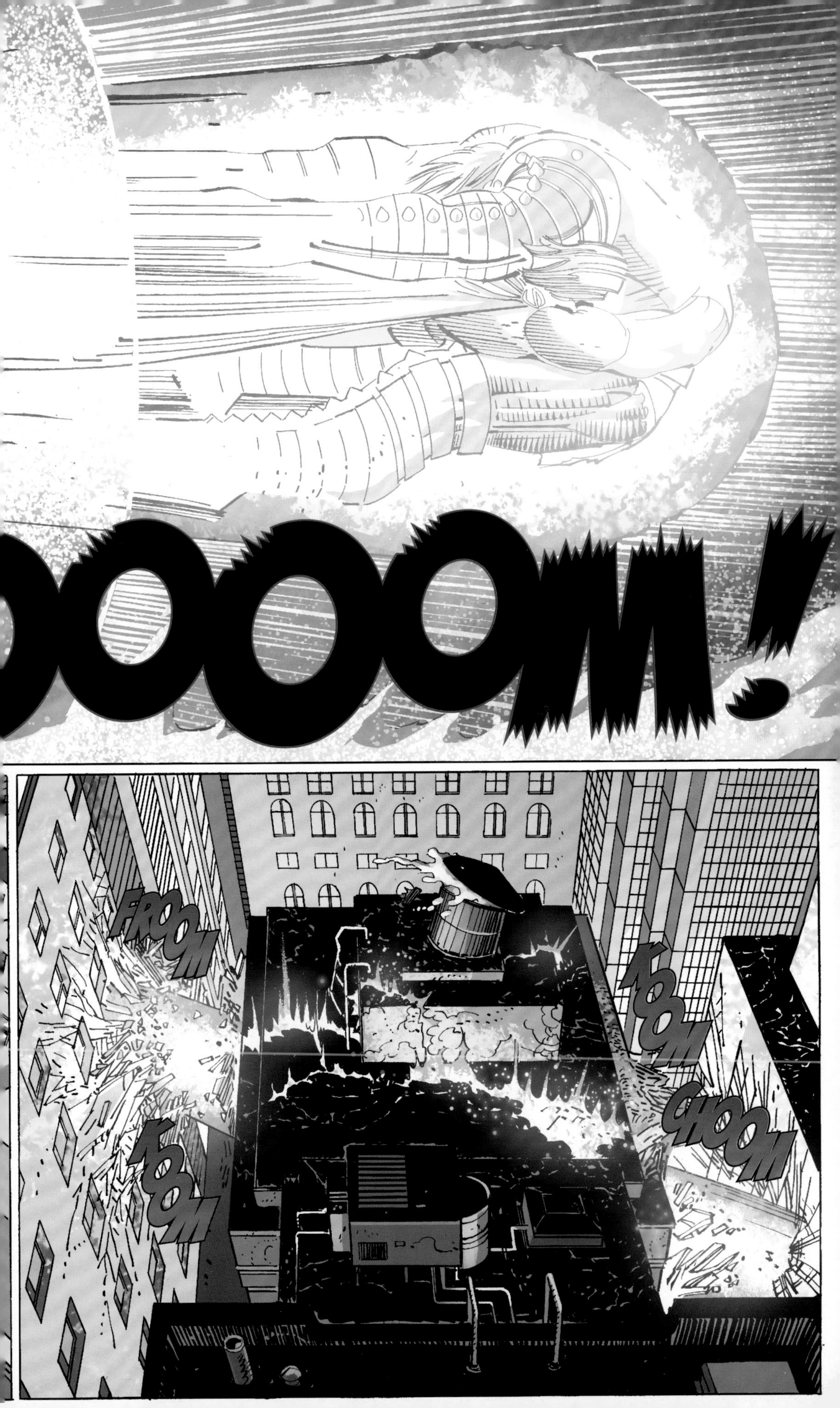
OOOM!
FROOM
KOOM
KOOM
CHOOM

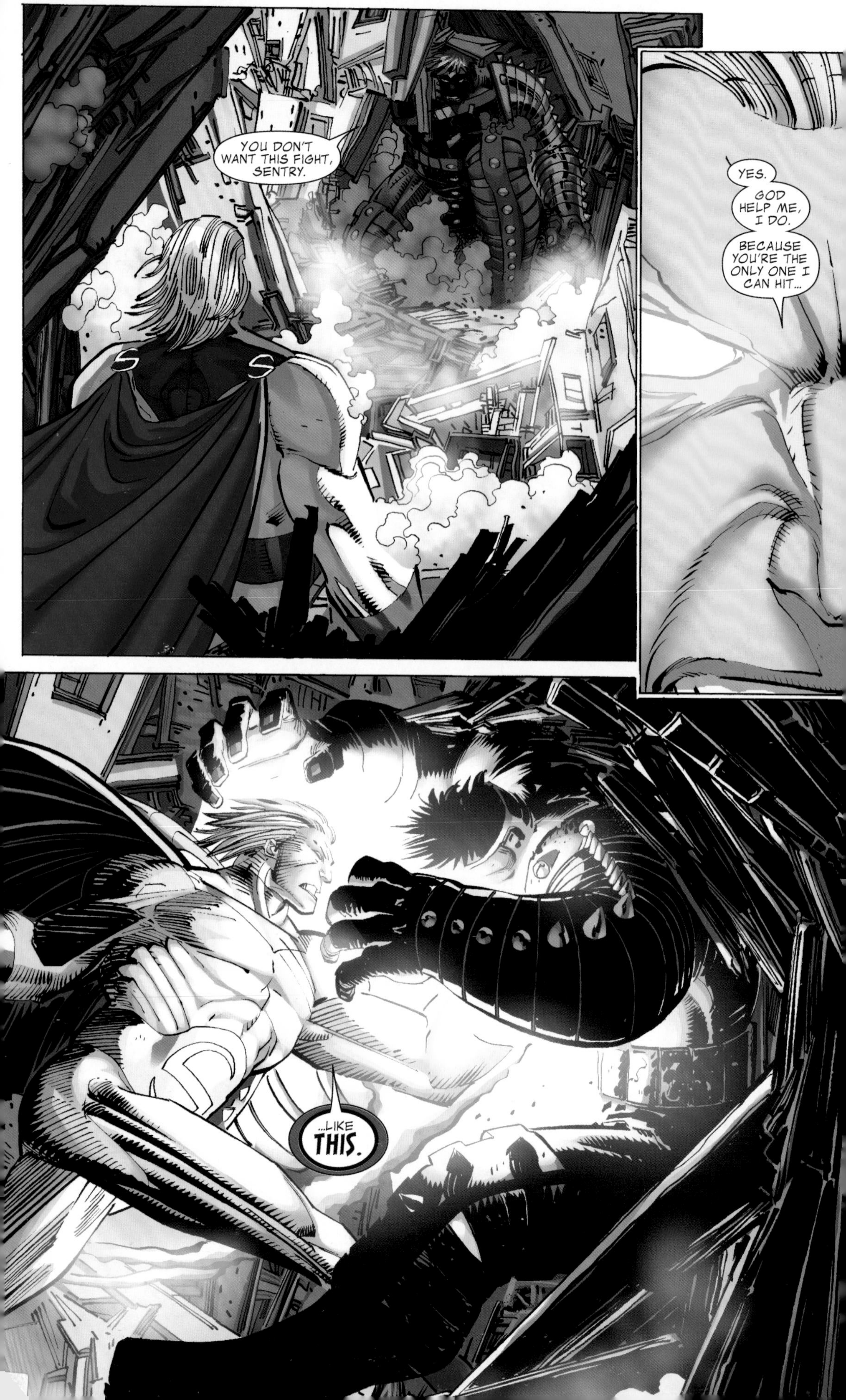
YOU DON'T WANT THIS FIGHT, SENTRY.
YES.
GOD HELP ME, I DO.
BECAUSE YOU'RE THE ONLY ONE I CAN HIT...
...LIKE THIS.

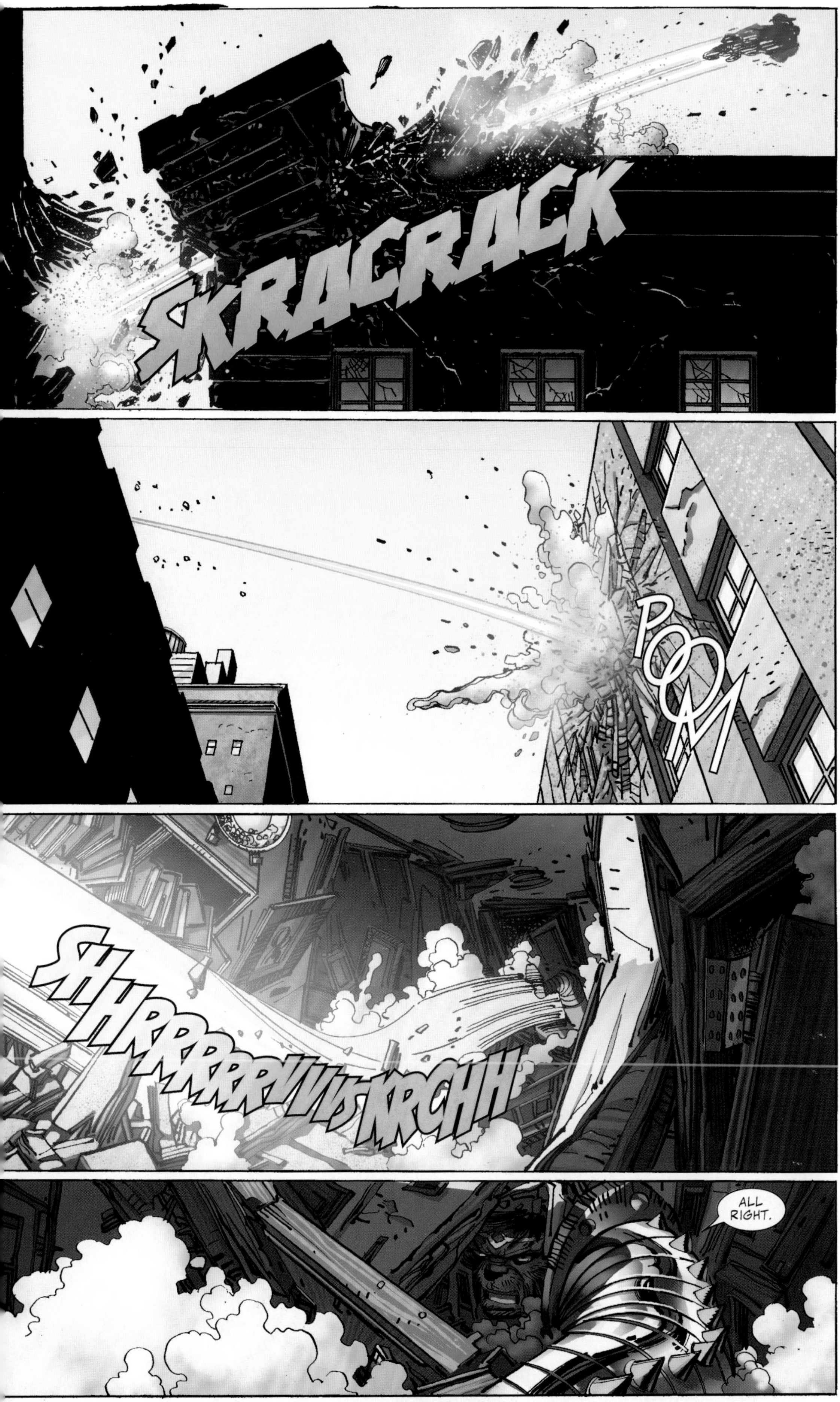
SKRACRACK
POOM
SHHRRRRRVVVS KRCHH
ALL RIGHT.

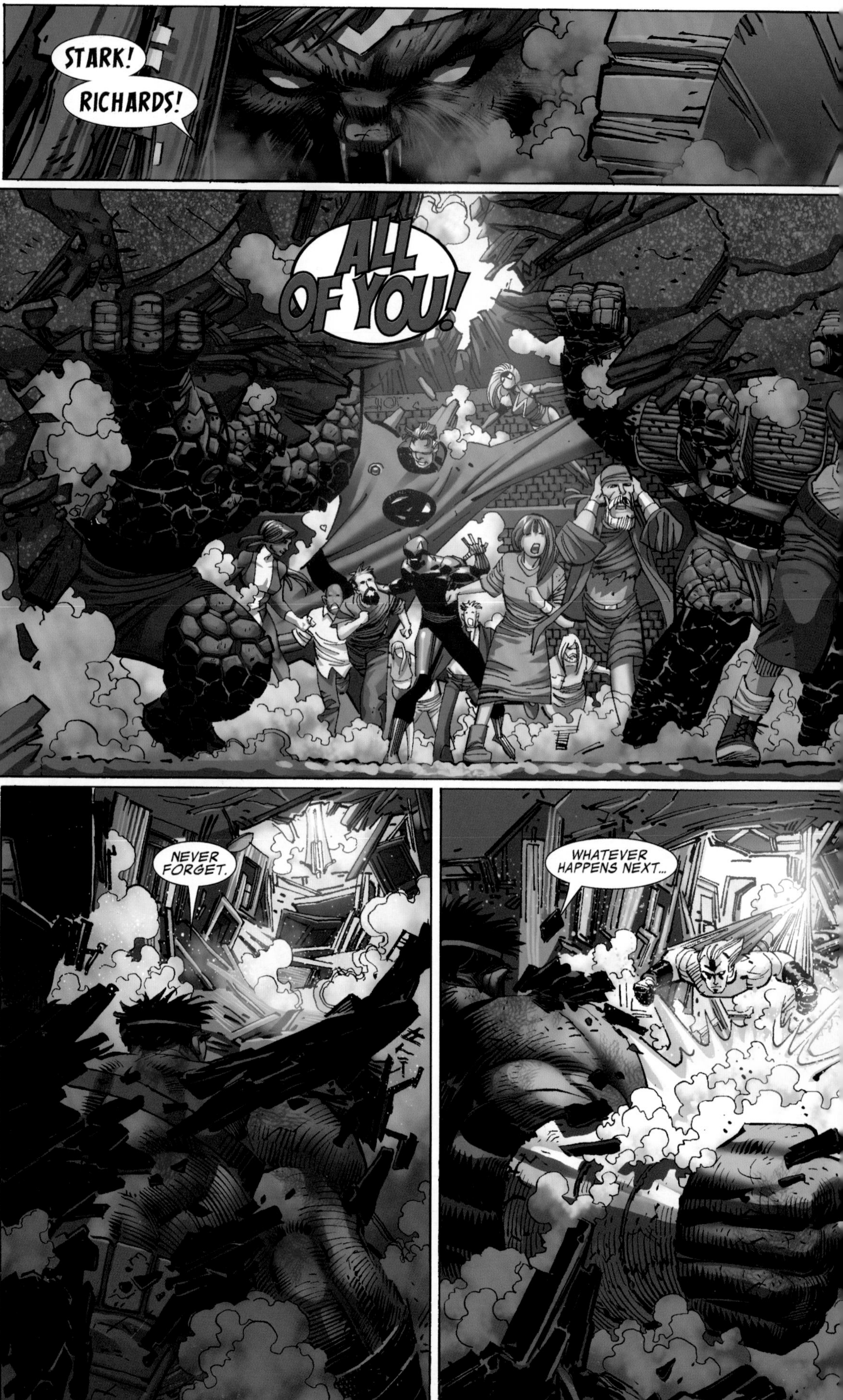
STARK!
RICHARDS!
ALL OF YOU!
NEVER FORGET.
WHATEVER HAPPENS NEXT...

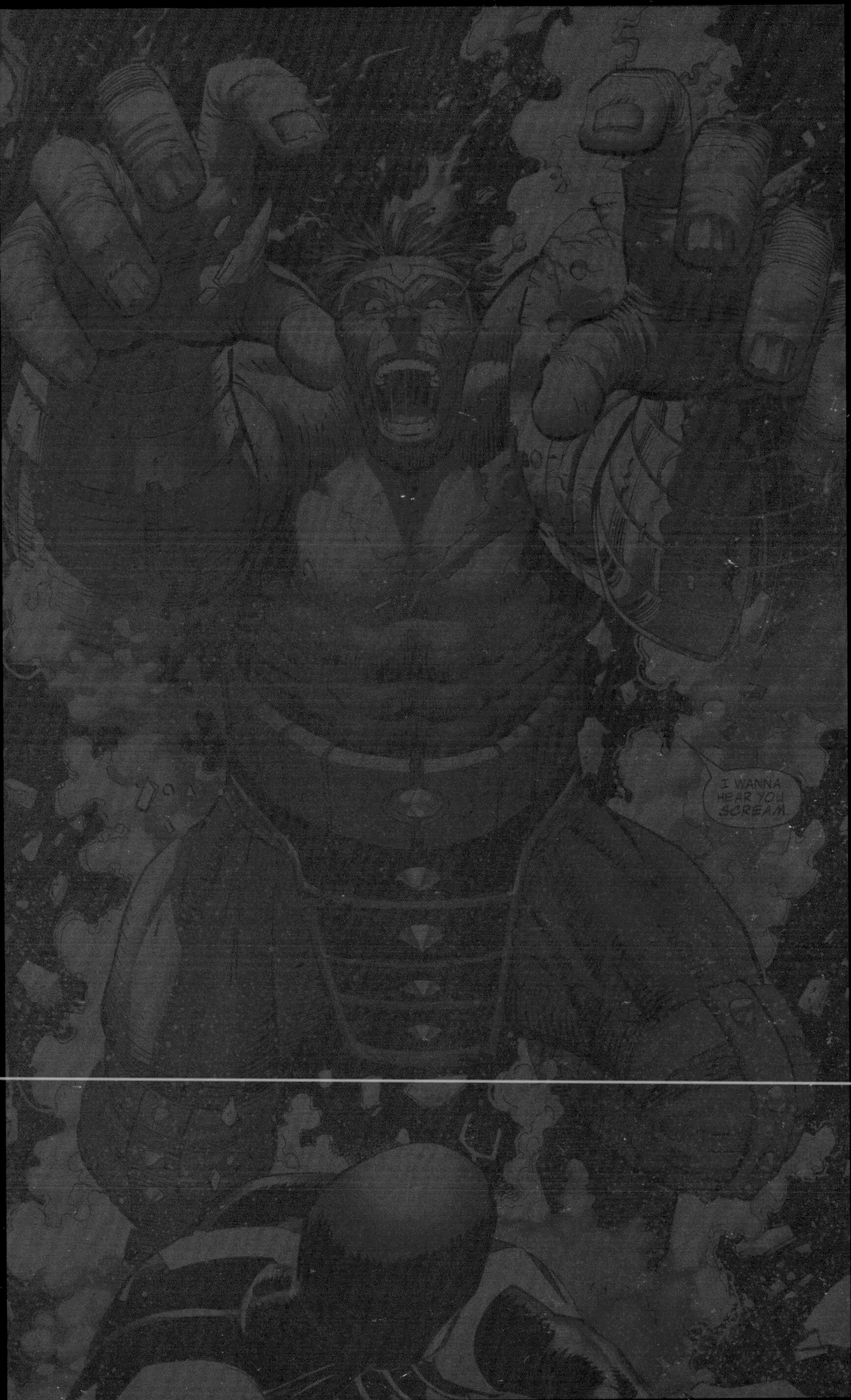
I WANNA HEAR YOU SCREAM.

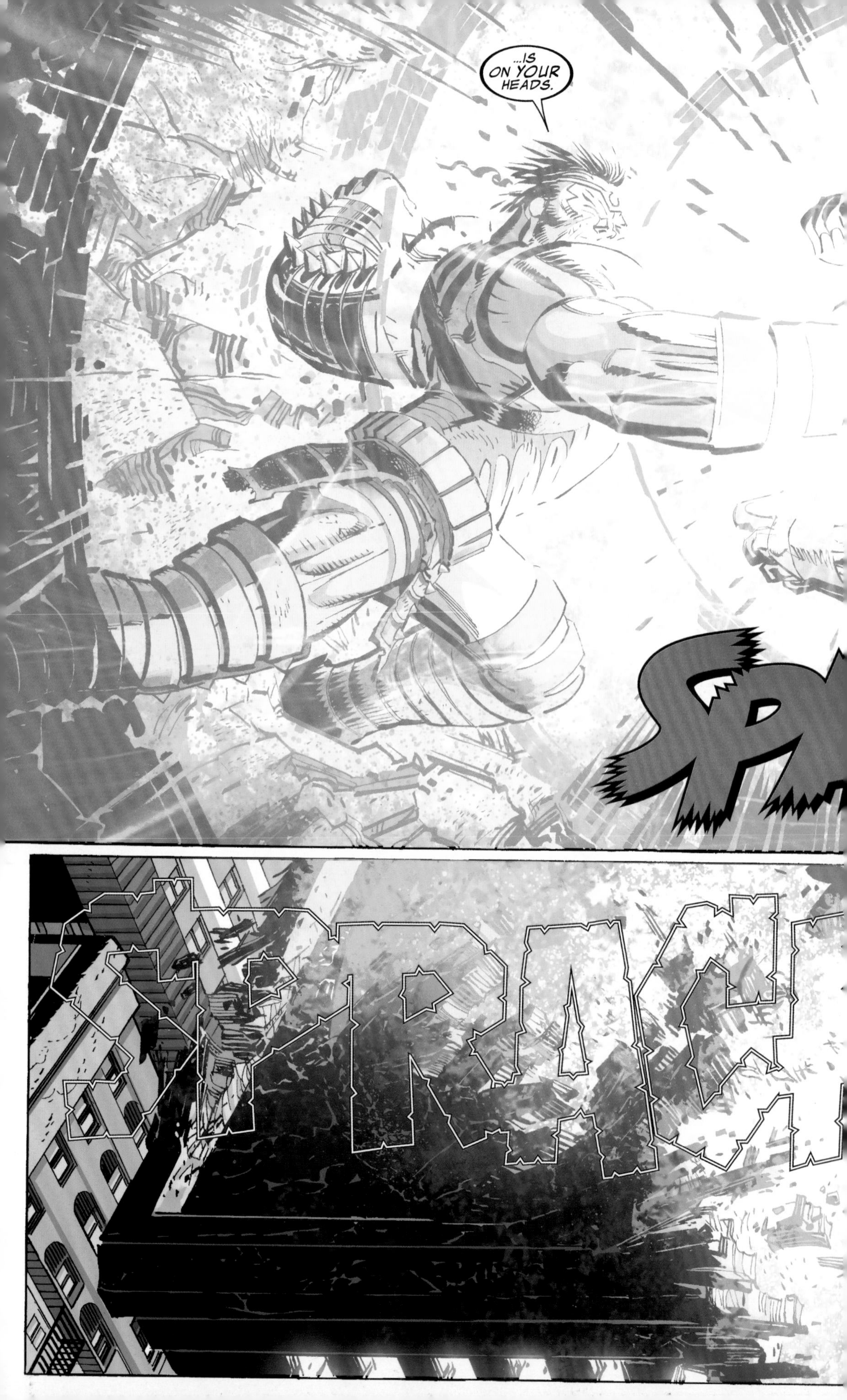
...IS ON YOUR HEADS.

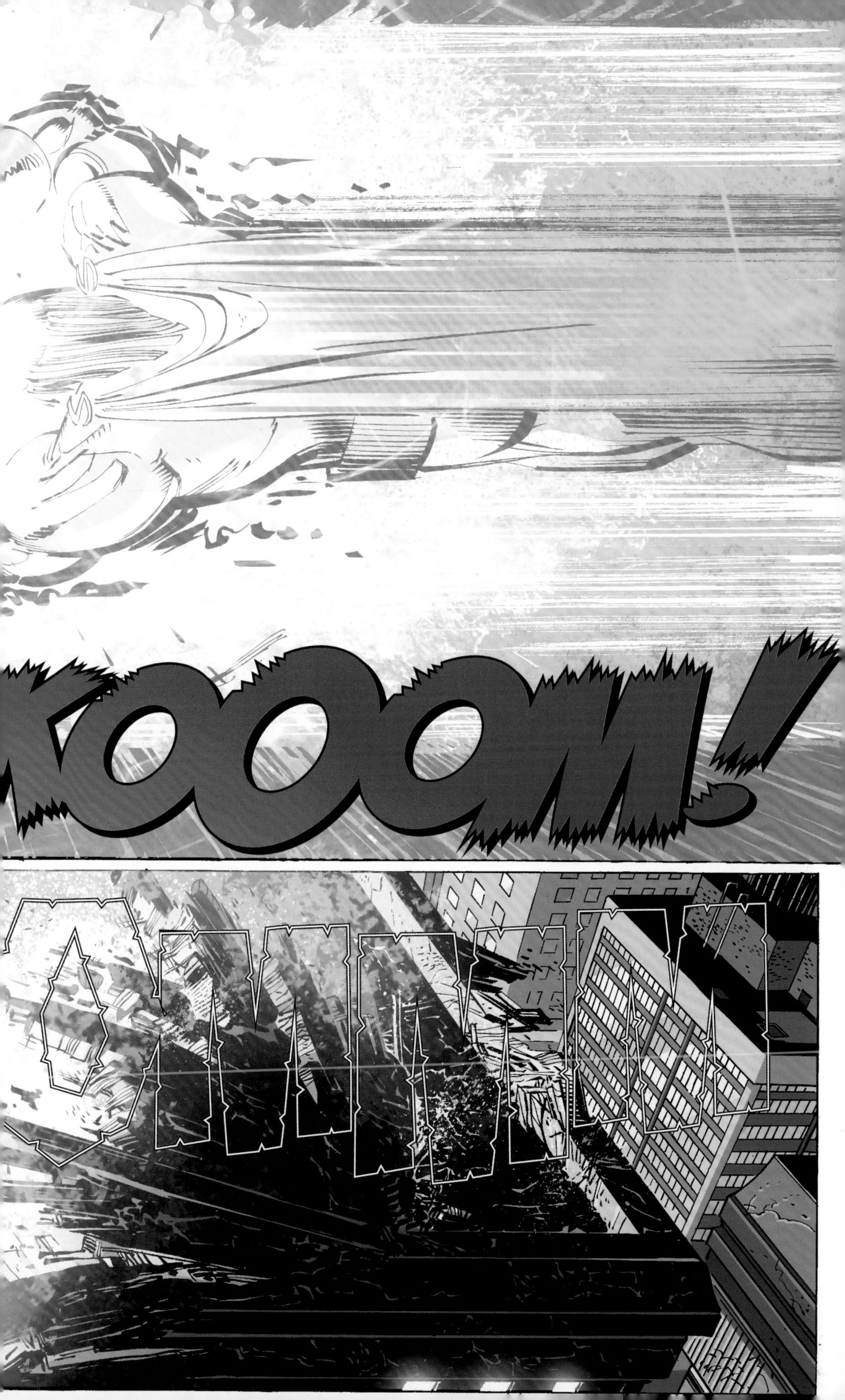
OOOM!

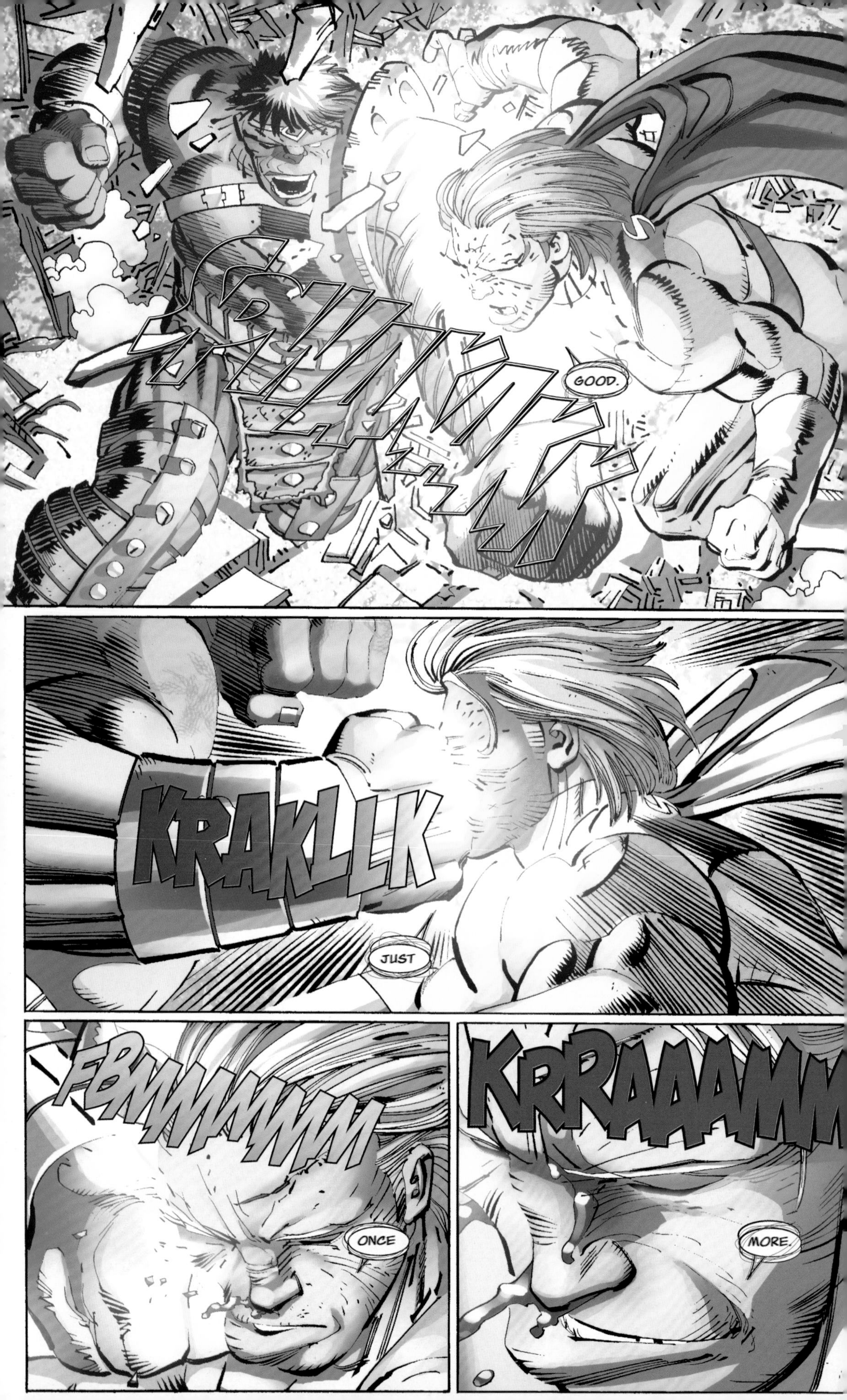
GOOD.
KRAKLLK
JUST
ONCE
MORE.

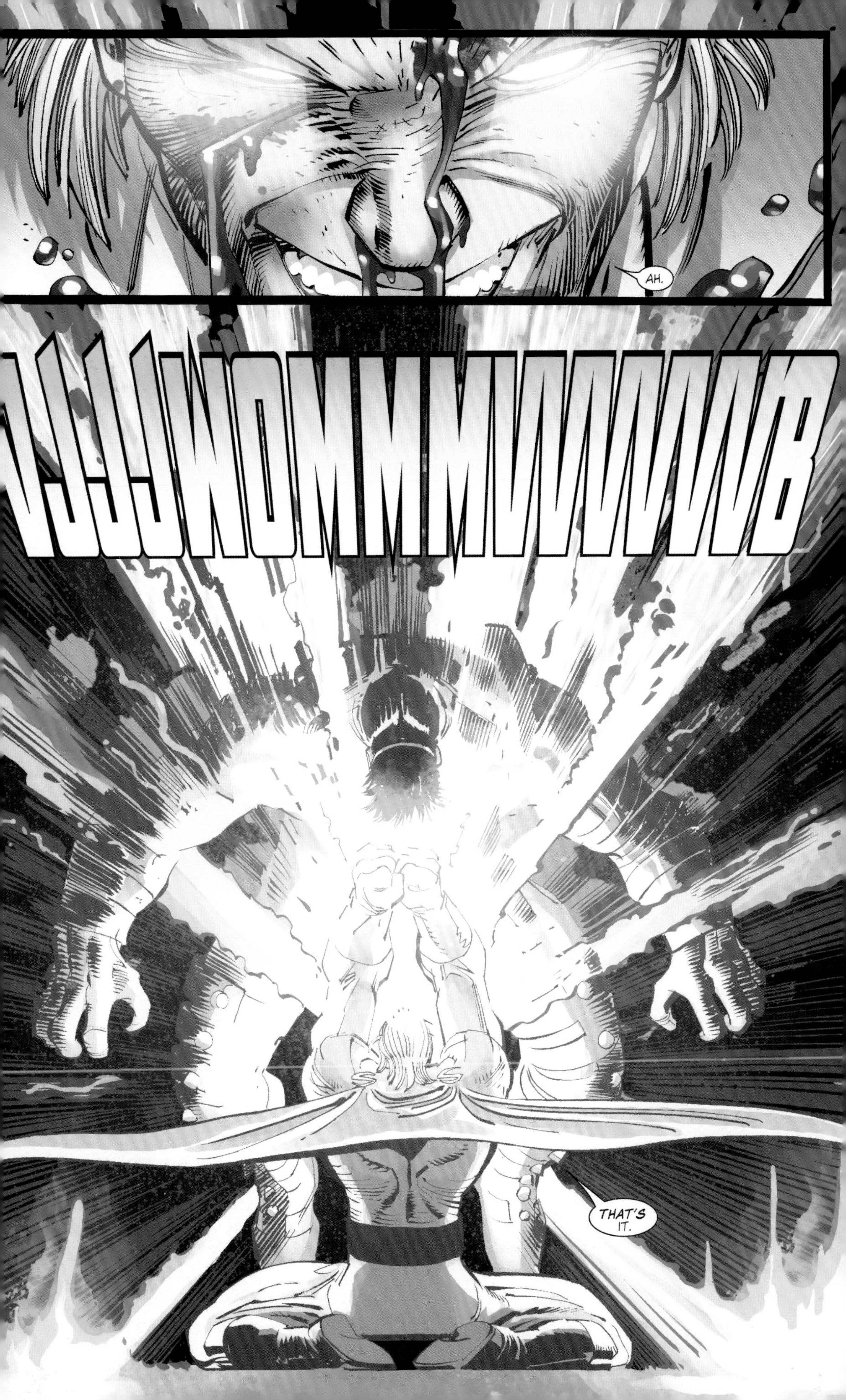
AH.
THAT'S IT.

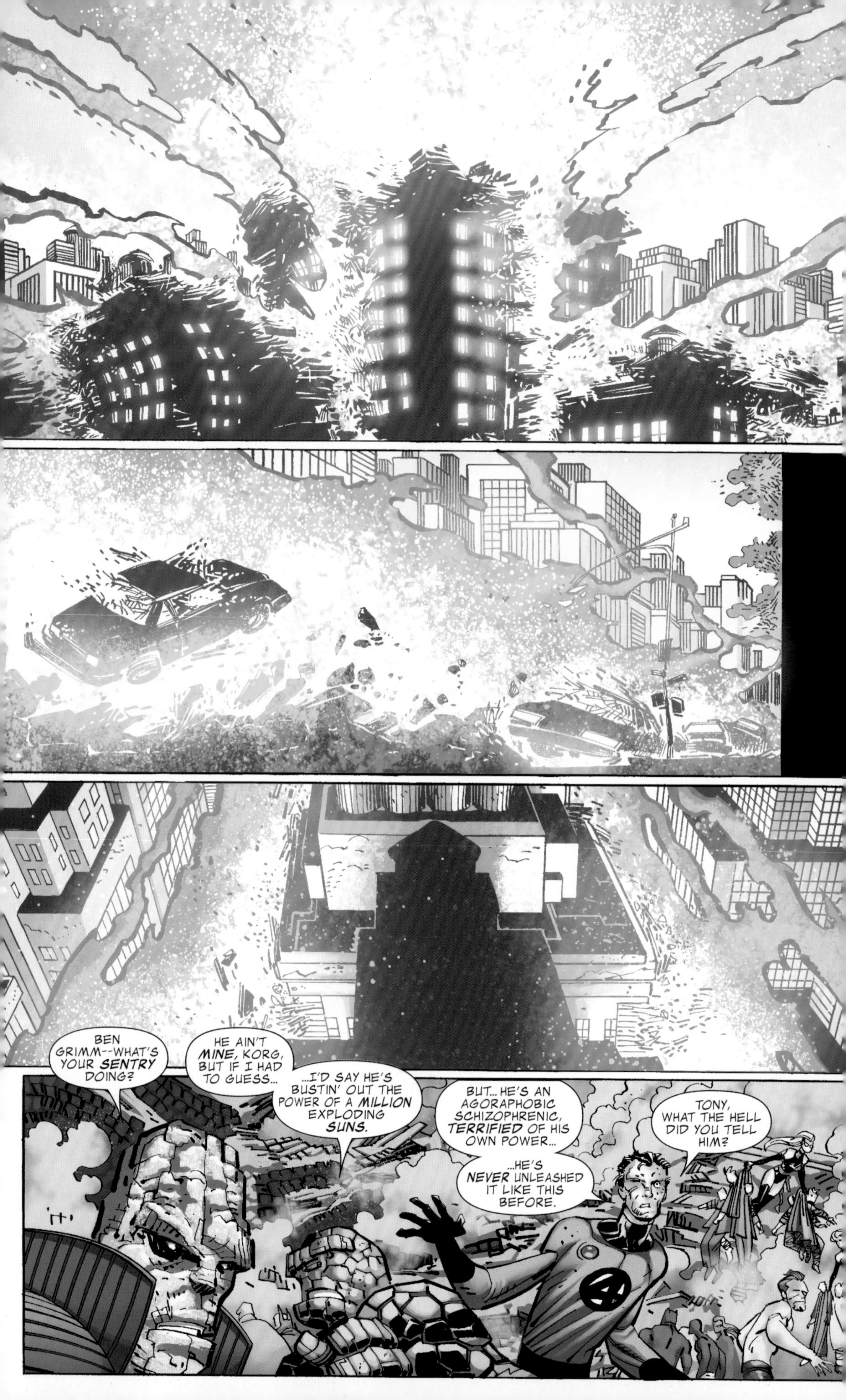
BEN GRIMM--WHAT'S YOUR SENTRY DOING?
HE AIN'T MINE, KORG, BUT IF I HAD TO GUESS...
...I'D SAY HE'S BUSTIN' OUT THE POWER OF A MILLION EXPLODING SUNS.
BUT... HE'S AN AGORAPHOBIC SCHIZOPHRENIC, TERRIFIED OF HIS OWN POWER...
...HE'S NEVER UNLEASHED IT LIKE THIS BEFORE.
TONY, WHAT THE HELL DID YOU TELL HIM?

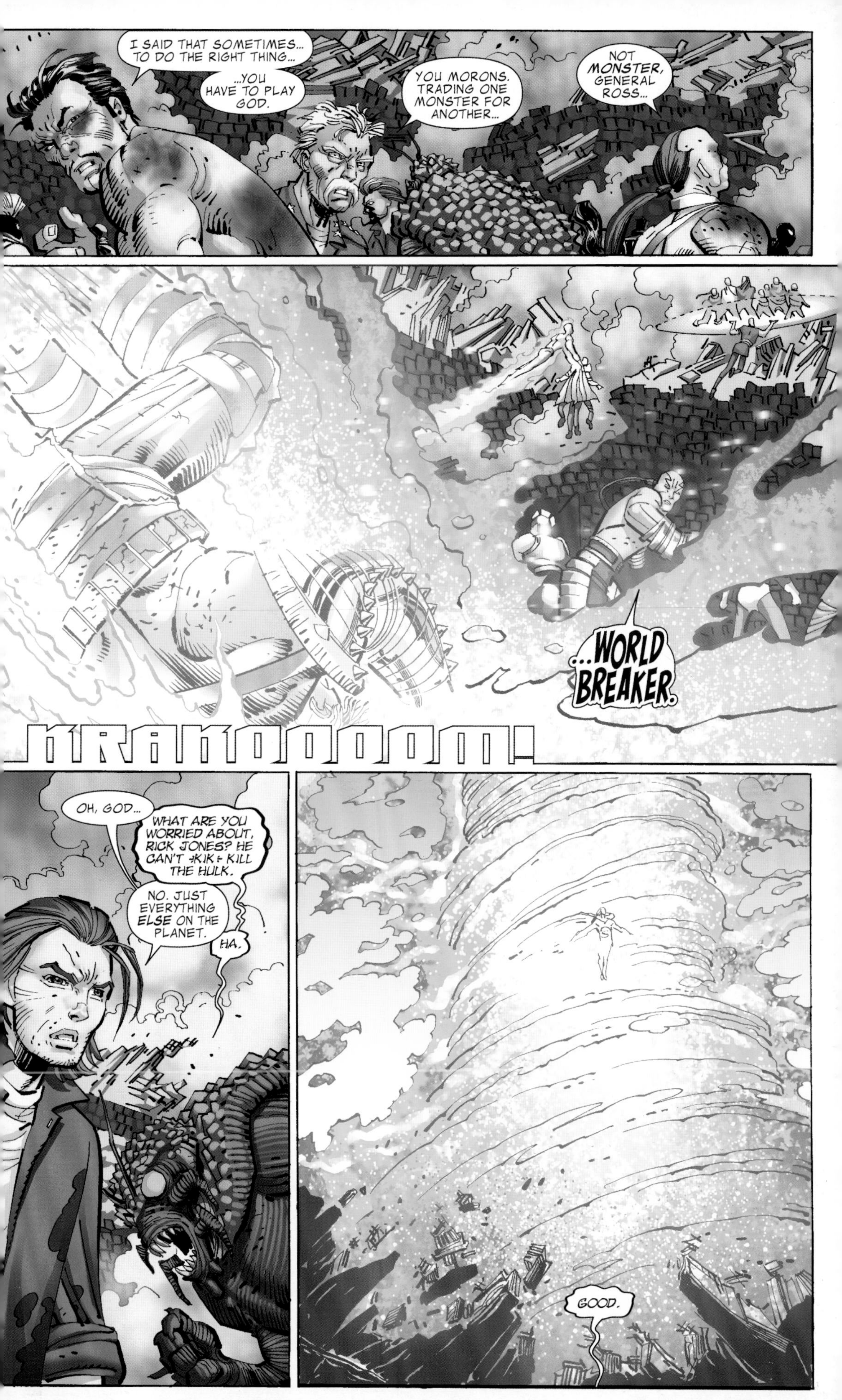
I SAID THAT SOMETIMES... TO DO THE RIGHT THING...
...YOU HAVE TO PLAY GOD.
YOU MORONS. TRADING ONE MONSTER FOR ANOTHER...
NOT MONSTER, GENERAL ROSS...
...WORLD BREAKER.
KRAKOOOOOM!
OH, GOD...
WHAT ARE YOU WORRIED ABOUT, RICK JONES? HE CAN'T *KIK* KILL THE HULK.
NO. JUST EVERYTHING ELSE ON THE PLANET.
HA.
GOOD.

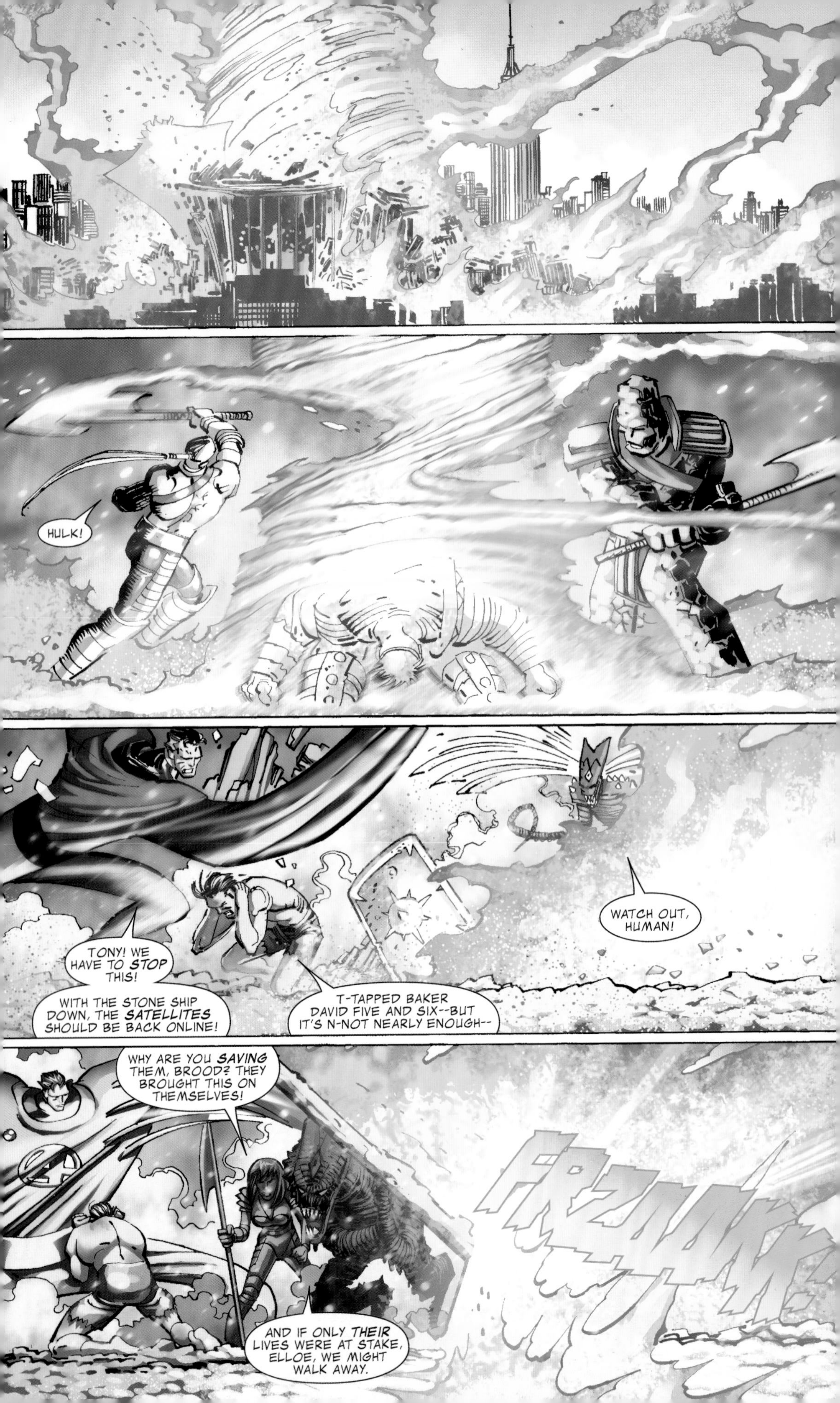
HULK!
TONY! WE HAVE TO STOP THIS!
WITH THE STONE SHIP DOWN, THE SATELLITES SHOULD BE BACK ONLINE!
T-TAPPED BAKER DAVID FIVE AND SIX--BUT IT'S N-NOT NEARLY ENOUGH--
WATCH OUT, HUMAN!
WHY ARE YOU SAVING THEM, BROOD? THEY BROUGHT THIS ON THEMSELVES!
AND IF ONLY THEIR LIVES WERE AT STAKE, ELLOE, WE MIGHT WALK AWAY.

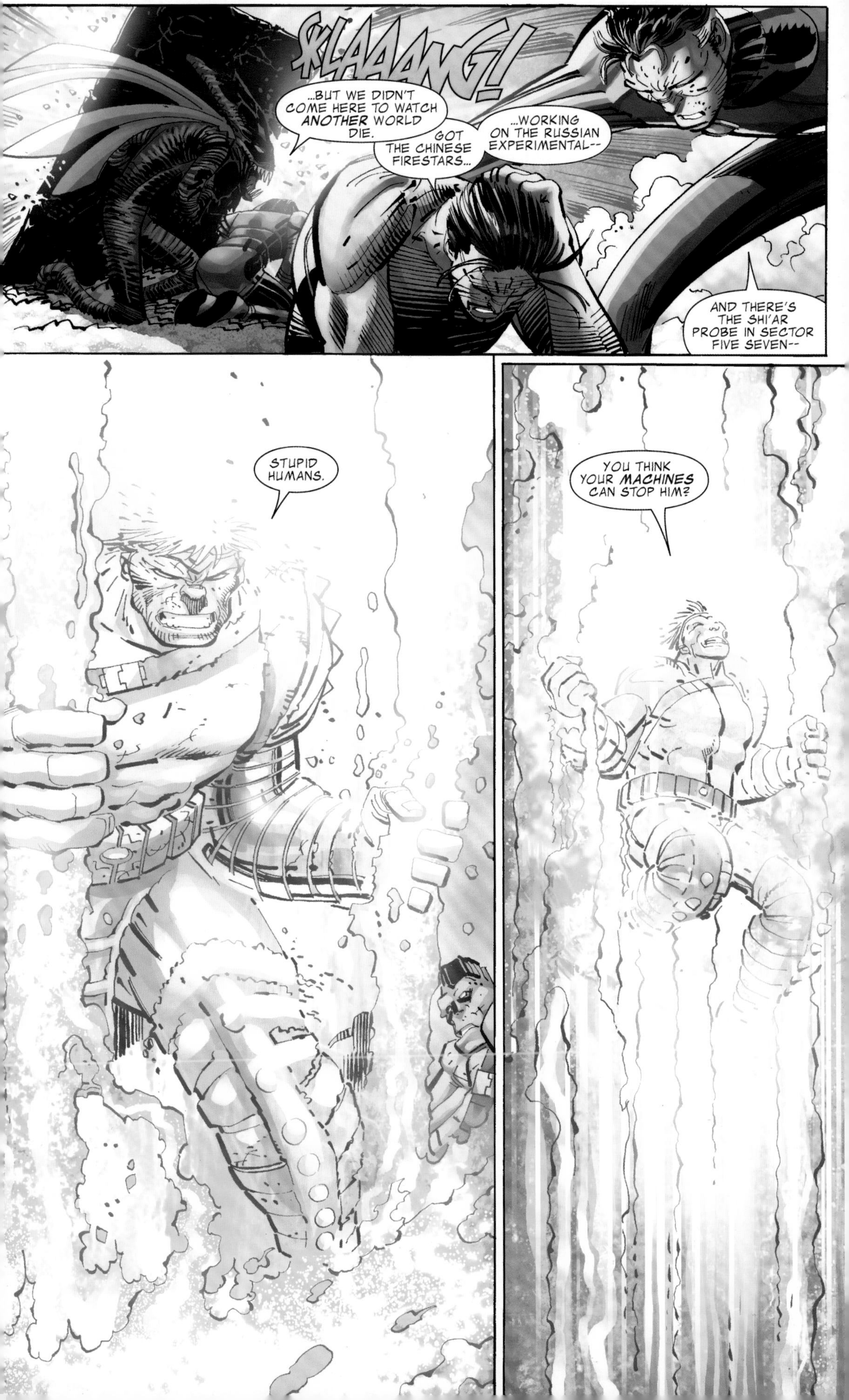
SKLAAANG!
...BUT WE DIDN'T COME HERE TO WATCH ANOTHER WORLD DIE.
GOT THE CHINESE FIRESTARS...
...WORKING ON THE RUSSIAN EXPERIMENTAL--
AND THERE'S THE SHI'AR PROBE IN SECTOR FIVE SEVEN--
STUPID HUMANS.
YOU THINK YOUR MACHINES CAN STOP HIM?

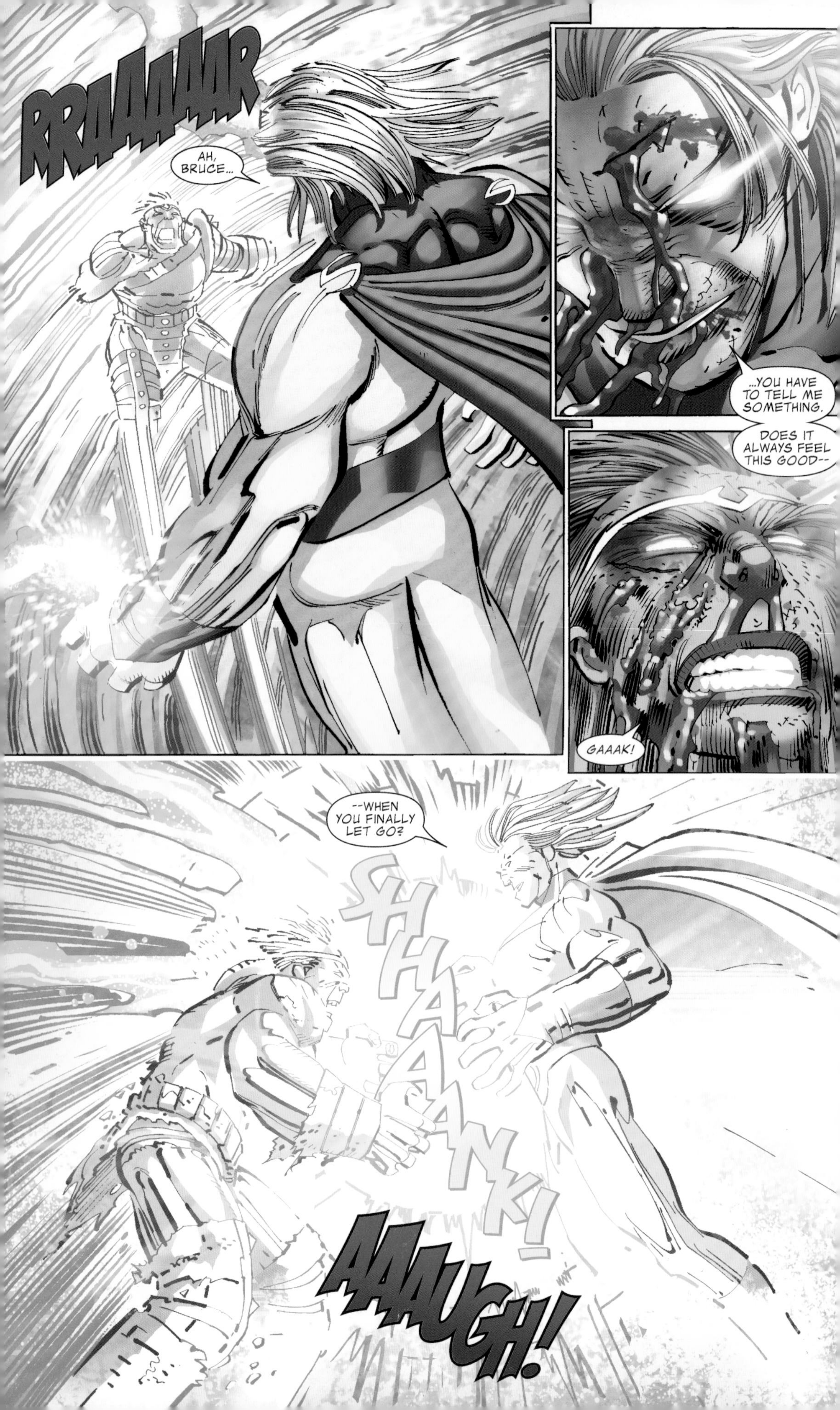
RRAAAAAR
AH, BRUCE...
...YOU HAVE TO TELL ME SOMETHING.
DOES IT ALWAYS FEEL THIS GOOD--
GAAAK!
--WHEN YOU FINALLY LET GO?
SHHAAANK!
AAAUGH!

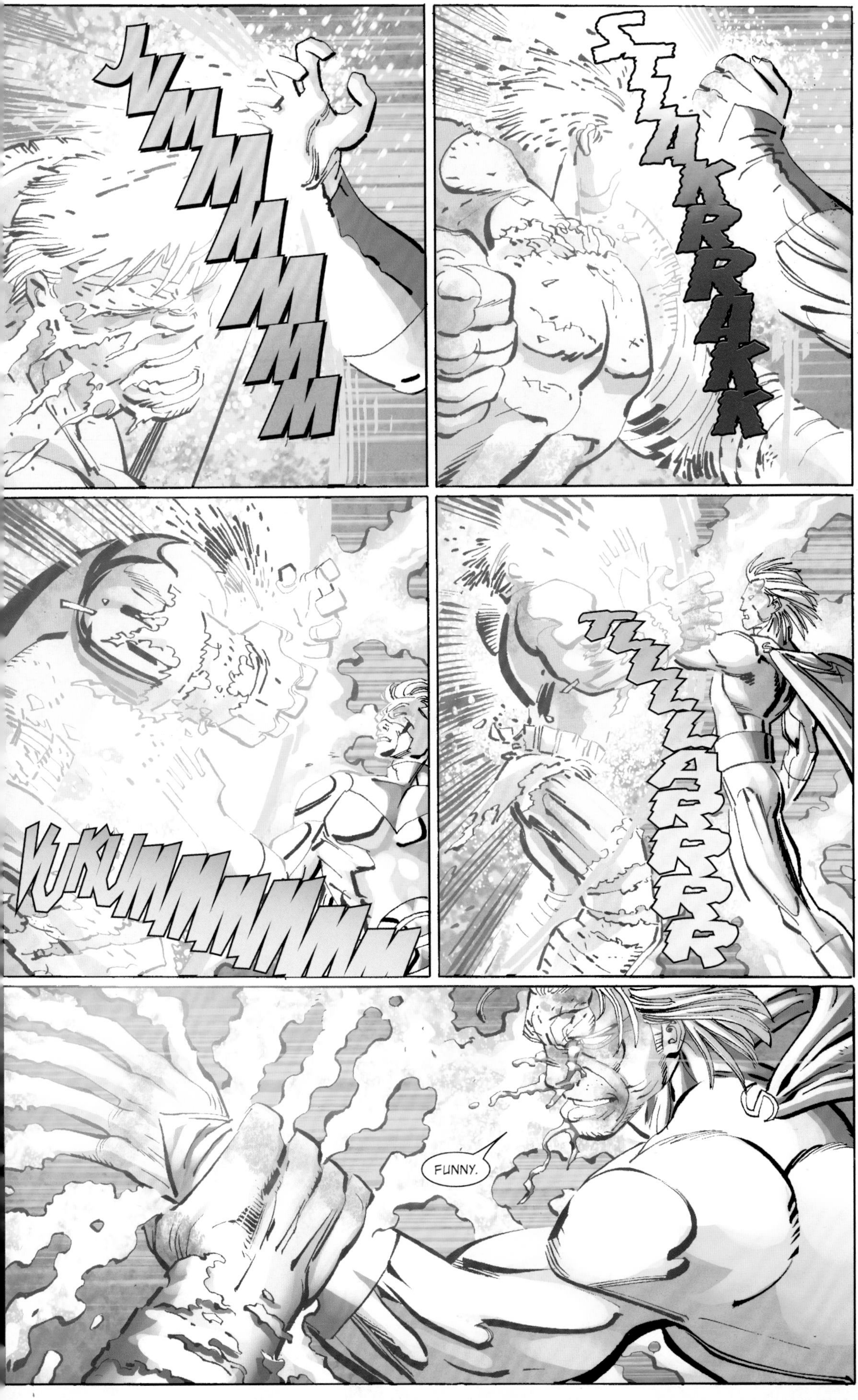
JVMMMMMM
STAKRRAKK
VUKUMMMMMMMM
TLLLLARRR
FUNNY.

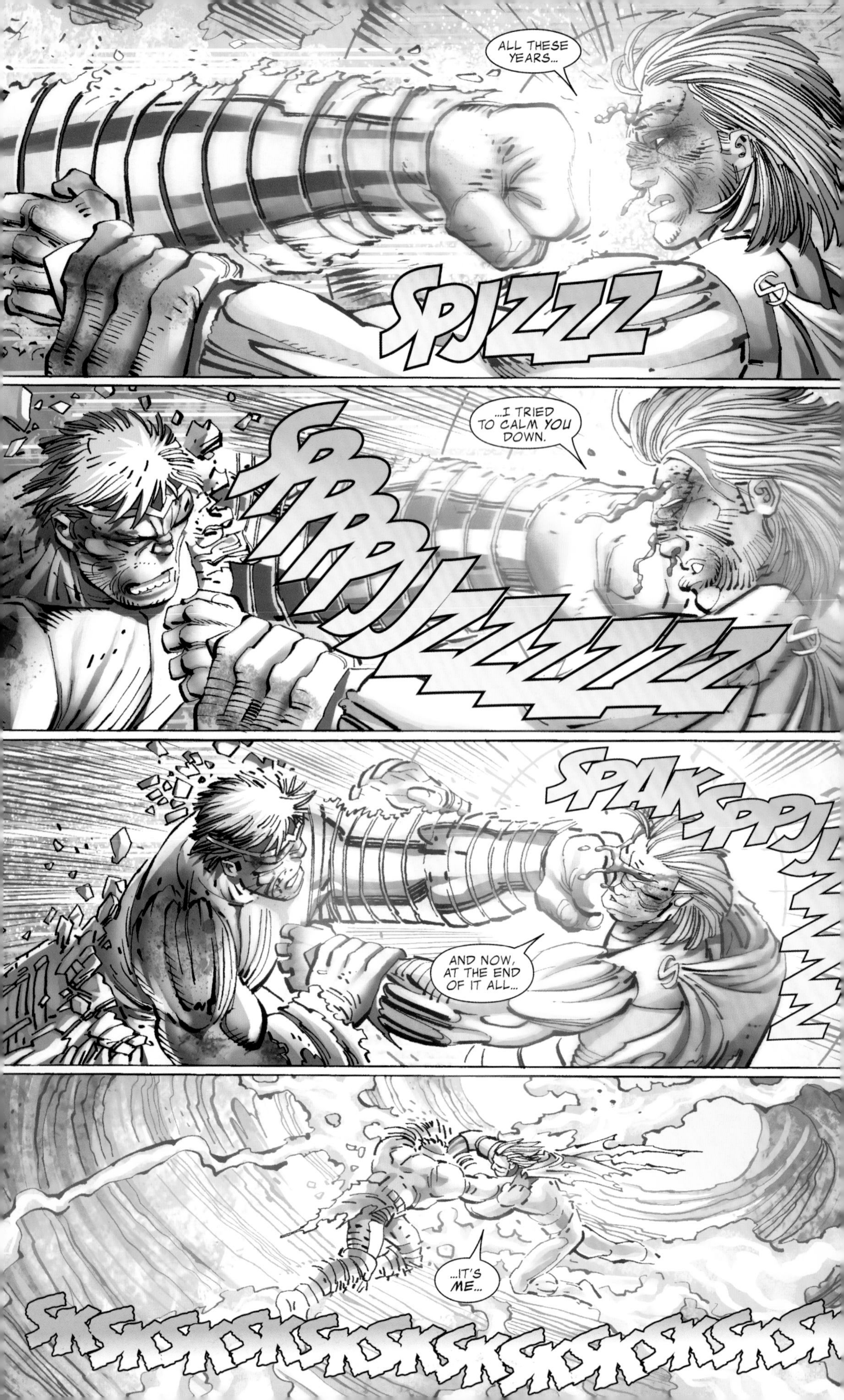

ALL THESE YEARS...
SPJZZZ
...I TRIED TO CALM YOU DOWN.
SPPPJZZZZZZ
SPAK
AND NOW, AT THE END OF IT ALL...
...IT'S ME...

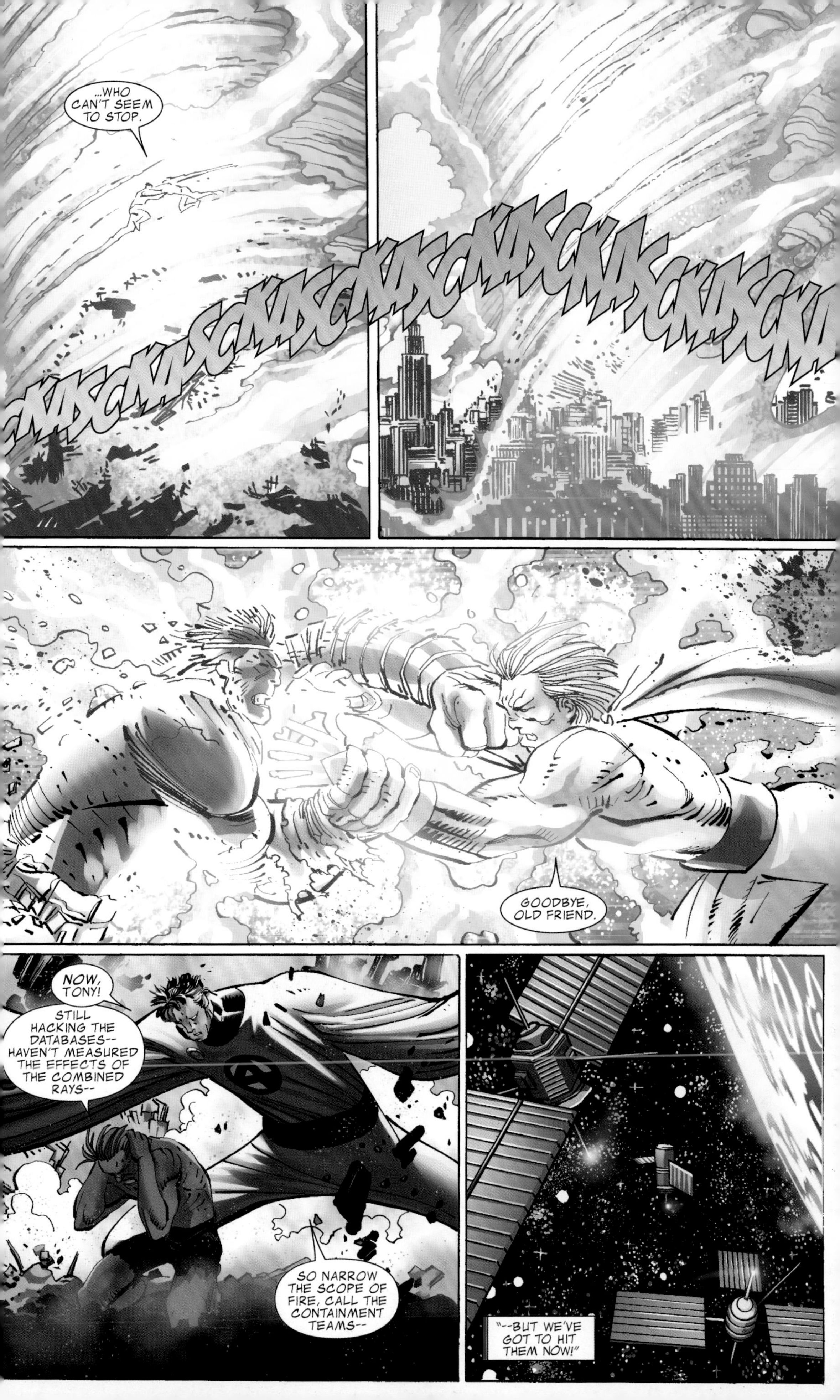
...WHO CAN'T SEEM TO STOP.
SCKASCKASCKASCKASCKASCKASCKASCKASCKASCKA
GOODBYE, OLD FRIEND.
NOW, TONY!
STILL HACKING THE DATABASES-- HAVEN'T MEASURED THE EFFECTS OF THE COMBINED RAYS--
SO NARROW THE SCOPE OF FIRE, CALL THE CONTAINMENT TEAMS--
"--BUT WE'VE GOT TO HIT THEM NOW!"

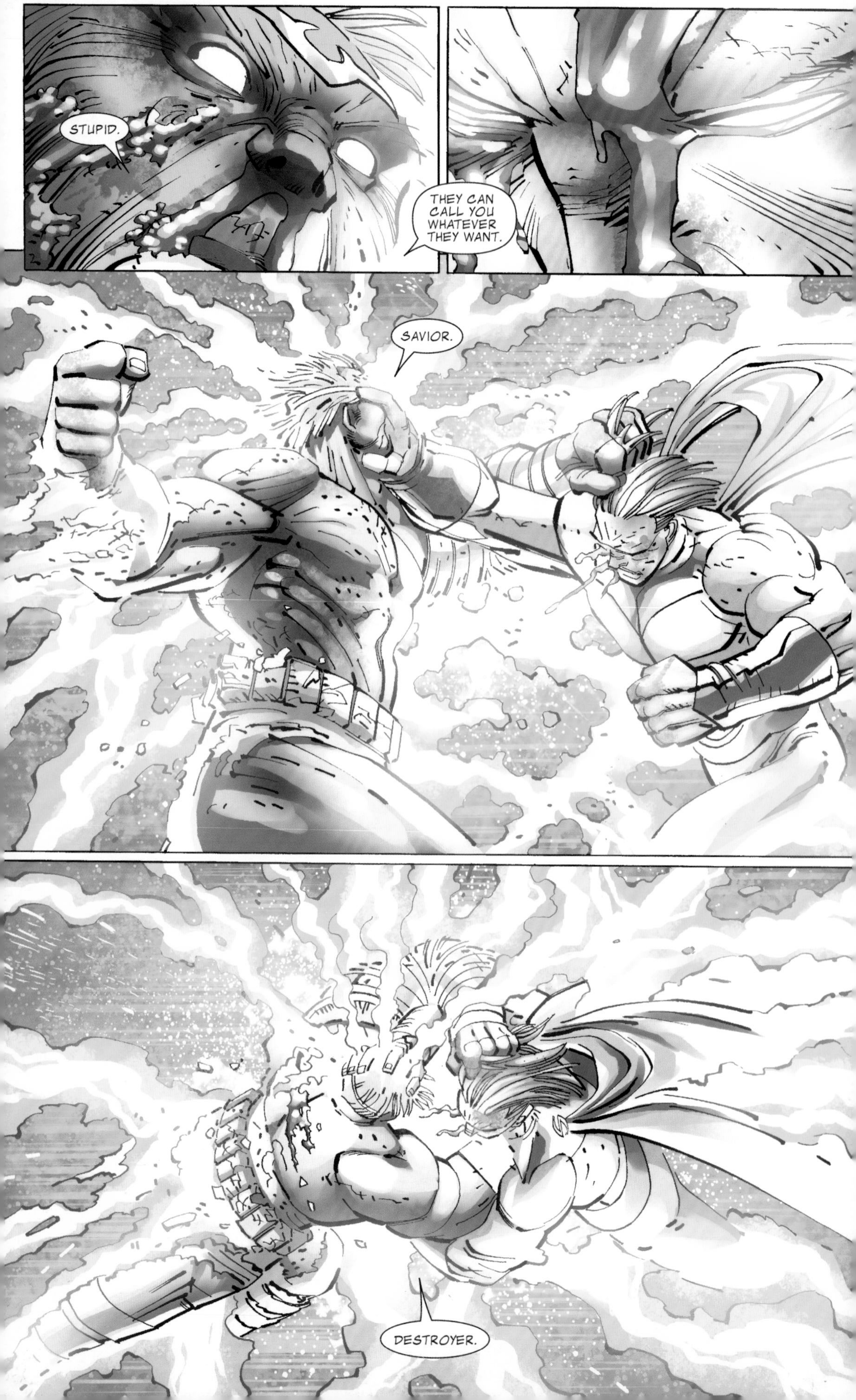
STUPID.
THEY CAN CALL YOU WHATEVER THEY WANT.
SAVIOR.
DESTROYER.

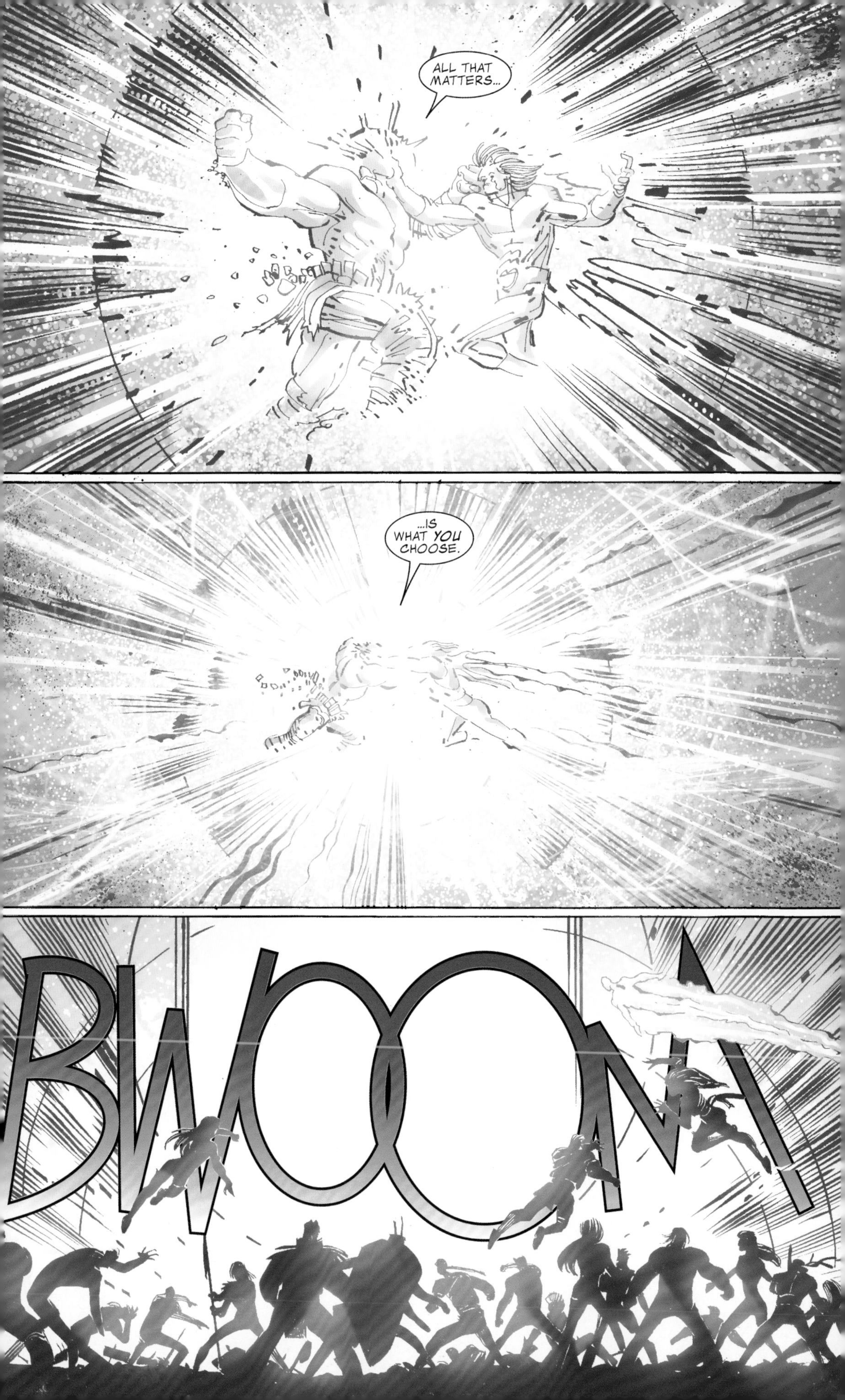
ALL THAT MATTERS...
...IS WHAT YOU CHOOSE.
BWOOM!

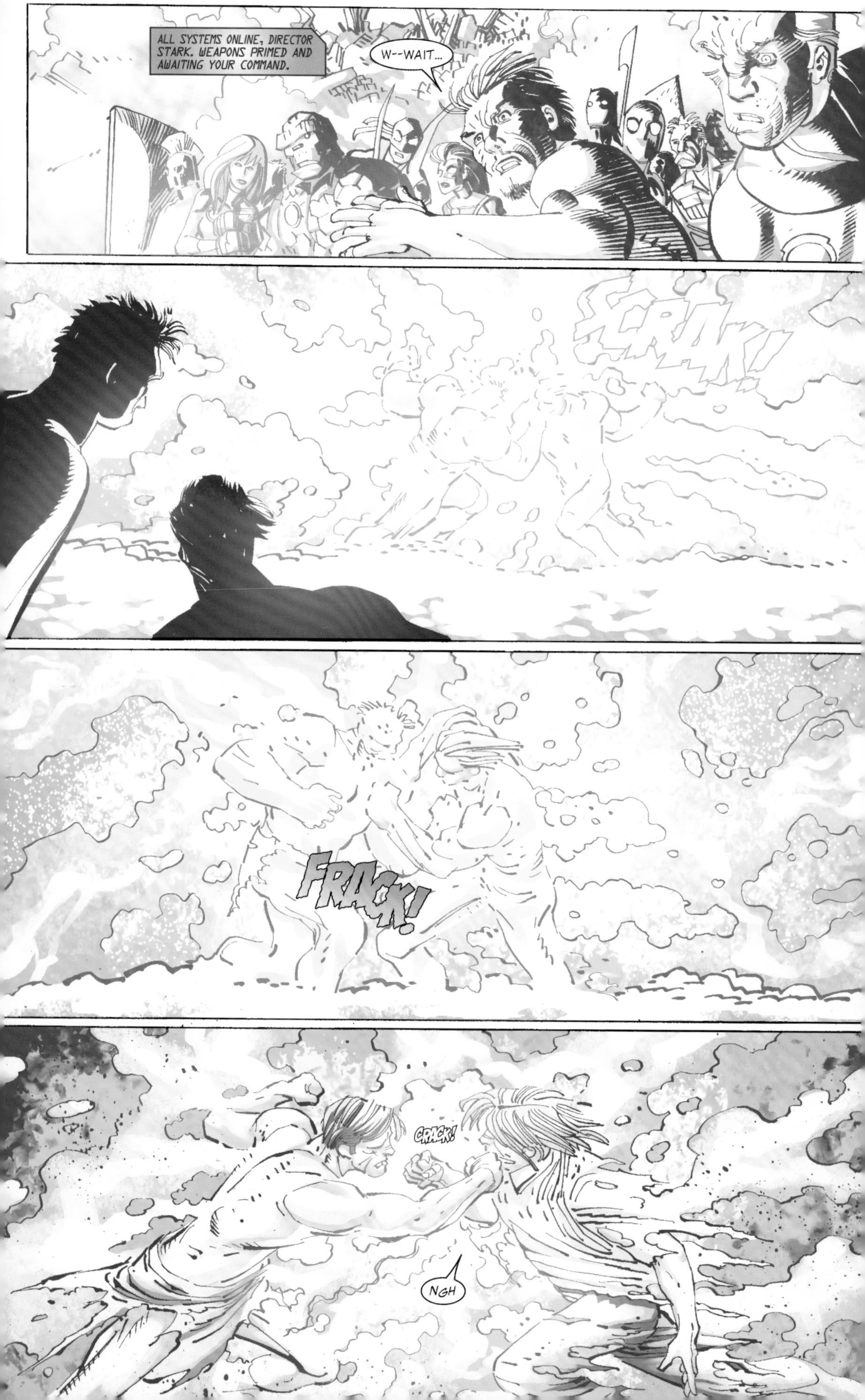
ALL SYSTEMS ONLINE, DIRECTOR STARK. WEAPONS PRIMED AND AWAITING YOUR COMMAND.
W--WAIT...
SCRAK!
FRACK!
CRACK!
NGH

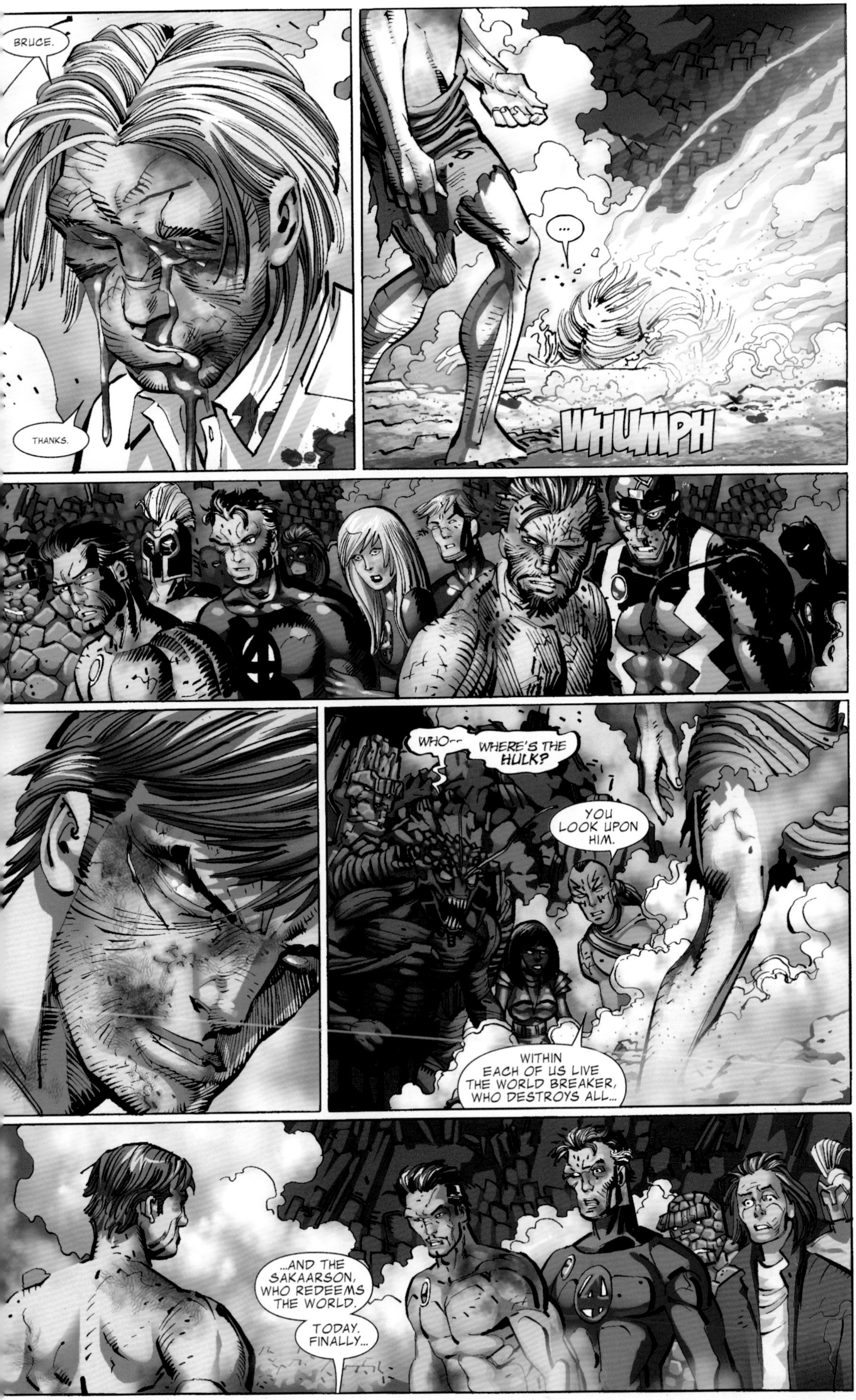
BRUCE.
THANKS.
...
WHUMPH
WHO--
WHERE'S THE HULK?
YOU LOOK UPON HIM.
WITHIN EACH OF US LIVE THE WORLD BREAKER, WHO DESTROYS ALL...
...AND THE SAKAARSON, WHO REDEEMS THE WORLD.
TODAY. FINALLY...

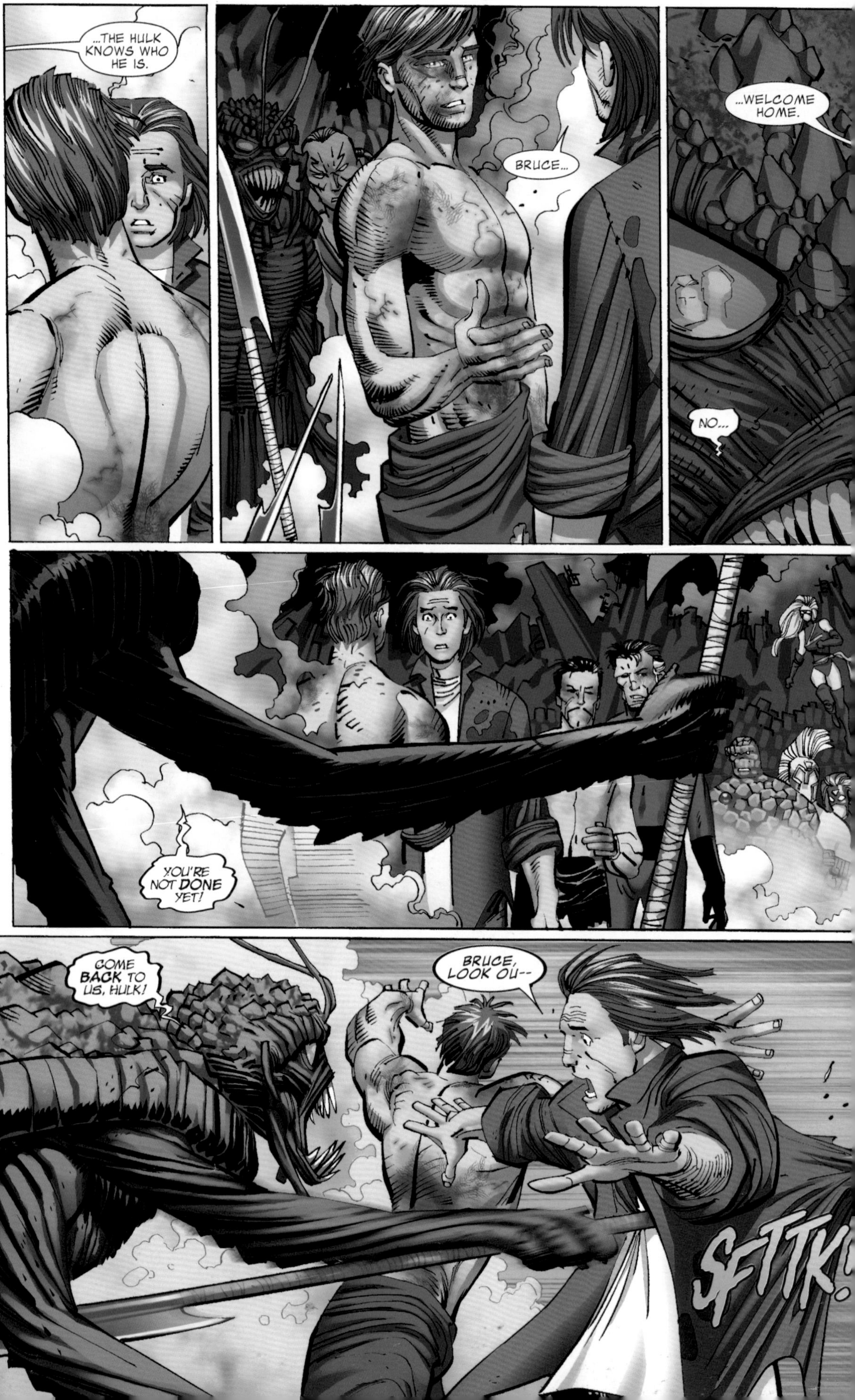
...THE HULK KNOWS WHO HE IS.
BRUCE...
...WELCOME HOME.
NO...
YOU'RE NOT DONE YET!
COME BACK TO US, HULK!
BRUCE, LOOK OU--
SFTTK!

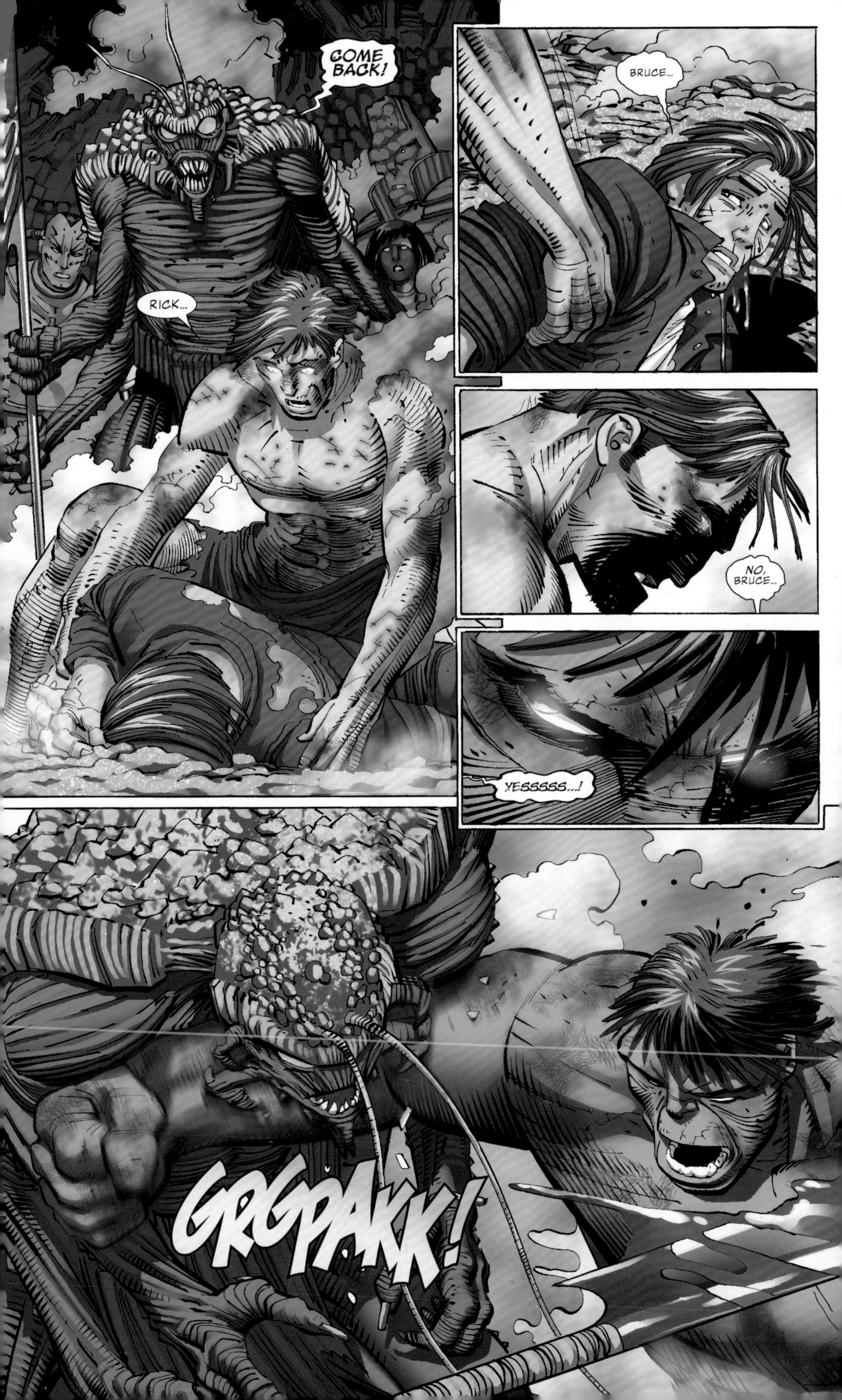
COME BACK!
RICK...
BRUCE...
NO, BRUCE...
YESSSSS...!
GRGPAKK!

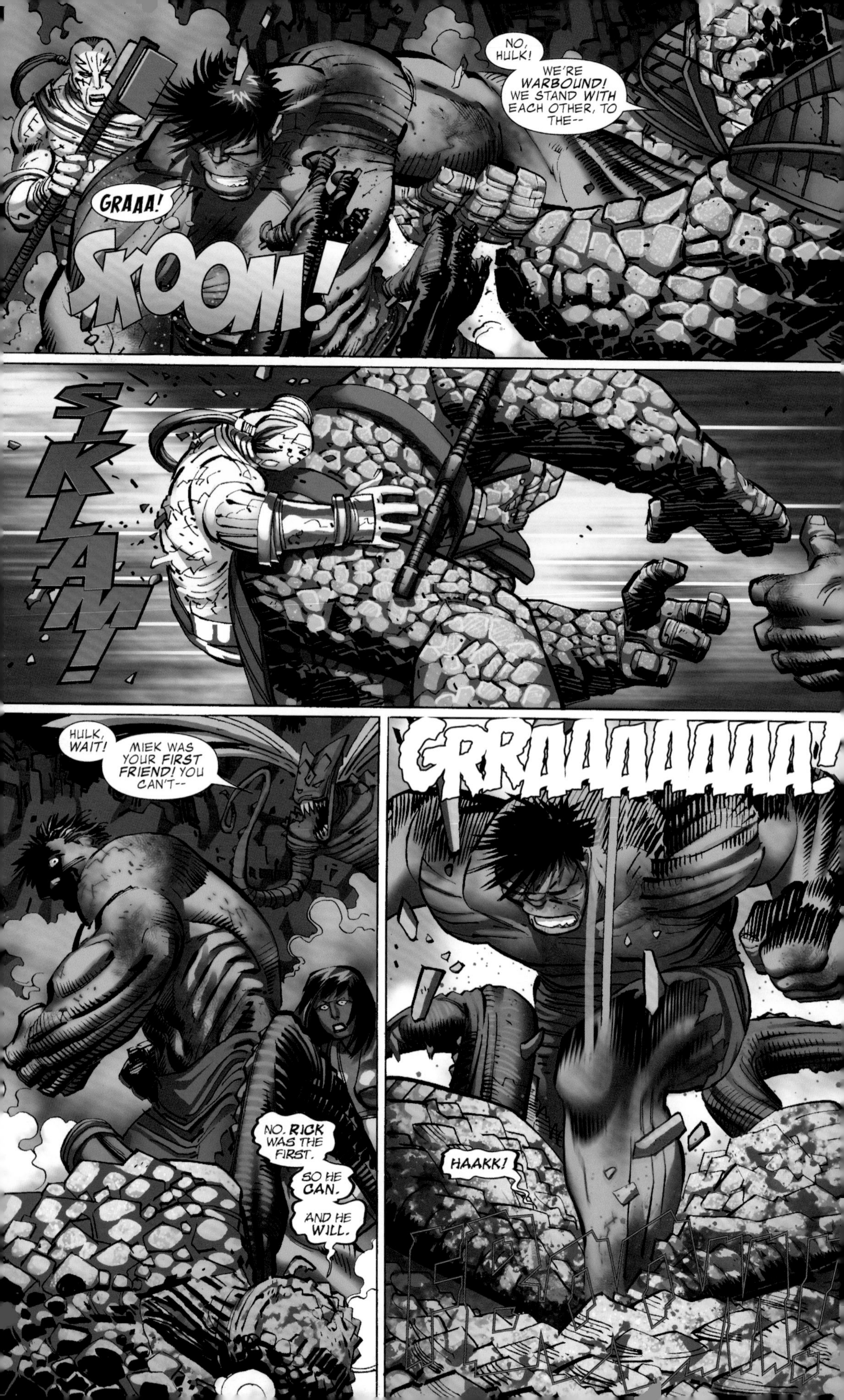
NO, HULK!
WE'RE WARBOUND! WE STAND WITH EACH OTHER, TO THE--
GRAAA!
SKOOM!
SKLAM!
HULK, WAIT!
MIEK WAS YOUR FIRST FRIEND! YOU CAN'T--
NO. RICK WAS THE FIRST.
SO HE CAN.
AND HE WILL.
GRRAAAAAAAA!
HAAKK!

BECAUSE THIS--

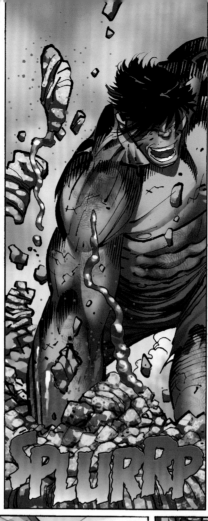

--IS WHAT YOU WERE MADE FOR.

DON'T LET THEM STOP YOU, HULK.

"NEVER ⚡KIK⚡ STOP MAKING THEM PAY."

THAT'S WHAT YOU TAUGHT ME.

THAT'S WHY I ⚡KIK⚡ KILLED THEM.

THAT'S WHY YOU'LL KILL ME. AND THEN--

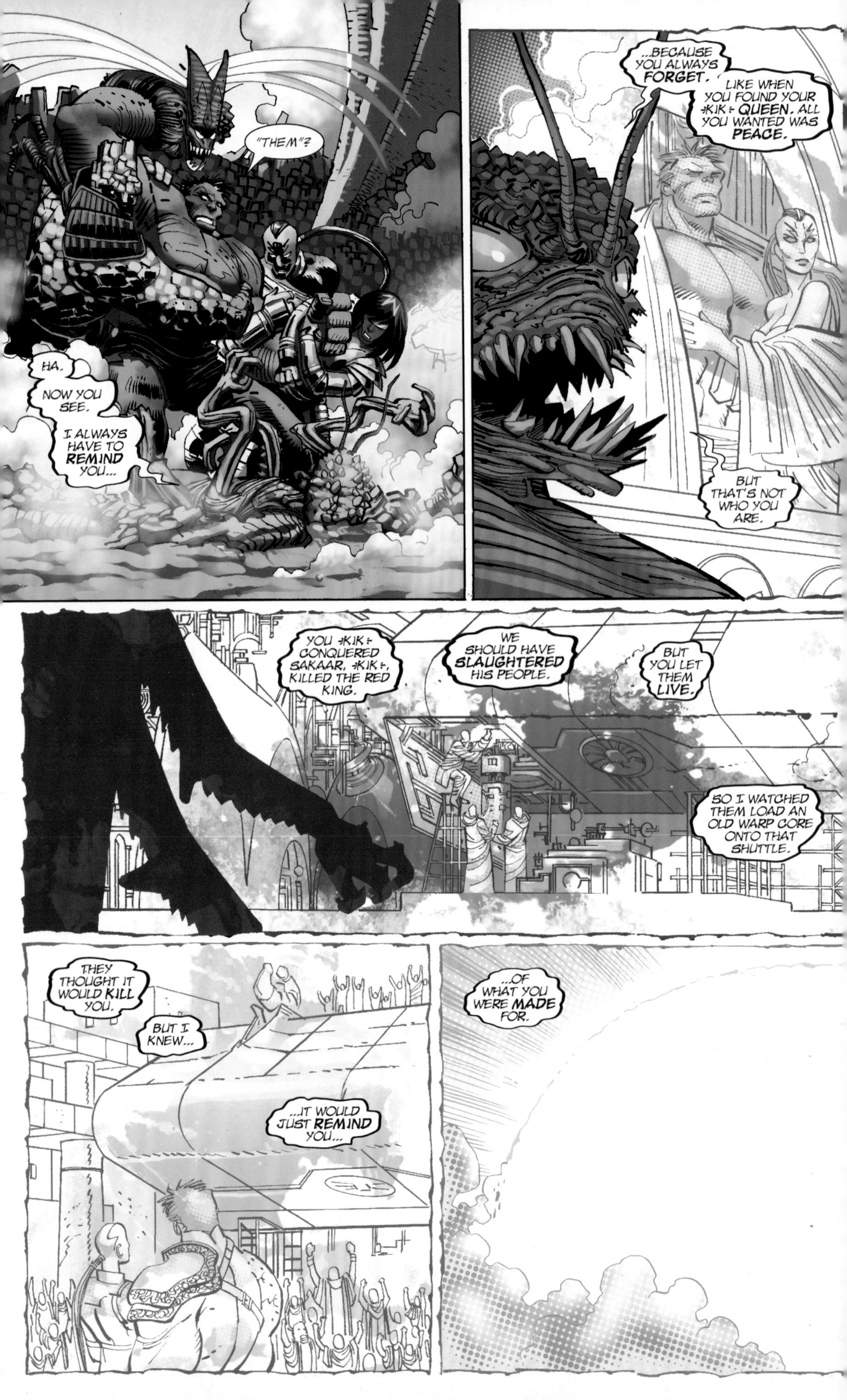
"THEM"?
HA.
NOW YOU SEE.
I ALWAYS HAVE TO REMIND YOU...
...BECAUSE YOU ALWAYS FORGET.
LIKE WHEN YOU FOUND YOUR ‡KIK‡ QUEEN. ALL YOU WANTED WAS PEACE.
BUT THAT'S NOT WHO YOU ARE.
YOU ‡KIK‡ CONQUERED SAKAAR, ‡KIK‡, KILLED THE RED KING.
WE SHOULD HAVE SLAUGHTERED HIS PEOPLE.
BUT YOU LET THEM LIVE.
SO I WATCHED THEM LOAD AN OLD WARP CORE ONTO THAT SHUTTLE.
THEY THOUGHT IT WOULD KILL YOU.
BUT I KNEW...
...IT WOULD JUST REMIND YOU...
...OF WHAT YOU WERE MADE FOR.

SHLISSS!
AAGH!
THE CH-- CHILDREN!
YOUR OWN BROTHER HIVELINGS!
KIK KIK
A M-- MILLION SOULS!
WE ALL KIK KIK MUST DIE.
ALL THIS KIK PASSING, SO THE NEXT KIK THING CAN COME...
...SO THE WORLD BREAKER...
...CAN FINALLY MAKE AN END.
HULK...
SMMRRCCRKKKKK

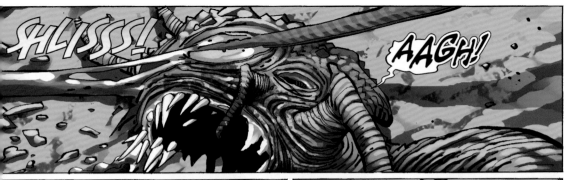

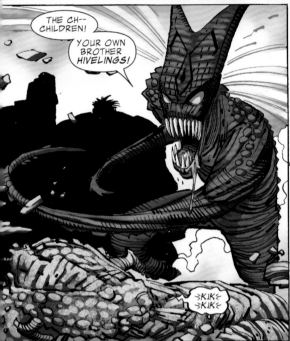

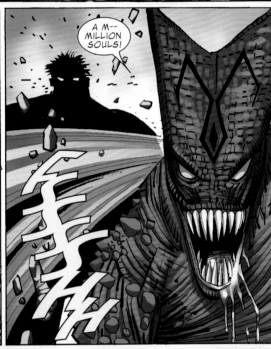

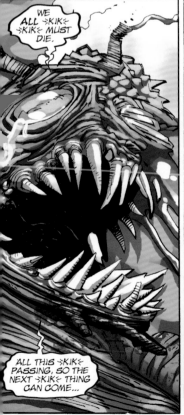

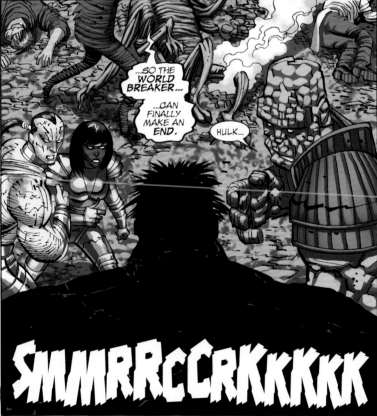

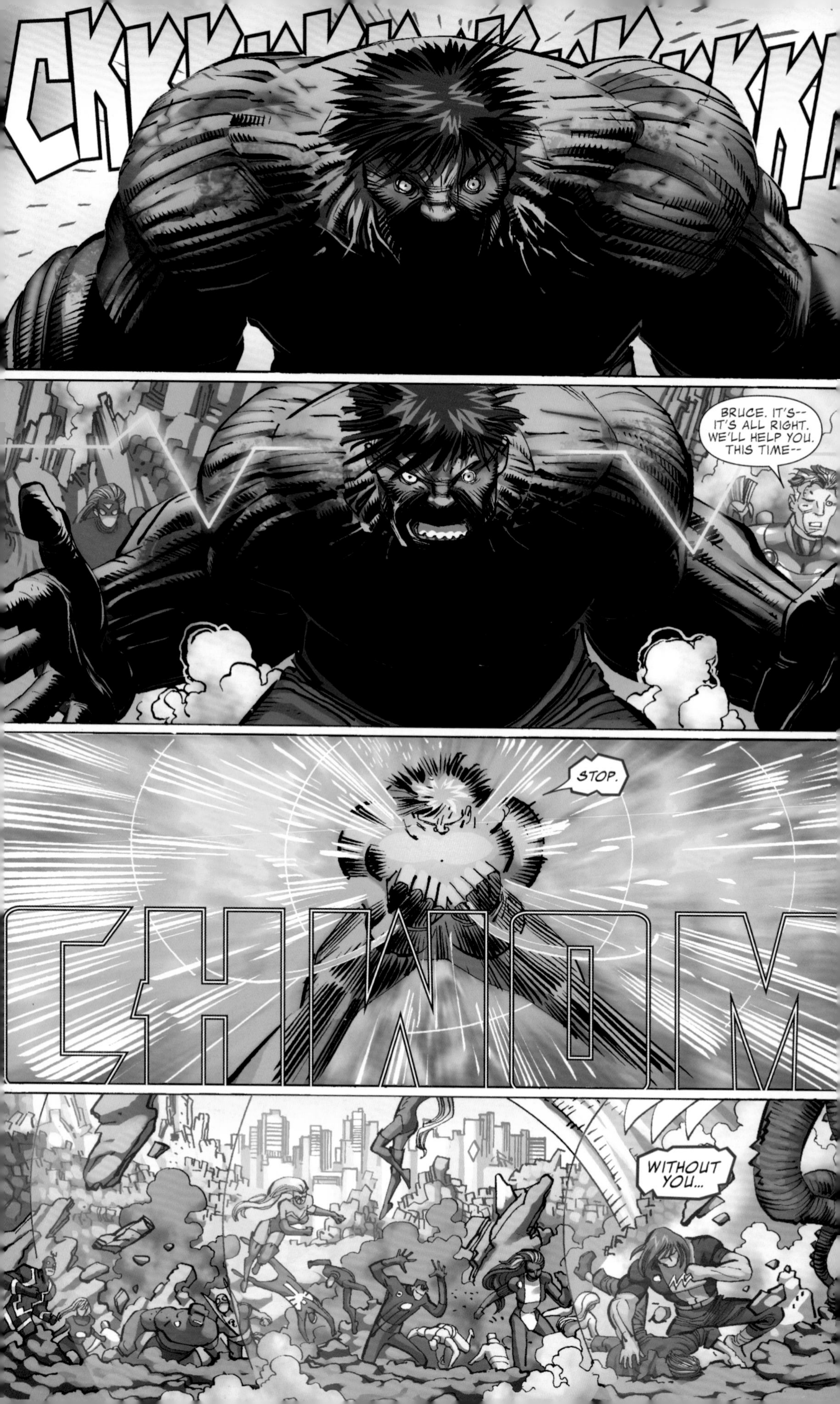
BRUCE. IT'S-- IT'S ALL RIGHT. WE'LL HELP YOU. THIS TIME--
STOP.
WITHOUT YOU...

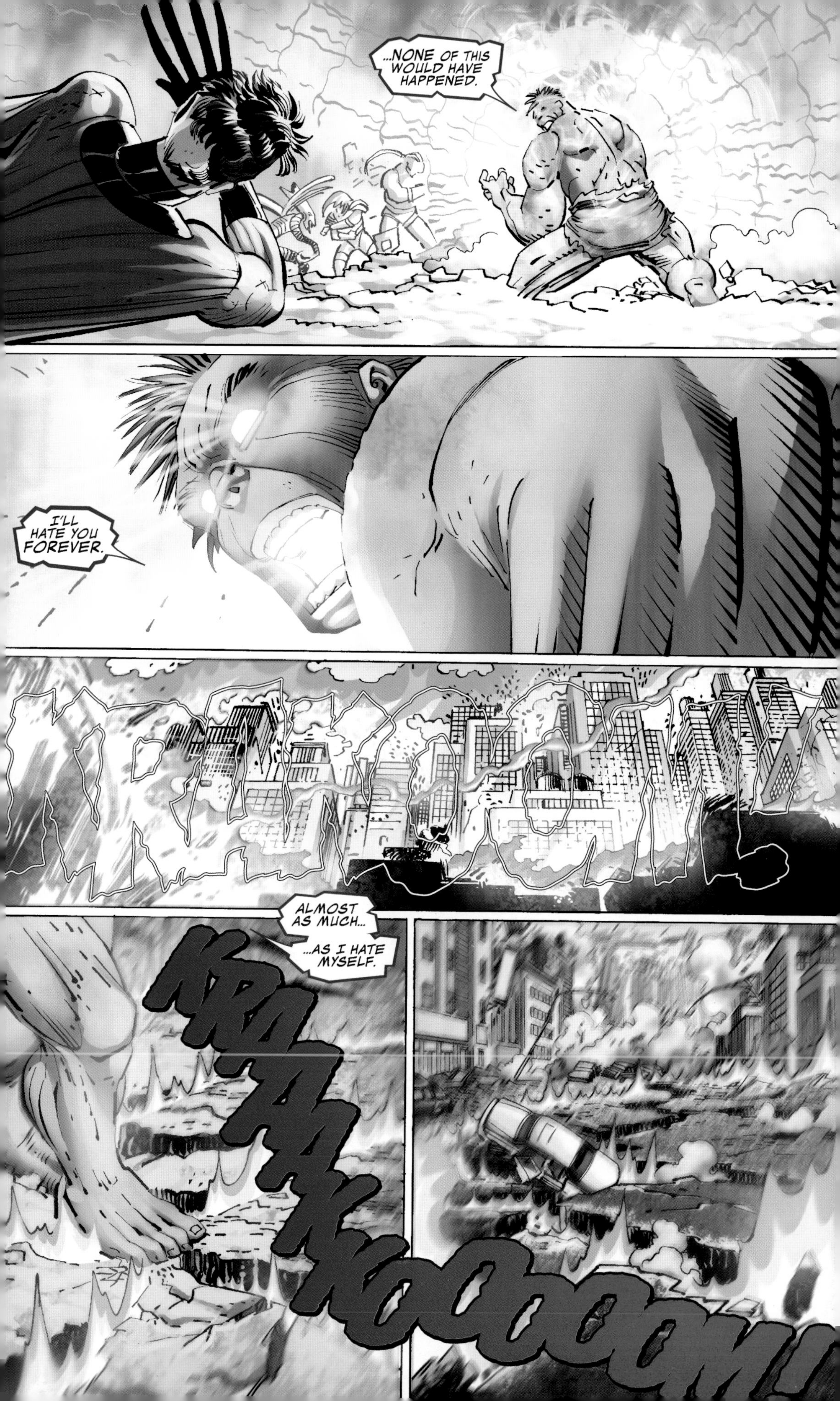
...NONE OF THIS WOULD HAVE HAPPENED.
I'LL HATE YOU FOREVER.
ALMOST AS MUCH...
...AS I HATE MYSELF.

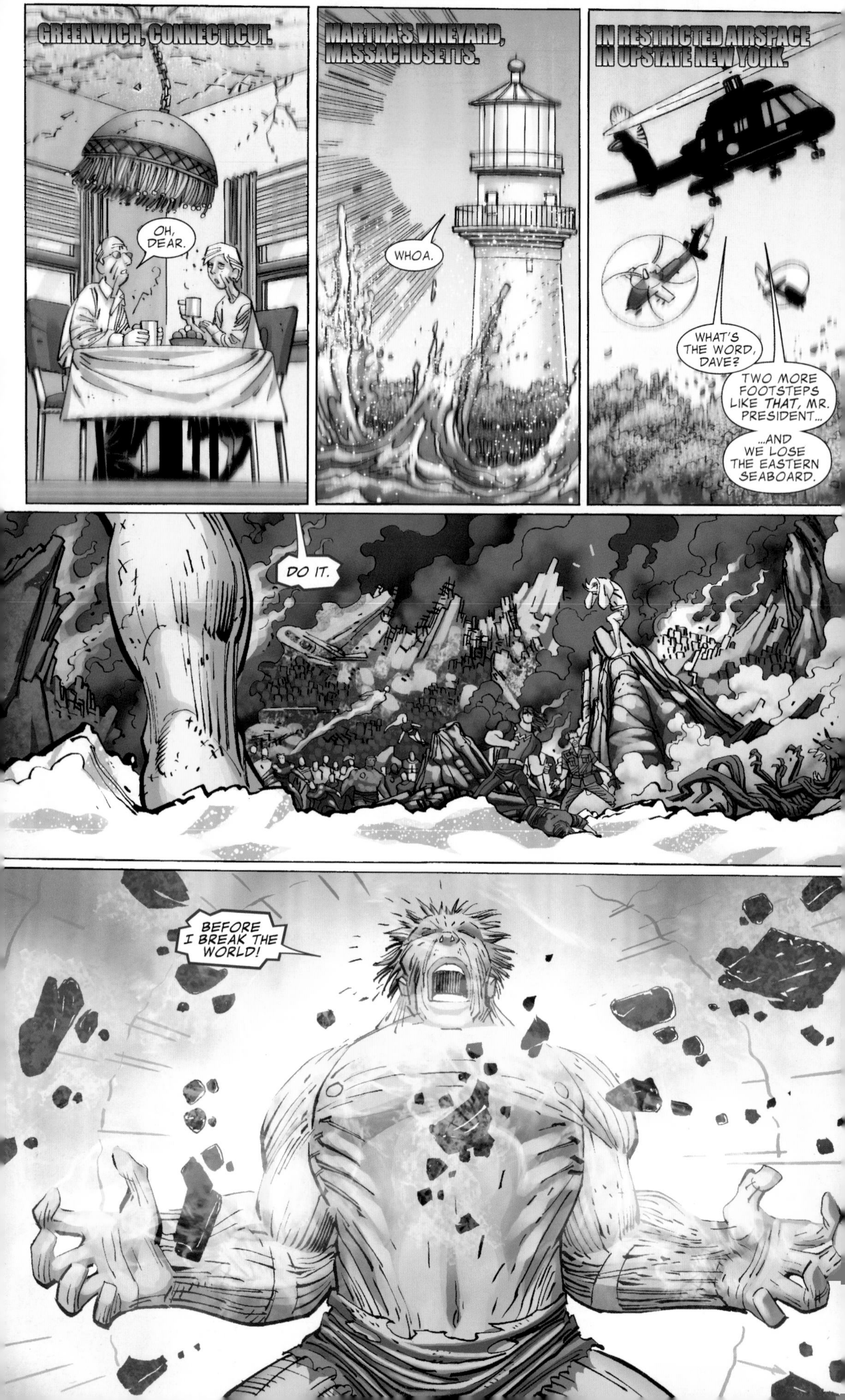
GREENWICH, CONNECTICUT.
OH, DEAR.
MARTHA'S VINEYARD, MASSACHUSETTS.
WHOA.
IN RESTRICTED AIRSPACE IN UPSTATE NEW YORK.
WHAT'S THE WORD, DAVE?
TWO MORE FOOTSTEPS LIKE THAT, MR. PRESIDENT...
...AND WE LOSE THE EASTERN SEABOARD.
DO IT.
BEFORE I BREAK THE WORLD!

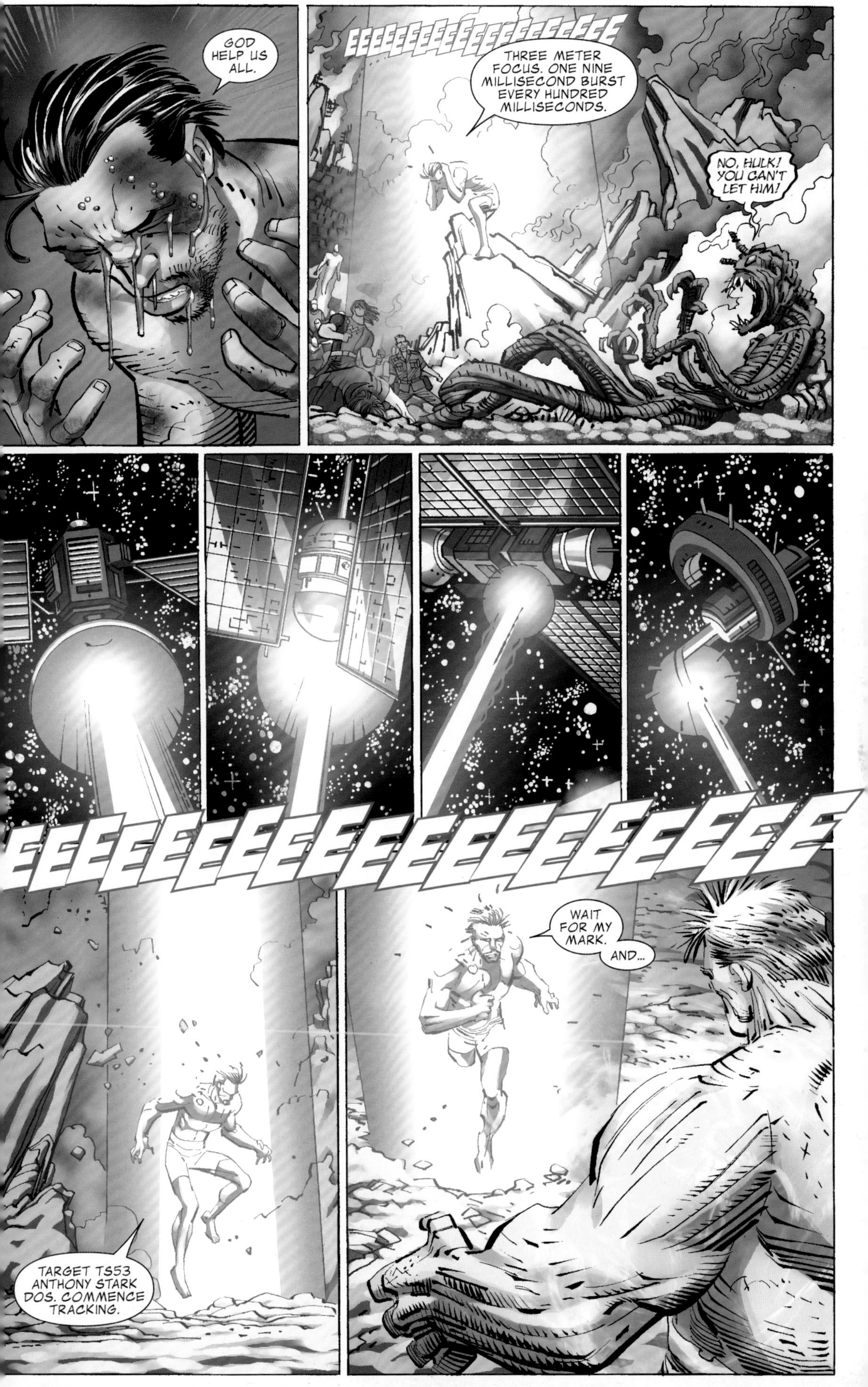
GOD HELP US ALL.
EEEEEEEEEEEEEEEEEE
THREE METER FOCUS. ONE NINE MILLISECOND BURST EVERY HUNDRED MILLISECONDS.
NO, HULK! YOU CAN'T LET HIM!
EEEEEEEEEEEEEEEEEEE
TARGET TS53 ANTHONY STARK DOS. COMMENCE TRACKING.
WAIT FOR MY MARK.
AND...

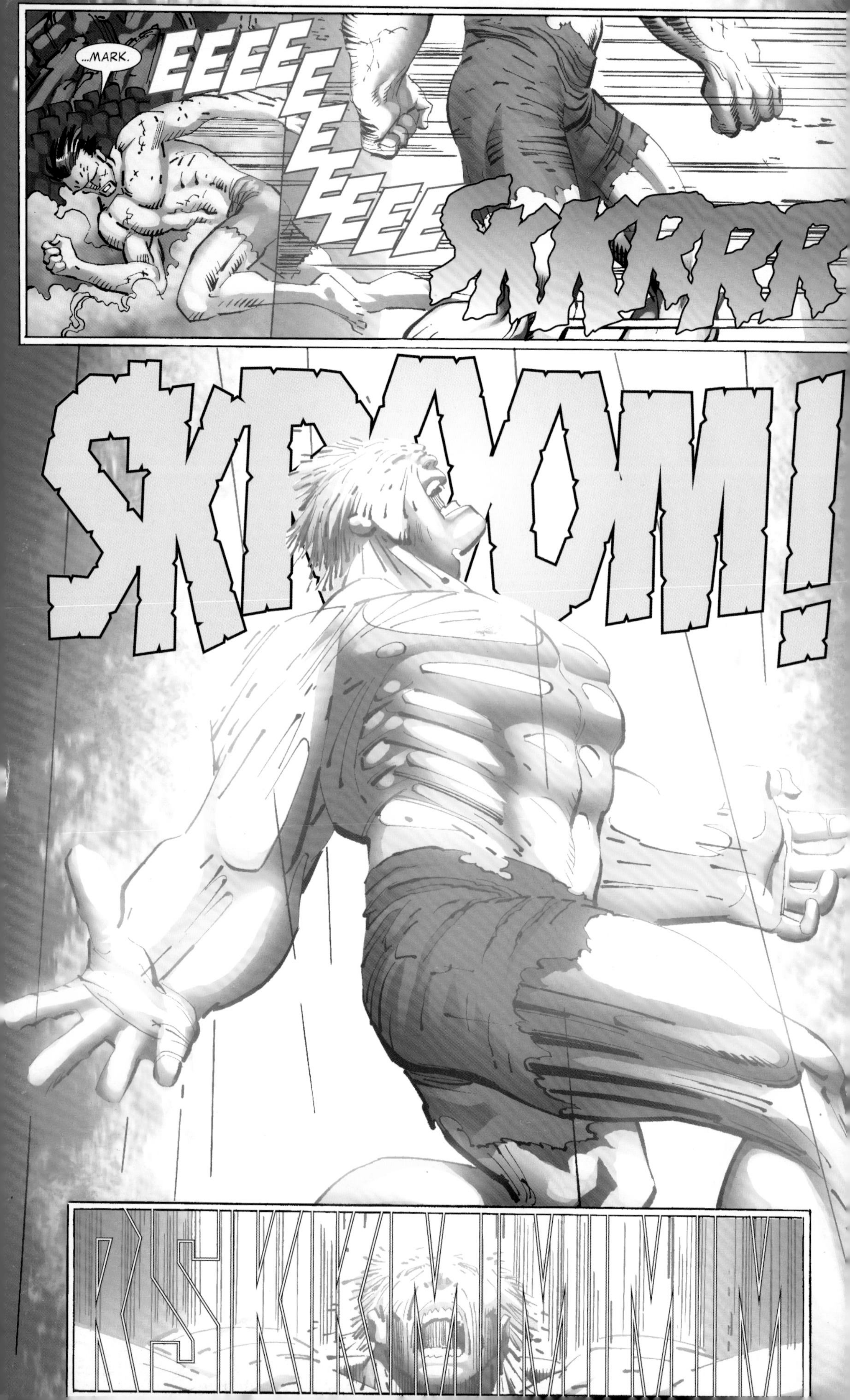
...MARK.

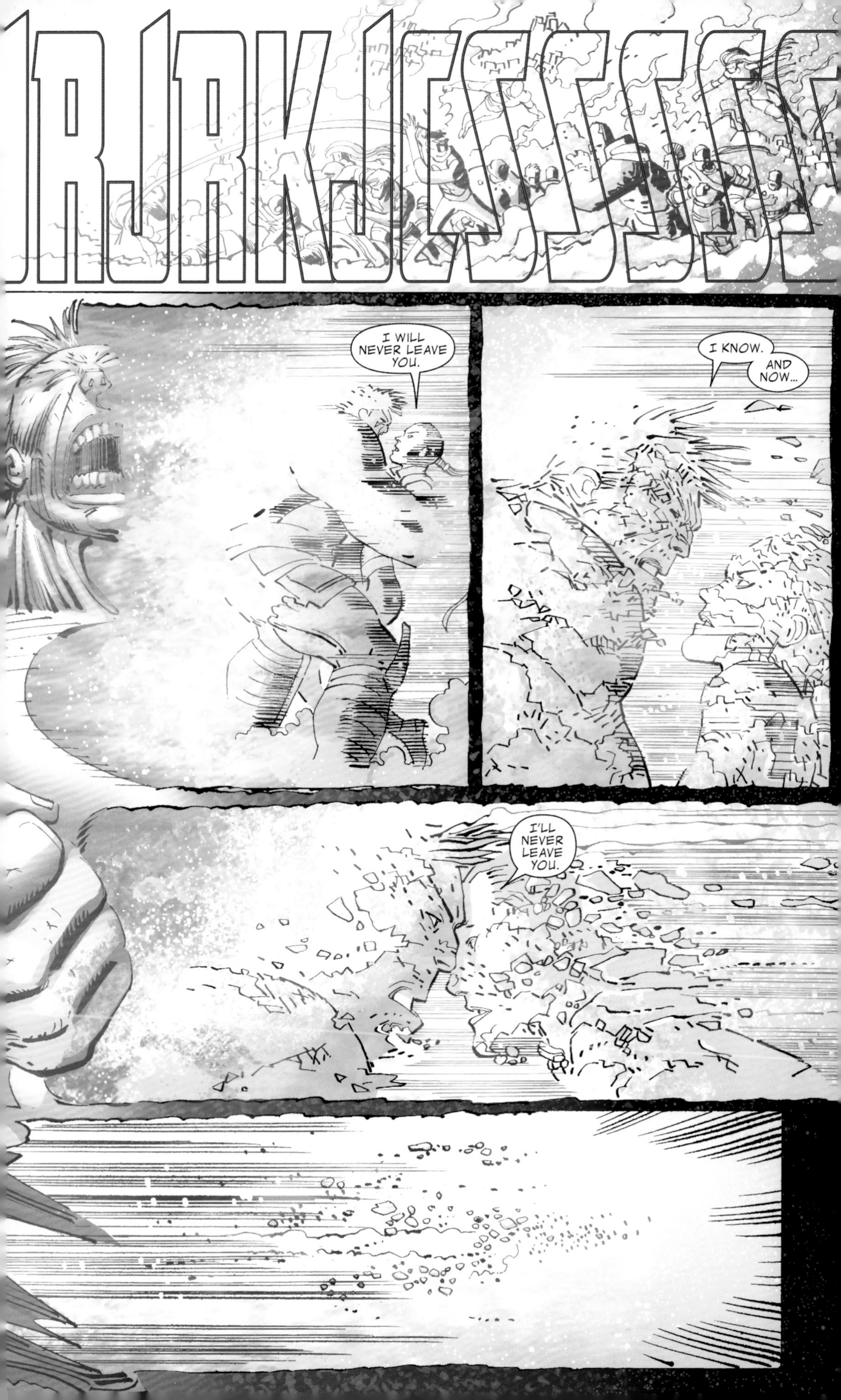
I WILL NEVER LEAVE YOU.
I KNOW.
AND NOW...
I'LL NEVER LEAVE YOU.

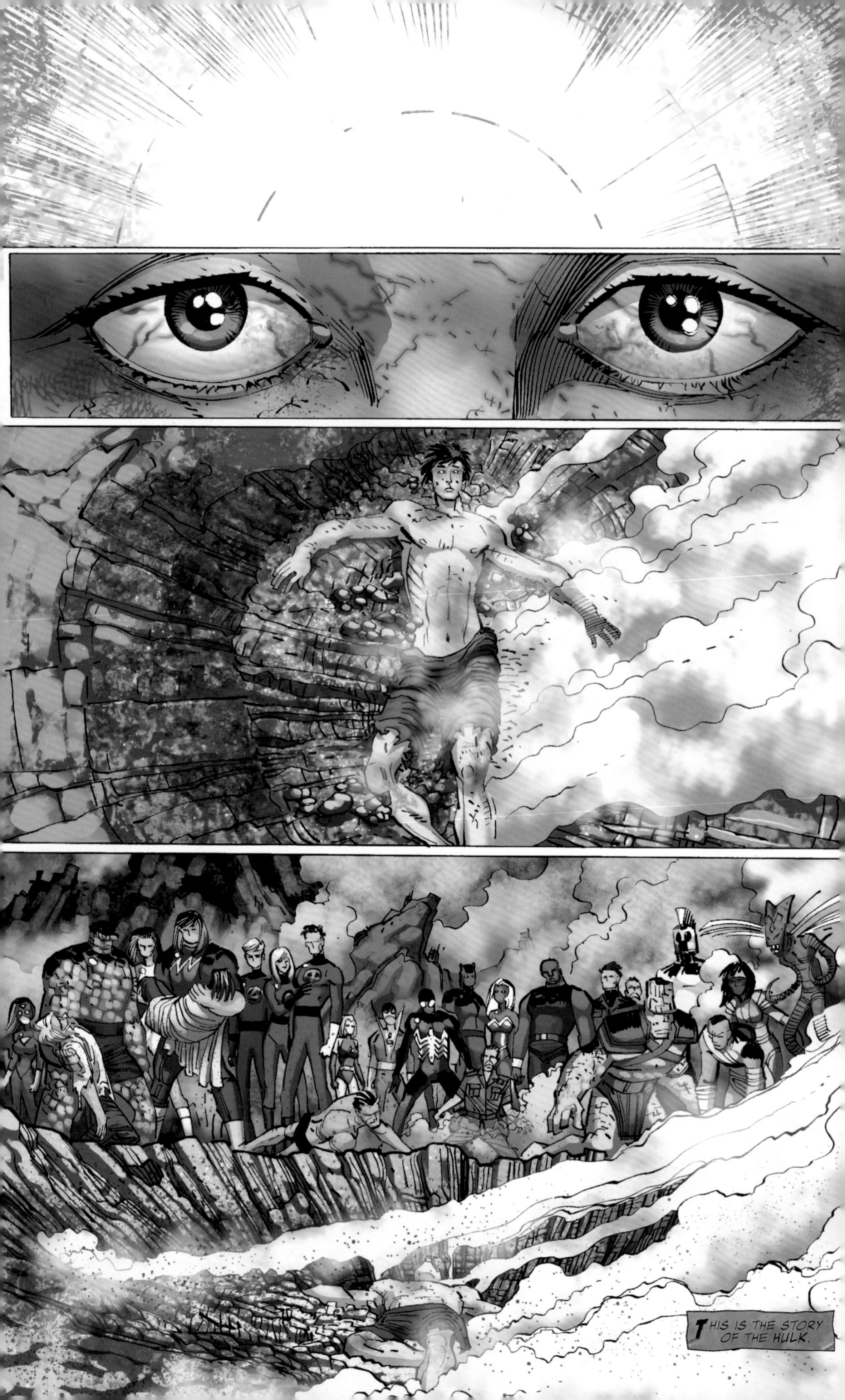
THIS IS THE STORY OF THE HULK.

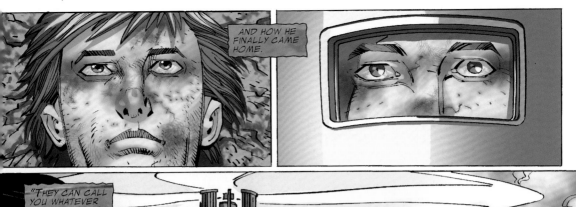
AND HOW HE FINALLY CAME HOME.

"THEY CAN CALL YOU WHATEVER THEY WANT," HE SAID.

S.H.I.E.L.D.

"SAVIOR.

"DESTROYER.

"ALL THAT MATTERS...

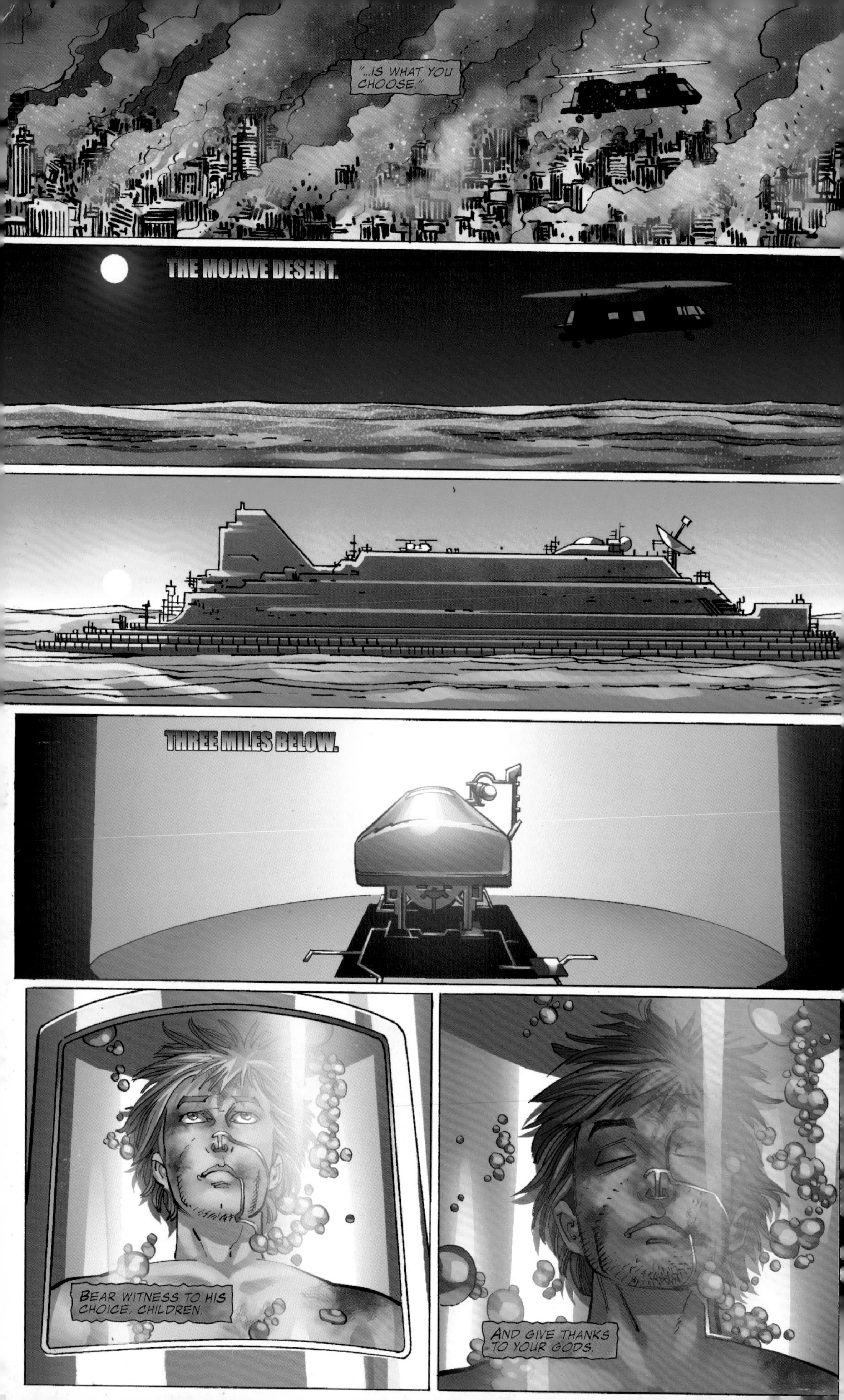
"...IS WHAT YOU CHOOSE."
THE MOJAVE DESERT.
THREE MILES BELOW.
BEAR WITNESS TO HIS CHOICE, CHILDREN.
AND GIVE THANKS TO YOUR GODS.

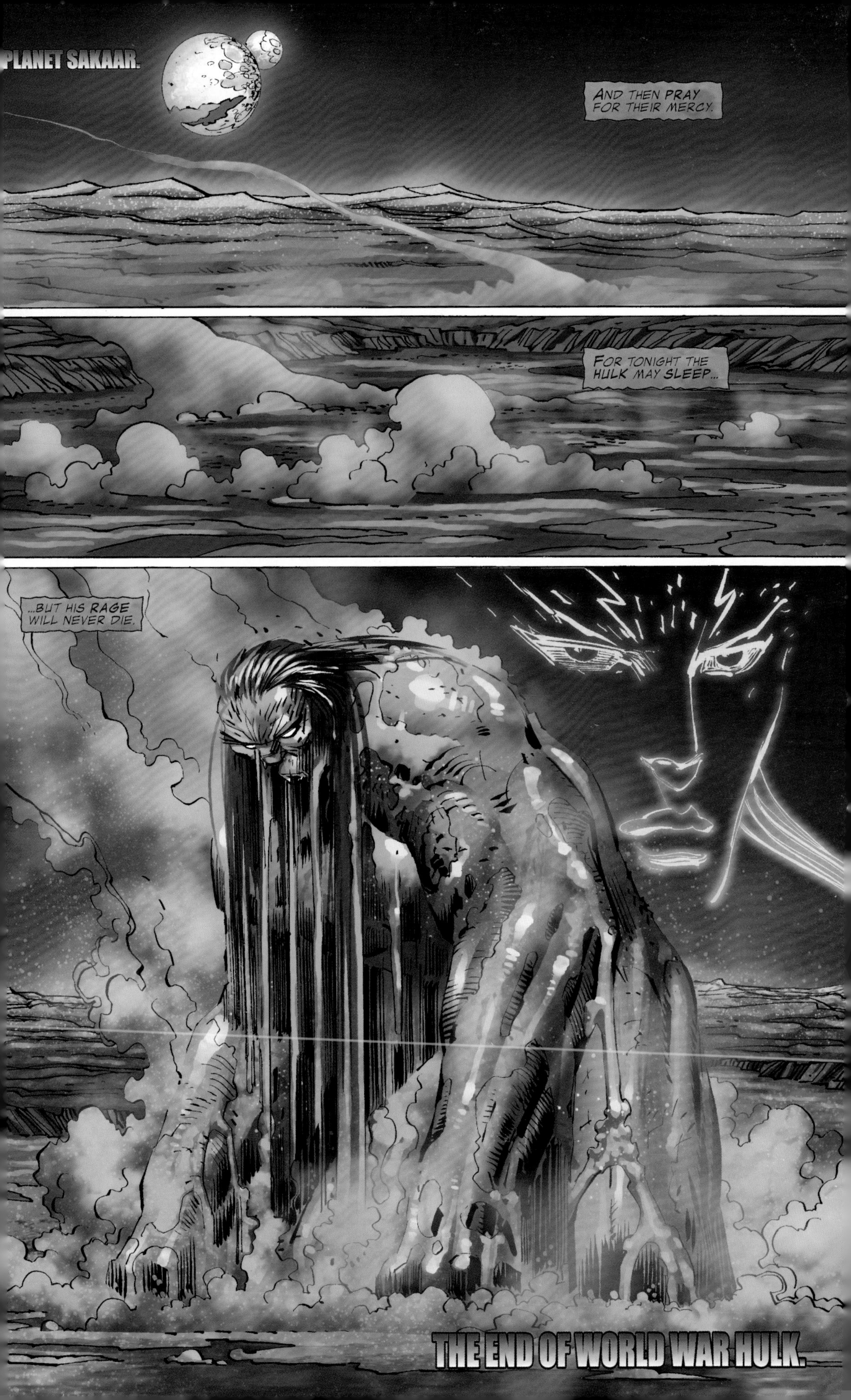

PLANET SAKAAR.
AND THEN PRAY FOR THEIR MERCY.
FOR TONIGHT THE HULK MAY SLEEP...
...BUT HIS RAGE WILL NEVER DIE.
THE END OF WORLD WAR HULK.

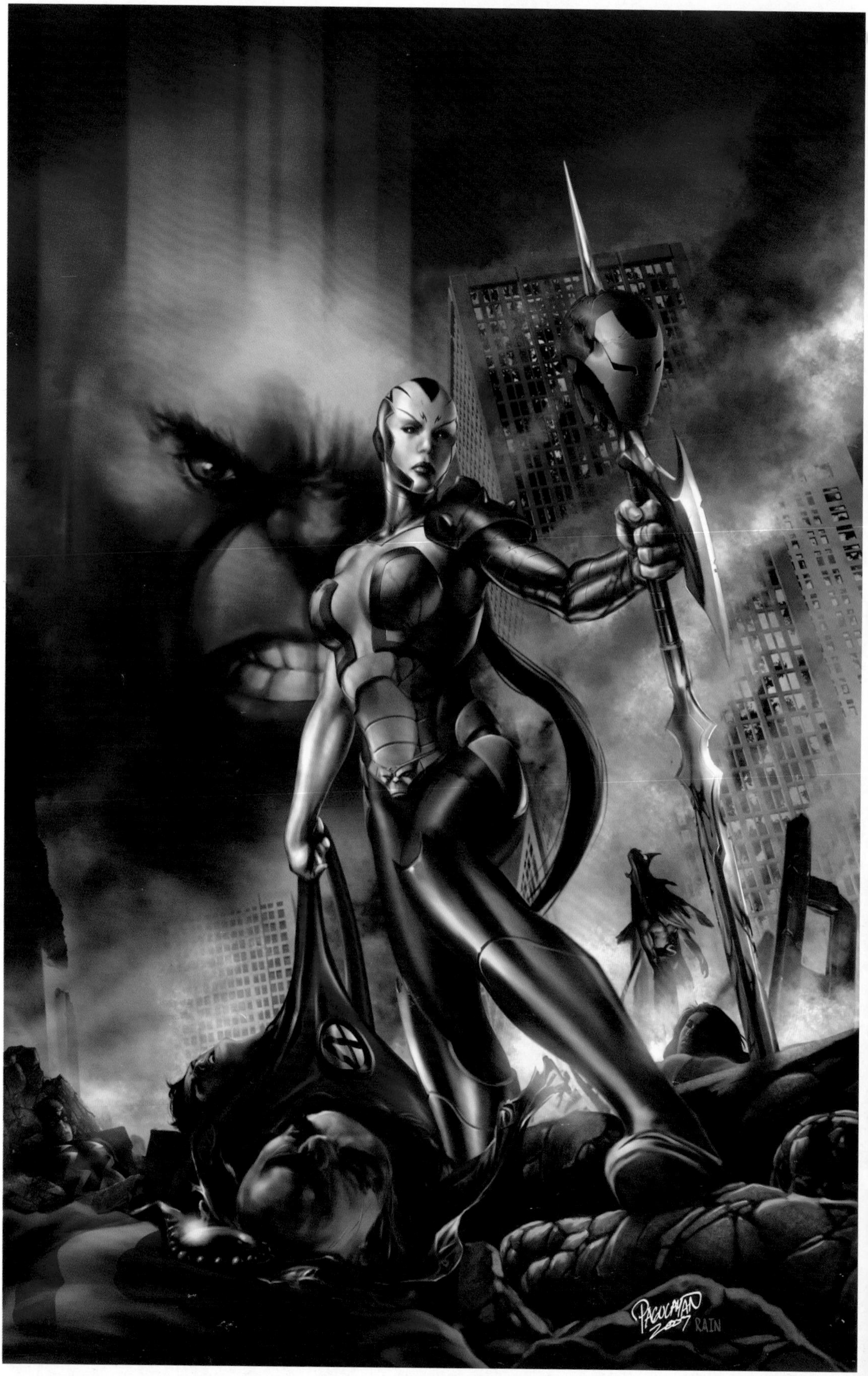
PACQUALAN 2007
RAIN

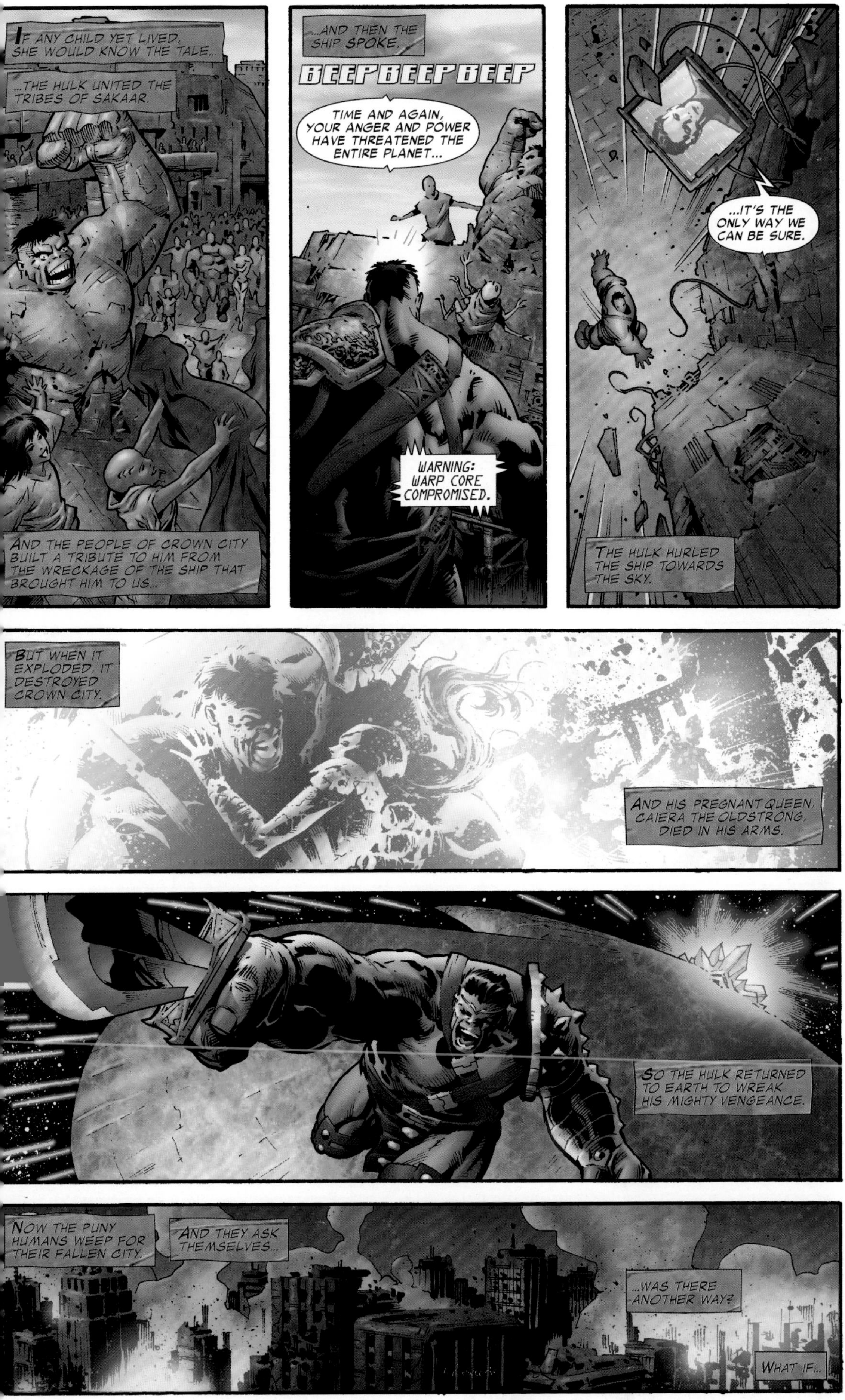

IF ANY CHILD YET LIVED, SHE WOULD KNOW THE TALE...
...THE HULK UNITED THE TRIBES OF SAKAAR.
AND THE PEOPLE OF CROWN CITY BUILT A TRIBUTE TO HIM FROM THE WRECKAGE OF THE SHIP THAT BROUGHT HIM TO US...
...AND THEN THE SHIP SPOKE.
BEEPBEEPBEEP
TIME AND AGAIN, YOUR ANGER AND POWER HAVE THREATENED THE ENTIRE PLANET...
WARNING: WARP CORE COMPROMISED.
...IT'S THE ONLY WAY WE CAN BE SURE.
THE HULK HURLED THE SHIP TOWARDS THE SKY.
BUT WHEN IT EXPLODED, IT DESTROYED CROWN CITY.
AND HIS PREGNANT QUEEN, CAIERA THE OLDSTRONG, DIED IN HIS ARMS.
SO THE HULK RETURNED TO EARTH TO WREAK HIS MIGHTY VENGEANCE.
NOW THE PUNY HUMANS WEEP FOR THEIR FALLEN CITY.
AND THEY ASK THEMSELVES...
...WAS THERE ANOTHER WAY?
WHAT IF...

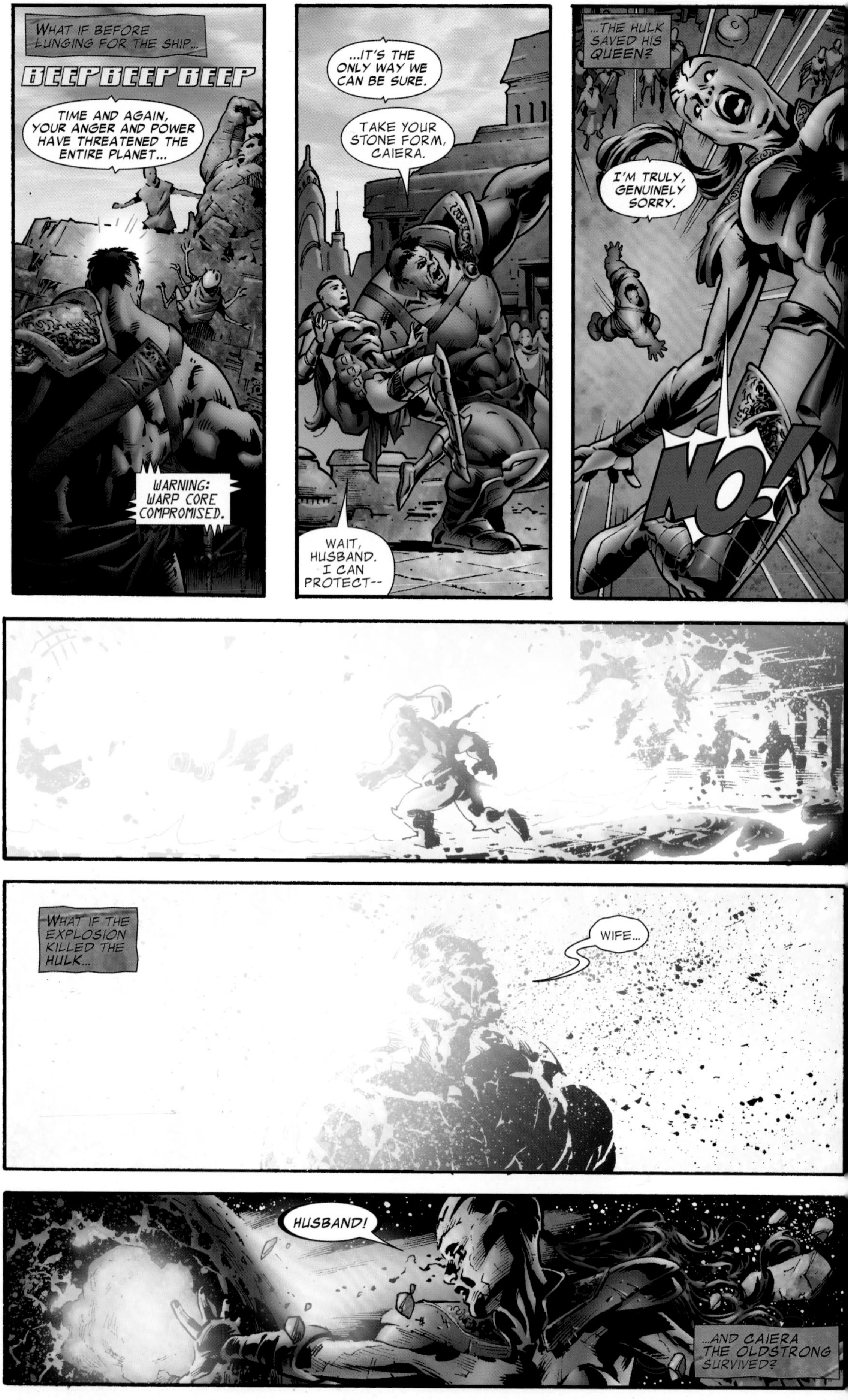

WHAT IF BEFORE LUNGING FOR THE SHIP...
BEEP BEEP BEEP
TIME AND AGAIN, YOUR ANGER AND POWER HAVE THREATENED THE ENTIRE PLANET...
WARNING: WARP CORE COMPROMISED.
...IT'S THE ONLY WAY WE CAN BE SURE.
TAKE YOUR STONE FORM, CAIERA.
WAIT, HUSBAND. I CAN PROTECT--
...THE HULK SAVED HIS QUEEN?
I'M TRULY, GENUINELY SORRY.
NO!
WHAT IF THE EXPLOSION KILLED THE HULK...
WIFE...
HUSBAND!
...AND CAIERA THE OLDSTRONG SURVIVED?

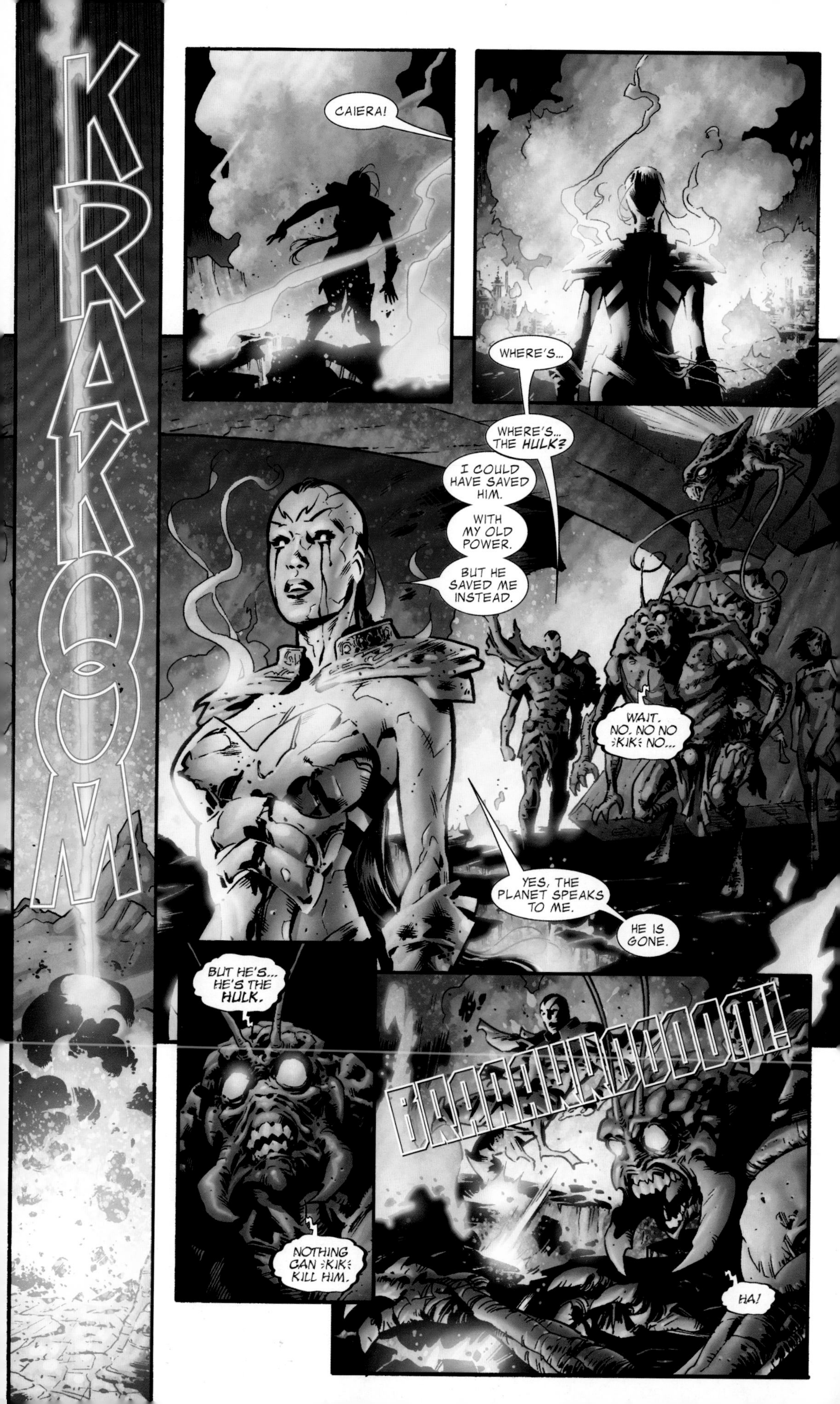
KRAKOOM
CAIERA!
WHERE'S...
WHERE'S... THE **HULK**?
I COULD HAVE SAVED HIM.
WITH MY OLD POWER.
BUT HE SAVED ME INSTEAD.
WAIT. NO. NO NO ≶KIK≶ NO...
YES, THE PLANET SPEAKS TO ME.
HE IS GONE.
BUT HE'S... HE'S THE **HULK**.
NOTHING CAN ≶KIK≶ KILL HIM.
BRAAKKKOOOOM!
HA!

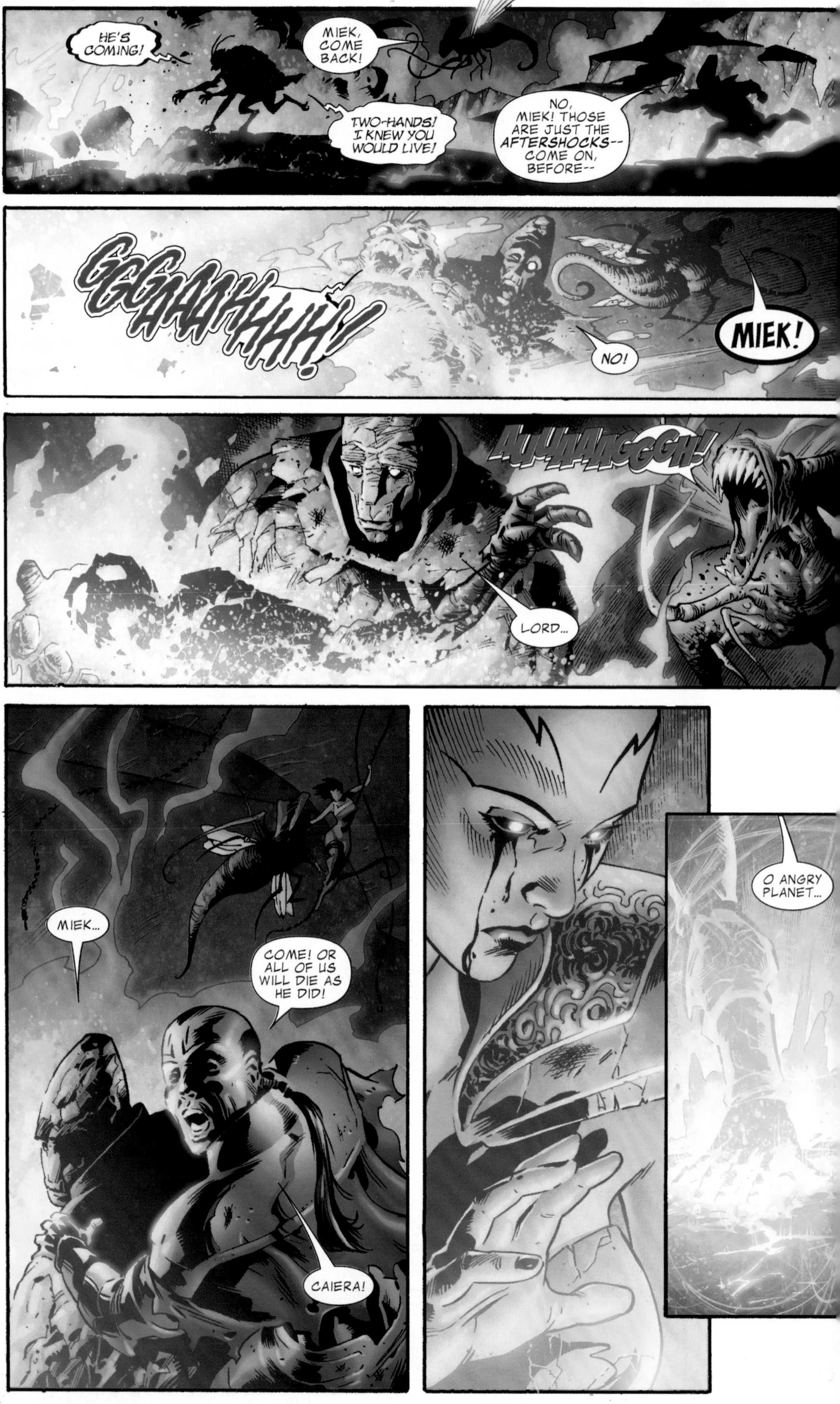
HE'S COMING!
MIEK, COME BACK!
TWO-HANDS! I KNEW YOU WOULD LIVE!
NO, MIEK! THOSE ARE JUST THE AFTERSHOCKS-- COME ON, BEFORE--
GGGAAAHHHH!
NO!
MIEK!
AUUUAAAGGGH!
LORD...
MIEK...
COME! OR ALL OF US WILL DIE AS HE DID!
CAIERA!
O ANGRY PLANET...

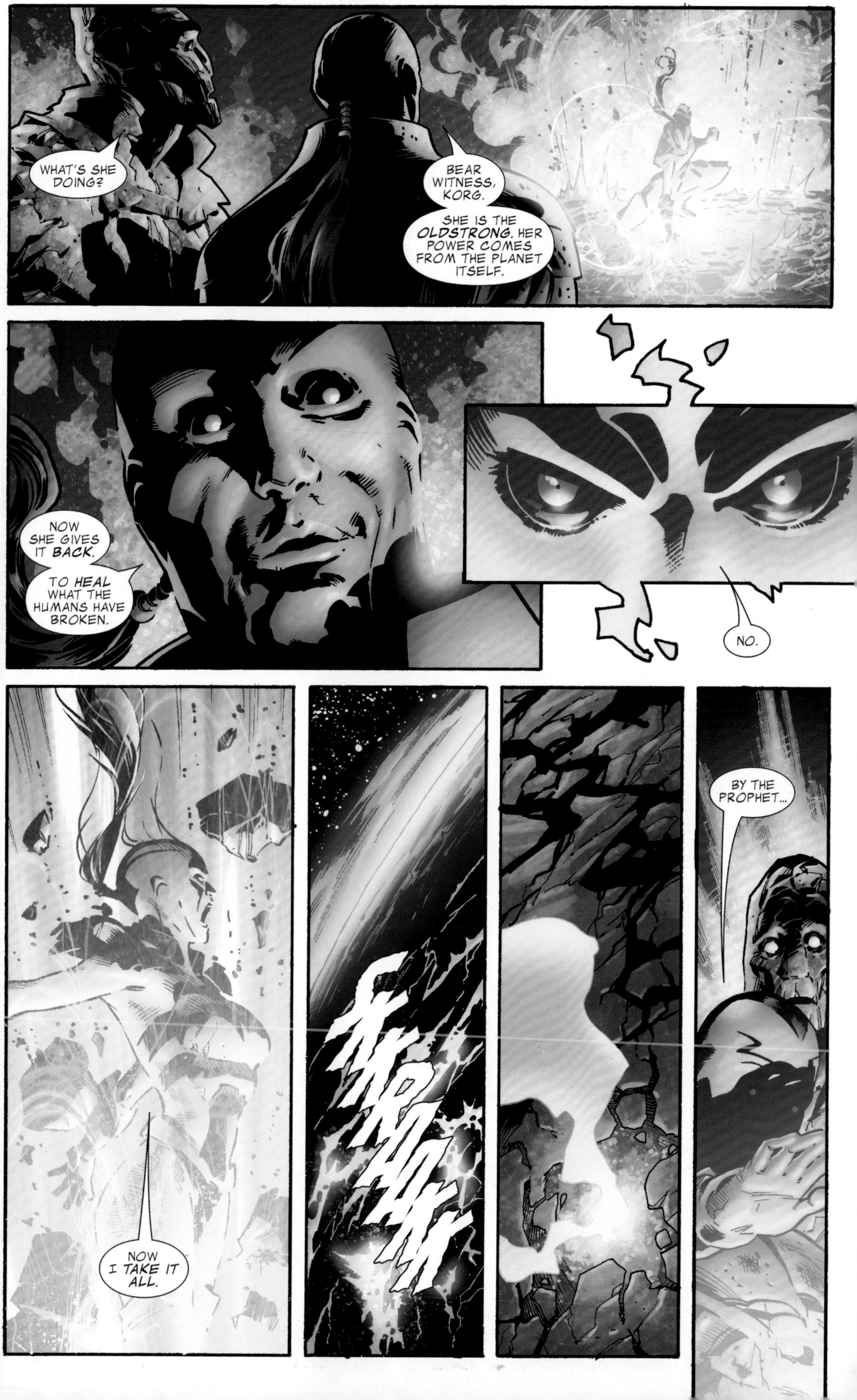

WHAT'S SHE DOING?
BEAR WITNESS, KORG.
SHE IS THE *OLDSTRONG*. HER POWER COMES FROM THE PLANET ITSELF.
NOW SHE GIVES IT *BACK*.
TO *HEAL* WHAT THE HUMANS HAVE BROKEN.
NO.
NOW I *TAKE IT ALL*.
KRAKAKK
BY THE PROPHET...

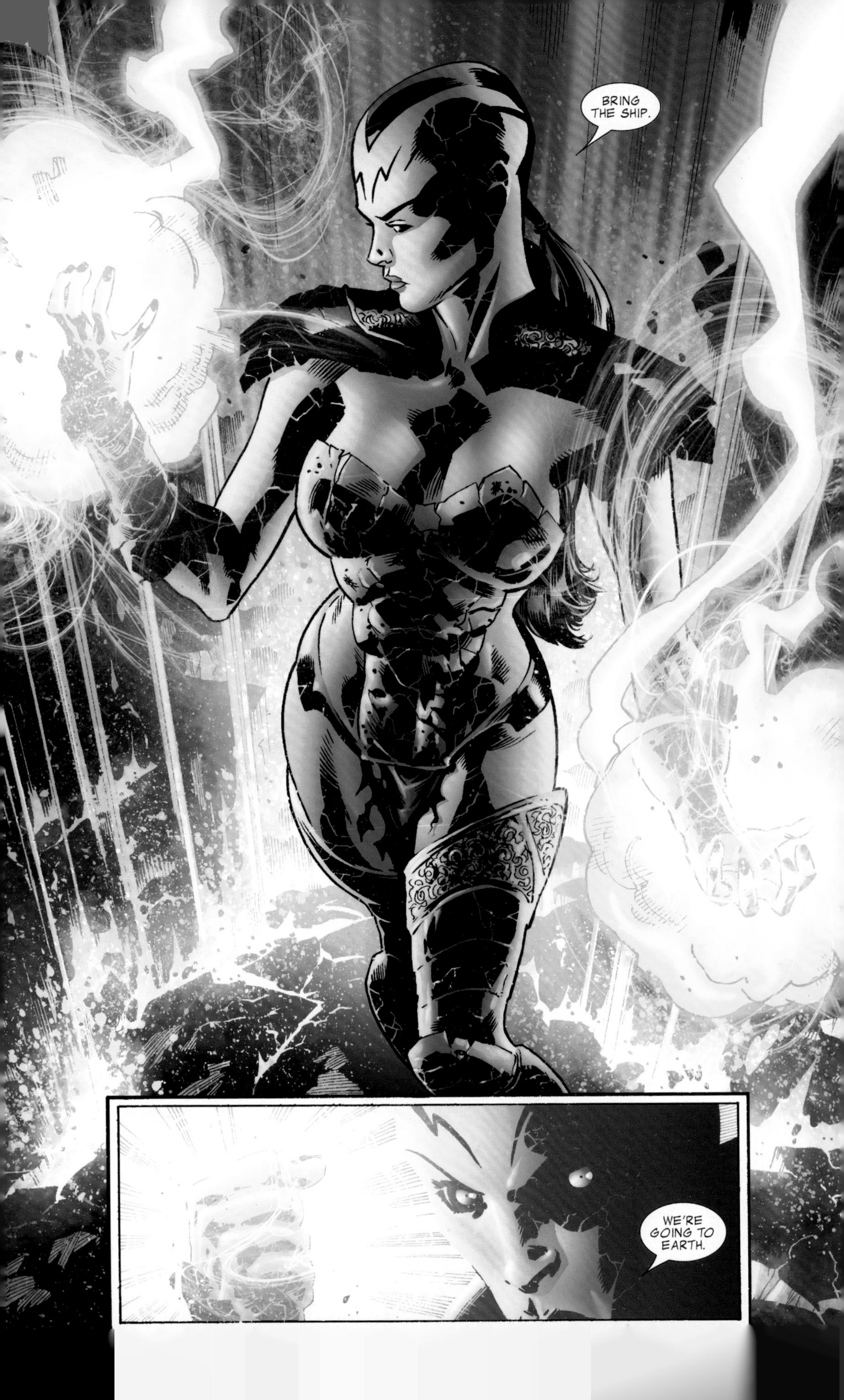
BRING THE SHIP.
WE'RE GOING TO EARTH.

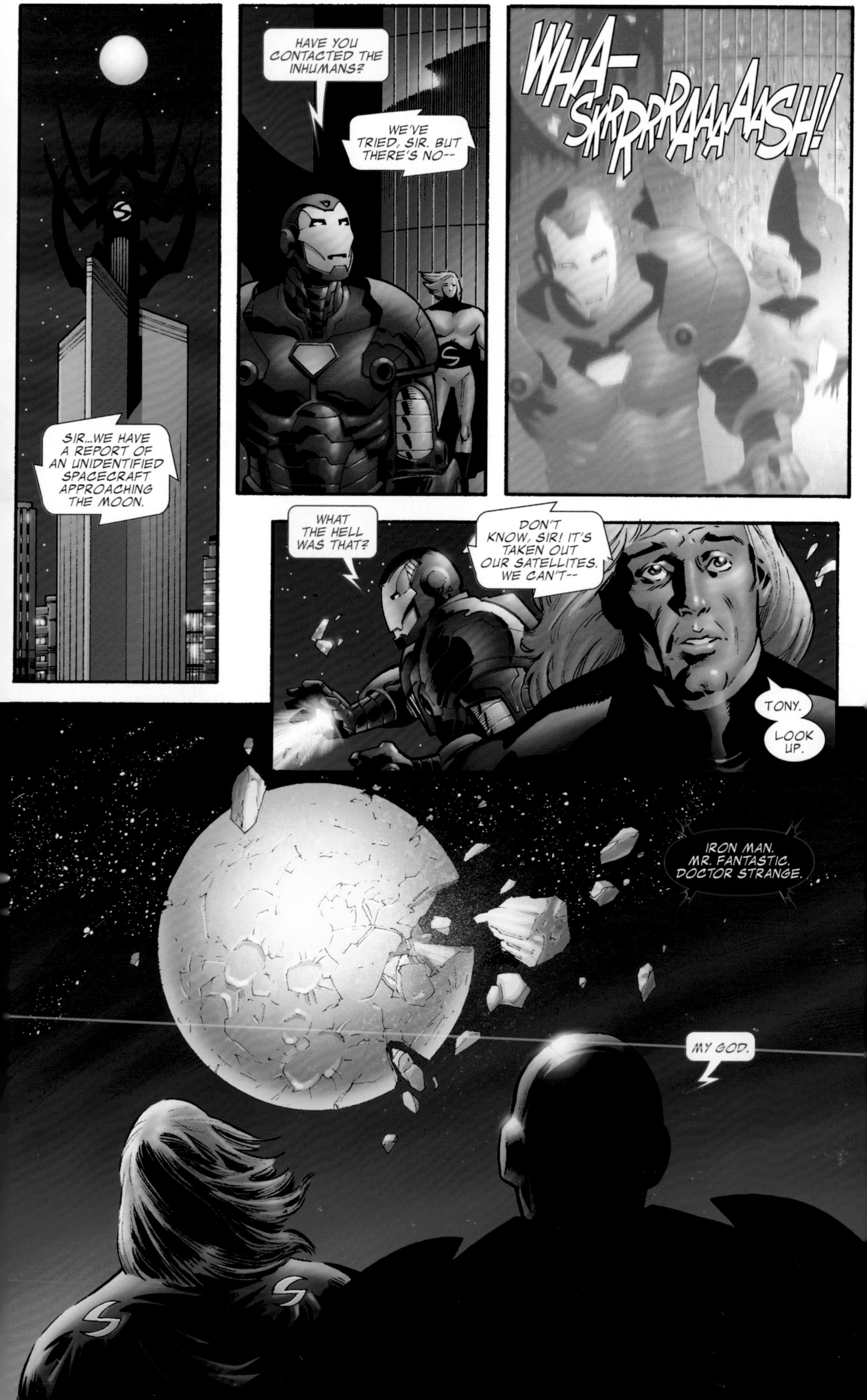
SIR...WE HAVE A REPORT OF AN UNIDENTIFIED SPACECRAFT APPROACHING THE MOON.
HAVE YOU CONTACTED THE INHUMANS?
WE'VE TRIED, SIR. BUT THERE'S NO--
WHA-SKRRRRAAAAASH!
WHAT THE HELL WAS THAT?
DON'T KNOW, SIR! IT'S TAKEN OUT OUR SATELLITES. WE CAN'T--
TONY.
LOOK UP.
IRON MAN. MR. FANTASTIC. DOCTOR STRANGE.
MY GOD.

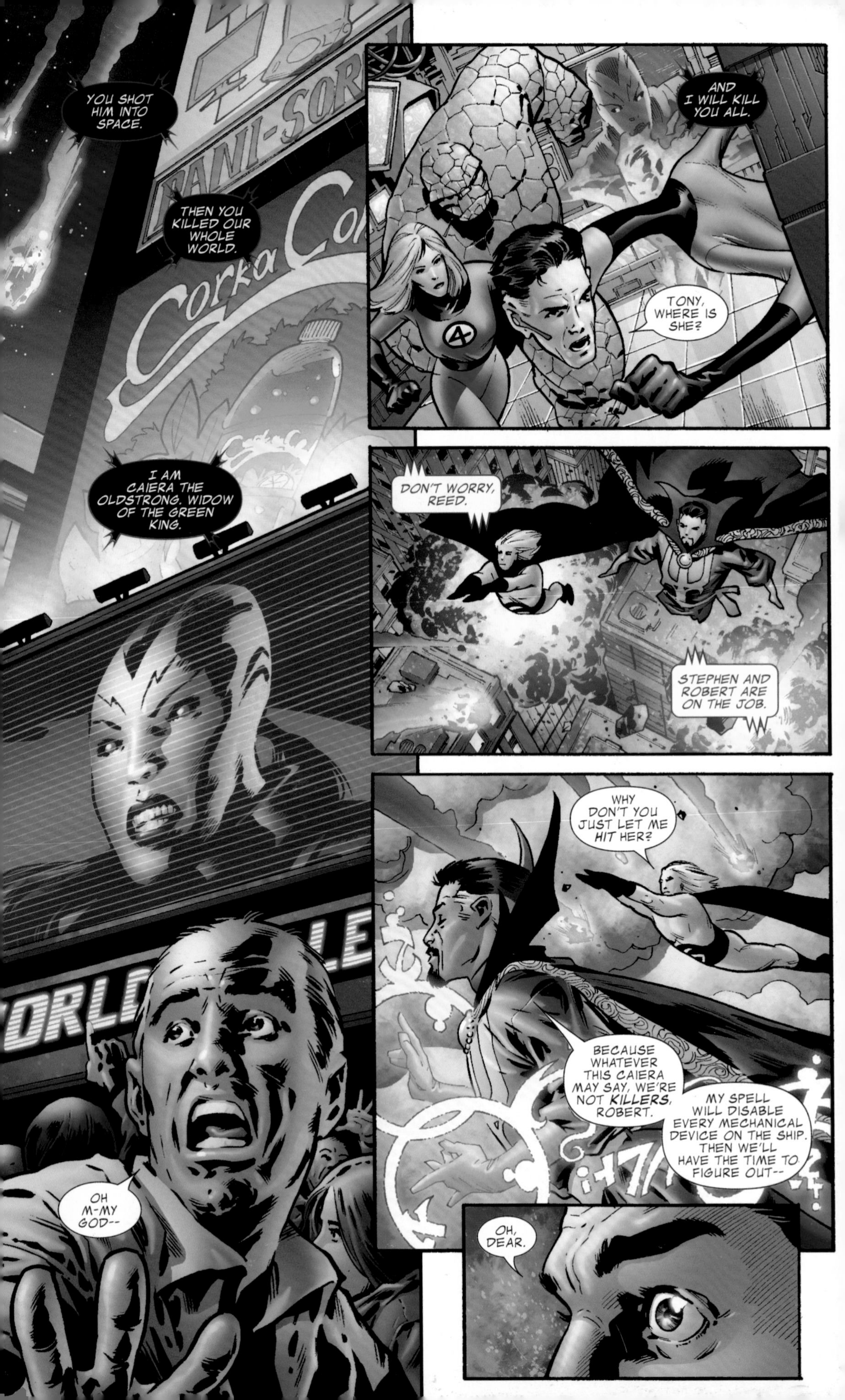
YOU SHOT HIM INTO SPACE.
THEN YOU KILLED OUR WHOLE WORLD.
I AM CAIERA THE OLDSTRONG. WIDOW OF THE GREEN KING.
OH M-MY GOD--
AND I WILL KILL YOU ALL.
TONY, WHERE IS SHE?
DON'T WORRY, REED.
STEPHEN AND ROBERT ARE ON THE JOB.
WHY DON'T YOU JUST LET ME HIT HER?
BECAUSE WHATEVER THIS CAIERA MAY SAY, WE'RE NOT KILLERS, ROBERT.
MY SPELL WILL DISABLE EVERY MECHANICAL DEVICE ON THE SHIP. THEN WE'LL HAVE THE TIME TO FIGURE OUT--
OH, DEAR.

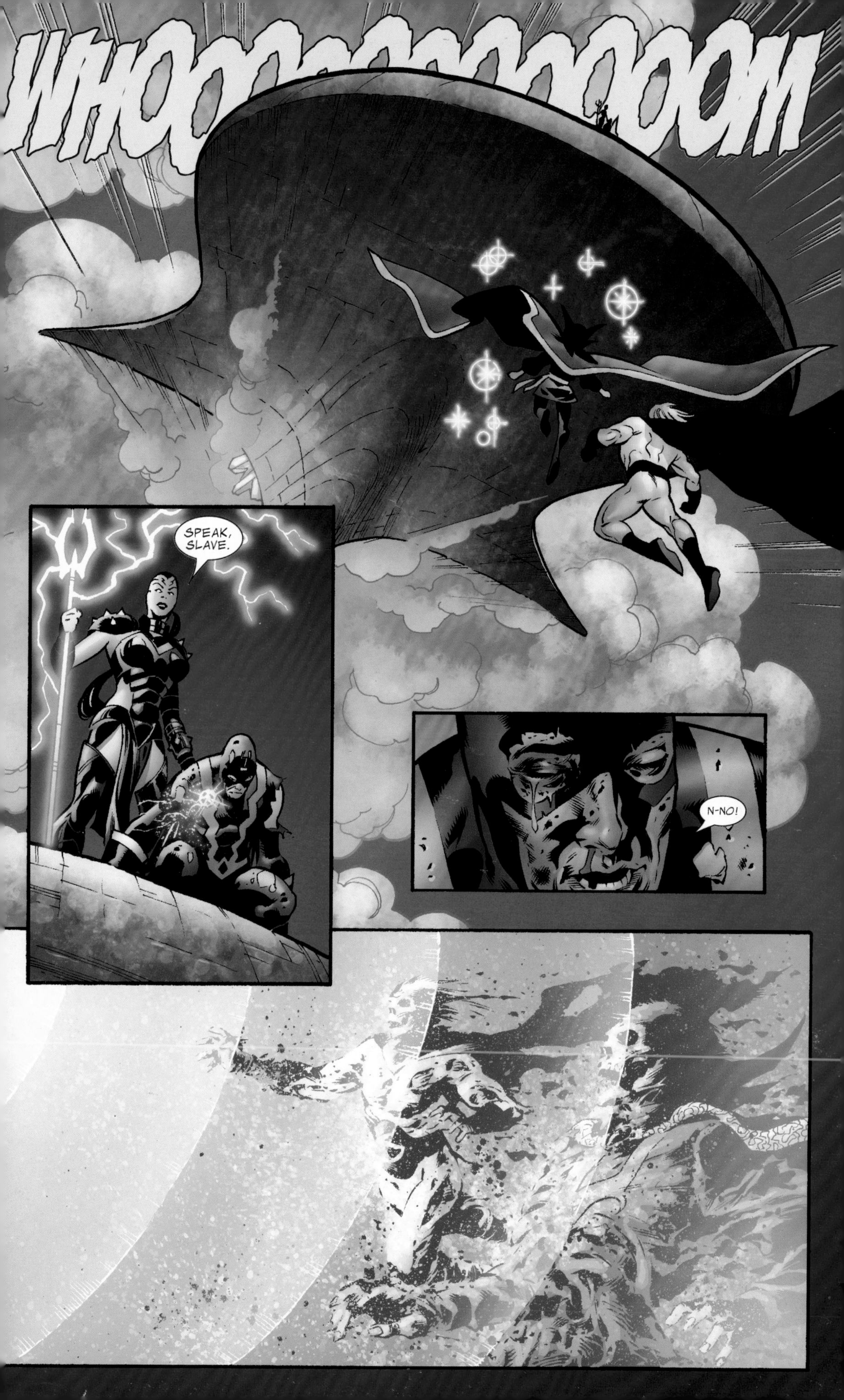
WHOOOOOOOOOOM
SPEAK, SLAVE.
N-NO!

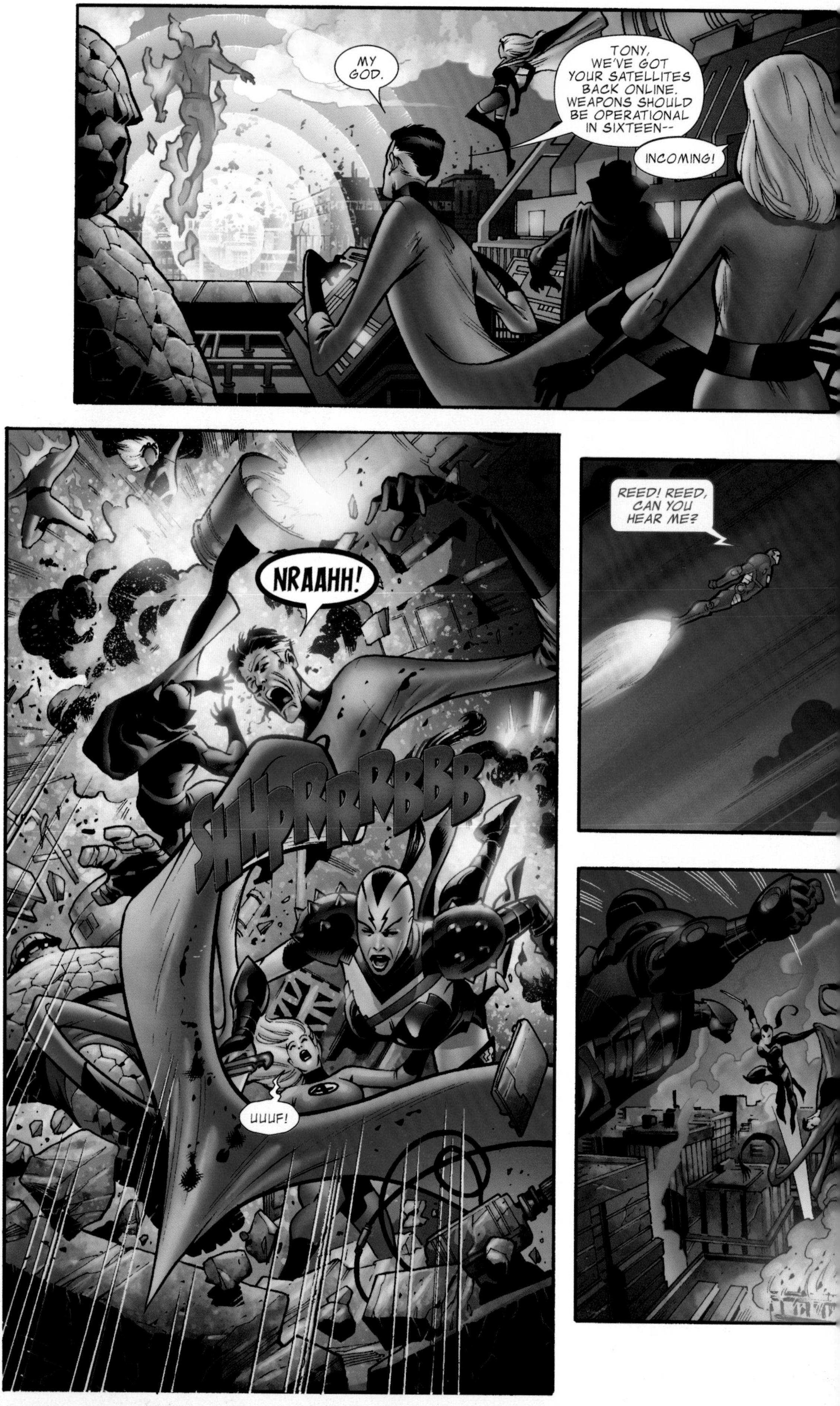
MY GOD.
TONY, WE'VE GOT YOUR SATELLITES BACK ONLINE. WEAPONS SHOULD BE OPERATIONAL IN SIXTEEN--
INCOMING!
NRAAHH!
SHHPRRRRBBB
UUUF!
REED! REED, CAN YOU HEAR ME?

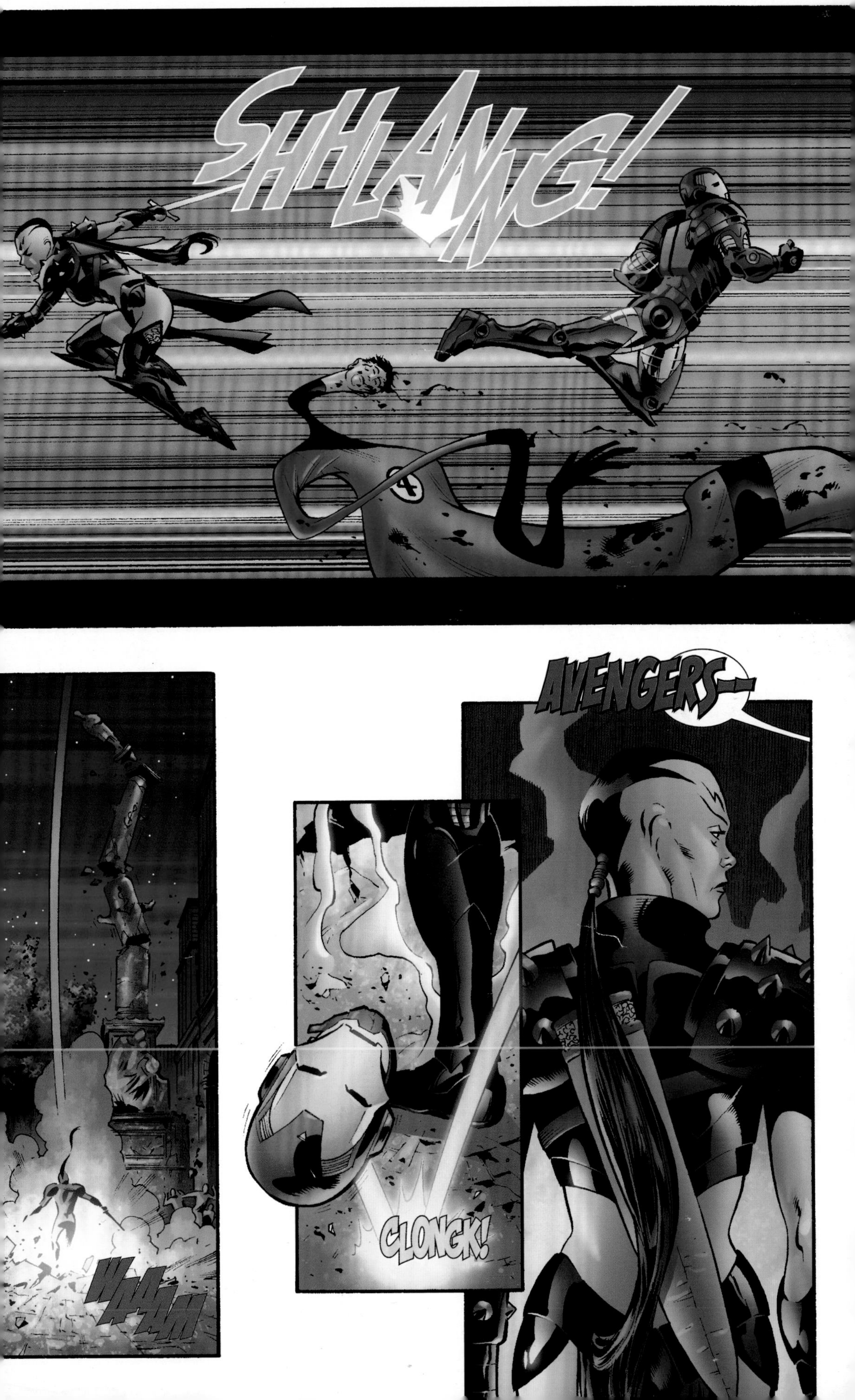
SHHLANNG!
WHAAM
CLONGK!
AVENGERS--

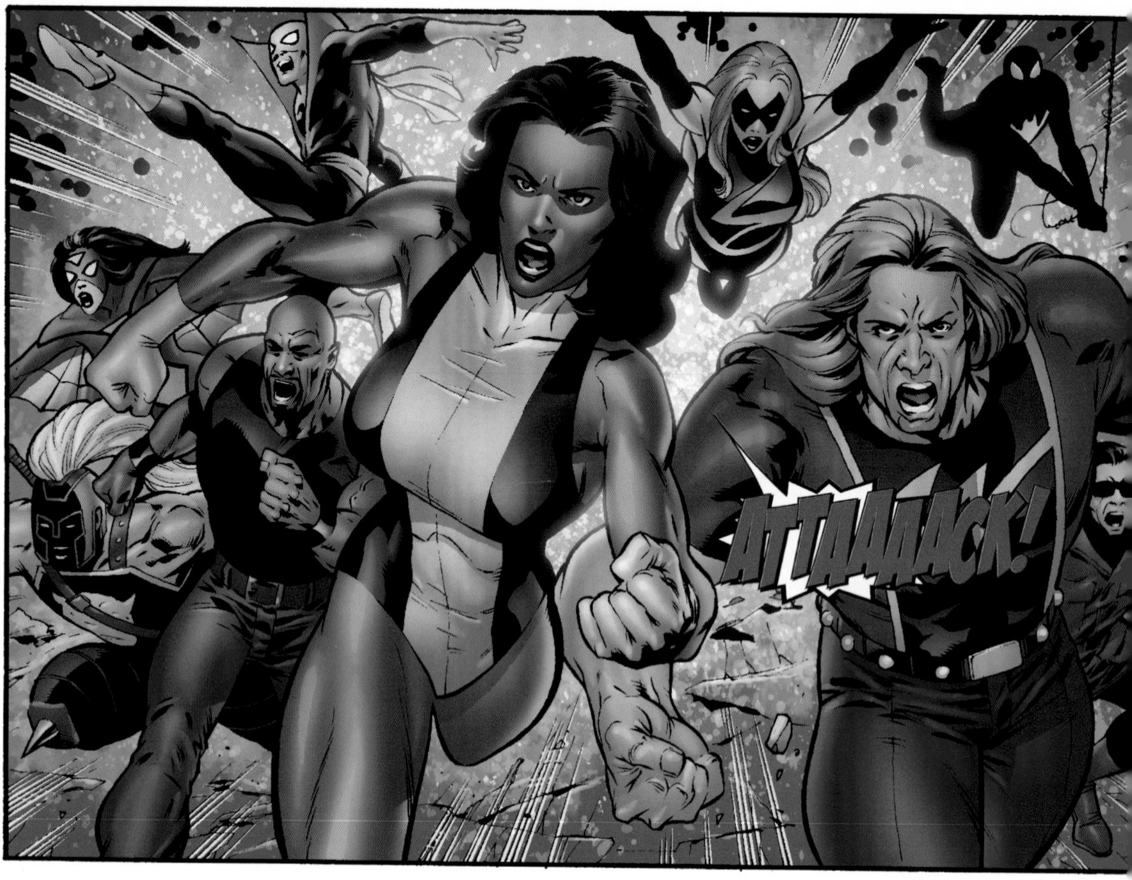
ATTAAAACK!

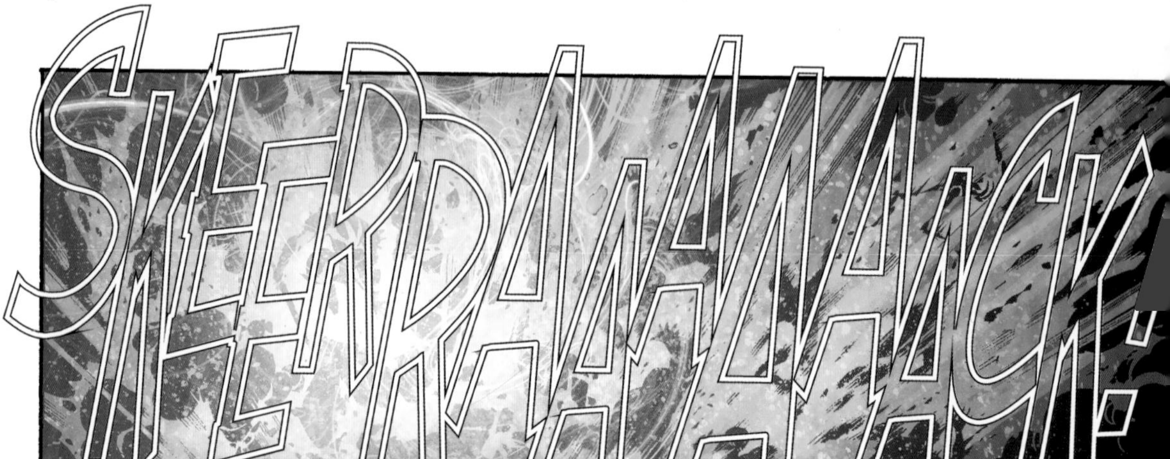
SKEERDAAAAAACK!

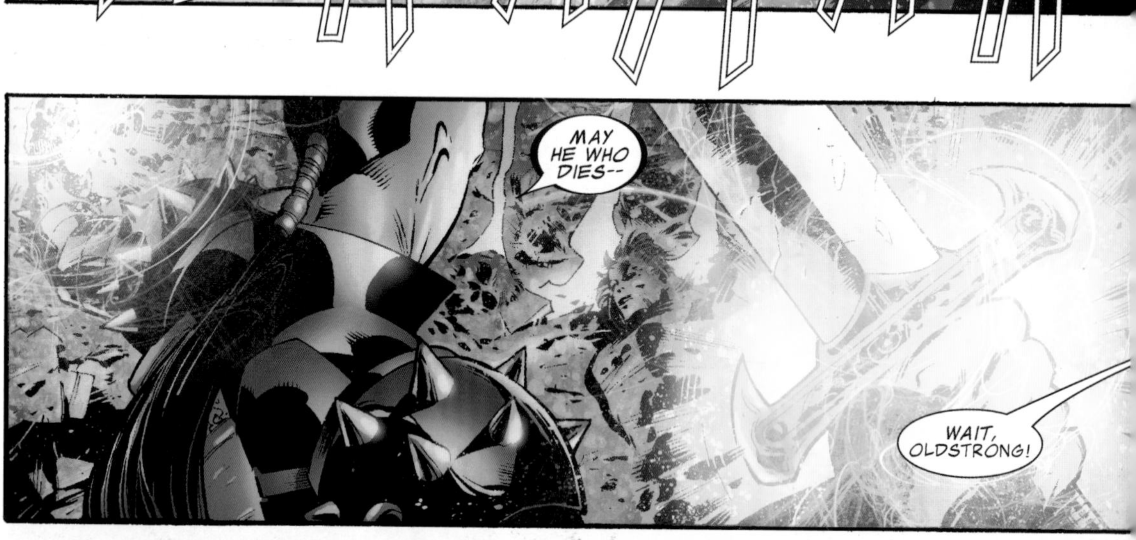
MAY HE WHO DIES--
WAIT, OLDSTRONG!

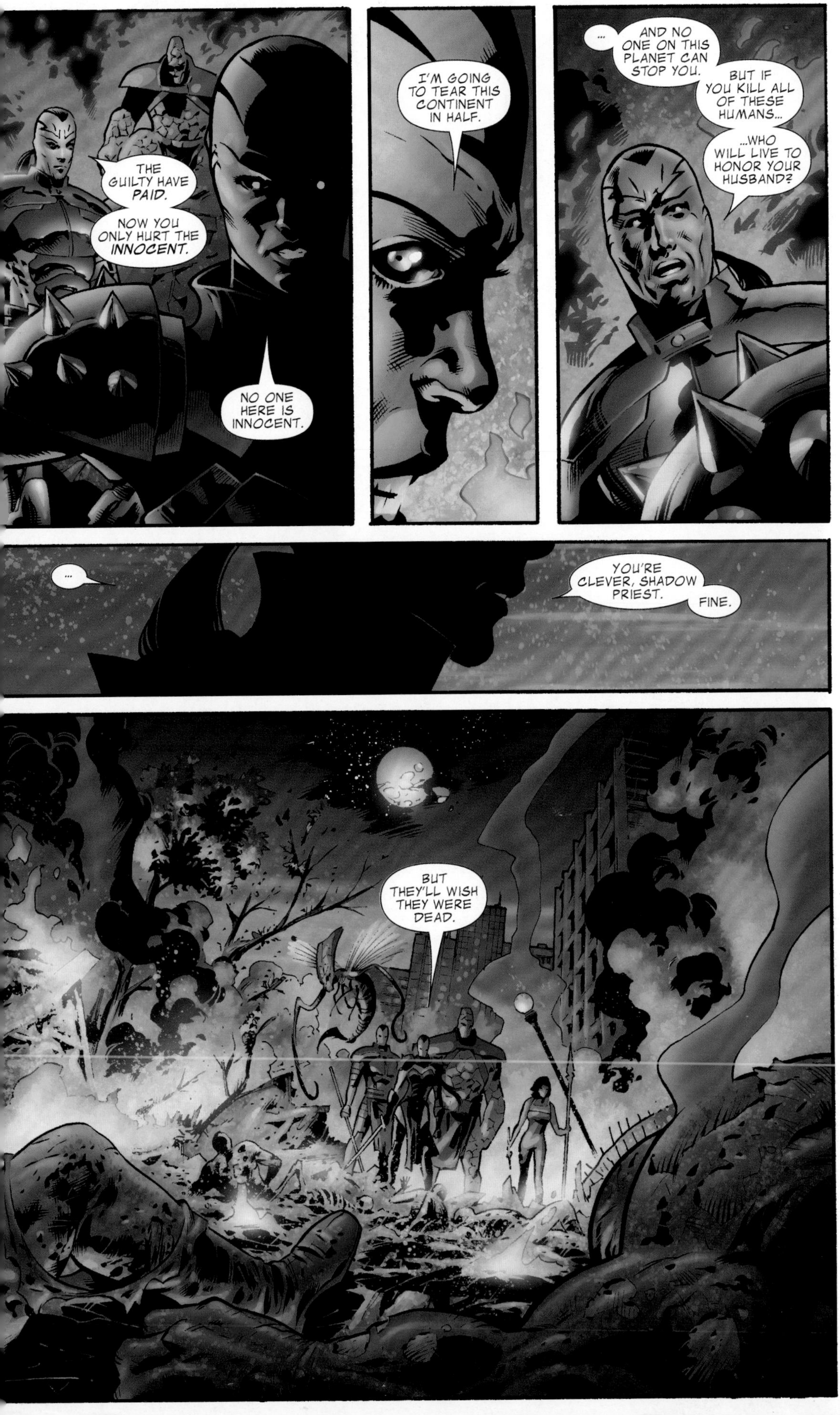
THE GUILTY HAVE PAID.
NOW YOU ONLY HURT THE INNOCENT.
NO ONE HERE IS INNOCENT.
I'M GOING TO TEAR THIS CONTINENT IN HALF.
...
AND NO ONE ON THIS PLANET CAN STOP YOU.
BUT IF YOU KILL ALL OF THESE HUMANS...
...WHO WILL LIVE TO HONOR YOUR HUSBAND?
...
YOU'RE CLEVER, SHADOW PRIEST.
FINE.
BUT THEY'LL WISH THEY WERE DEAD.

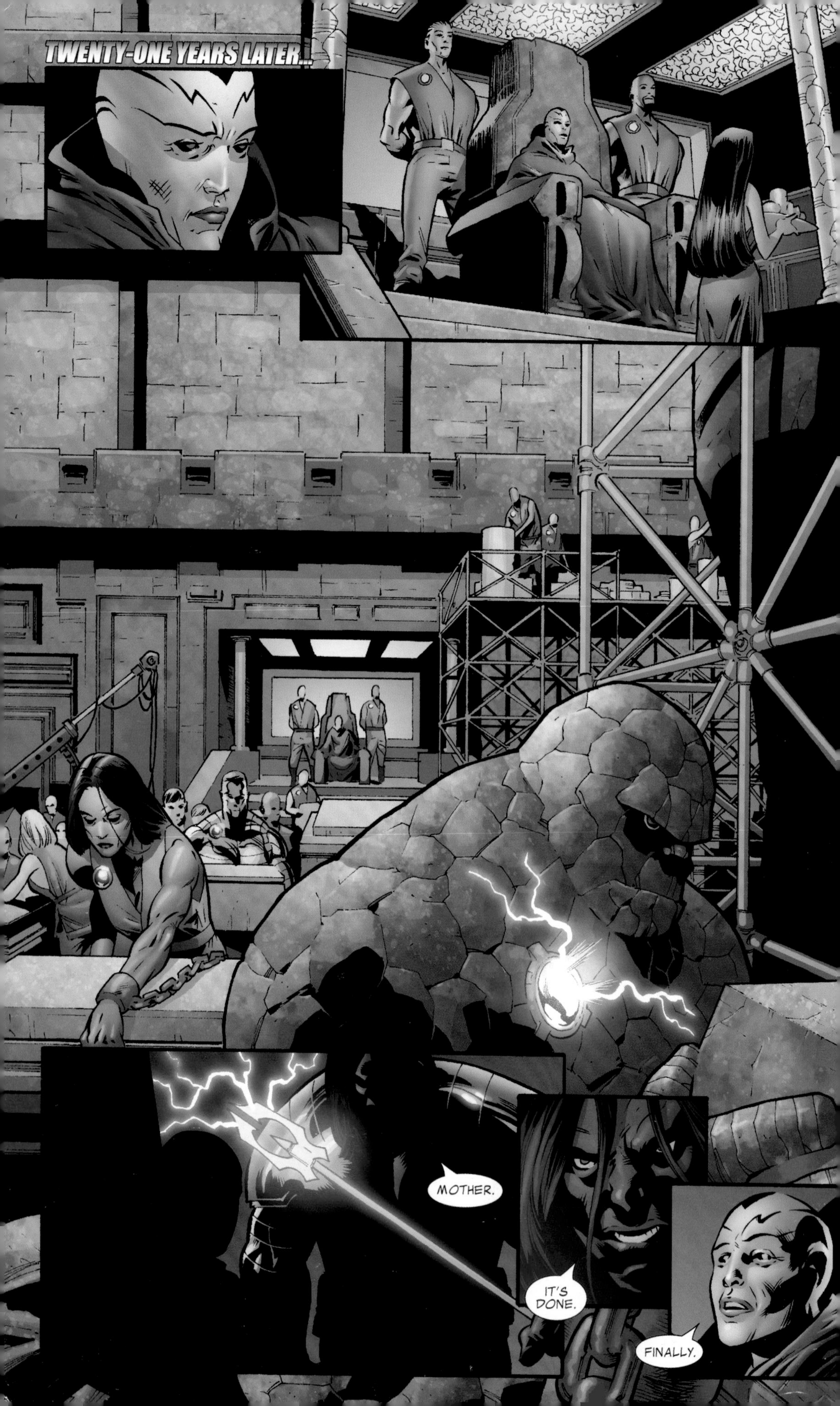

TWENTY-ONE YEARS LATER...
MOTHER.
IT'S DONE.
FINALLY.

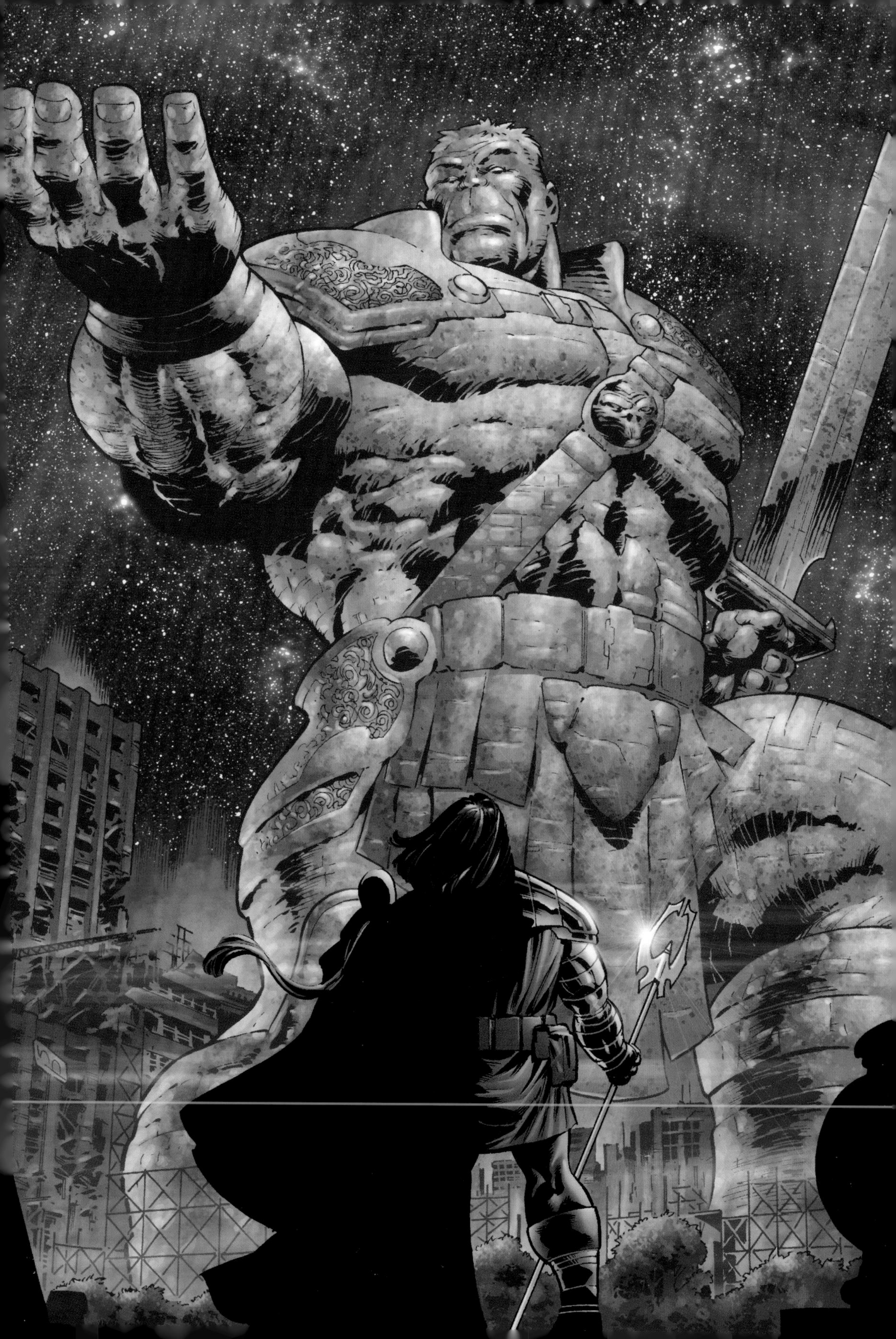

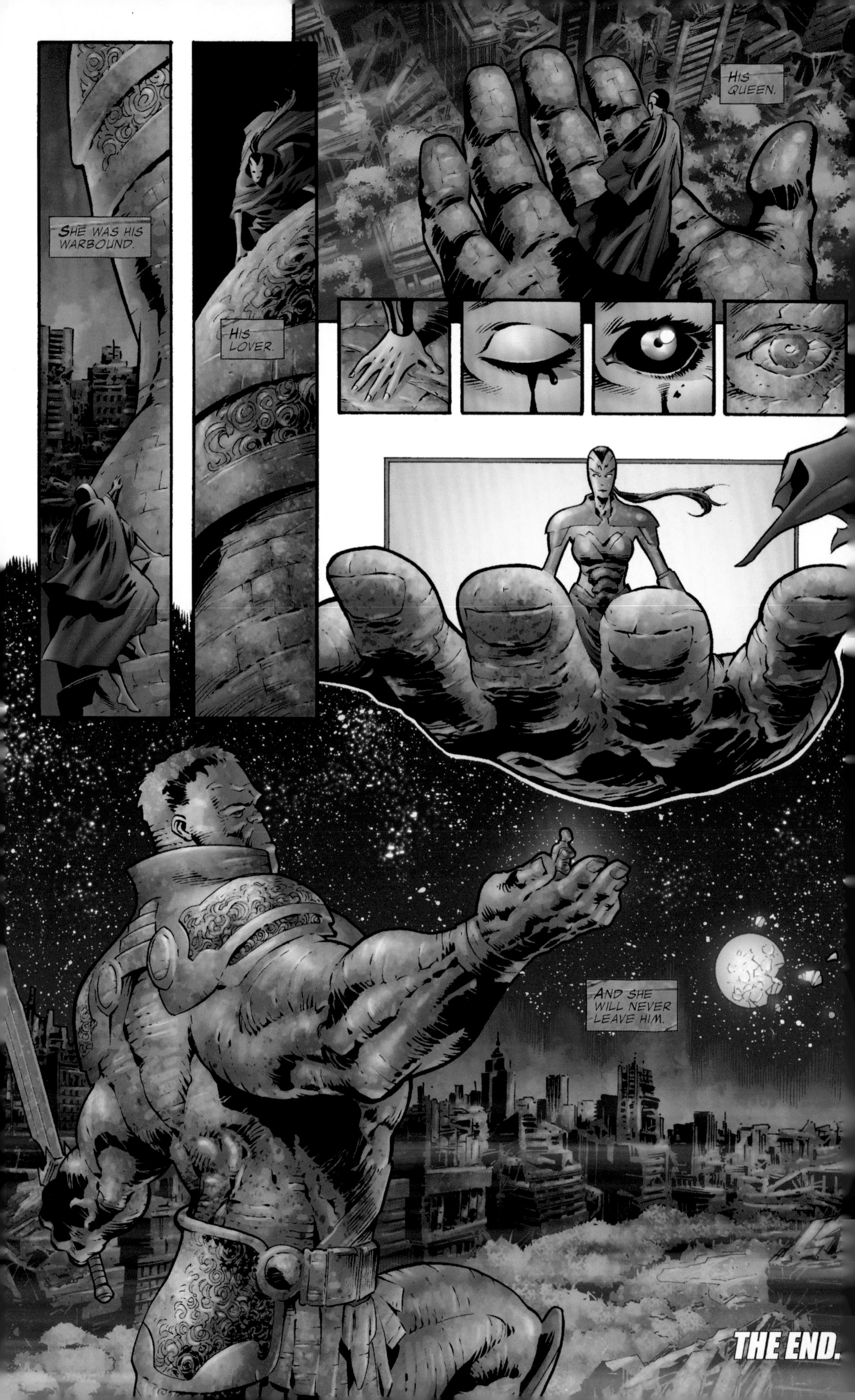
SHE WAS HIS WARBOUND.
HIS LOVER.
HIS QUEEN.
AND SHE WILL NEVER LEAVE HIM.
THE END.

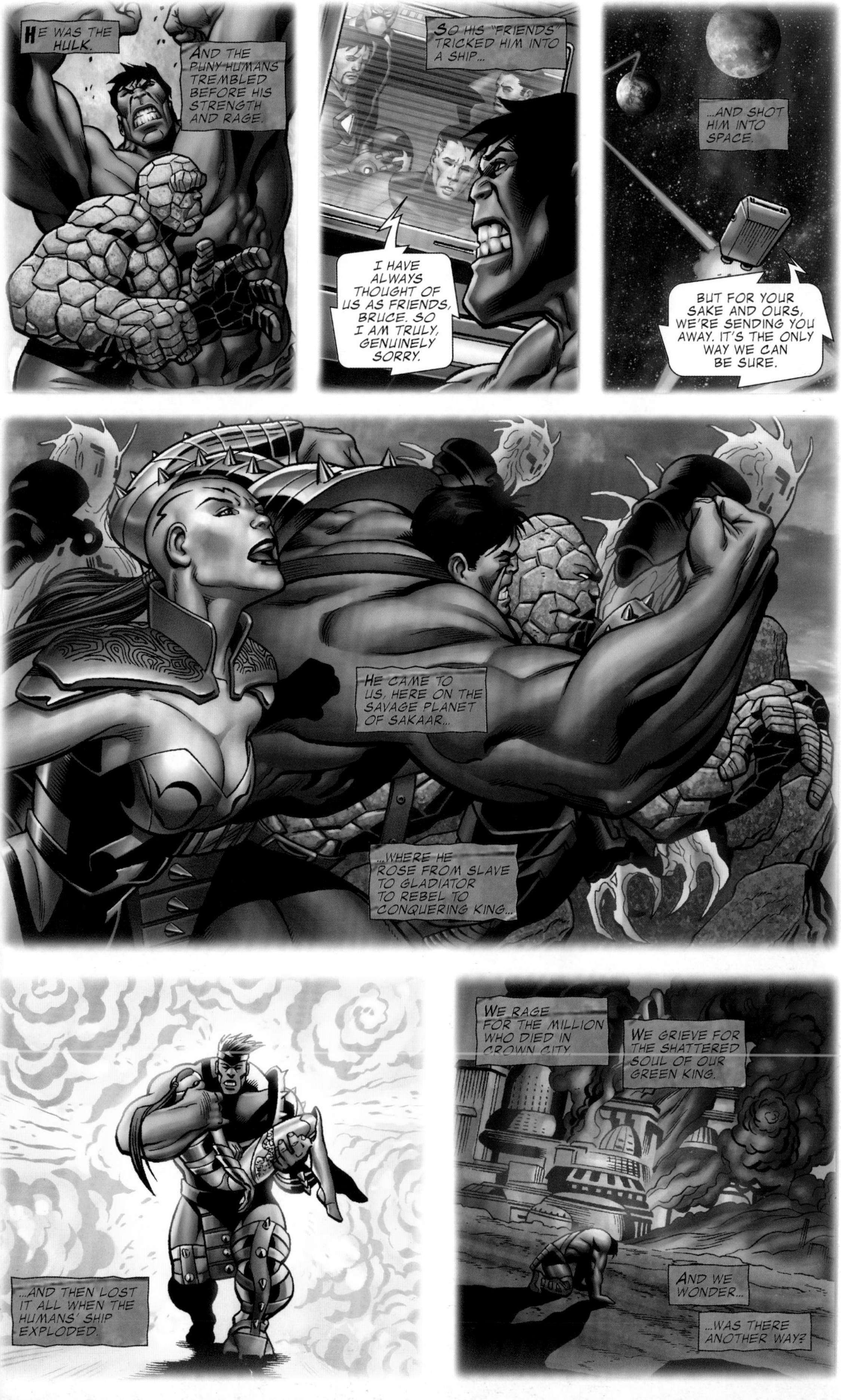
HE WAS THE HULK.
AND THE PUNY HUMANS TREMBLED BEFORE HIS STRENGTH AND RAGE.
SO HIS "FRIENDS" TRICKED HIM INTO A SHIP...
I HAVE ALWAYS THOUGHT OF US AS FRIENDS, BRUCE. SO I AM TRULY, GENUINELY SORRY.
...AND SHOT HIM INTO SPACE.
BUT FOR YOUR SAKE AND OURS, WE'RE SENDING YOU AWAY. IT'S THE ONLY WAY WE CAN BE SURE.
HE CAME TO US, HERE ON THE SAVAGE PLANET OF SAKAAR...
...WHERE HE ROSE FROM SLAVE TO GLADIATOR TO REBEL TO CONQUERING KING...
...AND THEN LOST IT ALL WHEN THE HUMANS' SHIP EXPLODED.
WE RAGE FOR THE MILLION WHO DIED IN CROWN CITY.
WE GRIEVE FOR THE SHATTERED SOUL OF OUR GREEN KING.
AND WE WONDER...
...WAS THERE ANOTHER WAY?

THE PUNY HUMANS NEVER INTENDED TO SEND THE HULK TO SAKAAR...

...THEY HAD A COMPLETELY DIFFERENT WORLD IN MIND FOR HIM.

WE PICKED YOUR DESTINATION CAREFULLY. A LUSH PLANET. FULL OF VEGETATION AND GAME.

BUT NO INTELLIGENT LIFE-FORMS.

THERE WILL BE NO ONE THERE TO HURT YOU...

WHEN THE HULK RIPPED OPEN THE SHIP, HE THREW IT OFF COURSE.

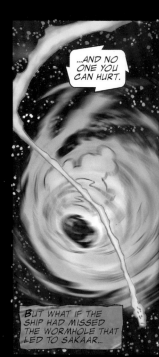

...AND NO ONE YOU CAN HURT.

BUT WHAT IF THE SHIP HAD MISSED THE WORMHOLE THAT LED TO SAKAAR...

YOU ALWAYS SAID YOU WANTED TO BE LEFT ALONE...

WHAT IF IT HAD CONTINUED ON COURSE?

...MAY YOU FINALLY FIND PEACE.

WHAT IF THE HULK LANDED ON THE PEACEFUL PLANET THAT REED RICHARDS PROMISED?

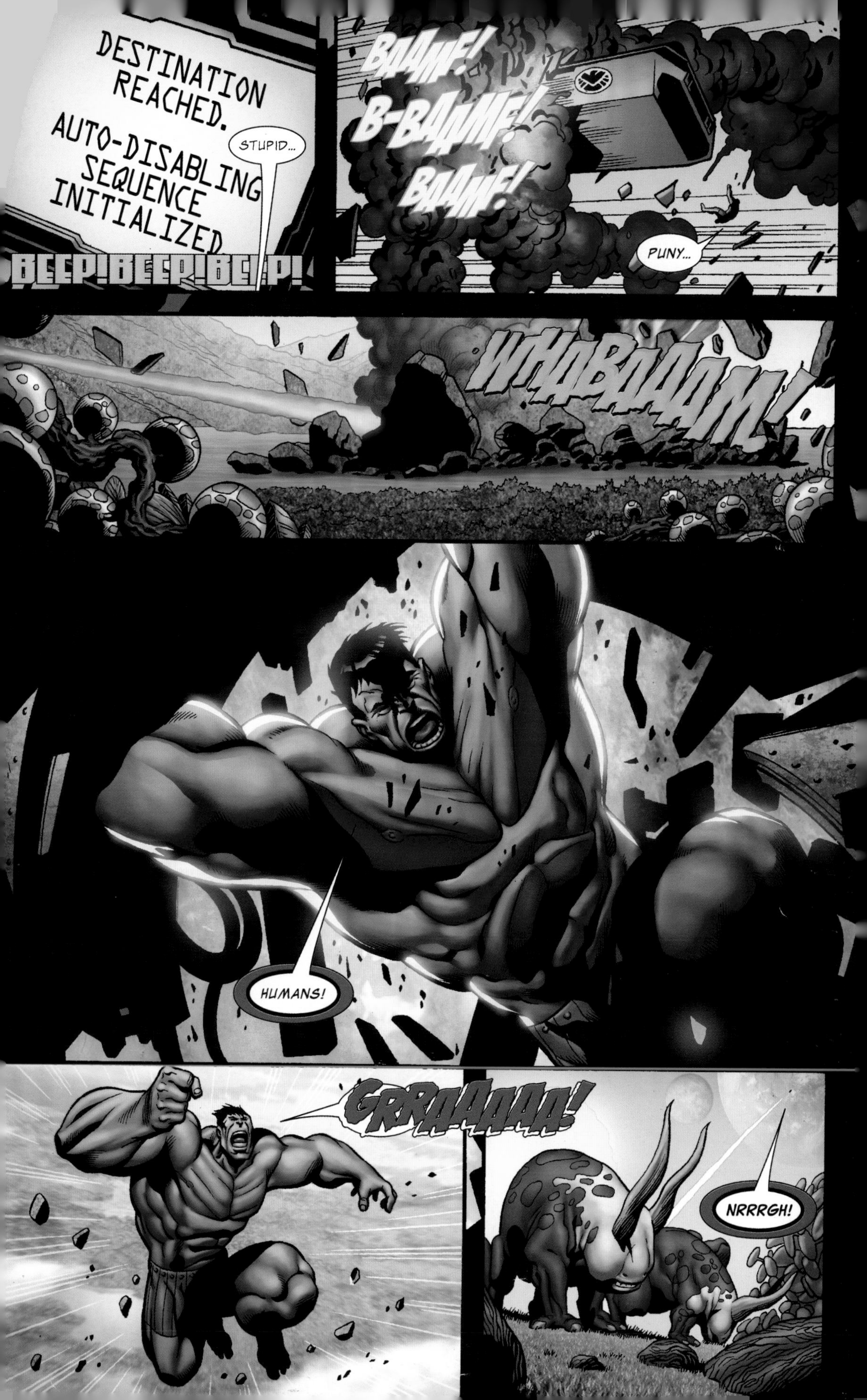
DESTINATION REACHED.
AUTO-DISABLING SEQUENCE INITIALIZED
STUPID...
BEEP! BEEP! BE P!
BAAMF!
B-BAAMF!
BAAMF!
PUNY...
WHABAAAM!
HUMANS!
GRRAAAAAA!
NRRRGH!

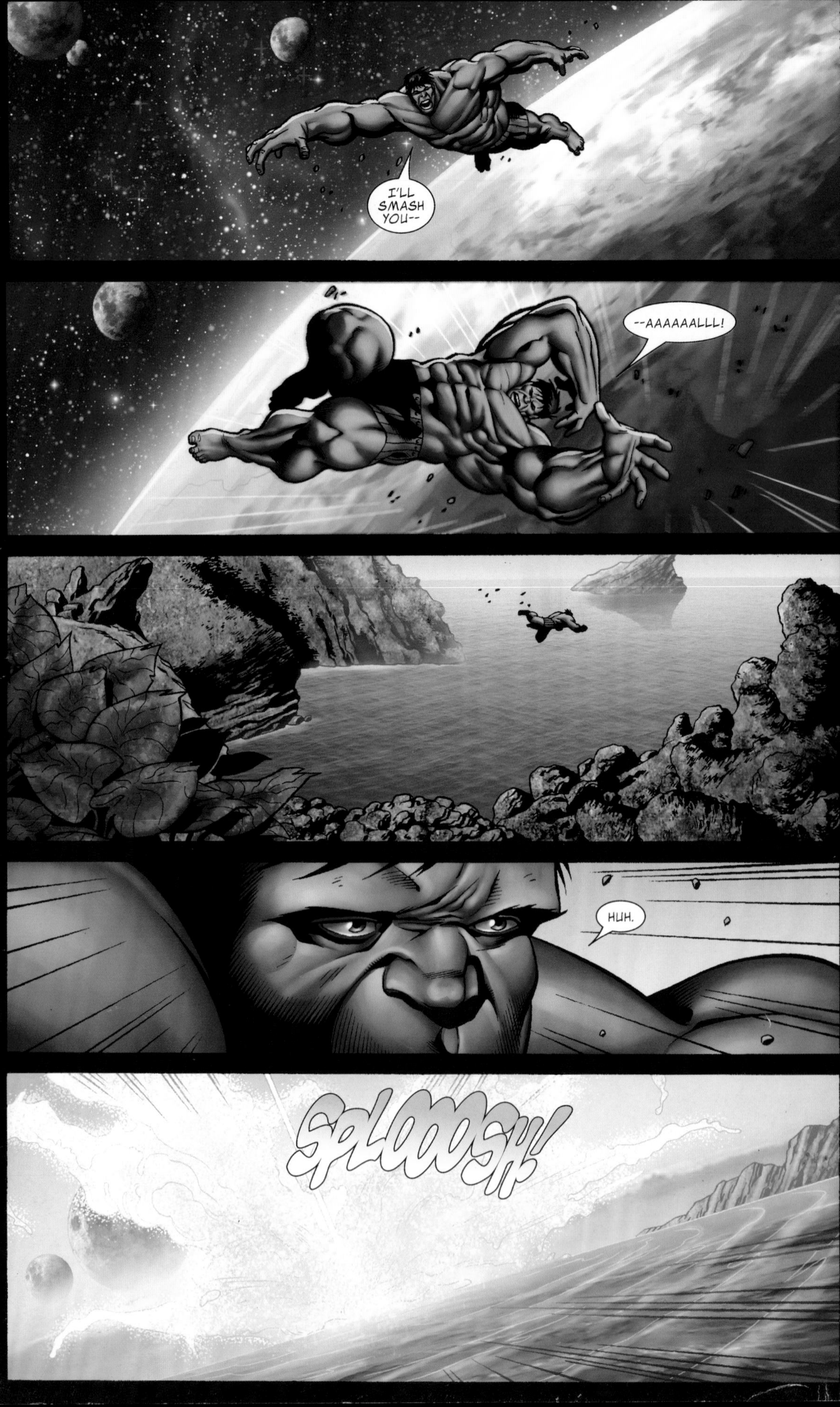
I'LL SMASH YOU--
--AAAAAALLL!
HUH.
SPLOOOSH!

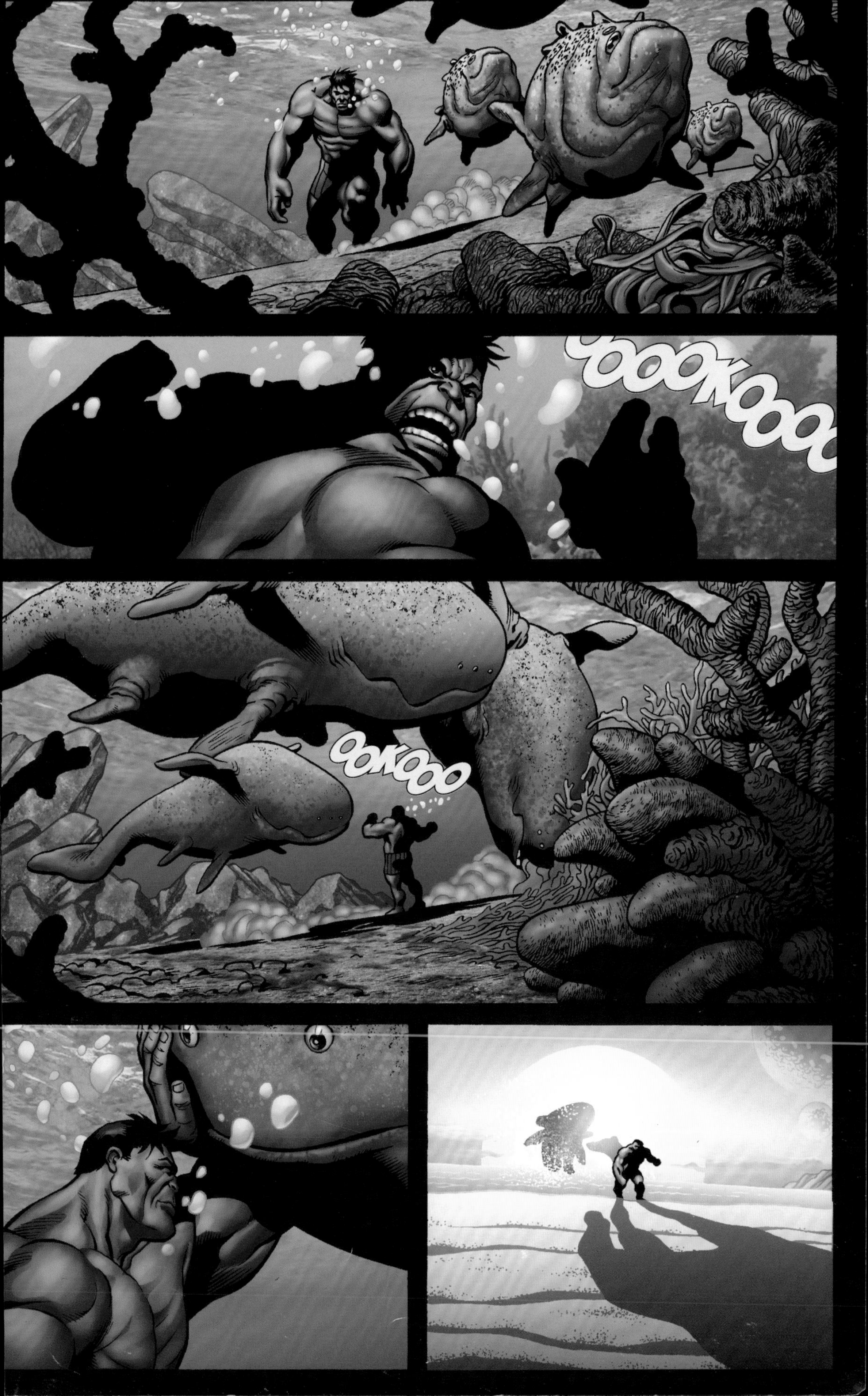
OOOOKOOOO
OOKOOO

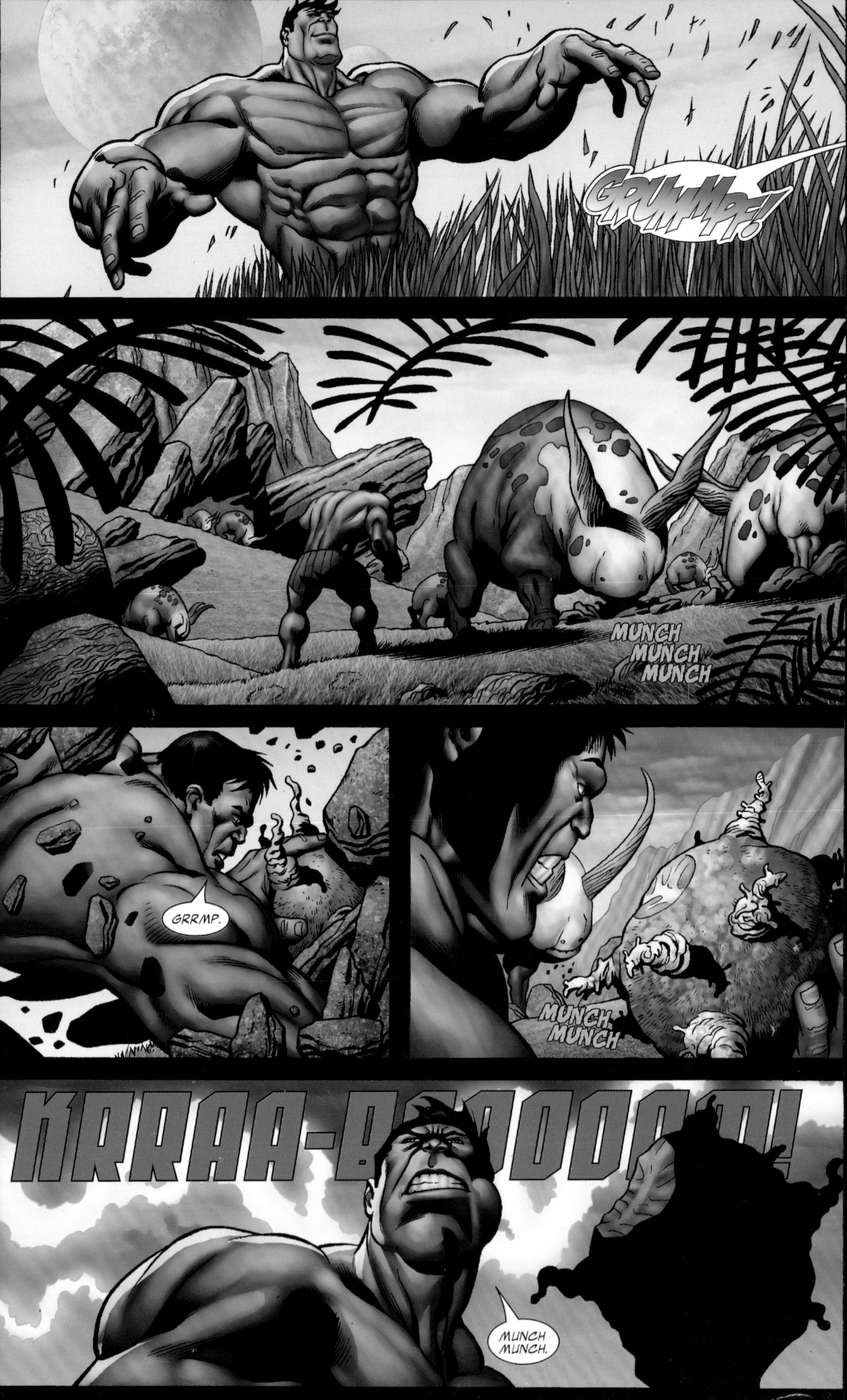
GRUMMPF!
MUNCH MUNCH MUNCH
GRRMP.
MUNCH MUNCH
KRRAA-
MUNCH MUNCH.

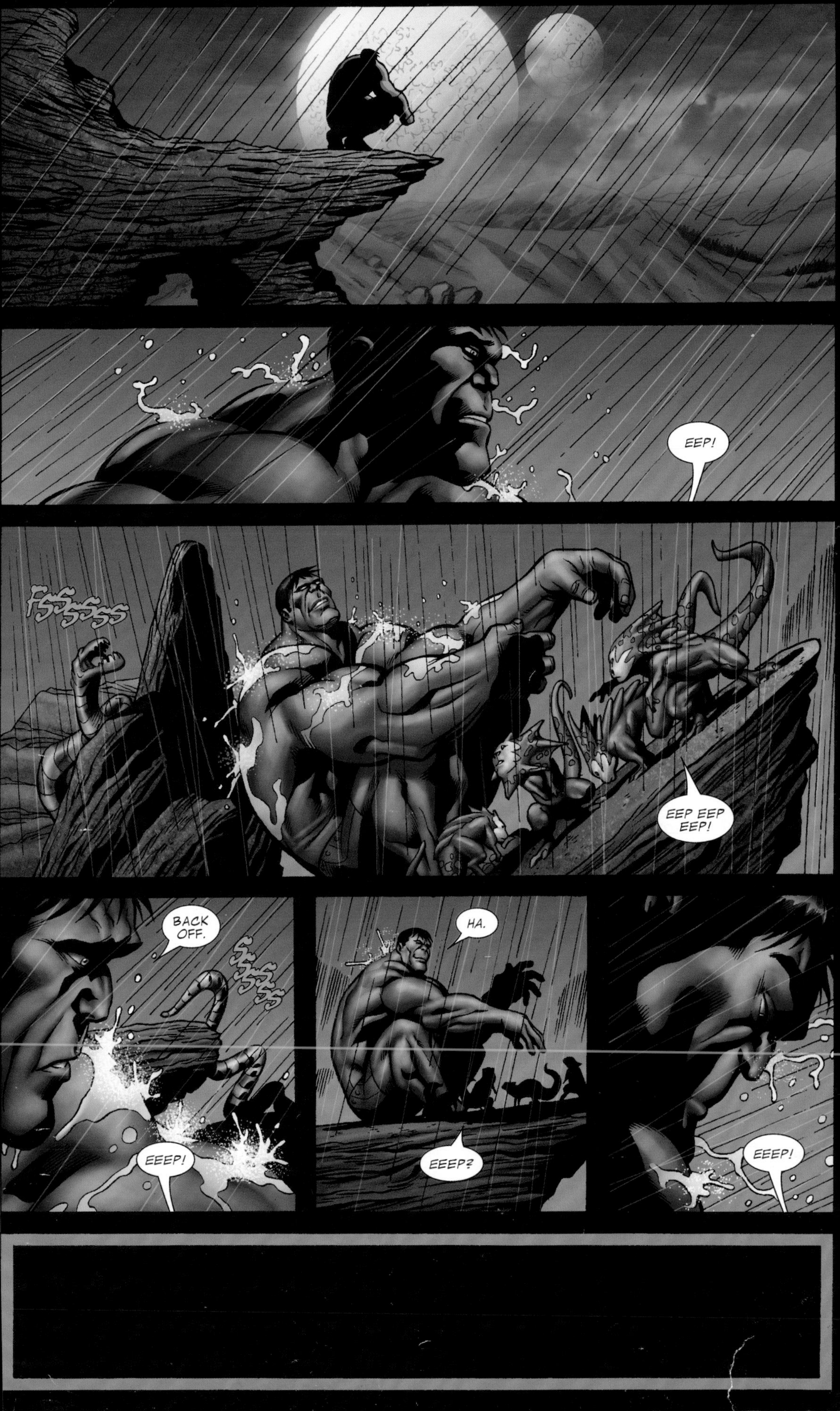
EEP!
FSSSSSS
EEP EEP EEP!
BACK OFF.
SSSSS
EEEP!
HA.
EEEP?
EEEP!

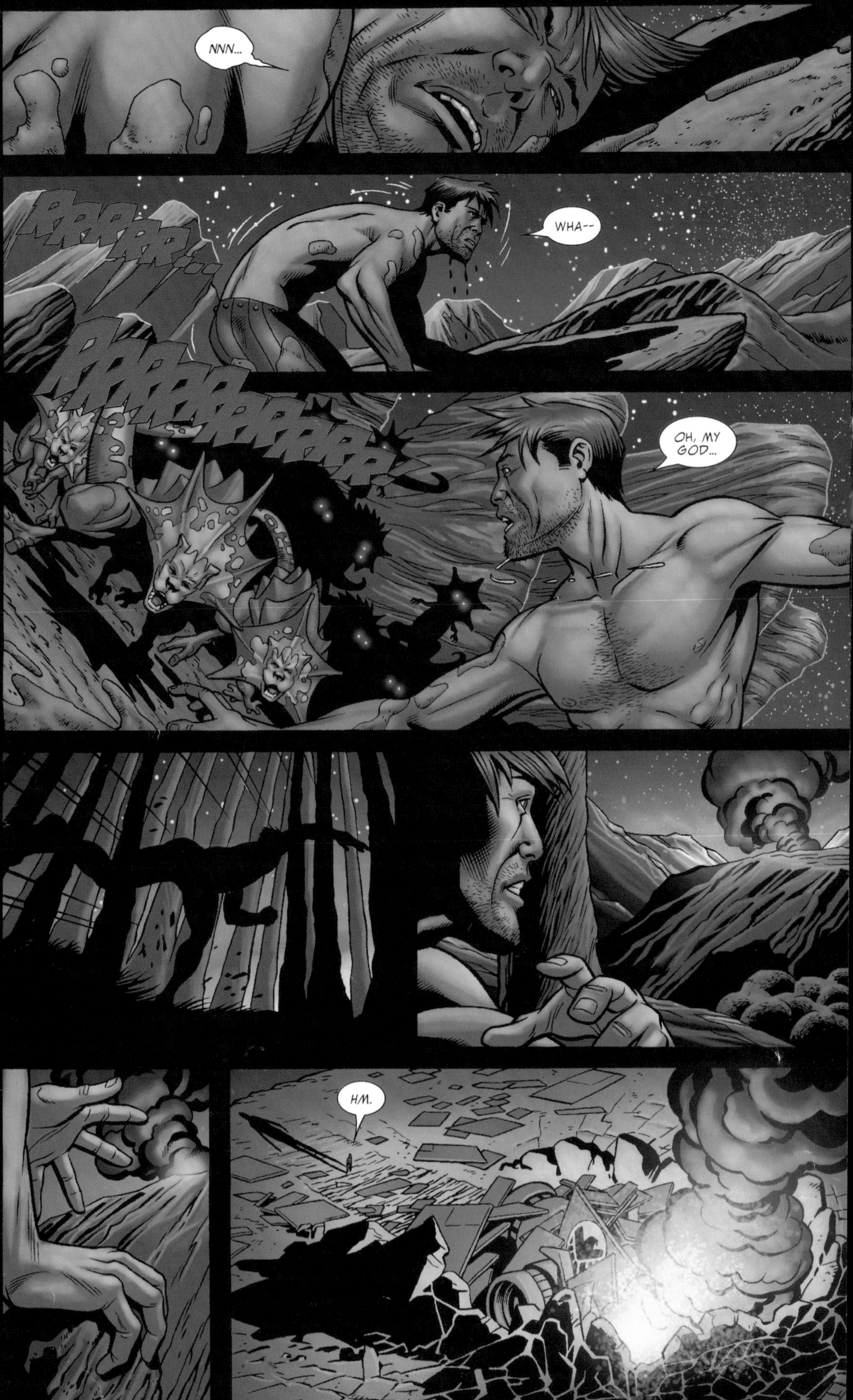

NNN...
RRRRRR...
WHA--
RRRRRRRRRRRRRRR!
OH, MY GOD...
HM.

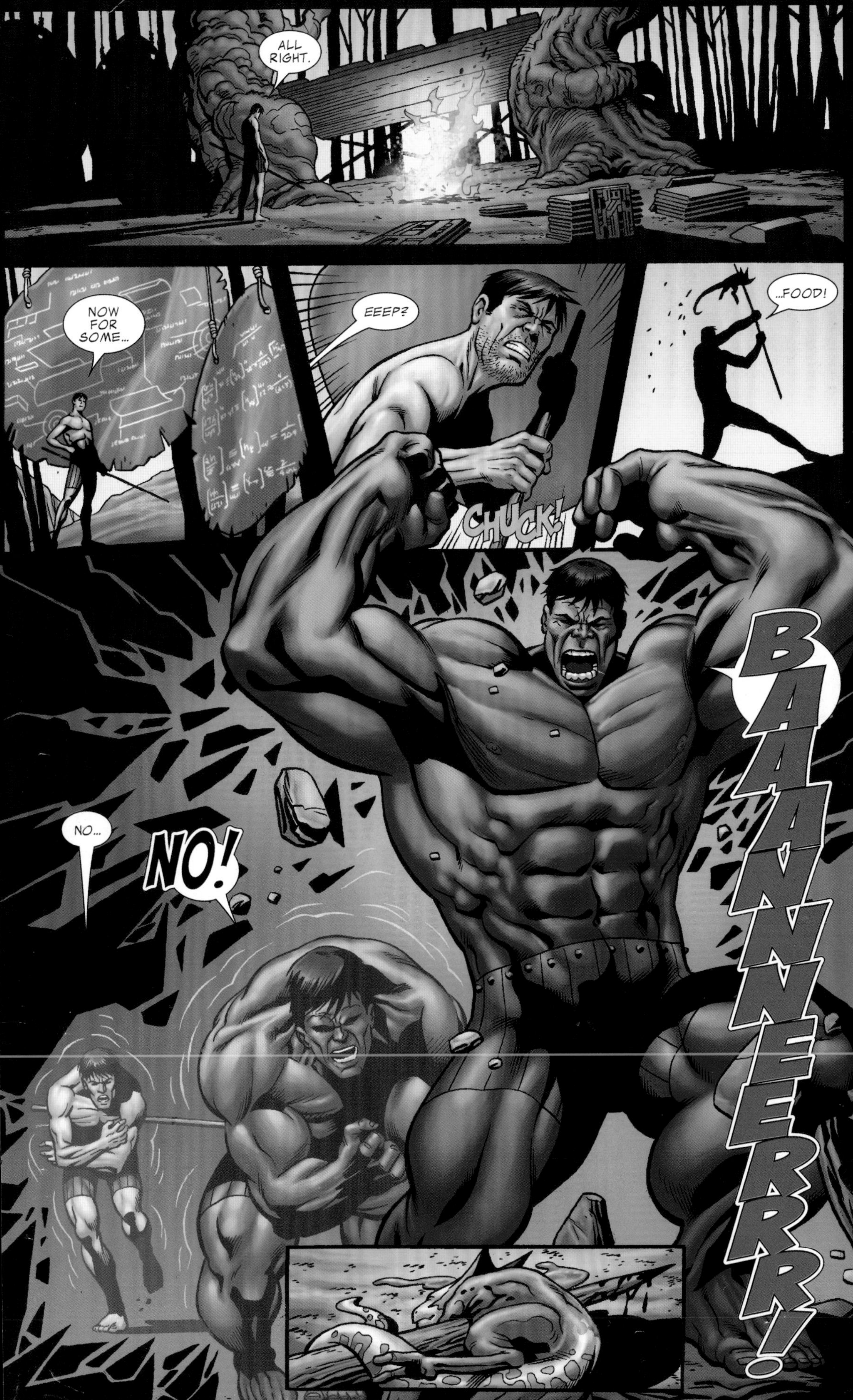
ALL RIGHT.
NOW FOR SOME...
EEEP?
...FOOD!
CHUCK!
BANNERRR!
NO...
NO!

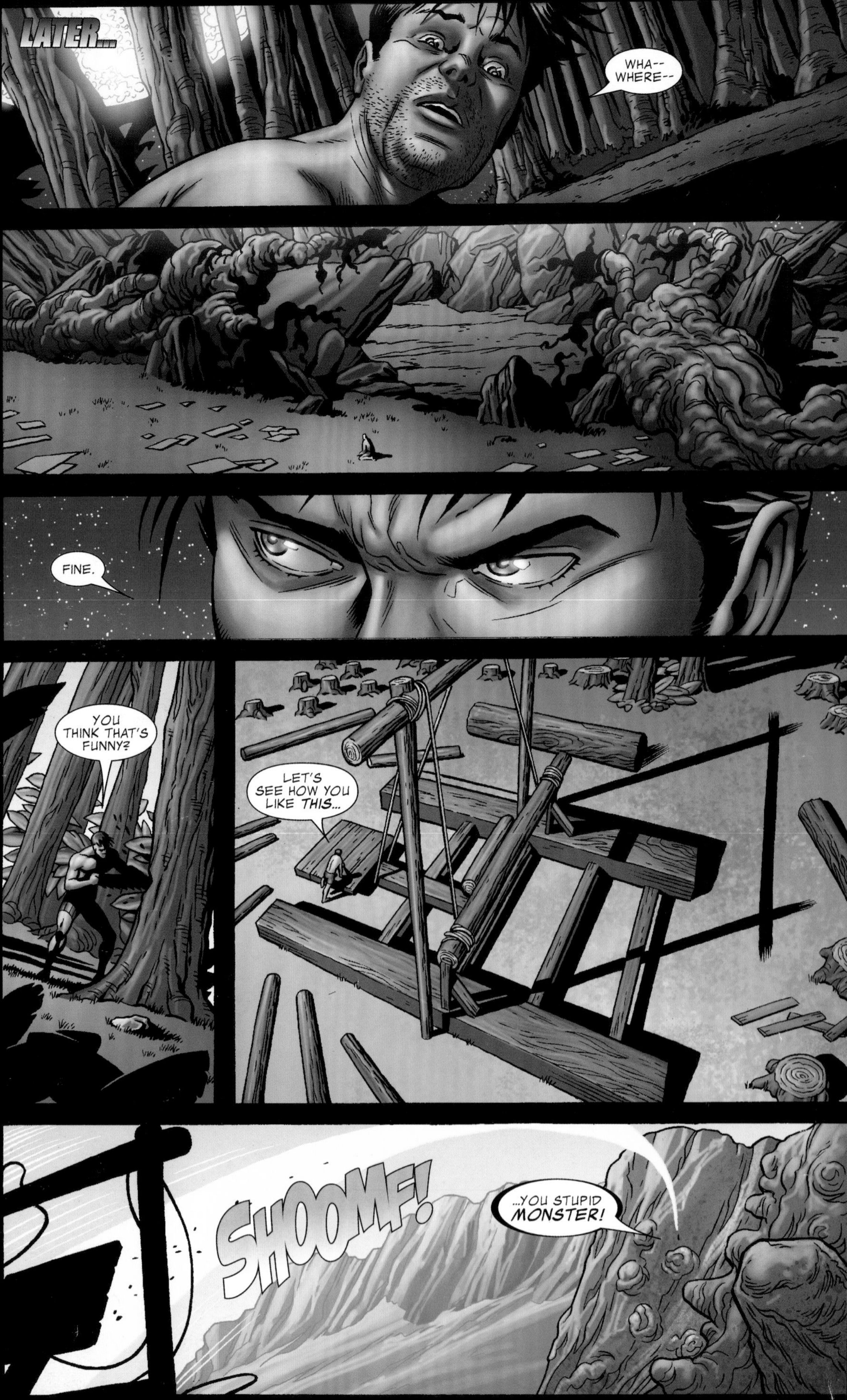
LATER...
WHA-- WHERE--
FINE.
YOU THINK THAT'S FUNNY?
LET'S SEE HOW YOU LIKE THIS...
SHOOMF!
...YOU STUPID MONSTER!

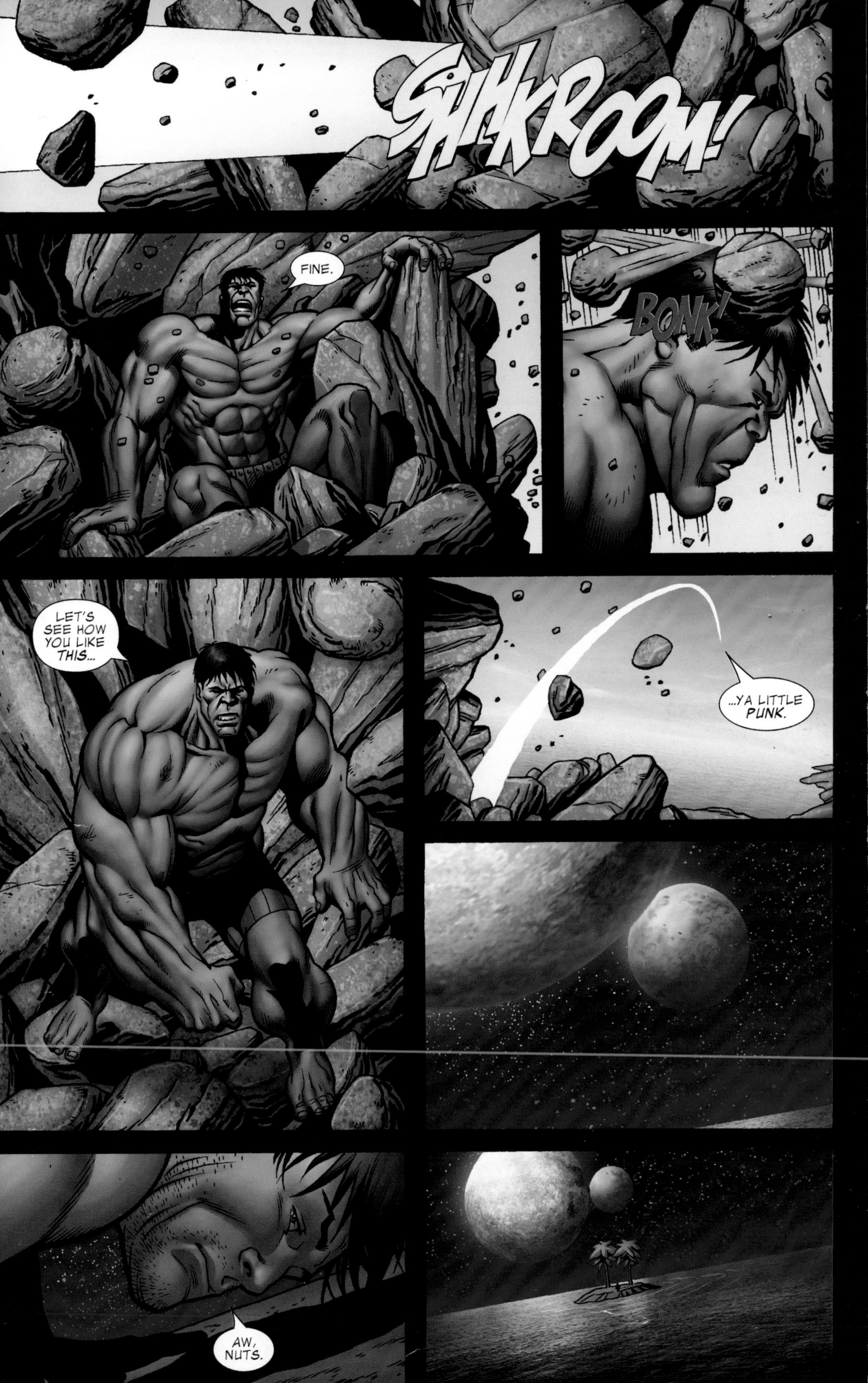
SHHKROOM!
FINE.
BONK!
LET'S SEE HOW YOU LIKE THIS...
...YA LITTLE PUNK.
AW, NUTS.

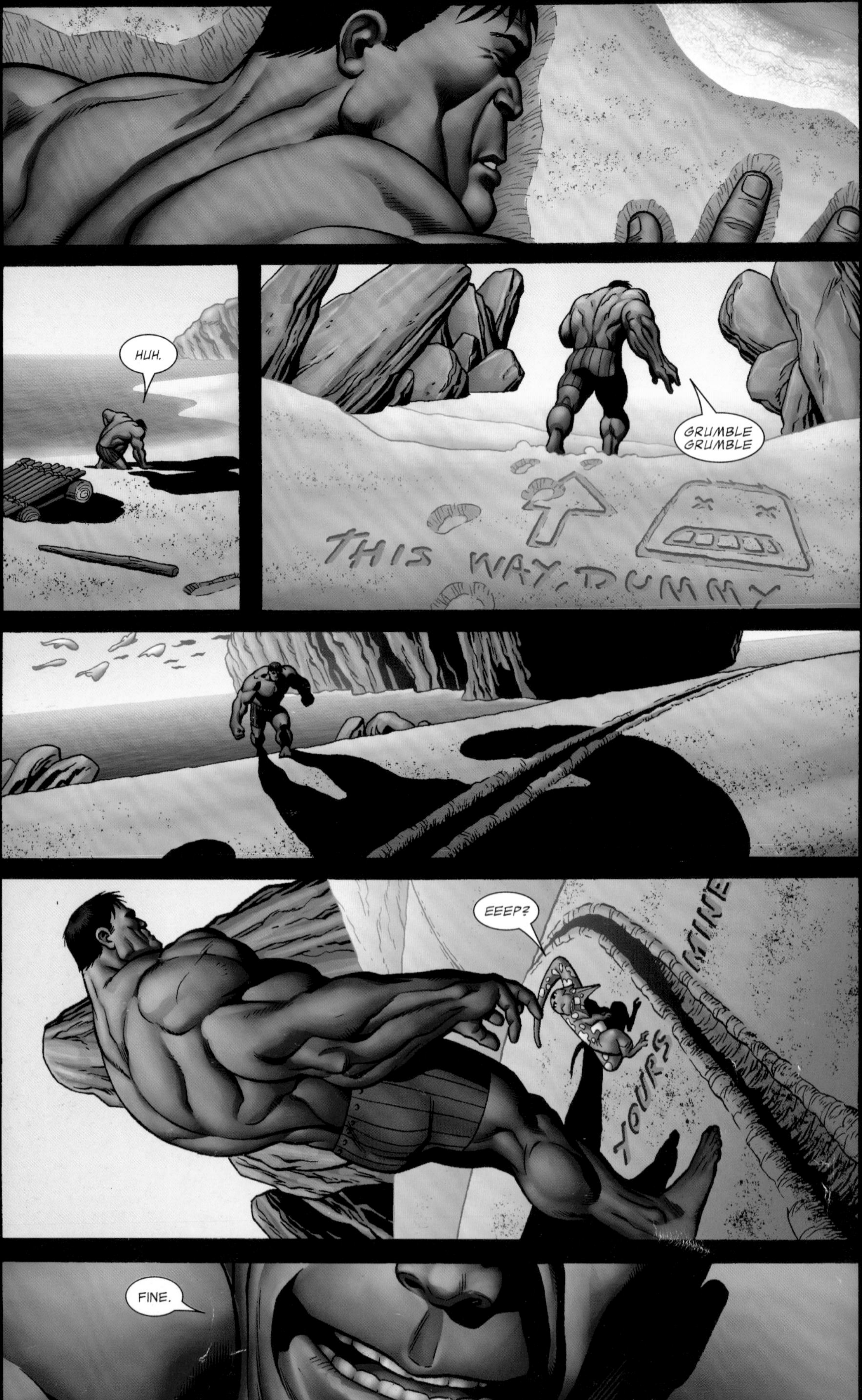
HUH.
GRUMBLE GRUMBLE
THIS WAY, DUMMY
EEEP?
MINE
YOURS
FINE.

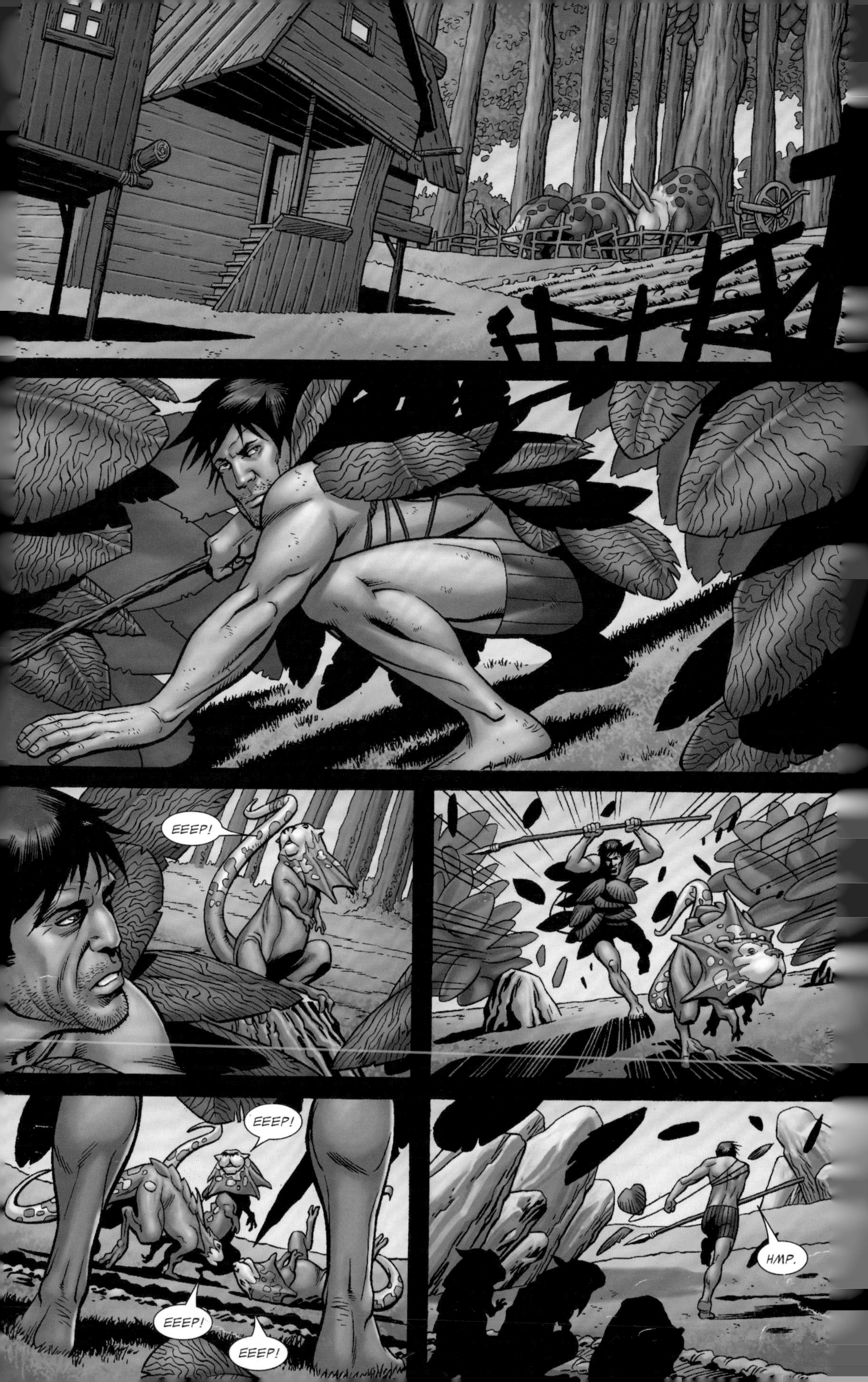
EEEP!
EEEP!
EEEP!
EEEP!
HMP.

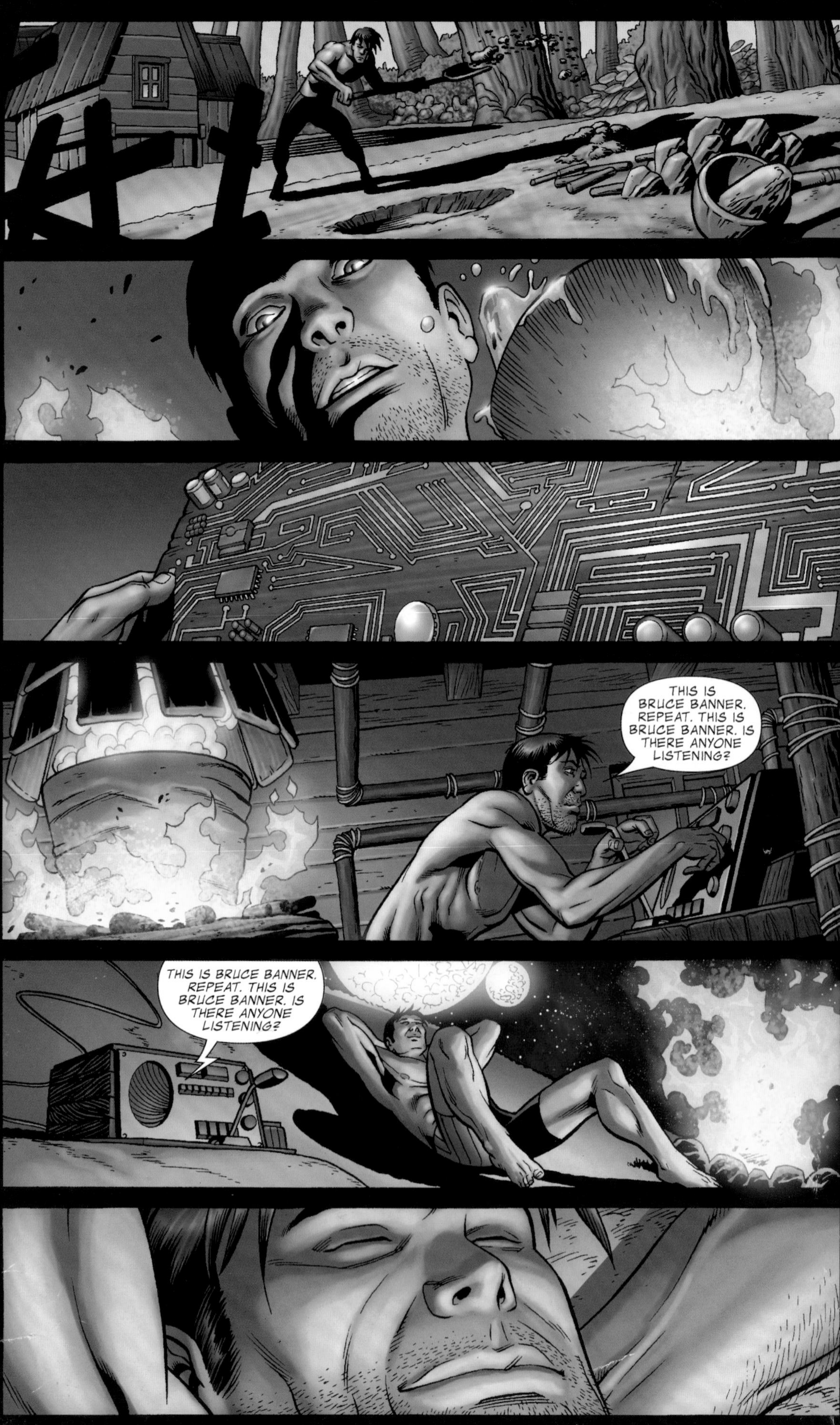
THIS IS BRUCE BANNER. REPEAT. THIS IS BRUCE BANNER. IS THERE ANYONE LISTENING?
THIS IS BRUCE BANNER. REPEAT. THIS IS BRUCE BANNER. IS THERE ANYONE LISTENING?

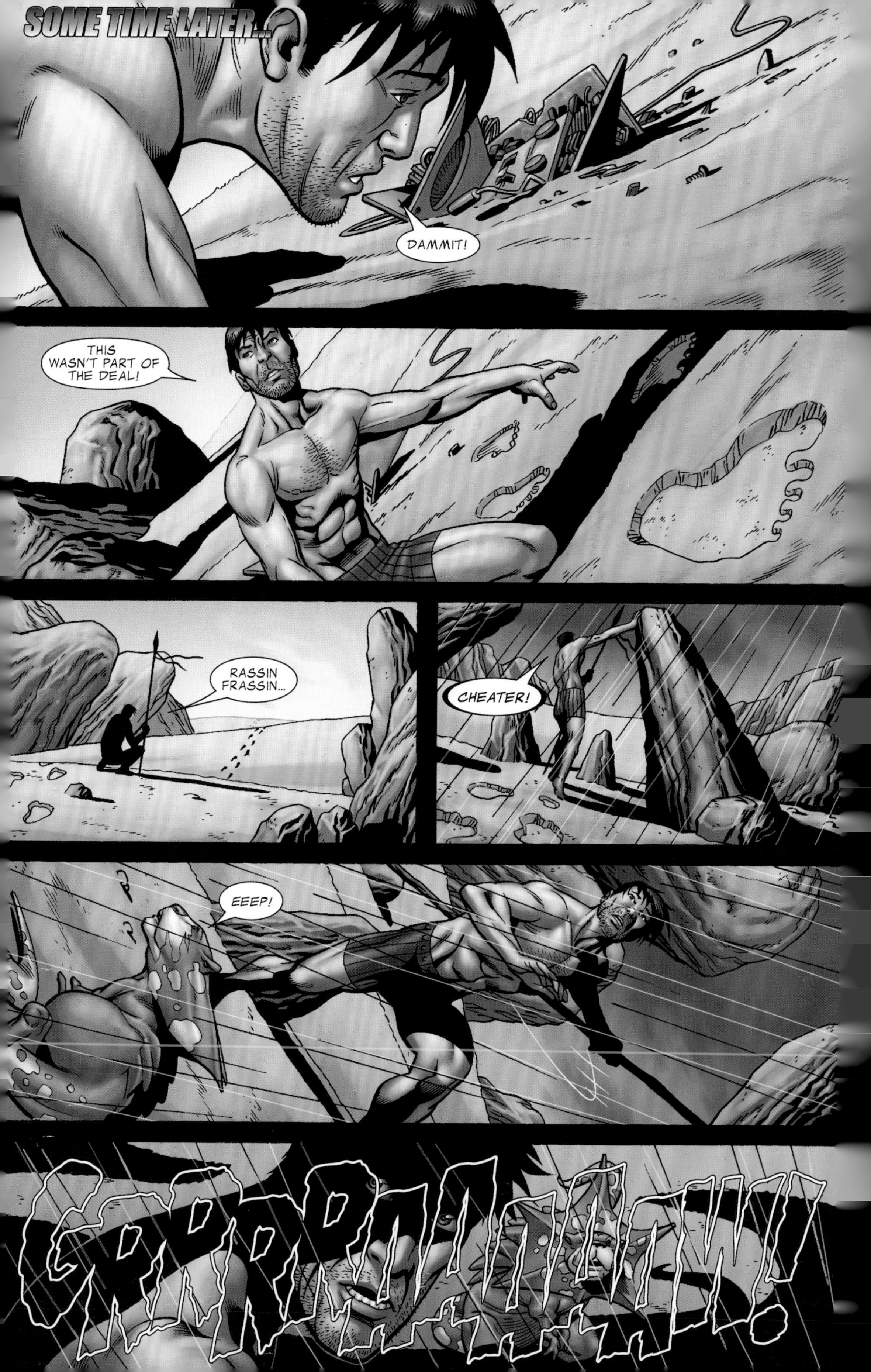
SOME TIME LATER...
DAMMIT!
THIS WASN'T PART OF THE DEAL!
RASSIN FRASSIN...
CHEATER!
EEEP!
GRRRAAAAAWW!

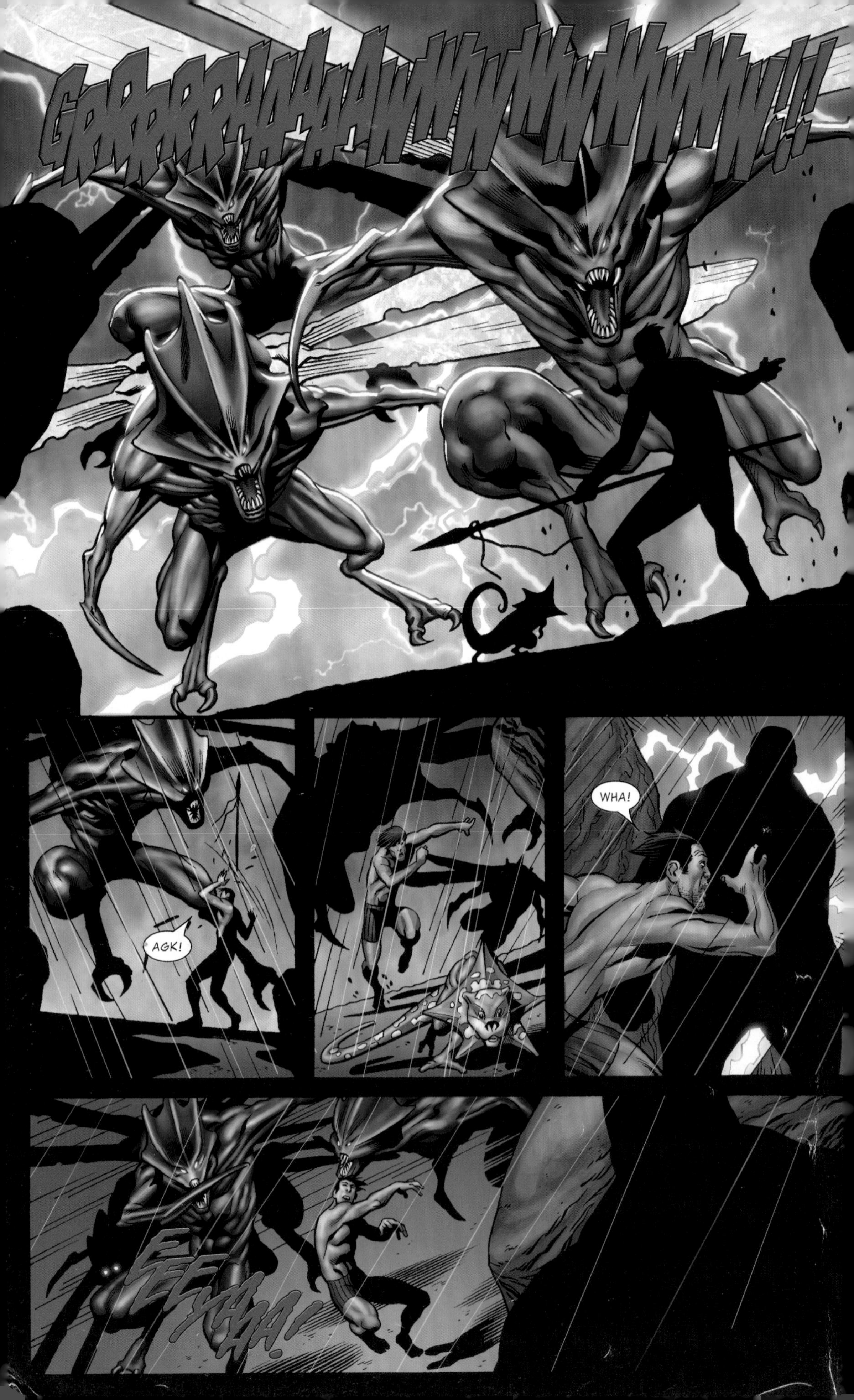
GRRRRAAAAAWWWWWWWWWW!!!
AGK!
WHA!
EEEYAAA!

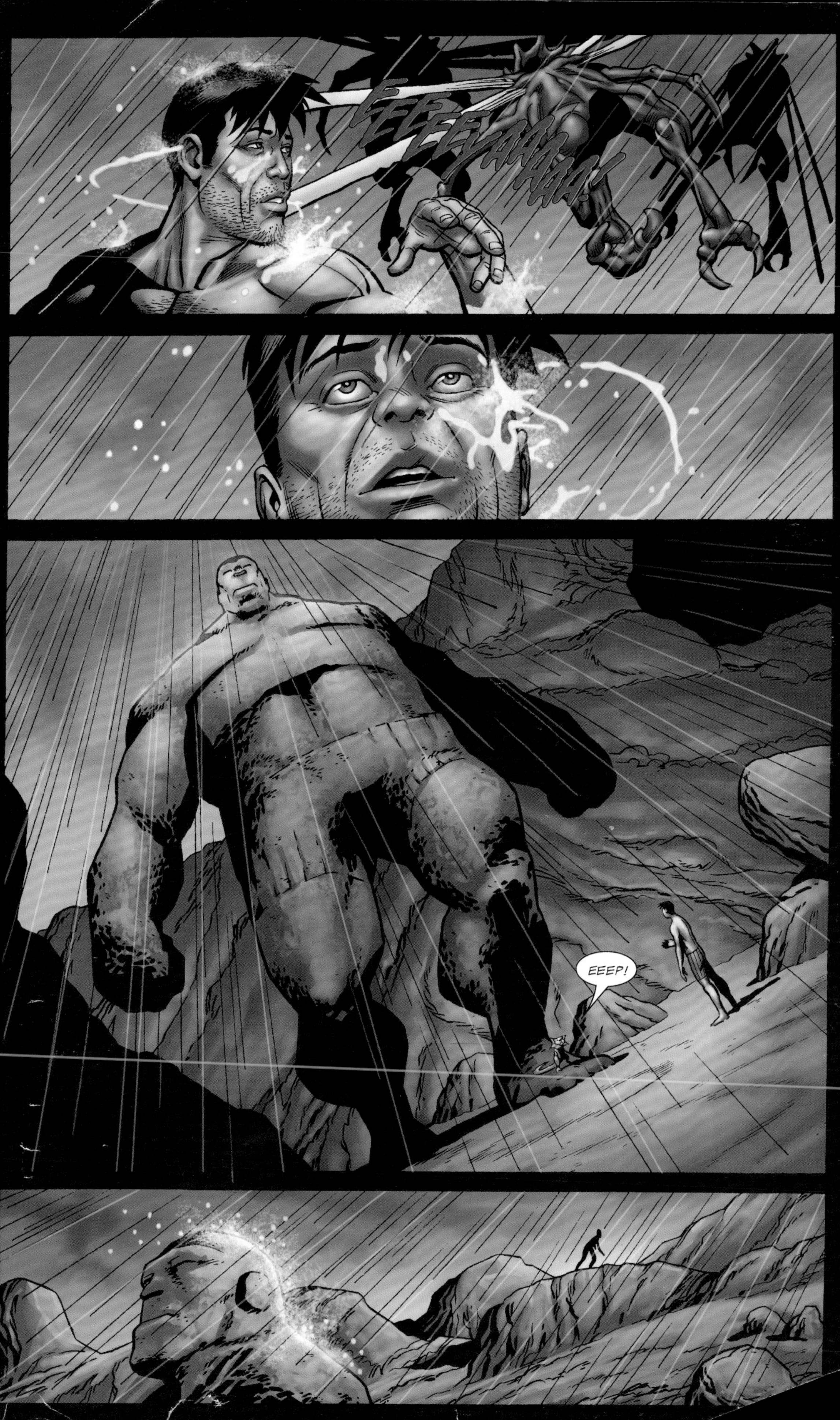

EEEEEYAAAAAAAAA!
EEEP!

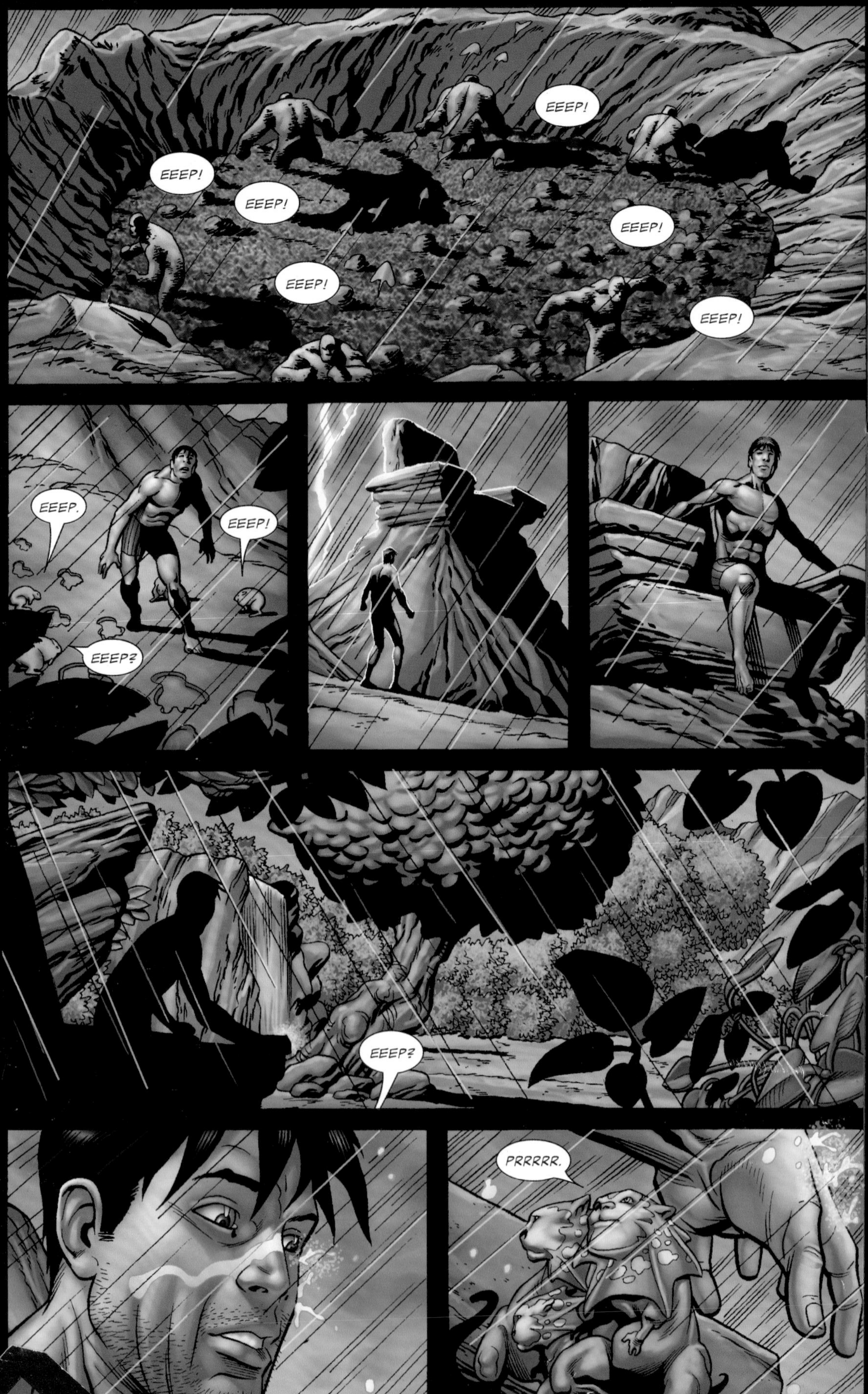
EEEP!
EEEP!
EEEP!
EEEP!
EEEP!
EEEP!
EEEP.
EEEP!
EEEP?
EEEP?
PRRRRR.

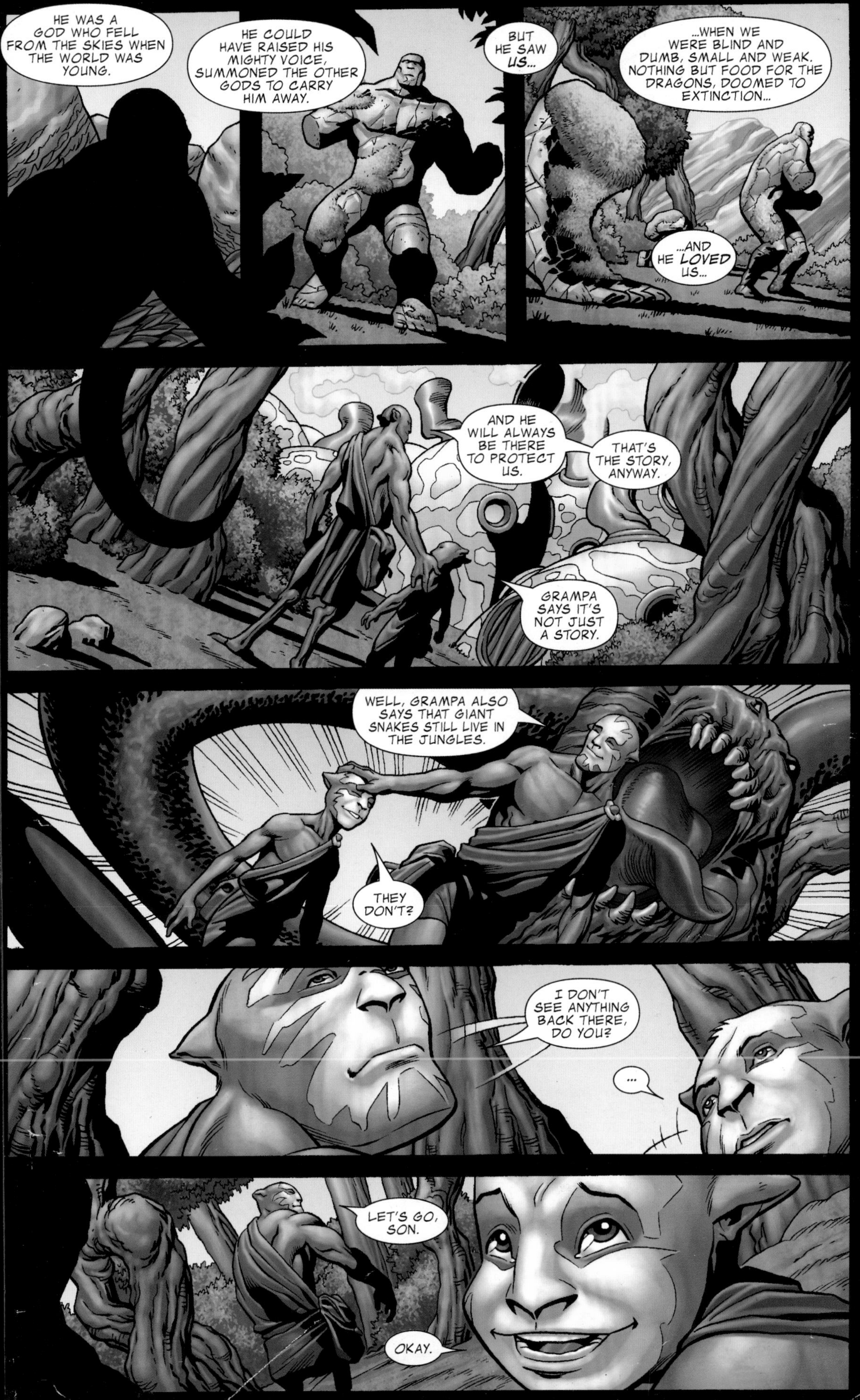
HE WAS A GOD WHO FELL FROM THE SKIES WHEN THE WORLD WAS YOUNG.
HE COULD HAVE RAISED HIS MIGHTY VOICE, SUMMONED THE OTHER GODS TO CARRY HIM AWAY.
BUT HE SAW US...
...WHEN WE WERE BLIND AND DUMB, SMALL AND WEAK. NOTHING BUT FOOD FOR THE DRAGONS, DOOMED TO EXTINCTION...
...AND HE LOVED US...
AND HE WILL ALWAYS BE THERE TO PROTECT US.
THAT'S THE STORY, ANYWAY.
GRAMPA SAYS IT'S NOT JUST A STORY.
WELL, GRAMPA ALSO SAYS THAT GIANT SNAKES STILL LIVE IN THE JUNGLES.
THEY DON'T?
I DON'T SEE ANYTHING BACK THERE, DO YOU?
...
LET'S GO, SON.
OKAY.

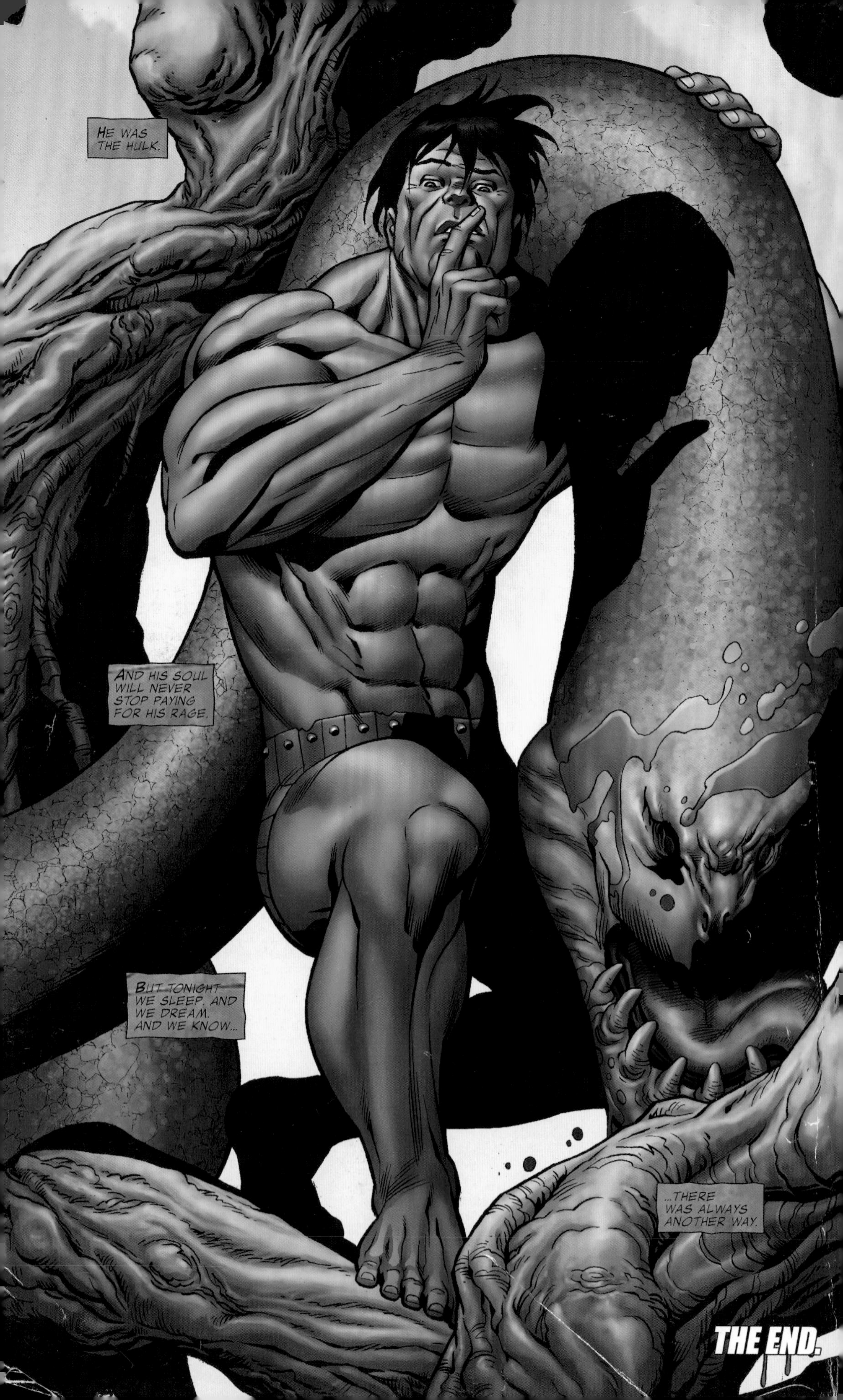
HE WAS THE HULK.
AND HIS SOUL WILL NEVER STOP PAYING FOR HIS RAGE.
BUT TONIGHT WE SLEEP. AND WE DREAM. AND WE KNOW...
...THERE WAS ALWAYS ANOTHER WAY.
THE END.

VARIANT COVER GALLERY
by JOHN ROMITA JR and MICHAEL TURNER

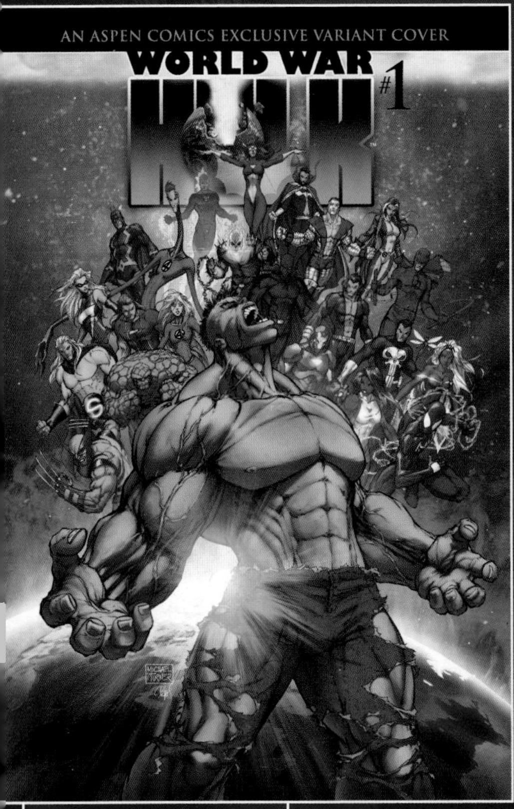
AN ASPEN COMICS EXCLUSIVE VARIANT COVER
WORLD WAR
#1

WORLD WAR HULK #1

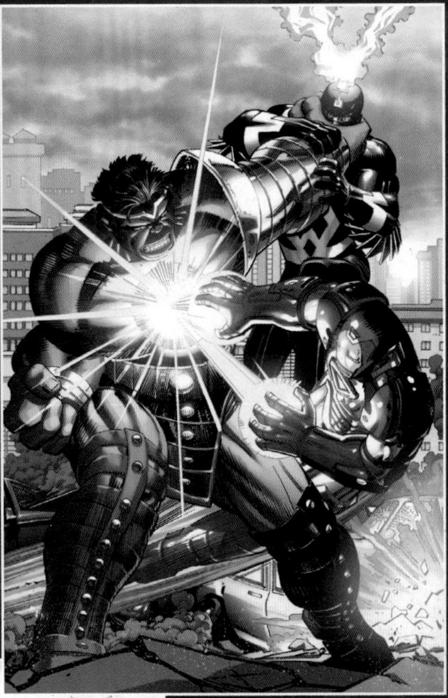

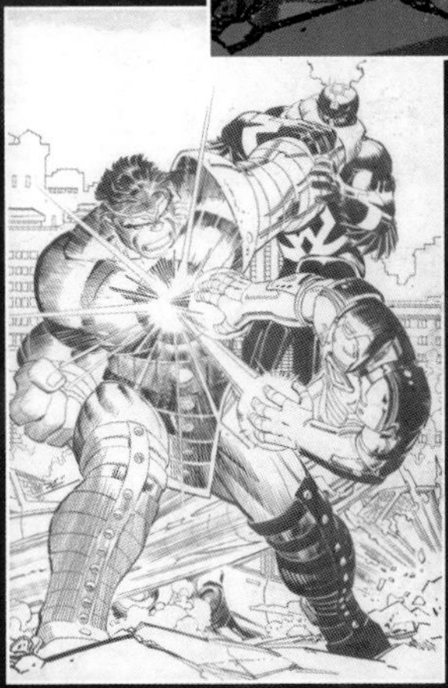

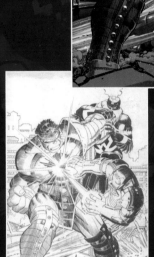

WORLD WAR HULK #2

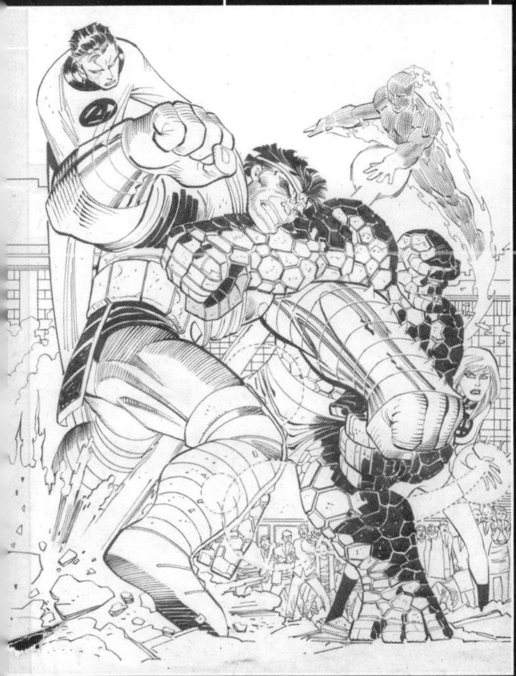

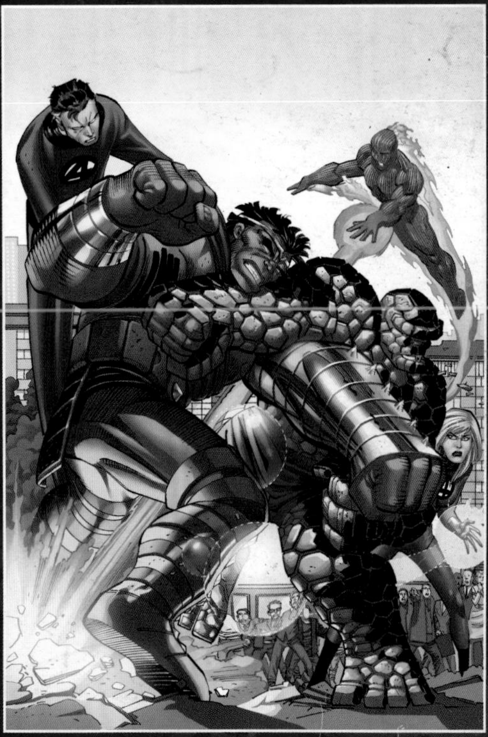

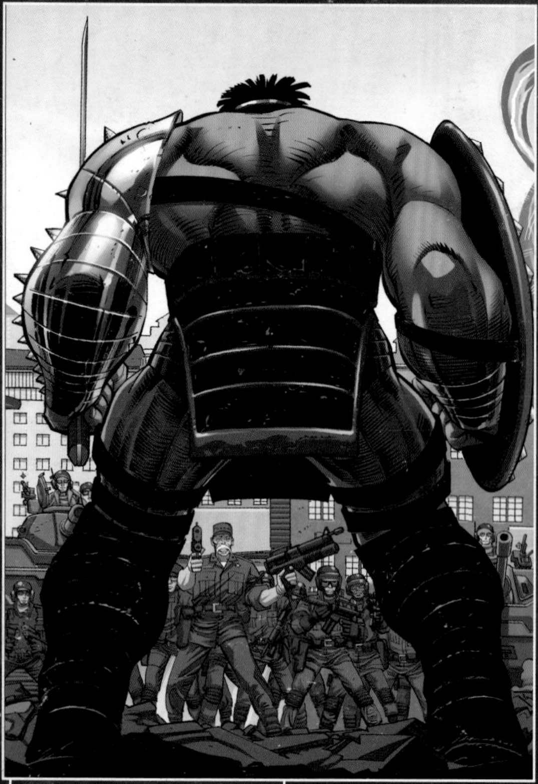

WORLD WAR HULK #3

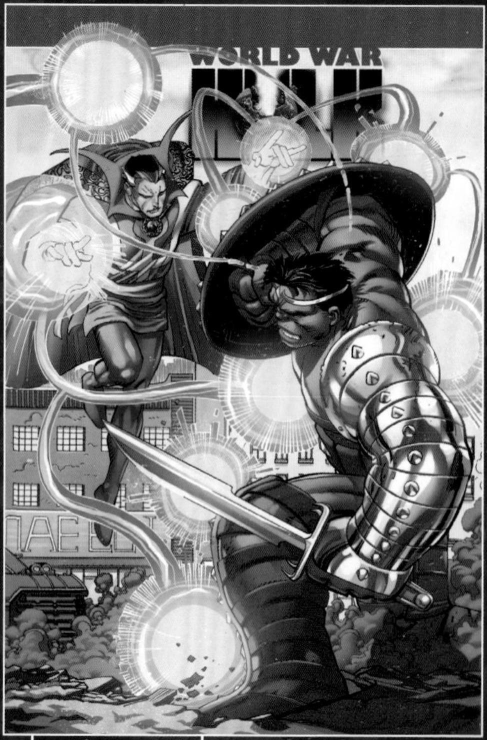
WORLD WAR

WORLD WAR HULK #4

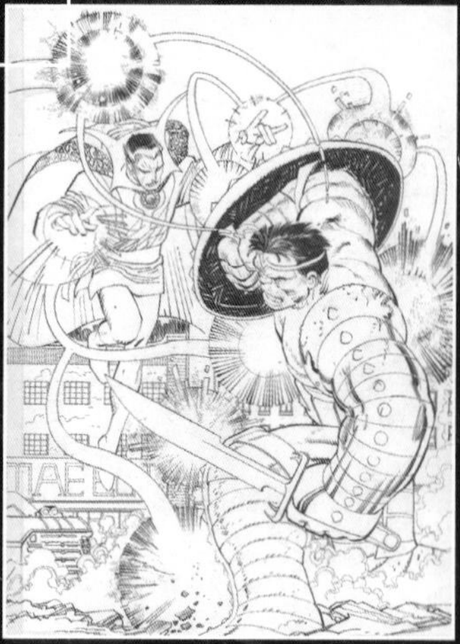

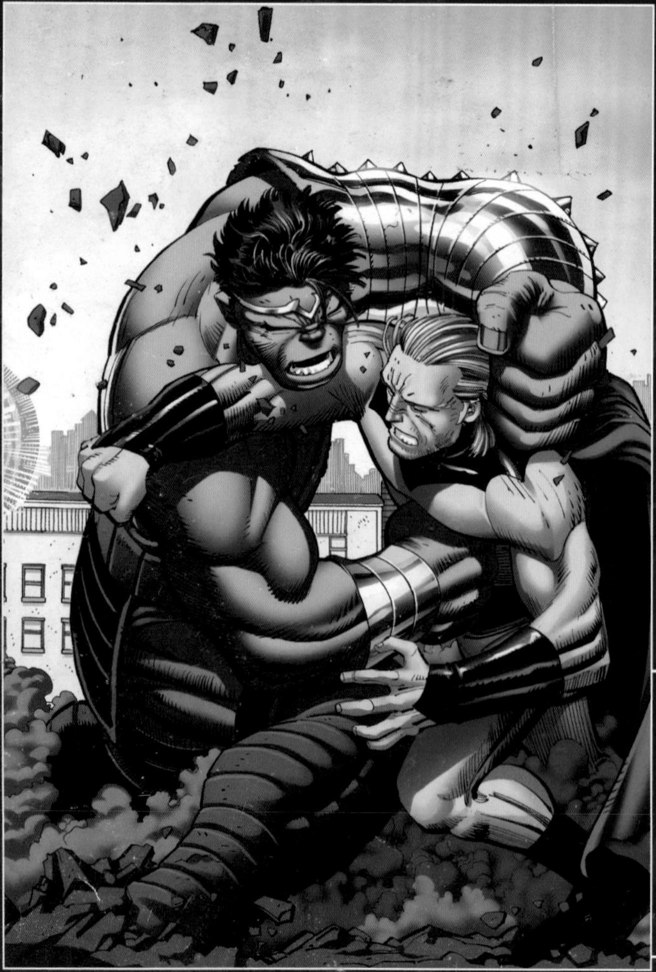

WORLD WAR HULK #5

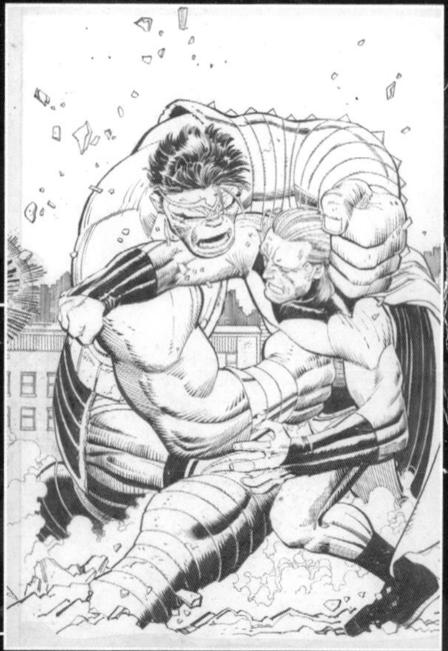